MAUI
HANDBOOK

MAUI
HANDBOOK
INCLUDING MOLOKAI AND LANAI
FIFTH EDITION

J.D. BISIGNANI
COMPILED AND REVISED
BY ROBERT NILSEN

MOON
TRAVEL
HANDBOOKS

MAUI HANDBOOK
FIFTH EDITION

Published by
Moon Publications, Inc.
P.O. Box 3040
Chico, California 95927-3040, USA

Printed by
Colorcraft

ISBN: 1-56691-138-9
ISSN: 1099-8772

Editors: Deana Corbitt Shields, Pauli Galin
Copy Editor: Deana Corbitt Shields
Production & Design: Rob Warner
Cartography: Eric Allen and Allen Leech
Index: Sondra Nation

Front cover photo: Protea flower; by Douglas Peebles

All photos by J.D. Bisignani unless otherwise noted.
All illustrations by Bob Race unless otherwise noted.

Distributed in the United States and Canada by Publishers Group West

Printed in China

Please send all comments,
corrections, additions,
amendments, and critiques to:

**MAUI HANDBOOK
MOON TRAVEL HANDBOOKS
P.O. BOX 3040
CHICO, CA 95927-3040, USA
e-mail: travel@moon.com
www.moon.com**

Printing History
1st edition—1986
5th edition—June 1999
5 4 3 2 1 0

To Sylvester T.,
the best long-distance man
there ever was

CONTENTS

MAPS

ABBREVIATIONS

A.F.B.—Air Force Base
B.Y.O.—Bring Your Own
4WD—Four-wheel Drive
HVB—Hawaii Visitors Bureau

OHA—Office of Hawaiian Affairs
PADI—Professional Association
    of Dive Instructors
Rt.—Route

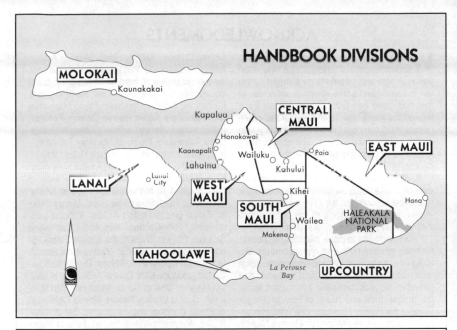

HANDBOOK DIVISIONS

MOLOKAI
Kaunakakai

LANAI
Lanai City

CENTRAL MAUI

Kapalua
Honokowai
Kaanapali
Lahaina
Wailuku
Paia
Kahului

EAST MAUI

WEST MAUI

SOUTH MAUI

Kihei

Wailea

Makena

La Perouse Bay

HALEAKALA NATIONAL PARK

Hana

UPCOUNTRY

KAHOOLAWE

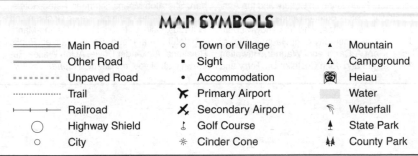

MAP SYMBOLS

═══ Main Road	○ Town or Village	▲ Mountain
── Other Road	▪ Sight	⌂ Campground
═ ═ ═ Unpaved Road	• Accommodation	🛕 Heiau
⋯⋯ Trail	✈ Primary Airport	Water
├─┼─┤ Railroad	✈ Secondary Airport	🖋 Waterfall
○ Highway Shield	⚑ Golf Course	▲ State Park
○ City	✳ Cinder Cone	♠♠ County Park

ACKNOWLEDGMENTS

Writing the acknowledgments for a book is supercharged with energy. It's a time when you look forward, hopefully, to a bright future for your work, and a time when you reflect on all that has gone into producing it. Mostly it's a time to say thank you. Thank you for the grace necessary to carry out the task, and thank you to all the wonderful people whose efforts have helped so much along the way. To the following people, I offer my most sincere thank you.

Firstly, to the Moon staff, professionals every one. As time has passed, and one book has followed another, they've become amazingly adept at their work, to the point where their mastery is a marvel to watch.

I would also like to thank the following people for their special help and consideration: Dr. Greg Leo, an adventurer and environmentalist who has done remarkable field research and provided me with invaluable information about the unique flora and fauna of Hawaii; Roger Rose of the Bishop Museum; Lee Wild, Hawaiian Mission Houses Museum; Marilyn Nicholson, State Foundation on Culture and the Arts; the Hawaii Visitors Bureau; Donna Jung, Donna Jung and Associates, who has shown confidence in me since day one; Haunani Vieira, Dollar Rent A Car; Keoni Wagner, Hawaiian Airlines; Jim and John Costello; Dr. Terry and Nancy Carolan; Aubrey Hawk, Bozelle Advertising; Constance Wright, Molokai Visitors Assoc.; Barbara Schonley, of Molokai; Elisa Josephsohn, Public Relations; Faith Ogawa, for helping me keep the faith; Joyce Matsumoto, Halekulani Hotel; Bernie Caalim-Polanzi, Hilton Hotels; Nancy Daniels, Outrigger Hotels; Donn Takahashi, Regional Manager Prince Hotels; Alvin Wong, Hawaii Prince Hotel Waikiki; Martin Kahn, Kahn Galleries; Allison Kneubuhl, Kahala Mandarin Oriental; Matt Bailey, Manele Bay Hotel; Kurt Matsumoto, Lodge at Koele; Stephanie Reid, Princeville Hotel; Margy Parker, Poipu Beach Resort Assoc.; Yvonne Landavazo, Ritz-Carlton Kapalua; Catherine Sharpe, Stryker Weiner; Adi Kohler, Percy Higashi, and Jon Fukuda, Mauna Kea Beach Hotel and Hapuna Prince Hotel; Donna Kimura, Orchid at Mauna Lani; Denise Anderson, Hawaiian Regent; Dennis Costa, Maui Hill; Kim Marshall, Grand Wailea Resort; Sheila Donnelly, of Sheila Donnelly and Associates; Sandi Kato-Klutke, Aston Kauai Beach Villa; Barbara Sheehan, Sheraton Moana Surfrider; Aston Hotels; Norm Manzione, Suntrips; Renee Cochran and Will Titus, Colony Resorts; Linda Darling-Mann, a helpful Kauai friend; Sonia Franzel, Public Relations; Alexander Doyle, Aston Wailea Resort. To all of you, my deepest *aloha*.

HELP MAKE THIS A BETTER BOOK

In today's world, things change so rapidly that it's impossible for one person to keep up with everything happening in any one place. This is particularly true in Hawaii, where situations are always in flux. Travel books are like automobiles: they require fine tuning and frequent overhauls to keep in shape. Help us keep this book in shape! We require input from our readers so that we can continue to provide the best, most current information available. Please write to let us know about any inaccuracies, new information, or misleading suggestions. Although we try to make our maps as accurate as possible, errors do occur. If you have any suggestions for improvement or places that should be included, please let us know about them.

We especially appreciate letters from female travelers, visiting expatriates, local residents, and hikers and outdoor enthusiasts. We also like hearing from experts in the field as well as from local hotel owners and individuals wishing to accommodate visitors from abroad.

If you take a photograph during your trip that you feel might be included in future editions, please send it to us. Send only good slide duplicates or glossy black-and-white prints. Drawings and other artwork are also appreciated. If we use your photo or drawing, you'll be mentioned in the credits and receive a free copy of the book. Keep in mind, however, that the publisher cannot return any materials unless you include a self-addressed, stamped envelope. Moon Publications will own the rights on all material submitted. Address your letter to:

Maui Handbook
Moon Travel Handbooks
P.O. Box 3040
Chico, CA 95927-3040 USA
e-mail: travel@moon.com

INTRODUCTION

The *Kumulipo,* the ancient genealogical chant of the Hawaiians, sings of the demigod Maui, a half-human mythological sorcerer known and revered throughout Polynesia. Maui was a prankster on a grand scale who used guile and humor to create some of the most amazing feats of derring-do ever recorded. A Polynesian combination of Paul Bunyan and Hercules, Maui's adventures were known as "strifes." He served mankind by fishing up the islands of Hawaii from the ocean floor, securing fire from a tricky mud hen, lifting the sky so humans could walk upright, and slowing down the sun god by lassoing his genitals with a braided rope of his sister's pubic hair. Maui accomplished this last feat on the summit of the great mountain Haleakala ("House of the Sun"), thus securing more time in the day to fish and to dry tapa. Maui met his just but untimely end between the legs of the great goddess, Hina. This final prank, in which he attempted to crawl into the sleeping goddess's vagina, left his feet and legs dangling out, causing uproarious laughter among his comrades, a band of warrior birds. The noise awakened Hina, who saw no humor in the situation. She unceremoniously squeezed Maui to death. The island of Maui is the only island in Hawaii and throughout Polynesia named after a god. With such a legacy the island couldn't help but become worthy of the moniker *"Maui no ka oi"* ("Maui is the best!").

AN OVERVIEW

In a land of superlatives, it's quite a claim to call your island *the* best, but Maui has a lot to back it up. Maui has more miles of swimmable beach than any of the other islands. Haleakala, the massive mountain that *is* East Maui, is the largest dormant volcano in the world, and its hardened lava rising over 30,000 feet from the sea floor makes it one of the heaviest concentrated masses on the face of the earth. There are legitimate claims that Maui grows the best onions and potatoes, but the boast of the best *pakalolo* may only be a pipe dream, since all islands have great soil, weather, and many enterprising gardeners. Some even claim that Maui gets more sunshine than the other islands, but that's hard to prove.

West Maui
If you look at the silhouette of Maui on a map, it looks like the head and torso of the mythical demigod bent at the waist and contemplating the

West Maui Mountains

ROBERT NILSEN

uninhabited island of Kahoolawe. The head is West Maui, and its profile is that of a wizened old man whose wrinkled brow and cheeks are the West Maui Mountains. The highest peak here is **Puu Kukui,** at 5,788 feet, located just about where the ear would be. If you go to the top of the head you'll be at Kapalua, a resort community recently carved from pineapple fields. Fleming Beach begins a string of beaches that continues down over the face, stopping at the chin, and picking up again on the chest, which is South Maui. Kaanapali is located at the forehead; its massive beach continues almost uninterrupted for four miles, an area that in comparison would take in all of Waikiki, from Diamond Head to Ala Moana. Sugarcane fields fringe the mountain side of the road, while condos are strung along the shore. The resorts here are cheek to jowl, but the best are tastefully done with uninterrupted panoramic views and easy and plentiful access to the beach.

Lahaina is located at the Hindu "third eye." This town is where it's "happening" on Maui, with concentrations of craftspeople, artists, museums, historical sites, restaurants, and nightspots. Used in times past by royal Hawaiian *ali'i* and then by Yankee whalers, Lahaina has always been somewhat of a playground, and the good-times mystique still lingers. It's from Lahaina, across the waters of the Auau Channel, better known as the "Lahaina Roads," that people can catch a glimpse of the island of Lanai. At the tip of the nose is Olowalu, where a lunatic Yankee trader, Simon

Metcalf, decided to slaughter hundreds of curious Hawaiians paddling toward his ship just to show them he was boss. From Olowalu you can see four islands: Molokai, Lanai, Kahoolawe, and a faint hint of Hawaii far to the south. The back of Maui's head is an adventurer's paradise. Back here are tremendous coastal views, bird sanctuaries, *heiau,* and Kahakuloa, a tiny fishing village reported to be a favorite stomping ground of great Maui himself.

Central Maui: The Isthmus
A low, flat isthmus planted primarily in sugarcane is the neck that connects the head of West Maui to the torso of East Maui, which is Haleakala. The Adam's apple is the little port of Maalaea, which has a good assortment of pleasure and fishing boats as well as the new Maui Ocean Center; Maalaea provides an up-close look at a working port not nearly as frenetic as Lahaina. The nape of the neck is made up of the twin cities of Wailuku, the county seat, and Kahului, where visitors arrive at Maui's airport. These towns are where the "people" live. Some say the isthmus, dramatically separating east and west, is the reason Maui is called "The Valley Isle." Head into Iao Valley from Wailuku, where the West Maui Mountains have been worn into incredible peaked monolithic spires. This stunning valley area played a key role in Kamehameha's unification of the Hawaiian Islands, and geologically seems to be a more fitting reason for Maui's nickname.

East Maui/Haleakala

Once you cross the isthmus you're on the immensity of Haleakala, the one mountain that makes up the entire bulging, muscled torso of the island. A continent in microcosm, its geology encompasses alpine terrain, baking desert, moonscape, blazing jungle, pastureland, and lava-encrusted wasteland. The temperature, determined by altitude, ranges from subfreezing to subtropical. If you head east along the spine, you'll find world-class sailboarding beaches, artist villages, last-picture-show towns, and a few remaining family farms planted in taro. Route 360, the only coastal road, rocks and rolls you over more than 600 curves and shows you more waterfalls and pristine pools than you can count. After crossing more than 50 bridges, you come to Hana. Here, the dream Hawaii that people seek still lives. Farther along is Kipahulu, and Oheo Gulch known for its fantastic pools and waterfalls. Close by is where Charles Lindbergh is buried, and many celebrities have chosen the surrounding hillsides for their special retreats and hideaways.

On Haleakala's broad chest are macho cowboy towns complete with Wild West rodeos contrasting with the gentle but riotous colors of carnation and protea farms. Polipoli Spring State Park is here, a thick forest canopy with more varieties of imported trees than anywhere else in Oceania. A weird cosmic joke places Kihei just about where the armpit would be. Kihei is a mega-growth condo area ridiculed as an example of what developers shouldn't be allowed to do. Oddly enough, Wailea, just down the road, exemplifies a reasonable and aesthetic planned community and is highly touted as a "model" development area. Just at the belly button, close to the Kundalini, is Makena, long renowned as Maui's alternative beach, but rapidly losing its status as the island's last "free" beach.

Finally, when you pilgrimage to the summit of Haleakala, it'll be as if you've left the planet. It's another world: beautiful, mystical, raw, inspired, and freezing cold. When you're alone on the crater rim with the world below garlanded by the brilliance of sunrise or sunset, you'll know that you have come at last to great Maui's heart.

THE LAND

The modern geological theory concerning the formation of the Hawaiian Islands is no less fanciful than the Polynesian legends sung about it. Science maintains that 30 million years ago, while the great continents were being geologically tortured into their rudimentary shapes, the Hawaiian Islands were a mere ooze of bubbling magma 20,000 feet below the surface of the primordial sea. For millions of years this molten rock flowed up through fissures in the sea floor. Slowly, layer upon layer of lava was deposited until an island rose above the surface of the sea. The island's great weight then sealed the fissures, whose own colossal forces progressively crept in a southwesterly direction, then burst out again and again to build the chain. At the same time the entire Pacific plate was afloat on the giant sea of molten magma, and it slowly glided to the northwest, carrying the newly formed islands with it.

In the beginning the spewing crack formed Kure and Midway islands in the extreme northwestern sector of the Hawaiian chain. Today, more than 130 islands, islets, and shoals make up the Hawaiian Islands, stretching 1,600 miles across an expanse of the North Pacific. Geologists maintain that the hot spot now primarily under the Big Island remains relatively stationary, and that the 1,600-mile spread of the Hawaiian archipelago is due to a northwestern drifting effect of about three to five inches per year. Still, with the center of activity under the Big Island, Mauna Loa and Kilauea volcanoes regularly add more land to the only state in the Union that is literally still growing. About 20 miles southeast of the Big Island is Loihi Seamount, waiting 3,000 feet below the waves. Frequent eruptions bring it closer and closer to the surface; one day it will emerge as the newest Hawaiian island and later, perhaps, merge with the Big Island itself.

Mountains

After the Big Island of Hawaii, Maui is the second largest and second youngest of the main Hawaiian Islands. The land was formed from two volcanoes: the **West Maui Mountains** and **Haleakala**.

MAUI

Maui

Kauai
Niihau
Oahu
Molokai
Lanai
Kahoolawe
Maui
Hawaii

Alenuihaha Channel

Hana
360
31
East Maui
Wailua
Keanae
Nahiku
Kaapahu Bay
Kipahulu
HALEAKALA NATIONAL PARK
Koupo
Mt. Haleakala (10,023 ft.)
378
31
Waipio Bay
Ulumalu
360
Makawao
Olinda
365
390
377
Haiku
36
Hali'imaile
Kula
Paia
37
Pukalani
Waiakoa
37
Ulupalakua Ranch
Makilo Bay
311
Pu'unene
Kihei
31
Wailea
KAHULUI
32
38
Waikapu
Makena
30
Maalaea
Maalaea Bay
La Perouse Bay
Kahakuloa
Mokeehia Island
Waiehu
320
Waihee
Molokini Island
Alalakeiki Channel
Honokohau Bay
Poelua Bay
Iao Needle
West Maui
Olowalu
30
Kapalua
Napili
Pu'u Kukui (5,788 ft.)
Lahaina
Kahana
Honolua Bay
Honokowai
1,477 ft.
Kahoolawe Island
Pailolo Channel
Au Au Channel

5 mi
5 km
0
0

© J.D. BISIGNANI AND MOON PUBLICATIONS, INC.

The West Maui Mountains are geologically much older than Haleakala, but the two were joined by subsequent lava flows that formed a connecting low, flat isthmus. **Puu Kukui,** at 5,788 feet, is the tallest peak of the West Maui Mountains. It's the lord of a mountain domain whose old weathered face has been scarred by a series of deep crags, verdant valleys, and inhospitable gorges. Rising over 30,000 feet from the ocean floor, **Haleakala** is by comparison an adolescent with smooth, rounded features looming 10,023 feet above sea level, with a landmass four times larger than West Maui. The two parts of Maui combine to form 727 square miles of land with 120 linear miles of coastline. At its widest, Maui is 26 miles from north to south and 48 miles east to west. The coastline has the largest number of swimmable beaches in Hawaii, and the interior is a miniature continent with almost every conceivable geological feature evident.

Island Builders

The Hawaiians worshipped Madame Pele, the fire goddess whose name translates equally well as "Volcano," "Fire Pit," or "Eruption of Lava." When she was angry, she complained by spitting fire, which cooled and formed land. Volcanologists say that the Islands are huge mounds of cooled basaltic lava surrounded by billions of polyp skeletons that have formed coral reefs. Maui, like all the Hawaiian Islands, is in essence a shield volcano that erupted rather gently, creating an elongated dome much like a turtle shell. Once above sea level, its tremendous weight seals the fissure below. Eventually the giant tube that carried lava to the surface sinks in on itself and forms a caldera, like atop Haleakala, whose huge depression could hold all of Manhattan Island. Wind and water take over and relentlessly sculpt the raw lava into deep crevices and cuts that become valleys. The once-smooth West Maui Mountains are now a mini-mountain range due to this process. Great Haleakala is being chiseled, too, as can be seen in the Kaupo Gap and the valleys of Kipahulu and Keanae.

Lava

Lava flows in two distinct types, for which the Hawaiian names have become universal geological terms: **a'a** and **pahoehoe.** They're easily distinguished in appearance, but chemically they're

lava flow

the same. A'a is extremely rough and spiny, and will quickly tear up your shoes if you do much hiking over it. Also, if you have the misfortune to fall down, you'll immediately know why they call it a'a. Pahoehoe, a billowy, ropy lava resembling burned pancake batter, can mold into fantastic shapes. Examples of both are frequently encountered on various hikes throughout Maui. Other lava oddities that you may spot are peridots (green gemlike stones called "Pele's Diamonds"); clear feldsparlike, white cotton candy called "Pele's Hair"; and gray lichen known as "Hawaiian snow" covering the older flows.

Rivers and Lakes

Maui has no navigable rivers but there are hundreds of streams. Two of the largest are **Palikea Stream,** which runs through Kipahulu Valley forming Oheo Gulch, and **Iao Stream,** which has sculpted the amazing monoliths in Iao Valley. The longest, at 18 miles, is Kalialinui-Waiale Stream, which starts just below the summit of Haleakala, runs through Pukalani, and empties into the ocean near Kahului Airport. A few reservoirs dot the island, but the two largest natural bodies of water are the 41-acre **Kanaha Pond,** on the outskirts of Kahului, and 500-acre **Kealia Pond,** on the southern shore of the isthmus, both major bird and wildlife sanctuaries. Hikers should be aware of the countless streams and rivulets that can quickly turn from trickles to torrents, causing flash floods in valleys that were the height of hospitality only minutes before.

Tsunamis

"Tsunami" is the Japanese word for "tidal wave." It ranks up there with the worst of them in sparking horror in human beings. But if you were to count up all the people in Hawaii who have been swept away by tidal waves in the last 50 years, the toll wouldn't come close to those killed on bicycles in only a few Mainland cities in just five years. A Hawaiian tsunami is actually a seismic sea wave that has been generated by an earthquake that could easily have originated thousands of miles away in South America or Alaska. Some waves have been clocked at speeds up to 500 mph. The safest place during a tsunami, besides high ground well away from beach areas, is out on the open ocean where even an enormous wave is perceived only as a large swell. A tidal wave is only dangerous when it is opposed by land. The worst tsunami to strike Maui in modern times occurred on April 1, 1946. The Hana coast bore the brunt with a tragic loss of many lives as entire villages were swept away. The same tsunami also struck Halawa Valley on the eastern end of Molokai, destroying the valley community.

Earthquakes

These rumblings are also a concern in Hawaii and offer a double threat because they can generate tsunamis. If you ever feel a tremor and are close to a beach, get as far away as fast as possible. Maui very rarely experiences earthquakes, but like the other islands has an elaborate warning system against natural disasters. You will notice loudspeakers high atop poles along many beaches and coastal areas; these warn of tsunamis, hurricanes, and earthquakes. The loudspeakers are tested at 11 a.m. on the first working day of each month. All island telephone books contain a civil defense warning and procedures section with which you should acquaint yourself—note the maps showing which areas traditionally have been inundated by tsunamis, and what procedures to follow in case an emergency occurs.

Environmental Resource Groups

Anyone interested in Hawaii's environmental issues can contact the following for more information: **Earthjustice Legal Defense Fund** (formerly Sierra Club Legal Defense Fund), 223 S. King St., 4th Fl., Honolulu, HI 96813, tel. (808) 599-2436, e-mail: eajushi@igc.apc.org; **Greenpeace,** 1807 Waianuenue Ave., Hilo, HI 96720, tel. (808) 969-9910, Web site www.greenpeace.org; **The Nature Conservancy,** 1116 Smith St., Suite 201, Honolulu, HI 96817, tel. (808) 537-4508, e-mail: TNCH1@aol.com, Web site: www.tnc.org/hawaii; **Rainforest Action Network,** 301 Broadway, Suite A, San Francisco, CA 94133, tel. (415) 398-4404, e-mail: rainforest@ran.org, Web site www.ran.org; **Sierra Club Hawaii Chapter,** 233 Merchant St., 2nd Fl., Honolulu, HI 96813, tel. (808) 538-6616, fax 537-9019, Web site www.hi.sierraclub.org; **Earth Trust,** 25 Kaneohe Bay Dr., Suite 205, Kailua, HI 96734, tel. (808) 254-2866, fax 254-6409, Web site: www.earthtrust.org.

A savvy monthly newsletter that focuses on environmental and political issues facing Hawaii today is *Environment Hawai'i,* 200 Kanoelehua Ave., Suite 103-325, Hilo, HI 96720, tel. (808) 934-0115, fax 934-8321, e-mail: pattum@aloha.net, individual subscription rate $35 per year. The well-researched and concisely written newsletter attempts to be fair to all parties concerned, explaining both sides to most controversies. Short on preaching and long on common sense, *Environment Hawai'i* is an excellent resource for anyone interested in sociopolitical and environmental issues.

For organizations offering environment-conscious tours in Hawaii, see "Ecotourism in Hawaii" under "Other Tours" in the "Getting Around" section of the Out and About chapter.

CLIMATE

Maui has similar weather to the rest of the Hawaiian islands, though some aficionados claim that it gets the most sunshine of all. The weather on

Maui depends more on where you are than on what season it is. The average daily temperature along the coast is about 78° F (25.5° C) in summer and during winter is about 72° F (22° C). On Haleakala summit, the average is 43-50° F (6-10° C). Nights are usually no more than 10 degrees Fahrenheit cooler than days. Since Haleakala is a main feature on Maui, you should remember that altitude drastically affects the weather. Expect an average drop of three degrees for every 1,000 feet of elevation, so at the top, Haleakala is about 30 degrees cooler than at sea level. The lowest temperature ever recorded on Maui was atop Haleakala in 1961, when the mercury dropped well below freezing to a low, low 11° F. In contrast, sunny Kihei has recorded a blistering 98° F.

Maui has wonderful weather and because of near-constant breezes the air is usually clear and clean. Traffic and weather conditions never create smog, but because of burning cane fields Maui air will at times become smoky, a condition that usually rectifies itself in a day when the winds are blowing. On rarer occasions, a volcanic haze, known as VOG, will filter over the island, being blown in from the Big Island. If it's hazy, doesn't smell of smoke, and nothing has been burning, it's probably VOG.

Precipitation

Rain on Maui is as much a factor as it is elsewhere in Hawaii. On any day, somewhere on Maui it's raining, while other areas experience drought. A dramatic example of this phenomenon is a comparison of Lahaina with Puu Kukui mountain, both on West Maui and separated by only seven miles. Lahaina, which translates as "Merciless Sun," is hot, arid, and gets only 15 inches of rainfall annually, while Puu Kukui can receive close to 500 inches (40 *feet!*) of precipitation. This rivals Mt. Waialeale on Kauai as the wettest spot on earth. Other leeward towns get a comparable amount of rain to Lahaina, but as you move upcountry and around the north coast, the rains become greater. Finally, in Hana, rainfall is about five times as great as on the leeward side, averaging over 80 inches a year. The windward (wet) side of Maui, outlined by the Hana Road, is the perfect natural hothouse. Here, valleys sweetened with blossoms house idyllic waterfalls and pools that visitors treasure when they happen upon them. On the leeward (dry) side are Maui's best beaches: Kapalua, Kaanapali, Kihei, Wailea, and Makena. They all sit in Haleakala's rain shadow. If it happens to be raining at one, just move a few miles down the road to the next. Anyway, the rains are mostly gentle and the brooding sky, especially at sundown, is even more spectacular than normal.

A consequence of the rains are the gorgeous rainbows. Because it's always raining somewhere on Maui, these arched bands of color can be seen anywhere on the island. Caused by light diffused through raindrops or mist in the air, rainbows are usually seen after or during a rain, but may also be spotted in a waterfall. A few lucky ones may also have the fortune of

MAUI AVERAGE
HIGH/LOW TEMPERATURE AND RAINFALL

TOWN		JAN.	MARCH	MAY	JUNE	SEPT.	NOV.
Lahaina	high	80	81	82	83	84	82
	low	62	63	68	68	70	65
	rain	3	1	0	0	0	1
Hana	high	79	79	80	80	81	80
	low	60	60	62	63	65	61
	rain	9	7	2	3	5	7
Kahului	high	80	80	84	86	87	83
	low	64	64	67	69	70	68
	rain	4	3	1	0	0	2

Note: Rainfall in inches; temperature in °F

seeing a full-round rainbow from a helicopter. As lovely as these daytime polychrome bands of color are, nighttime "moonbows," caused by light from the moon are also attractive but somehow ethereal, a real treat.

"So Good" Weather

The ancient Hawaiians had words to describe climatic specifics such as rain, wind, fog, and even snow, but they didn't have a general word for "weather." The reason is that the weather is just about the same throughout the year and depends more on where you are on any given island than on what season it is. The Hawaiians did distinguish between *kau* (summer, May-Oct.) and *hoo'ilo* (winter, Nov.-April), but this distinction included social, religious, and even navigational factors, far beyond a mere distinction of weather variations.

The Trade Winds

Temperatures in the 50th state are both constant and moderate because of the trade winds, a breeze from the northeast that blows at about 5-15 miles per hour. These breezes are so prevailing that the northeast sides of the islands are always referred to as **windward,** regardless of where the wind happens to blow on any given day. You can count on the trades to be blowing on an average of 300 days per year, hardly missing a day during summer, and occurring half the time in winter. While usually calm in the morning, they pick up during the heat of the afternoon, then weaken at night. Just when you need a cooling breeze, there they are, and when the temperature drops at night, it's as if someone turned down a giant fan.

The trade winds are also a factor in keeping down the humidity. They will suddenly disappear, however, usually in winter, and might not resume for a few weeks. The tropic of Cancer runs through the center of Hawaii, yet the latitude's famed oppressively hot and muggy weather is joyfully absent in the islands. Honolulu, on the same latitude as sweaty Hong Kong and Havana, has only a 50-60% daily humidity factor.

Kona Winds

"Kona" means "leeward" in Hawaiian, and when the trades stop blowing, these southerly winds often take over. To anyone from Hawaii, "kona wind" is a euphemism for bad weather, for it brings in hot, sticky air. Luckily, kona winds are most

WHAT IS A HURRICANE?

Tropical Depression: low-pressure system or cyclone with winds below 39 mph.

Tropical Storm: cyclone with winds 39-73 mph.

Hurricane: cyclone with winds over 74 mph. These winds are often accompanied by torrential rains, destructive waves, and storm surges.

The National Weather Service issues a Hurricane Watch if hurricane conditions are expected in the area within 36 hours. A Hurricane Warning is issued when a hurricane is expected to strike within 24 hours. The state of Hawaii has an elaborate warning system against natural disasters. You will notice loudspeakers high atop poles along many beaches and coastal areas; these warn of tsunamis, hurricanes, and earthquakes. As the figures below attest, property damage has been great but the loss of life has, thankfully, been minimal.

Major Hurricanes Since 1950

NAME	DATE	ISLANDS AFFECTED	DAMAGES
Hiki	Aug. 1950	Kauai	1 death
Nina	Dec. 1957	Kauai	—
Dot	Aug. 1959	Kauai	$5.5 million
Fico	July 1978	Hawaii	—
Iwa	Nov. 1982	Kauai, Oahu	1 death; $234 million
Estelle	July 1986	Maui, Hawaii	$2 million
Iniki	Sept. 1992	Kauai, Oahu	8 deaths; $1,900 million

common Oct.-April, when they appear roughly half the time. The temperatures drop slightly during the winter so these hot winds are tolerable, and even useful for moderating the thermometer. In the summer they are awful, but luckily—again—they hardly ever blow during this season.

A "kona storm" is another matter. These subtropical low-pressure storms develop west of the Hawaiian Islands, and as they move east they draw winds up from the south. Usual only in winter, they can cause considerable damage to crops and real estate. There is no real pattern to kona storms—some years they come every few weeks while in other years they don't appear at all.

Severe Weather

With all this talk of ideal weather it might seem as if there isn't any bad. Read on. When a storm does hit an island, conditions can be bleak and miserable. The worst storms occur in the fall and winter and often have the warped sense of humor to drop their heaviest rainfalls on areas that are normally quite dry. It's not infrequent for a storm to dump more than three inches of rain an hour; this can go as high as 10, making Hawaiian rainfalls some of the heaviest on earth.

Hawaii has also been hit with some walloping hurricanes in the last few decades. There haven't been many but they've been destructive. The vast majority of hurricanes originate far to the southeast off the Pacific coasts of Mexico and Latin America; some, particularly later in the season, start in the midst of the Pacific Ocean near the equator south of Hawaii. Hurricane season is generally considered June-November. Most pass harmlessly south of Hawaii but some, swept along by kona winds, strike the islands. The most recent and destructive was Hurricane Iniki, which battered the islands in 1992, killing eight people and causing an estimated $2 billion in damage. It had its greatest effect on Niihau, the Poipu Beach area of Kauai, and the leeward coast of Oahu.

FLORA AND FAUNA

THE MYSTERY OF MIGRATION

Anyone who loves a mystery will be intrigued by the speculation about how plants and animals first came to Hawaii. Most people's idea of an island paradise includes swaying palms, dense mysterious jungles ablaze with wildflowers, and luscious fruits just waiting to be plucked. In fact, for millions of years the Hawaiian chain consisted of raw and barren islands where no plants grew and no birds sang. Why? Because they are geological orphans that spontaneously popped up in the middle of the Pacific Ocean. The islands, more than 2,000 miles from any continental landfall, were therefore isolated from the normal ecological spread of plants and animals. Even the most tenacious travelers of the flora and fauna kingdoms would be sorely tried in crossing the mighty Pacific. Those that made it by pure chance found a totally foreign ecosystem. They had to adapt or perish. The survivors evolved quickly, and many plants and birds became so specialized that they were not only limited to specific islands in the chain but to habitats that frequently encompassed a single isolated valley. It was as if after traveling so far, and finding a niche, they never budged again. Luckily, the soil of Hawaii was virgin and rich, the competition from other plants or animals was nonexistent, and the climate was sufficiently varied and nearly perfect for most growing things.

The evolution of plants and animals on the isolated islands was astonishingly rapid. A tremendous change in environment, coupled with a limited gene pool, accelerated natural selection. For example, many plants lost their protective thorns and spines because there were no grazing animals or birds to destroy them. Before settlement, Hawaii had no fruits, vegetables, coconut palms, edible land animals, conifers, mangroves, or banyans. Tropical flowers, wild and vibrant as we know them today, were relatively few. In a land where thousands of orchids now brighten every corner, there were only four native varieties, the least in any of the 50 states. Today, the indigenous plants and animals have the highest rate of extinction anywhere on earth. By the beginning of this century, native plants growing below 1,500 feet in elevation were almost completely extinct or totally replaced by introduced species. The land and its living things have been greatly transformed by humans and their agriculture. This inexorable process began when Hawaii was the domain of its original Polynesian settlers, then greatly accelerated when the land was inundated by Western peoples.

The indigenous plants and birds of Maui have suffered the same fate as those of the other Hawaiian Islands; they're among the most endangered species on earth and disappearing at an alarming rate. There are some sanctuaries on Maui where native species still live, but they must be vigorously protected. Do your bit to save them; enjoy but do not disturb.

PLANTS, FLOWERS, AND TREES

Hawaii's indigenous and endemic plants, flowers, and trees are both fascinating and beautiful, but unfortunately, like everything else that was native, they are quickly disappearing. The majority of flora considered exotic by visitors was introduced either by the original Polynesians or by later white settlers. The Polynesians who colonized Hawaii brought foodstuffs, including coconuts, bananas, taro, breadfruit, sweet potatoes, yams, and sugarcane. They also carried along gourds to use as containers, *awa* to make a basic intoxicant, and the ti plant to use for offerings or to string into hula skirts. Non-Hawaiian settlers over the years have brought mangos, papayas, passion fruit, pineapples, and the other tropical fruits and vegetables associated with the islands. Also, most of the flowers, including protea, plumeria, anthuriums, orchids, heliconia, ginger, and most hibiscus, have come from every continent on earth. Tropical America, Asia, Java, India, and China have contributed their most beautiful and delicate blooms. Hawaii is blessed with national and state parks, gardens, undisturbed rainforests, private reserves, and commercial nurseries that offer an exhaustive botanical survey of the island. The following is a sampling of the common native and introduced flora that add dazzling color and exotic tastes to the landscape.

Native Trees

Koa and **ohia** are two indigenous trees still seen on Maui. The koa, a form of acacia, is Hawaii's finest native tree. It can grow to over 70 feet high and has a strong, straight trunk that can measure more than 10 feet in circumference. Koa is a quickly growing legume that fixes nitrogen in the soil. It is believed that the tree originated in Africa, where it was very damp. It then migrated to Australia, where it was very dry, which caused the elimination of leaves so that all that was left were bare stems that could survive in the desert climate. When koa came to the Pacific islands, instead of reverting to the true leaf, it just broadened its leaf stem into sickle-shaped, leaflike foliage that produces an inconspicuous, pale yellow flower. When the tree is young or damaged it will revert to the original feathery, fernlike leaf that evolved in Africa millions of years ago. Koa does best in well-drained soil in deep forest areas, but scruffy specimens will grow in poorer soil. The Hawaiians used koa as the main log for their dugout canoes, and elaborate ceremonies were performed when a log was cut and dragged to a canoe shed. Koa wood was also preferred for paddles, spears, even surfboards. Today it is still, unfortunately, considered an excellent furniture wood; and although fine specimens can be found in the reserve of Hawaii Volcanoes National Park on the Big Island, loggers elsewhere are harvesting the last of the big trees.

The ohia is a survivor and therefore the most abundant of all the native Hawaiian trees. Coming in a variety of shapes and sizes, it grows as miniature trees in wet bogs or as 100-foot giants on cool, dark slopes at higher elevations. This tree is often the first life in new lava flows. The ohia produces a tuftlike flower—usually red, but occasionally orange, yellow, or white, the latter being very rare and elusive—that resembles a natural pompon. The flower was considered sacred to Pele; it was said that she would cause a rainstorm if you picked ohia blossoms without the proper prayers. The flowers were fashioned into lei that resembled feather boas. The strong, hard wood was used to make canoes, poi bowls, and especially temple images. Ohia logs were also used as railroad ties and shipped to the Mainland from Pahoa. It's believed that the golden spike linking rail lines between the U.S. East and West Coasts was driven into a Puna ohia log when the two railroads came together in Ogden, Utah.

Silversword

Maui's official flower is a tiny pink rose called a *lokelani*. The island's unofficial symbol, however, is the silversword. The Hawaiian name for silversword is *ahinahina*, which translates as "gray gray," and the English name derives from a silverfish, whose color the plant is said to resemble. The silversword belongs to a remarkable plant family that claims 28 members, with five in the specific silversword species. It's kin to the common sunflower, and botanists say the entire family evolved from a single ancestral species. Hypothetically, the members of the silversword family can interbreed and produce remarkable hybrids. Some plants are shrubs, while others are climbing vines, and some even become trees. They grow anywhere from desert conditions to steamy jungles. On Maui, the silversword is only found on Haleakala, above the 6,000-foot level, and is especially prolific in the crater. Each plant lives from five to 20 years and ends its life by sprouting a gorgeous stalk of hundreds of purplish-red flowers. It then withers from a majestic six-foot plant to a flat gray skeleton. An endangered species, silverswords are totally protected. They protect themselves, too, from radiation and lack of moisture by growing fuzzy hairs all over their swordlike stalks. You can see them along the Haleakala Park Road at **Kalahaku Overlook,** or by hiking along **Silversword Loop** on the floor of the crater.

silversword

DIANA LASICH HARPER

Protea

These exotic flowers are from Australia and South Africa. Because they come in almost limitless shapes, sizes, and colors, they captivate everyone who sees them. They are primitive, almost otherworldly in appearance, and they exude a life force more like an animal than a flower. The slopes of leeward Haleakala between 2,000 and 4,000 feet are heaven to protea—the growing conditions could not be more perfect. Here are found the hardiest, highest-quality protea in the world. The days are warm, the nights are cool, and the well-drained volcanic soil has the exact combination of minerals on which protea thrive. Haleakala's crater even helps by creating a natural air flow that produces cloud cover, filters the sun, and protects the flowers. Protea make excellent gifts that can be shipped anywhere. As fresh-cut flowers they are gorgeous, but they have the extra benefit of drying superbly. Just hang them in a dark, dry, well-ventilated area and they do the rest. You can see protea, along with other botanical specialties, at the gardens, flower farms, and gift shops in Kula.

Carnations

If protea aren't enough to dazzle you, how about fields of carnations? Most Mainlanders think of carnations stuck in a groom's lapel, or perhaps have seen a table dedicated to them in a hothouse, but not fields full of carnations! The Kula area produces carnations that grow outside nonchalantly, in rows, like cabbages. They fill the air with their unmistakable perfume, and they are without doubt a joy to behold. You can see family and commercial plots throughout the upper Kula area.

Prickly Pear Cactus

Interspersed in countless fields and pastures on the windward slope of Haleakala, adding that final nuance to cattle country, are clusters of prickly pear cactus. The Hawaiians call them *panini,* which translates as "very unfriendly," undoubtedly because of the sharp spines covering the flat, thick leaves. These cactus are typical of those found in Mexico and the southwestern United States. They were introduced to Hawaii before 1810 and established themselves, coincidentally, in conjunction with the cattle being brought in at that time. It's assumed that Don Marin, a Spanish advisor to Kamehameha I, was responsible for importing the plant. Perhaps the early *paniolo* felt lonely without them. The *panini* can grow to heights of 15 feet and are now considered a pest, but nonetheless look as if they belong. They develop small pear-shaped fruits that are quite delicious. Hikers who decide to pick them should be careful of small yellowish bristles that can burrow under the skin and become very irritating. The fruits turn into beautiful yellow and orange flowers. An attempt is being made to control the cactus in *paniolo* country. *El cosano rojo,* the red worm found in the bottom of Mexican tequila, has been introduced to destroy the plant. It burrows into the cactus and eats the hardwood center, causing the plant to wither and die.

prickly pear cactus

DIANA LASICH HARPER

Lobelia

More species of lobelia grow in Hawaii than anywhere else in the world. A common garden flower elsewhere, in Hawaii it grows to tree height. You'll see some unique species covered with hair or with spikes. The lobelia flower is tiny and resembles a miniature orchid with curved and pointed ends, like the beak of the native *'i'iwi.* This bird feeds on the flower's nectar; it's obvious that both evolved in Hawaii together and exhibit the strange phenomenon of nature mimicking nature.

Tropical Rainforests

When it comes to pure and diverse natural beauty, the U.S. is one of the finest pieces of real estate on earth. As if purple mountains' majesty and fruited plains weren't enough, it even received a tiny, living emerald of tropical rainforest. A tropical rainforest is where the earth takes a breath and exhales pure sweet oxygen through its vibrant green canopy. Located in the territories of Puerto Rico and the Virgin Islands, and in the state of Hawaii, these forests comprise only one-half of one percent of the world's total, and they must be preserved. The U.S. Congress passed two bills in 1986 designed to protect the unique biological diversity of its tropical areas, but their destruction has continued unabated. The lowland rainforests of Hawaii, populated mostly by native ohia, are being razed. Landowners slash, burn, and bulldoze them to create more land for cattle and agriculture, and, most distressingly, for wood chips to generate electricity! Introduced wild boar gouge the forest floor, exposing sensitive roots and leaving tiny

fetid ponds where mosquito larvae thrive. Feral goats roam the forests like hoofed locusts and strip all vegetation within reach. Rainforests on the higher and steeper slopes of mountains have a better chance as they are harder for humans to reach. One unusual feature of Hawaii's rainforests is that they are "upside down." Most plant and animal species live on the forest floor, rather than in the canopy as in other forests.

Maui's Nature Conservancy Preserve in Waikamoi has managed to fence in a speck of this forest, keeping it safe from these animals for the time being. Almost half the birds classified in the U.S. as endangered live in Hawaii, and almost all of these make their homes in the rainforests. For example, Maui's rainforests have yielded the *poouli,* a new species of bird discovered only in 1974. Another forest survey in 1981 rediscovered the Bishop's *'o'o,* a bird thought to be extinct at the turn of the century. We can only lament the passing of the rainforests that have already fallen to ignorance, but if this ill-fated destruction continues on a global level, we will be lamenting our own passing. We must nurture the rainforests that remain, and with simple enlightenment, let them be.

BIRDS

One of the great tragedies of natural history is the continuing demise of Hawaiian birdlife. Perhaps only 15 original species of birds remain of the more than 70 native families that thrived before the coming of humans. Since the arrival of Captain Cook in 1778, 23 species have become extinct, with 31 more in danger. And what's not known is how many species were wiped out before the coming of white explorers. Experts believe that the Hawaiians annihilated about 40 species, including seven other species of geese besides the *nene,* a rare one-legged owl, ibis, lovebirds, sea eagles, and hunting creepers—all gone before Captain Cook arrived. Hawaii's endangered

BOTANICAL GARDENS
AND FOREST AREAS OF MAUI

Kula Botanical Gardens, tel. (808) 878-1715, has nearly 2,000 varieties of tropical and semitropical plants, including orchids, bromeliads, fuchsia, protea, *kukui* and sandalwood trees, and numerous ferns, on over five acres. Located at 3,300 feet in elevation near the junction of Rt. 377 (Kekaulike Ave.) and Rt. 37 at the south end, this privately owned garden is open daily 0 a.m.–4 p.m. for self-guided tours; $4 entrance fee.

Enchanting Floral Gardens, tel. (808) 878-2531, is located along Rt. 37 just south of Pukalani at mile marker 10. This private garden features about 1,500 species of native Hawaiian plants as well as exotic plants from around the world on eight acres. Open 9 a.m.-5 p.m. for self-guided tours; admission $4.

University of Hawaii Experimental Station offers 20 acres of constantly changing, quite beautiful plants, although the grounds are uninspired, scientific, rectangular plots. Located on Mauna Place just off Copp Rd. above Rt. 37 in Kula, this garden is open Mon.-Thurs. 7:30 a.m.-3:30 p.m., closed for lunch. Although admission is free, visitors should check in with the station manager.

Keanae Arboretum, above Keanae Peninsula on the Hana Hwy. (Rt. 360), is always open. In a natural setting with walkways, many identifying markers, and mosquitoes, this six-acre arboretum is split into two sections: ornamental tropical plants and Hawaiian domestic plants. The native forest swathes the surrounding hillsides. No fee.

Kahanu Gardens, tel. (808) 284-8912, a branch of the Pacific Tropical Botanical Gardens, is located on the rugged lava coast east of Hana at the site of Piilanihale Heiau. In this 120-acre garden, you'll find stands of breadfruit and coconut trees, a pandanus grove, and numerous other tropical plants from throughout the world. Open for two-hour guided tours daily at 1 p.m. for $10 per person; call for reservations.

Polipoli Spring State Recreation Area is the finest Upcountry camping and trekking area on Maui. At the south end of Rt. 377, turn onto Waipoli Rd. for 10 miles of bad road. Overnight camping is recommended. Native and introduced birds, and magnificent stands of redwoods, eucalyptus, conifers, ash, cypress, cedar, and *sugi* and other pines may be found here. This area is known for delicious methley plums, which ripen in early June. For camping information contact Division of State Parks in Wailuku, tel. (808) 984-8109.

Hosmer Grove, within Haleakala National Park at 6,800 feet in elevation, is an experimental forest project from the early 20th century. Here are fine examples of introduced trees like cedar, pine, fir, juniper, and *sugi* pine that were originally planted in hopes of finding a commercial, economically marketable wood for Hawaii. A short trail now winds through the no-longer-orderly stands of trees. Ranger-guided tours are offered periodically. For more information, contact the Haleakala National Park Headquarters, tel. (808) 572-9306.

birds account for 40% of the birds officially listed as endangered or threatened by the U.S. Fish and Wildlife Service. In the last 200 years, more than four times as many birds have become extinct in Hawaii as in all of North America. These figures unfortunately suggest that a full 40% of Hawaii's endemic birds no longer exist. Almost all of Oahu's native birds are gone and few indigenous Hawaiian birds can be found on any island below the 3,000-foot level.

Native birds have been reduced in number because of multiple factors. The original Polynesians helped wipe out many species. They altered large areas for farming, and used fire to destroy patches of pristine forests. Also, bird feathers were highly prized for the making of lei, for featherwork in capes and helmets, and for the large *kahili* fans that indicated rank among the *ali'i*. Introduced exotic birds and the new diseases they carried are another major reason for reduction of native bird numbers, along with predation by the mongoose and rat—especially upon ground-nesting birds. Bird malaria and bird pox were also devastating to the native species. Mosquitoes, unknown in Hawaii until a ship named the *Wellington* introduced them at Lahaina in 1826 through larvae carried in its water barrels, infected most native birds, causing a rapid reduction in birdlife. Feral pigs rooting deep in the rainforests knock over ferns and small trees, creating fetid pools in which mosquito larvae thrive. However, the most damaging factor by far is the assault upon native forests by agriculture and land developers. The vast majority of Hawaiian birds evolved into specialists. They lived in only one small area and ate a very limited number of plants or insects, which once removed or altered soon killed the birds.

You'll spot birds all over Maui, from the coastal areas to the high mountain slopes. Some are found on other islands as well, but the ones listed below are found only or mainly on Maui. Every bird listed is either threatened or endangered.

Maui's Endangered Birds

Maui's native birds are disappearing. The island is the last home of the crested honeycreeper *(akohe'kohe)*, which lives only on the windward slope of Haleakala from 4,500 to 6,500 feet. It once lived on Molokai, but no longer. It's rather a large bird, averaging over seven inches long, and predominantly black. Its throat and breast are tipped with gray feathers, and it has bright orange on its neck and underbelly. A distinctive fluff of feathers forms a crown. It primarily eats ohia flowers, and it's believed that the crown feathers gather pollen and help to propagate the ohia. The parrotbill is another endangered bird, found only on the slopes of Haleakala above 5,000 feet. It has an olive-green back and a yellow body. Its most distinctive feature is its parrotlike bill, which it uses to crack branches and pry out larvae.

Two waterbirds found on Maui are the Hawaiian stilt *(ae'o)* and the Hawaiian coot *(alae ke'oke'o)*. The stilt is about 16 inches tall and lives on Maui at Kanaha and Kealia ponds. Primarily black with a white belly, its sticklike legs are pink. The adults will pretend to be hurt, putting on an excellent performance of the "broken wing" routine, in order to lure predators away

from their nests. The Hawaiian coot is a webfooted waterbird that resembles a duck. It's found on all the main islands but mostly on Maui and Kauai. Mostly a dull gray, it has a white bill and tail feathers. It builds a large floating nest and vigorously defends its young.

The dark-rumped petrel is slightly different from other primarily marine birds. This petrel is found around the visitors center at Haleakala Crater about one hour after dusk from May through October. The *amakihi* and the *'i'iwi* are endemic birds that aren't endangered at the moment. The *amakihi* is one of the most common native birds. It's yellowish-green, and it frequents the high branches of ohia, koa, and sandalwood looking for insects, nectar, or fruit. It's less specialized than most other Hawaiian birds, the main reason for its continued existence. The *'i'iwi* is a bright red bird with a salmon-colored hooked bill. It's found on Maui, Hawaii, and Kauai in forests above 2,000 feet. It, too, feeds on a variety of insects and flowers. The *'i'iwi* is known for its harsh voice, which sounds like a squeaking hinge, but it is also capable of a melodious song.

The *poouli* is a dark brown, five-inch bird with a black mask and dark brown feet. Its tail is short, and it sports a conical bill. It was saved from extinction through efforts of the Sierra Club and Audubon Society, who successfully had it listed on the Federal List of Endangered Species. The bird has one remaining stronghold deep in the forests of Maui.

Other indigenous birds found on Maui are the wedge-tailed shearwater, the white-tailed tropic bird, the black noddy, the American plover, and a large variety of escaped exotic birds.

Pueo

This Hawaiian owl is found on all of the main islands, but mostly on Maui, especially in Haleakala Crater. The *pueo* is one of the oldest examples of an *aumakua* (family-protecting spirit) in Hawaiian mythology. It was an especially benign and helpful guardian. Old Hawaiian stories abound where a *pueo* came to the aid of a warrior in distress or a defeated army, which would head for a tree in which a *pueo* had alighted. Once there, they were safe from their pursuers and were under the protection of "the wings of an owl." There are many introduced barn owls in Hawaii, easily distinguished from a *pueo* by their distinctive heart-shaped faces. The *pueo* is about 15 inches tall with a mixture of brown and white feathers. The eyes are large, round, and yellow, and the legs are heavily feathered, unlike a barn owl. *Pueo* chicks are a distinct yellow color.

The *Nene*

The *nene*, or Hawaiian goose, deserves special mention because it is Hawaii's state bird and is making a comeback from the edge of extinction. The *nene* is found only on the slopes of Mauna Loa, Hualalai, and Mauna Kea on the Big Island, and in Haleakala Crater on Maui. It was extinct on Maui until a few birds were returned there in 1957, but some experts maintain that the *nene* lived naturally only on the Big Island. *Nene* are raised at the Wildfowl Trust in Slimbridge, England, which placed the first birds at Haleakala, and at the Hawaiian Fish and Game Station at Pohakuloa, along the Saddle Road on Hawaii. By the 1940s, fewer than 50 birds lived in the wild. Now approximately 125 birds live on Haleakala and 500 on the Big Island. Although the birds can be raised successfully in captivity, their life in the wild is still in question.

The nene (Hawaiian goose and the state bird) lives only on Haleakala and on the slopes of Mauna Loa and Mauna Kea on the Big Island.

The *nene* is believed to be a descendant of the Canada goose, which it resembles. Geese are migratory birds that form strong kinship ties, mating for life. It's speculated that a migrating goose became disabled and, along with its loyal mate, remained in Hawaii. The *nene* is smaller than its Canadian cousin, has lost a great deal of webbing in its feet, and is perfectly at home away from water, foraging and nesting on rugged and bleak lava flows. The *nene* is a perfect symbol of Hawaii: let it be, and it will live.

OTHER HAWAIIAN ANIMALS

Hawaii had only two indigenous mammals, the monk seal or *'ilio holu I ka uaua* (found throughout the islands) and the hoary bat (found primarily on the Big Island); both are threatened or endangered. Recently, a second species of bat (now extinct) was identified from bone fragments taken from caves on four of the Hawaiian Islands. The remainder of Maui's mammals are transplants. But like anything else, including people, that has been in the islands long enough, they take on characteristics that make them "local." There are no native amphibians or reptiles, ants, termites, or cockroaches. All are imported.

The **Hawaiian hoary bat** *(ope'ape'a)* is a cousin of the Mainland bat, a strong flier that made it to Hawaii eons ago and developed its own species. Its tail has a whitish coloration, hence the name. Small populations of the bat are found on Maui and Kauai, but most are on the Big Island. The hoary bat has a 13-inch wingspan and, unlike other bats, is a solitary creature, roosting in trees. It gives birth to twins in early summer and can often be spotted darting over a number of bays just around sundown.

Feral dogs *(ilio)* are found on all the islands but especially on the slopes of Mauna Kea on the Big Island, where packs chase feral sheep. Poisoned and shot by local ranchers, the *ilio* population is diminishing. Black dogs, thought to be more tender, are still eaten in some Hawaiian and Filipino communities.

Drosophila, the Hawaiian Fly

Most people hardly pay attention to flies, unless one lands on the plate lunch. But geneticists from throughout the world, and especially from the University of Hawaii, make special pilgrimages to the volcano area of the Big Island and to Maui just to study the native Hawaiian drosophila. This critter is related to the fruit fly and housefly, but there are hundreds of native species that are singularly unique—over one-third of the world's estimated total. The Hawaiian ecosystem is very simple and straightforward, so geneticists can trace the evolutionary changes from species to subspecies through mating behavior. The scientists compare the species between the two islands and chart the differences. Major discoveries in evolutionary genetics have been made through these studies.

Coral

Whether you're an avid scuba diver or novice snorkeler, you'll become aware of Maui's underwater coral gardens and grottoes whenever you peer at the fantastic seascapes below the waves. Although there is plenty of it, the coral in Hawaii doesn't do as well as in other more equatorial areas because the water is too wild and it's not quite as warm. Coral looks like a plant fashioned from colorful stone, but it's the skeleton of tiny animals, zoophytes, which need algae in order to live. Coral grows best on the west side of Maui where the water is quite still, the days more sunny, and where the algae can thrive. Many of Hawaii's reefs have been dying in the last 20 years, and no one seems to know why. Pesticides, used in agriculture, have been pointed to as a possible cause.

WHALES

Perhaps it's their tremendous size and graceful power, coupled with a dancer's delicacy of movement, that render whales so esthetically and emotionally captivating. In fact, many people claim that they even feel a spirit-bond to these obviously intelligent mammals that at one time shared dry land with us and then re-evolved into creatures of the great seas. Experts often remark that whales exhibit behavior akin to the highest social virtues. For example, whales rely much more on learned behavior than on instinct, the sign of a highly evolved intelligence. Gentle mothers and protective escort males join to teach the young to survive. They display loyalty and bravery in times of distress, and innate gentleness and curiosity. Their songs, especially those of the humpbacks, fascinate scientists and are considered a unique form of communication in the animal kingdom. Humpback whales migrate to Hawaii every year Nov.-May. Here, they winter, mate, give birth, and nurture their young until returning to food-rich northern waters in the spring. It's hoped that mankind can peacefully share the oceans with these magnificent giants forever. Then, perhaps, we will have taken the first step in saving ourselves.

Evolution and Socialization

Many millions of years ago, for an unknown reason, animals similar to cows were genetically triggered to leave the land and readapt to the sea—their closest land relative is the hippo. Known as cetaceans, this order contains about 80 species of whales, porpoises, and dolphins. Being mammals, cetaceans are warm-blooded and maintain a body temperature of 96°, only 2.5 degrees lower than humans. After a gestation period of about one year, whales give birth to fully formed young, which usually enter the world tail first. The mother whale spins quickly to snap the umbilical cord, then places herself under the newborn and lifts it to the surface to take its first breath. A whale must be taught to swim or it will drown like any other air-breathing mammal. The baby whale, nourished by its mother's rich milk, becomes a member of an extended family, or pod, through which it's cared for, socialized, and protected by many "nannies."

Physiology

The best way to spot a whale is to look for its spout, a misty spray forced from a blowhole—really the whale's nostrils, which have moved from its snout to just behind its head. The spray from the spout is not water, but highly compressed air heated by the whale's body and expelled with such force that it condenses into a fine mist. A whale's tail is called a fluke; unlike the vertical tail of fish, a whale's tail is horizontal. The fluke, a marvelous appendage for propelling the whale through the water, is a vestige of the pelvis. It's so powerful that a 40-ton humpback can lift itself completely out of the water with only three strokes of its fluke. A whale's flippers are used to guide it through the water. The bones in the flippers closely resemble those of the human arm and hand; small delicate bones at the ends of the flippers look like fingers and joints. On a humpback the flippers can be one-third as long as the body and supple enough to bend over its back, like a human reaching over the shoulder to scratch an itch.

A whale's eyes are functional but very small and not the primary sensors. Instead, the whale has developed keen hearing; the ears are small holes about as big around as the lead of a pencil. They have protective wax plugs that build up over the years. Like the growth rings in a tree, the ear plugs can be counted to determine the age of a whale; its life span is about the same as that of a human being. Because of strong ocean currents, and because of the myriad dangers inherent to being at sea, whales enjoy a very light sleep, more like a rest similar to humans just awakening, a state that is not fully conscious but aware. Dolphins are the smallest cetaceans and spend only 30% of their time feeding, with the rest given to leisure and social activities. They have evolved sleep patterns even further, and almost *never* sleep. In a constant soothing and revitalizing alpha wave state, much like meditation, they refresh themselves with only two or three minutes in a 24-hour period of what we would call sleep. And even then, they sleep literally with one eye open, resting the corresponding half of their brain, while the other eye and half of their brain stay alert for danger.

Types of Whales

Although all whales, dolphins, and porpoises are cetaceans, they are arbitrarily divided according to length. Whales are all those animals longer than 30 feet; dolphins range from six to 30 feet; and porpoises are less than six feet long. There are basically two types of whales: toothed, which includes the sperm, killer, and pilot whales, as well as porpoises and dolphins; and baleen, including the blue, minke, right, fin, and humpback. Toothed whales feed by capturing and tearing their prey with their teeth. The killer whale or orca is the best known of the toothed whales. With its distinctive black-and-white markings and propensity for aquabatics, it's a favorite at marine parks around the world. The orca hunts other cetaceans, oftentimes attacking in packs to overcome larger whales. A killer whale in the wild lives about four times as long as one in captivity, even if it is well cared for. A baleen whale eats by gliding through the water with its mouth open, sucking in marine plankton and tiny shrimplike creatures called krill. The whale then expels the water and captures the food in row after row of a prickly, fingernail-like substance called baleen.

Hawaiian Whales and Dolphins

The role of whales and dolphins in Hawaiian culture seems quite limited. Unlike fish, which were intimately known and individually named, only two generic names described whales: *kohola* (whale) and *palaoa* (sperm whale). Dolphins were all lumped together under one name, *nai'a;* Hawaiians were known to harvest dolphins on occasion by herding them onto a beach. Whale jewelry was worn by the ali'i. The most coveted ornament came from a sperm whale's tooth, called a *lei niho palaoa,* which was carved into one large curved pendant. Sperm whales have upward of 50 teeth, ranging in size from four to 12 inches and weighing up to two pounds. One whale could provide numerous pendants. The most famous whale in Hawaiian waters is the humpback, but others often sighted include the sperm, killer, false killer, pilot, Cuvier's, Blainville's, and pygmy killer. There are technically no porpoises, but dolphins include the common, bottlenose, spinner, white-sided, broad- and slender-beaked, and rough-toothed. The mahimahi, a favorite eating fish found on many menus, is commonly referred to as a dolphin but is unrelated and is a true fish, not a cetacean.

The Humpbacks of Maui

Humpbacks get their name from their style of exposing their dorsal fin when they dive, which gives them a humped appearance. Their dorsal fin also puts them into the **roqual** family. There are about 10,000 humpback whales alive today, down from an estimated 100,000 at the turn of the century. The remaining whales are divided into three separate global populations: North Atlantic, North Pacific, and South Pacific groups. About 2,000 North Pacific hump-

the humpback whale

backs migrate from coastal Alaska beginning in November. Migration peaks in February, when humpbacks congregate mostly in the waters off Maui, with smaller groups heading for the waters off the other islands. In 1992, the **Hawaiian Islands Humpback Whale National Marine Sanctuary** was designated, encompassing waters off all six major islands. This will hopefully ensure a perpetual safe haven for the whales.

Adult humpbacks average 45 feet long and weigh in at a svelte 40 tons (80,000 pounds) or more. They come to Hawaii mainly to give birth to 2,000-pound, relatively blubberless calves, most of which are born by the end of January. They nurse their calves for about one year and become impregnated again the next. While in Hawaiian waters humpbacks generally don't eat. They wait until returning to Alaska, where they gorge themselves on krill. It's estimated that they can live off their blubber without peril for six months. They have an enormous mouth filled with over 600 rows of baleen stretching one-third the length of their bodies. Humpbacks have been known to blow air underwater to create giant bubble-nets that help corral krill. They rush in with mouths agape and dine on their catch.

Like other baleen whales, humpbacks feed in relatively shallow waters and sound (dive) for periods lasting a maximum of about 25 minutes. In comparison, the sperm whale, a toothed bottom-feeder, can stay down for over an hour. On the surface a humpback will breathe about once every two minutes. They also sleep on the surface or just below it for two hours.

A distinctive feature of the humpback is the 15-foot flipper that it can bend over its back. The flippers and tail flukes have white markings that differ between individuals, much like human fingerprints. These markings are used to identify individual migrating humpbacks. Scientists photograph the distinctive tails and send prints to Seattle, Washington, a center of whale research. There a computer analysis is done to identify the individual or to record it as a new specimen. Thereafter, any sightings become part of its life history. The humpback is the most aquabatic of all whales, and it is a thrilling sight to see one of these agile giants leap from the water and create a monumental splash.

The Humpback's Song

Humpbacks have a special ability to sing unlike other whales. They create their melodies by grunt-ing, shrieking, and moaning. No one knows exactly what the songs represent, but it's clear they're a definite form of communication. The singers appear to be escort males that tag along with, and seem to guard, a mother and her calf. Some scientists believe that these are lone males and perhaps the song is territorial, or a mating call. The songs are exact renditions that last 20 minutes or longer and are repeated for hours. Amazingly, all the whales know and sing the same song, and the song changes from year to year. The notes are so forceful that they can be heard above and below the water for miles. Some of the deep bass notes will even carry underwater for 100 miles.

Good recordings of the humpbacks' songs can be heard aboard the *Carthaginian II,* a restored 19th-century square-rigged ship just to the right of the loading dock in Lahaina Harbor. It serves as a floating museum dedicated to whales and whaling. As you descend into the ship's hold and bright sunlight fades to cool shadow, you become a visitor in the watery world of the humpback whale. The mysterious songs of the humpback provide the background music and set the mood. Sit on comfortable captain's chairs and watch the excellent audiovisual display. The photos of whales are by Flip Nicklin, courtesy of the National Geographic Society.

Whaling History

Humans have known about whales for many thousands of years. A Minoan palace on the island of Crete depicts whales on a 5,000-year-old mural. The first whalers were probably Norwegians who used stone harpoon heads to capture their prey over 4,000 years ago. Inuit have long engaged in whaling as a means of survival, and for centuries many peoples living along coastal waters have harpooned migrating whales that ventured close to shore. The Basques had a thriving medieval whaling industry in the 12th century centered in the Bay of Biscay, until they wiped out all the Biscayan right whales. The height of the classic whaling industry that inspired Melville's *Moby Dick* occurred 1820-60. The international whaling capital perfectly situated in the center of the winter whaling grounds was Lahaina, Maui. At that time 900 sailing ships roamed the globe in search of whales. Of these, 700 were American, and they started the trend away from coastal to pelagic whaling by bringing their try-pots (blubber pots) aboard ship.

Although the killing was great during these years, every part of the whale was needed and used: blubber, meat, bone, teeth. Whale oil, the main product, was a superior lighting fuel and lubricant unmatched until petroleum came into general use in the mid-19th century. Today, every single whale by-product can be manufactured synthetically and there's absolutely no primary need to justify slaughtering whales.

During the great whaling days, the whales actually had a fighting chance. After all, they were hunted by men in wooden sailing ships that depended upon favorable winds. Once sighted by a sailor perched high in the rigging using a low-powered telescope, a small boat heaved off; after desperate rowing and dangerous maneuvering, the master harpooner threw his shaft by hand. When the whale was dead it took every able-bodied man to haul it in.

Today, however, modern methods have wiped out every trace of daring and turned the hunt into technologically assisted slaughter. Low-flying aircraft radio the whales' location to huge factory-ships that track them with radar and sonar. Once the pod is spotted, super-swift launches tear into them, firing cannon-propelled harpoons with lethal exploding tips. The killer launches keep firing until every whale in the pod is dead, and the huge factory boat follows behind merely scooping up the lifeless carcasses and hauling them aboard with diesel winches.

Many pirate whalers still roam the seas. The worst example perpetrated by these vultures occurred in the Bahamas in 1971. A ship that ironically carried the name of *the* classic conservation group, the *Sierra,* succeeded in wiping out every single humpback whale that wintered in Bahamian waters. Since 1971 not one whale has been sighted in the Bahamas, and whalewatchers lament that they will never return.

The Last Whalers

Thanks to world opinion, and the efforts of benign but aggressive organizations such as Greenpeace and Earth Trust, the **International Whaling Commission** (IWC), a voluntary group of 17 nations, now sets standards and passes quotas on the number and species of whales that can be killed. Over the last 18 years the blue, right, gray, bowhead, and humpback have become totally protected. However, many great whales such as the sperm, minke, sei, and fin are still hunted. Also, the IWC has no power of enforcement except for public opinion and possible voluntary economic sanction.

The Japanese and Norwegians still hunt for whale, their operations often thinly disguised as "research." Native American Inuit and a few other indigenous peoples of the world, like the villagers of Lamalera on Lembata in Indonesia, hunt whale, but the numbers of whales taken from these groups is minuscule. The Japanese technically stay within their quotas, but they hire and outfit these and other nationals to hunt whales for them. Their main argument is that whaling is a traditional industry upon which they rely for food and jobs. This is patently false. Hardly more than 100 years old, pelagic whaling is a new industry to the Japanese. Much of the Japanese whale meat becomes pet food anyway, which is mainly exported.

Amazingly, a recent poll taken in Japan by the Whale and Dolphin Society of London found that 69% of the people opposed whaling. Finally, through the efforts of **ICEARCH** (International Cetacean Education And Research Conference), the first pillars of a bridge were laid between Japanese and Western scientists who are dedicated to finding a way for mankind and the great whales to live in harmony. On Maui in April 1993, these scientists came together for the first time to discuss the issue.

Whalewatching

If you're in Hawaii from late November to early May, you have an excellent chance of spotting a humpback. March is perhaps the best month. You can often see a whale from a vantage point on land, but this is nowhere near as thrilling as seeing them close-up from a boat. Either way, binoculars are a must. Telephoto and zoom lenses are also useful, and you might even get a nifty photo in the bargain. But don't waste your film unless you have a fairly high-powered zoom: fixed-lens cameras give pictures with a lot of ocean and a tiny black speck. If you're lucky enough to see a whale breach (jump clear of the water), keep watching—they often repeat this a number of times. If a whale dives and lifts its fluke high in the air, expect it to be down for at least 15 minutes and not come up in the same spot. Other times they'll dive shallowly, then bob up and down quite often. From shore you're likely to see whales anywhere along Maui's south coast. If you're staying at any of the hotels or condos along Kaanapali or Kihei and have an ocean view, you can spot them from your lanai or window. Two good vantage spots are Papawai Point and McGregor Point along Rt. 30 just west of Maalaea. During whalewatching season, a Pacific Whale Foundation naturalist may be at one of these spots to help people locate whales and answer questions. In addition, a free talk on whales is sometimes conducted by a naturalist on the ocean observatory deck at the Kealia Beach Plaza weekdays around noon. Maalaea Bay is another favorite nursing ground for female whales and their calves; there you also can see a small working harbor up close. Another excellent viewpoint is Makena Beach, on the spit of land separating Little and Big Beach-

es. If you time your arrival near sunset, even if you don't see a whale you'll enjoy a mind-boggling light show.

To learn more about whales and the Hawaiian Islands Humpback Whale National Marine Sanctuary stop by the office at 726 S. Kihei Rd., Kihei, HI 96753, tel. (800) 831-4888, Web site: www .t-link.net/~whale. The office is open Mon.-Fri. 9 a.m.-3 p.m., grounds open dawn to dusk. Another good source of information is the **Pacific Whale Foundation,** 101 N. Kihei Road, Kihei, HI 96753, tel. (808) 879-8860, Web site: www.pacificwhale.org.

Note: For whalewatching cruises see "Ocean Tours" under "Sports and Recreation" in the Out and About chapter.

HISTORY

THE ROAD FROM TAHITI

Until the 1820s, when New England missionaries began a phonetic rendering of the Hawaiian language, the past was kept vividly alive only by the sonorous voices of special *kahuna* who chanted the sacred *mele*. The chants were beautiful, flowing word pictures that captured the essence of every aspect of life. These *mele* praised the land *(mele aina),* royalty *(mele ali'i),* and life's tender aspects *(mele aloha).* Chants were dedicated to friendship, hardship, and favorite children. Entire villages sometimes joined together to compose a *mele*—every word was chosen carefully, and the wise old *kapuna* would decide if the words were lucky or unlucky. Some *mele* were bawdy or funny on the surface but contained secret meanings, often with biting sarcasm, that ridiculed an inept or cruel leader. But the most important chants took the listeners back into the dim past, even before people lived in Hawaii. From these genealogies *(ko'i-honua),* the *ali'i* derived the right to rule, since these chants went back to the gods Wakea and Papa from whom the *ali'i* were directly descended.

The *Kumulipo*
The great genealogies, finally compiled in the late 1800s by order of King Kalakaua, were collectively known as *The Kumulipo, A Hawaiian Creation Chant,* basically a Polynesian account of

Genesis. Other chants related to the beginning of this world, but the *Kumulipo* sums it all up and is generally considered the best. The chant relates that after the beginning of time, there is a period of darkness. The darkness, however, mysteriously brims with spontaneous life; during this period plants and animals are born, as well as Kumulipo, the man, and Po'ele, the woman. In the eighth chant darkness gives way to light and the gods descend to earth. Wakea is "the sky father" and Papa is "the earth mother," whose union gives birth to the islands of Hawaii. First born is Hawaii, followed by Maui, then Kahoolawe. Apparently, Papa becomes bushed after three consecutive births and decides to vacation in Tahiti. While Papa is away recovering from postpartum depression and working on her tan, Wakea gets lonely and takes Kaula as his second wife; she bears him the island-child of Lanai. Not fully cheered up, but getting the hang of it, Wakea takes a third wife, Hina, who promptly bears the island of Molokai. Meanwhile, Papa gets wind of these shenanigans, returns from Polynesia, and retaliates by taking up with Lua, a young and virile god. She soon gives birth to the island of Oahu. Papa and Wakea finally decide that they really are meant for each other and reconcile to conceive Kauai, Niihau, Kaula, and Nihoa. These two progenitors are the source from which the *ali'i* ultimately traced their lineage, and from which they derived their god-ordained power to rule.

Basically, there are two major genealogical families: the **Nana'ulu,** who became the royal *ali'i* of Oahu and Kauai, and the **Ulu,** who provided the royalty of Maui and Hawaii. The best sources of information on Hawaiian myth and legend are Martha Beckwith's *Hawaiian Mythology* and the monumental three-volume opus *An Account of the Polynesian Race,* compiled by Abraham Fornander 1878-85. Fornander, after settling in Hawaii, married an *ali'i* from Molokai and had an illustrious career as a newspaperman, Maui circuit judge, and finally Supreme Court justice. For years Fornander sent scribes to every corner of the kingdom to listen to the elder *kapuna.* They returned with firsthand accounts, which he dutifully recorded.

The Great Navigators

No one knows exactly when the first Polynesians arrived in Hawaii, but the great "deliberate migrations" from the southern islands seem to have taken place A.D. 500-800, though anthropologists keep pushing the date backward in time as new evidence becomes available. Even before that, however, it's reasonable to assume that the first people to set foot on Hawaii were probably fishermen, or perhaps defeated warriors whose canoes were blown hopelessly northward into unfamiliar waters. They arrived by a combination of extraordinary good luck and an uncanny ability to sail and navigate without instruments, using the sun by day and the moon

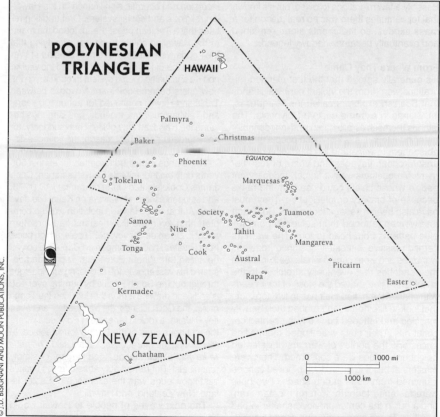

POLYNESIAN TRIANGLE

HAWAII

Palmyra

Baker   Christmas

Phoenix   EQUATOR

Tokelau   Marquesas

Society   Tuamoto

Samoa   Niue   Tahiti

Tonga   Cook   Mangareva

Austral   Pitcairn

Rapa

Kermadec   Easter

NEW ZEALAND

Chatham

0   1000 mi

0   1000 km

and rising stars by night. They could feel the water and determine direction by swells, tides, and currents. The movements of fish and cloud formations were also utilized to give direction. Since their arrival was probably an accident, they were unprepared to settle on the fertile but barren lands, having no stock animals, plant cuttings, or women. Forced to return southward, undoubtedly many lost their lives at sea, but a few wild-eyed stragglers must have made it home to tell tales of a paradise to the north where land was plentiful and the sea bounteous. This is affirmed by ancient navigational chants from Tahiti, Moorea, and Bora Bora, which passing from father to son revealed how to follow the stars to the "heavenly homeland in the north." Possibly a few migrations followed, but it's known that for centuries there was no real reason for a mass exodus, so the chants alone remained and eventually became shadowy legend.

From Where They Came

It's generally agreed that the first planned migrations were from the violent cannibal islands that Spanish explorers called the Marquesas, 11 islands in extreme eastern Polynesia. The islands themselves are harsh and inhospitable, breeding a toughness into these people that enabled them to withstand the hardships of long, unsure ocean voyages and years of resettlement. Marquesans were a fiercely independent people whose chiefs could rise from the ranks because of bravery or intelligence. They must have also been a savage-looking lot. Both men and women tattooed themselves in complex blue patterns from head to foot. The warriors carried massive, intricately designed ironwood war clubs and wore carved whale teeth in slits in their earlobes that eventually stretched to the shoulders. They shaved the sides of their heads with sharks' teeth, tied their hair in two topknots that looked like horns, and rubbed their heavily muscled and tattooed bodies with scented coconut oils. Their cults worshiped mummified ancestors; the bodies of warriors of defeated neighboring tribes were consumed. They were masters at building great double-hulled canoes launched from huge canoe sheds. Two hulls were fastened together to form a catamaran, and a hut in the center provided shelter in bad weather. The average voyaging canoe was 60-80 feet long and could comfortably hold an ex-tended family of about 30 people. These small family bands carried all the staples they would need in the new lands.

The New Lands

For five centuries the Marquesans settled and lived peacefully on the new land, as if Hawaii's *aloha* spirit overcame most of their fierceness. The tribes coexisted in relative harmony, especially since there was no competition for land. Cannibalism died out. There was much coming and going between Hawaii and Polynesia as new people came to settle for hundreds of years. Then, it appears that in the 12th century a deliberate exodus of warlike Tahitians arrived and subjugated the settled islanders. They came to conquer. This incursion had a terrific significance on the Hawaiian religious and social system. Oral tradition relates that a Tahitian priest, Paao, found the mana of the Hawaiian chiefs to be low, signifying that their gods were weak. Paao built a *heiau* at Waha'ula on the Big Island, then introduced the warlike god Ku and the rigid *kapu* system through which the new rulers became dominant. Voyages between Tahiti and Hawaii continued for about 100 years, and Tahitian customs, legends, and language became the Hawaiian way of life. Then suddenly, for no recorded or apparent reason, the voyages discontinued and Hawaii returned to total isolation.

The islands remained forgotten for almost 500 years until the indomitable English seaman, Capt. James Cook, sighted Oahu on January 18, 1778, and stepped ashore at Waimea on Kauai two days later. At that time Hawaii's isolation was so complete that even the Polynesians had forgotten about it. On an earlier voyage, Tupaia, a high priest from Raiatea, had accompanied Captain Cook as he sailed throughout Polynesia. Tupaia demonstrated his vast knowledge of existing archipelagos throughout the South Pacific by naming over 130 islands and drawing a map that included the Tonga group, the Cook Islands, the Marquesas, and even tiny Pitcairn, a rock in far eastern Polynesia where the mutinous crew of the *Bounty* found solace. In mentioning the Marquesas, Tupaia said, *"he ma'a te ka'ata,"* which means "food is man" or simply "cannibals!" But remarkably absent from Tupaia's vast knowledge was the existence of Easter Island, New Zealand, and Hawaii.

The next waves of people to Hawaii would be white men, and the Hawaiian world would be changed quickly and forever.

THE WORLD DISCOVERS HAWAII

The late 18th century was an extraordinary time in Hawaiian history. Monumental changes seemed to happen all at once. First, Capt. James Cook, a Yorkshire farm boy fulfilling his destiny as the all-time greatest Pacific explorer, found Hawaii for the rest of the world. For better or worse, it could no longer be an isolated Polynesian homeland. For the first time in Hawaiian history, a charismatic leader, Kamehameha, emerged, and after a long civil war he united all the islands into one centralized kingdom. The death of Captain Cook in Hawaii marked the beginning of a long series of tragic misunderstandings between whites and natives. When Kamehameha died, the old religious system of *kapu* came to an end, leaving the Hawaiians in a spiritual vortex. Many takers arrived to fill the void: missionaries after souls, whalers after their prey and a good time, traders and planters after profits and a home. The islands were opened and devoured like ripe fruit. Powerful nations, including Russia, Great Britain, France, and the United States, yearned to bring this strategic Pacific jewel under their own influence. The 19th century brought the demise of the Hawaiian people as a dominant political force in their own land and with it the end of Hawaii as a sovereign monarchy. An almost bloodless yet bitter military coup followed by a brief Hawaiian Republic ended in annexation by the United States. As the U.S. became completely entrenched politically and militarily, a new social and economic order was founded on the plantation system. Amazingly rapid population growth occurred with the importation of plantation workers from Asia and Europe, which yielded a unique cosmopolitan blend of races like nowhere else on earth. By the dawning of the 20th century, the face of old Hawaii had been altered forever; the "sacred homeland in the north" was hurled into the modern age. The attack on Pearl Harbor saw a tremendous loss of life and brought Hawaii closer to the U.S. by a baptism of blood. Finally, on August. 21, 1959, after 59 years as a territory, Hawaii officially became the 50th state of the Union.

Captain Cook Sights Hawaii

In 1776 Capt. James Cook set sail for the Pacific from Plymouth, England, on his third and final expedition into this still vastly unexplored region

Captain James Cook

HAWAII STATE ARCHIVES

of the world. On a fruitless quest for the fabled Northwest Passage across the North American continent, he sailed down the coast of Africa, rounded the Cape of Good Hope, crossed the Indian Ocean, and traveled past New Zealand, Tasmania, and the Friendly Islands (where an unsuccessful plot was hatched by the "friendly" natives to murder him). On January 18, 1778, Captain Cook's 100-foot flagship HMS *Resolution* and its 90-foot companion HMS *Discovery* sighted Oahu. Two days later, they sighted Kauai and went ashore at the village of Waimea on January 20, 1778. Though anxious to get on with his mission, Cook decided to make a quick sortie to investigate this new land and reprovision his ships. He did, however, take time to remark in his diary about the close resemblance of these newfound people to others he had encountered as far south as New Zealand, and marveled at their widespread habitation across the Pacific.

The first trade was some brass medals for a mackerel. Cook also stated that he had never before met natives so astonished by a ship, and that they had an amazing fascination for iron, which they called *toe*, Hawaiian for "adze." There is even some conjecture that a Spanish ship under one Captain Gaetano had landed in Hawaii as early as the 16th century, trading a few scraps of iron that the Hawaiians valued even more than the Europeans valued gold. It was also noted that the Hawaiian women gave themselves freely to the sailors with the apparent good wishes of the island men. This was actually a ploy by the *kahuna* to test if the newcomers were gods or men—gods didn't need women. These sailors proved immediately mortal. Cook, who was also a physician, tried valiantly to keep the 66 men (out of 112) who had measurable cases of venereal disease away from the women. The task proved impossible as women literally swarmed the ships; when Cook returned less than a year later, it was logged that signs of VD were already apparent on some natives' faces.

Cook was impressed with the Hawaiians' swimming ability and with their well-bred manners. They had happy dispositions and sticky fingers, stealing any object made of metal, especially nails. The first item stolen was a butcher's cleaver. An unidentified native grabbed it, plunged overboard, swam to shore, and waved his booty in triumph. The Hawaiians didn't seem to care for beads and were not at all impressed with a mirror. Cook provisioned his ships by trading chisels for hogs, while common sailors gleefully traded nails for sex. Landing parties were sent inland to fill casks with fresh water. On one such excursion a Mr. Williamson, who was eventually drummed out of the Royal Navy for cowardice, unnecessarily shot and killed a native. After a brief stop on Niihau, the ships sailed away, but both groups were indelibly impressed with the memory of each other.

Cook Returns

Almost a year later, when winter weather forced Cook to return from the coast of Alaska, his discovery began to take on far-reaching significance. Cook had named Hawaii the Sandwich Islands, in honor of one of his patrons, John Montague, the Earl of Sandwich. On this return voyage, he spotted Maui on November 26, 1778. After eight weeks of seeking a suitable harbor, the ships bypassed it, but not before the coastline was duly drawn by Lt. William Bligh, one of Cook's finest and most trusted officers. (Bligh would find his own drama almost 10 years later as commander of the infamous HMS *Bounty*.) The *Discovery* and *Resolution* finally found safe anchorage at Kealakekua Bay on the Kona coast of the Big Island. It is very lucky for history that on board was Mr. Anderson, ship's chronicler, who left a handwritten record of the strange and tragic events that followed. Even more important were the drawings of John Webber, ship's artist, who rendered invaluable impressions in superb drawings and etchings. Other noteworthy men aboard were George Vancouver, who would lead the first British return to Hawaii after Cook's death and introduce many fruits, vegetables, cattle, sheep, and goats; and James Burney, who would become a long-standing leading authority on the Pacific.

The Great God Lono Returns

By all accounts Cook was a humane and just captain, greatly admired by his men. Unlike many other supremacists of that time, he was known to have a respectful attitude toward any people he discovered, treating them as equals and recognizing the significance of their cultures. Not known as a violent man, he would use his superior weapons against natives only in an absolute case of self-defense. His hardened crew had been at sea facing untold hardship for almost three years; returning to Hawaii was truly like reentering paradise.

A strange series of coincidences sailed with Cook into Kealakekua Bay on January 16, 1779. It was *makahiki* time, a period of rejoicing and festivity dedicated to the fertility god of the earth, Lono. Normal *kapu* days were suspended and willing partners freely enjoyed each other sexually, along with dancing, feasting, and the islands' version of Olympic games. It was long held in Hawaiian legend that the great god Lono would return to earth. Lono's image was a small wooden figure perched on a tall, mastlike crossbeam; hanging from the crossbeam were long, white sheets of tapa. Who else could Cook be but Lono, and what else could his ships with their masts and white sails be but his sacred floating *heiau*? This explained the Hawaiians' previous fascination with his ships, but to add to the remarkable coincidence, Kealakekua Harbor happened to be considered Lono's private sacred harbor. Natives from throughout the land prostrated themselves and paid homage to the returning god. Cook was taken ashore and brought to Lono's sacred temple, where he was afforded the highest respect. The ships badly needed fresh supplies so the Hawaiians readily gave all they had, stretching their own provisions to the limit. To the sailors' delight, this included full measures of the *aloha* spirit.

The Fatal Misunderstandings

After an uproarious welcome and generous hospitality for over a month, it became obvious that the newcomers were beginning to overstay their welcome. During the interim a seaman named William Watman died, convincing the Hawaiians that the *haole* were indeed mortals, not gods. Watman was buried at Hikiau Heiau, where a plaque commemorates the event to this day. Incidents of petty theft began to increase dramatically. The lesser chiefs indicated it was time to leave by "rubbing the Englishmen's bellies." Inadvertently many *kapu* were broken by the Englishmen, and once-friendly relations became strained. Finally, the ships sailed away on February 4, 1779.

After plying terrible seas for only a week, *Resolution's* foremast was badly damaged. Cook sailed back into Kealakekua Bay, dragging the mast ashore on Feb. 13. The natives, now totally hostile, hurled rocks at the sailors. Orders were given to load muskets with ball; firearms had previously been loaded only with shot and a light charge. Confrontations increased when some Hawaiians stole a small boat and Cook's men set after them, capturing the fleeing canoe which held an ali'i named Palea. The English treated him roughly; to the Hawaiians horror, they even smacked him on the head with a paddle. The Hawaiians then furiously attacked the marines, who abandoned the small boat.

Cook Goes Down

Next the Hawaiians stole a small cutter from the *Discovery* that had been moored to a buoy and partially sunk to protect it from the sun. For the first time Captain Cook became furious. He ordered Captain Clerk of the *Discovery* to sail to the southeast end of the bay and stop any canoe trying to leave Kealakekua. Cook then made a fatal error in judgment. He decided to take nine armed marines ashore in an attempt to convince the venerable King Kalaniopuu to accompany him back aboard ship, where he would hold him for ransom in exchange for the cutter. The old king agreed, but his wife prevailed upon him not to trust the *haole*. Kalaniopuu sat down on the beach to think while the tension steadily grew.

Meanwhile, a group of marines fired upon a canoe trying to leave the bay, and a lesser chief, Nookemai, was killed. The crowd around Cook and his men reached an estimated 20,000, and warriors outraged by the killing of the chief armed themselves with clubs and protective straw-mat armor. One bold warrior advanced on Cook and struck him with his *pahoa* (dagger). In retaliation, Cook drew a tiny pistol lightly loaded with shot and fired at the warrior. His bullets spent themselves on the straw armor and fell harmlessly to the ground. The Hawaiians went wild. Lt. Molesworth Phillips, in charge of the nine marines, began a withering fire; Cook himself slew two natives.

Overpowered by sheer numbers, the marines headed for boats standing offshore, while Lieutenant Phillips lay wounded. It is believed that Captain Cook, the greatest seaman ever to enter the Pacific, stood helplessly in knee-deep water instead of making for the boats because he could not swim! Hopelessly surrounded, he was knocked on the head, then countless warriors passed a knife around and hacked and mutilated his lifeless body. A sad Lieutenant King lamented in his diary, "Thus fell our great and excellent commander."

The Final Chapter

Captain Clerk, now in charge, settled his men and prevailed upon the Hawaiians to return Cook's body. On the morning of February 16 a grisly piece of charred meat was brought aboard: the Hawaiians, according to their custom, had afforded Cook the highest honor by baking his body in an underground oven to remove the flesh from the bones. On February 17, a group of Hawaiians in a canoe taunted the marines by brandishing Cook's hat. The Englishmen, strained to the limit and thinking that Cook was being desecrated, finally broke. Foaming with blood-lust, they leveled their cannons and muskets on shore and shot anything that moved. It is believed that Kamehameha the Great was wounded in this flurry, along with four *ali'i*; 25 *maka'ainana* (commoners) were killed. Finally, on Feb. 21, 1779, the bones of Capt. James Cook's hands, skull, arms, and legs were returned and tearfully buried at sea. A common seaman, one Mr. Zimmerman, summed up the feelings of all who sailed under Cook when he wrote, ". . . he was our leading star." The English sailed next morning after dropping off their Hawaiian girlfriends who were still aboard.

Captain Clerk, in bad health, carried on with the fruitless search for the Northwest Passage. He died and was buried at the Siberian village of Petropavlovisk. England was at war with upstart colonists in America, so the return of the expedition warranted little fanfare. The *Resolution* was converted into an army transport to fight the pesky Americans; the once-proud *Discovery* was reduced to a convict ship ferrying inmates to Botany Bay, Australia. Mrs. Cook, the great captain's steadfast and chaste wife, lived to the age of 93, surviving all her children. She was given a stipend of 200 pounds per year and finished her days surrounded by Cook's mementos, observing the anniversary of his death to the very end by fasting and reading from the Bible.

THE UNIFICATION OF OLD HAWAII

Hawaii was already in a state of political turmoil and civil war when Cook arrived. In the 1780s the islands were roughly divided into three kingdoms: venerable Kalaniopuu ruled Hawaii and the Hana District of Maui; wily and ruthless warrior-king Kahekili ruled Maui, Kahoolawe, Lanai, and later Oahu; and Kaeo, Kahekili's brother, ruled Kauai. War ravaged the land until a remarkable chief, Kamehameha, rose and subjugated all the islands under one rule. Kamehameha initiated a dynasty that would last for about 100 years, until the independent monarchy of Hawaii forever ceased to be. To add a zing to this brewing political stew, Westerners and their technology were beginning to come in ever-increasing numbers. In 1786, Captain Jean de François La Pérouse and his French exploration party landed in what's now La Perouse Bay near Lahaina, foreshadowing European attention to the islands. In 1786 two American captains, Portlock and Dixon, made landfall in Hawaii. Also, it was known that a fortune could be made on the fur trade between the Pacific Northwest and Canton, China; stopping in Hawaii could make it feasible. After this was reported, the fate of Hawaii was sealed.

Hawaii under Kamehameha was ready to enter its "golden age." The social order was medieval, with the *ali'i* as knights, owing their military allegiance to the king, and the serflike *maka'ainana* paying tribute and working the lands. The priesthood of *kahuna* filled the posts of advisors, sorcerers, navigators, doctors, and historians. This was Polynesian Hawaii at its apex. But like the uniquely Hawaiian silversword, the old culture blossomed, and as soon as it did, began to wither. Ever since, all that was purely Hawaiian has been supplanted by the relentless foreign influences that began bearing down upon it.

Young Kamehameha

The greatest native son of Hawaii, Kamehameha, was born under mysterious circumstances in the Kohala District, probably in 1753. He was royal born to Keoua Kupuapaikalaninui, the chief of Kohala, and Kekuiapoiwa, a chieftess from Kona. Accounts vary, but one claims that before his birth, a *kahuna* prophesied that this child would grow to be a "killer of chiefs." Because of this, the local chiefs conspired to murder the infant. When Kekuiapoiwa's time came, she secretly went to the royal birthing stones near Mookini Heiau and delivered Kamehameha. She entrusted her baby to a manservant and instructed him to hide the child. He headed for the rugged and remote coast around Kapaau. Here Kamehameha was raised in the mountains, mostly by men. Always alone, he earned the nickname, "the Lonely One."

Kamehameha was a man noticed by everyone; there was no doubt he was a force to be reckoned with. He had met Captain Cook when the *Discovery* unsuccessfully tried to land at Hana on Maui. While aboard, he made a lasting impression, distinguishing himself from the multitude of natives swarming the ships by his royal bearing. Lt. James King, in a diary entry, remarked that Kamehameha was a fierce-looking man, almost ugly, but that he was obviously intelligent, observant, and very good-natured. Kamehameha received his early military training from his uncle Kalaniopuu, the great king of Hawaii and Hana who fought fierce battles against Alapai, the usurper who stole his hereditary lands. After regaining Hawaii, Kalaniopuu returned to his Hana District and turned his attention to conquering all of Maui. During this period young Kamehameha distinguished himself as a ferocious warrior and earned the nickname of "the Hard-shelled Crab," even though old Kahekili, Maui's king, almost annihilated Kalaniopuu's army at the sand hills of Wailuku.

When the old king neared death, he passed on the kingdom to his son Kiwalao. He also, however, empowered Kamehameha as the keeper of the family war god Kukailimoku: Ku of the Bloody Red Mouth, Ku the Destroyer. Oddly enough, Kamehameha had been born not 500 yards from Ku's great *heiau* at Kohala, and had heard the chanting and observed the ceremonies dedicated to this fierce god from his first breath. Soon after Kalaniopuu died, Kamehameha found himself in a bitter war that he did not seek against his two cousins, Kiwalao and his brother Keoua, with the island of Hawaii at stake. The skirmishing lasted nine years until Kamehameha's armies met the two brothers at Mokuohai in an indecisive battle in which Kiwalao was killed. The result was a shaky truce with Keoua, a much-embittered enemy. During this fighting, Kahekili of Maui conquered Oahu, where he built a house of the skulls and bones of his adversaries as a reminder of his omnipotence. He also extended his will to Kauai by marrying his half-brother to a high-ranking chieftess of that island. A new factor would resolve this stalemate of power—the coming of the *haole*.

The Olowalu Massacre

In 1790 the American merchant ship *Ella Nora,* commanded by Yankee Capt. Simon Metcalfe, was looking for a harbor after its long voyage from the Pacific Northwest. Following a day behind was the *Fair American,* a tiny ship sailed by Metcalfe's son Thomas and a crew of five. Simon Metcalfe, perhaps by necessity, was a stern and humorless man who would brook no interference. While his ship was anchored at Olowalu, a beach area about five miles east of Lahaina, some natives slipped close in their canoes and stole a small boat, killing a seaman in the process. Metcalfe decided to trick the Hawaiians by first negotiating a truce and then unleashing full fury upon them. Signaling he was willing to trade, he invited canoes of innocent natives to visit his ship. In the meantime, he ordered that all cannons and muskets be readied with scatter shot. When the

canoes were within hailing distance, he ordered his crew to fire at will. Over 100 people were slain; the Hawaiians remembered this killing as "the Day of Spilled Brains." Metcalfe then sailed away to Kealakekua Bay and in an unrelated incident succeeded in insulting Kameiamoku, a ruling chief, who vowed to annihilate the next *haole* ship that he saw.

Fate sent him the *Fair American* and young Thomas Metcalfe. The little ship was entirely overrun by superior forces. In the ensuing battle, the mate, Isaac Davis, so distinguished himself by open acts of bravery that his life alone was spared. Kameiamoku later turned over both Davis and the ship to Kamehameha. Meanwhile, while harbored at Kealakekua, the senior Metcalfe sent John Young to reconnoiter. Kamehameha, having learned of the capture of the *Fair American,* detained Young so he could not report, and Metcalfe, losing patience, marooned his own man and sailed off to Canton. (Metcalfe never learned of the fate of his son Thomas, and was later killed with another son while trading with the Native Americans along the Pacific coast of the Mainland.) Kamehameha quickly realized the significance of his two captives and the *Fair American* with its brace of small cannons. He appropriated the ship and made Davis and Young trusted advisors, eventually raising them to the rank of chief. They would all play a significant role in the unification of Hawaii.

Kamehameha the Great

Later in 1790, supported by the savvy of Davis and Young and the cannons from the *Fair American* (which he mounted on carts), Kamehameha invaded Maui, using Hana as his power base. The island's defenders under Kalaniekupule, son of Kahekili who was lingering on Oahu, were totally demoralized, then driven back into the deathtrap of Iao Valley. There, Kamehameha's forces annihilated them. No mercy was expected and none given, although mostly commoners were slain with no significant *ali'i* falling to the victors. So many were killed in this sheer-walled, inescapable valley that the battle was called Ka Pani Wai, which means "the Damming of the Waters"—literally with dead bodies.

While Kamehameha was fighting on Maui, his old nemesis Keoua was busy running amok back on Hawaii, again pillaging Kamehameha's lands. The great warrior returned home flushed with victory, but in two battles he could not subdue Keoua. Finally, Kamehameha had a prophetic dream in which he was told that Ku would lead him to victory over all the lands of Hawaii if he would build a *heiau* to the war god at Kawaihae. Even before the temple was finished, old Kahekili attempted to invade Waipio, Kamehameha's stronghold. But Kamehameha summoned Davis and Young, and with the *Fair American* and an enormous fleet of war canoes defeated Kahekili at Waimanu. Kahekili had no choice but to accept the indomitable Kamehameha as the king of Maui, although he himself remained the administrative head until his death in 1794.

Kamehameha by Louis Choris

HAWAII STATE ARCHIVES

Now only Keoua remained in the way and he would be defeated not by war, but by the great mana of Ku. While Keoua's armies were crossing the desert on the southern slopes of Kilauea, the fire goddess Pele trumpeted her disapproval and sent a huge cloud of poisonous gas and mud-ash into the air. It descended upon and instantly killed the middle legions of Keoua's armies and their families. The footprints of this ill-fated army remain to this day outlined in the mud-ash as clearly as if they were deliberately encased in wet cement. Keoua's intuition told him that the victorious mana of the gods had swung to Kamehameha and that his own fate was sealed. Kamehameha sent word that he wanted Keoua to meet with him at Ku's newly dedicated temple in Kawaihae. Both knew that Keoua must die. Riding proudly in his canoe, the old nemesis came gloriously outfitted in the red-and-gold feathered cape and helmet signifying his exalted rank. When he stepped ashore he was felled by Kamehameha's warriors. His body was ceremoniously laid upon the altar along with 11 others who were slaughtered and dedicated to Ku, of the Maggot-dripping Mouth.

Increasing Contact

By the time Kamehameha had won the Big Island, Hawaii was becoming a regular stopover for numerous ships seeking the lucrative sandalwood trade with China. In February 1791, Capt. George Vancouver, still seeking the Northwest Passage, returned to Kealakekua where he was greeted by a throng of 30,000. The captain at once recognized Kamehameha, who was wearing a Chinese dressing gown that he had received in tribute from another chief who in turn had received it directly from the hands of Cook himself. The diary of a crewmember, Thomas Manby, relates that Kamehameha, missing his front teeth, was more fierce-looking than ever as he approached the ship in an elegant double-hulled canoe sporting 46 rowers. The king invited all to a great feast prepared for them on the beach. Kamehameha's appetite matched his tremendous size. It was noted that he ate two sizable fish, a king-sized bowl of poi, a small pig, and an entire baked dog. Kamehameha personally entertained the English by putting on a mock battle in which he deftly avoided spears by rolling, tumbling, and catching them in midair, all the while hurling his own spear a great distance. The English reciprocated by firing cannon bursts into the air, creating an impromptu fireworks display. Kamehameha requested from Vancouver a full table setting with which he was provided, but his request for firearms was prudently denied. Captain Vancouver became a trusted advisor of Kamehameha, and told him about the white man's form of worship. He even interceded for Kamehameha with his headstrong queen, Kaahumanu, and coaxed her from her hiding place under a rock when she sought refuge at Pu'uhonua O Honaunau. The captain gave gifts of beef cattle, fowl, and breeding stock of sheep and goats. The ship's naturalist, Archibald Menzies, was the first *haole* to climb Mauna Kea; he also introduced a large assortment of fruits and vegetables. The Hawaiians were cheerful and outgoing, and showed remorse when they indicated that the remainder of Cook's bones had been buried at a temple close to Kealakekua. John Young, by this time firmly entrenched into Hawaiian society, made no request to sail away with Vancouver. During the next two decades of Kamehameha's rule, the French, Russians, English, and Americans discovered the great whaling waters off Hawaii. Their increasing visits shook and finally tumbled the ancient religion and social order of *kapu*.

Finishing Touches

After Keoua was laid to rest, it was only a matter of time until Kamehameha consolidated his power over all of Hawaii. In 1794 the old warrior Kahekili of Maui died and gave Oahu to his son, Kalanikupule, while Kauai and Niihau went to his brother Kaeo. In wars between the two, Kalanikupule was victorious, though he did not possess the grit of his father nor the great mana of Kamehameha. He had previously murdered a Captain Brown, who had anchored in Honolulu, and seized his ship, the *Jackal*. With the aid of this ship, Kalanikupule now determined to attack Kamehameha. However, while en route, the sailors regained control of their ship and cruised to the Big Island to inform and join with Kamehameha. An army of 16,000 was raised and sailed for Maui, where they met only token resistance, destroyed Lahaina, pillaged the countryside, and subjugated Molokai in one bloody battle.

The war canoes sailed next for Oahu and the final showdown. The great army landed at Waikiki, and though defenders fought bravely, giving up Oahu by the inch, they were steadily driven into the surrounding mountains. The beleaguered army made its last stand at Nuuanu Pali, a great precipice in the mountains behind present-day Honolulu. Kamehameha's warriors mercilessly drove the enemy into the great abyss. Kalanikupule, who hid in the mountains, was captured after a few months and sacrificed to

Ku, the Snatcher of Lands, thereby ending the struggle for power.

Kamehameha put down a revolt on Hawaii in 1796. The king of Kauai, Kaumuali, accepting the inevitable, recognized Kamehameha as supreme ruler without suffering the ravages of a needless war. Kamehameha, for the first time in Hawaiian history, was the undisputed ruler of all the islands of "the heavenly homeland in the north."

Kamehameha's Rule

Kamehameha was as gentle in victory as he was ferocious in battle. Under his rule, which lasted until his death on May 8, 1819, Hawaii enjoyed a peace unlike any the warring islands had ever known. The king moved his royal court to Lahaina, where in 1803 he built the Brick Palace, the first permanent building of Hawaii. The benevolent tyrant also enacted the "Law of the Splintered Paddle." This law, which protected the weak from the exploitation of the strong, had its origins in an incident of many years before. A brave defender of a small overwhelmed village had broken a paddle over Kamehameha's head and taught the chief—literally in one stroke—about the nobility of the commoner.

However, just as Old Hawaii reached its golden age, its demise was at hand. The relentless waves of *haole* both innocently and determinedly battered the old ways into the ground. With the foreign ships came prosperity and fanciful new goods after which the *ali'i* lusted. The *maka'ainana* were worked mercilessly to provide sandalwood for the China trade. This was the first "boom" economy to hit the islands, but it set the standard of exploitation that would follow. Kamehameha built an observation tower in Lahaina to watch for ships, many of which were his own returning laden with riches from the world at large. In the last years of his life Kamehameha returned to his beloved Kona coast, where he enjoyed the excellent fishing renowned to this day. He had taken Hawaii from the darkness of warfare into the light of peace. He died true to the religious and moral *kapu* of his youth, the only ones he had ever known, and with him died a unique way of life. Two loyal retainers buried his bones after the baked flesh had been ceremoniously stripped away. A secret burial cave was chosen so that no one could desecrate the remains of the great chief, thereby absorbing his mana. The tomb's whereabouts remain unknown, and disturbing the dead remains one of the strictest *kapu* to this day. The Lonely One's kingdom would pass to his son, Liholiho, but true power would be in the hands of his beloved but feisty wife Kaahumanu. As Kamehameha's spirit drifted from this earth, two forces sailing around Cape Horn would forever change Hawaii: the missionaries and the whalers.

MISSIONARIES AND WHALERS

The year 1819 was of the utmost significance in Hawaiian history. It marked the death of Kamehameha, the overthrow of the ancient *kapu* system,

MAUI MUSEUMS AND HISTORICAL SOCIETIES

Alexander and Baldwin Sugar Mill Museum, at the corner of Puunene Ave. and Hanson Rd. in Puunene, tel. (808) 871-8058, is a small but highly informative museum on the history and culture of sugar and sugar production on the island, set next to a functioning sugar mill. Open Mon.-Sat. 9:30 a.m.-4:30 p.m.; $4 admission.

Baldwin Home, on Front St. across from the harbor in Lahaina, tel. (808) 661-3262, is the two-story home of medical missionary Rev. Dwight Baldwin. This showcase museum is the oldest stone structure on the island, and it portrays the early days of the missions on Maui. Open daily 10 a.m.-4 p.m.; $3 admission. Next door to the Baldwin Home is the Master's Reading Room, a storehouse turned officers' club from the whaling days.

Carthaginian II is a floating museum anchored at the Lahaina Harbor. This ship is a replica of a 19th-century brig, featuring whaling artifacts and exhibits on the humpback whale. Open daily 10 a.m.-4 p.m.; $4 admission.

Hale Pa'i is a printing house located on the grounds of Lahainaluna school on the hillside above Lahaina. It has an operational relic of an original printing press, original Lahainaluna press publications, and an exhibit of Lahainaluna school past and present. Open Mon.-Fri. 10 a.m.-3 p.m.

Lahaina Restoration Foundation was begun in 1962. This privately funded organization seeks to preserve and maintain the flavor and authenticity of Lahaina and its old buildings and artifacts. Its office is in the Master's Reading Room at the Baldwin Home, tel. (808) 661-3262.

Bailey House Museum, at 2375 Main St., Wailuku, is a repository of Hawaiian historical objects, artifacts from the early days of the missionaries on Maui, and the paintings of Edward Bailey. Once Bailey's home, it also served at one time as a dormitory for the Wailuku Female Seminary boarding school. Open Mon.-Sat. 10 a.m.-4 p.m.; $4 admission.

Maui Historical Society is housed in the lower level of the Bailey House Museum. This society promotes interest in and knowledge of the history of Hawaii and Maui County. Free lectures during the year.

Hana Cultural Center, tel. (808) 248-8622, is located across from the entrance to Hana Bay. It preserves and restores historical artifacts, photos, and documents from the Hana area. On the grounds are a restored courthouse and jail. This cultural center also has four traditional-style buildings and maintains an ethnobotanical garden. Open daily 10 a.m.-4 p.m.; admission by donation.

Whalers Village Museum, at the Whalers Village mall in Kaanapali, displays whaling artifacts and portrays the history and culture of whaling in Hawaii. A second gallery seeks to explain the evolution and natural history of whales. In the courtyard is a 30-foot sperm whale skeleton. Self-guided learning experience while you shop. Open daily; free.

the great Queen Kaahumanu, by ship's artist Louis Choris, from the Otto Von Kotzebue expedition, c. 1816

the arrival of the first "whaler" in Lahaina, and the departure of Calvinist missionaries from New England determined to convert the heathen islands. Great changes began to rattle the old order to its foundations. With the *kapu* system and all of the ancient gods abandoned (except for the fire goddess Pele of Kilauea), a great void permeated the souls of the Hawaiians. In the coming decades Hawaii, also coveted by Russia, France, and England, was finally consumed by America. The islands had the first American school, printing press, and newspaper *(The Polynesian)* west of the Mississippi. Lahaina, in its heyday, became the world's greatest whaling port, accommodating over 500 ships during its peak years.

The Royal Family

Maui's Hana District provided Hawaii with one of its greatest queens, Kaahumanu, born in 1768 in a cave within walking distance of Hana Harbor. At the age of 17 she became the third of Kamehameha's 21 wives and eventually the love of his life. At first she proved to be totally independent and unmanageable, and was known to openly defy her king by taking numerous lovers. Kamehameha placed a *kapu* on her body and even had her attended by horribly deformed hunchbacks in an effort to curb her carnal appetites, but she continued to flaunt his authority. Young Kaahumanu had no love for her great, lumbering,

unattractive husband, but in time (even Captain Vancouver was pressed into service as a marriage counselor) she learned to love him dearly. She in turn became his favorite wife, although she remained childless throughout her life. Kamehameha's first wife was the supremely royal Keopuolani, who so outranked even him that the king himself had to approach her naked and crawling on his belly. Keopuolani produced the royal children Liholiho and Kauikeaouli, who became King Kamehameha II and III, respectively. Just before Kamehameha I died in 1819 he appointed Liholiho his successor, but he also had the wisdom to make Kaahumanu the *kuhina nui* or queen regent. Initially, Liholiho was weak and became a drunkard. Later he became a good ruler, but he was always supported by his royal mother Keopuolani and by the ever-formidable Kaahumanu.

Kapu Is *Pau*

Kaahumanu was greatly loved and respected by the people. On public occasions, she donned Kamehameha's royal cloak and spear: so attired and infused with the king's mana, she demonstrated that she was the real leader of Hawaii. For six months after Kamehameha's death, Kaahumanu counseled Liholiho on what he must do. The wise *kuhina nui* knew that the old ways were *pau* (finished) and that Hawaii could not hope to function in a rapidly changing world under the *kapu* system. In November 1819, Kaahumanu and Keopuolani prevailed upon Liholiho to break two of the oldest and most sacred *kapu* by eating with women and by allowing women to eat previously forbidden foods such as bananas and certain fish. Heavily fortified with strong drink and attended by other high-ranking chiefs and a handful of foreigners, Kaahumanu and Liholiho ate together in public. This feast became known as Ai Noa ("Free Eating"). As the first morsels passed Kaahumanu's lips, the ancient gods of Hawaii tumbled. Throughout the land, revered *heiau* were burned and abandoned and the idols knocked to the ground. Now the people had nothing but their weakened inner selves to rely on. Nothing and no one could answer their prayers; their spiritual lives were empty and in shambles.

Missionaries

Into this spiritual vortex sailed the brig *Thaddeus* on April 4, 1820. It had set sail from Boston on October 23, 1819, lured to the Big Island by Henry Opukahaia, a local boy born at Napoopoo in 1792. Coming ashore at Kailua-Kona, the Reverends Bingham and Thurston were granted a one-year trial missionary period by King Liholiho. They established themselves on the Big Island and Oahu and from there began the transformation of Hawaii. The missionaries were people of God, but also practical-minded Yankees. They brought education, enterprise, and most importantly (unlike the transient seafarers), a commitment to stay and build. By 1824 the new faith had such a foothold that Chieftess Keopuolani climbed to the fire pit atop Kilauea and defied Pele. This was even more striking than the previous breaking of the food *kapu* because the strength of Pele could actually be seen. Keopuolani ate forbidden *ohelo* berries and cried out, "Jehovah is my God." Over the next decades the governing of Hawaii slipped away from the Big Island and moved to the new port cities of Lahaina on Maui and, later, Honolulu.

Rapid Conversions

The year 1824 also marked the death of Keopuolani, who was given a Christian burial. She had set the standard by accepting Christianity, and a number of the *ali'i* had followed the queen's lead. Liholiho had sailed off to England, where he and his wife contracted measles and died. Their bodies were returned by the British in 1825, on the HMS *Blonde* captained by Lord Byron, cousin of *the* Lord Byron. During these years, Kaahumanu allied herself with Reverend Richards, pastor of the first mission in the islands, and together they wrote Hawaii's first code of laws based upon the Ten Commandments. Foremost was the condemnation of murder, theft, brawling, and the desecration of the Sabbath by work or play. The early missionaries had the best of intentions, but like all zealots they were blinded by the single-mindedness that was also their greatest ally. They weren't surgically selective in their destruction of native beliefs. *Anything* native was felt to be inferior, and they set about wiping out all traces of the old ways. In their rampage they reduced the Hawaiïan culture to ashes, plucking self-will and determination from the hearts of a once-proud people. More so than the whalers, they terminated the Hawaiian way of life.

The Early Seamen

A good portion of the common seamen of the early 19th century came from the dregs of the Western world. Many a whoremongering drunkard had awoken from a stupor and found himself on the pitching deck of a ship, discovering to his dismay that he had been "pressed into naval service." For the most part these sailors were a filthy, uneducated, lawless rabble. Their present situation was dim, their future hopeless, and they would live to be 30 if they were lucky and didn't die from scurvy or a thousand other miserable fates. They snatched brief pleasure in every port and jumped ship at every opportunity, especially in an easy berth like Lahaina. They displayed the worst elements of Western culture—which the Hawaiians naively mimicked. In exchange for *aloha* they gave drunkenness, sloth, and insidious death by disease. By the 1850s the population of native Hawaiians tumbled from the estimated 300,000 reported by Captain Cook in 1778 to barely 60,000. Common conditions such as colds, flu, venereal disease, and sometimes smallpox and cholera decimated the Hawaiians, who had no natural immunities to these foreign ailments. By the time the missionaries arrived, *hapa haole* children were common in Lahaina streets.

The earliest merchant ships to the islands were owned or skippered by lawless opportunists who had come seeking sandalwood after first filling their holds with furs from the Pacific Northwest. Aided by *ali'i* hungry for manufactured goods and Western finery, they raped Hawaiian forests of this fragrant wood so coveted in China. Next, droves of sailors came in search of whales. The whalers, decent men at home, left their morals back in the Atlantic and lived by the slogan "no conscience east of the Cape." The delights of Hawaii were just too tempting for most.

Two Worlds Tragically Collide

The 1820s were a time of confusion and soul-searching for the Hawaiians. When Kamehameha II died the kingdom passed to Kauikeaouli (Kamehameha III), who made his lifelong residence in Lahaina. The young king was only nine years old when the title passed to him, but his power was secure because Kaahumanu was still a vibrant *kuhina nui*. The young prince, more so than any other, was raised in the cultural confusion of the times. His childhood was spent during the very cusp of the change from old ways to new, and he was often pulled in two directions by vastly differing beliefs. Since he was royal born, he was bound by age-old Hawaiian tradition to mate and produce an heir with the highest-ranking *ali'i* in the kingdom. This mate happened to be his younger sister, the Princess Nahienaena. To the old Hawaiian advisors, this arrangement was perfectly acceptable and encouraged. To the increasingly influential missionaries, incest was an unimaginable abomination in the eyes of God. The problem was compounded by the fact that Kamehameha III and Nahienaena were drawn to each other and were deeply in love.

Kamehameha III

The young king could not stand the mental pressure imposed by conflicting worlds. He became a teenage alcoholic too royal to be restrained by anyone in the kingdom, and his bouts of drunkenness and womanizing were both legendary and scandalous.

Meanwhile, Nahienaena was even more pressured because she was a favorite of the missionaries, baptized into the church at age 12. She too vacillated between the old and the new. At times a pious Christian, at others she drank all night and took numerous lovers. As the prince and princess grew into their late teens, they became even more attached to each other and hardly made an attempt to keep their relationship from the missionaries. Whenever possible, they lived together in a grass house built for the princess by her father.

In 1832, the great Kaahumanu died, leaving the king on his own. In 1833, at the age of 19, Kamehameha III announced that the "regency" was over and that all the lands in Hawaii were his personally, and that he alone was the ultimate law. Almost immediately, however, he decreed that his half-sister Kinau would be "premier," signifying that he would leave the actual running of the kingdom in her hands. Kamehameha III fell into total drunken confusion, until one night he attempted suicide. After this episode he seemed to straighten up a bit and mostly kept a low profile. In 1836, Princess Nahienaena was convinced by the missionaries to take a husband. She married Leleiohoku, a chief from the Big Island, but continued to sleep with her brother. It is uncertain who fathered the child, but Nahienaena gave birth to a baby boy in September 1836. The young prince survived for only a few hours, and Nahienaena never recovered from her convalescence. She died in December 1836 and was laid to rest in the mausoleum next to her mother, Keopuolani, on the royal island in Mokuhina Pond (still in existence in modern-day Lahaina). After the death of his sister, Kamehameha III became a sober and righteous ruler. Often seen paying his respects at the royal mausoleum, he ruled longer than any other king until his death in 1854.

The Missionaries Prevail
In 1823, the first mission was established in Lahaina under the pastorage of Reverend Richards and his wife. Within a few years, many of the notable *ali'i* had been, at least in appearance, converted to Christianity. By 1828 the cornerstones for Wainee Church, the first stone church on the island, were laid just behind the palace of Kamehameha III. The struggle between missionaries and whalers centered around public drunkenness and the servicing of sailors by native women. The normally God-fearing whalers had signed on for perilous duty that lasted up to three years, and when they anchored in Lahaina they demanded their pleasure. The missionaries were instrumental in placing a curfew on sailors and prohibiting native women from boarding ships, which had become customary. These measures certainly did not stop the liaisons between sailor and *wahine*, but they did impose a modicum of social sanction and tolled the end of the wide-open days. The sailors were outraged; in 1825 the crew from the *Daniel* attacked the home of the meddler, Reverend Richards. A year later a similar incident occurred. In 1827, confined and lonely sailors from the whaler *John Palmer* fired their cannons at Reverend Richards' newly built home.

Slowly the tensions eased, and by 1836 many sailors were regulars at the Seamen's Chapel adjacent to the Baldwin home. Unfortunately, even the missionaries couldn't stop the pesky mosquito from entering the islands through the port of Lahaina. The mosquitoes arrived from Mexico in 1826 aboard the merchant ship *Wellington.* They were inadvertently carried as larvae in the water barrels and democratically pestered everyone in the islands from that day forward, regardless of race, religion, or creed.

Lahaina Becomes a Cultural Center
By 1831, Lahaina was firmly established as a seat of Western influence in Hawaii. That year marked the founding of Lahainaluna School, the first *real* American school west of the Rockies.

Virtually a copy of a New England normal school, it attracted the best students, both native and white, from throughout the kingdom. By 1834, Lahainaluna had an operating printing press publishing the islands' first newspaper, *The Torch of Hawaii,* starting a lucrative printing industry centered in Lahaina that dominated not only the islands but also California for many years.

An early native student was David Malo. He was brilliant and well educated, but more importantly, he remembered the "old ways." One of the first Hawaiians to realize his native land was being swallowed up by the newcomers, Malo compiled the first history of precontact Hawaii and the resulting book, *Hawaiian Antiquities,* became a reference masterpiece which has yet to be eclipsed. David Malo insisted that the printing be done in Hawaiian, not English. Malo is buried in the mountains above Lahainaluna where, by his own request, he is "high above the tide of foreign invasion." By the 1840s, Lahaina was firmly established as the "Whaling Capital of the World"; the peak year 1846 saw 395 whaling ships anchored here. A census in 1846 reported that Lahaina was home to 3,445 natives, 112 permanent *haole,* 600 sailors, and over 500 dogs. The populace was housed in 882 grass houses, 155 adobe houses, and 59 relatively permanent stone and wooden-framed structures. Lahaina would probably have remained the islands' capital, had Kamehameha III not moved the royal capital to the burgeoning port of Honolulu on the island of Oahu.

Foreign Influence
By the 1840s Honolulu was becoming the center of commerce in the islands; when Kamehameha III moved the royal court there from Lahaina, the ascendant fate of the new capital was guaranteed. In 1843, Lord Paulet, commander of the warship *Carysfort,* forced Kamehameha III to sign a treaty ceding Hawaii to the British. London, however, repudiated this act, and Hawaii's independence was restored within a few months when Queen Victoria sent Admiral Thomas as her personal agent of good intentions. The king memorialized the turn of events by a speech in which he uttered the phrase, *"Ua mau ke ea o ka aina i ka pono"* ("The life of the land is preserved in righteousness"), now Hawaii's motto. The French used similar bullying tactics to force an

unfavorable treaty on the Hawaiians in 1839; as part of these heavy-handed negotiations they exacted a payment of $20,000 and the right of Catholics to enjoy religious freedom in the islands. In 1842 the U.S. recognized and guaranteed Hawaii's independence without a formal treaty, and by 1860 over 80% of the islands' trade was with America.

The Great *Mahele*
In 1840 Kamehameha III ended his autocratic rule and instituted a constitutional monarchy. This brought about the Hawaiian Bill of Rights, but the most far reaching change was the transition to private ownership of land. Formerly, all land belonged to the ruling chief, who gave wedge-shaped parcels called *ahupua'a* to lesser chiefs to be worked for him. The commoners did all the real labor, their produce heavily taxed by the *ali'i*. The fortunes of war, the death of a chief, or the mere whim of a superior could force a commoner off the land. The Hawaiians, however, could not think in terms of "owning" land. No one could *possess* land; one could only *use* land, and its *ownership* was a strange foreign concept. (As a result, naive Hawaiians gave up their lands for a song to unscrupulous traders, which remains an integral, unrectified problem to this day.) In 1847 Kamehameha III and his advisors separated the lands of Hawaii into three groupings: crown land (belonging to the king), government land (belonging to the chiefs), and the people's land (the largest parcels). In 1848, 245 *ali'i* entered their land claims in the *Mahele Book,* assuring them ownership. In 1850 the commoners were given title in fee simple to the lands they cultivated and lived on as tenants, not including house lots in towns. Commoners without land could buy small *kuleana* (farms) from the government at 50 cents per acre. In 1850, foreigners were also allowed to purchase land in fee simple, and the ownership of Hawaii from that day forward slipped steadily from the hands of its indigenous people.

KING SUGAR

The sugar industry began at Hana, Maui, in 1849. A whaler named George Wilfong hauled four blubber pots ashore and set them up on a rocky hill in the middle of 60 acres he had planted in sugar. A team of oxen turned "crushing rollers" and the cane juice flowed down an open trough into the pots, under which an attending native kept a roaring fire burning. Wilfong's methods of refining were crude, but the resulting high-quality sugar turned a neat profit in Lahaina. The main problem was labor. The Hawaiians, who made excellent whalers, were basically indentured workers. They became extremely disillusioned with their contracts, which could last up to 10 years. Most of their wages were eaten up by manufactured commodities sold at the company store, and it didn't take long for them to realize that they were little more than slaves. At every opportunity they either left the area or just refused to work.

Imported Labor
The **Masters and Servants Act of 1850,** which allowed importation of laborers under the contract system, ostensibly guaranteed an endless supply of cheap labor for the plantations. Chinese laborers were imported, but were too enterprising to remain in the fields for a meager $3 per month. They left as soon as opportunity permitted, and went into business as small merchants and retailers. In the meantime, Wilfong had sold out, releasing most of the Hawaiians previously held under contract, and his plantation fell into disuse. In 1860 two Danish brothers, August and Oscar Unna, bought land at Hana to raise sugar. They solved the labor problem by importing Japanese laborers who were extremely hardworking and easily managed. The workday lasted 10 hours, six days a week, for a salary of $20 per month with housing and medical care thrown in. Plantation life was very structured, with stringent rules governing even bedtimes and lights out. A worker was fined for being late or for smoking on the job. Even the Japanese couldn't function under these circumstances, and improvements in benefits and housing were slowly gained.

Sugar Grows
The demand for "Sandwich Island sugar" grew as California was populated during the gold rush, and increased dramatically when the American Civil War demanded a constant supply. The only sugar plantations on the Mainland were small plots confined to the Confederate states, whose

products would hardly be bought by the Union and whose fields, later in the war, were destroyed. By the 1870s it was clear to the planters, still mainly New Englanders, that the U.S. was their market; they tried often to gain closer ties and favorable tariffs. The Americans also planted rumors that the British were interested in annexing Hawaii; this put pressure on the U.S. Congress to pass the long-desired **Reciprocity Act,** which would exempt sugar from import duty. It finally passed in 1875, in exchange for U.S. long-range rights to the strategic naval port of Pearl Harbor, among other concessions. These agreements gave increased political power to a small group of American planters whose outlooks were similar to those of the post-Civil War South, where a few powerful whites were the virtual masters of a multitude of dark-skinned laborers. Sugar was now big business and the Hana District alone exported almost 3,000 tons per year. All of Hawaii would have to reckon with the "sugar barons."

Changing Society
The sugar plantation system changed life in Hawaii physically, spiritually, politically, and economically. Now boatloads of workers came not only from Japan, but from Portugal, Germany, and even Russia. The white-skinned workers were most often the field foremen *(luna).* With the immigrants came new religions, new animals and plants, unique cuisines, and a plantation language known as pidgin, or better yet, *da'kine.* Many Asians and, to a lesser extent the other groups, including the white plantation owners, intermarried with Hawaiians. A new class of people properly termed "cosmopolitan" but more familiarly and aptly known as "locals" was emerging. These were the people of multiple race backgrounds who couldn't exactly say *what* they were but it was clear to all just *who* they were. The plantation owners became the new "chiefs" of Hawaii who could carve up the land and dispense favors. The Hawaiian monarchy was soon eliminated.

A KINGDOM PASSES

The fate of Lahaina's Wainee Church through the years has been a symbol of the political and economic climate of the times. Its construction heralded the beginning of missionary dominance in 1828. It was destroyed by a tornado or "ghost wind" in 1858, just when whaling began to falter and the previously dominant missionaries began losing their control to the merchants and planters. In 1894, Wainee Church was burned to the ground by royalists supporting the besieged Queen Liliuokalani. Rebuilding was begun in 1897—while Hawaii was a republic ruled by the sugar planters—with a grant from H.P. Baldwin. It wasn't until 1947 that Wainee was finally completed and remodeled.

The Beginning of the End
Like the Hawaiian people themselves, the Kamehameha dynasty in the mid-1800s was dying from within. King Kamehameha IV (Alexander Liholiho) ruled 1854-63; his only child died in 1862. He was succeeded by his older brother Kamehameha V (Lot Kamehameha), who ruled until 1872. With his passing the Kamehameha line ended. William Lunalilo, elected king in 1873 by popular vote, was of royal, but not Kamehameha, lineage. He died after only a year in office, and being a bachelor left no heirs. He was succeeded by David Kalakaua, known far and wide as "the Merrie Monarch," who made a world tour and was well received wherever he went. He built Iolani Palace in Honolulu and was personally in favor of closer ties with the U.S., helping push through the Reciprocity Act. Kalakaua died in 1891 and was replaced by his sister Lydia Liliuokalani, last of the Hawaiian monarchs.

The Revolution
When Liliuokalani took office in 1891, the native population was at a low of 40,000 and she felt that the U.S. had too much influence over her homeland. She was known to personally favor the English over the Americans. She attempted to replace the liberal constitution of 1887 (adopted by her pro-American brother) with an autocratic mandate in which she would have had much more political and economic control of the islands. When the McKinley Tariff of 1890 brought a decline in sugar profits, she made no attempt to improve the situation. Thus, the planters saw her as a political obstacle to their economic growth; most of Hawaii's American planters and

Queen Liliuokalani

pendence, would be outraged by the overthrow and would come to her aid. Incoming president Grover Cleveland *was* outraged and Hawaii wasn't immediately annexed as expected. When queried about what she would do with the conspirators if she were reinstated, Liliuokalani said that they would be hung as traitors. The racist press of the times, which portrayed the Hawaiians as half-civilized, bloodthirsty heathens, publicized this widely. Since the conspirators were the leading citizens of the land, the queen's words proved untimely. In January 1895 a small, ill-fated counterrevolution headed by Liliuokalani failed, and she was placed under house arrest in Iolani Palace. Officials of the republic insisted that she use her married name (Mrs. John Dominis) to sign the documents forcing her to abdicate her throne. She was also forced to swear allegiance to the new republic. Liliuokalani went on to write *Hawaii's Story* and the lyric ballad "Aloha O'e." She never forgave the conspirators and remained "queen" to the Hawaiians until her death in 1917.

Annexation

The overwhelming majority of Hawaiians opposed annexation and desired to restore the monarchy. But they were prevented from voting by the new republic because they couldn't meet the imposed property and income qualifications—a transparent ruse by the planters to control the majority. Most *haole* were racist and believed that the "common people" could not be entrusted with the vote because they were childish and incapable of ruling themselves. The fact that the Hawaiians had existed quite well for 1,000 years before white people even reached Hawaii was never considered. The Philippine theater of the Spanish-American War also prompted annexation. One of the strongest proponents was Alfred Mahon, a brilliant naval strategist who, with support from Theodore Roosevelt, argued that the U.S. military must have Hawaii in order to be a viable force in the Pacific. In addition, Japan, victorious in its recent war with China, protested the American intention to annex, and in so doing prompted even moderates to support annexation for fear that the Japanese themselves coveted the prize. On July 7, 1898, President McKinley signed the annexa-

merchants were in favor of a rebellion. She would have to go! A central spokesperson and firebrand was Lorrin Thurston, a Honolulu publisher who, with a central core of about 30 men, challenged the Hawaiian monarchy. Although Liliuokalani rallied some support and had a small military potential in her personal guard, the coup was ridiculously easy—it took only one casualty. Captain John Good shot a Hawaiian policeman in the arm and that did it. Naturally, the conspirators could not have succeeded without some solid assurances from a secret contingent in the U.S. Congress as well as outgoing president Benjamin Harrison, who favored Hawaii's annexation. Marines from the *Boston* went ashore to "protect American lives," and on January 17, 1893, the Hawaiian monarchy came to an end.

The provisional government was headed by Sanford B. Dole, who became president of the Hawaiian Republic. Liliuokalani surrendered not to the conspirators but to U.S. Ambassador John Stevens. She believed that the U.S. government, which had assured her of Hawaiian indetion agreement, and this "tropical fruit" was finally put into America's basket.

MODERN TIMES

Hawaii entered the 20th century totally transformed from what it had been. The old Hawaiian language, religion, culture, and leadership were all gone; Western dress, values, education, and recreation were the norm. Native Hawaiians were now unseen citizens who lived in dwindling numbers in remote areas. The plantations, new centers of social order, had a strong Asian flavor; more than 75% of their workforce was Asian. There was a small white middle class, an all-powerful white elite, and a single political party ruled by that elite. Education, however, was always highly prized, and by the turn of the century all racial groups were encouraged to attend school. By 1900, almost 90% of Hawaiians were literate (far above the national norm), and schooling was mandatory for all children ages 6-15. Intermarriage was accepted, and there was a mixing of the races like nowhere else on earth. The military became increasingly important to Hawaii. It brought in money and jobs, dominating the islands' economy. The Japanese attack on Pearl Harbor, which began U.S. involvement in WW II, bound Hawaii to America forever. Once the islands had been baptized by blood, the average Mainlander felt that Hawaii was American soil. A movement among Hawaiians to become part of the Union began to grow. They wanted a real voice in Washington, not merely a voteless delegate as provided under their territory status. Hawaii became the 50th state in 1959, and the jumbo-jet revolution of the 1960s made it easily accessible to growing numbers of tourists from all over the world.

Military History

A few military strategists realized the importance of Hawaii early in the 19th century, but most didn't recognize the advantages until the Spanish-American War. It was clearly an unsinkable ship in the middle of the Pacific from which the U.S. could launch military operations. Troops were stationed at Camp McKinley, at the foot of Diamond Head, the main military compound until it became obsolete in 1907. Pearl Harbor was first surveyed in 1872 by General Schofield. Later, a military base named in his honor, Schofield Barracks, was a main military post in central Oahu. It first housed the U.S. 5th Cavalry in 1909 and was heavily bombed by the Japanese at the outset of WW II. Pearl Harbor, first dredged in 1908, was officially opened on December 11, 1911. The first warship to enter was the cruiser *California.* Ever since, the military has been a mainstay of Hawaii's economy. Unfortunately, there has been long-standing bad blood between locals and military personnel. Each group has tended to look down upon the other.

Pearl Harbor Attack

On the morning of December 7, 1941, the Japanese carrier *Akagi,* flying the battle flag of the famed Admiral Togo of the Russo-Japanese War, received and broadcast over its PA system island music from Honolulu station KGMB. Deep in the bowels of the ship a radio man listened for a much different message, coming thousands of miles from the Japanese mainland. When the ironically poetic message "east wind rain" was received, the attack was launched. At the end of the day, 2,325 U.S. servicemen and 57 civilians were dead; 188 planes were destroyed; 18 major warships were sunk or heavily damaged; and the U.S. was in the war. Japanese casualties were ludicrously light. The ignited conflict would rage for four years until Japan, through Nagasaki and Hiroshima, was vaporized into total submission. At the end of hostilities, Hawaii would never again be considered separate from America.

Statehood

A number of economic and political reasons explain why the ruling elite of Hawaii desired statehood, but put simply, the vast majority of people who lived there, especially after WW II, considered themselves Americans. The first serious mention of making "The Sandwich Islands" a state was in the 1850s under President Franklin Pierce, but it wasn't taken seriously until the monarchy was overthrown in the 1890s. For the next 50 years statehood proposals were made repeatedly to Congress, but there was stiff opposition, especially from the southern states. With Hawaii a territory, an import quota system beneficial to Mainland producers could be enacted on produce, especially sugar. Also, there was prejudice against creating a state in a place where the majority of the populace was not white. This situation was illuminated by the infamous Massie Rape Case of 1931 (see "People," below), which went down as one of the greatest miscarriages of justice in American history.

During WW II, Hawaii was placed under martial law, but no serious attempt to intern the Japanese population was made, as in California. There were simply too many Japanese, who went on to gain the respect of the American people by their outstanding fighting record during the war. Hawaii's own 100th Battalion became the famous 442nd Regimental Combat Team, which gained notoriety by saving the Lost Texas Battalion during the Battle of the Bulge and went on to be *the* most decorated battalion in all of WW II. When these GIs returned home, *no one* was going to tell them that they were not loyal Americans. Many of these AJAs (Americans of Japanese Ancestry) took advantage of the GI Bill and received higher education. They were from the common people, not the elite, and they rallied grassroots support for statehood. When the vote finally occurred, approximately 132,900 voted in favor of statehood with only 7,800 votes against. Congress passed the Hawaii State Bill on March 12, 1959, and on August 21, 1960, President Eisenhower announced that Hawaii was officially the 50th state.

GOVERNMENT

The only difference between the government of the state of Hawaii and those of other states is that it's "streamlined," and in theory more efficient. There are only two levels of government: the state and the county. With no town or city governments to deal with, considerable bureaucracy is eliminated. Hawaii, in anticipation of becoming a state, drafted a constitution in 1950 and was ready to go when statehood came. Politics and government are taken seriously in the Aloha State, which consistently turns in the best national voting record per capita. For example, in the first state elections 173,000 of 180,000 registered voters voted—a whopping 94% of the electorate. In the election to ratify statehood, hardly a ballot went uncast, with 95% of the voters opting for statehood. The bill carried every island of Hawaii except Niihau, where, coincidentally, most of the people (total population 250 or so) are of relatively pure Hawaiian blood. The U.S. Congress passed the Hawaii State Bill on March 12, 1959, and on August 21, 1959, President Eisenhower proclaimed Hawaii the 50th state. Honolulu became the state capital. The present governor is Benjamin J. Cayetano, the second Hawaiian governor of the state, and the first with any Filipino heritage. Mr. Cayetano has held this office since 1994. He was elected to his second term in 1998, narrowly defeating a Republican challenge by former Maui mayor Linda Crockett Lingle. Lingle lost by a mere 5,200 votes, and Governor Cayetano said to Democrats, "This has been a wake-up call for all of us."

Maui County

The political boundaries of Maui County are a bit oddball. Maui County encompasses Maui island, as well as Lanai, Molokai, and the uninhabited island of Kahoolawe. One historical geographical oddity consisted of an arc on East Maui, from Makawao past Hana and along the south coast almost to Kihei, which was a "shared" political area, aligned culturally with the Kohala District of the Big Island since Polynesian times. As a traditional carryover, these two districts were joined with each other until political lines were redrawn in 1991, severing that political connection. The real strangeness occurs in Maui's 6th Senatorial District and the 7th and 12th Representative Districts. The 7th Representative District includes much of West Maui and the islands of Lanai and Molokai. The area of West Maui, with Kaanapali and Lahaina, is one of the most developed and financially sound areas in all of Hawaii. It's a favorite area with tourists and is one of the darlings of developers. On the other hand, Lanai has a tiny population, a growing tourist industry, and, in comparison, a minuscule economy. Molokai has the largest per capita concentration of native Hawaiians, a "busted economy" with a tremendous share of its population on welfare, and a grassroots movement deter-

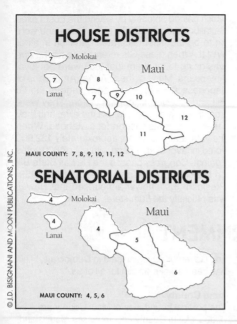

HOUSE DISTRICTS

Molokai

Maui

Lanai

MAUI COUNTY: 7, 8, 9, 10, 11, 12

SENATORIAL DISTRICTS

Molokai

Maui

Lanai

MAUI COUNTY: 4, 5, 6

© J.D. BISIGNANI AND MOON PUBLICATIONS, INC.

mined to preserve the historical integrity of the island and the dignity of the people. The 12th Representative District, which takes in the eastern third of the island of Maui, and 6th Senatorial District, which encompasses Kihei, Wailea, Makena, half of Upcountry, and Hana, are paired with the north coast of Kauai, from Kapaa through Hanalei to the Na Pali coast, an area that has no traditional political or cultural bond with Maui. You'd have to be a political magician to fairly represent all of the constituents in these widely differing districts.

The current mayor is James "Kimo" Apana. When elected in 1998, at age 36, he became the youngest mayor in Maui's history. Although Maui, like the rest of the state, is overwhelmingly Democratic, Apana's win broke a 20-year Republican grip on the mayor's office. The mayor is assisted by an elected county council, one member from each council district around the county. Of the 25 State Senatorial Districts, Maui County is represented by three, all Democrats. Maui County has six of 51 seats in the State House of Representatives, all Democrats except for one Republican representing the area of Kihei, Wailea, and part of Upcountry.

ECONOMY

Hawaii's mid-Pacific location makes it perfect for two primary sources of income: tourism and the military. Tourists come in anticipation of endless golden days on soothing beaches, while the military is provided with the strategic position of an unsinkable battleship. Each economic sector nets Hawaii about $4 billion annually, money that should keep flowing smoothly and even increase in the foreseeable future. These revenues remain mostly aloof from the normal ups and downs of the Mainland U.S. economy. Together they make up 60% of the islands' income, and both attract either gung-ho enthusiasts or rabidly negative detractors. The remaining 40% comes in descending proportions from manufacturing, construction, and agriculture (mainly sugar and pineapples). As long as the sun shines and the balance of global power requires a military presence, the economic stability of Hawaii is guaranteed.

Maui's economy is a mirror image of the state's economy: it's based on tourism, agriculture, and

government expenditures. The primary growth is in tourism, with Maui being the second most frequently chosen Hawaiian destination after Oahu. Over 17,000 rooms are available on Maui in all categories, and they're filled 75% of the time. On average, Maui attracts about two million tourists per year, and on any given day there are about 40,000 visitors enjoying the island. The majority of the rooms are in Kihei-Wailea and the Kaanapali to Kapalua strip. With tourists finding Maui more and more desirable every year, and with agriculture firmly entrenched, Maui's economic future is bright.

TOURISM

"The earthly paradise! Don't you want to go to it? Why, of course!" This was the opening line of *The Hawaiian Guide Book* by Henry Whitney, which appeared in 1875. In print for 25 years, it sold for 60 cents during a time when a roundtrip sea voyage between San Francisco and Honolulu cost $125. The technique is a bit dated, but the human desires remain the same: some of us seek paradise, all seek escape, some are drawn to play out a drama in a beautiful setting. Tourists have been coming to Hawaii ever since steamship service began in the 1860s. Until WW II, luxury liners carried the financial elite on exclusive voyages to the islands. By the 1920s 10,000 visitors a year were spending almost $5 million—cementing the bond between Hawaii and tourism.

A $25,000 prize offered by James Dole of pineapple fame sparked a trans Pacific air race in 1927. The success of the aerial daredevils who answered the challenge proved that commercial air travel to Hawaii was feasible. Two years later, **Hawaiian Airlines** was offering regularly scheduled flights between all of the major islands. By 1950, airplanes had captured over 50% of the transportation market, and ocean voyages were relegated to "specialty travel" catering to the elite. By 1960 the large airbuses made their debut; 300,000 tourists arrived on eight designated airlines. The Boeing 747 began operating in 1969. These enormous planes could carry hundreds of passengers at reasonable rates, so travel to Hawaii became possible for the average-income person. In 1970, two million arrived, and by 1990 close to six million passengers arrived on 22 international air carriers.

Tourists: Who, When, and Where

Tourism-based income outstripped pineapples and sugar by the mid-'60s and the boom was on. Most visitors (54%) are Americans, and by far the largest numbers come from the West Coast. Sunseeking refugees from Alaska, however, make up the greatest proportional number, according to state population figures. The remaining arrivals are, in descending proportions, from Japan, Canada, Korea, Australia, Germany, England, and Taiwan. Europe, as a whole, sends proportionately fewer visitors than North America or Asia, while the fewest come from South America. The Japanese market is constantly growing, reaching about two million Japanese visitors per year in 1995. This is particularly beneficial to the tourist market because the average Western tourist spends about $135 per day, while a Japanese counterpart spends $340 per day. The average Japanese

tourist, however, stays only about six days as opposed to 10 days for westbound travelers. Up until very recently the Japanese traveled only in groups and primarily stayed on Oahu. Now the trend is to travel independently or to come with a group and then peel off, with a hefty percentage heading for the "Neighbor Islands" (all islands other than Oahu).

The typical visitor is slightly affluent, and female visitors outnumber males three to two. The average age (35) is a touch higher than in most vacation areas because it reflects an inflated proportion of retirees heading for Hawaii, especially Honolulu, to fulfill lifelong dream vacations. A typical stay lasts about 10 days, down from a month in the 1950s; a full 56% of tourists are repeat visitors. On any given day there are about 80,000 travelers on Oahu, 40,000 on Maui, 19,000 on Hawaii, and about 8,000 on Kauai. Molokai and Lanai get so few visitors, 1,400 and 1,000, respectively, that the figures are hardly counted. In 1964 only 10% of the islands' hotel rooms were on the Neighbor Islands, but by 1966 the figure jumped to 25%, with more than 70% of the tourists opting to visit the Neighbor Islands. Today four out of 10 hotel rooms are on the Neighbor Islands, and that figure should reach 50% shortly.

Joaquin Miller, the 19th-century poet of the Sierra, said, "I tell you my boy, the man who has not seen the Sandwich Islands, in this one great ocean's warm heart, has not seen the world." The times have certainly changed, but the sentiments of most visitors to Hawaii remain the same.

Tourism-Related Problems

Tourism is both a boon and blight to Hawaii. It is the root cause of two problems: one environmental, the other socioeconomic. The environmental impact is obvious, and is best described in the lament of songstress Joni Mitchell's "Big Yellow Taxi": "They paved paradise and put up a parking lot." Put simply, tourism can draw too many people to an area and overburden it. In the process, it stresses the land and destroys the natural beauty that attracted people in the first place. Tourists come to Hawaii for what has been called its "ambient resource": a balanced collage of indulgent climate, invigorating waters, intoxicating scenery, and exotic people all wrapped up neatly in one area which can both soothe and excite. It's in the best interest of Hawaii to preserve this resource.

Most point to Waikiki as a prime example of development gone mad. Actually two prime examples of the best and the worst development can be found on Maui's south shore at Kihei and Wailea, less than five miles apart. In the late '60s Kihei experienced a development-inspired "feeding frenzy" that made the real sharks offshore seem about as dangerous as Winnie the Pooh. Condos were slapped up as fast as cement can dry, their architecture reminiscent of a stack of shoeboxes. A coastline renowned for its beauty was overburdened, and the view was wiped out in the process. Anyone who had the bucks built, and now parts of Kihei look like a high-rise, low-income, federally funded housing project. You can bet that those who made a killing building here don't live here.

Conversely, just down the road is Wailea, a model of what development could (and should) be. The architecture is tasteful, low-rise, unobtrusive, and designed with people and the preservation of the scenery in mind . . . mostly. It's obviously more exclusive, but access points to the beaches are open to everyone, and the view is still there for all to enjoy. Wailea points the way for the development of the future.

THE MILITARY

Hawaii is the most militarized state in the U.S.: all five services are represented. Camp H.M. Smith, overlooking Pearl Harbor, is the headquarters of CINCPAC (Commander in Chief Pacific), which is responsible for 70% of the earth's surface, from California to the east coast of Africa and to both poles. The U.S. military presence dates back to 1887, when Pearl Harbor was given to the Navy as part of the Reciprocity Act. The sugar planters were given favorable duty-free treatment for their sugar, while the U.S. Navy was allowed exclusive rights to one of the best harbors in the Pacific. In 1894, when the monarchy was being overthrown by the sugar planters, the USS *Boston* sent a contingency of U.S. Marines ashore to "keep order," which really amounted to a show of force backing the revolution. The Spanish-American War saw U.S.

troops billeted at Camp McKinley at the foot of Diamond Head, and Schofield Barracks opened to receive the 5th Cavalry in 1909. Pearl Harbor's flames ignited WW II, and there has been no looking back since then.

The small military presence on Maui amounts to a tiny Army installation near Kahului and the Coast Guard facility at Maalaea.

The Military Has No *Aloha*

Not everyone is thrilled by the strong military presence in Hawaii. Two factions, native Hawaiians and antinuclear groups, are downright angry. Radical contingencies of native Hawaiian-rights groups consider Hawaii an independent country, besieged and "occupied" by the U.S. government. They date their loss of independence to Liliuokalani's overthrow in 1894. The vast majority of ethnic Hawaiians, though they consider themselves Americans, are concerned about the loss of their rightful homelands with no financial reparation, and about continuing destruction of and disregard for their traditional religious and historical sites. A long list of grievances is cited by native Hawaiian action groups, but the best and clearest example was the controversy over the sacred island, Kahoolawe, which, until 1994, was used as a bombing target by the U.S. Navy.

A major controversy raised by the military presence focuses on Hawaii as a nuclear target. The ultimate goal of the antinuclear protesters is to see the Pacific, and the entire world, free from nuclear arms. They see Hawaii as a big target used by the international power merchants on the Mainland as both pawn and watchdog—if war breaks out, they say, the Hawaiian Islands will be reduced to cinders. The military naturally counters that a strong Hawaii is a deterrent to nuclear war and that Hawaii is not only a powerful offensive weapon, but one of the best-defended regions of the world. Unfortunately, when you are on an island there is no place to go: like a boxer in a ring, you can run, but you can't hide. Also, the military has been recently cited for disposing of stockpiles of chemical weapons by incineration on Johnston Island, a military installation southwest of the Big Island. Because there was no environmental impact study, scientists fear that wind and currents could carry the pollutants to the main Hawaiian Islands, destroying delicate coral reefs along the way.

AGRICULTURE

Agriculturally, Maui generates revenue through cattle, sugar, pineapples, and flowers, along with a substantial subculture economy in *pakalolo*. **Cattle grazing** occurs on the western and southern slopes of Haleakala, where 35,000 acres are owned by the Haleakala Ranch, and more than 23,000 acres by the Ulupalakua Ranch. The upper slopes of Haleakala around Kula are a gardener's dream. Delicious onions, potatoes, and all sorts of garden vegetables are grown, but are secondary to large plots of gorgeous flowers, mainly carnations and the amazing protea.

Sugar, actually in the grass family, is still very important to Maui's economy, but without federal subsidies it wouldn't be a viable cash crop. The largest acreage is in the central isthmus area, which is virtually all owned by the Alexander and Baldwin Company. There are also large sugarcane tracts along Kaanapali and the west coast that are owned by Amfac and Maui Land and Pineapple. Those lodging in Kaanapali will become vividly aware of the cane fields when they're burned off just prior to harvesting. Making these unsightly burnings even worse is the fact that the plastic pipe used in the drip irrigation of the fields is left in place. Not cost-efficient to recover, it is burned along with the cane, adding its noxious fumes to the air.

Pineapples grow in central east Maui between Paia and Makawao, where Alexander and Baldwin own most of the land, and substantial acres have been planted in Kapalua in the far northwest, where Maui Land and Pineapple controls most of the holdings.

Renegade entrepreneurs grow patches of *pakalolo* wherever they can find a spot that has the right vibes and is away from the prying eyes of the authorities. Deep in the West Maui Mountains and along the Hana coast are favorite areas.

THE "BIG FIVE"

Until statehood, Hawaii was ruled economically by a consortium of corporations known as the "Big Five": **C. Brewer and Co.,** sugar, ranching, and chemicals, founded in 1826; **Theo. H. Davies & Co.,** sugar, investments, insurance, and transportation, founded in 1845; **Amfac Inc.** (originally H. Hackfield Inc.—a German firm that changed its name and ownership during the anti-German sentiment of WW I to American Factors), sugar, insurance, and land development, founded in 1849; **Castle and Cooke Inc.,** (Dole) pineapple, food packing, and land development, founded in 1851; and **Alexander and Baldwin Inc.,** shipping, sugar, and pineapple, founded in 1895. This economic oligarchy ruled Hawaii with a velvet glove and a steel grip.

LEAF JOINT (COLLARS)

STALK

LEAF

INTERNODE

NODE

ROOTS

SEED PIECE

young sugarcane

LOUISE FOOTE

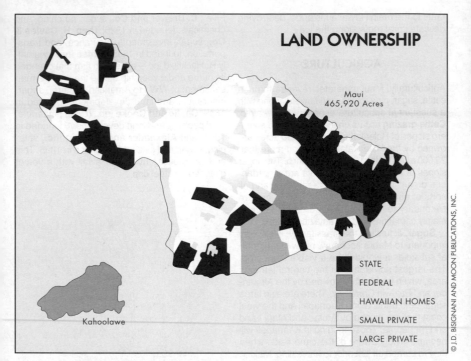

LAND OWNERSHIP

Maui
465,920 Acres

Kahoolawe

■ STATE

FEDERAL

HAWAIIAN HOMES

SMALL PRIVATE

LARGE PRIVATE

With members on all important corporate boards, they controlled all major commerce, including banking, shipping, insurance, hotel development, agriculture, utilities, and wholesale and retail merchandising. Anyone trying to buck the system was ground to dust, finding it suddenly impossible to do business in the islands. The Big Five were made up of the islands' oldest and most well-established *haole* families; all included bloodlines from Hawaii's own nobility. They looked among themselves for suitable husbands and wives, so that breaking in from the outside even through marriage was hardly possible. The only time they were successfully challenged prior to statehood was when Sears, Roebuck and Co. opened a store on Oahu. Closing ranks, the Big Five decreed that their steamships would not carry Sears' freight. When Sears threatened to buy its own steamship line, the Big Five relented.

Actually, statehood, and more to the point, tourism, broke their oligarchy. After 1960 too much money was at stake for Mainland-based corporations to ignore. Eventually the grip of the Big Five was loosened, but they are still enormously powerful and richer than ever. These days, however, they don't control everything; now their power is land. With only five other major landholders, they control 65% of the privately held land in Hawaii.

LAND OWNERSHIP

Landwise, Hawaii is a small pie, and its slices are not at all well divided. Of the state's 6,423 square miles of land, the six main inhabited islands make up 98% of it. This figure does not include Niihau, which is privately owned by the Robinson family and inhabited by some of the last remaining pure-blooded Hawaiians; nor does it include uninhabited Kahoolawe. Of the 4,110,966 acres that make up the inhabited islands, 34% is owned by the state and 16% by the federal government; the remaining 50% is in private hands. While only 40 owners, with 5,000 or more acres each, own 75% of all private lands, the top seven control 46% of it. To be more specific, Castle and Cooke Inc. owns 99% of Lanai, while 40-60% of Maui, Oahu, Molokai, Kauai, and Hawaii is owned by less than a dozen private parties. The largest private landowner, with over 336,000 acres or 8% of the total land area of the state, is the Kamehameha Schools/Bishop Estate, which recently lost a Supreme Court battle that ended with a ruling allowing the state of Hawaii to acquire privately owned land for "the public good."

More than in any other state, Hawaii's landowners tend to lease land instead of sell it, and many private homes are on rented ground. Many feel that with land prices going up all the time, only the very rich land developers will be able to purchase, and the "people" of Hawaii will become even more land-poor.

PEOPLE

Nowhere else on earth can you find such a kaleidoscopic mixture of people. Every major race is accounted for, and over 50 ethnic groups are represented throughout the islands, making Hawaii the most racially integrated state in the country. Its population of 1.2 million includes 100,000 permanently stationed military personnel and their dependents. It is the only state where whites are not the majority. About 56% of the people living in Hawaii were born there, 26% were born on the Mainland U.S., and 18% are foreign-born.

The population of Hawaii has been growing steadily in recent times, but it fluctuated wildly in times past. In 1876 it ebbed to its lowest, with only 55,000 permanent residents in the islands. This was the era of large sugar plantations; their constant demand for labor was the primary cause of the importation of various peoples from around the world, which is what led to Hawaii's racially integrated society. WW II saw Hawaii's population swell from 400,000 just prior to the war to 900,000 during the war. Naturally, 500,000 were military personnel who left at war's end, but many returned to settle after getting a taste of island living.

Of the 1.2 million people in the islands today (1995 est.), 870,000 live on Oahu, with slightly less than half of those living in the Honolulu Metropolitan Area. The rest of the population is distributed as follows: 137,000 on Hawaii, with 47,000 living in Hilo; 115,000 on Maui, with the largest concentration, 53,000, in Wailuku/Kahului; 56,000 on Kauai, including 230 pure-blooded Hawaiians on Niihau; 6,700 on Molokai; and just under 3,000 on Lanai. The population density, statewide, is 186 people per square mile, approximately that of California's. The population is not at all evenly distributed, with Oahu claiming about 1,430 people per square mile, Hawaii barely 34 residents per square mile. Statewide, city dwellers outnumber those living in the country by nine to one. For Maui County, 78% are urban while 22% live rurally.

Population Figures

With 115,000, Maui has the third-largest island population in Hawaii, about 9.5% of the state's total. Maui's population density is 158 people per square mile, with Molokai and Lanai at 26 and 20 per square mile, respectively. The Kahului/Wailuku area has the island's greatest density of population, with about 53,000 people. The Upcountry population is just over 33,000, while just fewer than 20,000 live along the west coast. Hana District registers a handful over 2,000 people. The ethnic breakdown of Maui's 115,000 people is as follows: 42% Caucasian, 19% Filipino, 18% Japanese, 14% Hawaiian, 2% Chinese, and 5% Other.

MAUI ETHNICITY

CAUCASIAN 42%
FILIPINO 19%
JAPANESE 18%
HAWAIIAN 14%
OTHER 5%
CHINESE 2%

© MOON PUBLICATIONS, INC.

THE HAWAIIANS

The study of the native Hawaiians is ultimately a study in tragedy because it ends in their demise as a viable people. When Captain Cook first sighted Hawaii in 1778, there were an estimated 300,000 natives living in perfect harmony with their ecological surroundings; within 100 years a scant 50,000 demoralized and dejected Hawaiians existed almost as wards of the state. Today, although more than 210,000 people claim varying degrees of Hawaiian blood, experts say that fewer than 1,000 are pure Hawaiian, and this is stretching it.

It's easy to see why people of Hawaiian lineage could be bitter over what they have lost, being strangers in their own land now, much like Native Americans. The overwhelming majority of "Hawaiians" are of mixed heritage, and the wisest take the best from all worlds. From the Hawaiian side comes simplicity, love of the land, and acceptance of people. It is the Hawaiian legacy of *aloha* that remains immortal and adds that special elusive quality that *is* Hawaii.

Polynesian Roots

The Polynesians' original stock is muddled and remains an anthropological mystery, but it's believed that they were nomadic wanderers who migrated from both the Indian subcontinent and Southeast Asia through Indonesia, where they learned to sail and navigate on protected waterways. As they migrated they honed their sailing skills until they could take on the Pacific, and as they moved, they absorbed people from other cultures and races until they had coalesced into what we now know as Polynesians.

Abraham Fornander, still considered a major authority on the subject, wrote in his 1885 *Account of the Polynesian Race* that he believed the Polynesians started as a white (Aryan) race that was heavily influenced by contact with the Cushite, Chaldeo-Arabian civilization. He estimated their arrival in Hawaii at A.D. 600, based on Hawaiian genealogical chants. Modern science seems to bear this date out, although it remains skeptical about his other surmises. According to others, the intrepid Polynesians who actually settled Hawaii are believed to have come from the Marquesas Islands, 1,000 miles southeast of Hawaii. The Marquesans were cannibals known

for their tenacity and strength, attributes that would serve them well.

The Caste System

Hawaiian society was divided into rankings by a strict caste system determined by birth, and from which there was no chance of escaping. The highest rank was the *ali'i,* the chiefs and royalty. The impeccable genealogies of the *ali'i* were traced back to the gods themselves, and the chants *(mo'o ali'i)* were memorized and sung by professionals (called *ku'auhau)* who were themselves *ali'i.* Ranking passed from both father and mother, and custom dictated that the first mating of an *ali'i* be with a person of equal status.

A *kahuna* was a highly skilled person whose advice was sought before any major project was undertaken, such as building a house, hollowing a canoe log, or even offering a prayer. The *mo'o kahuna* were the priests of Ku and Lono, and they were in charge of praying and following rituals. They were very powerful *ali'i* and kept strict secrets and laws concerning their various functions.

Besides this priesthood of *kahuna,* there were other *kahuna* who were not *ali'i* but commoners. The two most important were the healers *(kahuna lapa'au)* and the black magicians *(kahuna ana'ana),* who could pray a person to death. The *kahuna lapa'au* had a marvelous pharmacopoeia of herbs and spices that could cure over 250 diseases common to the Hawaiians. The *kahuna ana'ana* could be hired to cast a love spell over a person or cause his or her untimely death. They seldom had to send out a reminder of payment!

The common people were called the *maka'ainana,* "the people of land"—the farmers, artisans, and fishermen. The land that they lived on was owned by the *ali'i,* but they were not bound to it. If the local *ali'i* was cruel or unfair, the *maka'ainana* had the right to leave and reside on another's lands. The *maka'ainana* mostly loved their local *ali'i* much like a child loves a parent, and the feeling was reciprocal. *Maka'ainana* who lived close to the *ali'i* and could be counted on as warriors in times of trouble were called *kanaka no lua kaua,* "a man for the heat of battle." They were treated with greater favor than those who lived in the backcountry, *kanaka no hii kua,* whose lesser standing opened them up to discrimination and cruelty. All *maka'ainana* formed extended families called *ohana* who usually lived on the same section of land, called *ahupua'a.* Those farmers who

LOUISE FOOTE

The ali'i wore magnificent feathered capes that signified their rank. The noblest colors were red and yellow, provided by specialized hunters who snared and plucked just the right birds.

lived inland would barter their produce with the fishermen who lived on the shore, and thus all shared equally in the bounty of land and sea.

A special group called *kauwa* was a landless, untouchable caste confined to living on reservations. Their origins were obviously Polynesian, but they appeared to be descendants of castaways who had survived and become perhaps the aboriginals of Hawaii before the main migrations. It was *kapu* for anyone to go onto *kauwa* lands, and doing so meant instant death. If a human sacrifice was needed, the *kahuna* would simply summon a *kauwa,* who had no recourse but to mutely comply. To this day, to call someone *kauwa,* which now supposedly only means servant, is still considered a fight-provoking insult.

Kapu and Day-to-Day Life

Occasionally there were horrible wars, but mostly the people lived quiet and ordered lives based on a strict caste society and the *kapu* system. Famine was known but only on a regional level, and the population was kept in check by birth control, crude abortions, and the distasteful practice of infanticide, especially of baby girls. The Hawaiians were absolutely loving and nurturing parents under most circumstances, and would even take in a *hanai* (adopted child or oldster), a lovely practice that lingers to this day.

A strict division of labor existed among men and women. Men were the only ones permitted to have anything to do with taro: this foodstuff was so sacred that there were a greater number of *kapu* concerning taro than concerning man himself. Men pounded poi and served it to the women. Men also were the fishermen and the builders of houses, canoes, irrigation ditches, and walls. Women tended to other gardens and shoreline fishing, and were responsible for making tapa cloth. The entire family lived in the common house called the *hale noa.*

Certain things were *kapu* between the sexes. Primarily, women could not enter the *mua* (man's house), nor could they eat with men. Certain foods such as pork, coconut, red fish, and bananas were forbidden to women, and it was *kapu* for a man to have intercourse before going fishing, engaging in battle, or attending a religious ceremony. Young boys lived with the women until they underwent a circumcision rite called *pule ipu.* After this was performed, they were required to keep the *kapu* of men. A true Hawaiian settlement required a minimum of five huts: the men's eating hut; women's menstruation hut; women's eating hut; communal sleeping hut; and prayer hut. Without these five separate structures, Hawaiian "society" could not happen, since the *ia kapu* (forbidden eating between men and women) could not be observed.

Ali'i could also declare a *kapu,* and often did so. Certain lands or fishing areas were temporarily made *kapu* so that they could revitalize. Even today, it is *kapu* for anyone to remove all the *opihi* (a type of limpet) from a rock. The great King Kamehameha I even placed a *kapu* on the body of his notoriously unfaithful child bride, Kaahumanu. It didn't work! The greatest *kapu* (*kapu moe*) was afforded to the highest ranking *ali'i:* anyone coming into their presence had to prostrate themselves.

Lesser ranking *ali'i* were afforded the *kapu noho:* lessers had to sit or kneel in their presence. Commoners could not let their shadows fall upon an *ali'i* or enter an *ali'i's* house except through a special door. Breaking a *kapu* meant immediate death.

Fatal Flaws

Less than 100 years after Captain Cook's arrival, King Kalakaua found himself with only 48,000 Hawaiian subjects. Wherever the king went, he would beseech his people, *"hooulu lahui,"* "increase the race," but it was already too late. It was as if nature herself had turned her back on these once-proud people. Many of their marriages were barren; in 1874 when only 1,400 children were born, a full 75% died in infancy. The Hawaiians could do nothing but watch as their race faded from existence.

The Causes of Decline

The ecological system of Hawaii has always been exceptionally fragile and this included its people. When the first whites arrived they found a great people who were large, strong, and virile. But when it came to fighting off the most minor diseases, the Hawaiians proved as delicate as hot-house flowers. To exacerbate the situation, the Hawaiians were totally uninhibited toward sexual intercourse between willing partners, and they engaged in it openly and with abandon. Unfortunately, the sailors who arrived were full of syphilis and gonorrhea. The Hawaiian women brought these diseases home and, given the nature of Hawaiian society at the time, they spread like wildfire. By the time the missionaries came in 1820 and helped to halt the unbridled fornication, they estimated the native population at only 140,000, less than half of what it had been only 40 years since initial contact! In the next 50 years measles, mumps, influenza, and tuberculosis further ravaged the people. Furthermore, Hawaiian men were excellent sailors, and it's estimated that during the whaling years at least 25% of all able-bodied Hawaiian men sailed away, never to return.

But the coup de grace that really ended the Hawaiian race, as such, was that racial newcomers to the islands were attracted to the Hawaiians and the Hawaiians were in turn attracted to them. With so many interracial marriages, the Hawaiians literally bred themselves out of existence. By 1910, there were still twice as many full-blooded Hawaiians as mixed-bloods, but by 1940 mixed-blooded Hawaiians were the fastest-growing group, and full-blooded the fastest declining.

Hawaiians Today

Many of the Hawaiians who moved to the cities became more and more disenfranchised. Their folk society stressed openness and a giving nature, but downplayed the individual and the ownership of private property. These cultural traits made them easy targets for the users and schemers until they finally became either apathetic or angry. Most surveys reveal that although Hawaiians number only 13% of the population, they account for almost 50% of the financially destitute families and about half of all arrests and illegitimate births. Niihau, a privately owned island, is home to about

people of Lanai

J.D. BISIGNANI

230 pure-blooded Hawaiians, representing the largest concentration of them, per capita, in the islands. The Robinson family, which owns the island, restricts visitors to invited guests only.

The second-largest concentration is on Molokai, where 2,700 Hawaiians, living mostly on 40-acre kulcana of Hawaiian Homes Lands, make up 40% of that island's population. The majority of mixed-blooded Hawaiians, 80,000 or so, live on Oahu, where they are particularly strong in the hotel and entertainment fields. People of Hawaiian extraction are still a delight to meet, and anyone so lucky as to be befriended by one long regards this friendship as the highlight of his or her travels. The Hawaiians have always given their aloha freely to all the peoples of the world, and it is we who must acknowledge this precious gift.

THE CHINESE

Next to Yankees from New England, the Chinese are the oldest migrant group in Hawaii, and their influence has far outshone their meager numbers. They brought to Hawaii, along with their individuality, Confucianism, Taoism, and Buddhism, although many have long since become Christians. The Chinese population, at 68,000, makes up only 6% of the state's total, and the vast majority reside on Oahu. As an ethnic group they account for the least amount of crime, the highest per capita income, and a disproportionate number of professionals.

The First Chinese
No one knows his name, but an unknown Chinese immigrant is credited with being the first person in Hawaii to refine sugar. This Asian wanderer tried his hand at crude refining on Lanai in 1802. Fifty years later the sugar plantations desperately needed workers, and the first Chinese brought to Hawaii under the newly passed Masters and Servants Act were 195 coolies from Amoy, who arrived in 1852. These conscripts were contracted for three to five years and given $3 per month plus room and board. This was for 12 hours a day, six days a week, and even in 1852 these wages were the pits. The Chinese almost always left the plantations the minute their contracts expired. They went into business for themselves and promptly monopolized the restaurant and small-shop trades.

The Chinese Niche
Although many people in Hawaii considered all Chinese ethnically the same, they were actually quite different. The majority came from Guangdong Province in southern China. They were two distinct ethnic groups: the Punti made up 75% of the immigrants, and the Hakka made up the remainder. In China, they remained separate from each other, never mixing; in Hawaii, they mixed out of necessity. For one thing, hardly any Chinese women came over at first, and the ones who followed were at a premium and gladly accepted as wives, regardless of ethnic background. The Chinese were also some of the first groups who willingly intermarried with the Hawaiians, from whom they gained a reputation for being exceptionally caring spouses.

The Chinese accepted the social order and kept a low profile. For example, during the turbulent labor movements of the 1930s and '40s in Hawaii, the Chinese community produced not one labor leader, radical intellectual, or left-wing politician. When Hawaii became a state, one of the two senators elected was Hiram Fong, a racially mixed Chinese. Since statehood, the Chinese community has carried on business as usual as they continue to rise both economically and socially.

THE JAPANESE

Most scholars believe that (inevitably) a few Japanese castaways floated to Hawaii long before Captain Cook arrived, and might have introduced the iron with which the islanders seemed to be familiar before the white explorers arrived. The first official arrivals from Japan were ambassadors sent by the Japanese shogun to negotiate in Washington; they stopped en route at Honolulu in March 1860. But it was as plantation workers that the Japanese were brought en masse to the islands. A small group arrived in 1868, and mass migration started in 1885.

In 1886, because of famine, the Japanese government allowed farmers mainly from southern Honshu, Kyushu, and Okinawa to emigrate. Among these were members of Japan's little-talked-about untouchable caste, called eta or burakumin in Japan and chorinbo in Hawaii. They gratefully seized this opportunity to better their lot, an impossibility in Japan. The first Japanese migrants were almost all men. Between

The Japanese-American GIs returned as "our boys."

1897 and 1908 migration was steady, with about 70% of the immigrants being men. Afterward, migration slowed because of a "gentlemen's agreement," a euphemism for racism against the "yellow peril." By 1900 there were over 60,000 Japanese in the islands, constituting the largest ethnic group.

AJAs, Americans of Japanese Ancestry

Parents of most Japanese children born before WW II were *issei* (first generation), who considered themselves apart from other Americans and clung to the notion of "we Japanese." Their children, the *nisei* or second generation, were a different matter altogether. In one generation they had become Americans, and they put into practice the high Japanese virtues of obligation, duty, and loyalty to the homeland; that homeland was now unquestionably America. After Pearl Harbor was bombed, the FBI kept close tabs on the Japanese community, and the menace of the "enemy within" prompted the deci-

sion to place Hawaii under martial law for the duration of the war. It has since been noted that not a single charge of espionage or sabotage was ever reported against the Japanese community in Hawaii during the war.

AJAs as GIs

Although Japanese had formed a battalion during WW I, they were insulted by being considered unacceptable as American soldiers in WW II. Some Japanese-Americans volunteered to serve in labor battalions, and because of their flawless work and loyalty, it was decided to put out a call for a few hundred volunteers to form a combat unit. Over 10,000 signed up! AJAs formed two distinguished units in WW II: the 100th Infantry Battalion and later the 442nd Regimental Combat Team. They landed in Italy at Salerno and even fought from Guadalcanal to Okinawa. They distinguished themselves by becoming *the* most decorated unit in American military history.

The AJAs Return

Many returning AJAs took advantage of the GI Bill and received college educations. The "Big Five" corporations for the first time accepted former AJA officers as executives, and the old order was changed. Many Japanese became involved with Hawaiian politics and the first elected to Congress was Daniel Inouye, who had lost an arm fighting in WW II. Hawaii's past governor, George Ariyoshi, elected in 1974, was the country's first Japanese-American to reach such a high office. Most Japanese, even as they climb the economic ladder, tend to remain Democrats.

Today, one out of every two political offices in Hawaii is held by a Japanese-American. In one of those weird quirks of fate, it is now the Hawaiian Japanese who are accused by other ethnic groups of engaging in unfair political practices—nepotism and reverse discrimination. Many of these accusations against AJAs are undoubtedly motivated by jealousy, but the AJAs' record in social fairness issues is not without blemish; true to their custom of family loyalty, they do stick together.

There are now 250,000 people in Hawaii of Japanese ancestry, nearly one-quarter of the state's population. They are the least likely of any ethnic group in Hawaii to marry outside of their group—especially the men—and they enjoy a higher-than-average standard of living.

CAUCASIANS

White people have a distinction separating them from all other ethnic groups in Hawaii: they are lumped together as one. You can be anything from a Protestant Norwegian dockworker to a Greek Orthodox shipping tycoon, but if your skin is white, in Hawaii you're a *haole*. What's more, you could have arrived at Waikiki from Missoula, Montana, in the last 24 hours, or your *kama'aina* family can go back five generations, but again, if you're white, you're a *haole*.

The word *"haole"* has a floating connotation that depends upon the spirit in which it's used. It can mean everything from a derisive "honky" or "cracker" to nothing more than "white person." The exact Hawaiian meaning is clouded, but some say it meant "a man of no background," because white men couldn't chant a genealogical *kanaenae* telling the Hawaiians who they were. The word eventually evolved to mean "foreign white man" and today, simply "white person."

White History

Next to Hawaiians themselves, white people have the oldest stake in Hawaii. They've been there as settlers in earnest since the missionaries of the 1800s, and were established long before any other migrant group. From last century until statehood, old *haole* families owned and controlled everything, and although they were generally benevolent, philanthropic, and paternalistic, they were also racist. They were established *kama'aina* families, many of whom made up the boards of the Big Five corporations or owned huge plantations and formed an inner social circle that was closed to the outside. Many managed to find mates from among close family acquaintances.

Their paternalism, which they accepted with grave responsibility, at first extended only to the Hawaiians, who saw them as replacing their own *ali'i*. Asians were considered primarily instruments of production. These supremacist attitudes tended to drag on in Hawaii until quite recent times. They are today responsible for the sometimes sour relations between white and nonwhite people in the islands. Today, all individual white people are resented to a certain degree because of these past acts, even though they personally were in no way involved.

White Plantation Workers

In the 1880s the white landowners looked around and felt surrounded and outnumbered by Asians, so they tried to import white people for plantation work. None of their schemes seemed to work out. Europeans were accustomed to a much higher wage scale and better living conditions than were provided on the plantations. Although only workers and not considered the equals of the ruling elite, they still were expected to act like a special class. They were treated preferentially, which meant higher wages for the same jobs performed by Asians. Some of the imported workers included: 600 Scandinavians in 1881; 1,400 Germans 1881-85; 400 Poles 1897-98; and 2,400 Russians 1909-12. Many proved troublesome, like the Poles and Russians who staged strikes after only months on the job. Many quickly moved to the Mainland. A contingency of Scots, who first came as mule skinners, did become successful plantation managers and supervisors. The Germans and Scandinavians were well received and climbed the social ladder rapidly, becoming professionals and skilled workers.

The Depression years, not as economically bad in Hawaii as in the continental U.S., brought many Mainland whites seeking opportunity, mostly from the South and the West. These new people were even more racist toward brown-skinned people and Asians than the *kama'aina haole,* and they made matters worse. They also competed more intensely for jobs. The racial tension generated during this period came to a head in 1932 with the infamous Massie Rape Case.

The Massie Rape Case

Thomas Massie, a naval officer, and his young wife, Thalia, attended a party at the Officers Club in 1932. After drinking and dancing all evening, they got into a row and Thalia rushed out in a huff. A few hours later, Thalia was at home, confused and hysterical, claiming to have been raped by some local men. On the most circumstantial evidence, Joseph Kahahawai and four friends of mixed ethnic background were accused. In a highly controversial trial rife with racial tensions, the verdict ended in a hung jury.

While a new trial was being set, Kahahawai and his friends were out on bail. Seeking revenge, Thomas Massie and Grace Fortescue, Thalia's mother, kidnapped Joseph Kahahawai with a plan of extracting a confession from him. They were aided by two enlisted men assigned to guard Thalia. While questioning Joseph, they killed him and attempted to dump his body in the sea but were apprehended. Another controversial trial—this time for Mrs. Fortescue, Massie, and the accomplices—followed. Clarence Darrow, the famous lawyer, sailed to Hawaii to defend them. For killing Kahahawai, these people served *one hour* of imprisonment in the judge's private chambers. The other four, acquitted with Joseph Kahahawai, maintain innocence of the rape to this day. Later, the Massies divorced, and Thalia went on to become a depressed alcoholic who took her own life.

The Portuguese

The last time anyone looked, Portugal was still attached to the European continent, but for some anomalous reason the Portuguese weren't considered *haole* in Hawaii for the longest time. About 12,000 arrived between 1878 and 1887 and another 6,000 came between 1906 and 1913. Accompanied during this period by 8,000 Spanish, they were considered one and the same. Most of the Portuguese were illiterate peasants from Madeira and the Azores, and the Spanish hailed from Andalusia. They were very well received, and because they were white but not *haole,* they made a perfect "buffer" ethnic group. Committed to staying in Hawaii, they rose to be skilled workers—the *"luna* class" on the plantations. However, they de-emphasized education and became very racist toward Asians, regarding them as a threat to their job security.

By 1920, the 27,000 Portuguese made up 11% of the population. After that they tended to blend with the other ethnic groups and weren't counted separately. Portuguese men tended to marry within their ethnic group, but a good portion of Portuguese women married other white men and became closer to the *haole* group, while another large portion chose Hawaiian mates and grew further away. Although they didn't originate pidgin English (see "Language," below), the unique melodious quality of their native tongue did give pidgin that certain lilt it has today. Also, the ukulele was closely patterned after the *cavaquinho,* a Portuguese stringed folk instrument.

The White Population

Today Caucasians make up the largest racial group in the islands at 33% of the population. They are spread evenly throughout Kauai, Oahu, Maui, and the Big Island, with much smaller percentages on Molokai and Lanai. On Maui, there are heavy white concentrations on the Kihei and Kaanapali coasts. The white population is the fastest growing in the islands because most people resettling in Hawaii are white Americans predominantly from the West Coast.

FILIPINOS AND OTHERS

The Filipinos who came to Hawaii brought high hopes of amassing personal fortunes and returning home as rich heroes; for most it was a dream that never came true. Filipinos had been American nationals ever since the Spanish-American War of 1898, and as such weren't subject to immigration laws that curtailed the importation of other Asian workers at the turn of this century. The first to arrive were 15 families in 1906, but a large number came in 1924 as strikebreakers. The majority were illiterate peasants called Ilocanos from the northern Philippines, with about 10% Visayans from the central cities. The Visayans were not as hardworking or thrifty, but were much more sophisticated. From the first, Filipinos were looked down upon by all the other immigrant groups and were considered particularly uncouth by the Japanese. The value they placed on education was the least of any group, and even by 1930 only about half could speak rudimentary English, the majority remaining illiterate. They were billeted in the worst housing, performed the most menial jobs, and were the last hired and first fired.

One big difference between Filipinos and other groups was that the men brought no Filipino women to marry, so they clung to the idea of returning home. In 1930 there were 30,000 men and only 360 women. This hopeless situation led to a great deal of prostitution and homosexuality; many of these terribly lonely bachelors would feast and drink on weekends and engage in their gruesome but exciting pastime of cockfighting on Sundays. When some did manage to find wives, their mates were inevitably part Hawaiian. Today, there are still plenty of old Filipino bachelors who never managed to get home, and the Sunday cockfights remain a way of life.

The Filipinos constitute 15% of Hawaii's population (170,000), with almost 75% living on Oahu. Many visitors to Hawaii mistake Filipinos for Hawaiians because of their dark skin, and this is a minor irritant to both groups. Some streetwise Filipinos even claim to be Hawaiians, because being Hawaiian is "in" and goes over well with the tourists, especially the young women tourists. For the most part, these people are hardworking, dependable laborers who do tough work for little recognition. They remain low on the social totem pole and have not yet organized politically to stand up for their rights.

Other Groups

About 10% of Hawaii's population is made up of a conglomerate of other ethnic groups. Of these, one of the largest and fastest growing is Korean, with 25,000 people. About 8,000 Koreans came to Hawaii from 1903 until 1905, when their government halted emigration. During the same period about 6,000 Puerto Ricans arrived, but they have become so assimilated that only 4,000 people in Hawaii today consider themselves Puerto Rican. There were also two attempts made last century to import other Polynesians to strengthen the dying Hawaiian race, but they were failures. In 1869 only 126 central Polynesian natives could be lured to Hawaii, and from 1878 to 1885 2,500 Gilbert Islanders arrived. Both groups became immediately disenchanted with Hawaii. They pined away for their own islands and departed for home as soon as possible.

Today, however, 15,000 Samoans have settled in Hawaii, and with more on the way they are the fastest-growing minority in the state. For unexplainable reasons, Samoans and native Hawaiians get along extremely poorly and have the worst racial tensions and animosity of any groups. The Samoans ostensibly should represent the archetypical Polynesians that the Hawaiians are seeking, but it doesn't work that way. Samoans are criticized by Hawaiians for their hot tempers, lingering feuds, and petty jealousies. They're clannish and are often the butt of "dumb" jokes. This racism seems especially ridiculous, but that's the way it is.

Just to add a bit more exotic spice to the stew, there are about 27,000 blacks, 5,000 Native Americans, and 6,000 Vietnamese refugees living on the islands.

LANGUAGE

Hawaii is part of America and people speak English there, but that's not the whole story. If you turn on the TV to catch the evening news, you'll hear "Walter Cronkite" English, unless of course you happen to tune in to a Japanese-language broadcast designed for tourists from that country. You can easily pick up a Chinese-language newspaper or groove to the music on a Filipino radio station, but let's not confuse the issue. All your needs and requests at airports, car rental agencies, restaurants, hotels, or wherever you happen to travel will be completely understood, as well as answered, in English. However, when you happen to overhear Islanders speaking, what they're saying will sound somewhat familiar but you won't be able to pick up all the words, and the beat and melody of the language will be noticeably different.

Hawaii—like New England, the deep South, and the Midwest—has its own unmistakable linguistic regionalism. All the ethnic peoples who make up Hawaii have enriched the English spoken there with words, expressions, and subtle shades of meaning that are commonly used and understood throughout the islands. The greatest influence on English has come from the Hawaiian language itself, and words such as "aloha," "hula," and "muumuu" are familiarly used and understood by most Americans.

Other migrant peoples, especially the Chinese, Japanese, and Portuguese, influenced the local dialect to such an extent that the simplified plantation lingo they spoke has become known as "pidgin." A fun and enriching part of the "island experience" is picking up a few words of Hawaiian and pidgin. English is the official language of the state, business, education, and perhaps even the mind; but pidgin is the language of the people, the emotions, and life, while Hawaiian remains the language of the heart and the soul.

Note: Many Hawaiian words are commonly used in English, appear in English dictionaries, and therefore would ordinarily be subject to the rules of English grammar. The Hawaiian language, however, does not pluralize nouns by adding an "s"; the singular and plural are differentiated in context. For purposes of this book, and to highlight the Hawaiian culture, the Hawaiian style of pluralization will be followed for common Hawaiian words. The following are some examples of plural Hawaiian nouns treated this way in this book: *haole* (not haoles), hula, *kahuna,* lanai, lei, luau, and *nene.*

PIDGIN

The dictionary definition of pidgin is: a simplified language with a rudimentary grammar used as a means of communication between people speaking different languages. Hawaiian pidgin is a little more complicated than that. It had its roots during the plantation days of last century when white owners and *luna* (foremen) had to communicate with recently arrived Chinese, Japanese, and Portuguese laborers. It was designed as a simple language of the here and now, and was primarily concerned with the necessary functions of working, eating, and sleeping. It has an economical noun-verb-object structure (although not necessarily in that order).

Hawaiian words make up most of pidgin's non-English vocabulary. It includes a good smattering of Chinese, Japanese, and Samoan; the distinctive rising inflection is provided by the melodious Mediterranean lilt of the Portuguese. Pidgin is not a stagnant language. It's kept alive by hip new words introduced by people who are "so radical," or especially by slang words introduced by teenagers. It's a colorful English, like "jive" or "ghettoese" spoken by American blacks, and is as regionally unique as the speech of Cajuns from Louisiana's bayous. *Maka'ainana* of all socioethnic backgrounds can at least understand pidgin. Most islanders are proud of it, while some consider it a low-class jargon. The Hawaiian House of Representatives has given pidgin an official sanction, and most people feel that it adds a real local style and should be preserved.

Pidgin Lives

Pidgin is first learned at school where all students, regardless of background, are exposed to it. The pidgin spoken by young people today is "fo' real" different from that of their parents. It's no longer only plantation talk but has moved to the streets and picked up some sophistication. At one time there was an academic movement to exterminate it, but that idea died away with the same thinking that insisted on making left-handed people write with their right hand. It is strange,

---

CAPSULE PIDGIN

The following are a few commonly used words and expressions that should give you an idea of pidgin. It really can't be written properly, merely approximated, but for now, "Brah, study da' kine an' bimbye you be hele on, brah! Okay? Lesgo."

an' den—and then? big deal; what's next; how boring

bimbye—after a while; bye and bye. "Bimbye, you learn pidgin."

blalah—brother, but actually only refers to a large, heavy-set, good-natured Hawaiian man

brah—all the bros in Hawaii are brahs; brother; pal. Used to call someone's attention. One of the most common words used even among people who are not acquainted. After a fill-up at a gas station, a person would say "Tanks, brah."

cockaroach—steal; rip off. If you really want to find out what *cockaroach* means, just leave your camera on your beach blanket when you take a little dip.

da' kine—a catchall word of many meanings that epitomizes the essence of pidgin. *Da' kine* is easily used as a euphemism for pidgin and is substituted whenever the speaker is at a loss for a word or just wants to generalize. It can mean: you know? watchamacallit; of that type.

geev um—give it to them; give them hell; go for it. Can be used as an encouragement. If a surfer is riding a great wave, the people on the beach might yell, "Geev um, brah!"

hana ho—again. Especially after a concert the audience shouts "hana ho" (one more!).

hele on—right on! hip; with it; groovy

howzit?—as in "howzit brah?" what's happening? how is it going? The most common greeting, used in place of the more formal "How do you do?"

however, that pidgin has become the unofficial language of Hawaii's grassroots movement, when it actually began as a white owners' language that was used to supplant Hawaiian and all other languages brought to the islands.

Although hip young *haole* use pidgin all the time, it has gained the connotation of being the language of the nonwhite locals, and is part of the "us against them" way of thinking. All local people, *haole* or not, do consider pidgin their own island language, and don't really like it when it's used by *malihini* (newcomers). If you're in the islands long enough, you don't have to bother learning pidgin; it'll learn you. There's a book sold all over the islands called *Pidgin to da Max,* written by (you guessed it) a *haole* from Nebraska named Doug Simonson. You might not be able to understand what's being said by locals speaking pidgin (that's usually the idea), but you should be able to *feel* what's being meant.

HAWAIIAN

The Hawaiian language sways like a palm tree in a gentle wind. Its words are as melodious as a love song. Linguists say that you can learn a lot about people through their language; when you hear Hawaiian you think of gentleness and love, and it's hard to imagine the ferocious side so evident in Hawaii's past. With its many Polynesian root words easily traced to Indonesian and Malay, Hawaiian is obviously from this same stock. The Hawaiian spoken today is very different from old Hawaiian. Its greatest metamorphosis occurred when the missionaries began to write it down in the 1820s. There is a movement to reestablish the Hawaiian language, and courses in it are offered at the University of Hawaii. Many scholars have put forth translations of Hawaiian, but there are endless, volatile disagreements in the academic sector about the real meanings of Hawaiian words. Hawaiian is no longer spoken as a language except on Niihau, and the closest tourists will come to it is in place-names, street names, and words that have become part of common usage, such as *"aloha"* and *"mahalo."* A few old Hawaiians still speak at home and there are sermons in Hawaiian at some local churches. Kawaiahao Church in downtown Honolulu is the most famous of these. (See the Glossary for a list of commonly used Hawaiian words.)

---

hu hu—angry! You put the make on the wrong da' kine wahine brah, and you in da' kine trouble, if you get one big Hawaiian blalah plenty hu hu."

kapu—a Hawaiian word meaning forbidden. If *kapu* is written on a gate or posted on a tree it means "No trespassing." *Kapu*-breakers are still very unpopular in the islands.

lesgo—Let's go! Do it!

li'dis an' li'dat—like this or that; a catch-all grouping especially if you want to avoid details; like, ya' know?

lolo buggah—stupid or crazy guy (person). Words to a tropical island song go, "I want to find the lolo who stole my pakalolo."

mo' bettah—real good! great idea. An island sentiment used to be, "mo' bettah you *come* Hawaii." Now it has subtly changed to, "mo' bettah you *visit* Hawaii."

ono—number one! delicious; great; groovy. "Hawaii is ono, brah!"

pakalolo—literally "crazy smoke"; marijuana; grass; reefer. "Hey, brah! Maui-wowie da' kine ono pakalolo."

pakiki head—stubborn; bull-headed

pau—a Hawaiian word meaning finished; done; over and done with. *Pau hana* means end of work or quitting time. Once used by plantation workers, now used by everyone.

stink face—basically frowning at someone; using facial expression to show displeasure. Hard looks. What you'll get if you give local people a hard time.

swell head—burned up; angry

talk story—spinning yarns; shooting the breeze; throwing the bull; a rap session. If you're lucky enough to be around to hear *kapuna* (elders) "talk story," you can hear some fantastic tales in the tradition of old Hawaii.

tita—sister, but only used to describe a fun-loving, down-to-earth country girl

waddascoops—what's the scoop? what's up? what's happening?

THE ALPHABET.

—◦∗◦—

VOWELS.		SOUND.	
Names.		*Ex. in Eng.*	*Ex. in Hawaii.*
A a ---â	as in *father,*	la—sun.
E e ---ā	— *tele,*	hemo—cast off.
I i ---e	— *marine,*	marie—quiet.
O o ---o	— *over,*	ono—sweet.
U u ---oo	—*rule,*	nui—large.

CONSONANTS.	*Names.*	CONSONANTS.	*Names.*
B b	be	**N n**	nu
D d	de	**P p**	pi
H h	he	**R r**	ro
K k	ke	**T t**	ti
L l	la	**V v**	vi
M m	mu	**W w**	we

The following are used in spelling foreign words:

F f	fe	**S s**	se
G g	ge	**Y y**	yi

1

Cover page of the first Hawaiian primer, showing the phonetic rendering of the ancient Hawaiian language before five of the consonants were dropped.

Wiki Wiki Hawaiian

Thanks to the missionaries, the Hawaiian language is rendered phonetically using only 12 letters. They are the five vowels, a-e-i-o-u, sounded as they are in Italian, and seven consonants, h-k-l-m-n-p-w, sounded exactly as they are in English. Sometimes "w" is pronounced as "v," but this only occurs in the middle of a word and always follows a vowel. A consonant is always followed by a vowel, forming two-letter syllables, but vowels are often found in pairs or even triplets. A slight oddity about Hawaiian is the glottal stop. This is an abrupt break in sound in the middle of a word such as "oh-oh" in English, and is denoted with an apostrophe ('). A good example is *ali'i;* or even better, the Oahu town of Ha'iku, which actually means "Abrupt Break."

Pronunciation Key

For those unfamiliar with the sounds of Italian or other Romance languages, the vowels are sounded as follows:

A—in stressed syllables, pronounced as in "ah" (that feels good!). For example, Haleakala is pronounced "hah-lay-AH-kah-lah." Unstressed syllables are pronounced "uh" as in "again" or "above." For example, Kamehameha would be "kuh-MAY-huh-MAY-huh."

E—short "e" is "eh," as in "pen" or "dent" (thus *hale* is "HAH-leh"). Long "e" sounds like "ay" as in "sway" or "day." For example, the Hawaiian goose *(nene)* is a "nay nay," not a "knee knee."

I—pronounced "ee" as in "see" or "we" (thus *pali* is pronounced "PAH-lee").

O—pronounced as in "no" or "oh," such as "KOH-uh" (koa) or "OH-noh" (ono).

U—pronounced "oo" as in "do" or "stew"; for example, "KAH-poo" *(kapu)* or "POO-nuh" (Puna).

Diphthongs

There are also eight vowel pairs known as "diphthongs" (ae-ai-ao-au-ei-eu-oi-ou). These are the sounds made by gliding from one vowel to another within a syllable. The stress is placed on the first vowel. In English, examples would be soil and euphoria. Common examples in Hawaiian are lei and *heiau.*

Stress

The best way to learn which syllables are stressed in Hawaiian is by listening closely. It becomes obvious after a while. Also, some vowel sounds are held longer than others; these can occur at the beginning of a word, such as the first "a" in *"aina",* or in the middle of a word, like the first "a" in "lanai." Again, it's a matter of tuning your ear and paying attention. No one is going to give you a hard time if you mispronounce a word. It's good, however, to pay close attention to the pronunciation of street and place-names because many Hawaiian words sound alike and a misplaced vowel here or there could be the difference between getting where you want to go and getting lost.

RELIGION

The Lord saw fit to keep His island paradise secret from humans for a few million years, but once wo finally arrived we were awfully thankful. Hawaii sometimes seems like a floating tabernacle; everywhere you look there's a church, temple, shrine, or *heiau*. The islands are either a very holy place, or there's a powerful lot of sinning going on that would require so many houses of prayer. Actually, it's just America's "right to worship" concept fully employed in microcosm. All the peoples who came to Hawaii brought their own forms of devotion. The Polynesian Hawaiians praised the primordial creators, Wakea and Papa, from whom their pantheon of animistically inspired gods sprang. Obviously to a modern world these old gods would never do. Unfortunately for the old gods, there were too many of them, and belief in them was looked upon as superstition, the folly of semicivilized pagans. So the famous missionaries of the 1820s brought Congregational Christianity and the "true path" to heaven.

Inconveniently, the Catholics, Mormons, Reformed Mormons, Adventists, Episcopalians, Unitarians, Christian Scientists, Lutherans, Baptists, Jehovah's Witnesses, Salvation Army, and every other major and minor denomination of Christianity that followed in their wake brought their own brands of enlightenment and never quite agreed with each other. Chinese and Japanese immigrants established the major sects of Buddhism, Confucianism, Taoism, and Shintoism. Allah is praised, the Torah is chanted in Jewish synagogues, and nirvana is available at a variety of Hindu temples. If the spirit moves you, a Hare Krishna devotee will be glad to point you in the right direction and give you a free flower for only a dollar or two. If the world is still too much with you, you might find peace at a Church of Scientology, or meditate at a Kundalini yoga institute, or perhaps find relief at a local assembly of Baha'i. Anyway, rejoice, because in Hawaii you'll not only find paradise, you might even find salvation.

HAWAIIAN BELIEFS

The Polynesian Hawaiians worshipped nature. They saw its forces manifested in a multiplicity of forms to which they ascribed godlike powers, and based daily life on this animistic philosophy. Handpicked and specially trained storytellers chanted the exploits of the gods. These ancient tales, kept alive in a special oral tradition called *moolelo*, were recited only by day. Entranced listeners encircled the chanter; in respect for the gods and in fear of their wrath, they were forbidden to move once the tale was begun. This was serious business during which a person's life could be at stake. It was not like the telling of *kaao,* which were simple fictions, tall tales, and yarns of ancient heroes related for amusement and to pass the long nights. Any object, animate or inanimate, could be a god. All could be infused with mana, especially a dead body or respected ancestor.

Ohana had personal family gods called *aumakua* on whom they called in times of danger or strife. There were children of gods called *kupua* who were thought to live among humans and were distinguished either for their beauty and strength or for their ugliness and terror. It was told that processions of dead *ali'i,* called "Marchers of the Night," wandered through the land of the living and unless you were properly protected it could mean death if they looked upon you. There were simple ghosts known as *akua lapu* who merely frightened people. Forests, waterfalls, trees, springs, and a thousand forms of nature were the manifestations of *akua li'i,* "little spirits" who could be invoked at any time for help or protection. It made no difference who or what you were in old Hawaii; the gods were ever-present and they took a direct and active role in your life.

Behind all of these beliefs was an innate sense of natural balance and order. It could be interpreted as positive-negative, yin-yang, plus-minus, life-death, light-dark, whatever, but the main idea was that everything had its opposite. The time of darkness when only the gods lived was *po.* When the great gods descended to the earth and created light, this was *ao* and humanity was born. All of these *moolelo* are part of the *Kumulipo,* the great chant that records the Hawaiian version of creation. From the time the gods descended and touched the earth at Ku Moku on Lanai, the genealogies were kept. Unlike the

Bible, these included the noble families of female as well as male *ali'i*.

THE STRIFES OF MAUI

Of all the heroes and mythological figures of Polynesia, Maui is the best known. His "strifes" are like the great Greek epics, and they make excellent tales of daring that elders loved to relate to youngsters around the evening fire. Maui was abandoned by his mother, Hina of Fire, when he was an infant. She wrapped him in her hair and cast him upon the sea where she expected him to die, but he lived and returned home to become her favorite. She knew then that he was a born hero and had strength far beyond that of ordinary mortals. His first exploit was to lift the sky. In those days the sky hung so low that humans had to crawl around on all fours. A seductive young woman approached Maui and asked him to use his great strength to lift the sky. In fine heroic fashion, the big boy agreed, if the beautiful woman would euphemistically "give him a drink from her gourd." He then obliged her by lifting the sky, and he might even have made the earth move for her once or twice.

More Land

The territory of humankind was small at that time. Maui decided that more land was needed, so he conspired to "fish up islands." He descended into the land of the dead and petitioned an ancestress to fashion him a hook from her jawbone. She obliged and created the mythical hook, *Manai ikalani*. Maui then secured a sacred *alae* bird that he intended to use for bait and bid his brothers to paddle him far out to sea. When he arrived at the deepest spot, he lowered *Manai ikalani* baited with the sacred bird, and his sister, Hina of the Sea, placed it into the mouth of "Old One Tooth," who held the land fast to the bottom of the waters. Maui then exhorted his brothers to row, but warned them not to look back. They strained at the oars with all their might and slowly a great landmass arose. One brother, overcome by curiosity, looked back, and when he did so, the land shattered into all of the islands of Polynesia.

Further Exploits

Maui still desired to serve mankind. People were without fire, the secret of which was held by the sacred *alae* birds, who learned it from Maui's far-distant mother. Hina of Fire gave Maui her burning fingernails, but he oafishly kept dropping them into streams until all had fizzled out and he had totally irritated his generous progenitor. She pursued him, trying to burn him to a cinder; Maui chanted for rain to put out her scorching fires. When she saw that they were being quenched, she hid her fire in the barks of special trees and informed the mud hens where they could be found, but first made them promise never to tell humans. Maui knew of this and captured a mud hen, threatening to wring its scrawny, traitorous neck unless it gave up the secret. The bird tried trickery and told Maui first to rub together the stems of sugarcane, then banana, and even taro. None worked, and Maui's determined rubbing is why these plants have hollow roots today.

Finally, with Maui's hands tightening around the mud hen's gizzard, the bird confessed that fire could be found in the *hau* tree and also the sandalwood, which Maui named *ili aha* (fire bark) in its honor. He then rubbed all the feathers off the mud hen's head for being so deceitful, which is why their crowns are featherless today.

The Sun Is Snared

Maui's greatest deed, however, was in snaring the sun and exacting a promise that it would go slower across the heavens. The people complained that there were not enough daylight hours to fish or farm. Maui's mother could not dry her tapa cloth because the sun rose and set so quickly. She asked her son to help. Maui went to his blind grandmother, who lived on the slopes of Haleakala and was responsible for cooking the sun's bananas, which he ate every day in passing. She told him to personally weave 16 strong ropes with nooses from his sister's hair. Some say these came from her head, but other versions insist that it was no doubt Hina's pubic hair that had the power to hold the sun god. Maui positioned himself with the rope, and as each of the 16 rays of the sun came across Haleakala, he snared them until the sun was defenseless and had to bargain for his life. Maui agreed to free him if he promised to go more slowly. From that time forward the sun agreed to move slowly and Haleakala ("The House of the Sun") became his home.

HEIAU AND IDOLS

A *heiau* is a Hawaiian temple. The basic *heiau* was a masterfully built and fitted rectangular stone wall that varied in size from about as big as a basketball court to as big as a football field. Once the restraining outer walls were built, the interior was backfilled with smaller stones and the top dressing was expertly laid and then rolled, perhaps with a log, to form a pavementlike surface. All that remains of Hawaii's many *heiau* are the stone platforms. The buildings upon them, made from perishable wood, leaves, and grass, have long since disappeared.

Some *heiau* were dreaded temples where human sacrifices were made. Tradition says that this barbaric custom began at Waha'ula Heiau on the Big Island in the 12th century and was introduced by a ferocious Tahitian priest named Paao. Other *heiau,* such as Pu'uhonua o Honaunau, also on the Big Island, were temples of refuge where the weak, widowed, orphaned, and vanquished could find safety and sanctuary.

Idols

The Hawaiian people worshipped gods who took the form of idols fashioned from wood, feathers, or stone. The eyes were made from shells, and until these were inlaid, the idol was dormant. The hair used was often human hair, and the arms and legs were usually flexed. The mouth was either gaping or formed a wide figure-eight lying on its side, and more likely than not was lined with glistening dog teeth. Small figures made of woven basketry were expertly covered with feathers. Red and yellow feathers were favorites taken from specific birds by men whose only work was to roam the forests in search of them.

Ghosts

The Hawaiians had countless superstitions and ghost legends, but two of the more interesting involve astral travel of the soul and the "Marchers of the Night." The soul, *uhane,* was considered by Hawaiians to be totally free and independent of its body, *kino.* The soul could separate, leaving the body asleep or very drowsy. This disincorporated soul *(hihi'o)* could visit people and was considered quite different from a *lapu* or ordinary spirit of a dead person. A *kahuna* could immediately recognize if a person's *uhane* had left the body, and a special wreath was placed upon the head to protect the person and to facilitate reentry.

If confronted by an apparition, you could test to see if it was indeed dead or still alive by placing leaves of an *ape* plant upon the ground. If the leaves tore when they were walked upon, the spirit was merely human, but if they remained intact it was a ghost. Or you could sneak up and startle the vision, and if it disappeared it was a ghost. Also, if no reflection of the face appeared when it drank water from an offered calabash, it was a ghost. Unfortunately, there were no instructions to follow once you had determined that you indeed had a ghost on your hands. Maybe it was better not to know! Some people would sprinkle salt and water around their houses, but this kept away evil spirits, not ghosts.

There are also many stories of *kahuna* restoring a soul to a dead body. First they had to catch it and keep it in a gourd. They then placed beautiful tapa and fragrant flowers and herbs about the body to make it more enticing. Slowly, they would coax the soul out of the gourd until it reentered the body through the big toe.

Death Marchers

One inexplicable phenomenon that many people attest to is Ka Huakai o Ka Po, "Marchers of the Night." This march of the dead is fatal if you gaze upon it unless one of the marchers happens to be a friendly ancestor who will protect you. The peak time for "the march" is 7:30 p.m.-2 a.m. The marchers can be dead *ali'i* and warriors, the gods themselves, or the lesser *amakua.* When the *aumakua* march there is usually chanting and music. *Ali'i* marches are more somber. The entire procession, lit by torches, often stops at the house of a relative and might even carry him or her away. When the gods themselves march, there is often thunder, lightning, and heavy seas. The sky is lit with torches, and they walk six abreast, three gods and three goddesses. If you get in the way of a march, remove your clothing and prostrate yourself. If the marching gods or *amakua* happen to be ones to which you prayed, you might be spared. If it's a march of the *ali'i,* you might make it if you lie face upward and feign death. If you *do* see a death march, the last thing that you'll worry about is lying naked on the ground looking ridiculous.

MISSIONARIES ONE AND ALL

In Hawaii, when you say "missionaries," it's taken for granted you're referring to the small and determined band of Congregationalists who arrived aboard the brig *Thaddeus* in 1820, and the follow-up groups called "companies" or "packets" that reinforced them. They were sent from Boston by the American Board of Commissioners for Foreign Missions (ABCFM), which learned of the supposed sad and godless plight of the Hawaiian people through returning sailors and especially through the few Hawaiians who had come to America to study.

The person most instrumental in bringing the missionaries to Hawaii was a young man named Opukahaia. He was an orphan befriended by a ship's captain and taken to New England, where he studied theology. Obsessed with the desire to return home and save his people from certain damnation, Opukahaia wrote accounts of life in Hawaii that were published and widely read. These accounts were directly responsible for the formation of the Pioneer Company to the Sandwich Islands Missions in 1819. Unfortunately, Opukahaia died in New England from typhus the year before they left.

"Civilizing" Hawaii

The first missionaries had the straightforward task of bringing the Hawaiians out of paganism and into Christianity and civilization. They met with terrible hostility—not from the natives, but from the sea captains and traders who were very happy with the open debauchery and wanton whoremongering that was status quo in the Hawaii of

idol

1820. Many direct confrontations between these two factions even included the cannonading of missionaries' homes by American sea captains who were denied the customary visits of island women, thanks to meddlesome "do-gooders." The most memorable of these incidents involved "Mad Jack" Percival, the captain of the USS *Dolphin*, who bombed a church in Lahaina to show his rancor. In actuality, the truth of the situation was much closer to the sentiments of James Jarves, who wrote, "The missionary was a far more useful and agreeable man than his Catholicism would indicate; and the trader was not so bad a man as the missionary would make him out to be." The missionaries' primary aim might have been conversion, but the most fortuitous by-product was education, which raised the consciousness of every Hawaiian, regardless of religious affiliation. In 40 short years Hawaii was considered a civilized nation well on its way into the modern world, and the American Board of Missions officially ended its support in 1863.

Non-Christians

By the turn of the century, both Shintoism and Buddhism, brought by the Japanese and Chinese, were firmly established in Hawaii. The first official Buddhist temple was Hongpa Hongwanji, established on Oahu in 1889. All the denominations of Buddhism account for 17% of the islands' religious total, and there are about 50,000 Shintoists. The Hindu religion has perhaps 2,000 adherents, and about the same number of Jewish people live throughout Hawaii with only one synagogue, Temple Emanuel, on Oahu. The largest number of people in Hawaii (300,000) remain unaffiliated, and about 10,000 people are in new religious movements and lesser-known faiths such as Baha'i and Unitarianism.

ARTS AND MUSIC

Referring to Hawaii as "paradise" is about as hackneyed as you can get, but when you combine it into "artists' paradise" it's the absolute truth. Something about the place evokes art (or at least personal expression) from most people. The Islands are like a magnet: they not only draw artists to them, but they draw art *from* the artists.

The inspiration comes from the astounding natural surroundings. The land is so beautiful yet so raw, the ocean's power and rhythm are primal and ever-present; the riotous colors of flowers and fruit leap from the deep-green jungle background. Crystal water beads and pale mists turn the mountains into mystic temples, while rainbows ride the crests of waves. The stunning variety of faces begging to be rendered suggests that all the world sent delegations to the is-lands. And in most cases it did! Inspiration is everywhere, as is art, good or bad.

Sometimes the artwork is overpowering in itself and in its sheer volume. Though geared to the tourist's market of cheap souvenirs, there is hardly a shop in Hawaii that doesn't sell some item that falls into the general category of "art." You can find everything from carved monkey-face coconut shells to true masterpieces. The Polynesian Hawaiians were master craftspeople, and their legacy still lives in a wide variety of woodcarvings, basketry, and weavings. The hula is art in swaying motion, and the true form is rigorously studied and taken very seriously. There is hardly a resort area that doesn't offer the "bump and grind" tourist's hula, but even these revues are accompanied by proficient local musicians.

ART AND CRAFT INFORMATION

This section includes the names and addresses of organizations that dispense information on Hawaiian arts and crafts.

Bishop Museum, 1525 Bernice St., Honolulu, HI 96817, tel. (808) 847-3511, is the world's *best* museum covering Hawaii and Polynesia. Features include exhibits, galleries, archives, demonstrations of Hawaiian crafts, and a planetarium. On the premises, Shop Pacifica has a complete selection of books and publications on all aspects of Hawaiian art and culture.

Hawaii Craftsmen, P.O. Box 22145, Honolulu, HI 96823, tel. (808) 596-8128, increases awareness of Hawaiian crafts through programs, exhibitions, workshops, lectures, and demonstrations.

Honolulu Academy of Arts, 900 S. Beretania St., Honolulu, HI 96814, tel. (808) 532-8700, collects, preserves, and exhibits works of fine art, as well as offers public art education programs related to its collections. Also offered are tours, classes, lectures, films, and a variety of publications.

Maui Arts and Cultural Center, P.O. Box 338, Kahului, HI 96733, tel. (808) 242-7469, Web site: www.maui.net/~macc, is a new center that focuses on the performing arts, presenting concerts, exhibitions, and educational programs.

Pacific Handcrafters Guild, P.O. Box 29389, Honolulu, HI 96820-1789, tel. (808) 254-6788, focuses on developing and preserving handicrafts and fine arts of all mediums. The guild sponsors four major crafts fairs annually.

State Foundation on Culture and the Arts, 44 Merchant St., Honolulu, HI 96813, tel. (808) 586-0300, Web site: state.hi.us/sfca, was begun by the state legislature in 1965 to preserve and promote Hawaii's diverse cultural, artistic, and historical heritage. It manages grants and maintains programs in folk arts and art in public places.

Nightclubs offer "slack-key" balladeers; island music performed on ukuleles and on Hawaii's own steel guitars spills from many lounges.

Vibrant fabrics that catch the spirit of the islands are rendered into muumuu and aloha shirts at countless local factories. They're almost a mandatory purchase! Pottery, heavily influenced by the Japanese, is a well-developed craft at numerous kilns. Local artisans fashion delicate jewelry from coral and olivine, while some ply the whalers' legacy of etching on ivory, called scrimshaw. There are fine traditions of quilting, flower art in lei, and street artists working in everything from airbrush to glass.

ARTS OF OLD HAWAII

Since everything in old Hawaii had to be fashioned by hand, almost every object was either a genuine work of art or the product of a highly refined craft. With the "civilizing" of the natives, most of the "old ways" disappeared, including the old arts and crafts. Most authentic Hawaiian art exists only in museums, but with the resurgence of Hawaiian roots, many old arts are being revitalized, and a few artists are becoming proficient in them.

Magnificent Canoes

The most respected artisans in old Hawaii were the canoe makers. With little more than a stone adze and a pump drill, they built canoes that could carry 200 people and last for generations—sleek, well proportioned, and infinitely seaworthy. The main hull was usually a gigantic koa log, and the gunwale planks were minutely drilled and sewn to the sides with sennit rope. Apprenticeships lasted for years, and a young man knew that he had graduated when one day he was nonchalantly asked to sit down and eat with the master builders. Small family-sized canoes with outriggers were used for fishing and perhaps carried a spear rack; large oceangoing double-hulled canoes were used for migration and warfare. On these, the giant logs had been adzed to about two inches thick. A mainsail woven from pandanus was mounted on a central platform, and the boat was steered by two long paddles. The hull was dyed with plant juices and charcoal, and the entire village helped launch the canoe in a ceremony called "drinking the sea."

Carving and Weaving

Wood was a primary material used by Hawaiian craftsmen. They almost exclusively used koa because of its density, strength, and natural luster. It was turned into canoes, woodware, calabashes, and furniture used by the *ali'i*. Temple idols were also a major product of woodcarving. A variety of stone artifacts was turned out, including poi pounders, mirrors, fish sinkers, and small idols.

Hawaiians became the best basket makers and mat weavers in all of Polynesia. *Ulana* (mats) were made from *lau hala* (pandanus) leaves. Once split, the spine was removed and the leaves stored in large rolls. When needed they were soaked, pounded, and then fashioned into various floor coverings and sleeping mats. Intricate geometrical pattterns were woven in, and the edges were rolled and well fashioned. Coconut palms were not used to make mats in old Hawaii, but a wide variety of basketry was made from the aerial root *'ie'ie*. The shapes varied according to use. Some baskets were tall and narrow, some were cones, others were flat like trays, while many were woven around gourds and calabashes.

A strong tradition of weaving and carving has survived in Hawaii, and the time-tested material of *lau hala* is still the best, although much is now made from coconut fronds. You can purchase anything from beach mats to a woven hat, and all share the desirable qualities of strength, lightness, and ventilation.

Featherwork

This highly refined art was found only on the islands of Tahiti, New Zealand, and Hawaii, while the fashioning of feather helmets and idols was unique to Hawaii. Favorite colors were red and yellow, which came only in a very limited supply from a small number of birds such as the *'o'o, 'i'iwi, mamo,* and *apapane*. Professional bird hunters in old Hawaii paid their taxes to *ali'i* in prized feathers. The feathers were fastened to a woven net of *olona* cord and made into helmets, idols, and beautiful flowing capes and cloaks. These resplendent garments were made and worn only by men, especially during battle when a fine cloak became a great trophy of war. Featherwork was also employed in the making of *kahili* and lei which were highly prized by the noble *ali'i* women.

Tapa Cloth

Tapa, cloth made from tree bark, was common throughout Polynesia and was a woman's art. A few trees such as the *wauke* and *mamaki* produced the best cloth, but a variety of other types of bark could be utilized. First the raw bark was pounded into a feltlike pulp and beaten together to form strips (the beaters had distinctive patterns that also helped make the cloth supple). They were then decorated by stamping (using a form of block printing) and then were dyed with natural colors from plants and sea animals in shades of gray, purple, pink, and red. They were even painted with natural brushes made from pandanus fruit, with an overall gray color made from charcoal. The tapa cloth was sewn together to make bed coverings, and fragrant flowers and herbs were either sewn or pounded in to produce a permanent fragrance. Tapa cloth is still available today, but the Hawaiian methods have been lost, and most comes from other areas of Polynesia.

HULA AND LEI

The hula is more than an ethnic dance; it is the soul of Hawaii expressed in motion. It began as a form of worship during religious ceremonies and was danced only by highly trained men. It gradually evolved into a form of entertainment, but in no regard was it sexual. The hula was the opera, theater, and lecture hall of the islands all rolled into one. It was history portrayed in the performing arts. In the beginning an androgynous deity named Laka descended to earth and taught men how to dance the hula. In time the male aspect of Laka departed for the heavens, but the female aspect remained. The female Laka set up her own special hula *heiau* at Haena Point on the Na Pali coast of Kauai, where it still exists. As time went on women were allowed to learn the hula. Scholars surmise that men became too busy wrestling a living from the land to maintain the art form.

Men did retain a type of hula for themselves called *lua*. This was a form of martial art employed in hand-to-hand combat that evolved into a ritualized warfare dance called *hula kui*. During the 19th century, the hula almost vanished because the missionaries considered it vile and heathen. King Kalakaua is generally regarded as saving it during the 1800s, when he formed his own troupe and encouraged the dancers to learn the old hula. Many of the original dances were forgotten, but some were retained and are performed to this day. Although professional dancers were highly trained, everyone took part in the hula. *Ali'i*, commoners, young, and old all danced.

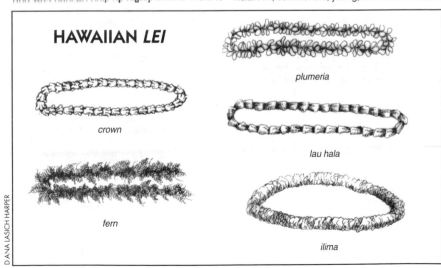

HAWAIIAN *LEI*

crown

plumeria

lau hala

fern

ilima

D.ANA LASICH HARPER

Today, hula *halau* (schools) are active on every island, teaching hula and keeping the old ways and culture alive. Performers still spend years perfecting their techniques. They show off their accomplishments during the fierce competition of the Merrie Monarch Festival in Hilo every April. The winning *halau* is praised and recognized throughout the islands.

Hawaiian hula was never performed in grass skirts; tapa or ti-leaf skirts were worn. Grass skirts came to Hawaii from the Gilbert Islands, and if you see grass and cellophane skirts in a "hula revue," it's not traditional. Almost every major resort offering entertainment or a luau also offers a revue. Most times, young island beauties accompanied by local musicians put on a floor show for the tourists. It'll be fun, but it won't be traditional. A hula dancer has to learn how to control every part of her/his body, including facial expressions, which help set the mood. The hands are extremely important and provide instant background scenery. For example, if the hands are thrust outward in an aggressive manner, this can mean a battle; if they sway gently overhead, they refer to the gods or to creation; they can easily become rain, clouds, sun, sea, or moon. Watch the hands to get the gist of the story, though in the words of one wiseguy, "You watch the parts you like, and I'll watch the parts I like!" The motion of swaying hips can denote a long walk, a canoe ride, or sexual intercourse. Foot motion can portray a battle, a walk, or any kind of conveyance. The overall effect is multidirectional synchronized movement. The correct chanting of the *mele* is an integral part of the performance. These story chants, accompanied by musical instruments, make the hula very much like opera; it is especially similar in the way the tale unfolds.

Lei-Making

Any flower or blossom can be strung into a lei, but the most common are carnations or the lovely smelling plumeria. Lei, like babies, are all beautiful, but special lei are highly prized by those who know what to look for. Of the different stringing styles, the most common is *kui*—stringing the flower through the middle or side. Most "airport-quality" lei are of this type. The *humuhumu* style, reserved for making flat lei, is made by sewing flowers and ferns to a ti, banana, or sometimes *hala* leaf. A *humuhumu* lei

makes an excellent hatband. *Wili* is the winding together of greenery, ferns, and flowers into short, bouquet-type lengths. The most traditional form is *hili,* which requires no stringing at all but involves braiding fragrant ferns and leaves such as *maile.* If flowers are interwoven, the *hili* becomes the *haku* style, the most difficult and most beautiful type of lei.

The Lei of the Land

Every major island is symbolized by its own lei made from a distinctive flower, shell, or fern. Each island has its own official color as well, though it doesn't necessarily correspond to the color of the island's lei. Maui is the pink island and its lei is the corresponding small pink rose called the *lokelani.* These flowers are not native, but were imported and widely cultivated at one time. In recent years they've fallen prey to a rose beetle, and sometimes when they're scarce, a *roselani* is substituted for Maui's lei.

THAT GOOD OLD ISLAND MUSIC

The missionaries usually take a beating when it's recounted how much Hawaiian culture they destroyed while "civilizing" the natives. However, they seem to have done one thing right. They introduced the Hawaiians to the diatonic musical scale and immediately opened a door to latent and superbly harmonious talent. Before the missionaries, the Hawaiians knew little about melody. Though sonorous, their *mele* were repetitive chants in which the emphasis was placed on historical accuracy and not on "making music." The Hawaiians, in short, didn't *sing.* But within a few years of the missionaries' arrival, they were belting out good old Christian hymns, and one of their favorite pastimes became group and individual singing.

Early in the 1800s, Spanish *vaqueros* from California were imported to teach the Hawaiians how to be cowboys. With them came guitars and moody ballads. The Hawaiian *paniolo* (cowboys) quickly learned how to punch cows and croon away the long lonely nights on the range. Immigrants who came along a little later in the 19th century, especially from Portugal, helped create a Hawaiian-style music. Their biggest influence was a small, four-stringed instrument called a *braga* or *cavaquinho*. One owned by Augusto Dias was the prototype of a homegrown Hawaiian instrument that became known as the ukulele. "Jumping flea," the translation of ukulele, is an appropriate name devised by the Hawaiians when they saw how nimble the fingers were as they "jumped" over the strings.

King Kalakaua (The Merrie Monarch) and Queen Liliuokalani were both patrons of the arts who furthered the Hawaiian musical identity at the turn of the century. Kalakaua revived the hula and was also a gifted lyricist and balladeer. He wrote the words to "Hawaii Pono," which became the national anthem of Hawaii and later the state anthem. Liliuokalani wrote the hauntingly beautiful "Aloha O'e," which is often pointed to as the "spirit of Hawaii" in music. Detractors say that its melody is extremely close to the old Christian hymn, "Rock Beside the Sea," but the lyrics are so beautiful and perfectly fitted that this doesn't matter.

Just prior to Kalakaua's reign a Prussian bandmaster, Capt. Henri Berger, was invited to head the fledgling Royal Hawaiian Band, which he turned into a very respectable orchestra lauded by many visitors to the islands. Berger was open-minded and learned to love Hawaiian music. He collaborated with Kalakaua and other island musicians to incorporate their music into a Western format. He headed the band for 43 years until 1915, and was instrumental in making music a serious pursuit of talented Hawaiians.

Popular Hawaiian Music

Hawaiian music has a unique twang, a special feeling that says the same thing to everyone who hears it: "Relax, sit back in the moonlight, watch the swaying palms as the surf sings a lullaby." This special sound is epitomized by the bouncy ukulele, the falsettos of Hawaiian crooners, and the smooth ring of the "steel" or "Hawaiian" guitar. The steel guitar is a variation originated by Joseph Kekuku in the 1890s. Stories abound of how Joseph Kekuku devised this instrument; the most popular versions say that Joe dropped his comb or pocketknife on his guitar strings and liked what he heard. Driven by the faint rhythm of an inner sound, he went to the machine shop at the Kamehameha Schools and turned out a steel bar for sliding over the strings. To complete the sound he changed the cat-gut strings to steel

and raised them so they wouldn't hit the frets. Voilà!—Hawaiian music as the world knows it today.

The first melodious strains of **slack-key guitar** *(ki ho'alu)* can be traced back to the time of Kamehameha III and the *vaqueros* from California. The Spanish had their way of tuning the guitar, and played difficult and aggressive music that did not sit well with Hawaiians, who were much more gentle and casual in their manners.

Hawaiians soon became adept at making their own music. At first, one person played the melody, but it lacked fullness. There was no body to the sound. So, as one *paniolo* tooled with the melody, another soon learned to play bass, which added depth. But, a player was often alone, and by experimenting he learned that he could get the right hand going with the melody, and at the same time could play the bass note with the thumb to improve the sound. Singers also learned that they could "open tune" the guitar to match their rich voices.

Hawaiians believed knowledge was sacred, and what is sacred should be treated with utmost respect—which meant keeping it secret, except from sincere apprentices. Guitar playing became a personal art form whose secrets were closely guarded, handed down only to family members, and only to those who showed ability and determination. When old-time slack-key guitar players were done strumming, they loosened all the strings so no one could figure out how they had them tuned. If they were playing, and some folks came by who were interested and weren't part of the family, the Hawaiians stopped what they were doing, put their guitars down, and put their feet across the strings to wait for the folks to go away. As time went on, more and more Hawaiians began to play slack key, and a common repertoire emerged.

Accomplished musicians could easily figure out the simple songs, once they had figured out how the family had tuned the guitar. One of the most popular tunings was the "open G." Old Hawaiian folks called it the "taro patch tune." Different songs came out, and if you were in their family and were interested in the guitar, they took the time to sit down and teach you. The way they taught was straightforward—and a test of your sincerity at the same time. The old master would start to play. He just wanted you to listen and get a feel for the music—nothing more than that. You brought your guitar and *listened.* When you felt it, you played it, and the knowledge was transferred. Today, only a handful of slack-key guitar players know how to play the classic tunes classically. The best-known and perhaps greatest slack-key player was Gabby Pahinui, with the Sons of Hawaii. He passed away recently, but left many recordings behind. A slack-key master still singing and playing is Raymond Kane. Raymond now teaches a handful of students his wonderful and haunting music. None of his students are from his own family, and most are *haole* musicians trying to preserve the classical method of playing.

Hawaiian music received its biggest boost from a remarkable radio program known as "Hawaii Calls." This program sent out its music from the Banyan Court of the Moana Hotel from 1935 until 1975. At its peak in the mid-1950s, it was syndicated on over 700 radio stations throughout the world. Ironically, Japanese pilots heading for Pearl Harbor tuned in island music as a signal beam. Some internationally famous classic tunes came out of the '40s and '50s. Jack Pitman composed "Beyond the Reef" in 1948; over 300 artists have recorded it and it has sold well over 12 million records. Other million-sellers include: "Sweet Leilani," "Lovely Hula Hands," "The Crosseyed Mayor of Kaunakakai," and "The Hawaiian Wedding Song."

By the 1960s, Hawaiian music began to die. Just too corny and light for those turbulent years, it belonged to the older generation and the good times that followed WW II. One man was instrumental in keeping Hawaiian music alive during this period. Don Ho, with his "Tiny Bubbles," became the token Hawaiian musician of the '60s and early '70s. He's persevered long enough to become a legend in his own time, and his Polynesian Extravaganza at the Hilton Hawaiian Village packed visitors in until the early 1990s. He's now at the Waikiki Beachcomber. Al Harrington, "The South Pacific Man," until his recent retirement had another Honolulu "big revue" that drew large crowds. Of this type of entertainment, perhaps the most Hawaiian is Danny Kaleikini, still performing at the Kahala Hilton, who entertains his audience with dances, Hawaiian anecdotes, and tunes on the traditional Hawaiian nose flute.

The Beat Goes On

Beginning in the mid-'70s islanders began to assert their cultural identity. One of the unifying factors was the coming of age of "Hawaiian" music. It graduated from the "little grass shack" novelty tune and began to include sophisticated jazz, rock, and contemporary rhythms. Accomplished musicians whose roots were in traditional island music began to highlight their tunes with this distinctive sound. The best embellish their arrangements with ukuleles, steel guitars, and traditional percussion and melodic instruments. Some excellent modern recording artists have become island institutions. The local people say that you know if the Hawaiian harmonies are good if they give you "chicken skin."

Each year special music awards, **Na Hoku Hanohano**, or Hoku for short, are given to distinguished island musicians. The following are recent Hoku winners considered by their contemporaries to be among the best in Hawaii. If they're playing on one of the islands while you're in Hawaii, don't miss them. **Barney Isaacs and George Kuo** won Instrumental Album of the year for *Hawaiian Touch.* **Na Leo Pilimehana** ("Flying With Angels") won Song of the Year, Album of the Year, Contemporary Album of the Year, and Group of the Year. **Robi Kahakalau**'s *Sistah Robi* earned Female Vocalist and Island Contemporary Album of the Year. "Friends in Me" won Single of the Year for **Brothers and Sister. Keali'i Reichel**'s *Lei Hali'a* was voted Popular Hawaiian Album of the Year (and the artist also won Male Vocalist of the Year and Favorite Entertainer of the Year). *Broken Hearts* earned **Darren Benitez** a Most Promising Artist of the Year award; **Sonny Kamahele** received a Lifetime Achievement Award; and **Ledward Ka'apana** is a Slack Key Award winner.

Past Hoku winners who have become renowned performers include: **Brothers Cazimero,** who are blessed with beautiful harmonic voices; **Krush,** who are highly regarded for their contemporary sounds; **The Peter Moon Band,** fantastic performers with a strong traditional sound; **Karen Keawehawai'i,** who has a sparkling voice and can be very funny when the mood strikes her; and **Henry Kapono,** formerly of Cecilio and Kapono, who keeps a low profile but is an incredible performer and excellent songwriter (his shows are noncommercial and very special). **Cecilio** is now teamed up with **Maggie Herron;** they are hot together and have a strong following in Honolulu. **The Beamer Brothers** are excellent performers, and can be seen at various nightspots. **Loyal Garner,** who was awarded Female Vocalist of the Year for *I Shall Sing,* is a truly wonderful artist. **Del Beazley** is a talented energized performer. **Makaha Sons Of Niihau** are the best traditional Hawaiian band and shouldn't be missed. **Hawaiian Style Band** is known for *Vanishing Treasures,* a terrific album filled with contemporary music.

Bryan Kessler & Me No Hoa Aloha perform songs like "Heiau," a haunting melody. **Susan Gillespie** and **Susi Hussong** are first-rate instrumentalists, and **Kealohi,** who recorded *Kealohi,* is very promising.

Other top-notch performers with strong followings are Ledward Kaapana; Mango; Oliver Kelly; Ka'eo; Freitas Brothers; Brickwood Galuteria, who won a double Hoku for Best Male Vocalist and Most Promising Artist; and Third Road Delite.

ON THE ROAD

SPORTS AND RECREATION

Maui won't let you down when you want to go outside and play. More than just a giant sandbox for big kids, its beaches and surf are warm and inviting, and there are all sorts of water sports from scuba diving to parasailing. You can fish, hunt, camp, or indulge yourself in golf or tennis to your heart's content. The hiking is marvelous and the horseback riding on Haleakala is some of the most exciting in the world. The information offered in this chapter is merely an overview to let you know what's available. Have fun!

CAMPING

A major aspect of the "Maui experience" is found in the simple beauty of nature and the outdoors. Some visitors come to Maui to luxuriate at resorts and dine in fine restaurants, but everyone heads for the sand and surf, and most are captivated by the lush mountainous interior. What better way to savor this natural beauty than by hiking slowly through it or pitching a tent in the middle of it? Maui offers a full range of hiking

but more limited camping, and most of it is easily accessible. Camping facilities are located both along the coast and amid the scenic forest areas of Haleakala. They range in amenities from housekeeping cabins to primitive hike-in sites. All require camping permits—inexpensive for the county parks, free for the state and national parks. Camping permits can be obtained by walk-in application to the appropriate office or by writing. Although there is usually no problem obtaining sites, when writing, request reservations well in advance, allowing a minimum of one month for letters to go back and forth.

General Information

Most campgrounds have pavilions, fireplaces, toilets (sometimes pit), and running water, but usually no individual electrical hookups. Pavilions may have electric lights, but sometimes campers appropriate the bulbs, so it's wise to carry your own. Drinking water is available at all except for the national park's Kipahulu Campground and two spots in Haleakala Crater, but brackish water may be used for flushing toilets and for showers, so read all signs regarding water. Never hike without an adequate supply of your own water. Cooking fires are allowed in established fire pits, but no wood is provided. Charcoal is a good idea. When camping in the mountains, be prepared for cold and rainy weather. Women, especially, should never hike or camp alone, and everyone should take precautions against theft.

Haleakala National Park

Camping at Haleakala National Park is free, but there is an automobile entrance fee of $10. Permits are not needed to camp at Hosmer Grove, just a short drive from park headquarters, or at Kipahulu Campground along the coastal road 10 miles south of Hana. Camping is on a first-come, first-served basis, and there's an official three-day stay limit, but it's a loose count, especially at Kipahulu, which is almost always empty. The case is much different at the campsites located inside Haleakala Crater proper. On the floor of the crater are two primitive tenting campsites, one

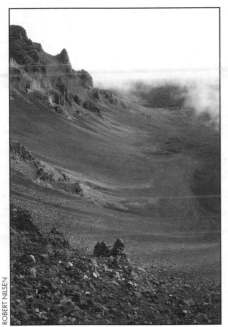

Haleakala crater

at Paliku on the east side and the other at Holua on the north rim. For these you'll need a wilderness permit from park headquarters. Because of ecological considerations, only 25 campers per night can stay at each site, and a three-night, four-day per month maximum stay is strictly enforced, with tenting allowed at any one site for only two consecutive nights. However, because of the strenuous hike involved, campsites are open most of the time. You must be totally self-sufficient and equipped for cold-weather camping to be comfortable at these two sites.

Also, Paliku, Holua, and another site at Kapalaoa on the south rim offer cabins. Fully self-contained with stoves, water, and nearby pit toilets, they can handle a maximum of 12 campers each. Bunks are provided, but you must have your own warm bedding. The same maximum-stay limits apply as in the campgrounds. Staying at these cabins is at a premium—they're popular with visitors and residents alike. Reservations for the cabins must be made at least 90 days in advance by mail using only a special cabin reservation request form. A lottery of the applicants chosen for sites keeps it fair for all. These cabins are geared toward groups, with rates at $40 for one to six people or $80 for up to the limit of 12. To have a chance at getting a cabin, write well in advance for complete information to: Haleakala National Park, P.O. Box 369, Makawao, HI 96768, or call (808) 572-9306.

State Parks

There are eight state parks on Maui, managed by the Department of Land and Natural Resources through the Division of State Parks. These facilities include everything from historical sites to wildland parks accessible only by trail. Some are only for looking at, some are restricted to day use, and two of them have overnight camping. **Polipoli Spring State Recreation Area** and **Waianapanapa** offer free tenting, and housekeeping cabins are available; reservations highly necessary. Permits are required at each, and RVs technically are not allowed.

Tent camping **permits** are free and good for a maximum stay of five nights at any one park. A permit to the same person for the same park is again available only after 30 days have elapsed. Campgrounds are open every day. You can arrive after 2 p.m. and you should check out by 11 a.m.

ROBERT NILSEN

MAUI CAMPGROUNDS AND PARKS

© J.D. BISIGNANI AND MOON PUBLICATIONS, INC.

The minimum age for park permits is 18, and anyone under that age must be accompanied by an adult. Alcoholic beverages are prohibited, as is nude sunbathing. Plants and wildlife are protected, but reasonable amounts of fruits and seeds may be gathered for personal consumption. Fires are on cookstoves or in designated pits only. Dogs and other pets must be under control at all times and are not permitted to run around unleashed. Hunting and freshwater fishing are allowed in season and only with a license, but ocean fishing is permitted, unless prohibited by posting. Permits are required for certain trails, so check at the state parks office.

Housekeeping cabins are available. As with camping, permits are required with the same five-day maximum stay (The cabin at Polipoli Spring is closed on Tuesday night). Reservations are absolutely necessary, especially at Wainapanapa, and a 50% deposit at time of confirmation is required. There's a three-day cancellation requirement for refunds, and payment is to be made in cash, by money order, certified check, or personal check, the latter only if it's received 30 days before arrival so that cashing procedures are possible. The balance is due on date of arrival. Cabins are $45 per night for up to four people, and $5 for each person up to the limit (six for Wainapanapa and 10 for Polipoli Spring). These are completely furnished down to the utensils, with heaters for cold weather and private baths.

Permits can be reserved up to one year in advance, but you must confirm at least seven days prior to arrival by writing a timely letter including your name, address, phone number, number of persons in your party, type of permit requested, and duration of your stay. They can be picked up on arrival with proof of identification. Office hours are Mon.-Fri. 8 a.m.-4 p.m. Usually, tent camping permits are no problem to secure on the day you arrive, but reserving ensures you a space and alleviates anxiety. The permits are available from the Maui (Molokai also) Division of State Parks, 54 S. High St., Wailuku, HI 96793, tel. (808) 984-8109.

County Parks

There are 16 county parks scattered primarily along Maui's coastline, and because of their locations, they're generally referred to as **beach parks.** Most are for day use only, where visitors fish, swim, snorkel, surf, picnic, and sunbathe, but only **Kanaha Beach Park** in Kahului has overnight camping. The rules governing use of these parks are just about the same as those for state parks. The main difference is that along with a use permit, county beach parks charge a fee for overnight use. Again, the differences between individual parks are too numerous to mention, but the majority have a central pavilion for cooking, restrooms, and cold-water showers, individual fire pits and picnic tables, with electricity usually only at the central pavilion. RVs are allowed to park in appropriate spaces. One safety point to consider is that beach parks are open to the general public, and most are used with regularity. This means that quite a few people pass through, and your chances of encountering a hassle or running into a rip-off are slightly higher in beach parks.

Camping **fees** are quite reasonable at $3 per night per person, 50 cents for children, with no more than three consecutive nights at the park. To get a permit and pay your fees, either write in advance or visit the following issuing office (Mon.-Fri. 9 a.m.-5 p.m.): Department of Parks and Recreation, Permit Office, 1580-C Kaahumanu Ave. (in the War Memorial Gym), Wailuku, HI 96793, tel. (808) 243-7389.

HIKING

The hiking on Maui is excellent; most times you have the trails to yourself, and the wide possibility of hikes ranges from a family saunter to a strenuous trek. Some restrictions to hiking apply because much of the land is privately owned, so you may need advance permission to hike. But plenty of public access trails along the coast and deep into the interior would fill the itineraries of even the most intrepid trekkers. If you enjoy the great outdoors on the Mainland, you'll be thrilled by these "mini-continents," where in one day you can go from the frosty summits of alpine wonderlands down into baking cactus-covered deserts and emerge through jungle foliage onto a sun-soaked subtropical shore.

Haleakala National Park

The most spectacular hikes on Maui are through Haleakala Crater's 30 miles of trails. **Halemauu**

Trail is 10 miles long, beginning three miles up the mountain from park headquarters. It quickly winds down a switchback descending 1,400 feet to the crater floor. It passes Holua Cabin and goes six more miles to Paliku Cabin, offering expansive views of Koolau Gap along the way. A spur leads to Sliding Sands Trail with a short walk to the visitors center. This trail passes Silversword Loop and the Bottomless Pit, two attractions in the crater. **Sliding Sands Trail** might be considered the main trail, beginning from the visitors center at the summit and leading 10 miles over the crater floor to Paliku Cabin. It passes Kapalaoa Cabin en route and offers the best walk through the crater, with up-close views of cinder cones, lava flows, and unique vegetation. **Kaupo Gap Trail** begins at Paliku Cabin and descends rapidly through the Kaupo Gap, depositing you in the semi-ghost town of Kaupo. Below 4,000 feet the lava is rough and the vegetation thick. You pass through the private lands of the Kaupo Ranch along well-marked trails. Without a pickup arranged at the end, this is a tough one because the hitching is scanty. (See also "Camping," above.)

West Maui Trails

The most frequented trails on West Maui are at Iao Needle. From the parking area you can follow the **Tableland Trail** for two miles, giving you beautiful panoramas of Iao Valley as you steadily climb to the tableland above, or you can descend to the valley floor and follow Iao Stream to a series of small but secluded swimming holes. **Waihee Ridge Trail** is a three-mile trek leading up the windward slopes of the West Maui Mountains. Follow Rt. 34 around the back side to Maluhia Road and turn up it to the Boy Scout camp. From here the trail rises swiftly to 2,560 feet. The views of Waihee Gorge are spectacular. The **Waihee Trail** runs into this narrow valley. North of the town of Waihee turn left at the Oki Place road sign. Proceed as far as you are able to drive, park your car, and walk up along the flume. This level track takes you over two suspension footbridges, through a bamboo forest, and under huge banyan trees until you reach the head dam. By crossing the river here, you can follow a smaller trail farther up the valley. **Kahakuloa Valley Trail** begins from this tiny fishing village on Maui's backside along Rt. 34. Start from the schoolhouse, passing burial

caves and old terraced agricultural sites. Fruit trees line the way to trails ending two miles above the town. The **Lahaina Pali Trail** is a Na Ala Hele (Hawaii Trail and Access System) trail. Five miles in length, it starts near mile marker 11, about one half mile west of the Lahaina Tunnel, follows an old established trail that crosses the Kealaloloa Ridge at 1,600 feet, and descends to an access road that meets the highway near the junction of Highways 30 and 380. This trail is hot and dry so bring plenty of water, and wear a hat and sturdy hiking boots. A number of markers along the way indicate cultural and historical sites.

Kula and Upcountry Trails

Most of these trails form a network through and around Polipoli Spring State Park, and are all accessible from the camping area at 6,200 feet. **Redwood Trail,** 1.7 miles, passes through a magnificent stand of redwoods, past the ranger station and down to an old Civilian Conservation Corps camp at 5,300 feet where there's a rough old shelter. **Tie Trail,** one-half mile, joins Redwood Trail with **Plum Trail,** so named because of its numerous plum trees, which bear during the summer. **Skyline Trail,** 6.5 miles, starts atop Haleakala at 9,750 feet, passing through the southwest rift and eventually joining the **Haleakala Ridge Trail,** 1.6 miles, at the 6,500-foot level, then descends through a series of switchbacks. You can join with the Plum Trail or continue to the shelter at the end. Both the Skyline and Ridge trails offer superb vistas of Maui.

Others throughout the area include: **Polipoli,** 0.6 miles, passing through the famous forests of the area; **Boundary Trail,** four miles, leading from the Kula Forest Reserve to the ranger's cabin, passing numerous gulches still supporting native trees and shrubs; **Waiohuli Trail** descending the mountain to join Boundary Trail and overlooking Keokea and Kihei with a shelter at the end; **Waiakoa Trail,** seven miles, beginning at the Kula Forest Reserve Access Road. It ascends Haleakala to the 7,800-foot level and then descends through a series of switchbacks, covering rugged territory and passing a natural cave shelter. It eventually meets up with the three-mile **Waiakoa Loop Trail.** All of these trails offer intimate forest views of native and introduced trees, and breathtaking views of the Maui coastline far below.

Coastal Trails

Along Maui's southernmost tip the **King's Highway Coastal Trail,** 5.5 miles, leads from La Perouse Bay through the rugged and desolate lava flow of 1790, the time of Maui's last volcanic eruption. This trail gets extremely rugged and should not be attempted by car, but is easy on foot. It leads over smooth stepping stones that were at one time trudged by royal tax collectors. The trail heads inland and passes many ancient Hawaiian stone walls and stone foundation sites. Spur trails lead down to the sea, including an overview of Cape Hanamanloa and its Coast Guard lighthouse. The trail eventually ends at private land.

Hana Wainapanapa Coastal Trail is on the opposite side of East Maui. You start from Wainapanapa State Park or from a gravel road near Hana Bay and again you follow the flat, laid stones of the "King's Highway." The trail is well maintained but fairly rugged due to lava and cinders. You pass natural arches, a string of *heiau,* blowholes, and caves. The vegetation is lush, and long fingers of black lava stretch out into cobalt-blue waters. This trail should take about three hours. The trail does continue beyond Wainapanapa along the coast to the Hana Airport, another two hours.

Hiking Tours

Hike Maui, P.O. Box 330969, Kahului, Maui, HI 96733, tel. (808) 879-5270, fax 876-0308, Web site: www.hikemaui.com, e-mail: hike@hikemaui.com, as its name implies, offers walking tours to Maui's best scenic areas accompanied by Ken Schmitt, a professional nature guide. Ken has dedicated years to hiking Maui and has accumulated an unbelievable amount of knowledge about this awesome island. He's proficient in Maui archaeology, botany, geology, anthropology, zoology, history, oceanography, and ancient Hawaiian cosmology. Moreover, he is a man of dynamic and gracious spirit who has tuned in to the soul of Maui. He hikes every day and is superbly fit, but will tailor his hikes for anyone, though good physical conditioning is essential. Ken's hikes are actually workshops in Maui's natural history. As you walk along, Ken imparts his knowledge, but he never seems to intrude on the beauty of the site itself. Ken has finally expanded his operation to include a small handpicked staff of assistants, each trained in the sciences, with the soul of an adventurer and the heart of an environmentalist. His hikes require a minimum of four people and a maximum of eight. He offers gourmet breakfasts, lunches, and snacks with an emphasis on natural health foods. All special equipment is provided, but you are requested to wear comfortable walking/hiking shoes. His hikes take in sights from Hana to West Maui and to the summit of Haleakala, and range from the moderate to the hardy ability level. Half-day hikes last about five hours and all-day hikes go for eight hours or more. The rates vary from $75 ($55 for children) to $115 ($90 for children). A day with Ken Schmitt or one of his guides is a classic outdoor experience. You'll be in the hands of experts. Don't miss it!

Mango Mitch Ecotours is another well-established company (since 1984) that offers half-day, full-day, and overnight hikes, as well as multiple-day expeditions to other islands, for small groups. Half-day hikes and snorkel trips run $48-58; the full-day Hana-area hike and swim is $88. An overnight in Haleakala Crater runs $118. Call for info on multiday trips. For Maui tours, refreshments and some gear are provided; all meals and equipment are provided on the overnight tours. Aside from the hiking experience itself, Mango Mitch wants to impart knowledge about Hawaii's natural history and culture to all his guests. For more information contact P.O. Box 2511, Wailuku, HI 96793, tel. (808) 875-9106 or (800) 552-6541, e-mail: mangopik@maui.net.

Maui Hiking Safaris, P.O. Box 11198, Lahaina, HI 96761, tel. (808) 573-0168 or (888) 445-3963, fax (808) 572-3037, Web site: www.maui.net/~mhs, e-mail: mhs@maui.net, also offers organized group hikes for $49 a half day or $89 a full day, all gear, snacks, and beverages provided. Various hikes are offered through valleys and forests, to waterfalls, up along ridges, and onto lava flows, and each hike is narrated with special attention to history, botany, and/or volcanology. Tours led by Randy Weaver.

Paths in Paradise offers various hikes, easy to strenuous, from half day to full day, most on Haleakala and its slope, with an emphasis on natural history and birds. Fees run $75-115 with discounts for children. All food and necessary gear are provided. Hikes are led by Renate Gassmann-Duvall, Ph.D.; tours in German available. For information and reservations contact P.O. Box 667,

Makawao, HI 96768, tel. (808) 573-0094, fax 572-1584, Web site: www.maui.net/~corvusco, e-mail: corvusco@maui.net. **Soul Journeys to Paradise,** P.O. Box 612, Kula, HI 96790, tel. (808) 876-1629, Web site: www.maui.net/~journeys, e-mail: journeys@maui.net, runs easy to challenging half-day and full-day hikes for $85-120. Snacks and any equipment included. These hikes can be done in conjunction with rejuvenating retreats in Upcountry.

For hikes through tracts of Maui Land and Pineapple Company of West Maui, try **Kapalua Nature Society,** 800 Kapalua Dr., Kapalua, HI 96761, tel. (808) 669-8088, Web site: www.kapaluamaui.com/nature.htm. Two hikes are given, the private Maunalei Arboretum and Pu'u Ka'eo nature walk and the Manienie Ridge hike. Both $80, these hikes are moderate in endurance. All monies go to the maintenance of Pu'u Kukui Preserve, on the mountainside above.

EQUIPMENT, SAFETY, AND INFORMATION

Camping and Hiking Equipment

Like everything else you take to Maui, your camping and hiking equipment should be lightweight and durable. Camping equipment size and weight should not cause a problem with baggage requirements on airlines: if it does, it's a tip-off that you're hauling too much. One odd luggage consideration you might make is to bring along a small **styrofoam cooler** packed with equipment. Exchange the gear for food items when you get to Hawaii; if you intend to car-camp successfully and keep food prices down, you'll definitely need a cooler. You can also buy one on arrival for only a few dollars.

You'll need a lightweight **tent,** preferably with a rainfly and a sewn-in floor. This will save you from getting wet and miserable, and will keep out mosquitoes, cockroaches, ants, and the few stinging insects on Maui. In Haleakala Crater, where you can expect cold and wind, a tent is a must; in fact you probably won't be allowed to camp without one.

Sleeping bags are a good idea, although you can get along at sea level with only a blanket. Down-filled bags are necessary for Haleakala—you'll freeze without one. **Campstoves** are needed because there's very little wood in some volcanic areas, it's often wet in the deep forest, and open fires are often prohibited. If you'll be car-camping, take along a multiburner stove, and for trekking, a backpacker's stove will be necessary. The grills found only at some campgrounds are popular with many families that go often to the beach parks for an open-air dinner. You can buy a very inexpensive charcoal grill at many variety stores throughout Maui. It's a great idea to take along a **lantern.** This will give added safety for car-campers. Definitely take a **flashlight,** replacement batteries, and a few small **candles.** A complete **first-aid kit** can mean the difference between life and death and is worth the extra bulk. Hikers, especially those leaving the coastal areas, should take rain gear, a plastic ground cloth, utility knife, compass, safety whistle, mess kit, water purification tablets, canteen, nylon twine, and waterproof matches. (For additional suggestions, see "What to Take" later in this chapter.)

You can find only a few stores that sell or rent camping and hiking equipment on Maui. For sales in Kahului, try **The Bike Shop** at the Triangle Square mall in Kahului, open Tues.-Fri. 10 a.m.-6 p.m., Saturday 9 a.m.-5 p.m. **Sports Authority, Costco,** and **Kmart** also carry some equipment, but it's not usually as fine in quality. **Base Camp** across from the Makawao Steak House in Makawao has a full range of camping and hiking equipment, more than you'll find anywhere else on the island. Base Camp also rents exterior-frame backpacks at $35 a weekend; two-person tents at $35 a weekend; and sleeping bags for $25 the first night and $10 each night after that for a 20° bag for inside the crater, or $20 the first night and $5 additional nights for lighter-weight bags. Open Mon.-Fri. 10 a.m.-6 p.m., Saturday until 1 p.m.

Safety

There are two things on Maui that you must keep your eye on in order to remain safe: humans and nature. The general rule is, the farther you get away from towns, the safer you'll be from human-induced hassles. If possible, don't hike or camp alone, especially if you're a woman. Don't leave your valuables in your tent, and always carry your money, papers, and camera with you. Don't tempt the locals by being overly friendly or unfriendly, and make yourself scarce if they're drinking. While hiking, remember that many trails are well maintained, but trailhead markers are often missing. The trails themselves can be muddy, which can make them treacherously slippery and often knee-deep. Always bring food because you cannot, in most cases, forage from the land. Water in most streams is biologically polluted and will give you bad stomach problems if you drink it without purifying it first by boiling, filtering, or adding purification tablets. For your part, please don't use the streams as a toilet.

Precautions

Always tell a ranger or official of your hiking intentions. Supply an itinerary and your expected route, then stick to it. Twilight is short in the islands, and night sets in rapidly. In June sunrise and sunset are around 6 a.m. and 7 p.m.; in December these occur at 7 a.m. and 6 p.m. If you become lost at night, stay put, light a fire if possible, and stay as dry as you can. Hawaii is made of volcanic rock, which is brittle and crumbly. Never attempt to climb steep *pali* (cliffs). Every year people are stranded and fatalities have occurred. If lost, walk on ridges and avoid the gulches, which have more obstacles and make it harder for rescuers to spot you. Be careful of elevation sickness, especially on Haleakala. The best cure is to head down as soon and as quickly as possible.

Heat can cause you to lose water and salt. If you become woozy or weak, rest, take salt, and drink water as you need it. Remember, it takes much more water to restore a dehydrated person than to keep hydrated; take small frequent sips. Be mindful of flash floods. Small creeks can turn into raging torrents with upland rains. Never camp in a dry creek bed. Fog is encountered only at elevations of 1,500-5,000 feet, but be careful of disorientation. Generally, stay within your limits, be careful, and enjoy yourself.

Helpful Departments and Organizations

The **Department of Land and Natural Resources,** Division of Forestry and Wildlife, 1151 Punchbowl St., Honolulu, HI 96813, tel. (808) 587-0166, is helpful in providing trail maps, accessibility information, hunting and fishing regulations, and general forest rules. Although somewhat out of date, the Maui *Recreation Map* is still useful and free if you can secure a copy. On Maui, contact the DLNR, Division of Forestry and Wildlife, 54 S. High St., Room 101, Wailuku, HI

96793, tel. (808) 984-8100. The following organizations can provide general information on wildlife, conservation, and organized hiking trips although they are not based on Maui: **Hawaiian Audubon Society,** P.O. Box 22832, Honolulu, HI 96822, and **Sierra Club, Hawaii Chapter** P.O. Box 2577, Honolulu, HI 96803, tel. (808) 538-6616, Web site: www.hi.sierraclub.org.

Hiking and Camping Books

Two helpful camping books are Hawaii: A Camping Guide, by George Cagala, and Richard McMahon's *Camping Hawaii.*

For a well-written and detailed hiking guide complete with maps, check out *Maui Trails* by Kathy Morey. See also *Hawaiian Hiking Trails,* by Craig Chisholm, and Robert Smith's *Hawaii's Best Hiking Trails* and *Hiking Maui.*

Topographical Maps and Nautical Charts

For detailed topographical maps, write **U.S. Geological Survey, Information Services,** P.O. Box 25286, Denver, CO 80225, or call (800) USA-MAPS or (703) 648-4888, Web site: www.usgs.gov. Many types of maps are available at Borders Books at the Maui Marketplace mall in Kahului. Also useful, but not for hiking, are the University of Hawaii Press reference maps of each island. For nautical charts, write **National Ocean Service,** Riverdale, MD 20737-1199, tel. (301) 436-6990 or (800) 638-8972.

BEACHES AND PARKS

Since the island is blessed with 150 miles of coastline, over 32 of which are wonderful beaches, your biggest problem is to choose which one you'll grace with your presence. The following should help you choose just where you'd like to romp about. But before you romp, pick up and read the brochures *Maui Beach Safety Tips,* by the American Red Cross, and *Beach and Ocean Safety Information,* both found at most free information stands around the island.

West Maui Beaches

The most plentiful and best beaches for swimming and sunbathing are on West Maui, strung along 18 glorious miles from Kapalua to Olowalu. For all-purpose beaches you can't beat **H.T.**

REEF FISH

blue-spotted cowfish

Hawaiian lionfish

saddleback wrasse

manta ray

Potter's angelfish

bluestrip butterflyfish

mottled moray

manini

trumpetfish

moorish idol

lagoon
humu

red-lipped
parrotfish

threadfin
butterflyfish

Achilles
tang

uhu

Fleming Beach or **Kapalua Bay Beach** on Maui's western tip. They have everything: safe surf (except in winter), great swimming, snorkeling, and bodysurfing in a first-class, family-oriented area. Then comes **Kaanapali Beach** along Rt. 30, bordered by the hotels and condos. This is open to the public and "rights of way" pass just along hotel grounds. **Black Rock** at the Sheraton is the best for snorkeling. In Lahaina, **Lahaina Beach** is convenient but not private and just so-so. **Puamana** and **Launiupoko Beaches** have only fair swimming, but great views and picnic areas. **Olowalu** has very good swimming and is one of the best and most accessible snorkling spots on the island, while **Papalaua Wayside** offers seclusion on a narrow beach fringed by *kiawe* trees that surround tiny patches of white sand.

Kihei and Wailea Beaches

The 10 miles stretching from Maalaea to Wailea are dotted with beaches that range from poor to excellent. **Maalaea** and **Kealia Beaches** extend four miles from Maalaea to Kihei. These are excellent for walking, windsurfing, and enjoying the view, but little else. **Kamaole Beach I, II,** and **III** are at the south end of Kihei. Top-notch beaches, they have it all—swimming, snorkeling, and safety. **Keawakapu** is more of the same. Then come the great little beaches of Wailea, which get more secluded as you head south: **Mokapu, Ulua, Wailea,** and **Polo.** All are surrounded by the picture-perfect hotels of Wailea and all have public access. **Makena Beach,** down the road from Wailea, is very special. It's one of the island's best beaches. At one time, alternative-lifestyle people made Makena a haven, and it still attracts free-spirited souls. There's nude bathing here in secluded coves, unofficial camping, and freedom. It gets the highest compliment when locals and those staying at hotels and condos around Maui come here to enjoy themselves.

Wailuku and Kahului Area

Poor ugly ducklings! The beaches in town are shallow and unattractive, and no one spends any time there. However, **Kanaha Beach** near the airport isn't bad at all, and it's a favorite of beginning windsurfers. **H.P. Baldwin Beach** has a reputation for hostile locals protecting their turf, but the beach is good and you won't be hassled if you "live and let live." **Hookipa Beach** just east of Paia isn't good

for the average swimmer, but it is the "Sailboarding Capital" of Hawaii, and you should visit here just to see the exciting, colorful spectacle of people skipping over the ocean with bright sails.

Hana Beaches

Everything about Hana is heavenly, including its beaches. There's **Red Sand Beach,** small, but almost too pretty to be real. **Wainapanapa** black-sand beach is surrounded by the state park and good for swimming and snorkeling, even providing a legendary cave whose waters turn blood red. **Hana Bay** is well protected and safe for swimming. Just south of town is the white-sand **Hamoa Beach,** described by James Michener as looking like the South Pacific.

Freshwater Swimming

There are several places for freshwater swimming in various stream pools on the road to Hana. One of the very best is **Twin Falls,** up a short trail from Hoolawa Bridge. **Helio's Grave** is another good swimming spot between Hana and Oheo Gulch. Farther along at **Kipahulu** you'll find the paradise you've been searching for—gorgeous freshwater pools at the base of wispy waterfalls and fronted by a tremendous sea of pounding surf only a few yards away. Also, you can take a refreshing dip at **Iao Stream** when you visit Iao Needle or in the next large valley north of there in **Waihee Stream.**

SNORKELING AND SCUBA

Maui is as beautiful from under the waves as it is above. There is world-class snorkeling and diving at many coral reefs and beds surrounding the island. You'll find some of the best, coincidentally, just where the best beaches are: mainly from Kihei to Makena, up around Napili Bay and especially around Olowalu. Backside Maui is great (but mostly for experts), and for a total thrill, try diving Molokini, the submerged volcano, just peeking above the waves and designated a Marine Life Conservation District.

Great Underwater Spots

These are some of the best on Maui, but there are plenty more. Use the same caution when scuba diving or snorkeling as when swimming. Be mindful of currents. It's generally safer to enter the water in the center of a bay than at the sides where rips are more likely to occur. The following sites are suitable for beginners to intermediates: on Maui's western tip **Honolua Bay** and nearby **Mokuleia Bay,** known as "Slaughterhouse," but gentle, both part of a Marine Life Conservation District; Napili Bay for usually good and safe conditions; in Kaanapali you'll enjoy **Black Rock** at the Sheraton Hotel; at **Olowalu,** the ocean is very gentle with plenty to see; also try **Kamaole Parks II** and **III** in Kihei, and **Ulua, Polo,** and **Wailea Beaches** in Wailea. On the windward side **Baldwin Beach Park** in Paia and **Wainapanapa State Park** near Hana are both generally good. Under no circumstances should you miss taking a boat out to Molokini. It's worth every penny, even though it's getting rather crowded! Some boats also stop at **Turtle Town** off the south coast.

For **scuba divers,** there are underwater caves at **Nahuna ("Five Graves") Point,** just up from Makena landing; great diving at Molokini; magnificent caves out at the **Lanai Cathedrals;** and a sunken Navy sub, the USS *Bluegill,* to explore. *Only* advanced divers should attempt the back side of West Maui, the coast at Kipahulu, and beyond Pu'uiki Island in Hana Bay.

With a name like Chuck Thorne, what else can you expect but a world-class athlete of some kind? Well, Chuck is a diver who lives on Maui and receives the highest accolades from other people. He's written *The Divers' Guide to Maui,* the definitive book on all the best dive/snorkel spots on the island. He's a no-nonsense kind of guy who's out to show you some great spots, but never forgets about safety first. While he's no longer available as a guide, his book is still available at many scuba outlets, or you can write for it direct: Maui Dive Guide, P.O. Box 40, Hana, HI 96713. This book is an invaluable resource, well worth the money and the effort to check it out.

Equipment

Sometimes condos and hotels have snorkeling equipment free for their guests, but if you have to rent it, don't do it from a hotel or condo; go to a dive shop where it's much cheaper. Expect to spend $5-7 a day for mask, fins, and snorkel. One of the best snorkel deals is through **Snorkel Bob's,** tel. (808) 879-7449 Kihei or 661-4421 Lahaina (also in Napili). Old Snorkel Bob will dispense info and full snorkel gear for only $14 weekly; you can return it on a Neighbor Island for a mere $3 charge, if you'll be heading off Maui before the week is up. More expensive custom snorkel equipment, hard-bottom boogie boards, and flotation boards are also available for rent. **A & B Rentals and Sports wear,** in Honokowai in Da Rose Mall at 3481 Lower Honoapiilani Rd., tel. (808) 669-0027, open daily 9 a.m.-5 p.m., rents snorkel gear for $2.50 per day and $0 per week, as well as boogie boards. Numerous other shops on the island also rent snorkel gear at comparable but variable rates depending upon the quality of the equipment.

Scuba divers can rent gear for about $40 from most shops. All the shops listed below rent snorkel gear as well. In Lahaina rent from: **Lahaina Divers,** 143 Dickenson St., tel. (808) 667-7496, one of the best all-around shops/schools on Maui; **Maui Dive Shop,** Lahaina Cannery Mall, tel. (808) 661-5388; **Capt. Nemo's Scuba Shack,** 150 Dickenson, tel. (808) 661-5555; or **Maui Diving,** in Anchor Square in Lahaina, tel. (808) 667-0633.

In Kihei-Wailea all-around dive shops are **Maui Dive Shop,** 1455 S. Kihei Rd., tel. (808) 879-3388; **Dive and Sea Maui,** 1975 S. Kihei Rd., tel. (808) 874-1952; and **Pacific Dive Maui,** at 1993 S. Kihei Rd., tel. (808) 874-5332. You might also consider renting an underwater camera. Expect to spend $15-20, including film.

Scuba Certification

A number of Maui companies take you from your first dive to PADI, NAUI, or NASDS certification. Prices range from $50 for a quickie refresher dive up to $300-400 for a four- to five-day certification course. Courses or arrangements can be made with any of the dive shops listed above, or with **Ocean Activities Center,** tel. (808) 879-4485; **Beach Activities of Maui,** tel. (808) 661-5500; **Ed Robinson's Diving Adventures,** tel. (808) 879-3584; or **Maui Diving,** tel. (808) 667-0633. Most major hotels also contract for scuba instruction for their guests, and most of these providers have booths on the hotel property.

Snorkel and Scuba Excursions

Many boats will take you out snorkeling or diving. Prices range from $30 (half day, four hours) to $60 (full day, eight hours) for a snorkeling adventure, and $50-100 for scuba diving. Some of these boats also do deep-sea fishing, moonlight cruises, and other charters. All "activities centers" on the island can arrange these excursions for no extra charge. Although there is some crossover, typically boats leaving from Lahaina Harbor go to Lanai or to spots along the west and north Maui coast to dive; those out of Maalaea or Makena go to Molokini or along the south coast of Maui.

Mike Severns, tel. (808) 879-6596, is one of the most experienced and respected divers on Maui. As a marine scientist/explorer, he is extremely knowledgeable about Maui both above and below the waves. Mike has his own boat and accepts both beginning and advanced divers. He dives mostly along the south coast. Diving with Mike is an extraordinary educational experience.

Dive and Sea Maui, 1975 S. Kihei Rd., tel. (808) 874-1952, open Mon.-Sat. 7 a.m.-5 p.m., until noon on Sunday, is a full-service dive shop offering scuba dives, certification classes, air refills, equipment rentals, and dive/snorkel trips to Molokini Crater on a six-passenger Mako boat so that you are given individual attention and full value for the money.

The **Maui Dive Shop,** at Azeka Place II Shopping Center along S. Kihei Road, tel. (808) 891-0153 or (800) 542-3483 (with nine other locations on the island), Web site: www.mauidiveshop.com, is a full-service water sports store that also operates snorkel and scuba dives to Molokini Crater and the south shore, or to Lanai depending upon water conditions and harbor of departure.

For a magnificent day of sailing, exploring, and snorkeling, you can't beat **Trilogy Excursions,** tel. (808) 661-4743 or (800) 874-2666, whose sleek catamarans leave Lahaina Harbor for a day trip to Lanai or leave Maalaea Harbor for Molokini.

Capt. Nemo's Scuba Shack, tel. (808) 661-5555 or (800) 367-8088, located at 150 Dickenson St. (with two locations in Kihei), offers open-water certification classes, beach dives, and night dives. This full-service scuba/snorkel store does daily rentals on scuba and snorkel equipment, boogie boards, and other water gear, and also has a complete repair facility and air fill station for those already certified. Nitrox available. Snorkel tours also available to South Maui locations.

Lahaina Divers, 143 Dickenson St. next to Pacific Whale Foundation, tel. (808) 667-7496 or (800) 998-3483, Web site: www.lahainadivers.com, offers a snorkeling experience, various scuba dives, and certification courses. Lahaina Divers uses its own boats for all of the excursions and offers beverages and snacks on all trips. This company is well regarded.

Ed Robinson's Diving Adventures, tel. (808) 879-3584 or (800) 635-1273 Mainland, Web site: www.mauiscuba.com, e-mail: robinson@maui.net, offers a great deal for those staying in South Maui. The company operates a beach cabana at the Four Seasons Resort in Wailea and runs tours from its fully equipped boat to spots all over the island and to Molokini and Lanai. Offered are free daily scuba clinics at the hotel; introductory and refresher shore and boat dives; Wailea reef dives; 007 underwater scooter dives; one-, two-, and three-tank dives, and night dives. PADI certification runs $485 and includes everything.

Among the many other companies in South Maui check out **Provider,** tel. (808) 875-4004; **Reef Watchers,** tel. (808) 874-3467; **Makena Coast Charters,** tel. (808) 874-1273 or (800) 833-6483; or **Boss Frog's,** tel. (808) 875-4477. In West Maui, try **Tropical Divers Maui,** tel. (808) 667-7709, Web site: www.scubamaui.com; **Happy Maui Diving and Tours,** tel. (808) 669-0123; or **Maui Diving,** tel. (808) 667-0633.

For a pure snorkeling adventure besides those offered by the dive shops and tour boats above, try **Island Explorations,** tel. (808) 572-8437, with Ann Fielding, the naturalist author of *Hawaiian Reefs and Tide Pools* and *Underwater Guide to Maui,* which details many of the invertebrates and reef fish that you will encounter on one of her fantastic dives. Ms. Fielding will instruct you in snorkeling and in the natural history and biology of what you'll be seeing below the waves. She tailors the dive to fit the participants, and does scuba as well. A basic snorkel dive, about two hours, costs $40.

Snuba

No, that's not a typo. Snuba is half snorkeling and half scuba diving. You have a regulator, weight belt, mask, and flippers, and you're tethered to scuba tanks that float 20 feet above you on a seasled. The idea is that many people become anxious diving under the waves encumbered by tanks and all the scuba apparatus. Snuba frees you. You would think that being tethered to the sled would slow you down, but actually you're sleeker and can make better time than a normal scuba diver. If you would like to start diving, this is a wonderful and easy way to begin. Try **The Four Winds,** tel. (808) 879-8188, a snorkel-dive boat that goes to Molokini Crater, or **Island Scuba,** tel. (808) 661-3369. Only a few other outfits are now starting to offer snuba on Maui.

MORE WATER SPORTS

Bodysurfing

All you need are the right waves, conditions, and ocean bottom to have a ball bodysurfing. Always check conditions first as bodysurfing has led to some very serious neck and back injuries for the ill-prepared. The following are some decent beaches: Ulua, Wailea, Polo, or Makena, the north end of Kamaole Beach Park I in Kihei, Napili Bay, and Baldwin Park.

Surfing

While the north coast of Oahu is known as the best surfing area in Hawaii—and arguably the best in the world—Maui has a few decent spots for the enthusiast. For good surfing on Maui try: Honolua Bay, Napili Bay, Baldwin Park, and Hookipa Beaches. Many beginners stay at the more gentle beaches between Lahaina and Olowalu, Maalaea Beach, and the beaches in Kihei. Maui does have one spot, however, that has gained worldwide notoriety over the last several years. This is "Jaws." Jaws is a place where, on a good day, waves rise 30-50 feet high! The conventional method of catching a wave—paddling belly down on your board until you gain enough speed and momentum to slip down the front of the wave—doesn't work here because of the height and speed of these waves. Ingenious (and maybe a bit crazy) surfers have come up with a solution—use a jet ski to gain speed and tow the surfer to the right spot before dashing out of harm's way. Some surfers use the tow rope as a big slingshot to propel themselves even faster from behind the jet ski. Surfboards used at Jaws have straps for the feet similar to a sailboard. So far, no one has died in this highly risky endeavor, but it seems likely that over time someone will bite it big. Jaws is located about 10 minutes past Hookipa Beach on the road to Hana and then down a road toward the ocean. People are reluctant to give the exact location, although locals know the spot well. Some fear, and rightly so, that inexperienced surfers will give

this monster a try, but homeowners in the area just don't like the traffic and congestion. On a high surf day, there may be as many as 350 cars parked on the approach road.

Surfing Instruction and Gear

There are about three dozen shops on Maui that rent surfboards and perhaps a dozen or more companies and individuals that teach the basics of surfing. Some are listed below. You can get surfing lessons in groups or individually. Lessons generally run in the vicinity of $55-65 for a group lesson that lasts about two hours or about $80 for a private lesson. Many lessons are taught directly south of Lahaina Harbor, while some instruction is done at the beach parks between Lahaina and Olowalu or in Kihei.

The **Maui Surfing School,** Web site: www .mauisurf.com, offers lessons at the beach just to the side of Lahaina Harbor. Call (808) 875-0625 and ask for Andrea Thomas. Specializing in "beginners and cowards," the school guarantees results after one lesson. Another "learn in one day" guarantee is offered by **Nancy Emerson School of Surfing,** tel. (808) 244-7873, Web site: www.maui.net/~ncesurf. Also in Lahaina are **Goofy Foot,** tel. (808) 244-9283; **Surf Dog Maui,** tel. (808) 250-7873; and **Maui Surf Camp,** tel. (808) 000 0010. Give **Maui Waveriders a call** in Kihei, tel. (808) 875-4761.

A good place to rent or buy surfboards and clothing in Lahaina is **Harbor Surf and Dive** at 113 Prison St., tel. (808) 667-6165. Also in Lahaina try **West Maui Cycles,** tel. (808) 661-9005; **Local Motion,** tel. (808) 661-7873; or **Maui Boardriders,** tel. (808) 667-7978. **A & B Rentals and Sportswear,** at the Da Rose Mall in Honokowai, tel. (808) 669-0027, open daily 9 a.m.-5 p.m., rents boogie boards, surfboards, and even fishing poles per day or week for reasonable rates. Kahului has at least three big shops where you can buy and rent surfing equipment: **Extreme Sports Maui,** tel. (808) 871-7953; **Hi-Tech Surf Sports,** tel. (808) 877-2111; and **Hawaiian Island Surf and Sport,** tel. (808) 873-0689.

Sailboarding/Windsurfing

This is one of the world's newest sports, and, unlike surfing, which tends to be male-dominated, women, too, have taken up sailboarding. Hookipa Beach, just east of Paia, is the "Sail-

ROBERT NILSEN

Kihei is one of Hawaii's sailboarding meccas.

boarding Capital of the World," and the big-money O'Neill International Championship used to be held here every year in March and April. Today, the **Aloha Classic,** held in late October or early November, with prize money at $5,000-10,000, is as big as it gets. For details, ask at any of the big windsurfing shops on the island or call (808) 575-9151.

Kanaha Beach Park, in nearby Kahului, has perfect, gentle winds and waves for learning the sport, and Kealia Beach in north Kihei is the choice of many. Summer is best for windsurfing because of the characteristics of the winds. Mornings are good for the novice as winds are lighter. As winds pick up in the afternoon the more advanced board riders hit the water. Any sailboard shop will point you in the right direction for location and gear according to your skill level.

To rent equipment or take instructions, try: **Maui Windsurf Company,** tel. (808) 877-4816 or (800) 872-0999, Web site: www.maui.net/~hst-cadiz. It has rentals from $45 a day to $395 for two weeks, and lessons for about $60-70. Remember—start with a big board and a small sail!

Take lessons to save time and energy. Several others to try, with comparable rates for lessons and rentals, are **Hi-Tech,** tel. (808) 877-2111; **Maui Sails,** tel. (808) 877-7443; **Hawaiian Island Surf and Sports,** tel. (808) 873-0827; **Hawaii Sail and Sport,** tel. (808) 879-0178; **Sailboards Maui,** tel. (808) 871-7954; and **Windsurfing West Maui,** tel. (808) 871-8733.

THRILL CRAFT

A recent controversy has focused on what have been called "thrill craft." Usually this refers to jet skis, water-skiing boats, speedboats, parasailing, and even sailboards. The feeling among conservationists is that these craft disturb humans, and during whale season they disturb the whales that come to nest in the rather small Lahaina Roads. This is definitely a case of "one man's pleasure is another man's poison." On March 31, 1991, a law was passed that bans these type of crafts from operating in west and south Maui waters during whale season, December 15 through May 15. Although you might assume that this is due to the sound of the motors roaring through the waters—some research has also been done to determine if this too is a problem—the restriction was set in place because of the speed and unpredictable nature of these watercraft.

Jet Skis
To try this exciting sport, contact **Pacific Jet Sport,** tel. (808) 667-2066, open daily 9 a.m.-4 p.m., for use of jet skis and wave runners. Meet the shuttle boat on the beach in front of the Hyatt Hotel in Kaanapali and it will take you out to the pontoon boat and riding area where you'll get instruction on how to operate these water machines. Rates for either craft are $47 for a half hour or $68 an hour, and $10 extra for each additional person up to three for the wave runners.

Water-Skiing
Maui Beach Activities, tel. (808) 667-1964, does water-skiing for $50 a half hour for one or two people, or $90 an hour for up to four people. Pickup can be arranged in the Kaanapali or Lahaina area. Visit the company's booth in the Whalers Village mall in Kaanapali.

Parasailing

If you've ever wanted to soar like an eagle, here's your chance with no prior experience necessary. Basically a parasail is a parachute tethered to a speedboat. And away we go! The most dangerous part seems to be getting in and out of the shuttle boat that takes you to the powerboat from where you take off. On the powerboat is a special harness attached to a parachute. You're put in a life vest and strapped to the harness that forms a cradle upon which you sit while aloft. Make sure, once you're up, to pull the cradle as far under your thighs as you can. It's much more comfortable. Don't be afraid to loosen your steel grip on the guide ropes because that's not what's holding you anyway. In the air, you are as free as a bird and the unique view is phenomenal. You don't have time to fret about going up. The boat revs and you're airborne almost immediately. Once up, the feeling is very secure. The technology is simple, straightforward, and safe. Relax and have a ball. Cost is about $50 for a 10-minute joyride that lets out about 800 feet of line or $42 for a seven-minute ride where you are at the end of a 400-foot line. Boats leave from Mala wharf and off Kaanapali Beach. Try **West Maui Para-Sail**, tel. (808) 661-4060; **UFO Parasail**, tel. 661-7UFO; or **Para-Sail Kaanapali**, tel. (808) 669-6555.

Rental Boats

If you really want to drive one on your own, **SeaEscape U-Drive Boat Rental**, 1979 S. Kihei Rd., tel. (808) 879-3721, can rent you a boat. The inflatable seagoing Zodiac rafts go for $75 an hour and the 17-foot mono-hull Boston Whaler for $95 an hour. Both are Coast Guard-approved for six persons and rent for a minimum of two hours.

You can also pilot a rigid-hull, inflatable Zodiac raft by contacting **H2O Tropical Tours,** tel. (808) 665-0488. Rates are $95 an hour, up to $495 for eight hours.

OCEAN TOURS

You haven't really seen Maui unless you've seen it from the sea. Tour boats operating out of Lahaina and Maalaea Harbors take you fishing, sailing, whalewatching, dining, diving, and snorkeling. You can find powerboats, sailboats, catamarans, and Zodiac rafts that offer a combination of some or all of these options or just sail you around for pure pleasure—Maui presents one of the premier sailing venues in the Pacific. Many take day trips to Lanai. Others visit Molokini, a submerged volcano with only half the crater rim above water; it has been designated a Marine Life Conservation District. The majority of Maui's pleasure boats are berthed in Lahaina Harbor, and most have a booth right there on the wharf where you can sign up. A substantial number of other boats come out of Maalaea, and a few companies are based in Kihei. The following are basically limited to sailing/dining/touring activities, with snorkeling often part of the experience. If you're interested in other ocean activities such as scuba, see above; for fishing, see below.

Excursions/Dinner Sails

Sunset cruises are very romantic and very popular. They last for about two hours and cost $40-70 for the basic cruise, but for a dinner sail expect to spend $70-90. Remember, too, that the larger established companies are usually on Maui to stay, but that smaller companies come and go with the tide! The following are general tour boats that offer a variety of cruises.

Trilogy Excursions, tel. (808) 661-4743 or (800) 874-2666, founded and operated by the Coon Family, is a success in every way. Its Lanai Cruise is the best on Maui. Although the handpicked crews have made the journey countless times, they never forget that it's your first time. They run catamarans that carry up to 50 passengers to Lanai. Once aboard, you're served a mug of steaming Kona coffee, fresh juice, and Mama Coon's famous cinnamon rolls. Once at Lanai, you can frolic at Hulopoe Bay, which is great for swimming and renowned as an excellent snorkeling area. All gear is provided. While you play, the crew is busy at work preparing a delicious barbecue at the picnic facilities at Manele Harbor. You couldn't have a more memorable or enjoyable experience than sailing with Trilogy. But don't spoil your day; be sure to bring along (and use!) a wide-brim hat, sunglasses, sunscreen, a long-sleeve shirt, and a towel. For this full day's experience, adults pay $159, children (3-12) half price. Trilogy Excursions also runs a popular half-day trip to Molokini Crater, sailing daily from Maalaea Harbor at 6:30 a.m. (adults $75, children half price), which includes breakfast, lunch, and all snorkeling gear;

a five-hour midday picnic sail from Kaanapali Beach; and two-hour whalewatching sails during whale season, also from Kaanapali Beach.

If you've had enough of Front Street Lahaina, **Club Lanai,** tel. (808) 871-1144 or (800) 531-5262, is a Maui-based company that runs day excursions to its developed facilities on the east side of Lanai (whalewatches and cocktail cruises, too). Besides Trilogy Excursions, Club Lanai is the only company with permission to land on Lanai. You board your catamaran at Lahaina Harbor, leaving at 7:30 a.m. and returning at around 3:30 p.m. after a full day. En route you're served a breakfast. The boats cruise to Club Lanai's private beach just near old Halepaloa Landing, between the deserted villages of Keomuku and Naha, on Lanai's very secluded eastern shore. Awaiting you is an eight-acre oasis of green landscaped beach protected by a reef. Palm trees provide shade over manmade lagoons, and hammocks wait for true relaxation. The club provides you with snorkel gear, wave skis, kayaks with instruction, bicycles for your personal exploration of the area, horseshoes, volleyball, and even a guided historic wagon tour. Scuba diving can also be arranged at an extra charge. On the grounds are a gift shop and a Hawaiian village where you can learn handicrafts from local or visiting artists. The bar serves exotic drinks and is open all day, and lunch is buffet style. The entire day including sail, meals, and use of facilities is reasonably priced at $89, with child and senior rates. Family oriented with plenty of activities for children of all ages, Club Lanai lets you set your own pace . . . do it all, or do nothing at all.

The **Navatek II,** a snow-white manta ray, has risen from Maui's waters and is prepared to instantly skim in effortless grace the frothing waves. This state-of-the-art marvel, built on Oahu and engineered expressly for use in Hawaii, is actually a SWATH vessel (Small Water Plane Area Twin Hull) of revolutionary design that features two submerged hulls, remote-controlled submarines, connected by two half-moon arching struts that support the above-water superstructure. The design means that the $5 million, 82-foot-long, 36 foot-wide cruise ship handles the waves with amazing dexterity since no part of the above-water decks comes into actual contact with the waves. The result is the island's most steady, most nimble, and most comfortable craft. With the touch of a finger, ballast tanks in the submersibles can be either flooded or blown to balance the craft, while a joystick raises or lowers the bow, and a polished aluminum ship's wheel only the size of a hockey puck steers the agile SWATH. Fronting the pilothouse is stepped amphitheater seating, and behind is a tanning deck comfortable with lounge chairs, restrooms, and even hot showers, very welcome after a swim or snorkeling adventure. The glass-enclosed lower deck converts to a floating restaurant, with stage, dance floor, full table settings, kitchen, and complete bar. The *Navatek II* offers a Lanai snorkel and whalewatch for $125 adults, $95 juniors 12-17, and $75 children ages 5-11, leaving daily except Friday from Maalaea Harbor at 8 a.m. and returning at about 2 p.m. The cruise offers a delicious breakfast buffet, barbecue lunch, snorkeling, and sail to and from the lightly visited island of Lanai. The Sunset Dinner Cruise, adults $87, children 2-11 $55, departs Maalaea Harbor nightly around 5:30 p.m., returning at 7:30 p.m., and features *pu pu,* cocktail hour, and a complete three-course dinner and dessert served at your table by a professional waitstaff. The *Navatek II* also does a two-hour whalewatch tour daily except Friday January through mid-April, after it returns from Lanai—$39 adults, $26.50 children 2-11. For complete details contact *Navatek II,* a division of Royal Hawaiian Cruises, tel. (808) 661-8787 or (800) 852-4183.

Scotch Mist, tel. (808) 661-0386, has one racing yacht, *The Scotch Mist II.* It is the oldest sailing charter on Maui (since 1970) and claims to have the fastest sailboats in Lahaina Harbor, boasting the lightest boat, the biggest sail, and the best crew. A sail/snorkel to Lanai in the morning costs $55 per person; West Maui is the destination in the afternoon. Or take the sunset sail (25 passengers) complete with champagne for $45 per person. When the time is right, a moonlight/starlight sail and a whalewatching sail are offered, for $40 each.

Other sailing ships that do a variety of snorkel, sunset, or sailing tours include the following. The **Lavengro,** tel. (808) 879-8188, a 60-foot "Roaring 20s" pleasure craft that even saw coastal duty during WW II, offers a lovely sail on a tall, two-masted wooden ship. This ship and its glass-bottom catamaran companion, **Four Winds,** make morning snorkel runs to Molokini; $59 for the *Lavengro* and $69 for the

Four Winds. The sloops **Flexible Flyer,** tel. (808) 244-6655, and **Cinderella,** tel. (808) 244-0009, also leave from Maalaea Harbor. America's Cup contender **America II,** tel. (808) 667-2195, sails out of Lahaina Harbor, and **World Class,** tel. (808) 667-7733, leaves from Kaanapali Beach.

One of the least expensive cruises is a cocktail sail aboard the 44-foot catamaran **Frogman,** tel. (808) 667-7622. It departs from Maalaea Harbor and serves pu pu, mai tais, and beer on its tradewind sail. Also from Maalaea Harbor is the champagne sunset dinner sail offered by Ocean Activities Center, tel. (808) 879-4485, aboard the 65-foot catamaran **Wailea Kai.** It sails Tuesday, Thursday, Friday, and Saturday. Also out of Maalaea Harbor is the **Mahana Maia,** tel. (808) 871-8636, a 58-foot cat that'll carry 50 passengers out to Molokini.

The **Prince Kuhio,** tel. (800) 468-1287 or (808) 242-8777 on Maui, offers a different kind of trip altogether. Comfort, luxury, and stability come with this 92-foot ship. Departing from Maalaea Harbor daily, the Prince Kuhio does a four-hour snorkel cruise to Molokini ($75 adult, $40 children under 12) including a continental breakfast, buffet lunch, open bar, and champagne on the return voyage; in season an afternoon whalewatching trip is offered for $30.

The quickest way to Molokini, which means more time in the water, is aboard the catamaran **Kai Kanani,** tel. (808) 879-7218, which departs from in front of the Maui Prince Hotel in Makena. Equipment and food are provided.

Pacific Whale Foundation, tel. (808) 879-8811, runs **The Manutea,** a 50-foot catamaran, offering a deluxe dinner sail for $69 from Maalaea Harbor. Pacific Whale Foundation has three other boats, one more leaving from Maalaea Harbor and two from Lahaina, which do whale, dolphin, and turtle sails. **Zip-Purr,** tel. (808) 667-2299, one of Maui's newest catamarans, offers a morning snorkel sail, sunset sail, and whalewatch in season with an Earthtrust scientist aboard for interpretation (some money goes to Earthtrust)—this family-operated, 41-foot catamaran was built in Hawaii expressly for Hawaiian waters. The **Maui Princess,** tel. (808) 667-6165, offers dinner cruises aboard its sleek 118-foot motor yacht for $75 ($35 children), which includes open bar, dinner, entertainment, and dancing. **Windjammer,** tel. (808) 661-8600, also does a salmon and prime rib dinner cruise on

its three-masted schooner, with sailings daily at 5:30 and 7:30 p.m.

Some of the above companies offer a variety of cocktail sails and whalewatches for much cheaper prices, but many tend to pack people in so tightly that they're known derisively as "cattle boats." Don't expect the personal attention you'd receive on smaller boats, and always check the number of passengers when booking. Some boats going to Lanai may take passengers for a one-way trip. You won't participate in the snorkeling or the food, but the price (negotiable) should be in line with the cost of a ferry ticket. This extra service is offered only if there's room. Talk to the individual captains.

Unique Ocean Tours

For a totally different experience, try a rafting trip. Several rafting companies have sprung up in the last few years so there's plenty of competition. These rafts are small rigid-bottom crafts with a sun shade that mostly seat 6-24 people. The vessels are highly maneuverable, totally seaworthy, high-tech motorized rafts whose main features are their speed and ability to get intimate with the sea as the supple form bends with the undulations of the water. You're right on the water, so you'll get wet, and you often ride right on the inflatable rubber tubes. Like boat tours, these rafts do one or a combination of tours that involve whalewatching, snorkeling, sea caves, coastal cruises, or the circumnavigation of Lanai. For half-day rides, you can expect a charge of about $65. The first company in Maui waters was **Blue Water Rafting,** tel. (808) 879-7238, Web site: www.maui.net/~mark/BWR.html, which still departs from the Kihei Boat Ramp. **Ocean Riders,** tel. (808) 661-3586, departs from Mala Wharf in Lahaina for trips to Lanai and Molokai. Royal Hawaiian Cruises runs the Maui Nui Explorer out of Lahaina Harbor to Lanai. Other options are **Ocean Rafting,** tel. (808) 667-2191 or (888) 677-7238, Web site: www.maui.net/~ocnraftn; **Hawaiian Rafting Adventures,** tel. (808) 661-7333; and **Ultimate Rafting,** tel. (808) 667-5678, Web site: www.maui.net/~ecoraft.

Kayaking has also become quite popular over the last few years. Located in the Rainbow Mall at 2439 S. Kihei Rd., **South Pacific Kayaks,** tel. (808) 875-4848 or (800) 776-2326, Web site: www.mauikayak.com, open daily 8 a.m.-5 p.m., offers a half-day introductory trip (with drinks and snacks) for $59, or an advanced explorer trip along the remote coastline of southwest Maui (including drinks and full lunch) for $89. Both tours include lunch along with plenty of snorkeling opportunities as you glide in and out of tiny bays fashioned from jutting lava rock fingers. South Pacific Kayaks offers rentals of single kayaks at $25-40 and double kayaks at $35-45 per day. **Kelii's Kayak Tours,** tel. (808) 874-7652, has several tours to various sites around the island ranging $55-99. See also **Pacific Whale Foundation** whalewatching tours, tel. (808) 879-8811, Web site: pacificwhale.org, or **Makena Kayak,** tel. (808) 879-8426.

Undersea adventures have also come to Maui. With **Atlantis,** tel. (800) 548-6262, you can dive to more than 100 feet to view the undersea world through glass windows. The basic tour starts at $69; you must be at least three feet tall to board. The **Reefrider,** tel. (808) 667-2133, and **SeaView Adventures,** tel. (808) 661-5550, are both submersibles that let you view the underwater from the depth of no more than 10 feet. But it's a great view nonetheless. All tours leave from Lahaina Harbor.

Whalewatching

Anyone on Maui from November to April gets the added treat of watching humpback whales as they frolic just off Lahaina, one of the world's major wintering areas for the humpback. Almost every boat in the harbor runs a special whalewatch during this time of year.

Whales Alive Maui, tel. (808) 874-6855, is a fantastic organization of dedicated scientists and naturalists who have made a career of studying the magnificent humpback whale and who operate whalewatches every day in season. Whales Alive Maui operates two-hour trips for a reasonable $30 through the **Ocean Activities Center,** tel. (808) 879-4485 or (800) 798-0652. Part of the proceeds are donated to further the research of this fine organization. Whales Alive Maui leaves Maalaea Harbor twice daily in the afternoon on the *Makakai* and *Wailea Kai.* On each of these stable and seaworthy catamarans is a fully trained Whales Alive Maui naturalist who offers a very educational and entertaining interpretive narration. When one of these wonderful animals shows itself by breaching, spouting, or slapping a pectoral fin, the naturalist will make every effort to inform you of what's going on, and especially how it relates to the social pattern of whale life. Simply by taking people out to see these magnificent creatures and teaching them about their lives, Whales Alive staff hope everyone will become aware of the whale's delicate place in nature and learn to appreciate their significance as something to be protected. There is no better way to have a truly Hawaiian experience of sea, surf, and natural beauty than enjoying a whalewatch sail with Whales Alive Maui.

Another highly educational whalewatch is sponsored by the **Pacific Whale Foundation,** located at Kealia Beach Plaza, Suite 25, 101 N. Kihei Rd., Kihei, HI 96753, tel. (808) 879-8811, open daily 8 a.m.-5 p.m. A nonprofit organization founded in 1980, it is dedicated to research, education, and conservation, and is one of the only research organizations that has been able to survive by generating its own funds through membership, donations, and excellent whalewatch cruises. The foundation has one of the best whalewatches on the island aboard its own ships, berthed for your convenience at Maalaea and Lahaina Harbors. The scientists and researchers who make up the crew rotate shifts and come out on the whalewatch when they're not out in the Lahaina Roads getting up close to identify, and make scientific observations of, the whales. Most of the information that the other whalewatches dispense to the tourists is generated by the Pacific Whale Foundation. Departures from Maalaea and Lahaina Harbors are several times daily. The foundation also offers an "Adopt-a-whale Program" and various reef and snorkel cruises that run throughout the year; check out their Web site: www.pacificwhale.org.

GONE FISHING

Surrounding Maui are some of the most exciting and productive "blue waters" in all the world. Here you can find a sportfishing fleet made up of skippers and crews who are experienced professional anglers. You can also fish from jetties, piers, rocks, and from shore. If rod and reel don't strike your fancy, try the old-fashioned throw-net, or take along a spear when you go snorkeling or scuba diving. There's nighttime torch fishing that requires special skills and equipment.

Streams and irrigation ditches yield introduced trout, bass, and catfish, but there are no state-maintained, public freshwater fishing areas in Maui County. While you're at it, you might want to try crabbing for Kona and Samoan crabs, or working low-tide areas after sundown hunting octopus, an island delicacy.

Deep-Sea Fishing

Most game-fishing boats work the waters on the calmer leeward sides of the islands. Some skippers, carrying anglers who are accustomed to the sea, will also work the much rougher windward coasts and island channels where the fish bite just as well. Trolling is the preferred method of deep-sea fishing; this is done usually in waters of 1,000-2,000 fathoms (a fathom is six feet). The skipper will either "area fish," which means running in a crisscross pattern over a known productive area, or "ledge fish," which involves trolling over submerged ledges where the game fish are known to feed. The most advanced marine technology, available on many boats, sends sonar bleeps searching for

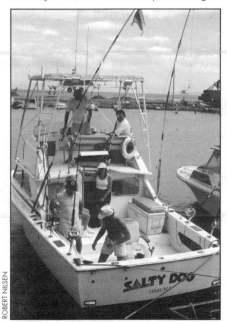

The Salty Dog

ROBERT NILSEN

fish. On deck, the crew and anglers scan the horizon in the age-old Hawaiian tradition—searching for clusters of seabirds feeding on baitfish pursued to the surface by the huge and aggressive game fish. "Still fishing" or "bottom fishing" with hand lines yields some tremendous fish.

The Game Fish

The most thrilling game fish in Hawaiian waters is marlin, generically known as billfish or a'u to the locals. The king of them is the blue marlin, with record catches of well over 1,000 pounds. There are also striped marlin and sailfish, which often go over 200 pounds. The best times for marlin are during spring, summer, and fall. The fishing tapers off in January and picks up again by late February. "Blues" can be caught year-round, but, oddly enough, when they stop biting it seems as though the striped marlin pick up. Second to the marlin are tuna. Ahi (yellowfin tuna) are caught in Hawaiian waters at depths of 100-1,000 fathoms. They can weigh 300 pounds, but between 25 and 100 pounds is common. There are also aku, skipjack tuna, and the delicious ono, which averages between 20 and 40 pounds.

Mahimahi is another strong, fighting, deep-water game fish abundant in Hawaii. These delicious fish can weigh up to 70 pounds. Shore-fishing and baitcasting yield papio, a jack tuna. Akule, a scad (locally called halalu), is a smallish schooling fish that comes close to shore and is great to catch on light tackle. Ulua are shore fish and can be found in tide pools. They're excellent eating, average two to three pounds, and are taken at night or with spears.

O'io are bonefish that come close to shore to spawn. They're caught by bait casting and bottom fishing with cut bait. They're bony, but they're a favorite for fish cakes and poki. Awa is a schooling fish that loves brackish water. It can get up to three feet long and is a good fighter; a favorite for throw-netters, it's even raised commercially in fishponds. Besides these, there are plenty of goatfish, mullet, mackerel, snapper, sharks, and even salmon.

Fishing Boats and Charters

The fishing around Maui ranges from very good to excellent. A sizable fleet of charter boats with skilled captains and tested crews is ready, willing, and competent to take you out. The majority are

GAME FISH

mahimahi

ono

uku

ulua

a'u

ahi

LOUISE FOOTE/DIANA LASICH HARPER

berthed at Lahaina Harbor while others are at Maalaea Harbor. The best times of year for marlin are July-Sept. and Jan.-March (when the generally larger females arrive). August is the optimum month. Rough seas can keep boats in for a few days during December and early January, but by February all are generally out.

You can hire a boat for a private or share charter, staying out for four, six, or eight hours. Some captains like to go for longer runs as there is a better chance of a catch and they can get farther into the water; some now do only private charters. Boat size varies, but four anglers per midsize boat is about average. No matter the size, most boats will take no more than six anglers. Although some provide it, be sure to bring food and drink for the day; no bananas, please—they're bad luck.

Deep-sea fishing on a share basis costs approximately $120 per half day (four hours) or $150 full day, per person. On a private basis, expect $500 per half day or up to $800 for a full day. If you're thinking of having a go at catching that "big one," go down to the harbor first and check out the boats, preferably in the afternoon when they're returning from sea. Be sure to talk with the captains and ask what success they've had lately, how they fish, where they try, and what happens to the fish.

Some of the best boats at Maalaea Harbor include: *Carol Ann,* tel. (808) 877-2181; *No Ka Oi III,* tel. (808) 879-4485, run by Ocean Activities Center; and *Makoa Kai,* tel. (808) 875-2251, captained by Dave Ventura, who does only private fishing charters. In Lahaina you can't go wrong with the *Judy Ann,* tel. (808) 667-6672; **Aerial Sportfishing,** tel. (808) 667-9089; *The Finest Kind* and *Reel Hooker,* tel. (808) 661-0338; or *Lucky Strike II,* tel. (808) 661-4606.

Coastal Fish

You don't have to hire a boat to catch fish! The coastline is productive too. Catch limits for 21 species of marine fish and eight crustaceans and shellfish are regulated, so check state guidelines. Also check state guidelines for Maui's four limited or prohibited areas of shore fishing: Molokini Marine Life Conservation District, Honolua-Mokuleia Marine Life Conservation District, Kahului Harbor, and Ahihi-Kinau Natural Reserve. If you need instruction or gear, contact one of the following companies: **Hawaiian Shoreline Fishing Adventures,** tel. (808) 573-0169; **Off-Road Shorefishing Expeditions,** tel. (808) 572-3470; or **Kawilani's Unique Tours,** tel. (808) 875-7305.

Freshwater Fish

Freshwater fishing on Maui is poor from an angler's point of view, but small populations of freshwater fish can be found in island streams and ponds. Hawaii has only one native freshwater game fish, the *o'opu.* This goby is an oddball with fused ventral fins. It grows to 12 inches and is found on all islands, especially Kauai. Introduced species include largemouth and small mouth bass, bluegills, catfish, *tucunare,* oscar, carp, and tilapia. The *tucunare* is a tough, fighting, good-tasting game fish introduced from South America, similar to the oscar from the same region. Both have been compared to bass, but are of a different family.

The tilapia is from Africa and has become common in Hawaii's irrigation ditches. It is a "mouth breeder"—the young will take refuge in their parents' protective jaws even a few weeks after hatching. The snakehead are eel-like fish that inhabit the reservoirs and are great fighters. The channel catfish can grow to over 20 pounds; it bites best after sundown. Or go for carp with its broad tails and tremendous strength, it's the poor man's game fish. All of these species are best caught with light spinning tackle, or with a bamboo pole and a trusty old worm. The catch limit of eight species of freshwater fish is regulated.

Fishing Licenses

A **Freshwater Game Fishing License** is good July 1-June 30. Licenses cost $7.50 for nonresidents, $3.50 for tourists (good for 30 days), $3.75 for residents over age 15 and military personnel and their dependents over age 15, $1.50 for children ages 9-15; they are free to senior citizens and children under age nine when accompanied by an adult with a license. You can pick up a license at sporting goods stores or at the Division of Aquatic Resources, 130 Mahalani St., Wailuku, tel. (808) 243-5294. Be sure to ask for the *Hawaii Fishing Regulations* and *Freshwater Fishing in Hawaii* booklets. Fishing is usually allowed in most State Forest Reserve Areas. Owner permission must be obtained to fish on private property. Shoreline and recreational fishing is permitted without a license.

HORSEBACK RIDING

Those who love sightseeing from the back of a horse are in for a big treat on Maui. Stables dot the island, so you have a choice of terrain for your trail ride: a breathtaking ride through Haleakala Crater, across rangeland, or a backwoods ride into the rainforest. There is no riding on the beach. Choose the stable by area or type of ride offered. Unfortunately, none of this comes cheap, but you won't be disappointed by either the quality of trailhand or scenery. It's advisable to wear jeans (jogging suit bottoms will do) and a pair of closed-toe shoes. Sunscreen and a hat are also recommended on most rides. All stables have age and weight restrictions, and some also have a height restriction, so be sure to check with them directly for all details.

Ironwood Ranch

You'll have your choice of rides at Ironwood Ranch: sunset, mountain, pineapple field, or extended rides for experienced riders. The West Maui Journey, for all skill levels, costs $75 for 90 minutes and runs through the foothills of the mountains. Also for all riders are the two-hour sunset ride for $100 and a two-hour Picnic in Paradise ride that also takes you on a short hike through a bamboo forest for $135. For the advanced rider, the Ironwood Odyssey takes you up the mountain for $125. No one over 220 pounds please. Horses are matched to the rider's experience level and all rides are escorted. Ironwood Ranch, 5095 Napilihau, Suite 308, Lahaina, HI 96761, tel. (808) 669-4991, is located at mile marker 29 along Rt. 30 above Napili. As all rides are conducted on private ranch land, meet at the pickup point across the highway from Napili Plaza.

Makena Stables

Makena Stables, tel. (808) 879-0244, is located at the end of Makena Alanui on La Perouse Bay; owners Helaine and Pat Borge will take you on a two-hour introductory ride through low-elevation rangeland, lava flows, and along the mountain trails of Ulupalakua Ranch; on three-hour morning or sunset rides; or on a five- to six-hour bay and lunch ride.

Haleakala and Environs

A few Upcountry companies offer trail rides through the crater or over the mountain. Wear *warm* clothes! **Charley's Trailride and Pack Trips** takes you on overnight camping rides to Haleakala, supplying all meals—in on Wednesday out on Thursday, or in on Saturday and out on Sunday. Contact Charles Aki, c/o Kaupo Store, Hana, HI 96713, tel. (808) 248-8209 (call before 10 a.m. or in the evening); rates on rides of more than two people are $250 per person per night, which includes food and camping equipment; $225 per night without food included. For only two people, the rate is $300 per person per day. Meet at Charley's residence in Kaupo for a 9 a.m. departure; early reservations are required, along with a $75 deposit well in advance. A hat, warm clothing, rain ponchos, and boots are recommended for all rides.

Pony Express Tours offers trail rides into Haleakala Crater—full day $160, partial day $130, lunch provided. One- and two-hour rides ($40-88) are also offered across Haleakala Ranch land at the 4,000-foot elevation on this volcanic mountain. Riders must be at least 10 years old, under 65, and not more than 235 pounds. Contact Pony Express Tours, P.O. Box 535, Kula, HI 96790, tel. (808) 667-2200, Web site: www.maui.net/~ponex, e-mail: ponex@maui.net.

Thompson Ranch Riding Stables, a family-operated stable that will even mount up children under 10, guides you over the slopes of Haleakala on one of Maui's oldest cattle ranches. Located at 3,700 feet, just outside of Keokea. Contact Thompson Stables, Thompson Rd., Kula, HI 96790, tel. (808) 878-1910.

Adventures On Horseback offers waterfall rides along the north coast over lands of a private estate in Haiku taking a maximum of six riders, who must be at least 16 years old and five feet tall, and not over 225 pounds. Bring your own swimming suit and towel. For reservations and information, call (808) 242-7445, or write P.O. Box 1419, Makawao, Maui, HI 96768.

Maui Mule Ride offers two-, five-, and six-hour rides into Haleakala Crater on these sure-footed beasts of burden, leaving from the visitors center parking lot near the top. Rates are $95, $155, and $190 per person, respectively. Long pants, shoes, and a jacket are a must, and it's best to bring sunglasses and a hat. A picnic lunch is provided on the longer rides, refreshments on all. For information and reservations call (808) 244-6853 or (808) 878-1743.

Hana District

The hotel guests are given priority for use of the horses at the **Hana Ranch Stables,** but you can call ahead to arrange a trail ride on this truly magnificent end of the island. The one-hour easy guided rides, two in the morning and one in the afternoon, go either along the coast or into the upper pastureland. Cost is $35 per person; riders must be seven years old. Private rides are given after 3 p.m. for $70 per person. For information, call (808) 248-0011.

In Kipahulu you'll find **Oheo Stables,** tel. (808) 667-2222. Two rides (10:30 and 11:30 a.m.) are given every day, both three hours on the trail, and the destination is the highland above Makahiku and Waimoku Falls in Haleakala National Park. Only six riders maximum per ride. Both rides include a continental breakfast, snacks, and drinks, while the later ride also includes lunch. The early ride is $119, the later ride $139.

Backside West Maui

Mendez Ranch and Trail Rides offers three-hour morning rides daily except Sunday over a small working ranch on the rugged north coast of Maui, $130 per person. Riders must be at least 11 years old and no more than 250 pounds. You'll have a look at the shoreline, pastureland, lush valleys, and waterfalls, and you round out the ride with a real *paniolo* barbecue picnic. This is a local experience led by real cowboys. Mendez Ranch is located just past mile marker 6 on Rt. 330 north of Wailuku. For reservations, call (808) 871-5222 or write P.O. Box 150, Wailuku, HI 96793.

Past mile marker 9 is **Seahorse Ranch,** which has three-hour trail rides over rangeland along the spectacular north coast. Lunch and drinks are served. Rides are $99, no one under 12 allowed. For reservations, call (808) 244-9862.

BICYCLING

Bicycle enthusiasts should be thrilled with Maui, but the few flaws might flatten your spirits as well as your tires. The countryside is great, the weather is perfect, but the roads are heavily trafficked and the most interesting ones are narrow and have bad shoulders. Pedaling to Hana will give you an up-close personal experience, but for bicycle safety this road is one of the worst. Haleakala is stupendous, but with a rise of more than 10,000 feet in less than 40 miles it is considered one of the most grueling rides in the world. And a paved bike path runs from Lahaina to Kaanapali that's tame enough for everyone. You may be better off bringing your own bike rather than renting. If you do rent, instead of a delicate road bike get a cruiser or mountain bike that can handle the sometimes-poor road conditions as well as open up the possibilities of offroad biking (mostly at Polipoli Spring State Recreation Area). In short, cycling on Maui as your primary means of transportation is not for the neophyte; because of safety considerations and the tough rides, only experienced riders should consider it.

Getting your bike to Maui from one of the Neighbor Islands is no problem. All of the interisland and commuter carriers will fly it for you for about $20 one-way on the same flight as you take—just check it in as baggage. Bikes must be packed in a box or hard case, supplied by the owner. Handlebars must be turned sideways and the pedals removed or turned in. Bikes go on a space available basis only—usually not a problem, except, perhaps, during bicycle competitions. In addition, a release of liability for damage must be signed before the airline will accept the bike. If you plan ahead, you can send your bike the previous day by air freight. The freight terminal at Kahului is just a few minutes' walk from the passenger terminal and opens at 7 a.m. You can also take your bike on the interisland ferry between Maui and Lanai. It will cost you $10 each way, but you don't need to pack it.

Getting your bike to Hawaii from the Mainland will depend upon which airline you take. Some will accept bicycles as baggage traveling with you (approximate additional charge of $30) if the bikes are properly broken down and boxed in a bicycle box, while others will only take them as air freight, in which case the rates are exorbitant. Check with the airlines well before you plan to go or explore the possibility of shipping it by sea through a freight company.

For general information on biking in Hawaii, contact **Hawaii Bicycling League,** P.O. Box 4403, Honolulu, HI 96812-4403. This nonprofit organization promotes biking as recreation, sport, and transportation, encourages safe biking practices, conducts biking education, and advocates for biking issues. It publishes a monthly newsletter, *Spoke-n-Words,* filled with news of the organization's business, its bicycle safety program for kids, and rides that are open to the public, as well as current bicycle issues and sponsored bicycle competitions throughout the state. If you are a bicycle rider living in the islands or simply want a subscription to the newsletter, write for membership information. For mountain biking and trail information on all the major islands, pick up a copy of *Mountain Biking the Hawaiian Islands* by John Alford.

For additional information, have a look at the *Bicycle Regulations and Illustrated Safety Tips* booklet put out by the Department of Transportation Services, City and County of Honolulu. Although written for the island of Oahu, the information is applicable to all the islands, except for a few minor details. From the Neighbor Islands or if coming from outside the state, write or call for a copy: Chris Sayers, Bicycle Coordinator, City and County of Honolulu, 711 Kapiolani Blvd., Suite 1200, Honolulu, HI 96813, tel. (808) 527-5044. Also very informative for rules of the road and common sense biking tips is the *Rights and Responsibilities for Hawai'i's Bicyclists* booklet. This booklet is available free from the State Bicycle/Pedestrian Coordinator, State Dept. of Transportation, 869 Punchbowl St., Honolulu, HI 96813, tel. (808) 587-2321, and may be available at city halls and tourist offices.

Bicycle Rentals

Some bicycle rental shops will tell you that the Park Service does not allow you to take your bike up to Haleakala National Park—horse pucky! You *cannot* ride the bike on the hiking paths, but going up the road (40 miles uphill) is okay if you have the steam. You are given this misinformation because the bike rental shops don't want the wear and tear on their bikes—but for the prices they charge, they shouldn't squawk.

South Maui Bicycles, 1993 S. Kihei Rd., tel. (808) 874-0068, open Mon.-Sat. 10 a.m.-6 p.m., Sunday until 2 p.m., is a rental and bike repair shop that boasts the largest fleet on Maui from which to choose. Rates are: street bikes $17 per day, $79 per week; mountain bikes $30 a day or $110 a week. Frank Hackett, the shop owner, will take time to give you tips including routes and the best times to travel.

West Maui Cycles, in Lahaina at 193 Lahainaluna Rd. with a sister store at the Kahana Manor Shops, is a full service bike sale and rental store that also carries other sporting equipment. The Lahaina store, tel. (808) 661-9005, has mostly road bikes; the Kahana store, tel. (808) 669-1169, mostly mountain bikes. Standard road bike rates run from $19 a day to $79 a week, more for a high-end bike or a tandem. Mountain bikes vary from $19 a day to $200 a week, depending on suspension.

For other bike rentals, try **A & B Rentals and Sportswear,** in Honokowai at 3481 Lower Honoapiilani Rd., tel. (808) 669-0027, open daily 9 a.m.-5 p.m., which rents basic mountain bikes at $15 for 24 hours, $60 per week. Aside from running bike tours, **Haleakala Bike Company,** tel. (808) 572-2200, in Haiku also rents mountain bikes, all equipment, and a rack if you need one for $29 the first day, $20 after that, or $110 a week. Upgraded suspension increases the cost. **The Island Biker,** tel. (808) 877-7744, 415 Dairy Rd. in Kahului, rents mostly mountain bikes along with its sales and repair services. They go for $25 a day, $85 a week, or $250 a month.

Haleakala Bicycle Tours

An adventure on Maui that's become famous is riding a specially equipped bike from the summit of Mt. Haleakala for 40 miles to the bottom at Paia. These bikes are mountain bikes or modified cruisers with padded seats, wide tires, and heavy-duty drum brakes, front and back. Typically, these tours take about eight hours with about three hours on the bike. Most offer a shuttle pickup and dropoff at your hotel. For tours that go to the top of the mountain for sunrise, expect to get picked up about 3 a.m.—get to bed early! Every bike rider on tours that ride through the national park must wear a full motorcycle helmet. Other tours that start outside the park will provide you with a regular bicycle helmet. Warm layered clothing is a must, long pants and closed-toe shoes recommended. Most bike companies have some guidelines—like no pregnant women, minimum age of 12, must be at least five feet tall—but each company's requirements may be slightly different, so check.

A pioneer in this field is **Maui Downhill,** 199 Dairy Rd., Kahului, tel. (808) 871-2155 or (800) 535-BIKE. Included in the bike ride for $115 you get two meals (continental breakfast, brunch or a gourmet picnic lunch), windbreakers, gloves, and helmets. To drench yourself in the beauty of a Haleakala sunrise, you have to pay your dues. You arrive at the base yard in Kahului at about 3:30 a.m. after being picked up at your condo by the courtesy van. Here, you'll muster with other bleary-eyed but hopeful adventurers and munch donuts and coffee, which at this time of the morning is more like a transfusion. Up the mountain, in the van, through the chilly night air takes about 90 minutes, with singing and storytelling along the way. Once atop, find your spot for the best natural light chow in the world: the sun goes wild with colors as it paints the sky and drips into Haleakala Crater. This is your first reward. Next comes your bicycle environmental cruise down the mountain with vistas and thrills every inch of the way, with stops for sightseeing, food, and to let cars pass. For the not-so-early risers, other mountain descent tours are available for $50-80.

Maui Mountain Cruisers of Makawao, tel. (808) 871-6014, and **Mountain Riders**, tel. (808) 242-9739, the other two of the "big three" bike touring companies, offer pretty much the same guided bike services at competitive rates.

A twist to this convoy guided bike tour is offered by **Haleakala Bike Company**, tel. (808) 572-2200, in Haiku. With this outfit, you meet at the bike store and get fitted with your bike and are given all necessary equipment. For the sunrise tours, the van leaves at about 4:15 a.m. and brings you to the top of the mountain in the park for your sunrise experience. When the riders start down the mountain, the company van stays with them until they are comfortable with the bikes and route and then lets them go the rest of the way by themselves, taking their time or zipping down the hill as they like, stopping when they want and eating where they desire. All that is required is that they return by about 4 p.m. It's bike freedom. Later in the morning, another dropoff goes to the crater rim. These rides are $59. Also leaving later in the morning, dropoffs at the park entrance go for $39.

Two other companies that do a go-at-your-own-pace tour are: **Haleakala Bike Adventures**, tel. (808) 573-2888, which does a summit sunrise trip for $58 and a day trip starting at the park entrance for $38; **Aloha Bicycle Tours**, tel. (808) 249-0911, does a run south on Routes 37 and 377 to Ulupalakua.

Chris's Bike Adventures, tel. (808) 871-BIKE, offers a variation on the theme, taking you on a mountain bike adventure down Haleakala including a tour of the Tedeschi Winery and a walk along the lava fields around La Perouse Bay, all for $99. Or you can take an afternoon ride, winding up at the winery where you can soothe your beaten bottom with a glass of *vino*.

Bicycle Touring

For those interested in bicycle touring, contact one of the following for their specialized bike trips. The owners and tour leaders of **Island Bicycle Adventures**, 560 Kapahulu Ave., Honolulu, HI 96815, tel. (808) 734-0700 or (800) 233-2226, are intimately familiar with bicycle touring and are members of the Hawaii Bicycling League. They offer tours to Maui, the Big Island, and Kauai. **Chris's Bike Adventures**, P.O. Box 869, Kula, HI 96790, tel. (808) 871-2453, runs two tours on Maui, one down Haleakala and the other on the backside of West Maui. Call for rates.

For those who like to strike out on their own, two routes are recommended. One takes you for a 50-mile loop from Wailuku (or Lahaina) up the Kaanapali coast and around the head of Maui back to Wailuku. The road starts out in good repair, but the traffic will be heavy until you pass Kapalua. Here the road begins to wind along the north coast. Since this road has been paved, traffic around the north end has picked up, so the road will not be just yours anymore. Around the north end there is no place to get service. Go prepared, and be on the lookout for cars.

The second route is from Kahului up to Kula or Pukalani via Pulehu Road and back down the mountainside via Paia, Haiku, or Ulumalu, taking you through irrigated cane fields, the cool Upcountry region, the lush, sculpted north slope of Haleakala, and along the back of Maui.

GOLF

Maui has 10 golf courses with 16 links; all but one have 18 holes. These range from modest municipal courses to world-class private clubs. Some are set along the coast, while others back against the mountain with sweeping views of the lowlands. The high-class resort areas of Kaanapali, Kapalua, and Wailea are built around golf courses.

MAUI GOLF COURSES

COURSE	PAR	YARDS	FEES	CART	CLUBS
Grand Waikapu **Resort Country Club** Wailuku, HI 96793 tel. (808) 244-7888	72	6,647	$200	Incl.	$30
Kaanapali Golf Courses Kaanapali, HI 96761 tel. (808) 661-3691					
North Course	71	6,136	$120	Incl.	$27
South Course	71	6,067	$120	Incl.	$27
Kapalua Golf Club Kapalua, HI 96791 tel. (808) 669-8044					
Bay Course	72	6,051	$140	Incl.	$35
Villa Course	71	6,001	$140	Incl.	$35
Plantation Course		73	$140	Incl.	$35
Makena Golf Courses Makena, HI 96753 tel. (808) 879-3344					
North Course	72	6,151	$140	Incl.	$35
South Course	36	6,168	$140	Incl.	$35
Maui Country Club Paia, HI 96779 tel. (808) 877-0616 (Monday only for visitors)	74	6,549	$45	Incl.	$10
Pukalani Country Club Pukalani, HI 96788 tel. (808) 572-1314	72	6,494	$55	Incl.	$20
Sandalwood Golf Course Wailuku, HI 96793 tel. (808) 242-4653	72	6,011	$75	Incl.	$30
Silversword Golf Club Kihei, HI 96753 tel. (808) 874-0777	71	6,404	$70	Incl.	$22
Waiehu Municipal Golf Course Waiehu, HI 96793 tel. (808) 243-7400	72	6,330	$25	$15	$25 (weekdays) $30 (weekends)
Wailea Golf Club Wailea, HI 96753 tel. (808) 875-5155, 875-5111					
Blue Course	72	6,152	$130	Incl.	$30
Gold Course	72	6,152	$115	Incl.	$30
Emerald Course	72	5,873	$140	Incl.	$30

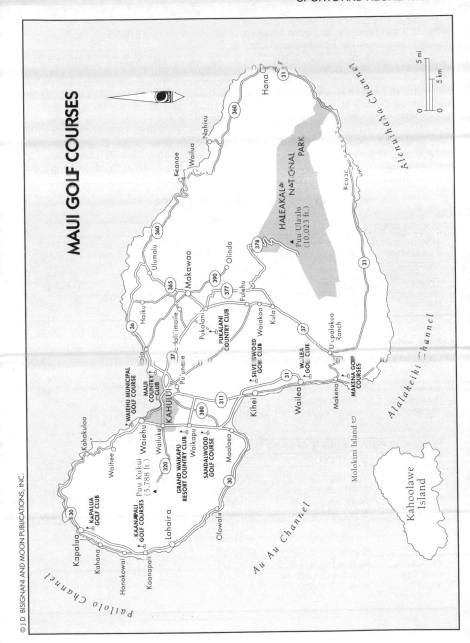

© J.D. BISIGNANI AND MOON PUBLICATIONS, INC.

MAUI GOLF COURSES

Municipal and public courses are open to everyone. Resort courses cater to the public as well as to resort guests. Private courses are strictly for members only and their guests. Most golf courses offer lessons. Many have driving ranges, some that are lighted. Virtually all have pro shops and clubhouses with restaurants and lounges. Greens fees listed in the chart are for non-Hawaii residents. Many courses offer reduced *kama'aina* rates, special time rates, and twilight hour rates. Be sure to ask about these rates as they often afford substantial savings.

TENNIS

There are many tennis courts on Maui, and plenty of them are free. County courts are under the control of the Department of Parks and Recreation, which maintains a combination of lighted and unlit courts around the island. No fees are charged for these public courts. Play is on a first-come first-served basis and limited to 45 minutes if there are people waiting. Weekends are often fairly busy, but it's relatively easy to get a court on weekdays. Court rules apply and

MAUI TENNIS COURTS

COUNTY COURTS

Under jurisdiction of the Department of Parks & Recreation, 200 High St., Wailuku, Maui, tel. (808) 244-7750; there are three additional locations around the island. Courts listed are in or near visitor areas and open to the public.

TOWN	LOCATION	NO. OF COURTS	LIGHTED
Haliimaile	Haliimaile Park	1	Yes
Hana	Hana Ball Park	2	Yes
Kahului	Kahului Community Center	2	Yes
Kihei	Kalami Park	4	Yes
	Waipulani Park	6	No
Lahaina	Lahaina Civic Center	5	Yes
	Malu-ulu-olele Park	4	Yes
Makawao	Eddie Tam Memorial Center	2	Yes
Pukalani	Pukalani Park	2	Yes
Wailuku	Wailuku War Memorial Complex	4	Yes
	Wells Park	7	Yes

HOTEL AND PRIVATE COURTS OPEN TO THE PUBLIC (FEES VARY)

TOWN	LOCATION	TEL. (808)	NO. OF COURTS	LIGHTED
Kaanapali	Hyatt Regency	661-1234	5	Yes
	Maui Marriott Resort	667-1200	5	No
	Royal Lahaina Hotel	661-3611	10	6
	Sheraton Maui Hotel	661-0031	3	Yes
	Whaler	661-5552	5	No
Kapalua	Kapalua Tennis Center	669-6200	10	5
	Kapalua Tennis Garden	669-6200	10	4
Makena	Makena Tennis Club	874-1111	6	2
Napili Bay	Napili Kai Beach Club	669-6271	2	No
Wailea	Wailea Tennis Club	875-7767	11	3

only soft-sole shoes are allowed. Also, some resort and private courts are open to the public for a fee, while others restrict play to members and guests only. The accompanying chart is a partial listing of what's available.

SPORTING CLAYS

An outgrowth of hunting, sporting clays is a sport that helps develop and maintain your hand-eye coordination. Shooting is done from different stations around a course, and the object is to hit a small round clay disk. Different than trap or skeet shooting, sporting clays relies upon moving targets that mimic different animals and birds, hopping along the ground as if a rabbit, springing off the ground like a teal, or flying high like a pheasant. Hawaii has about a half dozen sporting clay grounds; two are on Maui and one is on Lanai. Each is designed differently but all provide the same basic service. Although a variety of options are available for the beginner to the advanced shooter, a typical round with a 20-gauge shotgun would take about an hour and cost around $100. Open daily 8:30 a.m.-dusk, **Papaka Sporting Clays,** tel. (808) 879-5649, is located in Makena. Call for reservations and directions. **Westside Sporting Clays,** tel. (808) 669-7468, is located 3.3 miles beyond Office Rd. in Kapalua. Reservations recommended.

HUNTING

Most people don't think of Hawaii as a place for hunting, but actually it's quite good. Seven species of introduced game mammals and 15 species of game birds are regularly hunted—14 on Maui, 13 on Molokai, and 15 on Lanai. Some species of game animals are restricted on all islands, but every island offers hunting. Public game lands are located throughout Maui County; a license is required to take birds and game.

Information

Hunting rules and regulations are always subject to change. Also, environmental considerations often change bag limits and seasons. Make sure to check with the State Division of Forestry and Wildlife for the most current information. Request *Rules Regulating Game Bird Hunting, Rules Regulating Game Mammal Hunting,* and *Hunting in Hawaii.* Direct inquiries to: Department of Land and Natural Resources, Division of Forestry and Wildlife Office, 54 S. High St., Wailuku, HI 96793, tel. (808) 984-8100.

General Hunting Rules

Hunting licenses are mandatory in order to hunt on public, private, or military land anywhere in Hawaii. They're good for one year beginning July 1 and cost $15 residents and service personnel, $95 nonresidents, free to senior citizens. Licenses are available from sporting goods stores and from the various offices of the Division of Forestry and Wildlife. This government organization also sets and enforces the rules, so contact it with any questions. Generally, hunting hours are from a half hour before sunrise to a half hour after sunset. Checking stations are maintained, where the hunter must check in before and after hunting.

Rifles must have a muzzle velocity greater than 1,200-foot-pounds. Shotguns larger than .20 gauge are allowed, and muzzle-loaders must have a .45 caliber bore or larger. Bows must have a minimum draw of 40 pounds for straight bows, 35 pounds for a recursive bow, and 30 pounds for compounds. Arrows must be broadheads. The use of hunting dogs is permitted only for certain species of birds and game, and when dogs are permitted, only smaller caliber rifles and shotguns, and spears and knives, may be used—no big bore guns/shotguns. Hunters must wear orange safety cloth on front and back no smaller than a 12-inch square. Certain big-game species are hunted only by lottery selection; contact the Division of Forestry and Wildlife two months in advance. Guide service is not mandatory, but is advised if you're unfamiliar with hunting in Hawaii. You can hunt on private land only with permission, and you must possess a valid hunting license. Guns and ammunition brought into Hawaii must be registered with the chief of police of the corresponding county within 48 hours of arrival.

Game Animals

All game animals in Hawaii have been introduced. Some have adapted admirably and are becoming well-entrenched, while the survival of others is still precarious. **Axis deer** originated in India and were brought to Lanai and Molokai, where they're doing well. The small herd on Maui is holding its own. Their unique flavor makes them one of the best wild meats; they're hunted on Lanai from mid-February to mid-May by public lottery. **Mouflon sheep** are native to Corsica and Sardinia. They do well on the windswept slopes of Mauna Loa and Mauna Kea on the Big Island and on Lanai, where they're hunted Aug.-Oct., also by public lottery. **Feral pigs** are escaped domestic pigs and are found on all islands except Lanai. The stock is a mixture of original Polynesian pigs and subsequently introduced species. Hunted with dogs and usually killed with a spear or long knife, pig hunting is not recommended for the timid or tender-hearted. These beasts' four-inch tusks and fighting spirits make them tough and dangerous. **Feral goats** come in a variety of colors. Found on all islands except Lanai, they have been known to cause erosion and are considered a pest in some areas, especially on Haleakala. Openly hunted on all islands, their meat when properly cooked is considered delicious.

Game Birds

A number of game birds are found on most of the islands. Bag limits and hunting seasons vary, so check with the Division of Forestry and Wildlife

gray francolin

for details. **Ring-necked pheasants** are one of the best game birds, and found on all the islands. **Green pheasants** are found on Maui. **Francolins,** gray and black, from India and the Sudan, are similar to partridges. They are hunted with dogs and taste great roasted. There are also **chukar** from Tibet, found on the slopes of all islands; **quail,** including the Japanese and California varieties; **doves;** and the wild Rio Grande **turkey** to name a few.

SHOPPING

This chapter will provide general information about shopping on Maui for general merchandise, arts and crafts, food, and specialty items. Specific shops are listed in the "Shopping" section of each travel chapter. Here, you should get an overview of what's available and where, with enough information to get your pockets twitching and your credit cards smoldering! Happy bargain hunting!

SHOPPING CENTERS

Those who enjoy one-stop shopping will be happy with the choices in Maui's various malls. You'll

find regularly known department stores as well as small shops featuring island-made goods. The following are Maui's main shopping malls.

Kahului/Wailuku

Along Kaahumanu Avenue, you'll find **Kaahumanu Center,** the largest on the island. Here's everything from Sears and Liberty House to Sew Special, a tiny store featuring island fabrics. The mall is full-service with apparel stores, shoe stores, computer centers, art shops, music stores, gourmet coffee shop, and Waldenbooks. You can eat at numerous restaurants, buy ice cream cones, or enjoy a movie at Kaahumanu Theater.

Down the road is **Maui Mall**, featuring a photo center, Longs for everything from aspirin to film, another Waldenbooks, sports and swimwear shops, and numerous restaurants and food outlets. Sandwiched between these two modern facilities is **Kahului Shopping Center.** It's definitely "down-home" with old-timers sitting around outside. The shops here aren't fancy, but they are authentic and you can make some offbeat purchases while strolling through.

The past few years have seen a rapid expansion of mercantile outlets in Kahului. In the triangle by Kahana Pond is **Triangle Square** center, and many of its shops are dedicated to sports. Several small malls are strung along Dairy Road between Hana Highway and Hulilike Street. The newest and the second largest in town is the **Maui Marketplace Mall** on the south side of Dairy Road, where you can find Sports Authority, Eagle Hardware, OfficeMax, several banks, clothing shops, jewelry stores, and a Borders Books outlet.

Lahaina

You can't beat Lahaina's Front Street for the best, worst, most artistic, and tackiest shopping on Maui. This is where the tourists are, so this is where the shops are . . . shoulder to shoulder. The list is endless, but you'll find art studios and galleries, T-shirts galore, scrimshaw, jewelry, silks, boutiques, leathers, souvenir junk, eelskins, and even a permanent tattoo memory of Maui. No wimps allowed! Lahaina also has the best special-interest shopping on Maui in various little shops strung out along Front Street.

The following are the local malls: **The Wharf Cinema Center** on Front St. has a multitude of eating establishments, as well as stores and boutiques in its multilevel shopping facility. Nearly across the street are the **Pioneer Inn Shops,** again with a multitude of clothing and gift shops, but all on street level. **Lahaina Market Place,** tucked down an alley off Front St. near Lahainaluna Rd., features established shops along with open-air stalls. **Lahaina Square Shopping Center, Lahaina Shopping Center,** and **Anchor Square,** all set between Rt. 30 and Front St., have various shops and are the most *local* of the Lahaina malls. The **505 Front Street Mall** is at the south end of Front St. and offers distinctive and quiet shopping away from the frenetic activity.

The **Lahaina Cannery Mall,** on Lahaina's north end, features restaurants, boutiques, specialty shops, fast food, and plenty of bargains. It's the largest mall on West Maui and has some of the best shopping under one roof on the island. The newest mall in town is the open-air **Lahaina Center,** located along Front Street at Papalaua Street. Stores include Hilo Hattie, Liberty House, Banana Republic, Wet Seal, Maui Dive Shop, Hard Rock Café, and the Front Street Theaters.

Kaanapali to Kapalua

Whalers Village, the only mall in Kaanapali, is set right on the ocean and features a decent self-guided whaling museum. There are various eateries, upscale boutiques, art galleries, a bottle shop, film processing center, and a sundries store. It's a great place to stroll, buy, and learn a few things about Maui's past. The **Sheraton, Marriott, Westin Maui, Hyatt Regency,** and **Royal Lahaina** hotels all have shopping arcades. You'll need a suitcase stuffed with money to buy anything there, but it's a blast just walking around the grounds and checking out the big-ticket items.

Along Lower Honoapiilani Rd., the villages of Honokowai, Kahana, and Napili all have small local shopping malls, mostly for everyday items. Two new and larger malls have opened on Honoapiilani Hwy., however. At **Kahana Gateway Mall** is one of Maui's finest restaurants, a hardware store, a number of apparel shops, a laundromat, and even a sporting goods store. Farther along is the more recently opened **Napili Plaza** with restaurants, shops, and a food market.

Aside from the swanky arcade at the Ritz-Carlton, and **Honolua Store,** which has a mix of clothing, gifts, and deli foods, the only place to shop in Kapalua is at the **Kapalua Shops** attached to the Kapalua Bay Hotel. Here are high-end clothing retailers, an import store, art gallery, gift shop, and one restaurant.

Kihei and Wailea

Azeka Place, Azeka Place II, and **Longs Shopping Center** are all located in the center of Kihei along Kihei Road. Here there's food shopping, a multitude of clothing, gift, and specialty shops, with a few sporting goods stores, dive shops, and activities centers thrown in. Strung south along Kihei Road, one after another, are **Kukui**

Mall, Kihei Town Center, Kalama Village Marketplace, Dolphin Shopping Center, Kamaole Beach Center, Rainbow Mall, Kamaole Shopping Center, and Kai Nani Kai Village Plaza, where restaurants, food outlets, boutiques, and all manner of gift shops can be found. Aside from these larger malls, there are numerous small arcades and individual shops throughout the area.

The exclusive Wailea Shopping Village has an assortment of both chic and affordable boutiques and eateries near the Renaissance, Aston Wailea, Grand Wailea, The Four Seasons, and Kea Lani hotels, all of which have ritzy shopping arcades of their own.

The "Martinizing" of Maui

Maui has been "martinized:" Kmart is here in Kahului, along with Costco and OfficeMax, causing a bit of spindling, mutilating, and . . . folding of local small retail shops. But to some consumers, these shopping meccas have had a positive effect upon the island—sort of.

These retail behemoths have definitely lowered some prices and made more goods available, but with an eye toward corporate gain they've put the squeeze on local "mom and pop" shops, the island's traditional retailers. We have all been programmed to accept the dubious concept that "progress is our most important product," and in consequence the demise of the neighborhood store has been repeated countless times in towns and cities around the nation. However, in the encapsulated island economy of Hawaii, this brand of progress has been particularly devastating, since there is only a limited number of shoppers to go around, especially "tourist shoppers" whose dollars are the lifeblood of the small shops. In a free economy, all have the right to trade, and you may even feel that the coming of the "big boys" was inevitable. However, some of their business practices seem to be particularly aimed at crushing their small competitors. Since the "marts" have entered the retail scene, plenty of locally owned stores and boutiques have gone under. Keep this in mind when making that "special purchase," which can just as easily be bought from a local merchant tending his or her counter, as from a blue-smocked, name-tagged Assistant Manager in Training striding the antiseptic aisles.

FOOD MARKETS

If you're shopping for general food supplies and are not interested in gourmet, specialty items, or organic foods, you'll save money by shopping at the big-name supermarkets, located in Lahaina, Kahului, and Kihei, often in malls. Smaller towns have general stores, which are adequate but a bit more expensive. You can also find convenience items at commissaries in many condos and hotels, but these should be used only for snack foods or when absolutely necessary, because the prices are just too high.

Kahului and Wailuku

The greatest number of supermarkets is found in Kahului. Three are conveniently located along Kaahumanu Ave. in or adjacent to the three malls, one right after the other. Foodland, open daily until 10 p.m., is in the Kaahumanu Center. Just down the road in the Kahului Shopping Center is the ethnic Ah Fooks, open Mon.-Fri. until 7 p.m., closing early Saturday and Sunday, specializing in Japanese, Chinese, and Hawaiian foods. Farther along in the Maui Mall is Star Market, open every day until 9 p.m., except on Sunday until 7 p.m. Just behind the Maui Mall on E. Kamehameha Ave. is a Safeway. The biggest and most well-stocked in Wailuku is Ooka Supermarket. Along with the usual selection of items, it has a great ethnic food section. Open daily into the evening.

Kihei

In Kihei you've got your choice of Foodland in the Kihei Town Center, Star Market up the road, and Azeka's Market. Azeka's is an institution, and is very famous for its specially prepared (uncooked) ribs, perfect for a barbecue.

West Maui

In Lahaina you can shop at Foodland in the Lahaina Square Shopping Center. More interesting is Nagasako's across the street at the Lahaina Shopping Center. It has all you need, plus a huge selection of Chinese and Japanese items. Nagasako's is open Mon.-Sat. 7 a.m.-9 p.m., till 7 p.m. Sunday. If you're staying at a condo and doing your own cooking, the largest and generally least expensive supermarket on West Maui is the Safeway, open 24 hours daily, in the Lahaina Cannery Mall. North of Lahaina are the smaller but full service **Food Pantry** in Honokowai and the **Napili Market** in Napili Plaza. All others are smaller convenience stores with more limited selection and higher prices.

Around and About

Komoda's in Makawao is famous throughout Hawaii for its cream buns, which are sold out by 8 a.m. At **Pukalani Superette** in Pukalani, open seven days a week, you can pick up supplies and food to go, including sushi. Larger yet, with a greater selection, is **Foodland** in the Pukalani Terrace Center. In Pala try **Nagata's** or **Pala General Store** on the main drag. In Hana is the **Hana Store**, which carries all the necessities and even has a selection of health foods and imported beers; open daily 7:30 a.m.-6:30 p.m.

HEALTH FOOD

Those into organic foods, fresh vegetables, natural vitamins, and takeout snack bars have it made on Maui. At the island's fine health food stores you can have most of your needs met. In Kahului, **Down to Earth Natural Foods** is an excellent full service health food store complete with vitamins, minerals, and supplements, bulk foods, canned and boxed goods, and fresh vegetables and fruit. This store also has a deli counter, salad bar, and bakery. Open Mon.-Sat. 7 a.m.-9 p.m., Sunday 8 a.m.-8 p.m. The smaller **Maui Natural Foods,** in the Maui Mall in Kahului, is open daily and has a fair selection of fresh foods, refrigerated deli items, and a huge selection of vitamins, minerals, herbs, and supplements. **Westside Natural Foods and Deli** in Lahaina is located at the corner of Lahainaluna and Wainee Streets. Open daily, it's a full-service health food store, featuring bulk items, prepared goods, and a full selection of vitamins, minerals, and supplements. In Paia, at 49 Baldwin Ave., is **Mana Natural Foods,** open daily 8 a.m.-8 p.m. You can pick up at this old establishment whatever you need for your trip to Hana. It has a full range of bulk and packaged items, supplements, drinks, a deli counter, and picnic foods.

Farmers' Markets

For the best and freshest fruits, veggies, baked goods, flowers, and sometimes crafts and clothing, search out the farmers' markets. Gardeners from Kula bring their fresh vegetables to the Da Rose Mall in Honokowai on Monday and Thursday 6:30-11:30 a.m., and every Tuesday and Friday 1-5 p.m. in the parking lot of Suda's Store along the *mauka* (mountain) side at 61 S. Kihei Road. Be early for the best selection. In Kihei, Longs Shopping Center also hosts a farmers' market every Saturday 8 a.m.-noon. All along the road to Hana are family fruit and flower stands. Many times no one is in attendance and the very reasonably prices are paid on the honor system.

SPECIALTY SHOPS AND NEAT THINGS

Some truly nifty and distinctive stores are wedged in among Maui's run-of-the-mill shopping centers; however, for real treasures you'll find the solitary little shop the best. Lahaina's Front Street has the greatest concentration of top-notch boutiques, but others are dotted here and there around the island. The following is only a sampling of the best; many more are listed in the individual chapters.

Tattered sails on a rotted mast, tattooed seadogs in wide-striped jerseys, grim-faced Yankee captains squinting at the horizon, exotic (probably extinct) birds on the wing, flowers and weather-bent trees, and the beautiful, simple faces of Polynesians staring out from ancient days are faithfully preserved at **Lahaina Printsellers Ltd.,** one of the most unusual purveyors of art on Maui. Their three shops, like mini-museums, are hung with original engravings, drawings, maps, charts, and naturalist sketches ranging in age from 150 to 400 years. Each, marked with an authenticity label, can come from anywhere in the world, but the Hawaiiana collection is amazing in its depth. Many works feature a nautical theme, reminiscent of the daring explorers who opened the Pacific. The Lahaina Printsellers have been collecting for years, and are the largest collectors of material relating to Captain Cook in the entire Pacific Basin. Prices range from $25 for the smallest antique print up to $150,000 for a rare museum-quality work. The Lahaina Printsellers keep Maui's art alive by representing modern artists as well. The three shops are at the Whalers Village in Kaanapali, the Lahaina Cannery Mall, and at the Grand Wailea Resort.

For a unique memento of Maui have your photo taken along Front Street in front of the Pioneer Inn Shops. Here, you'll become the human perch for macaws and cockatoos. The birds are very tame, natural hams, and the only thing on Maui guaranteed to be more colorful than your Hawaiian shirt. For about $25, vendors take your picture and deliver your developed photos the next day.

Paia is quickly becoming an unofficial art center of Maui, along with being the windsurfing capital of Hawaii. Lahaina has slicker galleries, but you come much closer to the source in Paia. The **Maui Crafts Guild** is an exemplary crafts shop that displays the best in local island art. All artists must be selected by active members before their works can be displayed. All materials used must be natural, with an emphasis on those found only in Hawaii. Artists and craftspeople also work in Haiku and the vicinity, many with studios in the old Haiku or Pauwela canneries.

Upcountry's Makawao is a wonderful and crazy combination of old-time *paniolo,* matured hippies who now worry about drugs and their kids, those into alternative health practitioners, and up-and-coming artists. This hodgepodge makes for a town with tack shops, hardware stores, exclusive boutiques, art galleries, health food stores, and oriental health clinics, all strung along two Dodge City-like streets.

Kahului Swap Meet at Maui County Fairgrounds in Kahului, off Puunene Ave., is open every Saturday 8 a.m.-1 p.m. Great junk! Wailuku is Maui's **antique attic** turned out on the street. About half a dozen odd little shops on Market Street display every kind of knick-knack, curio, art treasure, white elephant, grotesque and sublime piece of furniture, jewelry, stuffed toy, game, or oddity that ever floated, sailed, flew, or washed up on Maui's beaches.

Whalers General Store and **ABC Discount Stores** are good places to look for sundries, but they can hardly be beat for prices on such things as snacks, bottles of liquor, beach towels, straw mats, straw hats, zoris, gift items, Hawaiian-made products, and postcards. Anywhere on the island, you can pick up ordinary postcards, three to five for $1. Large-size postcards go for 50 cents or $1 each, and exotic cards for various rates.

ARTS TO BUY

Wild Hawaiian shirts or bright muumuu, especially when worn on the Mainland, have the magical effect of making wearers "feel" like they're in Hawaii, while at the same time eliciting spontaneous smiles from passers-by. Maybe it's the colors, or perhaps it's just the "vibe" that signifies "party time" or "hang loose," but nothing says Hawaii like alohawear does. There are more than a dozen fabric houses in Hawaii turning out distinctive patterns, and many dozens of factories creating their own personalized designs. These factories often have attached retail outlets, but in any case you can find hundreds of shops selling alohawear. Aloha shirts were the brilliant idea of a Chinese merchant in Honolulu, who used to hand-tailor them and then sell them to the tourists who arrived by ship in the glory days before WW II. They were an instant success. Muumuu or "Mother Hubbards" were the idea of missionaries, who were appalled by Hawaiian women running about au naturel and insisted on covering their new Christian converts from head to foot. Now the roles are reversed, and it's Mainlanders who come to Hawaii and immediately strip down to as little clothing as possible.

Alohawear

At one time alohawear was exclusively made of cotton or from manmade, natural fiber-based rayon, and these materials are still the best for any tropical clothing. Beware, however: polyester has slowly crept into the market! No material could possibly be worse for the island climate, so when buying your alohawear make sure to check the label for material content. Muumuu now come in various styles and can be worn for the entire spectrum of social occasions in Hawaii. Aloha shirts are basically cut the same as always, but the patterns have undergone changes, and apart from the original flowers and ferns, modern shirts might depict an island scene in the manner of a silk-screen painting. A basic good-quality muumuu or aloha shirt is guaranteed to be worth its price in good times and happy smiles. The connoisseur might want to purchase *The Hawaiian Shirt, Its Art and History* by R. Thomas Steele. It's illustrated with more than 150 shirts that are now considered works of art by collectors the world over.

Scrimshaw

This art of etching and carving on bone and ivory has become an island tradition handed down from the times of the old whaling ships. Although scrimshaw can be found throughout Hawaii, the center remains in the old whaling capital of Lahaina. There along Front Street are a few shops specializing in scrimshaw. Today, pieces are carved on fossilized walrus ivory that is gathered by Inuit and shipped to Hawaii. It comes in a variety of shades from pure white to mocha, depending upon the mineral content of the earth in which it was buried. Elephant ivory or whale bone is no longer used because of ecological considerations, but there is a "gray market" in Pacific walrus tusks. Inuit can legally hunt the walrus. They then make a few minimal scratches on the tusks, which technically qualifief them to be "Native American art" and free of most governmental restrictions. The tusks are then sent to Hawaii as art objects, but the superficial scratches are immediately removed and the ivory is reworked by artisans. Scrimshaw is made into everything from belt buckles to delicate earrings and even into coffee-table centerpieces. The prices can go from a few dollars up into the thousands.

scrimshaw scene

Woodcarvings

One surviving Hawaiian art is woodcarving. Old Hawaiians used koa almost exclusively because of its density, strength, and natural luster, but koa is becoming increasingly scarce—though many items are still available—and costly milo and monkeypod are also excellent woods for carving and have largely replaced koa. You can buy tikis, bowls, and furniture at numerous shops. Countless inexpensive carved items are sold at variety stores, such as hula dancers or salad servers, but most of these are imported from Asia or the Philippines and can be bought at any variety store.

Weaving

The minute you arrive in Hawaii, you should shell out $2 for a woven beach mat. This is a necessity, not a frivolous purchase, but it definitely won't have been made in Hawaii. What is made in Hawaii is *lau hala*. This is traditional Hawaiian weaving from the leaves *(lau)* of the pandanus *(hala)* tree. These leaves vary greatly in length, with the largest over six feet, and they have a thorny spine that must be removed before they can be worked. The color ranges from light tan to dark brown. The leaves are cut into strips one-eighth- to one-inch wide and are then employed in weaving. Any variety of items can be made or at least covered in *lau hala*. It makes great purses, mats, baskets, and table mats.

Woven into a hat, it's absolutely superb but should not be confused with a palm-frond hat. A *lau hala* hat is amazingly supple and even when squashed will pop back into shape. A good one is expensive ($25) and with proper care will last for years. All *lau hala* should be given a light application of mineral oil on a monthly basis, especially if it's exposed to the sun. For flat items, iron over a damp cloth and keep purses and baskets stuffed with paper when not in use. Palm fronds also are widely used in weaving. They, too, are a great natural raw material, but not as good as *lau hala*. Almost any woven item, such as a beach bag woven from palm, makes a good authentic yet inexpensive gift or souvenir; a wide selection is available in countless shops.

Gift Items

Jewelry is always an appreciated gift, especially if it's distinctive, and Hawaii has some of the most original. The sea provides the basic raw materials of pink, gold, and black corals that are as beautiful and fascinating as gemstones. Harvesting coral is very dangerous work. The Lahaina beds off Maui have one of the best black coral lodes in the islands, but unlike reef coral, these trees grow at depths bordering the outer limits of a scuba diver's capabilities. Only the best can dive 180 feet after the black coral, and about one diver per year dies in pursuit of it. Conservationists have placed great pressure on the harvesters of these deep corals, and the state of Hawaii has placed strict limits and guidelines on the firms and divers involved.

Pink coral has long been treasured by humans. The Greeks considered it a talisman for good health, and there's even evidence that it has been coveted since the Stone Age. Coral jewelry is on sale at many shops throughout Hawaii. The value comes from the color of the coral and the workmanship.

Puka shells (with small, naturally occurring holes) and *opihi* shells are also made into jewelry. Many times these items are very inexpensive, yet they are authentic and are great purchases for the price. Hanging macramé planters festooned with seashells are usually quite affordable and are sold at roadside stands along with shells.

Hawaii produces some unique food items that are appreciated by most people. Various-sized jars of macadamia nuts and butters are great gifts, as are tins of rich, gourmet-quality Kona coffee, the only coffee produced in the United States. Guava, pineapple, passion fruit, and mango are often gift-boxed into assortments of jams, jellies, and spicy chutneys. And for that special person in your life, you can bring home island fragrances in bottles of perfumes and colognes in the exotic odors of gardenia, plumeria, and even ginger. All of the above items are reasonably priced, lightweight, and easy to carry.

FESTIVALS, HOLIDAYS, AND EVENTS

National holidays and Hawaiian state events are all celebrated and commemorated in Maui County, but several other unique happenings occur only on the Valley Isle, Molokai, and Lanai. If you happen to be visiting when any of the following are in progress, be sure to attend! For additional events of all sorts throughout the state, visit the calendar of events listing on the HVB Web site: www.gohawaii.com. For additional information of what's happening on the island, visit the State Foundation of Culture and the Arts calendar on the Web; featuring arts and cultural events, activities, and programs at www.state.hi.us/sfca/culturecalendar.html.

January
The **Makahiki Games,** tel. (808) 533-3876, are the ancient Hawaiian Olympics, plus food, arts, and crafts. The games are held at Kaunakakai Park on Molokai.

Late January brings the college all-star **Hula Bowl** football game, tel. (808) 244-3530, to the War Memorial Stadium in Kahului.

Maui Pro Surf Meet, tel. (808) 575-9264, holds surfing competitions for men and women at Hookipa Beach and Honolua Bay, with $40,000 in prize money.

March
The Valley Island Runners sponsor the **Maui Marathon,** tel. (808) 871-6441, in early March from Kaahumanu Center in Kahului to Whalers Village in Kaanapali.

Midmonth features feminine beauty, grace, and athletic ability at the **Miss Maui Pageant** at Baldwin High School, Wailuku.

Community Kite Flying is held in Lanai City.

The **East Maui Taro Festival,** tel. (808) 248-8892, Web site: www.hookele.com/tarofest, is celebrated in Hana with traditional ceremonies, music, food markets, symposiums, demonstrations, and exhibitions to honor one of the island's most basic food sources and the resurgence of Hawaiian cultural traditions.

April
The **Da Kine Hawaiian Pro Am** professional windsailing competition for men and women is held at Hookipa Beach, tel. (808) 575-9264.

The "Ulupalakua Thing," otherwise known as the **Maui Agricultural Trade Show,** tel. (808) 572-7543, is the largest event for displaying and promoting Maui-grown and -manufactured products. Held at the Ulupalakua Ranch; admission is charged.

May
Costumed pageants, canoe races, and a beard-judging contest commemorate times past at the **Lahaina Whaling Spree,** Lahaina.

A **May Day Program** is held at Lanai High, in Lanai City.

Maui's equestrians strut their stuff at the **Oskie Rice Polo Match** at Haleakala Ranch, Maui.

Music, song, and hula contests are the focus of the day at the **Molokai Ka Hula Piko,** tel.

(808) 553-3876, held at Papahako Beach Park on the west end of Molokai. This event, which includes craft and art demonstrations, is held to honor the birth of hula.

The annual **Molokai Challenge,** tel. (808) 545-1149, is a 38-mile kayak race from the west end of Molokai to Honolulu.

Ho'omanao Challenge, tel. (808) 661-3271, is an outrigger canoe championship that starts at Kaanapali Beach and ends at Waikiki Beach on Oahu.

June

The **Annual Upcountry Fair,** tel. (808) 242-2278, at the Eddie Tam Center, Makawao, is an old-fashioned farm fair right in the heart of Maui's *paniolo* country. Crafts, food, and competitions are all part of the fair.

July

Head for the coolness of Upcountry Makawao for the annual **4th of July rodeo.** *Paniolo* are an old and very important tradition in Hawaiian life. Held at the Oskie Rice Arena, this old-time Upcountry rodeo can't be beat for fun and entertainment anywhere in the country.

The 4th of July brings the **Pineapple Festival** to Lanai, when all the town gathers to enjoy music, crafts, demonstrations, and, of course, lots of pineapple.

Maui Onion Festival, at Whalers Village in Kaanapali, tel. (808) 661-4567, celebrates the island's most famous vegetable. All sorts of food and cooking related events take place.

August

Late July or early August offers *the* most difficult marathon in the world. **The Run to the Sun** takes runners from sea level to the top of Haleakala (10,023 feet), over 37 long grueling miles.

September

Labor Day weekend brings the well-respected **Maui Writers Conference,** tel. (808) 879-0061, usually held at one of the fancy hotels on the island.

Head back up to Makawao for another excellent **Maui County Rodeo** as well as plenty of good happenings during the statewide **Aloha Week.**

The **Molokai to Oahu Canoe Race** for women (men in October) takes off at the end of September from the remote Hale O Lono Beach on Molokai's west end to Fort DeRussy in Honolulu. In crossing, the teams must navigate the always-rough Kaiwi Channel.

October

Maui County Fair at the Wailuku War Memorial Complex brings out the kid in everyone. Held at the beginning of October; for information, call (808) 242-2721.

The **Molokai Hoe Outrigger Canoe Race** for men (women in September).

Visit the **Maui County Fair,** tel. (808) 875-0457, held at the fairgrounds in Kahului or the Wailuku War Memorial Complex. An old-fashioned fair with Western and homespun flavor, this event offers rides, booths, and games. Admission is $3.

Wild costumes and outlandish behavior set the mood island-wide for **Halloween** in Lahaina, the largest celebration of Halloween in Hawaii, often called the "Mardi Gras of the Pacific," tel. (808) 667-9175.

Lahaina's Pioneer Inn is headquarters for the **Lahaina Jackpot Fishing Tournament,** where the biggest marlin landed can bring big prize money.

The **Kaanapali Classic Senior PGA Golf Tournament** lures some of the game's living legends to the Kaanapali links.

November

The **Lincoln-Mercury Kapalua PGA Golf Tournament** brings golfers from around the world for this major event.

December

This month remembers Maui of old with the **Na Mele O Maui** festival in Lahaina and Kaanapali. Hawaiian music, dance, arts, and crafts are featured.

ACCOMMODATIONS

With about 18,000 rooms available, in some 225 properties, Maui is second only to Oahu in the number of visitors it can accommodate. There's a tremendous concentration of condos on Maui, approximately 9,000 units, predominating in the Kihei, Honokowai, and Kahana areas; plenty of hotels, the majority in Kaanapali and Wailea; and a growing number of bed and breakfasts. Camping is limited to a handful of parks, but what it lacks in number it easily makes up for in quality.

The Range

Over 90 hotels and condos have sprouted on West Maui, from Lahaina to Kapalua. The most expensive are strung along some of Maui's best beaches in **Kaanapali** and **Kapalua** and include the Hyatt Regency, Westin Maui, Sheraton, Kapalua Bay, and Ritz-Carlton. The older condos in Honokowai are cheaper, with a mixture of expensive and moderate as you head north. **Lahaina** itself offers only a handful of places to stay: condos at both ends of town, three renovated old-style inns, and a handful of bed and breakfasts. Most people find the pace a little too hectic, but you couldn't get more in the middle of *it* if you tried. **Maalaea Bay,** between Lahaina and Kihei, has 11 quiet condos. Prices are reasonable, the beach is fair, and you're within striking distance of the action in either direction.

Kihei is "condo row," with close to 100 of them along the six miles of Kihei Road, plus a few hotels. This is where you'll find top-notch beaches and the best deals on Maui. **Wailea** just down the road is expensive, but the hotels here are world-class and the secluded beaches are gorgeous. **Kahului** often takes the rap for being an unattractive place to stay on Maui. It isn't all that bad. You're smack in the middle of striking out to the best of Maui's sights, and the airport is minutes away for people staying only a short time. Prices are cheaper and Kanaha Beach is a sleeper, with great sand, surf, and few visitors. **Hana** is an experience in itself. You can camp, rent a cabin, or stay at an exclusive hotel. Always reserve in advance and consider splitting your stay on Maui, spending your last few nights in Hana. You can really soak up this wonderful area, and you won't have to worry about rushing back along the Hana Highway.

HOTELS

Even with the variety of other accommodations available, most visitors, at least first-timers, tend

Relax and enjoy the ocean air.

J.D. BISIGNANI

to stay in hotels. At one time, hotels were the only places to stay. Maui's Pioneer Inn dates from the turn of the century, and if you were Maui-bound, it and a handful that haven't survived were about all that were offered on Maui. Hotels come in all shapes and sizes, from 10-room, family-run affairs to high-rise giants. A recent trend turned some into condominiums. The Neighbor Islands have learned an aesthetic lesson from Waikiki, however, and build low rise resorts that don't obstruct the view and blend more readily with the surroundings.

Types of Hotel Rooms

Most readily available and least expensive is a bedroom with bath, the latter sometimes shared in the more inexpensive hotels. Some hotels can also offer you a studio, a large sitting room that converts to a bedroom; a suite, a bedroom with sitting room; or an apartment with full kitchen plus at least one bedroom. Kitchenettes are often available and contain a refrigerator, sink, and stove usually in a small corner nook or fitted together as one space-saving unit. Kitchenettes cost a bit more but save you a bundle by allowing you to prepare some of your own meals. To get that vacation feeling while keeping costs down, eat breakfast in, pack a lunch for the day, and go out to dinner. If you rent a kitchenette, make sure all the appliances work as soon as you arrive. If they don't, notify the front desk immediately, and if the hotel will not rectify the situation ask to be moved or ask for a reduced rate. Hawaii has cockroaches, so put all food away.

Amenities

All hotels have some of them, and some hotels have all of them. Air-conditioning is available in most, but under normal circumstances you won't need it. Balmy trade winds provide plenty of breezes, which flow through louvered windows and doors in many hotels. Casablanca room fans are better. TVs are often included in the rate, but not always. In-room phones are provided, but a service charge of up to 85 cents per call is often tacked on, even for local calls. Swimming pools are very common, even though the hotel may sit right on the beach. There is always a restaurant of some sort, a coffee shop or two, a bar, a cocktail lounge, and sometimes a sundries shop. Some hotels also offer tennis courts or golf courses either as part of the premises or affiliated with the hotel; usually an "activities desk" can book you into a variety of daily outings. Plenty of hotels offer laundromats on the premises, and hotel towels can be used at the beach. Bellhops get about a $1 tip per bag, and maid service is free, though maids are customarily tipped $1-2 per day and a bit more if kitchenettes are involved. Parking is free, and often valet parking is provided. Hotels can often arrange special services like baby sitters, all kinds of lessons, and special entertainment activities. A few even have bicycles and snorkeling equipment to lend. They'll receive and send mail for you, cash your traveler's checks, and take messages. For your convenience, each room should be equipped with a directory of hotel services and information, and some hotels also include information about area sights, restaurants, and activities.

Hotel Rates: Add 10% Room Tax

Every year Hawaiian hotels welcome in the New Year by hiking their rates by about 10%. A room that was $90 this year will be $99 next year, and so on. Hawaii, because of its gigantic tourist flow and tough competition, offers hotel rooms at universally lower rates than those at most developed resort areas around the world, so, even with the 10% room tax (6% transient accommodations tax, plus 4% state excise tax), there are still many reasonable rates to be had. Package deals, especially to Waikiki, almost throw in a week's lodging for the price of an air ticket. The basic **daily rate** is geared toward double occupancy; singles are hit in the pocketbook. Single rates are cheaper than doubles, but never as low as half the double rate; the most you get off is 40%. **Weekly and monthly** rates will save you approximately 10% off the daily rate. Make sure to ask because this information won't be volunteered. Many hotels will charge for a double and then add an additional charge ($3-25) for extra persons. Some hotels—not always the budget ones—let you cram in as many as can sleep on the floor with no additional charge, so again, ask. Others have a policy of **minimum stay,** usually three days, but their rates can be cheaper, and **business/corporate rates** are usually offered to anyone who can at least produce a business card. Senior citizens are sometimes offered special discount rates of 10-20%. This information will usually not be offered so you must inquire.

Hawaii's **peak season** runs from just before Christmas until after Easter, and then again in early summer. Rooms are at a premium, and peak-season rates are an extra 10% above the normal daily rate. Oftentimes they'll also suspend weekly and monthly rates during peak season. The **off-peak** season is late summer and fall, when rooms are easy to come by and most hotels offer off-peak rates. Subtract about 10% from the normal rate.

In Hawaiian hotels you always pay more for a good view. Terms vary slightly, but usually "oceanfront" means your room faces the ocean and mostly your view is unimpeded. "Ocean view" is slightly more vague. It could be a decent view, or it could require standing on the dresser and craning your neck to catch a tiny slice of the sea sandwiched between two skyscrapers. Rooms are also designated and priced upward as standard, superior, and deluxe. As you go up, this could mean larger rooms with more amenities, or can merely signify a better view.

Plenty of hotels offer the **family plan,** which allows children under a certain age to stay in their parents' room free, if they use the existing bedding. If another bed or crib is required, there is an additional charge. Only a limited number of hotels offer the **American plan,** where breakfast and dinner are included with the night's lodging. In many hotels, you're provided a refrigerator and a heating unit to make coffee and tea at no extra charge.

Paying, Deposits, and Reservations

The vast majority of Hawaiian hotels accept foreign and domestic traveler's checks, personal checks preapproved by the management, foreign cash, and most major credit cards. Reservations are always the best policy, and they're easily made through travel agents or directly by contacting the hotel. In all cases, bring documentation of your confirmed reservations with you in case of a mix-up.

Deposits are not always required to make reservations, but they do secure them. Some hotels require the first night's payment in advance. Reservations without a deposit can be legally released if the room is not claimed by 6 p.m. Remember too that letters "requesting reservations" are not the same as "confirmed reservations." In letters, include your dates of stay, type of room you want,

and price. Once the hotel answers your letter, *confirm* your reservations with a phone call or follow-up letter and make sure that the hotel sends you a copy of the confirmation. All hotels and resorts have **cancellation requirements** for refunding deposits. The time limit on these can be as little as 24 hours before arrival, to a full 30 days. Some hotels require full **advance payment** for your length of stay, especially during peak season or during times of crowded special events. Be aware of the time required for a cancellation notice *before* making your reservation deposit, especially when dealing with advance payment. If you have confirmed reservations, especially with a deposit, and there is no room for you, or one that doesn't meet prearranged requirements, you should be given the option of accepting alternate accommodations. You are owed the difference in room rates if there is any. If there is no room whatsoever, the hotel is required to find you one at a comparable hotel and to refund your deposit in full.

CONDOMINIUMS

The main qualitative difference between a condo and a hotel is in amenities. At a condo, you're more on your own. You're temporarily renting an apartment, so there won't be any bellhops and rarely a bar, restaurant, or lounge on the premises, though many times you'll find a sundries store. The main lobby, instead of having that grand-entrance feel of many hotels, is more like an apartment-house entrance, although there might be a front desk. Condos can be efficiencies (one big room), but mostly they are one- or multiple-bedroom affairs with a complete kitchen. Reasonable housekeeping items should be provided: linens, all furniture, and a fully equipped kitchen. Most have TVs and phones, but remember that the furnishings provided are up to the owner. You can find brand-new furnishings that are top of the line, right down to "garage sale" bargains. Inquire about the furnishings when you make your reservations. Maid service might be included on a limited basis (for example, once weekly), or you might have to pay extra for it.

Condos usually require a minimum stay, although some will rent on a daily basis, like hotels. Minimum stays when applicable are often three days, but seven is also commonplace, and during peak season two weeks isn't unheard of. Swimming pools are common, and depending on the "theme" of the condo, you can find saunas, weight rooms, jacuzzis, and tennis courts. Rates are about 10-15% higher than at comparable hotels, with hardly any difference between dou bles and singles. A nominal extra fee is charged for more than two people; condos can normally accommodate four to six guests. You can find clean, decent condos for as little as $200 per week, all the way up to exclusive apartments for well over $1,500. The method of paying for and reserving a condo is just about the same as for a hotel. However, requirements for deposit, final payments, and cancellation charges are much stiffer than in hotels. Make absolutely sure you fully understand all of these requirements when you make your reservations.

Their real advantage is for families, friends who want to share, and especially long-term stays, for which you will always get a special rate. The kitchen facilities save a great deal on dining costs, and it's common to find units with their own washers and dryers. Parking space is ample for guests, and like hotels, plenty of stay/drive deals are offered.

Hotel/Condominium Information

The best source of hotel/condo information is the **Hawaii Visitors Bureau.** While planning your trip, either visit one nearby or write to the bureau in Hawaii. (Addresses are given in the "Information and Services" section later in this chapter.) Request a copy of the current *Member Accommodation Guide* (free). This handy booklet lists all the hotel/condo members of the HVB, with addresses, phone numbers, facilities, and rates. General tips are also given.

Condo Booking and Reservations

The following is a partial list of booking agents handling a number of properties on Maui.

Aston Hotels and Resorts, 2250 Kuhio Ave., Honolulu, HI 96815, tel. (808) 931-1400 or (800) 922-7886 Mainland, (800) 445-6633 Canada, or (800) 321-2558 in Hawaii, Web site: aston-hotels.com

Marc Resorts Hawaii, 2155 Kalakaua Ave., Honolulu, HI 96815, tel. (808) 926-5900 or (800) 535-0085, Web site: marcresorts.com, e-mail: marc@aloha.net

Destination Resorts Hawaii, 3750 Wailea Alanui, Wailea, HI 96753, tel. (808) 879-1595 or (800) 367-5246, fax (808) 874-3554, Web site: www.destinationresortshi.com, rents condos in six separate luxury villages in Wailea.

Go Condo Hawaii, tel. (800) 452-3463, Web site: www.gocondohawaii.com

Maui Condominium and Home Realty, 2511 S. Kihei Rd., P.O. Box 1840 Kihei, Maui, HI 96753, tel. (808) 879-5445 or (800) 822-4409 Mainland and Canada, Web site: www.mauicondo .com, has over 300 listings in all price categories with most in the Kihei area.

Condo Rentals Hawaii, 362 Huku Li'i Place, #204, Kihei, HI 96753, tel. (800) 367-5242 Mainland (800) 663-2101 Canada, Web site: www.maui.net/~crh, e-mail: crh@maui.net

Maui Beachfront Rentals, 256 Papalaua St., Lahaina, HI 96761, tel. (808) 661-3500 or (888) 661-5200, fax (808) 661-5200, Web site: www.maui.net/~beachfrt, has high-end homes and condo units on West Maui.

AA Oceanfront Condo Rentals, 2439 S. Kihei Rd., Kihei, HI 96753, tel. (808) 879-7288, (800) 488-6004, has over three dozen units from Kihei to Makena.

Kihei Maui Vacations, P.O. Box 1055, Kihei, HI 96753, tel. (808) 879-7581 or (800) 541-6284 Web site: www.kmvmaui.com/home.html

Klahani Resorts, P.O. Box 11108, Lahaina, HI 96761, tel. (808) 667-2712 or (800) 628-6731, fax (808) 661-5875, offers units in half a dozen properties from Lahaina to Kahana.

Maalaea Bay Rentals, tel. (808) 244-7012 or (800) 367-6084, fax (808) 242-7476, handles over 100 units in a majority of the condos in Maalaea.

Unique Island Homes, tel. (808) 875-8808 or (800) 961-9196

BED AND BREAKFASTS

Bed-and-breakfast (B&B) inns are hardly a new idea. The Bible talks of the hospitable hosts who opened the gates of their homes and invited the wayfarer in to spend the night. B&Bs have a long tradition in Europe and were commonplace in Revolutionary America. Nowadays, lodging in private homes called bed and breakfasts is becoming increasingly fashionable throughout

America, and Hawaii is no exception, with about 100,000 B&B guests yearly. Not only can you visit Maui, you can "live" there for a time with a host family and share an intimate experience of daily life.

Points to Consider

The primary feature of bed and breakfasts is that every one is privately owned and therefore uniquely different from every other. The range of B&Bs is as wide as the living standards in America. You'll find everything from a semi-mansion in the most fashionable residential area to a little grass shack offered by a down-home fisherman and his family. This means that it's particularly important for the guest to choose a host family with whom his or her lifestyle is compatible.

Unlike at a hotel or a condo, you'll be living *with* a host (usually a family), although your room will be private, with private baths and separate entrances being quite common. You can make arrangements directly or you might want to go through an agency (listed below) which acts as a go-between, matching host and guest. Write to an agency and it will send you a booklet with a complete description of the B&B, its general location, the fees charged, and a good idea of the lifestyle of your host family. With the reservations application they'll include a questionnaire that will basically determine your profile: Are you single? Do you have children? Smoker? etc., as well as arrival and departure dates and all pertinent particulars.

Since B&Bs are run by individual families, the times that they will accept guests can vary according to what's happening in their lives. This makes it imperative to write well in advance: three months is good; earlier is too long and too many things can change. Four weeks is about the minimum time required to make all necessary arrangements. Expect a minimum stay (three days is common) and a maximum stay. B&Bs are not long-term housing, although it's hoped that guest and host will develop a friendship and that future stays can be as long as both desire.

B&B Agencies

A top-notch B&B agency with over 150 homes is **Bed and Breakfast Hawaii,** operated by Evelyn Warner and Al Davis. They've been running this service since 1978, and their reputation is excellent. B&B Hawaii has a membership fee of $10 yearly.

For this they mail you their *Directory of Homes,* a periodic "hot sheet" of new listings, and all pertinent guest applications; add $1 handling. Write Bed and Breakfast Hawaii, P.O. Box 449, Kapaa, HI 96746, tel. (808) 822-7771 or (800) 733-1632, Web site: www.planet-hawaii.com/bandb, e-mail: bandb@aloha.net.

One of the most experienced agencies, **Bed And Breakfast Honolulu Statewide,** at 3242 Kaohinanai Dr., Honolulu, HI 96817, tel. (808) 595-7533, (808) 595-2030, or (800) 288-4666, Web site: www.planet-hawaii.com/bnb-honolulu, e-mail: bnbshi@aloha.net, owned and operated by Marylee and Gene Bridges, began in 1982. Since then, they've become masters at finding visitors the perfect accommodations to match their desires, needs, and pocketbooks. Their repertoire of guest homes offers more than 350 rooms, with half on Oahu and the other half scattered around the state. When you phone, they'll match your needs to their computerized in-house guidelines.

Babson's Vacation Rentals and Reservation Service, 3371 Keha Dr., Kihei, Maui, HI 96753, tel. (808) 874-1166 or (800) 824-6409, is owned and operated by Ann and Bob Babson, a delightful couple who will try hard to match your stay with your budget. This is a statewide agency, and it accepts credit cards; car packages available.

Go Native Hawaii will send you a directory and all needed information if you write to 65 Halaulani Place, P.O. Box 11418, Hilo, HI 96721, tel. (808) 935-4178 or (800) 662-8483.

All Island Bed and Breakfast, 463 Iliwahi Loop, Kailua, HI 96734, tel. (808) 263-2342 or (800) 542-0344, Web site: planet-hawaii.com/all-island, e-mail: cac@aloha.net, can match your needs up with about 700 homes throughout the state.

Run by Susan Campbell, **Hawaii's Best Bed and Breakfast,** P.O. Box 563, Kamuela, HI 96743, tel. (808) 885-4550 or (800) 262-9912, fax (808) 885-0559, Web site: www.bestbnb.com, e-mail: bestbnb@aloha.net, is a smaller business but has listings all over the state.

Hawaiian Islands Vacation Rentals, 1277 Mokulua Dr., Kailua, HI 96734, tel. (808) 261-7895 or (800) 258-7895, is owned and operated by Rick Maxey, who can arrange stays on all islands and help with interisland flights and car rental.

Agencies specializing in beachfront villas, luxury condominiums, and exclusive estates are **Villas of Hawaii,** 4218 Waialae Ave., Suite 203,

Honolulu, HI 96816, tel. (808) 735-9000; and **Vacation Locations Hawaii,** P.O. Box 1689, Kihei, HI 96753, tel. (808) 874-0077.

HOSTELS

Maui has two reasonably priced hostels operating at this time, both in Wailuku. **Banana Bungalow,** 310 N. Market St., Wailuku, HI 96793, tel. (808) 244-5090, (800) 846-7835, or (800) 746-7871, fax (808) 846-3678, has office hours 7 a.m.-11 p.m. This laid back hostel has bunks for $14 a night and rooms for $20 single or $30.5 double. Extras include shuttle service, tours, on-site kitchen, and a jacuzzi in the garden. Just up the street and around the corner at 2080 Vineyard St. is the **Northshore Inn,** tel. (808) 242-8999, fax 244-5004. Look for the row of international flags on the streetfront balcony. Northshore offers most of the same amenities as Banana Bungalow.

Bunks are $13.65, rooms $26.95 single and $39.95 double.

HOME EXCHANGES

One other method of staying in Hawaii, open to homeowners, is to offer the use of your home for use of a home in Hawaii. This is done by listing your home with an agency that facilitates the exchange and publishes a descriptive directory. To list your home and to find out what is available, contact one of the following agencies:

Vacation Exchange Club (Affiliate of Homelink, Int'l), P.O. Box 650, Key West, FL 33041, tel./fax (305) 294-1448 or (800) 638-3841

Intervac U.S., P.O. Box 590504, San Francisco, CA 04159, tel. (415) 535-3497, fax 435-7440

Worldwide Home Exchange Club, 806 Brantford Ave., Silver Spring, MD 20904, tel. (301) 680-8950

FOOD AND DRINK

Hawaii is a gastronome's Shangri-La, a sumptuous smorgasbord in every sense of the word. The varied ethnic groups that have come to Hawaii in the last 200 years have each brought their own special enthusiasm and culture—and lucky for all, they didn't forget their cook pots, hearty appetites, and exotic taste buds. The Polynesians who first arrived found a fertile but barren land. Immediately they set about growing taro, coconuts, and bananas, and raising chickens, pigs, fish, and even dogs, though consumption of the latter was reserved for the nobility. The harvests were bountiful and the islanders thanked the gods with the traditional feast called the luau. The underground oven, the *imu,* baked most of the food. Participants were encouraged to feast while relaxing on straw mats and enjoying the hula and various entertainments. The luau is as popular as ever, and a treat that's guaranteed to delight anyone with a sense of eating adventure.

The missionaries and sailors came next; their ships' holds carried barrels of ingredients for the puddings, pies, dumplings, gravies, and roasts—the sustaining "American foods" of New England farms. The mid-1800s saw the arrival of

boatloads of Chinese and Japanese peasants, who wasted no time making rice instead of bread the staple of the islands. The Chinese added their exotic spices, cooking complex Sichuan dishes as well as workers' basics like chop suey. The Japanese introduced *shoyu* (soy sauce), sashimi, boxed *(bento)* lunches, delicate tempura, and rich, filling noodle soups. The Portuguese brought their luscious Mediterranean dishes of tomatoes, peppers, and plump, spicy sausages; nutritious bean soups; and mouthwatering sweet treats like *malasadas* (holeless donuts) and *pao dolce* (sweet bread). Koreans carried crocks of zesty kimchi and quickly fired up grills for *pulgogi,* a marinated beef cooked over a fire. Filipinos served up their delicious *adobo* stews—fish, meat, or chicken in a rich sauce of vinegar and garlic.

Recently, Thai and Vietnamese restaurants have been offering their irresistible dishes next door to restaurants serving fiery burritos from Mexico and elegant marsala cream sauces from France. The ocean breezes of Hawaii not only cool the skin but waft with them some of the most delectable aromas on earth, to make the taste buds tingle and the spirit soar.

HAWAIIAN CUISINE

Hawaiian cuisine, the oldest in the islands, consists of wholesome, well-prepared, and delicious foods. All you have to do on arrival is notice the size of some of the local boys (and women) to know immediately that food to them is indeed a happy and serious business. An oft-heard island joke is that "local men don't eat until they're full; they eat until they're tired." Many Hawaiian dishes have become standard fare at a variety of restaurants, eaten at one time or another by anyone who spends time in the islands. Hawaiian food in general is called *kaukau;* cooked food is *kapahaki,* and something broiled is called *kaola.* Any of these prefixes on a menu will let you know that Hawaiian food is served. Usually inexpensive, it will definitely fill you and keep you going.

Traditional Favorites
In old Hawaii, although the sea meant life, many more people were involved in cultivating beautifully tended garden plots of taro, sugarcane, breadfruit, and various sweet potatoes *(uala)* than with fishing. They husbanded pigs and barkless dogs *(ilio),* and prized *moa* (chicken) for their feathers and meat, but found eating the eggs repulsive. Their only farming implement was the *o'o,* a sharpened hardwood digging stick. The Hawaiians were the best farmers of Polynesia, and the first thing they planted was taro, a tuberous root that was created by the gods at the same time as humans. This main staple of the old Hawaiians was made into poi. Every luau will have poi, a glutinous purple paste made from pounded taro root. It comes in liquid consistencies referred to as one-, two-, or three-finger poi. The fewer fingers you need to eat it, the thicker it is. Poi is one of the most nutritious carbohydrates known, but people unaccustomed to it find it bland and tasteless. Some of the best, fermented for a day or so, has an acidic bite. Poi is made to be eaten *with* something, but locals who love it pop it in their mouths and smack their lips. Those unaccustomed to it will suffer constipation if they eat too much.

A favorite popular dessert is *haupia,* a custard made from coconut. *Limu* is a generic term for edible seaweed, which many people still gather from the shoreline and eat as a salad, or mix with ground *kukui* nuts and salt as a relish. A favorite Hawaiian snack is *opihi,* small shellfish (limpets) that cling to rocks. Those who gather them always leave some on the rocks for the future. Cut from the shell and eaten raw by all peoples of Hawaii, *opihi* sell for $150 per gallon in Honolulu—a testament to their popularity. A general term that has come to mean hors d'oeuvres in Hawaii is *pu pu.* Originally the name of a small shellfish, it is now used for any finger food. A traditional liquor made from ti root is *okolehao.* It literally means "iron bottom," reminiscent of the iron blubber pots used to ferment it.

Hawaiian family eating poi, by A. Plum c. 1846 engraving

HAWAII STATE ARCHIVES

Pacific Rim Specialties
(a.k.a. "Hawaiian Regional" Cuisine)

At one time the "tourist food" in Hawaii was woeful. Of course, there has always been a handful of fine restaurants, but for the most part the food lacked soul, with even the fine hotels opting to offer second-rate renditions of food more appropriate to large Mainland cities. Surrounded by some of the most fertile and pristine waters in the Pacific, you could hardly find a restaurant offering fresh fish, and it was an ill-conceived boast that even the fruits and vegetables lying limply on your table were "imported." Beginning with a handful of extremely creative and visionary chefs in the early 1980s, who took the chance of perhaps offending the perceived simple palates of visitors, a delightfully delicious new cuisine was born. Based upon the finest traditions of continental cuisine—including, to a high degree, its sauces, pastas, and presentations—the culinary magic of Pacific Rim boldly adds the pungent spices of Asia, the fantastic fresh vegetables, fruits, and fish of Hawaii, and, at times, the earthy cooking methods of the Southwest. The result is a cuisine of fantastic tastes, subtle yet robust, and satiating but health-conscious—the perfect marriage of fresh foods prepared in a fresh way. Now restaurants on every island proudly display menus labeled "Hawaiian Regional." As always, some are better than others, but the general result is that the "tourist food" has been vastly improved and everyone benefits. Many of these exemplary chefs left lucrative and prestigious positions at Hawaii's five-diamond hotels and opened signature restaurants of their own, making this fine food much more available and affordable.

Luau

The luau is an island institution. For a fixed price of about $60, you get to gorge yourself on a tremendous variety of island foods, sample a few island drinks, and have a night of entertainment as well. Generally, luau run from about 5:30-8:30 p.m. On your luau day, eat a light breakfast, skip lunch, and do belly-stretching exercises! Luau food is usually served buffet-style, although one or two do it family-style. All luau have pretty much the same format, although the type of food and entertainment differ. Following is a list of the luau presently available on Maui.

Old Lahaina Luau, on the beach at its new location near the Mala Wharf, tel. (808) 667-1998, has an excellent reputation because it is as close to authentic as you can get. Seating is Mon.-Sat. 5:30-8:30 p.m., but reserve at least three to six days in advance to avoid disappointment, especially during peak season. The luau, featuring a "local's favorite," all-you-can-eat buffet and all-you-can-drink bar, costs $57 adults, children 3-12 half price. The traditional hula dancers use ti-leaf skirts, and the music is *fo' real.* The Old Lahaina Luau is one of the oldest and best luau on the island.

Renaissance Wailea Beach Resort, tel. (808) 879-4900, recounts tales of old Hawaii with its very authentic and professional hula show and luau every Tuesday, Thursday, and Saturday at 5:30 p.m. Hawaiian music, hula, drumming, and a fire dancer entertain as you dine through the evening on a wonderful assortment of foods expertly prepared by the chefs. Price includes open bar at $57 adults, $28 children 5-12. Reservations are required.

The **Royal Lahaina Resort,** tel. (808) 661-9119, has been offering a nightly luau and entertainment for years in their Luau Gardens. The show is still spectacular and the food offered is authentic and good. Prices are $62 adults, children $29; reservations suggested.

Wailea's Finest Luau, tel. (808) 879-1922, at the Aston Wailea Resort, has garnered awards for its luau fare and Polynesian show, and its fire/knife dancer has won an international award for his skill three years in a row. Held Monday, Tuesday, Thursday, and Friday 5-8 p.m., $58 adults, children 6-12 $26.

Hyatt Regency Maui's **Drums of the Pacific,** tel. (808) 667-4720, is held every evening 5-8 p.m., for $62 adults, $39 children 13-20, $25 kids 6-12.

Legends of Makena Luau, tel. (808) 874-1111, is put on every Sunday 5:30-8:30 p.m. at the Maui Prince Hotel in Makena, charging $55 adults and $27 children ages 6-12. Food here is served family style, not buffet style as at most.

The **Maui Marriott** also presents its version of the luau and Polynesian show, starting the night with some Polynesian games and activities. The evening starts at 5 p.m. and runs until 8 p.m. Cost is $60 adults, $28 children 6-12. Call (808) 661-5828 for reservations.

TROPICAL FRUITS AND VEGETABLES

Some of the most memorable taste treats from the islands require no cooking at all: the luscious tropical and exotic fruits and vegetables sold in markets and roadside stands or just found hanging on trees, waiting to be picked. Make sure to experience as many as possible. The general rule in Hawaii is that you are allowed to pick fruit on public lands, but the amount should be limited to personal consumption. The following is a sampling of some of Hawaii's best produce.

Bananas

No tropical island is complete without them. There are over 70 species in Hawaii, with hundreds of variations. Some are for peeling and eating while others are cooked. A "hand" of bananas is great for munching, backpacking, or picnicking. Available everywhere—and cheap.

common banana

Avocados

Brought from South America, avocados were originally cultivated by the Aztecs. They have a buttery consistency and nutty flavor. Hundreds of varieties in all shapes and colors are available fresh year-round. They have the highest fat content of any fruit next to the olive.

Coconuts

What tropical paradise would be complete without coconuts? Indeed, these were some of the first plants brought by the Polynesians. When a child was born, a coconut tree was planted to provide fruit for the child throughout his or her lifetime. Truly tropical fruits, coconuts know no season. Drinking nuts are large and green, and when shaken you can hear the milk inside. You get about a quart of fluid from each. It takes skill to open one, but a machete can handle anything. Cut the stem end flat so that it will stand, then bore a hole into the pointed end and put in a straw or hollow bamboo. Coconut water is slightly acidic and helps balance alkaline foods. Spoon meat is a custard-like gel on the inside of drinking nuts. Sprouted coconut meat is also an excellent food. Split open a sprouted nut, and inside is the yellow fruit, like a moist sponge cake. "Millionaire's salad" is made from the heart of a coconut palm. At one time an entire tree was cut down to get to the heart, which is just inside the trunk below the fronds and is like an artichoke heart except that it's about the size of a watermelon. In a downed tree, the heart stays good for about two weeks.

Breadfruit

This island staple provides a great deal of carbohydrates, but many people find the baked, boiled, or fried fruit bland. It grows all over the islands and is really thousands of little fruits growing together to form a ball.

Mangos

These are some of the most delicious fruits known to humans. They grow wild all over the islands; the ones on the leeward sides of the islands ripen April-June, while the ones on the windward sides can last until October. They're found in the wild on trees up to 60 feet tall. The problem is to stop eating them once you start!

Papayas

This truly tropical fruit has no real season but is mostly available in the summer. Papayas grow on branchless trees and are ready to pick as soon as any yellow appears. Of the many varieties, the "solo papaya," meant to be eaten by one person, is the best. Split them in half, scrape out the seeds, and have at them with a spoon.

Passion Fruit

Known by their island name of *lilikoi,* passion fruit make excellent juice and pies. The small yellow fruit (similar to lemons but smooth-skinned) is mostly available in summer and fall. Many grow wild on vines, waiting to be picked. Slice off the stem end, scoop the seedy pulp out with your tongue, and you'll know why they're called "passion fruit."

Guavas

These small, round, yellow fruits are abundant in the wild, where they ripen from early summer

DIANA LASICH HARPER

to late fall. They're considered a pest—so pick all you want. A good source of vitamin C, they're great for juice, jellies, and desserts.

Macadamia Nuts
The king of nuts was brought from Australia in 1882. Now it's the state's fourth-largest agricultural product, producing 90% of the world's output. Available plain, roasted, candied, or buttered.

Litchis
Called nuts but really small fruit with thin red shells, litchis have sweet, juicy white flesh when fresh and appear nutlike when dried.

Potpourri
Along with the above, you'll find pineapples, oranges, limes, kumquats, thimbleberries, and blackberries in Hawaii, as well as carambolas, wild cherry tomatoes, and tamarinds.

FISH AND SEAFOOD

Anyone who loves fresh fish and seafood has come to the right place. Island restaurants specialize in seafood, and it's available everywhere. Pound for pound, seafood is one of the best dining bargains on Maui. You'll find it served in many kind of restaurant, and often the fresh catch of the day is proudly displayed on ice in a glass case. The following is a sampling of the best.

Mahimahi
This excellent eating fish is one of the most common and least expensive in Hawaii. It's referred to as "dolphin" but is definitely a fish, not a mammal. Mahimahi can weigh 10-65 pounds; the flesh is light and moist. This fish is broadest at the head. When caught it's a dark olive color, but after a while the skin turns iridescent shades of blue, green, and yellow. It can be served as a main course or as a patty in a fish sandwich.

A'u
This true island delicacy is a broadbill swordfish or marlin. It's expensive even in Hawaii because the damn thing's so hard to catch. The meat is moist and white and truly superb. If it's offered on the menu, order it. It'll cost a bit more, but you won't be disappointed.

Ono
Ono means "delicious" in Hawaiian so that should tip you off to the taste of this wahoo, or king mackerel. Ono is regarded as one of the finest eating fishes in the ocean, and its flaky white meat lives up to its name.

Manini
These five-inch fish are some of the most abundant in Hawaii and live in about 10 feet of water. They school and won't bite a hook but are easily taken with spear or net. Not often on menus, but they're favorites with local people who know best.

Ulua
This member of the crevalle jack family ranges 15-100 pounds. Its flesh is white and has a steak-like texture. Delicious and often found on the menu.

Uku
This gray snapper is a favorite with local people. The meat is light and firm and grills well.

Ahi
A yellowfin tuna with distinctive pinkish meat, ahi is a great favorite cooked or served raw in sushi bars.

Moi
This is the Hawaiian word for "king." The fish has large eyes and a sharklike head. Considered one of the finest eating fishes in Hawaii, it's best during the autumn months.

Seafood Potpourri
Other island seafood found on menus include opihi, a small shellfish (limpet) that clings to rocks and is considered one of the best island delicacies, eaten raw; aloalo, similar to tiny lobsters; crawfish, plentiful in taro fields and irrigation ditches; ahipalaka, albacore tuna; various octopuses and squid (calamari); and sharks of various types.

A'ama are the ubiquitous little black crabs that you'll spot on rocks and around pier areas. They're everywhere. For fun, local fishermen will try to catch them with poles, but the more efficient way is to throw a fish head into a plastic bucket and wait for the crabs to crawl in and trap themselves. The a'ama are about as big as two fingers and make delicious eating.

Limu is edible seaweed that has been gathered as a garnish since precontact times and is frequently found on traditional island menus. There's no other seaweed except *limu* in Hawaii. Because of this, the heavy, fishy-ocean smell that people associate with the sea but which is actually that of seaweed is absent in Hawaii.

UNIQUE ISLAND DRINKS

To complement the fine dining in the islands, bartenders have been busy creating their own tasty concoctions. The full range of beers, wines, and standard drinks is served in Hawaii, but for a real treat you should try mixed drinks inspired by the islands. Most look very innocent because they come in pineapples, coconut shells, or tall frosted glasses. They're often garnished with little umbrellas or sparklers, and most have enough fruit in them to give you your vitamins for the day. Rum is used as the basis of many of them; it's been an island favorite since it was introduced by the whalers of last century. Here are some of the most famous: mai tai, a mixture of light and dark rum, orange curaçao, orange and almond flavoring, and lemon juice; chi chi, a simple concoction of vodka, pineapple juice, and coconut syrup—a real sleeper because it tastes like a milk shake; Blue Hawaii, vodka and blue curaçao; Planter's Punch, light rum, grenadine, bitters, and lemon juice—a great thirst quencher; and Singapore sling, a sparkling mixture of gin and cherry brandy with lemon juice (and/or pineapple, lime, and orange juices).

Drinking Laws

There are no state-run liquor stores; all kinds of spirits, wines, and beers are available in markets and shops, generally open during normal business hours, seven days a week. The drinking age is 21, and no towns are "dry." Legal hours for serving drinks depend on the type of establishment. Hours generally are: hotels, 6 a.m.-4 a.m.; discos and nightclubs where there is dancing, 10 a.m.-4 a.m.; bars and lounges where there is no dancing, 6 a.m.-2 a.m. Most restaurants serve alcohol, and in many that don't, you can bring your own.

Coffee

Kona coffee is the only coffee grown in the United States. It originates from the Kona District of the Big Island and it is a rich, aromatic, truly fine coffee. Within the past decade or so, coffee farms have been started on Maui, Molokai, and Kauai, and these operations have become large commercial concerns, surpassing in output the Big Island coffee companies.

MUNCHIES AND ISLAND TREATS

Certain finger foods, fast foods, and island treats are unique to Hawaii. Some are meals in themselves, others are snacks. Here are some of the best and most popular.

Some of the best island treats come from small roadside stands.

J.D. BISIGNANI

Pu Pu

Pronounced as in "Winnie the Pooh Pooh," these are little finger foods and hors d'oeuvres. They can be anything from crackers to cracked crab. Often, they're given free at lounges and bars and can even include chicken drumettes, fish kebabs, and tempura. At a good display of them you can have a free meal.

Crackseed

A sweet of Chinese origin, crackseed is preserved and seasoned fruits and seeds. Favorites include coconut, watermelon, pumpkin seeds, mango, plum, and papaya. Distinctive in taste, they take some getting used to, but make great trail snacks. Available in all island markets. Also look for dried fish (cuttlefish) on racks, usually near the crackseed. Nutritious and delicious, it makes a great snack.

Shave Ice

This real island institution makes the Mainland "snow cone" melt into insignificance. Special machines literally shave ice to a fluffy consistency. It's mounded into a paper cone, and your choice from dozens of exotic island syrups is generously poured over it. Given a straw and spoon, you just slurp away.

Malasadas and Pao Dolce

Two sweets from the Portuguese, malasadas are holeless donuts and pao dolce is sweet bread. Sold in island bakeries, they're great for breakfast or as treats.

Lomi Lomi Salmon

This salad of salmon, tomatoes, and onions with garnish and seasonings often accompanies "plate lunches" and is featured at buffets and luau.

MONEY-SAVERS

Only one thing is better than a great meal: a great meal at a reasonable price. The following are island institutions and favorites that will help you eat well and keep prices down.

Kaukau Wagons

These are lunch wagons, but instead of slick, stainless-steel jobs, most are old delivery trucks converted into portable kitchens. Some say they're a remnant of WW II, when workers had to be fed on the job; others say that the meals they serve were inspired by the Japanese bento, a boxed lunch. You'll see the wagons parked along beaches, in city parking lots, or on busy streets. Usually a line of local people will be placing their orders, especially at lunchtime—a tip-off that the wagon serves delicious, nutritious island dishes at reasonable prices. They might have a few tables, but basically they serve food to go. Most of their filling meals are about $3.50, and they specialize in the "plate lunch."

Plate Lunch

One of the best island standards, these lunches give you a sampling of authentic island food that can include teriyaki chicken, mahimahi, lau lau, and lomi salmon, among others. They're on paper or Styrofoam plates, are packed to go, and usually cost less than $3.50. Standard with a plate lunch is "two-scoop rice" and a generous dollop of macaroni or other salad. Full meals, they're great for keeping down food costs and for instant picnics. Available everywhere, from kaukau wagons to restaurants.

Saimin

Special "saimin shops," as well as restaurants, serve this hearty, Japanese-inspired noodle soup. Saimin is a word unique to Hawaii. In Japan, these soups would be called ramin or soba, and it's as if the two were combined into saimin. A large bowl of noodles in broth, stirred with meat, chicken, fish, or vegetables, costs only a few dollars and is big enough for an evening meal. The best place to eat saimin is in a local hole-in-the-wall shop run by a family.

Tips

Even some of the island's best restaurants in the fanciest hotels offer "early bird specials"—the regular-menu dinners offered to diners who come in before the usual dinner hour, which is approximately 6 p.m. You pay as little as half the normal price, and can dine in luxury on some of the best foods. The specials are often advertised in the "free" tourist books, which might also include coupons for two-for-one meals or limited dinners at much lower prices. Just clip them out.

GETTING THERE

With the number of visitors each year over six million—and double that number of travelers just passing through—the state of Hawaii is one of the easiest places in the world to get to . . . by plane. About half a dozen large U.S. airlines (and other small ones) fly to and from the islands. About the same number of foreign carriers, mostly from Asia and Oceania, also touch down on a daily basis. In 1978 airlines were "deregulated." In 1984, the reign of the Civil Aeronautics Board (CAB), which controlled exactly which airlines flew where and how much they could charge, ended. Routes, prices, and schedules were thrown open to free competition. Airlines that had previously monopolized preferred destinations found competitors prying loose their strangleholds. Thus, Hawaii is now one of the most hotly contested air markets in the world. The competition among carriers is fierce, and this makes for "sweet deals" and a wide choice of fares for the money-wise traveler. It also makes for pricing chaos. It's impossible to quote airline prices that will hold true for more than a month, if that long. But it's comforting to know that flights to Hawaii remain relatively cheap, and mile for mile are one of the best travel bargains in the industry. Familiarize yourself with the alternatives at your disposal so you can make an informed travel selection. Now more than ever, you should work with a sharp travel agent who's on your side.

Almost all travelers to Maui arrive by air. A few lucky ones come by private yacht, the interisland ferry from Lanai, or the cruise ship SS *Independence,* which docks at Kahului. Maui, the Hawaiian destination second only to Oahu, attracts over a million visitors per year. A limited number of direct air flights from the Mainland U.S.A., Canada, and Japan are offered, but most airlines servicing Hawaii, both domestic and foreign, land at Honolulu International Airport and then carry on to Maui or offer connecting flights on "interisland carriers." In most cases they're part of the original ticket price with no extra charge. Different airlines have "interline" agreements with different Hawaiian carriers so check with your travel agent. All major and most smaller interisland carriers service Maui from throughout Hawaii with over 100 flights per day in and out of Kahului Airport and less than a dozen a day to Kapalua-West Maui airport.

When to Go
The prime tourist season starts two weeks before Christmas and lasts until Easter. It picks up again with summer vacation in early June and ends once more in late August. Everything is usually booked solid and prices are inflated. Hotel, airline, and car reservations, which are a must, are often hard to coordinate at this time of year. You can save 10-50% and a lot of hassling if you go in the artificially created "off season," September to early December, and mid-April (after Easter) until early June. Recently, the reduction in number of tourists during the off season has not been nearly as substantial as in years past, indicating the increasing popularity of the island at this time of year, but you'll still find the prices better and the beaches, trails, campgrounds, and even restaurants less crowded. The people will be happier to see you, too.

BY AIR

There are two categories of airlines that you can take to Hawaii: **domestic,** meaning American-owned, and **foreign**-owned. An American law, penned at the turn of the century to protect American shipping, says that "only" an American carrier can transport you to and from two American cities. In the airline industry, this law is still very much in effect. It means, for example, that if you want a roundtrip between San Francisco and Honolulu, you *must* fly on a domestic carrier, such as United or American. If, however, you are flying from San Francisco to Tokyo, you are at liberty to fly a "foreign" airline such as Japan Air Lines, and you may even have a stopover in Hawaii, but you must continue to Tokyo or some other foreign city and cannot fly JAL back to San Francisco. Canadians have no problem flying Canadian Pacific roundtrip from Toronto to Honolulu because this route does not connect two American cities, and so it is with all foreign travel to and from Hawaii. Travel agents know this, but if you're planning

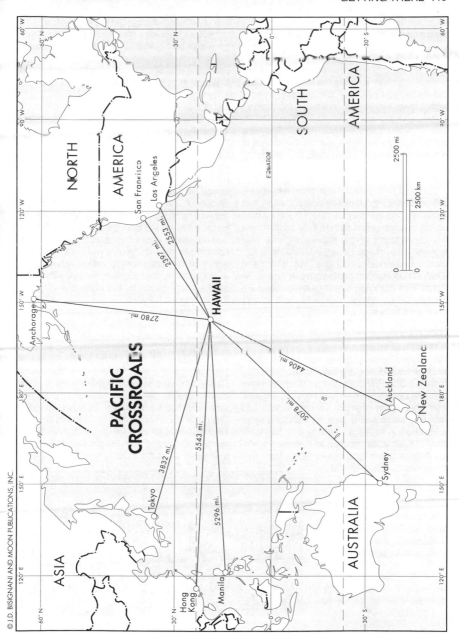

PACIFIC
CROSSROADS

your own trip be aware of this fact; if you're traveling roundtrip it must be on a domestic carrier.

Kinds of Flights

The three kinds of flights are the "milk run," direct, and nonstop. Milk runs are the least convenient. On these, you board a carrier—say, in your home town—fly it to a gateway city, change planes and carriers, fly on to the West Coast, change again, and then fly to Hawaii. They're a hassle—your bags have a much better chance of getting lost, you waste time in airports, and to top it off, they're not any cheaper. Avoid them if you can.

On direct flights you fly from point A to point B without changing planes; it doesn't mean that you don't land in between. Direct flights do land usually once to board and deplane passengers, but you sit cozily on the plane along with your luggage and off you go again. Nonstop is just that, but can cost a bit more. You board and when the doors open again you're in Hawaii. All flights from the West Coast gateway cities are nonstop "God willing"—because there is only the Pacific in between!

Nonstop Flights

Until recently, United Airlines was the only carrier that offered nonstop flights from the Mainland to Maui. United flies one daily nonstop to Maui from both San Francisco and Los Angeles. Now, Delta Air Lines flies once daily from Los Angeles, with other flights originating in Los Angeles and San Francisco going through Honolulu at no extra charge. American Airlines also flies daily from Los Angeles nonstop to Kahului. Hawaiian Airlines offers four weekly flights from San Francisco and Seattle to Maui.

Stopover Flights

All the major carriers have arrangements for getting you to Maui. American carriers such as Continental and Northwest, along with foreign carriers like Canadian Airlines, Qantas, and Japan Air Lines land at Honolulu. There they have an interline agreement with island carriers, including Hawaiian Airlines and

Aloha Airlines, which then take you to Maui. This sometimes involves a plane change, but your baggage can be booked straight through. Although Hawaiian Airlines has nonstop flights from San Francisco and Seattle to Maui, other flights go to Oahu, with connections in Honolulu to Kahului. They offer the added convenience of dealing with just one airline.

Travel Agents

At one time people went to a travel agent the same way they went to a barber or beautician, loyally sticking with one. Most agents are reputable professionals who know what they're doing. They should be members of the American Society of Travel Agents (ASTA) and licensed by the Air Traffic Conference (ATC). Most have the inside track on the best deals, and they'll save you countless hours calling 800 numbers and listening to elevator music while on hold. Unless you require them to make very special arrangements, their services are free—they are paid a commission by the airlines and hotels that they book for you.

If you've done business with a travel agent in the past and were satisfied with the services and prices, by all means stick with him or her. If no such positive rapport exists, then shop around. Ask friends or relatives for recommendations; if you can't get any endorsements go to the Yellow Pages. Call two or three travel agents to compare prices. Make sure to give all of them the same information and to be as precise as possible. Tell them where and when you want to go, how long you want to stay, which class you want to travel, and any special requirements. Write down their information. It's amazing how confusing travel plans can be when you have to keep track of flight numbers, times, prices, and all the preparation info. When you compare, don't look only for the cheapest price. Check for convenience in flights, amenities of hotels, and any other fringe benefits that might be included. Then make your choice of agent, and if he or she is willing to give you individualized service, stick with that agent from then on.

Agents become accustomed to offering the same deals to many clients because they're familiar with the arrangements and because the deals have worked well in the past. Sometimes these are indeed the best, but if they don't suit you, don't be railroaded into accepting them. Any good agent will work with you. After all, it's your trip and your money.

Package Tours

For the independent traveler, practical package deals that include only flight, car, and lodging are okay. Agents put these together all the time and they just might be the best, but if they don't suit you, make arrangements separately. A package *tour* is totally different. On these you get your hand held by an escort, eat where they want you to eat, go where they want you to go, and watch Hawaii slide by your bus window. For some people, especially groups, this might be the way to do it, but everyone else should avoid the package tour. You'll see Hawaii best on your own, and if you want a tour you can arrange one there, often more cheaply. Once arrangements have been made with your travel agent, make sure to take all receipts and letters of confirmation (hotel, car) with you to Hawaii. They probably won't be needed, but if they are, nothing will work better in getting results.

Mainland and International Fares

There are many categories of airline fares, but only three apply to the average traveler: first class, coach, and excursion (APEX). Traveling **first class** seats you in the front of the plane, gives you free drinks and movie headsets, a wider choice of meals, more leg room, and access to VIP lounges, if they exist. There are no restrictions, no penalties for advance-booking cancellations or rebooking of return flights, and no minimum-stay requirements.

Coach, the way that most people fly, is totally adequate. You sit in the plane's main compartment behind first class. Your seats are comfortable, but you don't have as much legroom or as wide a choice of meals. Movie headsets and drinks cost you a few dollars, but that's about it. Coach offers many of the same benefits as first class and costs about 30% less. You can buy tickets up until takeoff, you have no restrictions on minimum or maximum stays; you receive liberal stopover privileges, and you can cash in your return ticket or change your return date with no penalties.

Excursion or advance payment excursion (APEX) fares are the cheapest. You are accommodated on the plane exactly the same as if you were flying coach. There are, however, some restrictions. You must book and pay for your ticket in advance (usually 7-14 days). At the same time, you must book your return flight, and under most circumstances you can't change either without paying a penalty. Also, your stopovers are severely limited and you will have a minimum/maximum stay period. Only a limited number of seats on any one plane are set aside for APEX fares, so book as early as you can. Also, if you must change travel plans, you can go to the airport and get on as a standby passenger using a discounted ticket, even if the airline doesn't have an official standby policy. There's always the risk that you won't get on, but you do have a chance, as well as priority over an actual standby customer.

Standby is exactly what its name implies: you go to the airport and wait around to see if any flights going to Hawaii have an empty seat. You can save some money, but you cannot have a firm itinerary or limited time. Since Hawaii is such a popular destination, standbys can wait days before catching a plane.

Charters

Charter flights were at one time only for groups or organizations that had memberships in travel clubs. Now they're open to the general public. A charter flight is an entire plane or a block of seats purchased at a quantity discount by a charter company and then sold to customers. Because they are bought at wholesale prices, charter fares can be the cheapest available. As in package deals, only take a charter flight if it is a "fly only," or perhaps includes a car. You don't need one that

INTERISLAND AIR ROUTES

includes a guide and a bus. Most importantly, make sure that the charter company is reputable. It should belong to the same organizations (ASTA and ATC) as most travel agents. If not, check into the company at the local chamber of commerce.

More restrictions apply to charters than to any other flights. You must pay in advance. If you cancel after a designated time, you can be penalized severely or lose your money entirely. You cannot change departure or return dates and times. However, up to 10 days before departure the charter company is legally able to cancel, raise the price by 10%, or change time and dates. It must return your money if cancellation occurs, or if changed arrangements are unacceptable to you. Mostly charter companies are on the up-and-up and flights go smoothly, but there are horror stories. Be careful. Be wise. Investigate!

Tips

Flights from the West Coast take about five hours; you gain two hours over Pacific standard time when you land in Hawaii. From the East Coast it takes about 11 hours and you gain five

hours over eastern standard time. Flights from Japan take about seven hours and there is a five-hour difference between the time zones. Travel time between Sydney, Australia, or Auckland, New Zealand, and Hawaii is about nine hours. They are ahead of Hawaii time by 20 and 22 hours, respectively. Try to fly Mon.-Thurs., when flights are cheaper and easier to book. Pay for your ticket as soon as your plans are firm. If prices go up there is no charge added, but merely booking doesn't guarantee the lowest price. Make sure that airlines, hotels, and car agencies get your phone number too—not only your travel agent's—in case any problems with availability arise (travel agents are often closed on weekends). It's not necessary, but it's a good idea to call and reconfirm flights 24-72 hours in advance.

First-row (bulkhead) seats are good for people who need more legroom, but bad for watching the movie. Airlines will give you special meals (vegetarian, kosher, low cal, low salt) often at no extra charge, but you must notify them in advance. If you're "bumped" from an overbooked flight, you're entitled to a comparable flight to your destination within one hour. If more than an hour elapses, you get denied-boarding compensation which goes up proportionately with the amount of time you're held up. Sometimes this is cash or a voucher for another flight to be used in the future. You don't have to accept what an airline offers on the spot, if you feel it isn't being fair.

Traveling with Children
Fares for children ages 2-12 are 50% of the adult fare; children under two not occupying a seat travel free. If you're traveling with an infant or active toddler, book your flight well in advance and request the bulkhead seat or first row in any section and a bassinet if available. Many carriers have fold-down cribs with restraints for baby's

safety and comfort. Toddlers appreciate the extra space provided by the front-row seats. Be sure to reconfirm, and arrive early to ensure this special seating. On long flights you'll be glad that you took these extra pains.

Although most airlines have coloring books, puppets, etc., to keep your child busy, it's always a good idea to bring your own. These can make the difference between a pleasant flight and a harried ordeal. Also, remember to bring baby bottles, formula, diapers, and other necessities, as many airlines may not be equipped with exactly what you need. Make all inquiries ahead of time so you're not caught unprepared.

Baggage
You are allowed two free pieces of luggage—one large, the other small—and a carry-on bag. The

© J.D. BISIGNANI AND MOON PUBLICATIONS, INC.

two main pieces can weigh up to 70 pounds each; an extra charge is levied for extra weight. The larger bag can have an overall added dimension (height plus width plus length) of 62 inches; the smaller, 55 inches. Your carry-on must fit under your seat or in the overhead storage compartment. Purses and camera bags are not counted as carry-ons and may be taken aboard. Surfboards and bicycles are about $15 extra. Although they make great mementos, remove all previous baggage tags from your luggage; they can confuse handlers. Attach a sturdy holder with your name and address on the handle, or use a stick-on label on the bag itself. Put your name and address inside the bag, and the address where you'll be staying in Hawaii if possible. Carry your cosmetics, identification, money, prescriptions, tickets, reservations, change of underwear, camera equipment, and perhaps a change of shirt or blouse in your carry-on.

Visas

Entering Hawaii is like entering anywhere else in the United States. Foreign nationals must have a current passport and proper visa, an ongoing or return air ticket, and sufficient funds for the proposed stay in Hawaii. Canadians do not need a visa or passport but must have proper identification such as passport, driver's license, or birth certificate.

Agricultural Inspection

Everyone visiting Hawaii must fill out a "Plant and Animal Inspection Form" and present it to the appropriate official upon arrival in the state. Anyone carrying any of the listed items must have those items inspected by an agricultural inspection agent at the airport.

Remember that before you leave Hawaii for the Mainland, all of your bags are again subject to an agricultural inspection, a usually painless procedure taking only a minute or two. To facilitate your departure, leave all bags unlocked until after inspection. There are no restrictions on beach sand from below the high-water line, coconuts, prepackaged sugarcane, dried flower arrangements, fresh flower lei, pineapples, certified pest-free plants, seashells, seed lei, and wood roses. However, avocado, litchi, and papaya must be treated before departure. Some other restricted items are berries, fresh garde-

nias, roses, jade plants, live insects, snails, cotton, plants in soil, soil itself, and raw sugarcane. Raw sugar cane is okay, however, if it is cut between the nodes, has the outer covering peeled off, and is split into fourths. For any questions pertaining to plants that you want to take to the Mainland, call the Agricultural Quarantine Inspection office, tel. (808) 877-5261 in Kahului.

Maui's Airports

There are three commercial airports on Maui, but the vast majority of travelers will be concerned with **Kahului Airport,** which accommodates 95% of the flights in and out of Maui. Kahului Airport is only minutes from Kahului city center, on the north-central coast of Maui. A full-service facility with all amenities, it has a few gift and snack shops, a restaurant, two tourist information booths, a newsstand, display cases of Hawaiian arts and crafts, a lost and found office, luggage storage office, bathrooms, public telephones, car rental agencies, and limited private transportation. As you face the terminal building, the departure lounge is on your right, the arrival lounge is on your left, and splitting the two is an upper level courtyard with shops. For your entertainment, a hula and music show is performed here for two hours at midday. A few steps beyond the rental car booths at the front of the arrival building is the commuter terminal, and on the far side of the runway is the heliport. **Island Air, Paragon, Pacific Wings,** and **Scenic Air** operate flights from the commuter terminal. Public parking at the airport costs $1 for the first half hour, $1 for each additional hour, or $7 maximum per day. The Kahului Airport has recently undergone a major expansion that allows it to land the biggest commercial planes and handle a great increase in traffic, including direct international flights. Major roads lead from Kahului Airport to all primary destinations on Maui.

Hawaiian Airlines opened the one-strip **Kapalua-West Maui Airport** in early 1987. You fly in over pineapple fields. This facility is conveniently located between Kaanapali and the Kapalua resort areas, on the *mauka* side of the Honoapiilani Hwy. at Mahinahina just a few minutes from the major Kaanapali hotels and condos of Honokowai and Kahana. As convenient as it is to this area of West Maui, it is not heavily used. Hawaiian Airlines no longer operates connecting flights to West Maui with the rest of Hawaii, and for now only Island Air schedules flights and has a booth here. The small terminal is user-friendly with a snack bar, sundries shop, and courtesy phones for car rental pickup, but there is only fee parking.

The third airstrip is Hana Airport, an isolated runway with a tiny terminal on the northeast coast just west of Hana. It has no amenities aside from a bathroom and telephone, and transportation is available only to the Hotel Hana-Maui via the hotel shuttle. People flying into Hana Airport generally plan to vacation in Hana for an extended period and have made prior arrangements for being picked up. The only rental cars available in Hana can be arranged by calling Dollar Rent A Car at (808) 248-8237—call before you come!

DOMESTIC CARRIERS

The following are the major domestic carriers to and from Hawaii. The planes used are primarily DC-10s and 747s, with a smaller 727 flown now and again. A list of the "gateway cities" from which they fly direct and nonstop flights is given, but "connecting cities" are not. All flights, by all carriers, land at Honolulu International Airport except the limited direct flights to Maui and Hawaii. Only the established companies are listed. Entrepreneurial small airlines such as the defunct Hawaii Express pop up now and again and specialize in dirt-cheap fares. There is a hectic frenzy to buy their tickets and business is great for a while, but then the established companies lower their fares and the gamblers fold.

Hawaiian Airlines
One of Hawaii's own domestic airlines has entered the Mainland market. It operates daily flights from Los Angeles, San Francisco, Las Vegas (via Los Angelos), Seattle, and Portland to Honolulu, with four weekly flights from San Francisco and Seattle to Kahului, Maui, which continue on to Honolulu. The "common fare" ticket price includes an ongoing flight to any of the Neighbor Islands, and if you're leaving Hawaii, a free flight from a Neighbor Island to the link-up in Honolulu. Se-

nior-citizen discounts for people age 60 or older are offered on trans-Pacific and interisland flights. Scheduled flights to the South Pacific run between Honolulu and Pago Pago three-times a week and once a week on Saturdays to Papeete, Tahiti. Hawaiian Airlines offers special discount deals with Dollar rental cars and select major-island hotels. Contact Hawaiian Airlines at (800) 367-5320 Mainland and Canada, (800) 882-8811 in Hawaii.

United Airlines
Since its first island flight in 1947, United has become top dog in flights to Hawaii. Its Mainland routes connect over 100 cities to Honolulu. The main gateway cities of San Francisco, Los Angeles, and Chicago have direct flights to Honolulu; flights from all other cities connect through these. United also offers direct flights to Maui from San Francisco and Los Angeles, from San Francisco and Los Angeles to Kona on the Big Island, and from Los Angeles to Lihue, Kauai. Continuing through Honolulu, United flights go to Tokyo, where connections can be made for other Asian cities. United offers a number of packages, including flight and hotel on Oahu, and flight, hotel, and car on the Neighbor Islands. It interlines with Aloha Airlines and deals with Hertz rental cars. United is the "big guy" and it intends to stay that way—the packages are hard to beat. Call (800) 241-6522.

American Airlines
American offers direct flights to Honolulu from Los Angeles, San Francisco, Dallas/Fort Worth, and Chicago. It also flies daily from Los Angeles direct to Maui. Call (800) 433-7300.

Continental Airlines
Flights from all Mainland cities to Honolulu connect via Los Angeles, Newark, and Houston. Also available are direct flights from Guam Johnston Island, Taipei, and Tokyo (Narita) to Honolulu. Call (800) 525-3273 or (800) 231-0856 for international information.

Northwest Airlines
Northwest flies into Honolulu from Los Angeles, San Francisco, Seattle, and Minneapolis. All flights to Maui

must go through Honolulu. There are onward flights to Tokyo, Osaka, Nagoya, Manila, Guam, Bangkok, Singapore, Hong Kong, Taipei, and Seoul. Call (800) 225-2525.

Delta Air Lines
In 1985, Delta entered the Hawaiian market; when it bought out Western Airlines its share became even bigger. It has nonstop flights to Honolulu from Dallas/Fort Worth, Los Angeles, San Francisco, and Atlanta, and a direct flight to Kahului, Maui, from Los Angeles. Call (800) 221-1212.

FOREIGN CARRIERS

The following carriers operate throughout Asia and Oceania but have no U.S. flying rights. This means that in order for you to vacation in Hawaii using one of these carriers, your flight must originate or terminate in a foreign city. You can have a stopover in Honolulu with a connecting flight to a Neighbor Island. For example, if you've purchased a flight on Japan Air Lines from San Francisco to Tokyo, you can stop in Hawaii, but you must then carry on to Tokyo. Failure to do so will result in a stiff fine, and the balance of your ticket will not be refunded.

Canadian Airlines International
Nonstop flights from Canada to Honolulu originate in Vancouver and Toronto. Canadian has an interisland agreement with Aloha Airlines for travel to the neighboring islands. Call (800) 426-7000 in the U.S. or (800) 665-7530 in Canada.

Air New Zealand
Flights link New Zealand, Australia, and numerous South Pacific islands to Honolulu, with continuing flights to Mainland cities. All flights run via Auckland, New Zealand. Call (800) 926-7255 or (800) 262-1234 in the U.S. and (800) 663-5494 in Canada for current information.

Japan Air Lines
The Japanese are the second-largest group, next to Americans, to visit Hawaii. JAL flights to Honolulu originate in Tokyo (Narita), Nagoya, Osaka (Kansai), Hiroshima, Sapporo, Sendai, and Fukuoka. In addition, there are flights between Tokyo (Narita) and Kona on the Big Is-

land. There are no JAL flights between the Mainland and Hawaii. Call (800) 525-3663.

All Nippon Airways
ANA is the second Japanese airlines that flies to the U.S. Daily flights connect Tokyo (Narita) and Nagoya to Honolulu. Call (800) 262-9266.

Qantas
Daily flights connect Sydney with Honolulu; all other flights feed through this hub. Call (800) 227-4500.

China Airlines
Routes to Honolulu with China Airlines are from Taipei direct three times a week or through Tokyo five times a week, but all flights may not be available year-round. Connections are available in Taipei to most Asian capitals. Call (800) 227-5118.

Korean Air
Korean Air offers some of the least expensive flights to Asia. All flights to/from Honolulu go directly to Seoul, with connections to many Asian cities. Call (800) 438-5000.

Other Airlines
Aside from the above airlines, large volume charter operators book flights to the various island with such carriers as **Canada 3000** and **American Trans Air.**

INTERISLAND CARRIERS

Getting to and from Maui via the other islands is easy and convenient. The only effective way for most visitors to travel between the Hawaiian Islands is by air. Luckily, Hawaii has excellent air transportation that boasts one of the industry's safest flight records. All interisland flights have a no smoking regulation. Items restricted on flights from the mainland and from overseas are also restricted on flights within the state. Baggage allowances are the same as anywhere, except that due to space contraints, carry-on luggage on the smaller prop planes may be limited in number and size.

The following airlines have competitive prices, with interisland flights at about $90 each way, with substantial savings for state residents. With both

Hawaiian and Aloha Airlines, you can save about $7 per ticket by purchasing a booklet of six one-way **flight coupons**. These are available only in state at any interisland airline ticket office or airport counter, and are *transferable*. Just book a flight as normal and present the filled-in voucher to board the plane. Perfect for families or groups of friends. Hawaiian Airlines coupons are good for six months, Aloha Airlines coupons for one year.

Additionally, each airlines offers passes that are good for unlimited travel anywhere that the airlines flies, but they are non-transferable and may only be used on consecutive days. You may purchase these passes in state or before you arrive in Hawaii. Hawaiian Airlines has the "Hawaiian Island Pass": 5 days at $299, 7 days at $315, 10 days at $369, and 14 days at $409. Aloha Airlines offers one "7-day Island Pass" for $315 with the same conditions.

Note: Although every effort has been made for up-to-date accuracy, remember that schedules are constantly changing. The following should be used only as a point of reference. Please call the airlines listed below for their latest schedules.

Hawaiian Airlines
The majority of flights from Hawaiian Airlines, tel. (800) 367-5320 Mainland and Canada, (800) 882-8811 statewide, or (808) 871-6132 on Maui, Web site: www.hawaiianair.com, are to and from Honolulu (average flight time 35 minutes), with about two dozen per day in each direction. Hawaiian Airlines flights to Kahului, Maui, from Honolulu begin at 5:30 a.m., with flights thereafter about every 30 minutes until 10 p.m. Flights from Kahului to Honolulu begin at 6:30 a.m. and go all day until 9 p.m. There are two flights to/from Hilo daily, one at midmorning and one in the late afternoon. Kona, also on the Big Island, is serviced with two flights from Kahului; one in the morning and one in the afternoon. Kahului and Lihue, Kauai, are connected by just over a dozen flights daily in each direction, beginning at 6:30 a.m. and going into the early evening. There is one daily direct flight between Maui and Molokai. Molokai and Lanai are connected by daily late afternoon flights.

Aloha Airlines
Aloha Airlines, tel. (800) 367-5250 Mainland, (800) 235-0936 Canada, (808) 244-9071 Maui, Web site: www.alohaair.com, with its all-jet fleet of 737s, offers more flights to Maui than any other interisland carrier. It flies from Honolulu to Maui about 30 times per day beginning at 5:15 a.m. with the last flight at 8 p.m.; return flights to Honolulu start at 6:12 a.m., with the last at 9 p.m. Multiple flights throughout the day from Kauai begin at 6:30 a.m. until 7 p.m.; to Kauai they start at 6:12 a.m. and continue throughout the day until 6:50 p.m. Flights to and from Hilo leave twice daily, one at midmorning and the second in the late afternoon. From Kona three flights leave between 9:30 a.m. and 5:37 p.m.; to Kona the flights are between 8:17 a.m. and 4:07 p.m.

Island Air
Formerly Aloha Island Air but now known simply as Island Air, tel. (800) 323-3345 nationwide, (800) 652-6541 statewide, (808) 877-5755 Kahului, Web site: www.alohaair.com, this airline offers daily flights connecting Maui with all the major islands. Along with the main airports of Honolulu and Kahului, it services the smaller and more out-of-the-way airports of Kapalua and Hana on Maui, Lanai City on Lanai, and Hoolehua and Kalaupapa on Molokai. About half the flights are on jet aircraft and half on Dash-8 turboprop airplanes. Seven flights a day connect Honolulu to Kahului, all making stops on either Molokai or Lanai, beginning at 7:05 a.m. (6:55 a.m. from Honolulu) and running until 6:35 p.m. (5:05 p.m. from Honolulu). Four daily flights run from Molokai to Kahului (6:55 a.m.-4:30 p.m.), with two of these carrying on to Hana. Direct flights to and from Honolulu and Kapalua-West Maui Airport run nine times daily from 7:20 a.m. to 5:15 p.m. The newest routes are direct daily flights from Kapalua-West Maui Airport to Kona, on the Big Island, and from Lanai to Kona. There are regular twice-daily flights to Kalaupapa on Molokai from Hoolehua on Molokai and from Honolulu, but only with sponsorship from a resident or a reservation on one of the organized Damien Tours.

Pacific Wings
A local company operating eight-seat, twin engine Cessna 402C planes, Pacific Wings, tel. (888) 575-4546, Web site: www.pacificwings.com, flies out of Kahului for Hana (three a day), Molokai (four a day), and Kamuela on the Big Island (one a day), as well as from Honolulu to those three destinations, no more than twice daily.

Charter Airlines

If you've got the bucks or just need to go when there's no regularly scheduled flight, try **Paragon Air,** tel. (808) 244-3356 or (800) 428-1231, Web site: www.maui.net/~wings/index.htm, for island-wide service. **Pacific Wings** also offers charter service throughout the state.

TRAVEL BY SHIP

American Hawaii Cruises

This American cruise ship company operates the 800-passenger SS *Independence*. This ship offers a seven-day itinerary that calls at five ports on the four main islands. For those who want just a taste of a cruise through the islands, three- and four-day trips are also offered. The seven-day fares start at $1,230 per person double occupancy, three- and four-day fares from $670 and 805, respectively. Fares go up from there according to the class and location of your cabin. Children under 18 are often given special rates and cruise free June-Sept. when they share a cabin with their parents. All cruises leave on Saturday from the Aloha Towers in Honolulu. After leaving Honolulu, the seven-day cruise first stops at Nawiliwili on Kauai, followed by Kahului on Maui, and Hilo and Kona on the Big Island, before returning to Honolulu. For the three-day cruise, you board in Honolulu and alight in Kahului. Those on the four-day trip board in Kahului and get off in Honolulu. The ship is a luxury seagoing hotel and gourmet restaurant; swimming pools, health clubs, movies, and nightclubs are all part of the amenities. Onshore excursions are offered at each port of call. Airfare to Hawaii, interisland air flights, rental cars, and accommodation on any island after your cruise can be arranged for you by American Hawaii Cruises. For details contact: American Hawaii Cruises, Robin St. Wharf, 1380 Port of New Orleans Place, New Orleans, LA 70130-1890, tel. (800) 765-7000, fax (504) 585-0690, Web site: www.cruisehawaii.com.

Alternatives

Other companies offering varied cruises include **P&O Lines,** which operates the *Sea Princess* through the South Pacific, making port at Honolulu on its way from the West Coast once a year.

Royal Cruise Line out of Los Angeles, or Auckland alternatively, sails the *Royal Odyssey,* which docks in Honolulu on its South Pacific and Orient cruise, $2,200-4,000.

The **Holland America Line** sails a year-long World Cruise, calling at Honolulu. Call (800) 426-0327.

Society Expeditions offers a 42-day cruise throughout the South Pacific departing from Honolulu. Fares range $3,000-9,000. Call (800) 426-7794.

Information

Most travel agents can provide information on the above cruise lines. If you're especially interested in traveling by freighter, contact: **Freighter Travel Club of America,** P.O. Box 12693, Salem, OR 97309; or **Ford's Freighter Travel Guide,** P.O. Box 505, 22151 Clarendon St., Woodland Hills, CA 91367.

TOUR COMPANIES

Many tour companies advertise packages to Hawaii in large city newspapers every week. They offer very reasonable airfares, car rentals, and accommodations. Without trying, you can get roundtrip airfare from the West Coast and a week in Hawaii for $400-500 using one of these companies. The following companies offer great deals and have excellent reputations. This list is by no means exhaustive.

SunTrips

This California-based tour and charter company sells vacations all over the world. It's primarily a wholesale company but will work with the general public. SunTrips often works with Rich International Air, tel. (305) 871-5113. When you receive your SunTrips tickets, you are given discount vouchers for places to stay that are convenient to the airport of departure. Many of these hotels have complimentary airport pickup service and will allow you to park your car, free of charge, for up to 14 days, which saves a considerable amount on airport parking fees. SunTrips does not offer assigned seating until you get to the airport. They recommend that you get there two hours in advance, and they ain't kidding! This is the price you pay for getting such inexpensive air travel. SunTrips usually has a deal with a car rental company. Remember that everyone on your incoming flight is offered the same deal, and all make a beeline for the rental car's shuttle van after landing and securing their baggage. If you have a traveling companion, work together to beat the rush by leaving your companion to fetch the baggage and heading directly for the van as soon as you arrive. Pick your car up, then return for your partner and the bags. Even if you're alone, you could zip over to the car rental center and then return for your bags without having them sit very long on the carousel. Contact SunTrips, 2350 Paragon Dr., P.O. Box 18505, San Jose, CA 95158, tel. (800) 786-8747 in California, (808) 941-2697 in Honolulu.

Council Travel Services
These full-service, budget-travel specialists are a subsidiary of the nonprofit Council on International Educational Exchange, and the official U.S. representative to the International Student Travel Conference. They'll custom-design trips and programs for everyone from senior citizens to college students. Bona fide students have extra advantages, however, including eligibility for the International Student Identification Card (CIIC), which often gets you discount fares and waived entrance fees. Groups and business travelers are also welcome. For full information, call (800) 226-8624, or write to Council Travel Services at one of these offices: 530 Bush St., San Francisco, CA 94108, tel. (415) 421-3473; or 205 E. 42nd St., New York, NY 10017, tel. (212) 661-1450. Other offices are in Austin, Berkeley, Boston, Davis, Long Beach, Los Angeles, Miami, Portland, San Diego, and Seattle.

Student Travel Network
STA Travel is a full-service travel agency specializing in student travel, regardless of age. Those under 26 do not have to be full-time students to get special fares. Older independent travelers can avail themselves of services, although they are ineligible for student fares. STA works hard to get you discounted or budget rates. STA's central office is at 7202 Melrose Ave., Los Angeles, CA 90046, tel. (213) 934-8722 or (800) 777-0112. STA maintains 39 offices throughout the U.S., Australasia, and Europe, along with **Travel Cuts,** a sister organization

operating in Canada. Many tickets issued by STA are flexible, allowing changes with no penalty, and are open-ended for travel up to one year. STA also maintains **Travel Help,** a service available at all offices designed to solve all types of problems that may arise while traveling. STA is a well-established travel agency with an excellent and well-deserved reputation.

Nature Expeditions International
These quality tours have nature as the theme. Trips are nine- or 15-day, four-island, natural-history expeditions, with emphasis on plants, birds, and geology. Their guides are experts in their fields and give personable and attentive service. Contact Nature Expeditions International at 6400 E. El Dorado, Suite 200, Tucson, AZ 85714, tel. (520) 721-6712 or (800) 869-0639.

Ocean Voyages
This unique company offers seven- and 10-day itineraries aboard a variety of yachts in the Hawaiian Islands. The yachts, equipped to carry 2-10 passengers, ensure individualized sail training. The vessels sail throughout the islands, exploring hidden bays and coves, and berth at different ports as they go. This opportunity is for anyone who wishes to see the islands in a timeless fashion, thrilling to sights experienced by the first Polynesian settlers and Western explorers. For rates and information contact Ocean Voyages, 1709 Bridgeway, Sausalito, CA 94965, tel. (415) 332-4681.

Pleasant Hawaiian Holidays
A California-based company specializing in Hawaii, Pleasant Hawaiian Holidays, 2404 Townsgate Rd., Westlake Village, CA 91361, tel. (800) 242-9244, makes arrangements for flights, accommodations, and transportation only.

Travelers with Disabilities
Accessible Vans of Hawaii (formerly Wheelers of Hawaii), 186 Mehani Circle, Kihei, HI 96753, tel. (808) 879-5521, (800) 303-3750 Hawaii, or (888) AVAVANS Mainland, fax (808) 879-0649, is a private company owned and operated by Dave McKown, who has traveled the world with his paraplegic brother. Dave knows firsthand the obstacles faced by disabled people, and his disabled associate does as well. Accessible

Vans of Hawaii provides a full-service travel agency, booking rooms, flights, and activities for the physically disabled. Wheelchair-lift-equipped vans are rented on Oahu, Maui, and the Big Island for $109 a day or $560 a week, plus tax. If a van is needed on Kauai, it must be shipped at the renter's expense. Dave and his associate are good sources of information for any traveler with disabilities.

Ecotours to Hawaii

Sierra Club Trips offers Hawaii trips for nature lovers who are interested in an outdoor experience. Various trips include hikes over Maui's Haleakala and, on Kauai, a kayak trip along the Na Pali Coast and a family camping spree in the Koke'e region. All trips are led by experienced guides and are open to Sierra Club members only ($35 per year to join). For information contact the Sierra Club Outing Department, 85 2nd St., 2nd Fl., San Francisco, CA 94105, tel. (415) 775-5500.

Earthwatch allows you to become part of an expeditionary team dedicated to conservation and the study of the natural environment. An expedition might include studying dolphins in Kewalo Basin Marine Mammal Laboratory, or diving Maui's threatened reefs. If you become an as-sistant field researcher, your lodgings may be a dorm room at the University of Hawaii, and your meals may come from a remote camp kitchen. Fees vary and are tax deductible. If you're interested in this learning experience, contact Earthwatch, 680 Mt. Auburn St., P.O. Box 403-P, Watertown, MA 02272, tel. (617) 926-8200.

Backroads, 801 Cedar St., Berkeley, CA 94710, tel. (510) 527-1555 or (800) 462-2848, fax (510) 527-1444, Web site: www.backroads .com, arranges easy-on-the-environment bicycle and hiking trips to the Big Island. Basic tours include a six-day hiking/camping tour ($698), a six-day hiking/inn tour ($1,295), and a five-day bicycle/camping tour ($649). Prices include hotel/inn accommodations or tent when applicable, most meals, and professional guide service. Airfare is not included, and bicycles and sleeping bags can be rented (B.Y.O. okay) for reasonable rates.

Crane Tours, 15101 Magnolia Blvd., Sherman Oaks, CA 91403, tel. (800) 653-2545, owned and operated by Bill Crane, has been taking people kayaking and backpacking to the Big Island, Maui, and Kauai since 1976. Basic prices for these eco-adventures start at $650, with the most expensive tour around $1,145 (airfare not included).

GETTING AROUND

If it's your intention to *see* Maui when you visit, and not just to lie on the beach in front of your hotel, the only efficient way is to rent a car. Limited public transportation, a few free shuttles, taxis, and the good old thumb are available, but all these are flawed in one way or another. Other unique and fun-filled ways to tour the island include renting a bike or moped, or hopping on a helicopter, but these conveyances are highly specialized and are more in the realm of sports than touring.

CAR RENTALS

Maui has about three dozen car rental agencies that can put you behind the wheel of anything from a Mercedes convertible to a used station wagon with chipped paint and torn upholstery. There are national companies, interisland firms, good local companies, and a few fly-by-nights that'll rent you a clunker. Eight companies are clustered in little booths at the Kahului Airport. None have booths at Kapalua-West Maui Airport or Hana Airport, but the Hana Hotel can arrange a car for you or you can do it yourself by calling Dollar at (808) 248-8237 *before* you arrive. The rest are scattered around the island, with a heavy concentration in Kahului, at the Kaanapali Transportation Center, and along S. Kihei Road. Those without an airport booth either have a courtesy phone or a number to call; they'll pick you up and shuttle you to their lots. Stiff competition tends to keep the prices more or less reasonable. Good deals are offered off season, with price wars flaring at any time and making for real savings. Even with all these companies, it's best to book ahead. You might not save money, but you can save yourself headaches.

Requirements

A variety of requirements are imposed on the renter by car agencies, but the most important clauses are common. Some of the worst practices being challenged are: no rentals to people under 25 and over 70, and no rentals to military personnel or Hawaiian residents! Before renting, check that you fulfill the requirements. Generally, you must be 21, although some agencies rent to 18-year-olds, while others still require you to be 25. You must possess a valid driver's license, with licenses from most countries accepted, but if you are not American, get an International Driver's License to be safe. You should have a major credit card in your name. This is the easiest way to rent a car. Some companies will take a deposit, but it will be very stiff. It could easily be $50 per day on top of your rental fees and sometimes much more. In addition, they may require a credit check on the spot, complete with phone calls to your employer and bank. If you damage the car, charges will be deducted from your deposit, and the car company itself determines the extent of the damages. Some companies *will not* rent you a car without a major credit card in your name, no matter how much of a deposit you are willing to leave.

When to Rent

On this one, you'll have to make up your own mind, because it's a "bet" that you can either win or lose big. But it's always good to know the odds before you plop down your money. You can reserve your car in advance when you book your air ticket, or play the field when you get there. If you book in advance, you'll obviously have a car waiting for you, but the deal that you made is the deal that you'll get—it may or may not be the best around. On the other hand, if you wait, you can often take advantage of excellent on-the-spot deals. However, you're betting that cars are available. You might be totally disappointed and not be able to rent a car at all, or you might make a honey of a deal.

If you're arriving during the peak seasons of Christmas, Easter, or late summer vacation, absolutely *book your car in advance.* They are all accounted for during this period, and even if you can find a junker from a fly-by-night, the company will price-gouge you mercilessly. If you're going off peak, you stand a good chance of getting the car you want at the price you want. It's generally best to book ahead, but the majority of car compa-

nies have toll-free 800 numbers (listed below). At least call them for an opinion of your chances of getting a car upon your intended arrival.

Rates

If you pick up a car rental brochure at a travel agency, notice that the prices for Hawaii rentals are about the lowest in the country. The two rate options for renting are mileage and flat rate. A third type, mileage/minimum, is generally a bad idea unless you plan to do some heavy-duty driving. Mileage rate costs less per day, but you are charged for every mile driven. Mileage rates are best if you drive less than 30 miles per day—but even on an island that isn't much! The flat rate is best, providing a fixed daily rate and unlimited mileage. With either rate, you buy the gas; don't buy the cheapest because the poor performance from low octane eats up your savings.

Discounts of about 10-15% for weekend, weekly, and monthly rates are available. It's sometimes cheaper to rent a car for the week even if you're only going to use it for five days. Both weekly and monthly rates can be split between Neighbor Islands.

The average price of a subcompact standard shift, without a/c, is $30 per day, $120 per week (add about $10 per day, $60 per week for an automatic), but rates vary widely. Luxury cars are about $10 per day more, with a comparable weekly rate. Most of the car companies, local and national, offer special rates and deals. These deals fluctuate too rapidly to give any hard-and-fast information. They are common, however, so make sure to inquire. Also, peak periods have "blackouts" where normally good deals no longer apply.

Warning: If you keep your car beyond your contract, you'll be charged the highest daily rate unless you notify the rental agency beforehand. *Don't keep your car longer than the contract without notifying the company.* Companies are *quick* to send out their repossession specialists. You might find yourself in a situation with your car gone, a warrant issued for your arrest, and an extra charge on your bill. A simple courtesy call giving notification of your intentions saves a lot of headaches and hassle.

What Wheels to Rent

The super-cheap rates on the eye-catcher brochures refer to subcompact standard shifts.

The price goes up with the size of the car and with an automatic transmission. As with options on a new car, the more luxury, the more you pay. If you can drive a standard shift, get one! They're cheaper to rent and operate, and a standard shift gives you greater control. AM/FM radios are good to have for entertainment and for weather and surf conditions. If you have the choice, take a car with cloth seats instead of sticky vinyl. Air-conditioning is nice, especially if you plan on being in Lahaina a lot.

Maui's main highways are broad and well paved, just like major roads on the Mainland, but the back roads, where all the fun is, are narrow twisty affairs. You'll appreciate the downshifting ability of standard transmissions on curves and steep inclines. If you get a big fatso luxury car, it'll be great for "puttin' on the ritz" at the resort areas, but you'll feel like a hippopotamus in the backcountry. If you've got that much money to burn, rent two cars!

Insurance

Before signing your car rental agreement, you'll be offered "insurance" for around $10 per day. Since insurance is already built into the contract (don't expect the rental agency to point this out), what you're really buying is a waiver on the deductible ($500-1000), in case you crack up the car. If you have insurance at home, you will almost always have coverage on a rental car—including your normal deductible—although not all policies are the same, so check with your agent. Also, if you haven't bought the waiver, and you have a mishap, the rental agencies will put a claim against your major credit card on the spot for the amount of deductible, even if you can prove that your insurance will cover. They'll tell you to collect from your insurance company because they don't want to be left holding the bag on an across-the-waters claim. If you have a good policy with a small deductible, it's hardly worth paying the extra money for the waiver, but if your own policy is inadequate, buy the insurance. Also, most major credit cards offer complimentary car rental insurance as an incentive for using their cards to rent the car. Simply call the toll-free number of your credit card company to see if this service is included.

Driving Tips

Protect your children as you would at home with car seats. Their rental prices vary considerably:

Alamo offers them free of charge; National charges $3 per day; Hertz needs 48 hours notice; Dollar gives them free but they're not always available at all locations. Almost all the agencies can make arrangements if you give them enough notice. Check before you go and if all else fails, bring one from home.

In most cases, you'll get only one key for your rental car. Don't lock it in your car. If you do, call AAA or another auto emergency service if you have one and ask for assistance. Failing that, a local locksmith can open your car for a fee, or the rental car agency can send out a second key by taxi, but both of these options can get quite pricey.

The State Department of Transportation has installed over two dozen solar-powered emergency call boxes on Maui highways that are linked directly to the 911 emergency telephone number. These boxes are located along major roadways, on the Hana Hwy., the Haleakala Hwy., and on the road around the north end of the island in Kahakuloa.

There are few differences between driving in Hawaii and on the Mainland. Just remember that many people on the roads are tourists and can be confused about where they're going. Since many drivers are from somewhere else, there's hardly a "regular style" of driving in the islands. A farmer from Iowa accustomed to poking along on back roads can be sandwiched between a frenetic New Yorker who's trying to drive over his roof and a super-polite but horribly confused Japanese tourist who normally drives on the left.

In Hawaii, drivers don't honk their horns except to say hello, or in an emergency. It's considered rude, and honking to hurry someone might earn you a knuckle sandwich. Hawaiian drivers reflect the climate: they're relaxed and polite. Oftentimes, they'll brake to let you turn left when they're coming at you. They may assume you'll do the same, so be ready, after a perfunctory turn signal from another driver, for him or her to turn across your lane. The more rural the area, the more apt this is to happen.

It may seem like common sense, but remember to slow down when you enter the little towns strung along the circle-island route. It's easy to bomb along on the highway and flash through these towns, missing some of Hawaii's best scenery. Also, rural children expect *you* to be watchful, and will assume that you are going to stop for them when they dart out into the crosswalks.

The mile markers on back roads are great for pinpointing sites and beaches. The lower number on these signs is the highway number, so you can always make sure that you're on the right road.

B.Y.O. Car

If you want to bring your own car, write for information to: Director of Finance, Division of Licenses, 1455 S. Beretania St., Honolulu, HI 96814. However, unless you'll be in Hawaii for a bare minimum of six months and will spend all your time on one island, don't even think about it. It's an expensive proposition and takes time and plenty of arrangements. From California, the cost is at least $600 to Honolulu, and an additional $100 to any other island. To save on rental costs, it would be better to buy and sell a car in Hawaii, or to lease for an extended period.

Auto Rental Companies

The following are major firms that have booths at Kahului Airport—exit the arrival terminal and go to you right. Many pre-booked cars are waiting at these booths, but if not, and if you want to rent a car upon arrival, you must take a company shuttle to the yard across the airport parking lot to arrange for your car.

Dollar, tel. (808) 877-6526 or 667-2651 in Kahului, (808) 248-8237 in Hana, (800) 342-7398 statewide, or (800) 800-4000 worldwide, has an excellent reputation and very competitive prices. Dollar rents all kinds of cars as well as jeeps and convertibles for great weekly rates, and all major credit cards are accepted.

Alamo has good weekly rates, tel. (800) 327-9633 or (808) 871-6235 in Kahului, (808) 661-7181 in Kaanapali.

National Car Rental, tel. (808) 871-8851 or 667-9737 in Kaanapali, or (800) 227-7368 nationwide, has cars, vans, jeeps, and station wagons.

Avis, tel. (808) 871-7575 or 661-4588 Kaanapali, (800) 321-3712 nationwide, features late-model GM cars as well as most imports and convertibles.

Budget, tel. (808) 244-4721, (800) 451-3600 statewide, or nationwide (800) 527-0700, offers competitive rates on a variety of late-model cars.

Hertz, tel. (808) 877-5167 or (800) 654-3011 nationwide, perhaps the best known company, offers a wide variety of vehicles with some special weekly rates.

The following local companies are based in Hawaii and either have booths at the airport or pickup services through courtesy phones. **Word of Mouth Rent a Used Car,** at 150 Hana Hwy., tel. (808) 877-2436, (800) 533-5929, pickup van provided, offers some fantastic deals on their used, but not abused, cars. All cars, standard shift or automatic, can go for as little as $90 per week with a three-day minimum or $15.95 per day, but expect to spend $119 per week for a nice four-door a/c late model car. Office open 8 a.m.-5 p.m., but they will leave a car at the airport at earlier or later hours with prior arrangement. Others include: **Andres,** tel. (808) 877-5378; **Kihei Rent A Car,** tel. (808) 879-7257 or (800) 251-5288; **Regency,** tel. (808) 871-6147; **Wheels R Us,** tel. (808) 667-7751 or (808) 871-6858; and **Maui Cruisers,** tel. (808) 249-2319, who will put you in a car that will make you "look local."

Four Wheel Drive

Though much more expensive than cars, some people might feel safer in 4WDs for completely circling Maui or driving some roads in Upcountry. Also unlike cars, the rental companies offering 4WDs put no restrictions on driving past Oheo Gulch or around the backside of West Maui. Four-wheel vehicles can be obtained from **Maui Rent A Jeep,** tel. (808) 877-6626 or (800) 701-JEEP; **Wheels R Us; Kihei Rent A Car;** or **Island Riders,** tel. (808) 661-9966. **Dollar** and a few other of the "big boys" also rent 4WD jeeps. Rates vary from company to company, but are mostly around $70 per day, dependent on availability and length of rental.

Vanity Vehicles

If you feel like stepping out in *style,* consider renting a flashy sports cars. **Island Riders,** tel. (808) 661-9966 in Lahaina or (808) 874-0311 in Kihei, rents a Dodge Viper, Ferrari 348TS and

328GTS, Cobra, Porsche, and Corvette. These cars are classy but they're not cheap. However, for that one night of luxury, it may be worth it to you. Rates run from $199 for five hours to $349 for 24 hours. **The Toy Store,** tel. (808) 661-1212, across from Safeway in Lahaina, also has a variety of these fancy cars.

Motorcycles

A few companies also rent motorcycles for the intrepid traveler. Rental bikes are all Harley-Davidson big hogs or sportsters. Rates vary but run around $100 for half a day and $140-160 for 24 hours; longer rentals can be arranged. All drivers must be 21 years old, have a valid motorcycle license, and be in possession of a major credit card. Insurance is available. Companies want you to stay on good paved roads and don't usually allow trips to Hana. Although it is not required by state law to wear them, helmets are available. For riding one of these big steeds, contact **Mavrik Motorcycles Maui,** tel. (808) 871-7118, at 370 Dairy Rd. in Kahului; tel. (808) 891-2299, 1215 S. Kihei Rd. in Kihei; or tel. (808) 661-3099, 10-1 Halawai Dr. in Kaanapali. Also try **Island Riders,** tel. (808) 661-9966 in Lahaina or (808) 874-0311 in Kihei, or **The Toy Store,** tel. (808) 661-1212, on Honoapiilani Hwy. across from Safeway at the north end of Lahaina.

Mopeds

Just for running around town or to the beach mopeds are great. Expect to pay about $15 for two hours, $25 for eight hours, or $125 for the week. Check with **A & B Rentals and Sportswear,** in Honokowai at the Da Rose Mall, tel. (808) 669-0027; **Kukui Activity Center** at 1819 S. Kihei Rd., tel. (808) 875-1151; or **Wheels R Us,** tel. (808) 667-7751 in Lahaina or 871-6858 in Kahului.

ALTERNATIVE TRANSPORTATION

Shuttle Service

There is no public bus service on Maui, but numerous shuttle services operate from the Kahului Airport to South Maui and West Maui, between South Maui and West Maui, and within the resort developments of Kaanapali and Wailea.

Speedi Shuttle, tel. (808) 875-8070, connects Kihei and Wailea to the Kahului Airport

daily 5 a.m.-9 p.m. Pickup can be from any hotel or condo in the area. Use the telephone next to the information booth in the baggage claim area when at the airport. Rates are $16 for one up to $51 for 10 people.

Airporter Shuttle, tel. (808) 877-7308 or (800) 231-6984, operated by TransHawaiian, runs a regular service to and from Lahaina and Kaanapali, with pickup and dropoff in Honokowai and Kahana by reservation only. Shuttles make 15 runs a day, starting from the Kahului Airport at 9 a.m., with the last run from West Maui at 5 p.m. A courtesy phone and ticket booth are available at Kahului Airport next to the tourist information booth in the baggage area. Fares are $19 roundtrip, $13.50 from the airport to West Maui, and $7 from West Maui to the airport.

The free **Kaanapali Trolley** runs along the Kaanapali strip about every half hour 9 a.m.-6 p.m., stopping at all major resorts, the golf course, and the Whalers Village shopping complex. Look for the green jitneys. Pick up free printed tourist literature or ask at any hotel desk for the schedule.

Also free is the **Lahaina Express** shuttle, which runs 9 a.m.-10 p.m. connecting various stops in Lahaina to Kaanapali. The major pickup point in Lahaina is at the rear of the Wharf Cinema Center along Front Street.

The **Wailea Shuttle** is a complimentary jitney that stops at all major hotels and condos in Wailea, the Wailea Shopping Village, and golf and tennis courts in Wailea every 20-30 minutes. It operates 6:30 a.m.-8:30 p.m. Be sure to check with the driver about the last pickup times if you are out in the evening. For information on the schedule and stops, call (808) 879-2828.

The **West Maui Shopping Express** runs two routes, both from Lahaina, one to Kaanapali and the other to Kapalua. Stops include the hotels in Kapalua and Kaanapali, the Whalers Village shopping mall in Kaanapali, and the Wharf Shopping Center, Hilo Hattie, and the Lahaina Cannery Mall in Lahaina. Buses run about every hour from midmorning until midevening. Cost is $1 per person each way.

The **Whalers Village Shuttle,** called Maui Shopping Express, makes three shopping runs each day from hotels and condos in Makena, Wailea, and Kihei to the Whalers Village shopping mall in Kaanapali. The one-way fare is $15 adult, $5 for a child, but the return is free with a receipt from one of the shops or restaurants. Call (808) 877-7308 for exact pickup times and locations.

The old-style trolley-like bus, **"Da Mall" Trolley,** connects Wailea and Kihei to Kaahumanu Center, the Maui Mall, and Maui Marketplace in Kahului for your shopping pleasure. This trolley operates every day except Tuesday and Wednesday, and makes three runs each way each day: 9 a.m., 11 a.m., and 2 p.m. from the south, and 10:15 a.m., 12:15 p.m., and 5 p.m. from Kahului. The fare is $6 per person each way, but the return trip is free with a proof of purchase receipt from one of the stores in those malls. Call (000) 070-7108 for information.

For those riding the Sugar Cane Train, free transportation aboard the **Sugar Cane Trolley** is available from Front Street and the Lahaina Harbor to the Lahaina Station. Another trolley connects the Whalers Village shopping mall to the Kaanapali platform.

To get to and from the Maui Ocean Center from either Whalers Village in Kaanapali or a number of the hotels and condos in the Kihei/Wailea area, ride the center's shuttle, $7 roundtrip. Starting at the Maui Prince Hotel, this shuttle runs to the center three times a day each way, once at midmorning, the second in late morning, and the last at midafternoon. Call (808) 270-7000 or talk to your hotel concierge for the exact schedule.

Taxis
About two dozen taxi companies on Maui more or less operate in a fixed area. Most, besides providing normal taxi service, also run tours all over the island. While sedans predominate, some minivans are being used as well. Taxis are expensive and metered by the distance traveled. For example, a ride from Kahului Airport to Kaanapali is $55, to Kapalua $70, and to Wailea about $40. Expect $5-10 in and around town. In the Kihei/Wailea area try: **Yellow Cab of Maui,** tel. (808) 877-7000; **Wailea Taxi,** tel. (808) 874-5000; or **Kihei Taxi,** tel. (808) 879-3000. **Kahului Taxi Service,** tel. (808) 877-5681, operates in central Maui. In West Maui, options include **Alii Cab,** tel. (808) 661-3688; **AB Taxi,** tel. (808) 667-7575; and **Island Taxi,** tel. (808) 667-5656.

Classy Taxi operates between Lahaina and Kapalua, using renovated old cars from the '20s and '30s. A ride from Lahaina to Kaanapali will run about $7 and from there to Kapalua about $14.

For those who desire private limo service, there are several companies on the island that can fill the bill. These are expensive rides, however, and will run, for example, over $120 one-way from the Kahului Airport to Kaanapali. Ask your hotel concierge for assistance in arranging for this service.

Hitchhiking
The old tried-and-true method of hitchhiking—with thumb out, facing traffic, a smile on your interesting face—is "out" on Maui! It's illegal, and if a policeman sees you, you'll be hassled, if not outright arrested. You've got to play the game. Simply stand on the side of the road facing traffic with a smile on your interesting face, but put away the old thumb. In other words, you can't actively solicit a ride. People know what you're doing; just stand there. You can get around quite well by hitchhiking if you're not on a schedule. The success rate of getting a ride to the number of cars that go by isn't that great, but you will get picked up. Locals and the average tourist with family will generally pass you by. Recent residents and single tourists will most often pick you up, and 90% of the time these will be white males. Hitching short hops along the resort beaches is easy. People can tell by the way you're dressed that you're not going far and will give you a lift. Catching longer rides to Hana or up to Haleakala can be done, but it'll be tougher because the driver will know that you'll be with him or her for the duration of the ride. Women under no circumstances should hitch alone.

BY INTERISLAND FERRY

Molokai-Maui Interisland Ferry
From time to time, ferry companies have operated in Hawaii, but very stiff competition generated by the airline industry and the notoriously rough waters of the Hawaiian channels have combined to scuttle their opportunity for success. During the mid-1990s, the 118-foot *Maui Princess* had a regular schedule ferrying passengers between Lahaina and Kaunakakai, Molokai. Alas, it has ceased this service, but now operates several day and overnight tours to Molokai, so you can still get there by boat. For information and reservations call (808) 661-8397 or (800) 833-5800. Perhaps some-

day this ferry or a state-funded operation will once again take passengers by water between these two islands.

Lanai-Maui Interisland Ferry

A passenger ferry, *Expeditions,* now plies the waters between Lahaina and Manele Bay on Lanai. This shuttle service is not luxury travel but offers a speedy, efficient, and convenient transportation alternative to the Pineapple Island. You are allowed to take luggage free of charge, but there's an extra $10 fee for a bicycle. The one-hour crossing leaves Lahaina's public launch pier daily at 6:45 a.m., 9:15 a.m., 12:45 p.m., 3:15 p.m., and 5:45 p.m.; from Manele Bay at 8 a.m., 10:30 a.m., 2 p.m., 4:30 p.m., and 6:45 p.m.; adults pay $25 one-way, and children 2-11 pay $20. *Kama'aina* rates available. It is best to reserve your place. For information and reservations contact Expeditions, P.O. Box 10, Lahaina, HI 96767, tel. (800) 695-2624 or (808) 661-3756.

SIGHTSEEING TOURS

Tours are offered that will literally let you cover Maui from head to foot; you can drive it, sail around it, fly over it, or see it from below the water. Almost every major hotel has a tour desk from which you can book, and there are many private booking agencies that will do the same. Some of these are listed below.

Note: For ocean, bicycling, and hiking tours, see the "Sports and Recreation" section above.

Booking Agencies

Ocean Activities Center, tel. (808) 879-4485, is one of the biggest and perhaps the best agency for booking any and all kinds of activities on Maui. For much of the fun events like snorkeling, scuba diving, whalewatching, sunset cruises, and deep-sea fishing, the center has its own facilities and equipment, which means it not only provides you with an excellent outing, but offers very competitive prices. Ocean Activities can also book you on helicopters, parasails, and land tours, and rent and sell boogie boards, snorkel equipment, sailboards, and surfboards. It has sun and surf store/booking agencies in the Kihei/Wailea area at the Kea Lani Hotel,

Mana Kai Maui Resort, and Maui Hill Resort; the Lahaina Cannery Mall in Lahaina; and the Maui Marriott in Kaanapali. Ocean Activities also runs a boat from the beach at the Maui Prince Hotel to the underwater fantasy of Molokini Crater. Prices on all of their activities are very reasonable, and the service is excellent. If you had to choose one agency for all your fun needs, this would be a good bet.

Another very reputable outfit with two booking offices is **Barefoot's Cashback Tours,** tel. (808) 661-8889, Web site: www.tombarefoot.com, e-mail: barefoot@maui.net, which gives you up to a 10% discount on all your activities. It too can set you up with virtually any activity around the island. In Lahaina, it's at 834 Front St., tel. (808) 661-8889; in Kihei, go to 2395 S. Kihei Rd. in the Dolphin Plaza, tel. (808) 879-4100.

Activity Warehouse can provide the same service, often with last-minute reservations, and it also rents some ocean equipment. You can find Activity Warehouse in Lahaina, tel. (808) 667-4000, and in Kihei, tel. (808) 875-4000.

In Lahaina along Front Street try any of the **Fantasy Island Activities and Tours** kiosks or call (808) 667-9740. Also try the **Activities Information Center** in the Wharf Shopping Complex, tel. (808) 662-3100, or at 888 Wainee St. in Anchor Square, tel. (808) 667-7777. These are legitimate venders with solid reputations. You will, however, find a horde of other activities desks up and down Front Street; you don't have to search for them—they'll find you, especially to make an exhausting high-pressured pitch for time shares! Avoid them—unless you want to listen to the rap in exchange for your reduced ticket price.

One of the easiest ways to book an activity and sightsee at the same time is to walk along the Lahaina Wharf—there's an information booth here operated by many of the companies who rent slips at the harbor. Check it out first, and then plan to be there when the tour boats return. Asking the passengers, right on the spot, if they've had a good time is about the best you can do. You can also check out the boats and do some comparative pricing of your own.

For boats and a full range of activities out of quiet Maalaea Harbor, contact the **Maalaea Activity Center,** tel. (808) 242-6982. The center does it all, from helicopters to horseback, but specializes in the boats berthed at Maalaea.

Land Tours

It's easy to book tours to Maui's famous areas such as Lahaina, Hana, Iao Valley, and Haleakala. Normally they're run on either half- or full-day schedules (Hana is always a full day) and range anywhere from $30 to $110 with hotel pickup included. Big bus tours are run by **Roberts Hawaii,** tel. (808) 871-6226, (800) 831-5541 in Hawaii, or (888) 472-4729. These tours are quite antiseptic—you sit behind tinted glass in an air-conditioned bus. Smaller companies, with smaller tour buses and vans, also hit the high points but have specialty tours. Try **Ekahi Tours,** tel. (808) 572 9775; **Polynesian Adventure Tours,** tel. (808) 877-4242; and **Valley Isle Excursions,** tel. (808) 661-8687.

Temptation Tours, tel. (808) 887-8888, operates the ultimate in luxury van tours for the discriminating traveler. The deluxe vans, more like limousines, seat each of the eight passengers in a comfortable captain's chair for trips to Hana and Haleakala. This outfit offers two tours: either down to or back from Hana by helicopter, with the van making the connection for the reverse trip; or fly to and from Hana by small plane from where you tour the Hana area by van.

A twist on the tour business is offered by **Quality Motorcycle Tours,** tel. (808) 242-1015, also known as Ride Maui, who take you down the highway on two wheels. All bikes are Hondas. This company offers various day-long tours, or can customize one for you. One- and two-day overnight treks are also an option. The day starts about 8 a.m. and goes until about 6 p.m. Day rides are $200 single and $140 double, more for overnighters. Food, drinks, helmets, and all equipment are provided. You must have a motorcycle validation on your license and be at least 25 years old. A major credit card is used for reservation; book two weeks in advance. For more information, write P.O. Box 728, Wailuku, HI 96793 or see their Web site: www.ridemaui.com.

For those who desire a go-at-your-own pace alternative to van tours, yet want the convenience of an escort, **Best of Maui Cassette Tours** may be for you. Rent a quality tape describing the Hana Highway for $20. This rental comes with a cassette player, a small guidebook of sights, history, and legends, a route map, coupons for free water equipment rental, and a discount lunch. For $25, you get all of the above plus a free tour video of the entire island. Pick up your cassettes 6 a.m.-1 p.m.; reservations are appreciated. Call Best of Maui at (808) 871-1555 or stop by the office at 333 Dairy Rd., Kahului.

Offering roughly the same service for the same price is **Hana Cassette Guide,** tel. (808) 572-0550. Pick up your tape and all the extras at their booth at the Shell gas station along Dairy Road near Maui Marketplace in Kahului.

For a personalized tour down the Hana Hwy. where a guide drives your car and takes you to "local" places, try **Hana Road Adventures,** tel. (808) 877-4042.

Air Tours

Maui is a spectacular sight from the air. A few small charter airlines, a handful of helicopter companies, and a hang gliding outfit swoop you around the island. These joyrides are literally the highlight of many people's experiences on Maui, but they are expensive. The excursions vary, but expect to spend at least $100 for a basic half-hour tour. The most spectacular ones take you over Haleakala Crater, or perhaps to the remote West Maui Mountains, where inaccessible gorges lie at your feet. Other tours are civilized; expect a champagne brunch after you visit Hana. Still others take you to nearby Molokai to view some of the world's most spectacular sea cliffs and remote beaches. Know, however, that many hikers and trekkers have a beef with the air tours: after they've spent hours, or maybe days, hiking into remote valleys in search of peace and quiet, out of the sky comes the mechanical whir of a chopper to spoil the solitude.

For a Maui joyride out of Kahului Airport, contact **Paragon Air,** tel. (808) 244-3356. Paragon offers several different options, like a flight to Molokai with a tour of Kalaupapa for $199 or a flight to Molokai coupled with the mule ride down to Kalaupapa for $259. Others include a Big Island volcano tour for $275, and a six-island tour for $425.

For hang gliding and motorized hang gliding, contact **Hang Gliding Maui,** at (808) 572-6557. The motorized flight runs $150, the tandem hang gliding flight $250.

Want to try paragliding off Haleakala? Contact **Proflight Hawaii Paragliding** at (808) 874-5433. They'll set you up on a tandem flight with a certified instructor.

Helicopter Tours

Most companies use a six-seat A-STAR helicopter. Each is air-conditioned and has a window ventilation system. For all, tours are narrated over specially designed earphones, and some companies offer a video of your helicopter tour of Maui as a souvenir at the end of the flight for an extra $20. On certain flights the craft will touch down for a short interlude, and on some flights a complimentary lunch will be served. Most companies will make special arrangements to drop off and pick up campers in remote areas, or design a package especially for you. What is particularly attractive about helicopter rides is that you can sightsee from a perspective not possible from the ground and you can get close to areas not accessible by foot. There may be a tradeoff, however. Steep turns, quick descents, and unstable pockets of air can cause some riders to get airsick. Chopper companies are competitively priced, with tours of West or East Maui at around $100-125, with a Hana/Haleakala flight at about $135. Circle-island tours are approximately $200, but the best might be to include a trip to Molokai at approximately $180 in order to experience the world's tallest sea cliffs along the isolated windward coast.

All flights leave from the heliport at the back side of Kahului Airport—access off Haleakala Hwy. extension road. Each company has an office here where you check in, pay your money, and receive your pre-flight instructions. There is a parking lot here: free the first 15 minutes, $1 for 15-30 minutes, $1 each additional hour, maximum of $7 a day.

Alex Air, tel. (808) 871-0792 or (888) 418-8458, Web site: mauigateway.com/~alexair, is a small personable company that runs a tight ship. It offers a wide variety of flights on two types of helicopters, ranging from the West Maui special at $69 to the deluxe circle-island tour for $240.

Sunshine Helicopter, tel. (808) 871-0722 or (800) 544-2520, Web site: www.sunshinehelicopters.com, is another local, family-run outfit. It flies the "Black Beauties." The seating is two-by-two, and owner and chief pilot Ross Scott goes out of his way to give you a great ride over Maui.

Air Maui, tel. (808) 877-7005, seems to be the "little guy" but it tries hard to please. A family-owned company, Air Maui offers all the standards and can customize a tour for you.

Hawaii Helicopter, tel. (808) 877-3900 or (800) 994-9099 in Hawaii, Web site: www.hawaiiheli.com, is a statewide company. Its helicopters have plush interiors for your comfort, but may squeeze four people in the back, so the two middle ones don't always get a good view. The helicopters have two engines.

Blue Hawaiian Helicopters, tel. (808) 871-8844, Web site: www.bluehawaiian.com, operates on Maui and the Big Island. It's a company that does lots of advertising, gets a lot of passengers, and has done work for film companies.

Alex Air helicopter

ROBERT NILSEN

OTHER TOURS

The Sugar Cane Train

The old steam engine puffs along from Lahaina to Puukolii platform in Kaanapali pulling old-style open-air passenger cars through cane fields and the Kaanapali golf course. The six miles of narrow-gauge track are covered in 25 minutes (each way) and the cost roundtrip is $14 adult and $7.50 for children 3-12. A free double-decker bus shuttles between Lahaina Station and the waterfront and from the Whalers Village Shopping Center to the Kaanapali Station to accommodate the most popular tour on Maui. The train runs throughout the day 8:55 a.m.-4:40 p.m. It's very popular so book in advance—over 400,000 ride the train every year. All rides are narrated and there will be a singing conductor. It's not just great fun for children; everybody has a good time. All kinds of combination tours are offered as well: some feature lunch, a tour of Lahaina with admission into the Baldwin House and the *Carthaginian II,* and even a cruise on a glass-bottom boat. They're tame, touristy, and fun. The price is right. Contact the Lahaina Kaanapali and Pacific Railroad at (808) 661-0089, Web site: www.maui.net/~choochoo/sugrcane.html.

Ecotourism in Hawaii

Ecotourism is economically, culturally, socially, and environmentally sensitive and sustainable tourism that helps promote local communities and organizations and works in harmony with nature. Although small potatoes yet in the Hawaiian (and worldwide) tourism economy, ecotourism and its goals are growing in importance and will become a major factor in the economic vitality of tourism in the state. For more information on ecotourism in Hawaii, contact the Hawaii Ecotourism Association, P.O. Box 61435, Honolulu, HI 96839, tel. (808) 956-2866, Web site: www.planet-hawaii.com/hea, e-mail: hea@aloha.net. In addition, the following organizations also can provide related information and contacts: Ecotourism Society International, P.O. Box 755, North Bennington, VT 05257, tel. (802) 447-2121, fax 447-2122, Web site: www.ecotourism.org, e-mail: ecotsocy@iga.apc.org; and the Center For Responsible Travel, P.O. Box 827, San Anselmo, CA 94979, tel. (415) 258-6594.

The following is a partial list of organizations and companies, both public and private, that offer environmentally sound tours and outings on Maui.

Hawaii Audubon Society, 212 Merchant St., Suite 320, Honolulu, HI 96813, tel. (808) 528-1432 (hiking and birding)

Haleakala National Park, P.O. Box 369, Makawao, HI 96768, tel. (808) 572-9306, Web site: www.nps.gov/hale (hikes and talks)

Sierra Club, P.O. Box 2000, Kahului, HI 96732, Web site: www.hi.sierraclub.org (hikes and service trips)

Hike Maui, P.O. Box 000000, Kahului, HI 96790, tel. (808) 879-5270, Web site: www.hike-maui.com (hiking)

Island Explorations, P.O. Box I 107, Makawao, HI 96768, tel. (808) 572-8437 (snorkeling)

Mango Mitch Ecotours, P.O. Box 2511, Wailuku, HI 96793, tel. (808) 875-9106 or (800) 552-6541 (hiking, camping, ocean tours)

Paths to Paradise, P.O. Box 667, Makawao, HI 96768, tel. (808) 573-0094, Web site: www.maui.net/~corvusco (hiking)

Nancy Emerson's School of Surfing, P.O. Box 463, Lahaina, HI 96767, tel. (808) 874-1183, Web site: www.maui.net/~ncesurf/ncesurf.html (surfing)

SPECIAL NEEDS

Help for the Handicapped

A handicapped or physically disabled person can have a wonderful time in Hawaii; all that's needed is a little pre-planning. The following is general advice that should help your planning.

Commission on Persons with Disabilities

This commission was designed with the express purpose of aiding handicapped people. It is a source of invaluable information and distributes self-help booklets free of charge. Any handicapped person heading to Hawaii should write first or visit its offices on arrival. For the *Aloha Guide To Accessibility* ($3) write or visit the head office at: Commission on the Handicapped, 500 Ala Moana Blvd., Honolulu, HI 96813, tel. (808) 586-8121; on Maui, 54 High St., Wailuku, Maui, HI 96793, tel. (808) 243-5441; on Kauai, 3060 Eiwa St. #207, Lihue, Kauai, HI 96766, tel. (808)

241-3308; on Hawaii, P.O. Box 1641, Hilo, HI 96820, tel. (808) 933-7747.

General Information

The key for a smooth trip is to make as many arrangements ahead of time as possible. Tell the transportation companies and hotels you'll be dealing with the nature of your handicap in advance so that they can make arrangements to accommodate you. Bring your medical records and notify medical establishments of your arrival if you'll be needing their services. Travel with a friend or make arrangements for an aide on arrival (see below). Bring your own wheelchair if possible and let airlines know if it is battery-powered; boarding interisland carriers requires steps. No problem: They'll board you early on special lifts, but they must know that you're coming. Many hotels and restaurants accommodate disabled persons, but always call ahead just to make sure.

Maui Services

On arrival at Kahului Airport, parking spaces are directly in front of the main terminal. The restaurant here has steps, so food will be brought to you in the cocktail lounge. There are no special emergency medical services, but visitor information is available at (808) 872-3893. There is no centralized medical service, but Maui Memorial Hospital in Wailuku will refer, tel. (808) 244-9056. Getting around can be tough because there is vir-

tually no public transportation on Maui, and most tour operators do not accommodate nonambulatory persons. However, both Hertz and Avis rental cars can be fitted with hand controls (both right and left), but some restrict these controls to certain size or type vehicles. They generally require prior arrangements, one or two days at least, preferably when making your advanced reservation. Rates are comparable with or the same as for standard rental cars. A private special shuttle company operating all over the island is **Hawaii Care Van Shuttle,** tel. (808) 669-2300 in Lahaina. It takes wheelchair-bound persons. **Accessible Vans of Hawaii,** tel. (808) 879-5521 or (800) 303-3750, fax (808) 879-0649, rents wheelchair-lift-equipped vans on Oahu, Maui, and the Big Island for $109 a day or $560 a week. This is a full-service travel agency and a good source of information on traveling with disabilities. Valid, out-of-state, **handicapped parking placards** may be used throughout the state of Hawaii. A Hawaiian **handicapped parking permit** can be obtained from the county drivers' licensing section at the War Memorial Complex in Wailuku, tel. (808) 243-7793.

For medical support services, contact: **Maui Center for Independent Living,** tel. (808) 242-4966; **Action Medical Personnel,** tel. (808) 875-8300; **CareResourse Hawaii,** tel. (808) 871-2115; or **Interim Healthcare,** tel. (808) 877-2676. Medical equipment is available **Gammie Homecare,** tel. (808) 877-4032.

HEALTH AND CONDUCT

In a survey published by *Science Digest,* Hawaii was cited as the healthiest state in the U.S. in which to live. Indeed, Hawaiian citizens live longer than anywhere else in America: men to 76 years and women to 82. Lifestyle, heredity, and diet help with these figures, but Hawaii is still an oasis in the middle of the ocean, and germs just have a tougher time getting there. There are no cases of malaria, cholera, or yellow fever. Because of a strict quarantine law, rabies is also nonexistent. On the other hand, tooth decay, perhaps because of a wide use of sugar and the enzymes present in certain tropical fruits, is 30% above the national average. With the perfect weather, a multitude of fresh-air activities, soothing negative ionization from the sea, and a

generally relaxed and carefree lifestyle, everyone feels better there. Hawaii is just what the doctor ordered: a beautiful, natural health spa. That's one of its main drawing cards. The food and water are perfectly safe, and the air quality is the best in the country.

Handling the Sun

Don't become a victim of your own exuberance. People can't wait to strip down and lie on the sand like beached whales, but the tropical sun will burn you to a cinder if you're silly. The burning rays come through easier in Hawaii because of the sun's angle, and you don't feel them as much because there's always a cool breeze. The worst part of the day is 11 a.m.-3 p.m. You'll just have to force yourself to go slowly. Don't worry; you'll be able to flaunt your best souvenir, your golden Hawaiian tan, to your green-with-envy friends when you get home. It's better than showing them a boiled lobster body with peeling skin! If your skin is snowflake white, 15 minutes per side on the first day is plenty. Increase by 15-minute intervals every day, which will allow you a full hour per side by the fourth day. Have faith; this is enough to give you a deep golden, uniform tan.

Haole Rot

A peculiar condition caused by the sun is referred to locally as *haole* rot. It's called this because it supposedly affects only white people, but you'll notice some dark-skinned people with the same condition. Basically, the skin becomes mottled with white spots that refuse to tan. You get a blotchy effect, mostly on the shoulders and back. Dermatologists have a fancy name for it, and they'll give you a fancy prescription with a not-so-fancy price tag to cure it. It's common knowledge throughout the islands that Selsun Blue shampoo has some ingredient that stops the white mottling effect. Just wash your hair with it and then make sure to rub the lather over the affected areas, and it should clear up.

Bugs

Everyone, in varying degrees, has an aversion to vermin and creepy crawlers. Hawaii isn't infested with a wide variety, but it does have its share. Mosquitoes were unknown in the islands until their larvae stowed away in the water barrels of the *Wellington* in 1826 and were introduced at Lahaina. They bred in the tropical climate and rapidly spread to all the islands. They are a particular nuisance in the rainforests. Be prepared, and bring a natural repellent like citronella oil, available in most health stores on the islands, or a commercial product available in all groceries or drugstores. Campers will be happy to have mosquito coils to burn at night as well. Cockroaches are very democratic insects. They hassle all strata of society equally. They breed well in Hawaii and most hotels are at war with them, trying desperately to keep them from being spotted by guests. One comforting thought is that in Hawaii they aren't a sign of filth or dirty housekeeping. They love the climate like everyone else, and it's a real problem keeping them under control.

WATER SAFETY

Hawaii has one very sad claim to fame: more people drown here than anywhere else in the world. Moreover, there are dozens of yearly swimming victims with broken necks and backs or with injuries from scuba and snorkeling accidents. These statistics shouldn't keep you out of the sea, because it is indeed beautiful—benevolent in most cases—and a major reason to go to Hawaii. But if you're foolish, the sea will bounce you like a basketball and suck you away for good. The best remedy is to avoid situations you can't handle. Don't let anyone dare you into a situation that makes you uncomfortable. "Macho men" who know nothing about the power of the sea will be tumbled into Cabbage Patch dolls in short order. Ask lifeguards or beach attendants about conditions, and follow their advice. If local people refuse to go in, there's a good reason. Even experts get in trouble in Hawaiian waters. Some beaches, such as Waikiki, are as gentle as a lamb and you would have to tie an anchor around your neck to drown there. Others, especially on the north coasts during the winter months, are frothing giants.

While beachcombing, or especially when walking out on rocks, never turn your back to the sea. Be aware of undertows (the waves drawing back into the sea). They can knock you off your feet. Before entering the water, study it for rocks, breakers, reefs, and riptides. Riptides are powerful currents, like rivers in the sea, that can drag you out. Mostly they peter out not too far from shore, and you can often see their choppy waters on the surface. If caught in a "rip," don't fight to swim directly against it; you'll lose and only exhaust yourself. Swim diagonally across it, while going along with it, and try to stay parallel to the shore. Don't waste all your lung power yelling, and rest by floating.

When bodysurfing, never ride straight in; come to shore at a 45-degree angle. Remember, waves come in sets. Little ones can be followed by giants, so watch the action awhile instead of plunging right in. Standard procedure is to duck under a breaking wave. You can survive even thunderous oceans using this technique. Don't try to swim through a heavy froth and never turn your back and let it smash you. Don't swim alone if possible, and obey all warning signs. Hawaiians want to entertain you and they don't put up signs just to waste money. The last rule is, "If in doubt, stay out."

Yikes!

Sharks live in all the oceans of the world. Most mind their own business and stay away from shore. Hawaiian sharks are well fed—on fish—and don't usually bother with unsavory humans. If you encounter a shark, don't panic! Never thrash around because this will trigger their attack instinct. If they come close, scream loudly.

Portuguese man-of-wars put out long, floating tentacles that sting if they touch you. Don't wash the sting off with fresh water, as this will only aggravate it. Hot salt water will take away the sting, as will alcohol (the drinking or the rubbing kind), after-shave lotion, and meat tenderizer (MSG), which can be found in any supermarket or Chinese restaurant.

Coral can give you a nasty cut, and it's known for causing infections because it's a living organism. Wash the cut immediately and apply an antiseptic. Keep it clean and covered, and watch for infection.

Poisonous sea urchins, such as the lacquer-black *wana,* can be beautiful creatures. They are found in shallow tide pools and will hurt you if you step on them. Their spines will break off, enter your foot, and burn like blazes. There are cures. Vinegar and wine poured on the wound will stop the burning. If not available, the Hawaiian solution is urine. It might seem ignominious to have someone pee on your foot, but it'll put the fire out. The spines will disintegrate in a few days, and there are generally no long-term effects.

Hawaiian reefs also have their share of moray eels. These creatures are ferocious in appearance but will never initiate an attack. You'll have to poke around in their holes while snorkeling or scuba diving to get them to attack. Sometimes this is inadvertent on the diver's part, so be careful where you stick your hand while underwater.

HAWAIIAN FOLK MEDICINE AND CURES

Hawaiian folk medicine is well developed, and its cures for common ailments have been used effectively for centuries. Hawaiian *kahuna* were highly regarded for their medicinal skills, and Hawaiians were by far some of the healthiest people in the world until the coming of the Europeans. Many folk remedies and cures are used to this day and, what's more, they work. Many of the common plants and fruits that you'll encounter provide some of the best remedies. When roots and seeds and special exotic plants are used, the preparation of the medicine is as painstaking as in a modern pharmacy. These prescriptions are exact and take an expert to prepare. They should never be prepared or administered by an amateur.

This "denizen of the deep" is much more afraid of you than you are of him.

HOWARD LENDEMAN

KUKUI (CANDLENUT)

LOUISE FOOTE

Reaching heights of 80 feet, the *kukui* (candlenut) was a veritable department store to the Hawaiians, who made use of almost every part of this utilitarian giant. Used as a cure-all, its nuts, bark, or flowers were ground into potions and salves and taken as a general tonic, applied to ulcers and cuts as an effective antibiotic, or administered internally as a cure for constipation or asthma attacks. The bark was mixed with water and the resulting juice was used as a dye in tattooing, tapa-cloth making, and canoe painting, and as a preservative for fishnets. The oily nuts were burned as a light source in stone holders, and ground and eaten as a condiment called *inamona*. Polished nuts took on a beautiful sheen and were strung as lei. Lastly, the wood itself was hollowed into canoes and used as fishnet floats.

Common Curative Plants

Arrowroot, for diarrhea, is a powerful narcotic used in rituals and medicines. The pepper plant *(Piper methisticum)* is chewed and the juice is spat into a container for fermenting. Used as a medicine for urinary tract infections, rheumatism, and asthma, it also induces sleep and cures headaches. A poultice for wounds is made from the skins of ripe bananas. Peelings have a powerful antibiotic quality and contain vitamins A, B, and C, phosphorous, calcium, and iron. The nectar from the plant was fed to babies as a vitamin juice. Breadfruit sap is used for healing cuts and as a moisturizing lotion. Coconut is used to make moisturizing oil, and the juice was chewed, spat into the hand, and used as a shampoo. Guava is a source of vitamins A, B, and C. Hibiscus has been used as a laxative. *Kukui* nut oil makes a gargle for sore throats and a laxative, plus the flowers are used to cure diarrhea. *Noni*, an unappetizing hand-grenade-shaped fruit that you wouldn't want to eat unless you had to, reduces tumors, diabetes, and high blood pressure, and the juice is good for diarrhea. Sugarcane sweetent many concoctions, and the juice of toasted cane was a tonic for sick babies. Sweet potato is used as a tonic during pregnancy, and juiced as a gargle for phlegm. Tamarind is a natural laxative and contains the most acid and sugar of any fruit on earth. Taro has been used for lung infections and thrush, and as suppositories. Yams are good for coughs, vomiting, constipation, and appendicitis.

HOSPITALS AND PHARMACIES

Maui Memorial Hospital is located at 221 Mahaluni St., Wailuku, tel. (808) 244-9056. **Kihei-Wailea Medical Center**, 41 E. Lipoa St., Kihei, tel. (808) 874-8100 (near Star Market) offers a number of physicians in varying specialties and a laboratory; open Mon.-Fri. 8 a.m.- 8 p.m., Saturday and Sunday until 5 p.m.

There are several clinics around the island, including the following. Upstairs in the Dolphin Mall in Kihei are **Kihei Clinic and Wailea Medical Services,** tel. (808) 879-0114, open Mon.-Fri. 8 a.m.-7 p.m., Saturday until 6 p.m., and Sunday and holidays 9 a.m.-2 p.m. **Kaiser Permanente** has a clinic in Kihei in Azeka Place II, tel. (808) 891-3000, in Lahaina at 910 Wainee, tel. (808) 661-7400, and in Wailuku at 80 Mahalani St., tel. (808) 243-6000; open Mon.-Fri. 8 a.m.-5 p.m., closed noon-1 p.m., weekends, and holidays. In the center of Wailuku at 2180 Main St., try **Maui Medical Group,** tel. (808) 242-6464. The **West Maui Healthcare Center** maintains an office at the Whalers Village shopping mall, tel. (808) 667-9721; open 8 a.m.-10 p.m. daily.

Of the numerous drugstores throughout the island, the following should meet your needs: **Longs Drug** in Kihei, tel. (808) 879-2033, Lahaina, tel. (808) 667-4390, and Kahului, tel. (808) 877-0068.

ILLEGAL DRUGS

The use and availability of illegal, controlled, and recreational drugs are about the same in Hawaii as throughout the rest of America. Cocaine constitutes the fastest growing recreational drug, and it's available on the streets of the main cities, especially Honolulu. Although most dealers are small-time, the drug is brought in by organized crime. The underworld here is mostly populated by men of Asian descent, and recently the Japanese *yakuza* is said to be displaying a heightened involvement in Hawaiian organized crime. Cocaine trafficking fans out from Honolulu.

Another drug menace hitting the streets is "ice." Ice is smokable methamphetamine that will wire a user for up to 24 hours. The high lasts longer and the drug is cheaper than cocaine or its derivative, "crack." Users become quickly dependent, despondent, and violent because ice robs them of their sleep, along with their dignity. Its use is particularly prevalent among late-night workers. Many of the violent deaths in Honolulu have been linked to the growing use of ice.

However, the main drug available and commonly used in Hawaii is marijuana, which is locally called *pakalolo*. There are also three varieties of psychoactive mushrooms that contain the hallucinogen psilocybin. They grow wild, but are considered illegal, controlled substances.

Pakalolo Growing
About 30 years ago, mostly *haole* hippies from the Mainland began growing pot in the more remote sections of the islands, such as Puna on Hawaii and around Hana on Maui. They discovered what legitimate planters had known for 200 years: plant a broomstick in Hawaii, treat it right, and it'll grow. *Pakalolo,* after all, is a weed, and it grows in Hawaii like wildfire. The locals quickly got into the act when they realized that they, too, could grow a "money tree." As a matter of fact, they began resenting the *haole* usurpers, and a quiet and sometimes dangerous feud has been going on ever since. Much is made of the viciousness of the backcountry "growers" of Hawaii. There are tales of

booby traps and armed patrols guarding their plants in the hills, but mostly it's a cat-and-mouse game between the authorities and the growers. If you, as a tourist, are tramping about in the forest and happen upon someone's "patch," don't touch anything. Just back off and you'll be okay. Pot has the largest monetary turnover of any crop in the islands, and as such, is now considered a major source of agricultural revenue. There are all kinds of local names and varieties of pot in Hawaii, the most potent being "Kona Gold," "Puna Butter," and "Maui Wowie." These names are all becoming passe. It's possible that a dealer will approach you. Their normal technique is to stroll by, and in a barely audible whisper say, "Buds?"

Hawaiian *pakalolo* is sold slightly differently than on the Mainland. The dealers package it in heat-sealed "Seal-a-Meal" plastic bags. The glory days are over, and many deals, especially on the streets, are rip-offs. All passengers leaving Hawaii are subject to a thorough "agricultural inspection," and you can bet they're not only looking for illegal papayas. In 1984 there was an uproar involving a particular post office on the Big Island. It turned out that a staggering 80% of the outgoing packages contained *pakalolo*. The authorities are getting wise.

THEFT AND HASSLES

From the minute you sit behind the wheel of your rental car, you'll be warned not to leave valuables unattended and to lock up your car tighter than a drum. Signs warning about theft at most major tourist attractions help fuel your paranoia. Many hotel rooms offer coin-operated safes, so you can lock your valuables away and relax while getting sunburned. Stories abound about purse snatchings and surly locals just itching to give you a hard time. Well, they're all true to a degree, but Hawaii's reputation is much worse than the reality. In Hawaii you'll have to observe two golden laws: if you look for trouble, you'll find it; and, a fool and his camera are soon parted.

Theft
The majority of theft in Hawaii is of the "sneak thief" variety. If you leave your hotel door unlocked, a camera sitting on the seat of your rental car, or valuables on your beach towel, you'll be

inviting a very obliging thief to pad away with your stuff. You have to learn to take precautions, but they won't be anything like those employed in rougher areas like South America or Southeast Asia, just normal American precautions.

If you must walk alone at night, stay on the main streets in well-lit areas. Always lock your hotel door and windows and place valuable jewelry in the hotel safe. When you leave your hotel for the beach, there is absolutely no reason to carry all your traveler's checks and credit cards or a big wad of money. Just take what you'll need for drinks and lunch. If you're uptight about leaving money in your beach bag, stick it in your bathing suit or bikini. American money is just as negotiable if it is damp. Don't leave your camera or portable stereo on the beach unattended. Ask a person nearby to watch them for you while you go for a dip. Most people won't mind at all, and you can repay the favor.

While sightseeing in your shiny new rental car, which immediately brands you as a tourist, again, don't take more than what you'll need for the day. Why people leave a camera sitting on the seat of their car is a mystery! Many people lock valuables in the trunk, but remember that most good car thieves can jimmy it open as quickly as you can open it with your key. If you must, for some reason, leave camera or valuables in your car, lock them in the trunk, stash them under a seat back that's been reclined, or consider putting them under the hood. Thieves usually don't look there, and on most modern cars you can only pop the hood with a lever inside the car. It's not fail-safe, but it's worth a try.

Campers face special problems because their entire scene is open to thievery. Most campgrounds don't have any real security, but who, after all, wants to fence an old tent or a used sleeping bag? Many tents have zippers that can be secured with a small padlock. If you want to go trekking and are afraid to leave your gear in the campground, take a large green garbage bag with you. Transport your gear down the trail and then walk off through some thick brush. Put your gear in the garbage bag and bury it under leaves and other light camouflage. That's about as safe as you can be. You can also use a variation on this technique instead of leaving your valuables in your rental car.

Hassles

Another self-perpetuating myth about Hawaii is that "the natives are restless." An undeniable animosity exists between locals (especially those with some Hawaiian blood) and *haole*. Fortunately, this prejudice is directed mostly at the group and not at the individual. The locals are resentful of those *haole* who came, took their land, and relegated them to second-class citizenship. They realize that this is not the average tourist and they can tell what you are at a glance. Tourists usually are treated with understanding and are given a type of immunity. Besides, Hawaiians are still among the most friendly, giving, and understanding people on earth.

Haole who live in Hawaii might tell you stories of their children having trouble at school. They could even mention an unhappy situation at some schools called "beat-up-a-*haole*" day, and you might hear that if you're a *haole* it's not a matter of "if" you'll be beaten up, but "when." Truthfully, most of this depends upon your attitude and your sensitivity. The locals feel infringed upon, so don't fuel these feelings. If you're at a beach park and there is a group of local people in one area, don't crowd them. If you go into a local bar and you're the only one of your ethnic group in sight, you shouldn't have to be told to leave. Much of the hassle involves drinking. Booze brings out the worst prejudice on all sides. If you're invited to a beach party, and the local guys start getting drunk, make this your exit call. Don't wait until it's too late.

Most trouble seems to be directed toward white men. White women are mostly immune from being beaten up, but they have to beware of the violence of sexual abuse and rape. Although plenty of local women marry white men, it's not a good idea to try to pick up a local girl. If you're known in the area and have been properly introduced, that's another story. Also, women out for the night in bars or discos can be approached if they're not in the company of local guys. If you are with your bikini-clad girlfriend, and a bunch of local guys are, say, drinking beer at a beach park, don't go over and try to be friendly and ask, "What's up?" You, and especially your girlfriend, just might find out. Maintain your own dignity and self-respect by treating others with dignity and respect. Most times you'll reap what you sow.

WHAT TO TAKE

It's a snap to pack for a visit to Maui. Everything is on your side. The weather is moderate and uniform on the whole, and the style of dress is delightfully casual. The rule of thumb is to pack lightly: few items, and light clothing both in color and weight. What you'll need will depend largely on your itinerary and your desires. Are you drawn to the nightlife, the outdoors, or both? If you forget something at home, it won't be a disaster. You can buy everything you'll need in Hawaii. As a matter of fact, Hawaiian clothing, such as muumuu and aloha shirts, is one of the best purchases you can make, both in comfort and style. It's quite feasible to bring only one or two changes of clothing with the express purpose of outfitting yourself while there. Prices on bathing suits, bikinis, and summer wear in general are quite reasonable.

Matters of Taste

A grand conspiracy in Maui adhered to by everyone—tourist, traveler, and resident—is to "hang loose" and dress casually. Best of all, alohawear is just about all you'll need for comfort and virtually every occasion. The classic muumuu is large and billowy, and aloha shirts are made to be worn outside the pants. The best of both are made of cool cotton. Rayon is a natural fiber that isn't too bad, but polyester is hot, sticky, and not authentic. Not all muumuu are of the "tent persuasion." Some are very fashionable and form-fitted with peek-a-boo slits up the side, down the front, or around the back. *Holomuu* are muumuu fitted at the waist with a flowing skirt to the ankles. They are not only elegant, but perfect for "stepping out."

In the Cold and Rain

Two occasions for which you'll have to consider dressing warmly are visits to mountaintops and boat rides where wind and ocean sprays are a factor. You can conquer both with a jogging suit (sweat suit) and a featherweight, water-resistant windbreaker. If you intend to visit Haleakala, it'll be downright chilly. Your jogging suit with a hooded windbreaker/raincoat will do the trick for all occasions. If you're going to camp or trek, you should add another layer, a woolen sweater being one of the best. Wool is the only natural fiber that retains most of its warmth-giving properties even if it gets wet. Several varieties of "fleece" synthetics currently on the market also have this ability. If your hands get cold, put a pair of socks over them. Tropical rain showers can happen at any time so you might consider a fold-up umbrella, but the sun quickly breaks through and the warming winds blow.

Shoes

Dressing your feet is hardly a problem. You'll most often wear zoris (rubber thongs) for going to and from the beach, leather sandals for strolling and dining, and jogging shoes for trekking and sightseeing. A few discos require dress shoes, but it's hardly worth bringing them just for that. If you plan on heavy-duty trekking, you'll definitely want your hiking boots. Lava, especially a'a, is murderous on shoes. Most backcountry trails are rugged and muddy, and you'll need those good old lug soles for traction. If you plan moderate hikes, you might want to consider bringing rubberized ankle supports to complement your jogging shoes. Most drugstores sell them, and the best are a rubberized sock with toe and heel cut out.

Specialty Items

Following is a list of specialty items that you might consider bringing along. They're not necessities but most will definitely come in handy. A pair of binoculars really enhances sightseeing—great for viewing birds and sweeping panoramas, and almost a necessity if you're going whalewatching. A folding, Teflon-bottomed travel iron makes up for cotton's one major shortcoming, wrinkles; you can't always count on hotels to have irons. Nylon twine and miniature clothespins are handy for drying garments, especially bathing suits. Commercial and hotel laundromats abound, but many times you'll get by with hand-washing a few items in the sink. A transistor radio/tape recorder provides news, weather, and entertainment, and can be used to record impressions, island music, and a running commentary for your slide show. A hair dryer can be useful: although the wind can be relied upon to dry wet hair, it leaves a bit to be desired in the styling department. An inflatable raft for riding waves, along with flippers, mask, and snorkel, can easily be bought in Hawaii but don't weigh much or take up much space in your luggage. If you'll be camping, trekking, or boating with only seawater available for bathing, take along "Sea Saver Soap," available from good sporting goods stores. This special soap will lather in seawater and rinse away the sticky salt residue with it.

For the Camper

If you don't want to take it with you, all necessary camping gear can be purchased or rented while in Hawaii. Besides the above, you should consider taking the following: framed backpack or the convertible packs that turn into suitcases, daypack, matches in a waterproof container, all-purpose knife, mess kit, eating utensils, flashlight (remove batteries), candle, nylon cord, and sewing kit (dental floss works as thread). Take a first-aid kit containing Band-Aids, all-purpose antiseptic cream, alcohol swabs, tourniquet string, cotton balls, elastic bandage, razor blade, Telfa pads, and a small mirror for viewing private nooks and crannies. A light sleeping bag is good, although your fleecy jogging suit with a ground pad and light blanket or even your rain poncho will be sufficient. Definitely bring a down bag for Haleakala or mountainous areas. In a film container pack a few nails, safety pins, fishhooks, line, and bendable wire. Nothing else does what these do and they're all handy for a million and one uses.

Basic Necessities

As previously mentioned, you really have to consider only two "modes" of dressing in Hawaii: beachwear and casual clothing. The following is designed for the midrange traveler carrying one suitcase or a backpack. Remember that there are laundromats and that you'll be spending a considerable amount of time in your bathing suit. Consider the following: one or two pairs of light cotton slacks for going out and about, and one pair of jeans for trekking, or better yet, corduroys which can serve both purposes; two or three casual sundresses—muumuu are great; three or four pairs of shorts for beachwear and for sightseeing; four to five short-sleeved shirts or blouses and one long-sleeved; three or four colored and printed T-shirts that can be worn anytime from trekking to strolling; a beach cover-up—the short terrycloth type is the best; a brimmed hat for rain and sun—the crushable floppy type is great for purse or daypack, or pick up a straw or woven hat here for about $10; two or three pairs of socks are sufficient, nylons you won't need; two bathing suits (nylon ones dry quickest); plastic bags to hold wet bathing suits and laundry; five to six pairs of underwear; towels (optional, because hotels provide them, even for the beach); a first-aid kit—pocket-size is sufficient; suntan lotion and insect repellent; a daypack or large beach purse. And don't forget your windbreaker, perhaps a shawl for the evening, and an all-purpose jogging suit.

Pets and Quarantine

Hawaii has a very rigid pet quarantine policy designed to keep rabies and other Mainland diseases from reaching the state. All domestic pets are subject to **120 days' quarantine** (a 30-day quarantine is allowed by meeting certain pre-arrival and post-arrival requirements—inquire). Unless you are contemplating a move to Hawaii, it is not feasible to take pets. For complete information, contact the Department of Agriculture, Animal Quarantine Division, 99-951 Halawa Valley St., Aiea, HI 96701, tel. (808) 483-7151.

INFORMATION AND SERVICES

HAWAII VISITORS BUREAU OFFICES

The **HVB,** Web site: www.gohawaii.com, is a top-notch organization providing help and information to all of Hawaii's visitors. Anyone contemplating a trip to Hawaii should visit or write the HVB and inquire about any specific information that might be required. The advice and excellent brochures on virtually every facet of living, visiting, or simply enjoying Hawaii are free. The material offered is too voluminous to list, but for basics, request individual island brochures (including maps), and ask for copies of *Member Accommodation Guide,* and *Member Restaurant Guide.* Allow two to three weeks for requests to be answered.

HVB Offices Statewide

The best information on Maui is dispensed by the **Maui HVB,** 1727 Wili Pa Loop, Wailuku, HI

96793, tel. (808) 244-3530, Web site: www.visitmaui.com.

Statewide offices include: **HVB Administrative Office,** Waikiki Business Plaza, 2270 Kalakaua Ave., Suite 801, Honolulu, HI 96815, tel. (808) 923-1811; **Big Island HVB, Hilo Branch,** 250 Keawe St., Hilo, HI 96720, tel. (808) 961-5797; **Big Island, Kona Branch,** 75-5719 W. Ali'i Dr., Kailua-Kona, HI 96740, tel. (808) 329-7787; **Kauai HVB,** 3016 Umi St., Suite 207, Lihue, HI 96766, tel. (808) 245-3971.

North American Offices
HVB New York, Empire State Bldg., 350 5th Ave., Suite 1827, New York, NY 10018, tel. (212) 947-0717
HVB Washington D.C., 3975 University Dr., #335, Fairfax, VA 22030, tel. (703) 691-1800
HVB San Diego, 11835 Carmel Mountain Rd., #1304-353, San Diego, CA 92128, tel. (619) 485-7278
HVB Canada, c/o Comprehensive Travel, 1260 Hornby St., #104, Vancouver, BC V6Z1W2, tel. (604) 669-6691

European Office
HVB United Kingdom, P.O. Box 208, Sunbury on Thames, Middlesex, England, TW165RJ, tel. (181) 941-4009

Asia/Pacific Offices
HVB Japan, Kokusai Bldg., #2F, 1-1, Marunouchi 3-chome, Chiyoda-ku, Tokyo 100, tel. (3) 3201-0430
HVB Korea, c/o Travel Press, Inc., Samwon Bldg., 10th Floor, 112-5, Sokong-dong, Chung-gu, Seoul 100-070, tel. (2) 773-6719
HVB New Zealand, c/o Walshes World, 87 Queen St., 2nd Fl., Dingwall Bldg., Auckland, tel. (9) 379-3708
HVB Taiwan, c/o Federal Transportation Co., 8th Fl., 61 Nanking E. Road, Section 3, Taipei, tel. (2) 507-8133

Other Tourism-Related Sources
The state operates two **visitors' kiosks** at Kahului Airport, one in the center building upper level and the other in the baggage claim area of the arrival terminal. Both are open daily 6:30 a.m.-10 p.m., tel. (808) 872-3892, offering plenty of practical brochures and helpful information. Also, scattered around the arrival terminal lower level are numerous racks of free brochures, magazines, and other tourist literature.

LOCAL RESOURCES

To summon **police, fire, or ambulance** anywhere on Maui, dial **911.**

Civil Defense: In case of natural disaster such as hurricanes or tsunamis on Maui, call (808) 243-7721.

Coast Guard: tel. (800) 331-6176.

Sexual Assault Crisis Line: tel. (808) 242-4357.

For any legal problems or advice while on Maui, contact **Legal Aid Society,** tel. (808) 244-3731.

Aloha Pages, tel. (808) 244-8934, is a free 24-hour "talking telephone" information service on a variety of topics including weather, news, sports, community service, and entertainment. For specific information, dial the above number, followed by a four-digit code number as directed, or check your local Hawaiian phone book for a complete listing of available topics.

Weather and Marine Reports

For recorded information on **local island weather-er,** call (808) 877-5111; for the **marine report,** call (808) 877-3477; and for conditions on Haleakala, call (808) 571-5054.

Consumer Protection

If you encounter problems with accommodations, bad service, or downright rip-offs, try the following: **Maui Chamber of Commerce,** 250 Ala Maha, Kahului, tel. (808) 871-7711; the Office of Consumer Protection, tel. (808) 984-8244; or the Better Business Bureau (Oahu), tel. (808) 941-5222.

Post Offices

Branch post offices are found in most major towns. Window service is offered Mon.-Fri. 8:30 a.m.-4 p.m.; some offices are open Saturday 10 a.m.-noon. The following are the main offices: Wailuku, tel. (808) 244-4815; Kahului, tel. (808) 871-4710; Kihei, tel. (808) 879-2403; Lahaina at the Lahaina Shopping Center, tel. (808) 661-0550; Lahaina at the Civic Center, tel. (808) 667-6611.

Laundromats

Laundromats are located in sizable towns on Maui, in Lanai City, and in Kaunakakai on Molokai. Hours are generally early morning to early evening. Some are a bit run-down, but several new laundromats have been built recently with the best machines. You'll find prices here about the same as on the Mainland, with a load of wash running $1.75 and 25 cents for about 10 minutes in a dryer. Little boxes of laundry soap go for 75 cents, and there is usually a change machine in the establishment. All machines take quarters only. Try **W & F Washerette,** 125 S. Wakea in Kahului, tel. (808) 877-0353; **Lipoa Laundry Center,** 41 E. Lipoa in Kihei, tel. (808) 875-9266; **Kwick N Kleen,** 845 Wainee in Lahaina, tel. (808) 661-7949; and **Kahana Koin-Op Laundromat,** in the Kahana Gateway Center, tel. (808) 669-1587.

Storage

While there are no storage lockers at the Kahului Airport, there is a baggage storage room. Open 6 a.m.-9:45 p.m., rates are $2, $5, or $10 per item, per day, depending upon the size. Payment in U.S. currency only. No perishables.

For guests of the Northshore Inn and Banana Bungalow in Wailuku, an alternative is to use the on-site storage rooms for everything from backpacks to surfboards and bicycles.

Reading Material

Free tourist literature is well done and loaded with tips, discounts, maps, happenings, etc. Found in hotels, restaurants, and street stands, they include: *This Week Maui* and *Guide to Maui,* weekly; *Maui Gold* and *Maui Magazine,* one for each season; and the monthly *Today Magazine* and *Pleasant Hawaii Magazine.* The weekly *Drive Guide,* with excellent maps and tips, is given out free by all car rental agencies. Both *Menu* and *Maui Menus* are all about food.

Both the *Honolulu Advertiser* and *Honolulu Star Bulletin* are available on Maui for 75 cents apiece. Aside from these two big Honolulu newspapers, local papers available on Maui include the *Maui News,* published Mon.-Fri., which has a good "Datebook" listing of local events. *Lahaina News* is a community paper of news, feature stories, and entertainment listings; 25 cents. It's a daily, as is the free *Maui Times.* The *South Maui Weekly* and *Haleakala Times* are weeklies, and *Gold Coast* and *MauiAina* are seasonal.

The main branch of the **library** is at 251 High St., Wailuku, tel. (808) 243-5945; other branches are in Kahului, Lahaina, Makawao, Kihei, and Hana. The libraries hold a hodgepodge of hours through the week and are usually closed Friday or Saturday.

OTHER INFORMATION

Telephone: All-Hawaii Area Code 808

Local calls from public telephones (anywhere on the same island is a local call) cost 25 cents. Calls from hotels, on the other hand, will usually result in a charge of up to 85 cents per call on your bill. Calling between islands is a long-distance toll call, and the price depends on when and from where you call and for how long you speak. Emergency calls are always free. As they do everywhere else in the U.S., long-distance rates go down at 5 p.m. and again at 11 p.m. until 8 a.m. the next morning. From Friday at 5 p.m. until Monday morning at 8 a.m. rates are cheapest. For directory assistance: local, 1-411; interisland, 1-555-1212; Mainland, 1-area code-555-1212; toll free 1-800-555-1212.

Time Zones

There is no daylight saving time in Hawaii. When daylight saving time is not observed on the Mainland, Hawaii is two hours behind the West Coast, four hours behind the Midwest, five hours behind the East Coast, and 11 hours behind Germany. Hawaii, being just east of the international date line, is almost a full day behind most Asian and Oceanic cities. Hours behind these countries and cities are: Japan, 19 hours; Singapore, 18 hours; Sydney, 20 hours; New Zealand, 22 hours; Fiji, 22 hours.

Electricity

The same electrical current is in use in Hawaii as on the U.S. Mainland and is uniform throughout the islands. The system functions on 110 volts, 60 cycles of alternating current (AC). Appliances from Japan will work, but there is some danger of burnout, while those requiring the normal European voltage of 220 will not work.

Distance, Weights, and Measures

Hawaii, like all of the U.S., employs the "English method" of measuring weights and distances. Basically, dry weights are in ounces and pounds; liquid measures are in ounces, quarts, and gallons; and distances are measured in inches, feet, yards, and miles. The metric system, based on units of 10, is known but is not in general use. The conversion chart at the back of the book should be helpful.

Island Radio

More than a dozen radio stations broadcast on Maui. Popular ones: KHPR 88.1 FM broadcasts from Honolulu and is the island's public radio station; KQMQ 93.1 FM plays Top 40 songs; KPOA 93.5 FM out of Lahaina does a mix of contemporary Hawaiian and standard rock; for easy listening tune to KUMU 94.7 FM; the format on KAOI 95.1 FM in Wailuku is mostly adult rock with a request line, and KAOI 1110 AM does news, talk, and sports; broadcasting from Honolulu, KRTR 96.3 FM and KPOI 97.5 FM both play rock and roll.

Maui Facts

Maui is the second youngest and second largest Hawaiian island after Hawaii. Its nickname is the Valley Island. Its color is pink and its flower is the *lokelani,* a small rose.

MONEY AND FINANCES

Currency

U.S. currency is among the drabbest in the world. It's all the same size and color; those unfamiliar with it should spend some time getting acquainted so that they don't make costly mistakes. U.S. coinage in use is: one cent, five cents, 10 cents, 25 cents, 50 cents, and $1 (uncommon); paper currency is $1, $2 (uncommon), $5, $10, $20, $50, $100. Bills larger than $100 are not in common usage.

Banks

Full-service banks tend to open slightly earlier than Mainland banks, at 8:30 a.m. Mon.-Fri., closing at 3 p.m., except for late hours on Friday when most banks remain open until 6 p.m. Of most value to travelers, banks sell and cash traveler's checks, give cash advances on credit cards, exchange and sell foreign currency, and have 24-hour ATM machines. Major banks on Maui are American Savings Bank, Bank of Hawaii, and First Hawaiian Bank. All have branches in Kahului, Wailuku, Kihei, Lahaina, and Pukalani. First Hawaiian has a branch in Napili, and Bank of Hawaii also has offices in Kahana, Paia, and Hana.

Traveler's Checks

Traveler's checks are accepted throughout Hawaii at hotels, restaurants, and car rental agencies, and in most stores and shops. However, to be readily acceptable they should be in American currency. Some larger hotels that often have Japanese and Canadians guests will accept their currency. Banks accept foreign-currency traveler's checks, but it'll mean an extra trip and inconvenience. It's best to get most of your traveler's checks in $20-50 denominations; anything larger will be hard to cash in shops and boutiques, though not in hotels.

Credit Cards

More and more business is transacted in Hawaii using credit cards. Almost every form of accommodation, shop, restaurant, and amusement accepts them. For renting a car they're almost a must. With "credit card insurance" readily available, they're as safe as traveler's checks and sometimes even more convenient. However, don't rely on them completely because some establishments won't accept them, or perhaps won't accept the kind that you carry.

tree fern

CENTRAL MAUI: THE ISTHMUS

KAHULUI

It is generally believed that Kahului means "The Winning," but perhaps it should be "The Survivor." Kahului suffered attack by Kamehameha I in the 1790s, when he landed his war canoes here in preparation for battle at Iao Valley. In 1900 it was purposely burned to thwart the plague, then rebuilt. Combined with Wailuku, the county seat just down the road, this area is home to 53,000 Mauians, nearly one-half the island population. Here's where the people live. It's a practical, homey town, the only deep-water port from which Maui's sugar and pineapples are shipped. Although Kahului was an established sugar town by 1880, it's really only grown up in the last 20 years. In the 1960s, Hawaiian Commercial and Sugar Co. began building low-cost housing for its workers, which became a model development for the whole of the U.S. Most people land at the airport, blast through for Lahaina or Kihei, and never give Kahului a second look. It's in no way a resort community, but it has the best general-purpose shopping on the island, a few noteworthy sites, and a convenient location to the airport.

SIGHTS

Kanaha Pond State Wildlife Sanctuary
This one-time royal fishpond is located between downtown and the airport at the junctions of Routes 36 and 38. It's on the migratory route of various ducks and Canada geese, but most importantly it's home to the endangered Hawaiian stilt *(ae'o)* and the Hawaiian coot *(alae ke'oke'o).* The stilt is a slender, 16-inch bird with a black back, white belly, and stick-like pink legs. The coot is a gray-black ducklike bird that builds large floating nests. An observation pavilion is maintained on the south edge of the pond, accessed by a short walkway from a small parking area. The observation stand is always open and free of charge. Bring binoculars.

Maui Community College
Just across the street from the Kaahumanu Center on Route 32, the college is a good place to check out the many bulletin boards for various activities,

items for sale, and cheaper long-term housing. The **Student Center** is conspicuous as you drive in, and is a good place to get most information. The library is adequate.

War Memorial

At the corner of Kaahumanu and Kanaloa Avenues is **Wailuku War Memorial Park and Center.** Here you'll find a football stadium, baseball field, gymnasium, swimming pool, tennis courts, track, and free hot showers. After years of being played at the Aloha Stadium in Honolulu, the college all-star Hula Bowl now takes place at the War Memorial Stadium and is scheduled to be played there at least until 2002. To the left, at the entrance to the gym, you can pick up county camping permits.

Going up the hill from there you'll find Baldwin High School, followed by the Aloha Bowling Center and Stillwell's Bakery. Toward the ocean are the new Kapiolani Park and the Maui Arts and Cultural Center, the new center of cultural activity, education, and entertainment for the island.

Hawaiian stilt

Alexander and Baldwin Sugar Mill Museum

The museum is located at the intersection of Puunene Ave. (Rt. 350) and Hanson Rd., about one-half mile from Dairy Rd. (Rt. 380), tel. (808) 871-8058. Hours are Mon.-Sat. 9:30 a.m.-4:30 p.m.; admission is $4 adults, $2 children, ages five and under admitted free. (Avoid the area around 3 p.m. when the still-working mill changes shifts.) This small but highly informative museum could easily be your first stop after arriving at Kahului Airport only 15 minutes away, especially if you're heading to Kihei. Once you get off the plane, you'll realize that you're in the midst of sugarcane fields. If you want to know the history of this crop and the people who worked and developed it, visit the museum. The vintage museum building was the home of the sugar mill supervisor, who literally lived surrounded by his work. Inside is a small but well-stocked bookstore and gift shop featuring Hawaiiana and handmade clothing and artifacts, with goodies like guava and coconut syrups and raw sugar.

As you begin your tour, notice the ancient refrigerator in the corner that the staff still uses. In the first room, you are given a brief description of the natural history of Maui, along with a rendition of the legends of the demigod Maui. Display cases explain Maui's rainfall and use of irrigation for a productive sugarcane yield. There is an old-fashioned copper rain gauge along with pragmatic artifacts from the building of the Haiku Ditch. A collection of vintage photos features the Baldwin and Alexander families, while a historical plaque recalls when workers lived in ethnic camps, each with its own euphemistic name (Chinese at Ah Fong, Japanese at Nashiwa, Portuguese at Cod Fish). This setup was designed to discourage competition (or cooperation) between the ethnic groups during labor disputes, and to ease the transition to the new land. These people are represented by everything from stuffed fighting cocks to baseball mitts from the '30s. Included is an educational video on the various methods of sugarcane production, and scale models show just how selected machinery works. The museum is in the shadow of the state's largest sugar mill, and you can hear the wheels turning and the mill grinding. It's not an antiseptic remembrance, but a vital one where the history still continues. No tours are given of the mill.

Kanaha Beach County Park

This is the only beach worth visiting in the area. Good for a swim and a picnic, the broad beach here is flanked by plenty of trees so you can get out of the sun. In this strip of trees are picnic tables, barbecue pits, bathrooms, and a pavilion. This beach is used by one of the outrigger canoe clubs on the island, and you'll see their canoes drawn up on shore when they're not out on the water practicing their strokes. It's also *the* best place to learn sailboarding. Rent your board in town. The wind is steady but not too strong, and the wave action is gentle. Many sailboard instructors bring their students here. From Kaahumanu Avenue or the Hana Highway, turn onto Hobron Avenue, and then immediately right onto Amala Street, and follow the signs to the park. Alternately, follow Route 38 to the airport. Swing back around and turn right on Ka'a Street. Pass the rental car agencies and carry on to Hobron. There are two entrances to the park and plenty of parking. The only drawback might be the frequent and noisy arrivals and departures of aircraft at the airport, which is only a few hundred yards away.

ACCOMMODATIONS

Kahului features three motel/hotels because most people are short-term visitors, heading to or from the airport. These accommodations are all bunched together next to Hoaloha Park on the harbor side of Kaahumanu Ave. (Rt. 32). The **Maui Beach Hotel,** tel. (808) 877-0051, and just across a parking lot, its sister hotel, **The Maui Palms,** tel. (808) 877-0071, are both Castle Resort and Hotel properties. On the lobby level of the Maui Beach are the front desk, small gift shop, and the Red Dragon Chinese restaurant. The Maui Beach has a pool on the second floor, open 9 a.m.-9 p.m. daily, and its daily buffets at the Rainbow Dining Room are good value. Cocktails and *pu pu* are served at the Rainbow Lounge near the dining room from 5 p.m. The central courtyard off the main foyer leads down to the narrow beach. The Maui Beach is more like a standard hotel—with a Polynesian-style roof over its lobby—while the Maui Palms has more the feel of an economical motel. Both are low-rise affairs. Rates for the Maui Beach are $93-115 for its standard to oceanfront rooms,

and $180 for an oceanfront suite. At the Maui Palms, these rates are $60-80 for the standard to deluxe rooms. Both offer the sixth night free or a free one-day rental car package. During a reconstruction phase at the Maui Palms, check-in will be handled at the Maui Beach Hotel. For reservations, call (800) 367-5004, interisland (800) 272-5275. These hotels offer a complimentary shuttle to the airport every half hour 6:30 a.m.-9 p.m.; reservations required.

The one other hotel, 100 yards to the east, is the **Maui Seaside,** tel. (808) 877-3311 or (800) 560-5552, Web site: www.sand-seaside.com, e-mail: sandsea@aloha.net, part of the Sand and Seaside Hotels, a small island-owned chain. Friendly and economical, this too is a low-rise fa-

WAILUKU-KAHULUI OVERVIEW

*(Map labels, reading across:)* PACIFIC OCEAN; Kahului Bay; KAHANA BEACH PARK; KAHULUI AIRPORT; To Hana, Paia; ALAHOO ST.; MAUI ARTS AND CULTURE CENTER; Kahului Harbor; AMALA ST.; KAHANA POND STATE WILDLIFE SANCTUARY; TERMINAL; EEHIA ST.; HOBRON AVE.; MAUI COMMUNITY COLLEGE; KAHULUI BEACH RD.; KAHULUI SHOPPING CENTER; 32B; 32A; MAUI MALL; KEOLANI; PAPALAHA RD.; HEMALOA ST. EXTENSION; KALA RD.; HELIPORT; FENA ST.; 36; 3400; 32; KAAHUMANU SHOPPING CENTER; KANA AVE.; COUNTY FAIRGROUNDS; POST OFFICE; 380; HALEAKALA HWY.; KAHULUI; KAMEHAMEHA; KAMAAINA ST.; ALAMAHA PL. RD.; HANA HWY.; HALEAKALA HWY.; 37; To Haleakala; ONEHEE AVE.; WAKEA AVE.; PUUNENE; LAIO PL. RD.; DAIRY RD.; 36; KAM AVE.; LANI AVE.; HINA AVE.; LAAU AVE.; MAUI MARKETPLACE; MOLOKAI HEMA AVE.; W. PAPA AVE.; 3500; KUIHELANI HWY.; SPANISH RD.; A & B SUGAR MILL MUSEUM; CENTRAL BOX PLANT RD.; HANSEN; 311; MCGERROW RD.; To Kihei; SUGAR MILL; To Lahaina; 380; 0 0.5 mi; 0 0.5 km

© J.D. BISIGNANI AND MOON PUBLICATIONS, INC.

cility with a swimming pool in the central courtyard, access to the beach, a guest activities desk, a lobby lounge, and Vi's Restaurant. All rooms hold two double beds or a king, have color TV, a small refrigerator, ceiling fan, and air-conditioning. Some kitchenettes are available. Rates are $80-140 or $110-170 with rental car. For central reservations, call (800) 367-7000.

FOOD

The Kahului area has some elegant dining spots as well as an assortment of inexpensive yet good eating establishments. Many are found in the shopping malls. Here are some of the best.

Inexpensive

Several basic restaurants and other food purveyors are located along Dairy Road. **Ma Chan's**, tel. (808) 877-7818, is a cement-floored, no-atmosphere restaurant at 199 Dairy Rd., located in the fading pink-on-green Maui Plantation Shops. Open daily for breakfast and lunch until 6 p.m., Ma Chan's has a variety of inexpensive sandwiches, burgers, and plate lunches, all with an island twist. The restaurant is a little worse for wear, but the staff is very friendly, and the food is very good.

Maui Bakery Bagelry and Deli, almost next door at 201 Dairy Rd., tel. (808) 871-4825, open daily 6:30 a.m.-5:30 p.m., makes fresh (preservative-, fat-, and cholesterol-free) rye, blueberry, whole wheat, garlic, poppy seed, sesame, and

© J.D. BISIGNANI AND MOON PUBLICATIONS, INC.

onion bagels. Choose a buttered bagel or one smothered with a layer of cream cheese and have it wrapped to go, or eat it at one of the tables. Or try a tasty deli sandwich, served on a bagel, French bread, or rye. The bakery also makes mouthwatering cinnamon and walnut coffee cake, fudge brownies, strudel, and loaves of French, rye, and whole wheat bread. A deli case also holds a variety of drinks and flavored cream cheese.

If you're looking for a wholesome, natural deli item, fresh salad, or freshly baked pastry try the deli counter at **Down to Earth Natural Foods,** 305 Dairy Road, tel. (808) 877-2661. It's open daily; as it's a full-service grocery store, you can also shop for all your food items here.

At the Dairy Center just up the road, you'll find the inexpensive eateries **Local Boys** for Hawaiian plate lunches, **Koko Ichiban-ya** for Japanese-inspired plate lunches, and **Piñata's** Mexican restaurant.

At 444 Dairy Road is **Maui Coffee Roasters,** tel. (808) 877-2877, for those who want a hot brew now or want take-home beans. Other drinks, sandwiches, soups, salads, veggie burgers, and baked goods are also available in this good-time, upscale, yuppie-ish place. Right next door is **Connoisseur Food and Wine.** All that its name implies, it handles high and wine, vinegar, cheese, pasta, spices, other foods, and a big selection of cigars.

Follow your nose in the Kaahumanu Shopping Center to **The Coffee Store,** tel. (808) 871-6860, open daily 7 a.m.-6 p.m., till 9 p.m. on Thursday and Friday, and Sunday 9 a.m.-3 p.m. Light lunches include savories like a hot croissant or a spinach roll pastry puff. Coffee by the cup is under $2.25, refills 35 cents. The coffees, roasted on the premises, are from over 20 gourmet varieties handpicked in Africa, South America, Indonesia, and of course Hawaii, and include exotic beans like Jamaican Blue Mountain. Gifts and giftwear too!

The **Maui Mall,** off of Puunene Ave., has a terrific selection of inexpensive eateries. **Matsu Restaurant** is a fast-food Japanese restaurant with an assortment of daily specials for under $6, or a steaming bowl of various types of saimin for $5. Very authentic, like a *soba-ya* in Japan. Japanese standards include *katsu don buri,* tempura, or curry rice. Adjacent is **Siu's Chinese Kitchen,** where most of their typical Chinese

dishes are under $5. **Stanton's,** tel. (808) 877-3711, is another gourmet coffee, food gift, and tobacco shop that offers a commodious setting for sipping fresh-brewed coffee and eating gourmet sandwiches. A good place for an inexpensive lunch with some atmosphere. **Luigi's Pasta and Pizzeria** serves up decent Italian food, and **SW Bar-B-Q** is a terrific indoor/outdoor fast food restaurant with Korean favorites, plate lunches under $5, and a delicious grilled chicken sandwich.

Around back at the Maui Mall is the **Wayfinders Cafe,** tel. (808) 877-8670, where you can have health-conscious food and drinks while you spend time on the Internet, send e-mail, or just play on the computer.

Others worth trying include **Shirley's Drive In** and **Dairy Queen,** near each other on Lono Avenue. Both serve good and inexpensive plate lunches and sandwiches, and Shirley's is open early mornings.

Finally, for those who need their weekly fix of something fried and wrapped in Styrofoam, Kahului's streets behind Maui Mall are dotted with McDonald's, Pizza Hut, Burger King, Taco Bell, Jack-in-the-Box, KFC, and other fast-food restaurants. Other fast-food outlets can be found in the food courts at Maui Marketplace and Kaahumanu Center.

Moderate

The Maui Beach Hotel's **Rainbow Dining Room** serves food in the second-floor dining room. You can fill up here at the breakfast buffet 7-9:30 a.m. for $8.75 or at the lunch buffet 11 a.m.-2 p.m. for $10.75. Order off the menu for dinner or choose the Japanese Imperial dinner buffet 5:30-8:30 p.m. for $18.75. On the lobby level, dine Wed.-Sun. 5:30-8:30 p.m. at the **Red Dragon Restaurant.** Featured is an all-you-can-eat buffet, $16 per person, where many of the dishes change nightly.

Vi's Restaurant, tel. (808) 871-6494, at the Maui Seaside Hotel, serves a standard American fare breakfast 7-9 a.m. for $5 or less and dinner 6-8 p.m. for $8-12. Vi's offers over 20 dinners, and breakfasts include omelettes, hotcakes, and other island favorites.

In the Kahului Shopping Center you'll find **Ichiban,** an authentic and inexpensive Japanese restaurant, tel. (808) 871-6977, open daily except Sunday 6:30 a.m.-2 p.m., dinner 5-9 p.m., featuring full and continental breakfast, along with Japanese, American, and local specialties. Much of the breakfast menu is typically American, like eggs and bacon, omelettes, and pancakes, most around $6. The lunch menu includes teriyaki chicken or shrimp tempura, chicken cutlet, *don buri* dishes, a variety of *udon,* and basic noodles, most under $7. Sandwiches are everything from a BLT to baked ham. Dinner features combination plates, with your choice of any two items like shrimp and vegetable tempura, sashimi, or teriyaki chicken for around $12, along with more expensive special combinations like steak and lobster, the most expensive item on the menu. The interior is basic American with a pinch of Japanese.

At the back of Kahului Shopping Center is the **Asain Sports Bar,** tel. (808) 877-7776. Open for lunch and dinner, this place serves Japanese and Korean food. For lunch, try the lunch box for $5.95, or the tempura *soba* or Bul Go Ki plate, both for $5.50. The dinner menu is a bit more extensive with items from barbecued chicken at $6.95 to sukiyaki for $16.95.

Another sports bar of sorts is **Koho Grill and Bar,** tel. (808) 877-5588, at the Kaahumanu Shopping Center. Koho combines appetizers and salads with burgers, plate lunches, a few Mexican and Italian dishes, plus fish and standard American meat entrees. It's an easygoing, good-time place, but not necessarily quiet when the big games are broadcast on the large screen TV in the bar.

At the corner of Dairy Road and the Hana Highway is **Marco's Grill and Deli,** tel. (808) 877-4446, a casual place with tuck-and-roll leather booths and marble tabletops, and high-backed cane chairs set around tiled tables. White and black predominate and you might hear Tony Bennett being played as background music. It's very Italian. For breakfast try chocolate cinnamon French toast for $6.95, pancakes, omelettes, or pastries. A quick lunch might be one of the many deli sandwiches or a hot sandwich from the grill, most for under $10. Among the usual Italian fare are Italian sausage and linguine at $15.95 and veal parmesan for $18.95. Other specialties are vodka rigatoni or ravioli at $15.95 and seafood pasta at $20.95. Takeout is available for anything on the menu, or choose something from the

deli case. A glass block wall separates the main dining area from the bar, so here too you can sit down and relax in the evening over a drink. Open 7:30 a.m.-10 p.m. daily.

Expensive

The **Chart House,** on Kahului Bay at 500 N. Puunene Ave., tel. (808) 877-2476, is a steak and seafood restaurant that's not too expensive. This is a favorite with businesspeople and island residents. The quality is good and the atmosphere is soothing. Set next to Hoaloha Park, the Chart House overlooks Kahului Bay, so you can eat in the dining room or out on the lanai overlooking the water. Dinners come with a salad, squash, bread, and rice pilaf. Most entrees run around $25. This Chart House is known for its salad bar. On Monday it has a prime rib special with salad bar for $19.95. Open for dinner only 5-10 p.m.

Sam Choy has opened another of his wonderful restaurants at the Kaahumanu Center. **Sam Choy's Kahului Restaurant,** tel. (808) 893-0366, serves breakfast 7-10:30 a.m., lunch 10:30 a.m-3 p.m., and dinner 5-9 p.m. (Friday and Saturday to 9:30). Choose a table in the back or a stool at the counter and watch the cooks prepare your food in the open kitchen. For breakfast try Sam's plantation-style breakfast, which is two eggs, your choice of meat, rice, hash browns, or home fries, and toast and jelly for $5.75, or such things as Makawao steak and eggs for $9.50, or Paia veggie moco at $6.95. Lunch offerings include sandwiches, plate lunches, and rice and noodle dishes, most below $7. Dinners are more expensive, $18.95-31.95, with such items as oven-roasted duck, veal osso bucco, and vegetarian lasagna, with the most pricey being the Hawaiian-style seafood bouillabaisse. Although Sam Choy's is decorated in a very pleasing manner, people come for the food. There are always large portions, and the presentation is as fine as the taste. It's always busy, so come early for lunch; dinner reservations recommended.

On the first floor of the Kahului Building at 33 Lono Ave. you'll find **Papa's N Chiles,** tel. (808) 871-2074, an upscale restaurant serving authentic Mexican cuisine. Specials are in the $12-17 range, seafood up to $19, with salads, soups, appetizers, and combination plates. Closed Monday; open Tues.-Fri. 11 a.m.-10 p.m., Saturday and Sunday 5-10 p.m. only.

Groceries

For basic grocery items try any of the following in Kahului: **Star Market** at the Maui Mall, **Ah Fooks** at the Kahului Shopping Center, **Foodland** at the Kaahumanu Center, **Safeway** at 170 E Kamehameha Ave. behind the Maui Mall, or **Down to Earth Natural Foods** at 305 Dairy Road across from the Maui Marketplace mall.

Liquor

Connoisseur Food and Wine, 444 Dairy Road, open Mon.-Sat. 9 a.m-7 p.m., is a good place for a high-end bottle of bubbly. For a quick stop at a basic bottle shop try **Ah Fooks** at the Kahului Shopping Center or **Star Market** at the Maui Mall.

ENTERTAINMENT

The six-plex **Kaahumanu Theater,** tel. (808) 873-3133, is at the Kaahumanu Center, and **The Maui Theater,** tel. (808) 877-3560, is to the side of the Kahului Shopping Center. In addition, live theater is offered by the **Maui Community Theater,** 68 N. Market St., Wailuku, tel. (808) 242-6969, in the remodeled Iao Theater building. Major productions occur four times a year.

Opened in 1994, the $32 million **Maui Arts and Cultural Center** is becoming a big draw for the island. Big name concerts are held here, as well as local art exhibitions, educational programs, and films. Call (808) 242-7469 for information or tickets.

SHOPPING

Because of the three malls right in a row along Kaahumanu Avenue and the new Maui Marketplace on Dairy Road, Kahului has the best all-around shopping on the island. Here you can find absolutely everything you might need. Combine this with the smaller shopping plazas, Kmart, Costco, and individual shops around town and you're in general shopping heaven. For something different, don't miss the **Aloha Maui Swap Meet,** tel. (808) 877-3100, at the fairgrounds on Puunene Ave. every Saturday 7 a.m.-noon.

You can also shop almost the minute you arrive or just before you leave at two touristy but good shops along Keolani Place. Less than a half mile from the airport are the **T-shirt Factory,** with original Maui designs and custom T-shirts for $5-25, all cotton, as well as Aloha shirts, sarongs, and pareau; and **Coral Factory,** for pink and black coral and jewelry set with semiprecious stones—the Coral Factory seems to be set up largely to cater to Japanese tour groups. When Keolani Place turns into Dairy Road you'll find **Airport Flower and Fruits,** which can provide you with produce that's pre-inspected and admissible to the Mainland. It also has a large selection of lei, which can be packed to go. On Dairy Road between Haleakala and Hana highways are the two huge stores housing Kmart and Costco. Mainland American mercantilism has invaded.

The two-story **Kaahumanu Center,** along Kaahumanu Avenue, is Kahului's largest mall and has the widest selection of stores. There's lots of free parking. The mall's central courtyard is covered with a big skylight and a huge sail-like expanse of canvas—a good way to let the light and breezes through. You'll find the big stores like **Liberty House, Sears,** and **JCPenney** anchoring this mall, with smaller chains, like **Shirokiya** and **Ben Franklin,** here as well. Numerous other apparel, shoe, jewelry, and specialty stores and a half dozen restaurants fill this center, and a dozen inexpensive International fast-food eateries are located in the food court. Several of the specialty shops are **Waldenbooks,** tel. (808) 871-6112, for one of the best selections of books on Maui; **GNC** for nutritional supplements, and **Fox Photo** for all your camera needs. A great place for a relaxing cup of coffee or light lunch is **The Coffee Store. Maui Dive Shop** has a full range of snorkel and scuba equipment for rent and sale. On the upper level, you can relax in the cool dark comfort of the **Kaahumanu Theater** and catch a movie. Local musicians perform at the center 6-8 p.m. on the first and last Mondays of the month.

The low-rise, open-air Maui Mall is more pedestrian, yet it has a nice ambiance as its buildings are set around courtyards filled with greenery. At the intersection of Hana Hwy. and Kaahumanu Ave., **Maui Mall** has **Longs** for everything from aspirin to film, **Star Market, Roy's Photo and Video,** another **Waldenbooks,** and other clothing and specialty shops.

At the **Kahului Shopping Center,** 47 Kaahumanu Ave., you will find **Ah Fooks,** specializing in Asian foods; **Burger King;** and the inexpensive but authentic **Ichiban Restaurant. Maui Organic Farmers Market** holds court here on Wednesday 8 a.m.-noon. This mall is less distinctive than the other two along Kaahumanu Ave. and seems to have suffered most because of the newer malls in town.

The Old Kahului Shopping Center, at 55 Kaahumanu Ave., just across from the Maui Mall, is just that, an old building from 1916 that held a bank and a series of shops that was modernized and brought back to life in the late '80s. Once full of boutiques and specialty shops, it's now mostly empty. Only two stores and a doctor's office remain. **Lightening Bolt** specializes in surfboards and surf attire, modern fashions, women's apparel, hats, and sunglasses. **Manniquin** carries women's clothes.

The newest mall in Kahului, with a style from Anywhere U.S.A., occupies a huge area along Dairy Road. This is the **Maui Marketplace Mall,** and here you'll find such stores as **Borders Books,** open until 10 p.m. daily; the **Sports Authority;** numerous clothing stores including **Hawaiian Island Creations;** the huge **Eagle Hardware and Garden** center for anything you might need for your house or yard; **OfficeMax** for your business needs; several jewelry stores; numerous other smaller shops; and a food court. For banking needs, try the **First Federal Savings Bank** or **Bank of Hawaii** along Dairy Road.

Also new is the **Triangle Square** mall, on Hwy. 36 across from Kahana Pond, where you'll find **Hi-Tech Surf Sports** and **Maui Sails** for all water sports equipment and information. For food, step into **Boomers** and order a burger, taco, or deli item.

On the corner across from Kmart is **Hawaiian Island Surf and Sport,** which also carries a multitude of water sports equipment, new and used, for sale and rental. Next door is **Island Bikery,** which sells and rents mountain bikes.

In **Dairy Center** on Dairy Road you'll find **Extreme Sports Maui, Piñata's** for reasonable

Mexican food, **Koko Ichiban-ya** Japanese restaurant for inexpensive plate lunches and noodle and rice dishes, a **Local Boys** restaurant for local grind plate lunches, and **Kinko's.** If you need to check your e-mail while on Maui, you can stop at Kinko's and use a computer for a reasonable fee. Extreme Sports rents the usual water equipment, plus skateboards and bikes. It also has a small climbing wall.

Just down the street and across from the new Maui Marketplace is **Down to Earth Natural Foods,** open Mon.-Sat. 7 a.m.-9 p.m., Sunday 8 a.m.-8 p.m. A full-service grocery with bulk items, canned and boxed goods, fresh vegetables and fruit, and vitamins, minerals, and supplements, the store also has a deli counter, salad bar, and bakery, so stop in for a wholesome lunch for under $10.

SERVICES

Kahului has numerous banks, most with ATM machines. There is a **Bank of Hawaii,** tel. (808) 871-8220, at 11 S. Puunene Ave.; **First Hawaiian Bank,** tel. (808) 877-2311, at 20 W. Kaahumanu Ave. and another branch at 86 Kamehameha Ave.; and an **American Savings Bank,** tel. (808) 871-5501, and a **City Bank,** tel. (808) 871-7761, at the Kaahumanu Center.

The Kahului **post office** is on Puunene Ave. (Rt. 350) just across the street from the fairgrounds, tel. (808) 871-4710.

The library, at 90 School St., tel. (808) 873-3097, has irregular hours.

The **W & F Washerette,** 125 S. Wakea, tel. (808) 877-0353, features video games to while away the time as well as a little snack bar. Open daily 6 a.m.-9 p.m.

For medical emergencies, try **Maui Memorial Hospital,** tel. (808) 244-9056, at 221 Mahalani. Clinics include **Kaiser Permanente,** tel. (808) 243-6000, at 20 Mahalani.

WAILUKU

Often, historical towns maintain a certain aura long after their time of importance has passed. Wailuku is one of these. Maui's county seat since 1905, the town has the feel of one that has been important for a long time. Wailuku earned its name, "Bloody Waters," from a ferocious battle fought by Kamehameha I against Maui warriors just up the road in Iao Valley. The slaughter was so intense that over four miles of the local stream literally ran red with blood. Last century the missionaries settled in Wailuku, and their architectural influences, such as a white-steepled church and the courthouse at the top of the main street, give an impression of a New England town. Later in the century, sugar came to town and this vast industry grew with muscle and pumped great vitality into the community. After the turn of the century, Wailuku strengthened its stance as the island's center of government, business, and industry, and the wealthy and influential built homes here. Wailuku maintained this strong position until the '60s when the sugar industry declined and the growth of tourism began to create other centers of population and industry on the island. Although still a vibrant government and population center, much of Wailuku's importance to the island's economy has been eclipsed.

While much of Wailuku is a pretty town, it's a mixed bag in the back streets. The historical town center lends it dignity, and much is being done to maintain and refurbish it. Comely rows of plantation-era bungalows are scattered here and there around town, yet fading sections past their prime also exist, not always too far from the new and modern developments. Built on the rolling foothills of the West Maui Mountains, this adds some character—unlike the often-flat layout of many other Hawaiian towns. You can "do" Wailuku in only an hour, though most people don't even give it that much time. They just pass through on their way to Iao Needle, where everyone goes, or through Happy Valley and on to Kahakuloa, around the back side.

You *can* see Wailuku's sights from the window of your car, but don't shortchange yourself this way. Definitely visit the Bailey House Museum, and while you're out, walk the grounds of **Kaahu-manu Church.** Clustered near these two are other historical buildings, several of which are listed on the Hawaii and national registers of historic places. These include the Circuit Courthouse (1907), Old County Building (1925), Territorial Building (1930), Wailuku Public Library (1928), Wailuku Union Church (1911), and the Wailuku Public School (1904). One block away is the Church of the Good Shepherd (1911), and beyond that the Iao Theater (1929). This theater is the last remaining of the 19 theaters that dotted the island in the era between the world wars. Market Street, between Main and Mill Streets, has a clutch of intriguing antique and curio shops that you can peek into while you're at it.

SIGHTS

Kaahumanu Church
It's fitting that Maui's oldest existing stone church is named after the resolute but loving Queen Kaahumanu. This rock-willed woman is the "Saint Peter" of Hawaii, upon whom Christianity in the islands was built. She was *the* most important early convert, often attending services in Kahului's humble grass-hut chapel. It is also worth noting that the church was erected on Maui king Kahekili's *heiau*—the squashing of one religion with the growing presence of another. In 1832 an adobe church was built on the same spot and named in her honor. Rain and time washed it away, to be replaced by the island's first stone structure in 1837. In 1876 the church went through its fourth metamorphosis, the church tower and clock being delayed until 1884, and what remains is the white and green structure we know today. Its construction was supervised by the missionary Edward Bailey, whose home stands to the rear. A three-year renovation project ended in 1976, bringing the church back to form. Oddly enough, the steeple was repaired in 1984 by Skyline Engineers, who hail from Massachusetts, the same place from which the missionaries came 150 years earlier! You can see the church sitting there on High Street (Rt. 30), but it's sometimes closed dur-

WAILUKU

HAPPY VALLEY

POST OFFICE

MAUI TOURIST BUREAU

330

ULEI

PL.

KAPOAI ST.

WILIPA LOOP RD

KALA ST.

MILL ST.

CENTRAL AVE.

KANIELA ST.

MISSION ST.

MooN

KONAHEA ST.

MAKUA ST.

KAHAWAI ST.

BANANA BUNGALOW

MOLINA'S

SIAM THAI

NORTHSHORE INN

RAMON'S

SAENG'S

N. MARKET ST.

NORTH ST.

CHURCH ST.

IAO THEATER

330

NANI ST.

OOKA SUPERMARKET

A SAIGON CAFE

N. HIGH ST.

VINYARD ST.

MAUI MEDICAL GROUP

STATE OFFICE BUILDING

KAAHUMANU CHURCH

BAILEY HOUSE MUSEUM

LIBRARY

COUNTY OFFICE BUILDING

HAMBURGER MARY'S

E. MAIN ST.

WELLS ST.

S. MARKET ST.

WELLS PARK

KANOA ST.

WALALE DR.

PAKAHI ST.

PALUA ST.

AUPUNI ST.

KOELI ST.

WAILUKU PUBLIC SCHOOL

KAOHU ST.

MALAKO ST.

KAHOOKELE ST.

OLD WAILUKU INN

KALUA ST.

MAKAHALA ST.

0   0.25 mi

0   0.25 km

© J.D. BISIGNANI AND MOON PUBLICATIONS, INC.

ing the week. Sunday services are at 9 a.m., when the Hawaiian congregation sings the Lord's praise in their native language. An excellent cultural and religious event to attend!

Bailey House Museum

This is the old Bailey House, built from 1833 to 1850, with various rooms added throughout the years. In the 1840s it housed the Wailuku Female Seminary, of which Edward Bailey was principal until it closed in 1849. After that, the Baileys bought the property and lived here until the 1890s. Bailey then went on to manage the Wailuku Sugar Company. More important for posterity, he became a prolific landscape painter of various areas around the island. Most of his paintings, 26 in the museum's holdings, record the period from 1866 through 1896 and are now displayed in the Bailey Gallery, once the sitting room of the house. The one-time seminary dining room, now housing the museum gift shop, was his studio. In July 1957 this old missionary homestead formally became the Maui Historical Society Museum, at which time it acquired the additional name of Hale Hoikeike, "House of Display." It closed in 1973, then was refurbished and reopened in July 1975.

You'll be amazed at the two-foot-thick walls the missionaries taught the Hawaiians to build, using goat hair as the binding agent. Years of whitewashing make them resemble new-fallen snow. The rooms inside are given over to various themes. **The Hawaiian Room** houses excellent examples of the often practical artifacts of pre-contact Hawaii; especially notice the fine displays of tapa cloth and calabashes. Hawaiian tapa, now a lost art, was considered Polynesia's finest and most advanced. Upstairs is the bedroom. It's quite large and dominated by a four-poster bed. There's a dresser with a jewelry box, other pieces of furniture, and clothes including fine lace gloves. Downstairs you'll discover the sitting room and kitchen, heart of the house: the "feelings" are strongest here. The lintel over the doorway is as stout as the spirits of the people who once lived here. The stonework on the floor is well laid and the fireplace is totally homey.

Go outside! The lanai runs across the entire front and down the side. Around back is the canoe shed, housing a refurbished Hawaiian-sewn sennit outrigger canoe from the late 1800s, as well as Duke Kahanamoku's redwood surfboard from about 1910. On the grounds you'll also see exhibits of sugarcane, sugar pots, *konane* boards, and various Hawaiian artifacts. The Bailey House Museum is open Mon.-Sat. 10 a.m.-4 p.m. Admission is well worth the $4 for adults, $3.50 seniors, and $1 for children 6-12. Upon arrival, a docent will introduce you to the house and then let you make a self-guided tour at your leisure. The bookstore/gift shop has a terrific selection of souvenirs, books, and Hawaiiana at better-than-average prices. All are done by Hawaiian artists and craftsmen, and many are created specifically for this shop. The office of the Maui Historical Society is in the basement, tel. (808) 244-3326. It seems

the Bailey House

appropriate that this society, which collects and preserves artifacts and disseminates information about the history and culture of Maui, should be located on the grounds where Kahekili, Maui's last king, had his compound.

Kepaniwai Park

As you head up Route 320 to Iao Valley, you're in for a real treat. Two miles after leaving Wailuku, you come across Kepaniwai Park and Heritage Gardens. Here the architect, Richard C. Tongg, envisioned and created a park dedicated to all of Hawaii's people. See the Portuguese villa and garden complete with an outdoor oven, a thatch-roofed Hawaiian grass shack, a New England "salt box," a Chinese pagoda, a Japanese teahouse with authentic garden, and a bamboo house—the little "sugar shack" that songs and dreams are made of. Admission is free and there are pavilions with picnic tables. This now-tranquil spot is where the Maui warriors fell to the invincible Kamehameha and his merciless patron war god, Ku. Kepaniwai means "Damming of the Waters"—literally with corpses. Kepaniwai is now a monument to man's higher nature: harmony and beauty.

Hawaii Nature Center

Located just above Kepaniwai Park is the Hawaii Nature Center, Iao Valley, a private, nonprofit educational and interactive science center—good for kids and grown-ups alike and highly recommended. Open 10 a.m.-4 p.m., $6 adults, $4 children, this center boasts 30 exhibits that will beg you to participate, challenge your mind, and teach you about all aspects of Hawaiian nature at the same time. This seems an appropriate spot for a nature center as the West Maui Mountains harbor 12 distinct plant communities, about 300 species of plants, of which 10 are endemic to this locale, and literally thousands of varieties of animals and insects. Daily nature walks are guided through the valley to bring you face to face with some of the wonders that this valley has to offer. Reservations are required for the walks; call (808) 244-6500.

The Changing Profile

Up the road toward Iao Valley you come to a scenic area long known as Pali Ele'ele, or Black Gorge. This stream-eroded amphitheater canyon has attracted attention for centuries. Amazingly,

after President Kennedy was assassinated, people noticed his likeness portrayed there by a series of large boulders; mention of a profile had never been noted or recorded there before. A pipe stuck in the ground serves as a rudimentary sighting instrument. Squint through it and there he is, with eyes closed in deep repose. The likeness is uncanny, and easily seen, unlike most of these formations, where you have to stretch your imagination to the breaking point. Recently, however, the powers that be (a committee of the State Department of Land and Natural Resources) have pronounced that this image is really that of the late-15th-century *kahuna* Kauaka'iwai. Legend has it that he was turned to stone to protect the *ali'i* buried in this valley. Go figure. You obviously see what you want to in these stones anyway.

Iao Valley State Park

This valley has been a sacred spot and a place of pilgrimage since ancient times. Before Westerners arrived, the people of Maui, who came here to pay homage to the "Eternal Creator," named this

Iao Needle

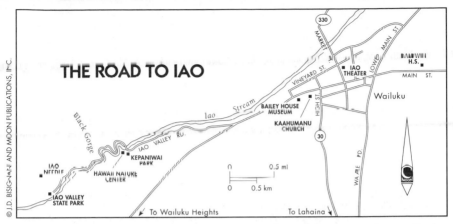

valley Iao, "Supreme Light." Facing almost directly east, the valley catches the warming morning sunlight. According to legend, the gods Maui and Hina raised their daughter Iao in this valley. As Iao grew, she became entranced with a half-man, half-fish god, and they became lovers. This arrangement did not please her father, who, in revenge, turned Iao's lover into a stone pinnacle, the peak we know as Iao Needle.

Historically, Iao Valley was a place set aside and did not belong to the traditional *ahupua'a* land division system. No commoners were allowed into the valley except on special occasions, and royalty were buried here in secret graves. During the Battle of Kepaniwai in 1790, when King Kamehameha defeated Maui's King Kahekili, this valley was valiantly defended but overrun. Countless commoners perished while the *ali'i* escaped over the mountains to Olowalu.

In the center of this velvety green amphitheater-like valley is a pillar of stone rising over 1,200 feet (actual height above sea level is 2,250 feet), its grassy plateau top at one time a natural altar and lookout for defense. Kuka'emoku, now commonly called "The Needle," is a tough basaltic ridge that remained after water swirled away the weaker stone surrounding it, leaving only a saddle that connects it to the valley wall, unseen from below. Iao Valley is actually the remnant of the volcanic caldera of the West Maui Mountains, whose grooved walls have been smoothed and enlarged by the restlessness of mountain streams. Robert Louis Stevenson had

to stretch poetic license to create a word for Iao when he called it "viridescent."

The road ends in a parking lot. Signs point you to paths, tame and well maintained, some even paved, with plenty of vantage points for photographers. If you take the lower path to the river below, you'll find a good-sized, popular swimming hole; but remember, these are the West Maui Mountains, and it can rain at any time. Puu Kukui, West Maui Mountains' tallest peak, lies on the western edge of this crater rim and gets about 400 inches of rain a year! You can escape the crowds even in this heavily touristed area by following a path up to the pavilion. As you head back, take the paved path that bears to the right. It soon becomes dirt, skirting the river, and the tourists magically disappear. Here are a number of pint-sized pools where you can take a refreshing dip. No real path continues up this valley so you'll have to make your way up through the stream or along the banks. About a mile up is a fork in the stream, beyond which it is not recommended to go.

Iao is for day use only; hours are 7 a.m.-7 p.m. On your way back to Wailuku you might take a five-minute side excursion up to Wailuku Heights. Look for the road on your right. There's little here besides a mid- to upper-end residential area, but the view below is tops!

Maui Tropical Plantation and Country Store

This attraction is somewhat out of the ordinary. The 60-acre Maui Tropical Plantation presents a model of a working plantation that you can tour by small tram. Most interesting is an up-close look at Maui's agricultural abundance. Displays of each of these products are situated around the taro patches at the plantation village. A 40-minute tram ride (optional, as you can also walk) takes you through fields of cane, banana, guava, mango, papaya, pineapple, coffee, and macadamia nuts; flowers here and there add exotic color. Leaving every 45 minutes 10 a.m.-4 p.m., this tram runs $8.50 for adults and $3.50 for children. The plantation, with its restaurant, gift shop, and tropical flower nursery, is in Waikapu, a small village along Rt. 30 between Wailuku and Maalaea. If you visit over the noon hour, stop by the Plantation Cafe for lunch, open 10:30 a.m-3 p.m. daily. The Country Store sells Maui-produced goods and can mail gift packages of fruits, nuts, and coffee, while the nursery will ship flowers to anywhere in the country. Look for the windmill! Open daily 9 a.m.-5 p.m., tel. (808) 244-7643.

ACCOMMODATIONS

Visitors to Wailuku mostly stay elsewhere on Maui because there really isn't any place to lodge in town except for a few very specialized and very humble hostels and one very comfortable and historic bed and breakfast inn.

The Old Wailuku Inn at Ulupono

The first, best, and only fine place to stay in Wailuku is at the attentively renovated Old Wailuku Inn, now on the Hawaii Register of Historic Places. Built in 1924 for the son and daughter-in-law of Maui's first bank president, this was the queen of homes in one of Maui's poshest neighborhoods. Refurbished in 1997, this house was brought back to its early-century charm, lovingly detailed, filled with period furniture that evokes the feeling of grandma's house, and decorated with Hawaiian and Asian antiques and artwork. It's a gem. Yet no modern amenity is left out. Each room has a TV, VCR, telephone, private bath, ceiling fan, and gorgeous Hawaiian quilt on its spacious bed. A fax machine, photocopier, and computer are also available for use. The house has central air-conditioning, but the cooling trade winds are generally enough to moderate the temperature. Catching the morning sun, the screened breakfast room looks out over the rear garden. The open-air front porch is a perfect spot for afternoon tea or reading a book from the extensive house library, and the living room a fine place to relax in the evening. Each of the seven guest rooms is named for a Hawaiian flower, and their color and design motifs follow. The four upstairs rooms are spacious and grand, with native hardwood floors and 10-foot ceilings. The downstairs rooms are cozier, and two have their own courtyards. A gourmet breakfast accompanies each night's stay and, no matter what the offering, is tasty, filling, nutritious, and well-presented. You'll be pampered. Born and raised on the island, the gracious and personable hosts, Tom and Janice Fairbanks, have intimate knowledge of what to do, what to see, and where to eat throughout the island and will gladly share their knowledge and recommendations with you. Rooms run $130-180 double occupancy, two nights minimum. Parking is on property. For information and reservations contact the Old Wailuku Inn at Ulupono, 2199 Kaho'okele St., Wailuku, HI 96793, tel. (800) 305-4899 or (808) 244-5897, fax (808) 242-9600, Web site: aitv.com/ulupono, e-mail: Mauibandb@aol.com.

Northshore Inn

This "hostel and hotel," 2080 Vineyard St., tel. (808) 242-8999, fax (808) 244-5004, Web site: http://macmouse.com/hostel/maui.html, is easily spotted with its row of international flags fluttering from the second-floor balcony. Enter via the alley sidewalk. With a capacity of about 45, this clean, light, and comfortable hostel caters mostly to young independent travelers and surfers. Skylights brighten the upstairs; potted plants add color to the walls; and the homey sitting room offers a place for the international guests to talk, listen to music, or watch television; the balcony is a fine place to catch the evening air; and a bulletin board is filled with helpful information about Maui and the other islands. Bunk rooms go for $13.65 a bed, single rooms $26.95, and double rooms $39.95, exclusive of tax; all rooms share four bathrooms. Not only is this an easygoing, well-cared-for place, the management is environmentally conscious. There are laundry facilities; a safe for valuables; storage facilities for sailboards, backpacks, and large items; free use of boogie boards and snorkel equipment; cheap moped, bicycle, and surfboard rental; a full communal kitchen, free morning coffee; inexpensive dinners nightly;

free evening movies; reasonable Internet rates; and a small garden in the back with an 80-year-old banyan tree and tropical fruit trees. The Northshore Inn also has a shuttle van with delivery service to the airport and daily island excursions. Ask about the deal with Word of Mouth Rental Cars for low daily rates. The Northshore Inn won the respect of the community for transforming the former fleabag Wailuku Grand Hotel into a viable business and dealing equitably with the locals.

Banana Bungalow

The Banana Bungalow is located only a few blocks away on the edge of Happy Valley at 310 N. Market St., Wailuku, HI 96793, tel. (808) 244-5090, (800) 846-7835, or (800) 746-7871, fax (808) 846-3678, Web site: home1.gte.net/bungalow, e-mail: Bungalow@gte.net; office hours are 7 a.m.-11 p.m. Until very recently, this too was a flophouse for locals who were down on their luck. Now it's a clean and spartan hostel, with a fresh coat of (yellow) paint, many new artistic decorations, and refurbished bathrooms up and down. Typically, you're liable to hear languages from a dozen countries, and if you're into sailboarding or just after a cross-cultural experience, this is the spot. The Banana offers basic accommodations, and if you care more about your experience than what your bedroom looks like, it's the place for you. Rates are $20 single, $35 double, or $14 ($10 the first night) for a bunk in a four- to six-person dorm. Extra services include a free and convenient airport/beach shuttle; low-cost adventure tours; free coffee, movies, and parties; laundry and storage facilities; a common room for conversation or TV; inexpensive morning and evening meals at the communal kitchen; a jacuzzi in the garden under tropical fruit trees; discounts on water equipment and lessons; and inexpensive car rental deals.

Molina's

The name Molina's Tropical Hideaway conjures up a different image than reality. Molina's, tel. (808) 244-4100, at 197 Market St. on the periphery of downtown Wailuku, offers utilitarian rooms at $35 a night, $125 a week, or $460 a month. Other rooms go for $45 a night, and a bunk in the dorm runs $15 per person. All rooms have bathrooms, TVs, and small refrigerators. The $25 key deposit is returned on exit. Although cleaned up in the last few years, Bogart playing a character with a five-

day-old beard and a hangover might still be comfortable waking up at this basic, clean, and friendly fleabag. Many renters are long-term, so be sure to call ahead to see if a room is available. Downstairs, Molina's Bar is a neighborhood joint with satellite TV and live jazz on Sunday evening.

The Bungalow

Two doors down from the Northshore Inn is the Bungalow, tel. (808) 244-3294. Rooms here are rented nightly for $18 single or $25 double, weekly at $120 single or $125 double, or monthly for $300 single and $360 double. Monthly stays require a $200 deposit. All rooms share a common bathroom.

FOOD

Downtown

Wailuku has some of the best and the most inexpensive restaurants on Maui. The establishments listed below are all in the bargain or reasonable range. The decor in most is basic and homey, with the emphasis placed on the food. Even here in this nontouristy town, however, some of the restaurants are sprucing up and becoming a bit gentrified.

Saeng's, 2119 Vineyard, tel. (808) 244-1567, serves excellent Thai food at great prices. Dishes include appetizers like Thai crisp noodles for $4.95, green papaya salad for $6.50, and shrimp salad at $8.50. The savory soups, enough for two, include spicy coconut shrimp soup for $8.50 and po teak, a zesty seafood combination soup for $10.95. Thai specialties such as pad Thai vegetables, cashew chicken, and eggplant shrimp are all under $10, while vegetarian selections like stir-fry vegetables and Evil Prince tofu are under $7.50. The best seating, although the interior is quite tasteful with linen tablecloths and paisley booths, is outside in a garden area where a small waterfall gurgles pleasantly. Open Mon.-Sat. for lunch 11 a.m.-3 p.m. and dinner nightly 5-9:30 p.m. Saeng's and its friendly competitor Siam Thai are the two best reasonably priced restaurants in town.

Siam Thai is a small restaurant painted black and white at 123 N. Market, tel. (808) 244-3817, open Mon.-Sat. 11:30 a.m.-2:30 p.m., daily 5-9:30 p.m. It serves excellent Thai food with an emphasis on vegetarian cuisine, at prices that are comparable with Saeng's. Extensive menu. **Ramon's,** 2101 Vineyard St., tel. (808) 244-7243, serves breakfast, lunch, and dinner; open 10 a.m.-9 p.m. daily (until 10 p.m. Friday and Saturday). It's one of the few places in town open for Sunday breakfast. As the name implies, its flavor is Mexican, but you can get many local dishes here as well. For breakfast, try an omelette, huevos rancheros, or a stack of pancakes. During the rest of the day, order burritos, tacos, enchiladas, tamales, chiles rellenos, or any number of combination plates on the Mexican side or various plate lunches from the Hawaiian side of the menu. No entree is more than $10. Dishes can be made vegetarian as no animal fat is used. Ramon's has a full-service bar, so you can accompany your meal with a frosty beer, glass of wine, or mixed drink. Fiesta Hour at the bar runs Mon.-Fri. 3-6 p.m.

Across the street at 2092 Vineyard St. is **Maui Bake Shop and Deli,** tel. (808) 242-0064, open weekdays 6 a.m.-5:30 p.m., Saturday 7 a.m.-3 p.m., closed Sunday. This establishment has a full selection of home-baked goods and sandwiches at very reasonable prices. Sandwich selections include turkey, ham, roast beef, pastrami, or veggie all for about $3.75, with soup du jour $5.95. Daily specials can be pizza, quiche, filled croissants, or even lox and bagels for under $5. Tantalizing baked goods include apple strudel, coconut macaroons, apricot twists, fruit tarts, homemade pies, and a menagerie of butter and cream pigs, rabbits, and frogs. Enjoy your selection with an espresso, cappuccino, or hot tea.

Underneath the Northshore Inn is **Restaurant Mushroom,** tel. (808) 244-7117, a clean and reasonably priced place serving local, American, and Japanese foods. You can get mostly soups and sandwiches here as well as saimin and other Asian noodle dishes. Lunch 10 a.m.-2 p.m., dinner 5-8:30 p.m. The **Applause Cafe** at the remodeled Iao Theater serves lunch daily and theme dinners on performance nights. About a block down Vineyard is the **Silk Road** restaurant, serving Chinese and Korean dishes. Open Mon.-Sat. 10 a.m.-9 p.m., tel. (808) 249-2399.

Hamburger Mary's, at the corner of N. Main and E. Market streets, tel. (808) 244-7776, open Mon.-Sat. 10 a.m.-2 a.m., is a very friendly bar and restaurant, where people of all sexual lifestyles are welcome, and where you can have a quiet beer or boogie the night away to video rock music. There's a $5 cover for dancing when a DJ spins discs. Thursday, Friday, and Saturday nights there's food until midnight, every other night until 10 p.m. The interior, like the inside of a big kid's toy box, is brightened with Pee Wee Herman riding a sled, the man in the moon hanging from the ceiling, a mannequin riding a horse, a winged mermaid floating in celestial bliss, Japanese fans, Hawaiiana from the 1940s, surfboards, a small mirrored dance floor, and cherubic angels and fairies perched here and there about the room. Start your day with a breakfast of Portuguese sausage and eggs for $6, create-your-own omelettes for $6, or Mary's short stack for $4.50. The lunch menu has *pu pu* like homefried melt for $4 and an assortment of fresh salads and homemade soups for under $6. Large two-fisted sandwiches and burgers include avocado burger for $6.75, meatless patty burger for $6.95, and the bird of paradise sandwich with cheddar cheese, sliced bacon, turkey, and avocado for $8.95. Hamburger Mary's claims to have the biggest burgers on the island and has been voted the best on a couple of occasions. You can also enjoy a gigantic charbroiled steak with salad for $11.25, or Mary's mahimahi or a breast of chicken for $10.25. Every day there's a lunch and dinner special. Happy hour, daily 3-6 p.m., features $2 well drinks and domestic beers, while Saturday special Bloody Marys are $3.

A little out of the way at 1792 Main St., but well worth the effort to find, is **A Saigon Cafe,** tel. (808) 243-9560. A great family place, clean but not fancy, this may be the best Vietnamese cuisine on the island. Although there's no large sign yet advertising its location, it's a favorite local stop, and you'll know why once you try. Start with spring rolls at $5.75 or shrimp pops for $7.25 and move on to one of the tasty soups like hot and sour fish soup for $9.20 or a green papaya salad for $5.50. Entrees, all under $10 except the Saigon fondue, which is cooked at your table, include a wide range of noodle, meat, fish, and vegetarian dishes, all with good portions. The menu is extensive. Open daily 10 a.m.-10 p.m. (Sunday until 9 p.m.), this restaurant is behind Ooka Supermarket, below the bridge.

Both **Wakamatsu** at 145 N. Market St. and **Nagasako Fish Market** on Lower Main offer a wide variety of fresh fish. For general grocery shopping, go to **Ooka Supermarket** at 1870 Main St., where you'll find not only the usual groceries but also many ethnic foods.

Food off the Main Drag

If you get out of downtown and take Mill Street and Lower Main, you'll be rewarded with some of the *most* local and *least* expensive restaurants on West Maui. They are totally unpretentious, and serve hefty portions of tasty, homemade local foods. If your aim is to *eat* like a local, search out one of these.

The **Tasty Crust Restaurant**, 1770 Mill St., tel. (808) 244-0845, opens daily 5:30 a.m.-11 p.m. (Friday and Saturday until midnight). Similar to a diner, with bar stools at the counter, booths, and a few tables, the welcome sign says "This is where old friends meet." If you have to carbo-load for a full day of sailing, snorkeling, or windsurfing, order the famous giant homemade hotcakes.

Sam Sato's, tel. (808) 244-7124, is at 1750 Wili Pa Loop Road in the Mill Yard. Sato's is famous for *manju*, a puff-like pastry from Japan usually filled with sweets, meats, or *adzuki* beans. One of those places that, if you are a local resident, you must bring Sato's *manju* when visiting friends or relatives off-island. Aside from the *manju* there are noodles, sandwiches, plate lunches, and side dishes. Most everything is under $6. Open Mon.-Sat. 7 a.m.-2 p.m., pickup until 4 p.m. A highly specialized place, but worth the effort.

Or try **Nazo's Restaurant**, 1063 Lower Main St., second floor of the Puuone Plaza, an older yellowish two-story building, tel. (808) 244-0529. Park underneath and walk upstairs. Daily specials cost under $8, but Nazo's is renowned for its oxtail soup, a clear-consommé broth with peanuts and water chestnuts floating around, a delicious combination of East and West.

Tokyo Tei, in the same complex, tel. (808) 242-9630, open daily 11 a.m.-1:30 p.m. for lunch, 5-8:30 p.m. dinner, open Sunday for dinner only, is another institution that has been around for decades serving Japanese dishes to a devoted clientele. Eating here is as consistent as eating at grandma's kitchen, with traditional Japanese dishes like tempura, various *don buri*,

and seafood platters. If you want to sample real Japanese food at affordable prices, come here!

Norm's Cafe, "Where food and people of good taste come together," is located at 740 Lower Main St., tel. (808) 242-1667. A place of local atmosphere in a no-nonsense part of town, the inside is pink, white, and yellow, with booths and a few tables. Breakfast starts at 5 a.m. and includes items like pancakes, omelettes, and loco moco. For lunch and dinner, try salads, sandwiches, or a more hardy dish like the bamboo-steamed ono. Nothing on the menu is over $7. Norm's is an institution.

For a different taste treat, try the *mochi* made fresh daily at Wailuku's **Shishido Manju Shop,** 758 Lower Main Street.

On the edge of town toward Kahului near the underpass is **Stillwell's Bakery and Cafe,** 1740 Kaahumanu Ave., tel. (808) 243-2243. Having established a fine reputation with locals, it's now becoming known to visitors. The surroundings are nothing special, but the food is worthy of the reputation and the baked goods are delicious—and served at some fine restaurants on the island. Stop in for a pastry or a full lunch.

If you're out at Maui Tropical Plantation or coming up from Lahaina and need to stop for a quick bite to eat on the way, try **Waikapu Stop** in Waikapu, a few miles south of Wailuku. Choose from many plate lunches, hamburgers, and sandwiches, most for under $6; open Mon.-Sat. 6 a.m.-1:30 p.m.

SHOPPING

Most shopping in this area is done in Kahului at the big malls. But for an interesting diversion try one of these, all on or around Main or Market Street.

Wailuku's attic closets are overflowing. Several discovery shops in a row hang like promnight tuxedos, limp with old memories. Each has its own style. Look for these shops along N. Market St., many on the elevated portion of the 100 block as you head toward Happy Valley. Here you'll find Bitterford's Antiques and Collectibles, tel. (808) 242-4313; Brown-Kobayashi, tel. (808) 242-0804, for Asian art and furniture; and Traders of the Lost Art, tel. (808) 242-7753, specializing in carvings from the Pacific, especially from New Guinea. Here as well are Memory Lane, tel. (808)

244-4196, for curios and collectibles; and Wailuku Gallery just a few doors away. Also along antique row search out Bird of Paradise, tel. (808) 242-7699, open Mon.-Sat. 9:30 a.m.-5:30 p.m., where owner Joe Myhand sells blue willow china, vintage bottles, Depression and carnival glass, license plates from around the world, and even a smattering of antique furniture.

St. Anthony's Thrift Shop on Lower Main is open Wednesday and Friday 8 a.m.-1 p.m., where you'll find used articles from irons to aloha shirts.

SERVICES

There's a **Bank of Hawaii** at 2105 Main, tel. (808) 871-8200, and a **First Interstate** at 2005 Main, tel. (808) 244-3951. The state office building, county office building, old courthouse, and **li-**brary, tel. (808) 243-5566, are along High Street in the center of town, and the new **post office,** tel. (808) 244-4815, is out in the Mill Yard near the **Maui HVB** office, tel. (808) 244-3530, on Wili Pa Loop Road.

For conventional health care, go to **Maui Memorial Hospital,** 221 Mahalani St. off Route 32, tel. (808) 244-9056, or **Kaiser Permanente, Wailuku Clinic,** tel. (808) 243-6000, near the hospital at the entrance to Mahalani Street. In the center of town at 2180 Main St. is **Maui Medical Group,** tel. (808) 242-6464.

Camping permits for county parks are available at the War Memorial Gym, Room 102, tel. (808) 243-7389. They cost $3 for adults, 50 cents for children, per person per night. State park permits can be obtained from the State Building, 54 S. High St., Wailuku, HI 96793, tel. (808) 984-8109.

KAHAKULOA—WEST MAUI'S BACK SIDE

To get around to the back side of West Maui you can head north from Kaanapali or northwest from Wailuku. A few short years ago, this road was in rugged shape, closed to all but local traffic, and forbidden to rental cars by their companies. It's still narrow and very windy in part, but now it's paved all the way. What once took three hours might now take only an hour. As many people drive it these days, there is more traffic, so it ⌐ ⌐ʹ has its hazards. Additionally, loose rock tumbles onto the roadway from embankments and *pali* (particularly after rainfalls), so be mindful and aware of debris. Drive slowly, drive carefully, and drive defensively. The road is the journey.

Before you start this 18-mile stretch, make sure you have adequate gas and water. Start heading north on Market Street, down toward the area of Wailuku called Happy Valley. As you head downhill, Rt. 330 meets Rt. 340, which you'll follow toward Kahakuloa Bay and all the way around. Just north of the bridge over Iao Stream, coming up Rt. 340 from Kahului, will be Kuhio Place on your left. Turn here and then again onto Hea Place to **Halekii and Pihana Heiau State Monument,** which sits on a bluff overlooking lower Iao Stream. This was a place of great prominence when Maui kings called Wailuku home and when a large population filled the surrounding land. Although uninspiring, this 10-acre site is historical and totally unvisited. Originally constructed for other reasons, these *heiau* were made temples of war by Kahekili, Maui's last king.

A short way north and down Lower Waiehu Road toward the water—a Shoreline Access sign will point the way—you'll reach **Waiehu Beach County Park.** This strip of sand meets the southern end of the Waiehu Golf Course and is a good place for sunbathing, as well as swimming when the water is calm.

Back on Route 340 you come shortly to **Waihee** ("Slippery Water"); there's a little store here. Turn at the Kiwanis Park (softball on Saturday) and follow the sign pointing you to **Waiehu Golf Course;** call (808) 243-7400 for tee times. Mostly local people golf here; it's full of kids and families on the weekend. The fairways, strung along the sea, are beautiful to play. **Waiehu Inn Restaurant** is an adequate little eatery at the golf course.

Like its sister on the south edge of the golf course, **Waiehu Beach County Park** is tucked into its northern corner. It too is secluded and frequented mostly by local people. Some come here to spear fish inside the reef. Although both parks are for day use only, they'd probably be okay for an unofficial overnight stay. To reach this

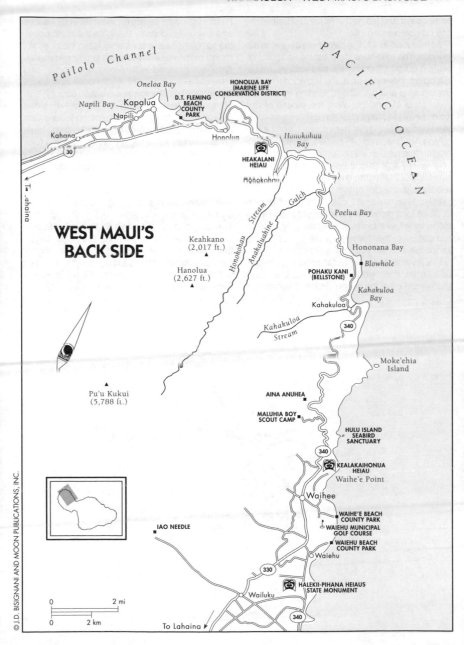

WEST MAUI'S BACK SIDE

Pailolo Channel

Oneloa Bay

Napili Bay Kapalua

Napili

Kahana

To Lahaina

30

D.T. FLEMING BEACH COUNTY PARK

HONOLUA BAY (MARINE LIFE CONSERVATION DISTRICT)

Honolua

Honokohau Bay

HEAKALANI HEIAU

Honokohau

PACIFIC OCEAN

Keahkano
(2,017 ft.)

Hanolua
(2,627 ft.)

Honokohau Stream

Anakaluahine Gulch

Poelua Bay

Hononana Bay

Blowhole

POHAKU KANI (BELLSTONE)

Kahakuloa Bay

Kahakuloa

340

Kahakuloa Stream

Pu'u Kukui
(5,788 ft.)

Moke'ehia Island

AINA ANUHEA

MALUHIA BOY SCOUT CAMP

340

HULU ISLAND SEABIRD SANCTUARY

KEALAKAIHONUA HEIAU

Waihe'e Point

Waihee

WAIHE'E BEACH COUNTY PARK

WAIEHU MUNICIPAL GOLF COURSE

WAIEHU BEACH COUNTY PARK

Waiehu

330

IAO NEEDLE

HALEKII-PIHANA HEIAUS STATE MONUMENT

Wailuku

340

To Lahaina

0   2 mi

0   2 km

park, go left and follow the fence just before the golf course parking lot.

At mile marker 11, the pavement begins to deteriorate. The road hugs the coastline and gains elevation quickly; the undisturbed valleys are resplendent. Here you pass the entrance to a Boy Scout camp and a trailhead leading up into the West Maui Mountains. With the paving of this road, several commercial establishments have been opened along this back route. One of these is **Aina Anuhea,** a private garden. While not spectacular, this garden is fine for a short stop. From here you're able to see not only the bay below but Haleakala off in the distance. Walkways take you through the diminutive gardens and a short path leads up to a small, quiet waterfall, a peaceful place for a picnic on the rocks or to sit in meditation for a few minutes. Smitty will greet you as you come up the driveway, collect your $4 entrance fee, and set you on the right path.

In a few miles you skirt a tall headland—easily seen from Paia and points along the north shore—and enter the fishing village of **Kahakuloa**

("Tall Hill"), with its dozen weatherworn houses and tiny green church. Being on the north coast, the turbulent waters constantly wash the beach of round black stones. Although a tiny community (you are greeted with Aloha, Welcome, and Farewell all on one sign), each house is well kept with pride. To cater to the increased through traffic, several fruit stands have popped up along the road. Overlooking Kahakuloa on the western side is a pullout and promontory where you have good views over the rugged coast. Here the road is at its absolute narrowest. The valley is very steep-sided and beautiful. Supposedly, great Maui himself loved this area.

Two miles past Kahakuloa, you come to **Pohaku Kani,** the bell stone. It's about six feet tall and the same in diameter, but graffiti spoils it. The seascapes along this stretch are tremendous. The surf pounds along the coast below and sends spumes skyward, roaring through a natural blowhole. The road becomes wider again but still curvy and you're soon at **Fleming Beach Park.** Civilization comes again too quickly.

Bone or shell was used as the cutting edge of the pump drill.

LOUISE FOOTE

WEST MAUI

LAHAINA

Lahaina ("Merciless Sun") is and always has been the premier town on Maui. It's the most energized town on the island as well, and you can feel it from the first moment you walk down Front Street. Maui's famed warrior-king Kahekili lived here and ruled until Kamehameha, with the help of newfound cannon power, subdued Kahekili's son in Iao Valley at the turn of the 19th century. When Kamehameha I consolidated the island kingdom, he chose Lahaina as his seat of power. It served as such until Kamehameha III moved to Honolulu in the 1840s. Lahaina is where the modern world of the West and the old world of Hawaii collided, for better or worse. The *ali'i* of Hawaii loved to be entertained here; the royal surf spot, mentioned numerous times as an area of revelry in old missionary diaries, is just south of the Small Boat Harbor. Kamehameha I built in Lahaina the islands' first Western structure in 1801, known as the Brick Palace; a small ruin still remains. Queens Keopuolani and Kaahumanu, the two most powerful

wives of the great Kamehameha's harem of over 20, were local Maui women who remained after their husband's death and helped to usher in the new order.

The whalers came preying for "sperms and humpbacks" in 1819 and set old Lahaina Town a-reelin'. Island girls, naked and willing, swam out to meet the ships, trading their favors for baubles from the modern world. Grog shops flourished, and drunken sailors with their brown-skinned doxies owned the debauched town. The missionaries, invited by Queen Keopuolani, came praying for souls in 1823. Led by the Reverends Stuart and Richards, they tried to harpoon moral chaos. In short order, there was a curfew, a *kapu* placed on the ships by wise but ineffectual old Governor Hoapili, and a jail and a fort to discourage the strong-arm tactics of unruly captains. The pagan Hawaiians transformed like willing children to the new order, but the Christian sailors damned the meddling missionaries. They even whistled a few cannonballs into the

WEST MAUI

Oneloa Bay
Honolua Bay
Kapalua Bay — Kapalua
Napili
Napili Bay
Kahana
D.T. FLEMING BEACH COUNTY PARK
HONOKOWAI BEACH COUNTY PARK
KAPALUA WEST MAUI AIRPORT
KAHEKILI BEACH PARK
Honokowai
To Kahului
Kaanapali
KAANAPALI GOLF COURSES
SUGAR CANE TRAIN
WAHIKULE STATE WAYSIDE
Pu'unoa Point
LAHAINALUNA HIGH SCHOOL
Lahaina
West Maui Mountains
PUAMANA BEACH COUNTY PARK
LAUNIUPOKO CO. WAYSIDE
Launiupoko Point
Pu'u Kukui (5,788 ft.)
KULANAOKALA BEACH
Hekili Point
Olowalu
KA'ILI'ILI BEACH
PUNAHOA BEACH
UKUMEHAME BEACH COUNTY PARK
To Kihei and Kahului
PAPALAUA CO. WAYSIDE
TUNNEL
MAALAEA
Parawai Point
LOOKOUT
KAPOLI BEACH COUNTY PARK
McGregor Point

0   3 mi
0   3 km

© J.D. BISIGNANI AND MOON PUBLICATIONS, INC.

"sugar town" dominated by the Pioneer Sugar Mill, which has operated since 1860. In 1901, the Pioneer Inn was built to accommodate inter-island ferry passengers, but no one *came* to Lahaina. In the 1960s, Amfac Inc. had a brilliant idea. It turned Kaanapali, a magnificent stretch of beach just west, into one of the most beautifully planned and executed resorts in the world. The Pioneer Sugar Mill had long used the area as a refuse heap, but now the ugly duckling became a swan, and Lahaina flushed with new life. With superb farsightedness, the Lahaina Restoration Foundation was begun in those years and almost the entire town was made a national historical landmark. Lahaina, subdued but never tamed, throbs with its special energy once again.

Parking

Traffic congestion is a problem that needs to be addressed. Be parked and settled 4:30-5:30 p.m., when traffic is heaviest. While there still are no traffic lights on Front Street, a spree of construction in the last several years has increased the number of lights on the highway from two to over half a dozen. The other thing to know to make your visit carefree is where to stash your car. The two lots along Dickenson Street are centrally located and charge a reasonable daily rate. A little more expensive but closer to Front Street is the lot behind Burger King. There are two smallish lots along Luakini Street, small lots behind the Baldwin Home and the Lahaina Hotel, and an underground lot below the 505 Front Street Mall. These lots charge $3-8 a day; exact fee only, no attendants on duty. The large lot at Prison and Front Streets is free but has a three-hour limit. The lots at Maluuluolele and Kamehameha Iki parks are also free and ostensibly for use by park users only, but people do park and walk into town from there. Aside from these public parking lots, all shopping centers in town have parking: some are free, some charge, and some offer reduced rates with validation. Most of the meters in town are a mere one hour, and the most efficient people on Maui are the "meter patrol!" ($15-20 per parking ticket). Your car will wind up in the pound if you're not careful! Those staying in Kaanapali should leave cars behind and take the Lahaina Express or West Maui Shopping Express shuttles for the day or hop on the Sugar Cane Train.

Lahaina homestead of Reverend Richards, hoping to send him speedily to his eternal reward. Time, a new breed of sailor, and the slow death of the whaling industry eased the tension.

Meanwhile, the missionaries built the first school and printing press west of the Rockies at Lahainaluna, in the mountains just above the town, along with downtown's Wainee Church, the first stone church on the island. Lahaina's glory days slipped by and it became a sleepy

LAHAINA

WAHIKULI COUNTY WAYSIDE PARK

FIRE STATION
POST OFFICE
LAHAINA CIVIC CENTER
POLICE STATION

WAI OLA
THE GUEST HOUSE
WAHIKULI RD

FLEMING ST.

LAHAINA ROADS CONDO

LAHAINALUNA HIGH SCHOOL

HALE PA'I

OLD LAHAINA LUAU
LAHAINA CANNERY MALL

MALA WHARF

LAHAINA JODO MISSION

SEAMEN'S HOSPITAL

TRAIN STATION

LAHAINALUNA RD

SEE "DOWNTOWN LAHAINA" MAP

ST.

Lahaina Harbor

SHAW ST.
BAMBULA INN

BELLADONNA COTTAGES
ALOHA LANI INN
OLD LAHAINA HOUSE

HONOAPIILANI HWY

0   0.5 mi

0   0.5 km

PUAMANA

PUAMANA BEACH COUNTY PARK

© J.D. BISIGNANI AND MOON PUBLICATIONS, INC.

SIGHTS

In short, strolling around Lahaina offers the best of both worlds. It's busy, but it's bite-sized. It's engrossing enough, but you can "see" it in half a day. The main attractions are mainly downtown within a few blocks of each other. Lahaina technically stretches, long and narrow, along the coast for about four miles, but you may only be interested in the central core, a mere mile or so. All along Front Street, the main drag, and the side streets running off it are innumerable shops, restaurants, and hideaways where you can browse, recoup your energy, or just wistfully watch the sun set. Go slowly and savor, and you'll feel the dynamism of Lahaina past and present all around you. Enjoy!

The Banyan Tree

The best place to start your tour of Lahaina is at this magnificent tree at the corner of Hotel and Front Streets. You can't miss it as it spreads its shading boughs over almost an entire acre. It is the largest banyan in the state. Use the benches to sit and reconnoiter while the sun, for which Lahaina is infamous, is kept at bay. Children love it, and it seems to bring out the Tarzan in everyone. Old-timers sit here chatting, and you might be lucky enough to hear Ben Victorino, a tour guide who comes here frequently, entertain people with his ukulele and endless repertoire of Hawaiian tunes. On Saturday and Sunday, members of the Lahaina Art Society gather here to display and sell their artwork under the tree's broad branches. This banyan was planted in April 1873 by Sheriff Bill Smith in commemoration of the Congregationalist Missions' golden anniversary. One hundred years later, a ceremony was held here and over 500 people were accommodated under this natural canopy. Just left of the banyan, down the lane toward the harbor, was a canal and the Government Market. All kinds of commodities, manufactured and human, were sold here during the whaling days, and it was given the apt name of "Rotten Row."

The Courthouse

Behind the banyan on Wharf Street is the Courthouse. Built in the late 1850s from coral blocks recycled from Kamehameha III's ill-fated palace,

Hale Piula ("House of Iron"), it also served as a post office, customs office, and the police station, complete with a jail in the basement. Until its most recent renovation, the jail was home to the **Lahaina Art Society,** where paintings and artifacts were kept behind bars, waiting for patrons to liberate them. As of this writing, the renovation project has not been completed and no decision has yet been made as to exactly what use the building will have in the future.

Adjacent is **The Fort,** built in the 1830s to show the sailors that they couldn't run amok in Lahaina. Even with its 20-foot-high walls, it was more for show than for force. When it was torn down, the blocks were hauled over to Prison Street to build the real jail, **Hale Pa'ahao.** A corner battlement of the fort was restored, but that's it, because restoring the entire structure would mean mutilating the banyan. The cannons, from a military vessel sunk in Honolulu harbor a few years prior and now set along the wharf in front of the courthouse, are in approximately the location that they had when they were fixtures on the fort wall.

Small Boat Harbor

Walking along the harbor stimulates the imagination and the senses. The boats waiting at anchor sway in confused syncopation. Hawser ropes groan and there's a feeling of anticipation and adventure in the air. Here you can board for all kinds of seagoing excursions. In the days of whaling there was no harbor; the boats tied up one to the other offshore in the "roads," at times forming an impromptu floating bridge. The whalers came ashore in their chase boats; with the winds always up, departure could be made at a moment's notice. The activity here is still dominated by the sea.

Just as today, the old commercial and whaling boats used a light to guide their way to port. Beyond the *Carthaginian II* anchored at the harbor's mouth is the site of the Lahaina's first lighthouse. In 1840, before any were built along what would later be the West Coast of the U.S., King Kamehameha III ordered a lighthouse to be constructed here. The original wooden nine-foot structure was rebuilt to 26 feet in 1869, and the present concrete structure installed in 1919. As might be expected, a whale oil lamp was first used for light, later to be supplanted by electricity.

The *Carthaginian II*

The masts and square rigging of this replica of the enterprising freighters that braved the Pacific tower over Lahaina Harbor. You'll be drawn to it . . . go! It's the only truly square-rigged ship left afloat on the seas. It replaced the *Carthaginian I* when that ship went aground in 1972 while being hauled to Honolulu for repairs. The Lahaina Restoration Foundation found this steel-hulled ship in Denmark; built in Germany in 1920 as a two-masted schooner, it tramped around the Baltic under converted diesel power. The foundation had it sailed 12,000 miles to Lahaina, where it underwent extensive conversion until it became the beautiful replica that you see today.

The *Carthaginian II* is a floating museum dedicated to whaling and to whales. It's open daily 10 a.m.-4 p.m., but arrive no later than 3:30 to see all the exhibits and videos. Admission is $4 adults, seniors $3, $5 for the whole family. Whale researchers Debra and Mark Ferrari narrate a video documenting the life of humpbacks. Belowdecks is the museum containing artifacts and implements from the whaling days. There's even a whaling boat that was found intact in Alaska in the 1970s. The light below decks is subdued, and while you sit in the little "captains' chairs" the humpbacks chant their peaceful hymns in the background. Flip Nicklin's sensitive photos adorn the bulkheads.

The Brick Palace

This rude structure was commissioned by Kamehameha I in 1801 and slapped together by two forgotten Australian exconvicts. It was the first Western structure in Hawaii, but unfortunately the substandard materials have for the most part disintegrated. Kamehameha never lived in it, but it was occupied and used as a storehouse until the 1850s. Just to the right of the Brick Palace site, as you face the harbor, is **Hauola Stone.** Formed like a chair, it was believed by the Hawaiians to have curative powers if you sat on it and let the ocean bathe you. Best view at low tide.

Pioneer Inn

This vintage inn, situated at the corner of Hotel and Wharf Streets, is just exactly where it belongs. Stand on its veranda and gaze out at the *Carthaginian II*. Presto . . . it's magic time! You'll see. It was even a favorite spot for actors like Errol Flynn and later Spencer Tracy, when he was in Lahaina filming *Devil at Four O'clock*. The green and white inn was built in 1901 to accommodate interisland ferry passengers, but its style seems much older. If ironwork had been used on the veranda, you'd think you were in New Orleans. A new wing was built behind it in 1965 and the two form a courtyard. Make sure to read the hilarious rules governing behavior that are posted in the main lobby. The inn is still functional and retains some character and atmosphere even though it has undergone a recent major remodeling.

Baldwin Home

One of the best attractions in Lahaina is the Baldwin Home, on the corner of Front and Dickenson Streets. It was occupied by Doctor/Reverend Dwight Baldwin, his wife Charlotte, and their eight children. He was a trained teacher, as well as the first doctor/dentist in Hawaii. The building served from the 1830s to 1868 as a dispensary, meeting room, and boarding home for anyone in need. The two-foot-thick walls are of

Carthaginian II

ROBERT NILSEN

cut lava, and the mortar made of crushed coral over which plaster was applied. As you enter, notice how low the doorway is, and that the doors inside are "Christian doors"—with a cross forming the upper panels and an open Bible at the bottom. The Steinway piano that dominates the entrance was built in 1859. In the bedroom to the right, along with all of the period furniture, is a wooden commode. Also notice the lack of closets; all items were kept in chests. Upstairs was a large dormitory where guests slept.

The doctor's fees are posted and are hilarious. Payment was by "size" of sickness: very big $50, diagnosis $3, refusal to pay $10! The Reverend Baldwin was 32 when he arrived in Hawaii from New England, and his wife was 25. She was supposedly sickly (eight children!), and he had heart trouble, so they moved to Honolulu in 1868 to receive better health care. The home became a community center, housing the library and meeting rooms. Today, the Baldwin Home is a showcase museum of the Lahaina Restoration Society. It's open daily 10 a.m.-4 p.m., admission $3 adult (or $5 for the Baldwin House and the *Carthaginian II*), $2 seniors, and $5 for the family.

The oldest coral-block house in Hawaii was built for Rev. William Richards and his family when they came to serve in Lahaina in the 1830s. Now gone, the house occupied the site of Campbell Park next door to the Baldwin Home.

Master's Reading Room

Originally a missionaries' storeroom, the Master's Reading Room was converted to an officers' club in 1834. Located next door to the Baldwin Home, these two venerable buildings constitute the oldest Western structures on Maui, and fittingly, this uniquely constructed coral-stone building is home to the Lahaina Restoration Foundation, tel. (808) 661-3262. The building is not really open to the public, but you can visit to pick up maps, brochures, and information about Lahaina; open weekdays 9 a.m.-4 p.m.

The **Lahaina Restoration Foundation,** begun in 1962 by Jim Luckey, a historian who knows a great deal about Lahaina and the whaling era, is now headed by Keoki Freeland, an old Maui resident and grandson of the builder of the Pioneer Inn. The main purpose of the foundation is to preserve the flavor and authenticity of Lahaina without stifling progress—especially

tourism. The foundation is privately funded and has managed to purchase many of the important historical sites in Lahaina. It owns two of the buildings mentioned, the restored Wo Hing Temple, and the land under the U.S. Seamen's Hospital, and it will own the plantation house next door to it in a few years. The 42 people on the board of directors come from all socioeconomic backgrounds. You don't get on the board by how much money you give but by how much effort and time you are willing to invest in the foundation; the members are extremely dedicated. Merchants approach the foundation with new ideas for business and ask how they can best comply with the building codes. The townspeople know that their future is best served if they preserve the feeling of old Lahaina rather than rush headlong into frenzied growth. The historic village of Williamsburg, Virginia, is often cited as Lahaina's model, except that Lahaina wishes to remain a "real" living, working town.

Hale Pa'ahao

This is Lahaina's old prison, located midblock on Prison Street, and its name literally means "Stuck-in-Irons House." It was constructed by prisoners in the 1850s from blocks of stone salvaged from the old defunct Fort. It had a catwalk for an armed guard and cells complete with shackles for hardened criminals, but most were drunks who yahooed around town on the Sabbath, wildly spurring their horses. The cells were rebuilt in 1959, the gatehouse in 1988, and the structure is maintained by the Lahaina Restoration Foundation. The cells, curiously, are made of wood, which shows that the inmates weren't that interested in busting out. It's open daily; admission is free but donations are accepted.

Malu Ulu O Lele Park

"The Breadfruit Shelter of Lele" park—Lele was the former name of Lahaina—is a nondescript area at the corner of Shaw and Front that was at one time the most important spot in Lahaina. Here was a small pond with a diminutive island in the center. The pond, Mokuhinia, was home to a *mo'o,* a lizard spirit. The tiny island, Mokuula, was the home of the Maui chiefs and the Kamehamehas when they were in residence. It became a royal mausoleum, but in the early years of the 20th century all the remains were taken away and the pond was filled and the ground leveled. King Kamehameha III and his sister Princess Nahienaena were raised together in Lahaina. They fell in love, but the new ways caused turmoil and tragedy. Instead of marrying and producing royal children, a favored practice only 20 years earlier, they were wrenched apart by the new religion. He, for a time, numbed himself with alcohol, while she died woefully from a broken heart. She was buried here, and for many years Kamehameha III could frequently be found at her grave, quietly sitting and meditating.

Kamehameha Iki Park

Across the street from Malu Ulu O Lele Park was the site of Hale Piula, a two-story royal stone palace built in the late 1830s for King Kamehameha III. Never finished, its stones were later used to construct the courthouse that now stands between the banyan tree and harbor. This mostly barren spot is now known as Kamehameha Iki Park. On this site the 62-foot double-hulled sailing canoe, Mo'o Kiha ("Sacred Lizard"), has been built by the cultural group Hui O Wa'a Kaulua, and is considered by them to be "Maui's flagship of Hawaiian culture and goodwill." Future plans for the park include additional canoes, canoe sheds, traditional-style buildings, landscaping, and educational and cultural training programs. Access to one of the two in-town beaches is here.

Wainee Church and Cemetery

The church itself is not impressive, but its history is. This is the spot where the first Christian services were held in Hawaii, in 1823. A church was built here in 1832 that could hold 3,000 people, but it was razed by a freak hurricane in 1858. Rebuilt, it survived until 1894, when it was deliberately burned by an angry mob, upset with the abolition of the monarchy in Hawaii and the islands' annexation by the United States. Another church was built, but it too was hit not only by a hurricane but by fire as well. The present structure was built in 1953. In the cemetery is a large part of Maui's history: buried here are Hawaiian royalty. Lying near each other are Queen Keopuolani, her star-crossed daughter, Princess Nahienaena, and old Governor Hoapili, their royal tomb marked by two large headstones surrounded by a wrought-iron fence. Other graves hold missionaries such as William Richards and many infants and children.

Churches and Temples

You may wish to stop for a moment at Lahaina's churches and temples dotted around town. They are reminders of the mixture of faiths and peoples that populated this village and added their particular cultural styles. **Holy Innocents Episcopal Church,** built in 1927, is on Front Street, near Kamehameha III school. Known for its "Hawaiian Madonna," its altar is resplendent with fruits, plants, and birds of the islands. Stop by on Sunday when the church is full and hear the sermon preached and hymns sung in Hawaiian. **The Episcopal Cemetery** on Wainee Street shows the English influence in the islands. Many of the royal family, including King Kalakaua, became Anglicans. This cemetery holds the remains of many early Maui families, and of Walter Murray Gibson, the notorious settler, politician, and firebrand of the 1880s (see the "History" section of the "Introduction" to the Lanai chapter). Just behind is **Hale Aloha,** "House of Love," a small structure built by Maui residents in thanksgiving for being saved from a terrible smallpox epidemic that ravaged Oahu but bypassed Maui in 1858. The structure was restored in 1974. Also on Wainee is **Maria Lanakila Church,** the site of the first Roman Catholic Mass in Lahaina, celebrated in 1841. The present structure dates from 1928. Next to the church's cemetery is the **Seamen's Cemetery** where many infirm from the ships that came to Lahaina were buried after failing to recover. Most stones have been obliterated by time, and only a few remain. Herman Melville came here to pay his last respects to a cousin buried in this yard. **Hongwanjii Temple** is also on Wainee, between Prison and Shaw. It's a Buddhist temple with the largest congregation in Lahaina and dates from 1910, though the present structure was raised in 1927. Down Luakini Street is the tall clapboard **Shingon Buddhist Temple,** a plantation-era structure.

The **Wo Hing Temple** on Front Street is the Lahaina Restoration Foundation's newest reconstruction. It was opened to the public in 1984 and shows the Chinese influence in Lahaina. Downstairs are displays, upstairs is the altar. In the cookhouse next door, you can see film clips of Hawaii taken by the Edison Company in 1899 and 1906. It's open daily 10 a.m.-4:15 p.m.; admission is by donation.

The **Lahaina Jodo Mission** is near Mala Wharf on Ala Moana Street. When heading west,

The Wo Hing Temple was restored by the Lahaina Restoration Foundation.

B. COWAN

you'll leave the main section of town and keep going until you see a sign over a building that reads "Jesus Coming Soon." Turn left toward the beach and you'll immediately spot the three-storied pagoda. Here the giant bronze Buddha sits exposed to the elements. The largest outside of Asia, it was dedicated in 1968 in commemoration of the centennial of the arrival of Japanese workers in Hawaii. The grounds are impeccable and serenely quiet. You may stroll around, but the buildings are closed to the public. If you climb the steps to peek into the temple, kindly remove your shoes. The entire area is quiet and a perfect spot for solitary meditation if you've had enough of frenetic Lahaina. The Pu-upia cemetery is across the street along the beach. It seems incongruous to see tombstones set in sand. There is beach access here between the temple and cemetery, at the end of Pu'unoa Place, and at the turnaround on Kai Pali Place, the next two streets in toward town.

Mala Wharf

Once an integral part of Lahaina commerce, the Mala Wharf now stands decaying at the northern end of town. It sports a boat launch ramp, which is used by some local fishermen and some ocean activities companies. There are restrooms here but no other amenities or services.

U.S. Seamen's Hospital

This notorious hospital was reconstructed by the Lahaina Restoration Foundation in 1982. Here is where sick seamen were cared for under the auspices of the U.S. State Department. Allegations during the late 1850s claimed that the care here extended past the grave! Unscrupulous medicos supposedly charged the U.S. government for care of seamen who had long since died. The hospital is located at Front and Baker, heading toward Kaanapali, near the Jodo Mission. While the stony exterior of this building has been maintained, the building now houses Paradise TV, a company that produces the visitor channel. In the front yard is a 10,000-pound, swivel-end Porter anchor, found off Black Rock in Kaanapali.

Lahainaluna

Head up the mountain behind Lahaina on Lahainaluna Road for approximately two miles. On your left you'll pass the **Pioneer Sugar Mill,** in operation since 1860. Once at Lahainaluna ("Above Lahaina") you'll find the oldest school west of the Rockies, opened by the Congregationalist missionaries in 1831. Children from all over the islands, and many from California, came here if their parents could afford to send them away to boarding school. Today, the school is West Maui's public high school, but many children still come here to board. The first students were not only given a top-notch academic education, but a practical one as well. They built the school buildings, and many were also apprentices in the famous **Hale Pa'i** ("Printing House"), which turned out Hawaii's first newspaper and made Lahaina famous as a printing center.

One look at Hale Pa'i and you think of New England. It's a white stucco building with blue trim and a wood-shake roof. It houses a replica printing press and copies of documents once printed here. It was restored in 1982 and is open Mon.-Fri. 10 a.m.-3 p.m. If you visit the campus when school is in session, you may go to Hale Pa'i, but if you want to walk around, please sign in at the vice principal's office. Lahainaluna High School in still dedicated to the preservation of Hawaiian culture. Every year, in April, it celebrates the anniversary of the death of one of its most famous students, David Malo. Considered Hawaii's first scholar, he authored the definitive *Hawaiian Antiquities.* His final wish was to be buried "high above the tide of foreign invasion," and his grave is close to the giant "L" atop Mount Ball, behind Lahainaluna. At graduation, students from the school follow a decades-old tradition of surrounding the "L" with lighted tiki torches, making quite a sight from town. On the way back down to town, you get a wide, impressive panorama of the cane fields, port, Lahaina Roads, and Lanai, and realize that Lahaina is not a big place as you can see it all easily from end to end.

Heading East

Five miles east of Lahaina along the coastal road (Ht. 30) is the little village of **Olowalu.** Today, little more than the Olowalu General Store and Chez Paul French Restaurant are here. This was the place of the Olowalu Massacre perpetrated by Captain Metcalf, whose far-reaching results greatly influenced Hawaiian history. Two American seamen, Young and Davis, were connected with this incident, and with their help Kamehameha I subdued all of Hawaii. Behind the general store a half-mile dirt track leads to **petroglyphs;** make sure you pass a water tower within the first few hundred yards because there are three similar roads here. You'll come to the remains of a wooden stairway going up a hill. There once was an HVB Warrior here, but it might be gone. Claw your way up the hill to the petroglyphs, which are believed to be 300 years old.

If you continue east on Route 30, you'll pass **Papawai** and **McGregor Point,** both noted for their vistas and as excellent locations to spot whales in season. The road sign merely indicates a scenic lookout. Near mile marker 14 there is good snorkeling.

BEACHES

The best beaches around Lahaina are just west of town in Kaanapali, or just east toward Olowalu. A couple of adequate places to spread your towel are right in Lahaina, but they're not quite on a par with the beaches just a few miles away.

In-Town Beaches

One beach stretches east of the harbor starting at Kamehameha Iki Park. It's crowded at times

Hale Pa'i, the oldest printing house west of the Rocky Mountains

ROBERT NILSEN

and there's plenty of "wash up." It's cleaner and quieter at the east end down by Lahaina Shores Hotel. Close to the old royal compound, it was a favorite with the *ali'i*. There are restrooms, the swimming is fair, and the snorkeling acceptable past the reef. **Lahaina Beach** is at the west end of town near Mala Wharf. Follow Front to Pu'unoa Place and turn down to the beach. This is a good place for families with tots because the water is clear, safe, and shallow.

Puamana Beach County Park

About two miles before you enter Lahaina from the southeast along Route 30, you'll see signs for this beach park, a narrow strip between the road and the sea. The swimming and snorkeling are only fair. The setting, however, is quite nice with picnic tables shaded by ironwood trees. The views are terrific and this is a great spot to eat your plate lunch only minutes from town.

Launiupoko Wayside Park

A mile farther southeast, this park has restrooms and showers, but only a small enclosed kiddie beach that's best at high tide when it fills with water. This is more of a picnic area than anything else, although many come to sunbathe on the grass below the coconut trees. Beginning surfers like this spot and some beginning surf lessons are taught here because the waves are gentle.

South of here you'll see lots of shore fishermen and others out for a quiet afternoon. Although not a designated park, the water is adequate for swimming. Find parking where you can under the trees.

East of Olowalu

Between Olowalu and the highway tunnel are **Ukumehame Beach County Park** and **Papalaua Wayside.** The first is a small park with picnic tables, barbecue pits, toilets, and a tiny lawn for sunbathing; swimming is okay. The second is an unimproved area with lots of ironwood trees for shade. This long narrow beach is a favorite of shore fishermen.

Wahikuli State Wayside

Along Route 30 between Lahaina and Kaanapali, this park is a favorite with local people and excellent for a picnic. With three parking areas, it's as if the park was split into three units. This wayside is very clean and well maintained. Tennis courts are located up across the street behind the main Lahaina post office.

Just up the highway, as if connected to this wayside park, is **Hanakaoo Beach County Park.** This beach runs north past some of the most exclusive hotels on the island. Often the local canoe club will put their canoes in the water here and at certain times of the year paddling events will be held at this beach.

ACCOMMODATIONS

Lodging in Lahaina is limited, surprisingly inexpensive, and an experience . . . of sorts. Most visitors head for Kaanapali, because Lahaina tends to be hot and hot to trot, especially at night. But you can find good bargains here, and if you want to be in the thick of the "action," you're in the right spot.

Pioneer Inn

This is the oldest hotel on Maui still accommodating guests. Located at 658 Wharf St., Lahaina, HI 96761, tel. (808) 661-3636 or (800) 457-5457, it has undergone more than a facelift. The semi-seedy old-timey essence has now been spiffed up and yuppified. Now a Best Western hotel, the Pioneer had half a million dollars poured into it in 1997-98—with more to come. For decades, the Pioneer Inn had absolutely no luxury whatsoever, only a double scoop of atmosphere. It was the place to come if you wanted to save money and be the star of your own movie with the Pioneer Inn as the stage set. Creaky stairways, threadbare carpets, low-light hallways, shared baths, and questionable merrymakers and occupants—the place had it all. Now the stairway doesn't creak anymore, new carpet has been laid, TVs installed—baths have shiny new tiles and fixtures, bedrooms have new furniture, the queen-size beds are comfortable and covered in Hawaiian quilts, and you can even have a room with air conditioning, although fans and louvered windows are also available. What does remain the same are the lanai, which, depending upon your room, look out over the banyan tree (nonsmoking rooms) or the hotel courtyard (smoking rooms) and the front desk with its many pigeonholes for keys, the posted house rules, and the old salt that stands at the

DOWNTOWN LAHAINA

To Kaanapali
To Kaanapali

KENUI ST.

PIZZA HUT

SEAMEN'S HOSPITAL

THE BAKERY

TRAIN DEPOT

BAKER ST.

HONOAPIILANI HWY.

KUHUA ST.

AKI ST.

PAE'OHI ST.

To Lahainaluna

KAISER PERMANENTE CLINIC

30

PARKING

FIRST HAWAIIAN BANK

LAHAINA CENTER

ST.

GAS

PAPALUA

POST OFFICE

GAS

ANCHOR SQUARE

BANK OF HAWAII

PIONEER MILL

LAHAINA SHOPPING CENTER

LAHAINA SQUARE

GAS

LAHAINALUNA RD.

WO HING TEMPLE

WESTSIDE NATURAL FOODS

DICKENSON ST.

LAHAINA INN

PARKING

FRONT ST.

PLANTATION INN

LAHAINA MARKETPLACE

SEAMEN'S CEMETERY

WAINE'E ST.

PACIFIC WHALE FOUNDATION

MARIA LANAKILA CHURCH

PARKING

PARKING

PARKING

MASTER'S READING ROOM

SHINGON BUDDIST TEMPLE

HAUOLA STONE

BALDWIN HOME

MAUI ISLANDER

BRICK PALACE

PIONEER INN SHOPS

EPISCOPAL CEMETERY

LIBRARY

HALE ALOHA

PIONEER INN

BANYAN TREE

COURTHOUSE

WHARF CINEMA CENTER

Au'au Channel

FORT RUINS

DAN'S GREENHOUSE

HALE PAAHAO (THE PRISON)

Lahaina Small Boat Harbor

KAMEHAMEHA III SCHOOL

PRISON ST.

PARKING

MAUI MEDICAL GROUP

30

LUAKINI ST.

EPISCOPAL CHURCH

LAHAINA HONGWANJII

WAINEE CHURCH

PARKING

MAUI ULO O LELE PARK

KAMEHAMEHA IKI PARK

PARKING

505 FRONT ST. MALL

SHAW ST.

HONOAPIILANI HWY.

LAHAINA SHORES

BAMBULA INN

FRONT ST.

BELLADONNA COTTAGES

OLD LAHAINA HOUSE

ALOHA LANI INN

KAUA'ULA ST.

30

To Maalaea, Kihei, and Kahului

0   0.25 mi

0   0.25 km

© J.D. BISIGNANI AND MOON PUBLICATIONS, INC.

This "old salt" guards the grog shop at the Pioneer Inn.

front door. Rooms run $90-130; AAA and Best Western Gold Club discounts available.

The Plantation Inn

If Agatha Christie were seeking inspiration for *the* perfect setting for one of her mysteries, this is where she would come. The neo-Victorian building is appointed with posted verandas, hardwood floors, natural wood wainscoting and trim counterpointed by floral wall coverings, bedspreads, and deep-cushioned furniture. Rays of sunlight stray through stained-glass windows and wide double doors. Each uniquely decorated room is comfortable, with four-poster beds and private tiled baths with bold porcelain and brass fixtures; most have sofas. The complete illusion is turn-of-the-century, but the modern amenities of a/c, remote TV and VCR, a fridge, daily maid service, and a soothing spa and pool are included. The back ad-

dition brings the total room count to 19. Most of the 12 new units have lanai overlooking the garden, pool, spa, and guest pavilion. Prices are a reasonable $135 standard, $155 superior, $175 deluxe, $215 suite (some with kitchenette and jacuzzi), and all include a filling breakfast buffet at poolside prepared by Gerard's, the fine French restaurant on the first floor. The Plantation Inn also has money-saving options for dinner at Gerard's, rental cars, and package deals. While now associated with the Kaanapali Beach Hotel in Kaanapali, it still maintains great autonomy. For full information contact the inn at 174 Lahainaluna Rd., Lahaina, HI 96761, tel. (808) 667-9225 or (800) 433-6815, fax (808) 667-9293, Web site: www.maui.net/~inn, e-mail: inn@maui.net. Set on a side street away from the bustle, it's simply one of the best accommodations that Maui has to offer.

Lahaina Inn

Just down the street is another reborn classic: the Lahaina Inn, 127 Lahainaluna Rd., Lahaina, HI 96761, tel. (808) 661-0577 or (800) 669-3444, fax (808) 667-9480, Web site: www.lahainainn.com, e-mail: inntown@aloha.net. Completely renovated and remodeled, this one-time dowdy orphan, the old, down-at-the-heels traveler's classic, Lahainaluna Hotel, emerged in 1989 as a lovely lady. Gone from this cockroach paradise are the weather-beaten linoleum floors, bare-bulbed musty rooms, and rusted dripping faucets. In their place are antique-stuffed, neo-Victorian, tastefully appointed rooms that transport you back to the late 1800s. Each room is individually decorated and nothing in any room is older than 1894. Period pieces include everything from wardrobes to nightstands, rugs, ceramic bowls, mirrors, pictures, lamps, and books. If you really fall in love with something and decide that you can't live without it, make the management an offer. All pieces are privately owned antiques and the owner has been known to part with some. The only deference to modernity are the bathrooms with their new-but-old-style fixtures, the air-conditioning, telephones, and safes—no TV. You can still peer from the balcony of this vintage hotel—each room has a lanai with two hardwood rocking chairs and a table—or observe the masses below from behind heavy drapes and lace curtains. The 12 units include three spacious suites. Rates are $99 for the rooms and $169 for the parlor suites, and include a complimentary continental breakfast, served every morning from about 7:30 a.m. at the sideboard at the end of the hall. For dinner, you might try downstairs at the renowned David Paul's Restaurant, which offers inn guests a discount. Children over 15 are welcome at the inn. The Lahaina Inn's only minor drawback is the lack of on-site parking. Hotel guests are charged $5 for 24 hours in an adjacent parking lot; this is much lower than regular rates.

Maui Islander

Located a few blocks away from the hubbub, at 660 Wainee St., Lahaina, HI 96761, tel. (808) 667-9766 or (800) 367-5226, the Maui Islander is a very adequate hotel offering rooms with kitchenettes, studios, and one- and two-bedroom suites. All have daily maid service, a/c and TV, plus a swimming pool, lighted tennis courts (hotel guests only), and a barbecue and picnic area. There is a laundry facility on premise. Low-rise design in a garden setting lends a homey atmosphere; activities are planned daily. Basic hotel rooms start at $92, studios $105-114, and suites $125-182. Rates are $10 cheaper for singles. Studios and suites all have kitchens. Even if you don't stay here, take a botanical walk through the garden, where plants are numbered and identified. This fine little hideaway is now an Aston property.

Lahaina Shores

This six-story condo was built before the Lahaina building code limited the height of new structures. Located at the east end of town, at 475 Front St., Lahaina, HI 96761, tel. (808) 661-4835 or (800) 628-6699, the condo has become a landmark for incoming craft. The Shores offers a swimming pool and spa and is the only accommodation in Lahaina located on a beach. From a distance, the Southern-mansion facade is striking; up close, though, it becomes painted cement blocks and false colonnades. The rooms, however, are good value for the money. The basic room contains a full bathroom, powder room, large color TV, and equipped kitchen. They're all light and airy, and the back side views of the harbor or front side of the mountains are the best in town. Studios are $130 mountain view and $165 ocean view; one-bedroom suites are $180 mountain view and $210 ocean view. The penthouse suites run $220 and $245 for mountain and ocean views, respectively. Reduced rates of about 20% are given during low

season. Other amenities include daily maid service, laundry facilities, and an activities desk.

Lahaina Roads

This condo/apartment is at the far west end of town at 1403 Front St., Lahaina, HI 96761, tel. (808) 661-3166 or (800) 624-8203. All units have fully equipped kitchens, TV, and maid service on request. One-bedroom units (for two) run $100, two-bedroom units (for four) are $180. There is a three-night minimum stay and a deposit required to hold your reservation. Select credit cards are honored. There is no beach as it sits right along the seawall, but there is a freshwater pool, and you couldn't have a better view, as every unit faces the ocean. Parking is on ground level below the rooms. Rentals are handled through Klahani Resorts, P.O. Box 11108, Lahaina, HI 96761, tel. (808) 667-2712 or (000) 628-6731, fax (808) 661-5875.

Puamana

A 28-acre private community of condos, located on the south edge of town along the ocean, Puamana is a quiet hideaway away from the hustle and bustle of town. The clubhouse (1923) here was the Pioneer Sugar Company's former plantation manager's residence, and it's a beauty. Surrounding it are broad lawns and the guesthouses. One-bedroom condo units run $100-175, two-bedroom units $140-250, and three-bedroom townhouses $300-350. Discounts are given for long stays. All units have fully equipped kitchens, all linens, TVs and VCRs, a/c, and outdoor barbecue grills. Puamana also features an oceanside swimming pool plus two others on property; a sauna, reading parlor, and lending library in the clubhouse; a guests-only tennis court; badminton and volleyball courts; and children's play areas. The only drawback is that it's wedged against the highway, but a thick hedge blocks out much of the noise. For rentals, contact Klahani Resorts, P.O. Box 11108, Lahaina, HI 96761, tel. (808) 667-2712 or (800) 628-6731, fax (808) 661-5875; or Whaler's Realty, tel. (808) 661-8777 or (800) 367-5632, fax (808) 661-8951.

B&Bs and Guesthouses

Aloha Lani Inn, 13 Kauaula Rd., Lahaina, HI 96761, tel. (808) 661-8040 or (800) 572-5642, fax (808) 661-8045, Web site: www.maui.net/~tony

/index.html, e-mail: tony@maui.net, off Front St., is a homey, cozy, and clean single-family home turned guesthouse. Located across from the neighborhood beach, this guest home is a few minutes' walk south of downtown Lahaina. The three guest rooms rent for $59 single, $69 double and share two baths; two nights minimum. Guests have use of the kitchen, the living room with its books, television, and sound system, laundry facilities, and the backyard lanai under a mango tree. Complimentary (strong) coffee is available all day, but no breakfast is served. For information and reservations, talk with Melinda.

Next door is John and Sherry Barbier's **Old Lahaina House,** P.O. Box 10355, Lahaina, HI 96761, tel. (808) 667-4663 or (800) 847-0761, fax (808) 667-5615. This big salmon-colored house, surrounded by a wall of the same color, has four rooms (two with private baths) that range $50-95. All rooms include a/c, telephone, TV, and access to the swimming pool, which occupies the front yard, and the garden; breakfast is included. Reduced rental car rates can be arranged. Old Lahaina House is a relaxing homey place, lived in by the family (so there are kids around). Web site: www.mauiweb.com /maui/olhouse; e-mail: olh@oldhouse.com).

Just down the road at 418 Front St. is **Belladona Cottages,** tel. (808) 661-0358 or (888) 889-7440, fax (808) 667-0394, Web site: www.mauigate.com/~belladon, e-mail: belladon @mauigate.com. Lush gardens surround this house, and a large swimming pool occupies the yard. Rooms have full baths, TV, a refrigerator and microwave. Rates are $82 a night per couple, $20 each additional person, $550 a week, or $2,000 a month.

In the streets behind, you'll find the **Bambula Inn Bed and Breakfast,** 518 Ilikahi St., Lahaina, HI 96761, tel. (808) 667-6753 or (800) 544-5524, fax (808) 667-0979, Web site: www.maui.net /~bambula, e-mail: bambula@maui.net. Here, the two studios are separated at the back of the house so you're more independent from the family. Each unit has a kitchen, private bath, TV, phone, and lanai. The detached cottage ($95) has a/c while the attached unit ($85) has a ceiling fan; $10 less in low season. Three nights minimum. Breakfast is brought to your room, and a complimentary sunset sail aboard the family sailboat *Bambula* is offered every evening,

weather permitting. Contact Pierre or Irene for information and reservations.

The **GuestHouse,** 1620 Ainakea Rd., Lahaina, HI 96761, tel. (808) 661-8085 or (800) 621-8942, fax (808) 661-1896, Web site: ourworld.compuserve.com/homepages/guesthouse, e-mail: GuestHouse@compuserv.com), is a well-appointed B&B where the host will provide free snorkel gear, and even scuba lessons for a fee. The GuestHouse caters largely to honeymooners and scuba enthusiasts. All rooms have queen beds, a/c, ceiling fans, TV, refrigerators, phones, and private lanai, and all but one have private baths. Full breakfast is provided. Everyone shares the living room, kitchen, barbecue, and laundry facility. Rates for the honeymoon suites run $95 a couple, $85 single, and $15 each additional guest. The room with the shared bath is $65 a couple or $55 single. For all five rooms with two people a room is $395 a night.

Just around the corner at 1565 Kuuipo is **Wai Ola Vacation Paradise,** tel./fax (808) 661-7901 or tel./fax (800) 4WAIOLA, Web site: www.maui .net/~tai/WaiOla.html, e-mail: tai@maui.net. This private home has three units. Located just off the pool, the large one-bedroom apartment is over 1,000 square feet, with full kitchen and amenities. It runs $135 a couple and $15 each extra person up to four. Newly remodeled, the studio apartment is about half as big but also has a full kitchen and all amenities. Located in the garden, it runs $115 a couple. The newest is the honeymoon Kuuipo Room, with its own private lanai and larger king bed. It goes for $120 a night. Low season rates are $20 less. All units have a/c, TV, VCR, and phones, and everyone has use of the laundry facilities and the swimming pool. As a vacation rental, no food is served. Contact Julie Frank at P.O. Box 12580, Lahaina, HI 96761, for information and reservations.

FOOD

Lahaina's menu of restaurants is gigantic; all palates and pocketbooks can easily be satisfied: there's fast food, sandwiches, sushi, happy hours, vegetarian, and elegant cosmopolitan restaurants. Because Lahaina is a dynamic tourist spot, restaurants and eateries come and go with regularity. The following is not an exhaustive list of Lahaina's food spots—it couldn't be. But there is plenty listed here to feed everyone at breakfast, lunch, and dinner. *Bon appétit!*

Fast Food and Snacks

Fanatics can get their fix at: **Burger King** on Front St. near the banyan tree, **Pizza Hut** at 127 Hinau St. near the Sugar Cane Train depot, or at the Lahaina Shopping Center, which has **McDonald's** and **Kentucky Fried Chicken.**

Lappert's Ice Cream, at the Pioneer Inn Mall, not only has ice cream, shave ice, and cookies, but also serves fat- and sugar-free ice cream, about the only thing on Maui that is fat-free! Down in front of the banyan tree, **Tropical Dreams Ice Cream** can also serve up your favorite flavor and probably others you're not familiar with.

A good one for a quick snack is **Mr. Sub** at 129 Lahainaluna Road. It features double-fisted sandwiches and packed picnic lunches.

Planet Juice and Java in the Lahaina Square Shopping Center is a relaxing place to stop for fresh fruit juices, smoothies, and coffee drinks. Also served are nutritious wraps, pitas, garden burgers, pizza, sandwiches, and salads. Eat in or take out.

Take Home Maui at 121 Dickenson St., mail order tel. (800) 545-MAUI, is a food store and delicatessen that specializes in packaging agriculturally inspected Maui produce such as pineapples, papayas, Maui onions, protea, potato chips, macadamia nut products, and even Kona coffee, which they will deliver to you at the airport before your departing flight. For an on-the-spot treat they prepare deli sandwiches like roast beef or ham for under $5.50, a variety of quiches, and sides of macaroni and potato salad. Take Home Maui is famous for its fresh-fruit smoothies, homemade soups, and picnic lunches. Choose a shaded spot on the veranda and enjoy your lunch while taking a break from the jostle of Front Street.

Try **Athens Greek Restaurant** in the Lahaina Cannery Mall food court for gyros, shish kebabs, moussaka, pita, falafel, or tabbouleh, and other Mediterranean specialties. Vegetarian plates available, as are Greek salad and spanakopita.

Your sweet tooth will begin to sing the moment you walk into **The Bakery** at 911 Limahana, near the Sugar Cane Train. You can't beat the stuffed croissants for under $3, or the sandwiches for under $5! Coffee is cheap and the pastries, breads, and pasta are gooood! Open daily 7 a.m.-5 p.m., until noon on Sunday, tel. (808) 667-9062.

Inexpensive

Smokehouse BBQ, 1307 Front St., tel. (808) 667-7005, serves baby back ribs, chicken, and fish smoked over a kiawe grill and smothered in special barbecue sauce. Also available for lunch are a variety of burgers and sandwiches, and always sides like rice, barbecued beans, and cole slaw. This is where local people and those in the know come for a very good but no-frills meal. If eating hearty without caring about the ambiance (actually the sunset view couldn't be better) is your aim, come here. Takeout available.

The **Thai Chef,** tel. (808) 667-2814, will please any Thai food lover who wants a savory meal at a good price. Search for this restaurant stuck in a corner at the Lahaina Shopping Center, open Mon.-Fri. 11 a.m.-2:30 p.m. for lunch, dinner nightly 5-10 p.m. As in most Thai restaurants vegetarians are well taken care of with plenty of spicy tofu and vegetable dishes. The extensive menu offers everything from scrumptious Thai soups with ginger and coconut for $7.25 (enough for two) to curries and seafood. Most entrees are under $10 with a good selection under $8. It's not fancy but food-wise you won't be disappointed. Takeout available. When in Kihei, visit Thai Chef's second restaurant in the Rainbow Mall.

Zushi's is a hole-in-the-wall, very reasonably priced Japanese restaurant selling sushi and various other Japanese dishes directly across the street from McDonald's on Wainee Street. Zushi's serves lunch (takeout too) 11 a.m.-2 p.m., dinner 5-9 p.m. Authentic with most items under $6. Also in the plaza next to the Activities Information Center is a small takeout window with the imaginative name of **Local Food,** which sells local food in the form of plate lunches. Basic, cheap, filling, and good.

The open-air **Cheeseburger in Paradise** at 811 Front St., tel. (808) 661-4855, open 10:30 a.m.-11 p.m., live music nightly, is a joint down by the sea overlooking the harbor out back. Served are a whole slew of burgers priced $6.95-7.95, the jumbo cheese dog covered with cheese and grilled onions for $5.95, or the Maui classic BLT for $5.95. Other selections include the aloha fish and seasoned fries at $9.95, a huge Upcountry salad for $6.95, or various sides for $3.50-6.50. Cheeseburger also has a full bar that sells a range of both imported and domestic beer, along with tropical concoctions. If you were going to pick one spot to have a beer, soak in the sights, and capture the flavor of old Lahaina, "the Burg" has all the trimmings.

Sunrise Cafe, open 6 a.m.-6 p.m. at 693 Front, tel. (808) 661-8558, is the kind of place that locals keep secret. It's a tiny little restaurant where you can have excellent coffee and a sandwich or more substantial gourmet food at down-home prices. The nutritious and wholesome food includes breakfast specials like freshly baked quiche or yogurt and cottage cheese $5.95, and lunch salads from Caesar to fresh island fruit all priced under $7. Heartier appetites can choose various hot or cold sandwiches for under $7, pasta, plate lunches, and a more substantial fish or seafood dinner meal for under $10. A deli case holds scrumptious award-winning pastries that are complemented by fine coffee selections always freshly brewed, and a good selection of herbal teas. Eat inside or out on the back patio and enjoy the nightly live entertainment.

The tiny yellow cinder block **Sushiya Deli** is a local plate lunch, *bento,* and saimin place on Prison Street just after you turn toward the mountains off Front Street. Look for it across the street from the public parking lot. Open weekdays 6 a.m.-4 p.m., they make their own sushi but are usually sold out by early afternoon. You can also choose from a full selection of plate lunches like beef teriyaki, or a hamburger plate. This is a very local restaurant with unbeatable prices.

Next door to the new Old Lahaina Luau venue near Mala Wharf is **Aloha Plate Lunch,** tel. (808) 661-3322, a great spot for a simple authentic meal and a cold drink. While noodle dishes, burgers, and sandwiches are on the menu, the specialties are the plate lunches. Available in three sizes, they run $2.95-9.95. Open 10:30 a.m.-10 p.m.; happy hour 3-7 p.m. Live Hawaiian music is performed on a regular schedule, with karaoke on Thursday, Friday, and Saturday 9 p.m.-1 a.m.

Also good for a filling local meal is **Local Boys** in the Lahaina Square Mall. Most items on the full menu are $6-7. Also in this shopping center is **Denny's,** which serves up standard American fare.

The Wharf Shopping Center at 658 Front St. includes the inexpensive **Blue Lagoon Tropical Bar and Grill** on the ground floor, open daily 9 a.m.-10 p.m. The surroundings in the courtyard are pleasant, and most everything on the menu is under $12. **Orange Julius** dispenses its famous drinks, along with hot dogs and sandwiches for a quick, cheap meal. To the rear on the opposite side is **Song's Oriental Kitchen.** This unpretentious restaurant is of the precooked hot plate variety, but you can stuff yourself on meals like beef stew for $3.95 or barbecued chicken, $3.85, all with two-scoop rice and macaroni salad. **Chun's Chinese Barbecue** on the second level offers plate lunches, *bento,* a full selection of Chinese food, and some Korean favorites. Also in this center are **Nanny's Kitchen** for hearty German food and **Pancho and Lefty's** Mexican restaurant.

Located over the ABC Store at the Wharf Cinema Center is **Il Bucaniere,** tel. (808) 661-3966. Open for lunch 11 a.m.-2:30 p.m. and dinner from 5:30 p.m., Il Bucaniere offers live entertainment nightly 6-10 p.m. A casual place that overlooks the big banyan tree at Lahaina Harbor, lunch might be soup and salad, pasta, sandwiches, burgers, or pizza, most for under $10. Dinner includes more pizza, salads, and a wider selection of pasta, meat, and fish for under $15. *Pu pu* can be ordered after dinner until closing. Full bar.

The Hard Rock Café, at the Lahaina Shopping Center on the corner of Front and Papalaua Streets, tel. (808) 667-7400, open daily from 11:30 a.m., is a large breezy, screened restaurant keeping the rock 'n' roll faith. Over the bar is a '59 Cadillac convertible woody, and on the walls are prints of rock stars and electric guitars including a Gibson autographed by The Grateful Dead. The floors have a shiny patina, and the raised stools and round-top tables give you a view of the street and the sea beyond. Menu prices are moderate, with homemade onion rings at $3.75, Caesar salad for $7.59, country club sandwich at $7.99, barbecued chicken for $8.95, and the natural veggie burger for $7.99. The bar serves house wine, champagne, domestic and imported beer, mixed drinks, soft drinks, and coffee. Sit inside at the bar or dining section or outside under the umbrellas. Food is served until 10 p.m. Sun.-Thurs., until 10:30 Friday and Saturday; the bar is open two hours longer every night.

Almost next door at 900 Front St. is **World Cafe,** tel. (808) 661-1515, basically a sports bar with pool and foosball tables. Food includes sandwiches, chicken wings, pizza, and burritos. Drinks are well prices and every night there is a special. Always music, but no dancing. The World Cafe is a good-time bar, a fine place for a little fun.

Aside from the full range of produce, vitamins, health foods, and bulk foods, the **Westside Natural Foods and Deli** on Lahainaluna St., tel. (808) 667-2855, has some reasonably priced and healthy prepared hot and cold foods and fruit drinks. Open daily until 9 p.m., 8 p.m. on Sunday.

Moderate

You won't be a pawn when you walk onto the black-and-white checkered floor at **Longhi's,** 888 Front St., tel. (808) 667-2288, open daily 7:30 a.m.-10 p.m. Longhi owns the joint and he's a character. He feels that his place has "healing vibes" and that man's basic food is air. Longhi's has been around since 1976 and it's many people's favorite. Prices at Longhi's may seem expensive but the portions are enormous and can easily fill two. Better yet, order a half-order. With all meals and salads comes a wonderful basket of jalapeño and pizza breads. Mornings you can order frittatas, like spinach, ham, and bacon, easily enough for two. A good lunch choice is pasta Siciliana with calamari, spicy with marinara sauce; for dinner, the prawns amaretto and shrimp Longhi are signature dishes. Save room for the fabulous desserts. It's hard not to have a fine meal here, and the wine list is a winner. There's always a line, reservations accepted, never a dress code, and always complimentary valet parking! Live music is provided only on Friday and Saturday evenings.

Kobe Japanese Steak House is at 136 Dickenson at the corner of Luakini, tel. (808) 667-5555, open daily for dinner from 5:30 p.m. Service is *teppan yaki*-style, which means that the chef comes to you. His sharp blade flashes through the air and thumps the table, keeping the culinary beat as it slices, dices, and minces faster than any Veg-o-matic you've ever seen. The delectables of marinated meat, chicken, and vegetables are then expertly flash-fried at your own grill, oftentimes with aplomb in a ball of sake-induced flame. The experience is fun, the food very good, and the interior authentic Japanese. *Teppan* meals come complete with rice, soup, and tea. Ex-

pect to spend at least $18 for an entree (less for the early bird specials), $10 for an appetizer, and $11 for four pieces of sushi. Complement your meal with a glass of sake or Japanese beer.

Pioneer Inn Grill and Bar, tel. (808) 661-3636, at the historic Pioneer Inn serves breakfast 6:30-11 a.m., offering buttermilk pancakes for $4.95, corned beef hash and eggs for $8.95, and a selection of side orders for under $1.50. From 11 a.m.-5:30 p.m., lunch is a hearty bowl of Portuguese soup for $5.95, romaine Caesar salad for $8.95, a full selection of sandwiches for under $9, or a variety of burgers for less than $11. Pioneer Inn also has ice cream, shaved ice, and a host of desserts. Dinner is also served at the hotel 5:30-10 p.m. Try the baby back rib appetizers for under $10 or soup and salad. Select dinner entrees are grilled beef filet for $21.95, shellfish for around $20.95, and herbed chicken at $15.95. Since the Pioneer Inn is the oldest hotel in town, and a true landmark with a great lanai from which you can view the harbor, the experience is really the history and the atmosphere.

Kimo's, 845 Front St., tel. (808) 661-4811, is friendly and has great harbor and sunset views on the lower level. If you're in Lahaina around 6 p.m. and need a break, head here to relax with some "Kimo therapy." Popular, but no reservations taken. Kimo's offers seafood from $16.95, with most entrees $15-20, and is known for the catch-of-the-day, usually the best offering on the menu; limited menu for children. Dine upstairs or down. The downstairs bar has top-notch well drinks featuring brand-name liquors.

Across the street, **Moose McGillycuddy's,** tel. (808) 667-7758, is almost an institution. A wild and zany place, there is music nightly (live on Friday and Saturday), daily specials, early bird specials (both breakfast and dinner), and a happy hour 3-6 p.m. The large portions are filling, and the menu reads like a book. Take a moment and have a look at all the stuff hanging on the walls.

Located at 839 Front St. is **Aloha Cantina,** tel. (808) 661-8788, with touches that might remind you of a Mexican restaurant or beach palapa. Serving breakfast, lunch, and dinner, the place is open 8 a.m.-10 p.m. (till 11:30 on Thursday and Friday), with live music most nights. Breakfast meals include omelettes and huevos rancheros for around $6.95, while a fajita lunch or sandwich costs a few dollars more. For dinner, it's especially known for the chicken, beef, or shrimp fajitas, which run about $15, but Aloha Cantina has most other items that you'd expect on the menu of a Mexican restaurant. To complement your entree, order a tropical drink or smoothie from the bar and watch the sunset off the back veranda.

The Lahaina Fish Company, 831 Front St., tel. (808) 661-3472, open daily from 11 a.m. for lunch and 5-10 p.m. for dinner, buys from local fishermen so the fish is guaranteed fresh. Belly up to the Hammerhead Bar, fashioned from glass and brass, or choose a table that looks directly out onto Lahaina Harbor. Notice the vintage Coca Cola vending machine and a display of knots that were tied by the old salts who visited Lahaina. Happy hour brings domestic beer, house wine, and well drinks for $2, while imports and exotic drinks are only $2.50. The limited lunch menu has burgers and other light foods, mostly for under $10. The evening dinner menu starts with dinner salads at $2.95, fried calamari at $8.95, or a bowl of fresh fish chowder for $3.95. Entrees can be island fish and chips at $8.95, fisherman's pasta with fish and vegetables for $12.95, or sautéed sea scallops for $16.95. Meat and poultry dishes include Hawaiian ginger chicken for $12.95, luau-style pork ribs for $15.95, or top sirloin steak for $12.95. The fresh fish, depending on what's caught that day, is grilled, oven broiled, or blackened Cajun style and offered at market price, and every day brings a chef's special that ranges $17.95-21.95.

The Old Lahaina Cafe is located at the 505 Front Street Mall and is famous for offering one of the best luau on Maui. The post-and-beam cafe, tel. (808) 661-3303, open daily 7:30 a.m.-10 p.m., happy hour noon-6 p.m., is blue-on-blue with shutters that open to the sea breezes. Breakfast entrees are served 7:30-11:30 a.m., with Sunday brunch 8 a.m.-3 p.m., and include the *paniolo* breakfast of two eggs, Portuguese sausage, pineapple sausage, bacon or papaya wedge, along with rice or home-fried potatoes for $6.95. You can build your own omelette from $5.95, or forget about your arteries and order a *loco moco*, two fried eggs over hamburger steak with gravy on a bed of rice for $6.95. Lunch, served noon-3:30 p.m., offers very reasonable selections like soup du jour for $3.75, a selection of sandwiches $6.95-9.95, and an assortment of plate lunches for under $7.95. Dinner entrees, served 5:30-10 p.m., include fresh island fish broiled over *kiawe* or sautéed in a papaya and ginger sauce, or the luau dinner (without the entertainment) that includes kalbi ribs, chicken long rice, *lomi lomi* salmon, sweet potatoes, rice, and kalua pork. There's also broiled lobster tail and a selection of beef and chicken entrees that are priced $12.95-23.95. The Old Lahaina Cafe has very good food at reasonable prices in a congenial atmosphere and is worth the money.

Next door is **Hecock's,** tel. (808) 661-8810, open daily 7 a.m.-10 p.m. for food service, bar open until 2 a.m., owned and operated by Tom and Nancy, a husband and wife team who bring you good food at reasonable prices. Hecock's breakfast could be ranch eggs with a grilled New York steak for $8.95, or a three-egg scampi omelette for $8.95, along with the classics like French toast or buttermilk pancakes with the trimmings for under $8. The lunch menu offers a chef salad for $8.95, assorted burgers and sandwiches priced under $8.25, and pasta dishes like cheese tortellini or fettuccine Alfredo for under $8.95. The dinner bill of fare includes fettuccine Alfredo $14.95, scampi for $20.95, and rack of lamb at $21.95. A children's menu, happy hour, daily specials, and an early bird special offered 5-6 p.m. help to keep prices down.

Pacific'O Cafe, tel. (808) 667-4341, at 505 Front St., is a newcomer to the restaurant scene in Lahaina but has garnered a solid reputation. Foods and flavors from the West, the East, and the Pacific are blended together, using only the freshest ingredients from the islands, to create a very delectable Pacific Rim cuisine. Start with a fine Kula mixed green salad for $4.50 and move on to a more substantial Caesar with roasted bell peppers, macadamia nuts, and anchovies for $7.50. Lunch entrees, like the seared fish sandwich or the penne pasta with smoked shrimp, sautéed tomatoes, and fresh basil, are all reasonable at less than $11. Dinner entrees run $21-25 and might be fish tempura wrapped in wakame, mushroom ravioli, or sesame-crusted lamb. Comfortable seating, attentive servers, and the views out over the ocean might tempt you to linger over your meal and savor an excellent bottle of wine. Open daily for lunch 11 a.m.-4 p.m. and dinner 5:30-10 p.m.; there's live jazz Thurs.-Sat. evenings.

Lahaina Coolers on Dickenson St. presents quick easy meals throughout the day in an open-air setting. Try pancakes, omelettes, or eggs Benedict for breakfast; salads, sandwiches, and burgers for lunch; and pasta, tortillas, fresh fish, steak, and burgers for dinner. Nothing on the evening menu is over $16.95, with most in the $12-15 range. Coolers is a late-night place; you can get food until midnight.

B.J.'s Pizzeria, tel. (808) 661-0700, on the second floor overlooking the seawall, is one of the newer places in town. Along with pizza, try the pasta, sandwiches, and a sesame chicken salad. Eat in or take out. B.J.'s has a large beer selection and live entertainment in the evenings. Close by is **Planet Hollywood**, serving California cuisine with a Hawaiian twist, and up the street is the movie-inspired **Bubba Gump's** for shrimp off the old wooden boat.

For a little bit of New York in Lahaina, try **Scaroles** for pizza—its main focus—salads, sandwiches, and pasta dishes. Done with thick crusts, the pizzas run $12-25; salads are about $6, sandwiches are less than $9, and the pasta dishes vary $7-13. Even with something from the bar, you can have an inexpensive lunch or dinner. Scaroles is located at 930 Wainee St. in Lahaina, tel. (808) 661-4466.

Compadres Mexican Bar and Grill, tel. (808) 661-7189, at the Lahaina Cannery Mall, has a full menu ranging from nacho appetizers through soups, salads, and sandwiches to a complete list of entrees, most in the $9-18 range. Sit down, relax, have a beer or margarita, and enjoy your meal and the surroundings.

Gourmet Dining

When you feel like putting a major dent in your budget and satisfying your desire for gourmet food, you should be pleased with one of the following.

Whoever said "East is East and West is West" would have whistled a different tune if only they had had the pleasure of dining at the **Avalon**, tel. (808) 667-5559, in the courtyard at 844 Front St., open daily for lunch and dinner. Owner/chef Mark Ellman has put together a uniquely blended Hawaiian regional cuisine menu. Here are dishes from Sausalito to Saigon, and from Mexico City to Tokyo, with a bit of Nebraska and Hong Kong thrown in for good measure. Moreover, Avalon has spiced, herbed, and garnished its delectables by mixing and matching the finest and most refined tastes from all the geographical areas, creating a culinary extravaganza. If you're tired of the same old appetizers, try Maui onion rings with tamarind-chipotle catsup, or don't resist the combination platter with a selection of the best appetizers for $16.95 (enough for two). Move on to mixed greens and crispy noodles tempting in a ginger sesame dressing, or *gado-gado* on a bed of brown rice turned sumptuous by a Balinese peanut sauce. Drift the Pacific through their grill selections like whole fresh *opakapaka* in Thai sauce. If you need more convincing, try the chili seared salmon, which is a layered dish of mashed potatoes, eggplant, salmon, greens, and island tomato salsa, or the mouthwatering Asian pasta like mama-*san* wished she could make. If only people could get along together as well as this food. Choose indoor seating where you dine in air-conditioned comfort, or dine alfresco in the courtyard. The Avalon boasts a fine wine list, or order one of its unique drinks, like the chocolate martini. The Avalon has only one dessert, caramel miranda, made fresh daily and sure to please. While here, have a look at the art on the walls.

Gerard's elegant restaurant is in the Plantation Inn, at 174 Lahainaluna Rd., tel. (808) 661-8939, open daily for dinner only 6-9 p.m., with validated free parking nearby. The epitome of neo-Victorian charm, the room is comfortable with puff-pillowed wicker chairs and always set with fine crystal atop starched linen. Fronting the building is a small dining garden, and inside the interior is rich with hardwood floors and oak bar. Chef Gerard Reversade, trained in the finest French culinary tradition since age 14, creates masterpieces. He feels that eating is *the* experience of life, around which everything else that is enjoyable revolves. Gerard insists that the restaurant's waiters and waitresses share his philosophy, so along with the excellent food comes excellent service. The menu changes, but it's always gourmet. Gerard's is not cheap but it's worth every penny as nothing on the menu is less than excellent. Appetizers range $8.50-18.50, entrees $26.50-32.50, and desserts are $7.50. Some superb salad choices are the island greens with Kiawe honey vinaigrette dressing, or spinach salad with grilled scallops, shaved parmesan cheese, and truffle sauce. Appetizers feature mouthwatering choices like shiitake and oyster mushrooms in a puff pastry. Full entrees like grilled rack of lamb with mint crust or savory stuffed breast of veal with spinach and herb sauce and glazed vegetables titillate the palate. Confit of duck with pommes frites served with mixed greens in a walnut-oil dressing is one of Gerard's superb signature dishes. Even if you possess great self control, you have less than an even chance of restraining yourself from choosing a luscious dessert like crème brûlée, chocolate mousse in cream puffs with raspberry sabayon, or even fresh strawberries glazed with suzette butter and macadamia nut cream.

David Paul's Lahaina Grill, 127 Lahainaluna Rd., tel. (808) 667-5117, open for dinner nightly 6-10 p.m., is one of Lahaina's finest gourmet restaurants. Here owner David Paul Johnson, famous for his sauces, presents "artwork on a plate." The dining room is quite lovely, with coved and molded ceilings from which hang punch-bowl chandeliers illuminating the starched white table settings. The restaurant has expanded from its once-crowded confines to incorporate a much larger and also well-appointed room, and its new chairs are more comfortable, meant for a long romantic evening of salubrious relaxation. The waiters and waitresses, professional, friendly, and well-dressed in black pants, white shirts, and ties, definitely give you attentive service. The menu is wonderful. Start with rich white bean soup, with roasted ham hock broth and goat cheese tortellini for $8, a Kona lobster-crab cake for $15, or a heart of romaine Caesar salad for $12. Entrees include David Paul's signature dish, the "seafood painted desert"—a savory creation of grilled seafood served on a bed of chardonnay and Gorgonzola sauce, and three pepper-flavored butters that David uses to paint cacti and a red setting sun—available on request. Other wonderfully prepared dishes are tequila shrimp and firecracker rice, another signature entree, made from tiger prawns marinated in chili oil, lemons, cilantro, cumin, and brown sugar in a blend of vanilla bean and chili rice for $28, or Kona coffee roasted lamb for $37. Vegetarians will find at least one meatless entree on each menu, and other dietary restrictions can be accommodated by the masterful chefs. No matter what is on the changing menu, you can be assured that the ingredients are the freshest

available. The very wicked dessert tray, with everything priced at $6, combined with a cup of rich roasted coffee, ends a wonderful meal.

Chez Paul, tel. (808) 661-3843, five miles east of Lahaina in Olowalu, is secluded, romantic, very popular, and French—what else! There are two seatings nightly at 6:30 and 8:30 p.m., by reservation only, credit cards accepted. Local folks into elegant dining give it two thumbs up. The wine list is tops, the desserts fantastic, and the food, *magnifique!* Start with luscious hors d'oeuvres like warm Maine lobster salad with a brandy cocktail sauce, homemade country pâté, or more simply with bay shrimp salad, and a bowl of soup du jour all priced $7-16. Entrees are delightful with fresh island fish poached in champagne, scampi smothered with fresh mushrooms, lobster in a cream bisque, veal in lemon butter, or a medley of island vegetables, all priced $22-34, except for *bloc de foie gras* at $36. Chez Paul is definitely worth the trip from Lahaina with a short stroll along the beach recommended as a perfect aperitif.

ENTERTAINMENT

Lahaina is one of those places where the real entertainment is the town itself. The best thing to do here is to stroll along Front Street and people-watch. As you walk along, it feels like a block party with the action going on all around you—as it does on Halloween. Some people duck into one of the many establishments along Front Street for a breather, a drink, or just to watch the sunset. It's all free, enjoyable, and safe.

Art Night
Friday night is Art Night in Lahaina. In keeping with its status as the cultural center of Maui, Lahaina opens the doors of its galleries, throws out the welcome mat, sets out food and drink, provides entertainment, and usually hosts a well-known artist or two for this weekly party. It's a fine social get-together where the emphasis is upon gathering people together to appreciate the arts and not necessarily on making sales. Take your time and stroll Front Street from one gallery to the next. Stop and chat with shopkeepers, munch the goodies, sip the wine, look at the pieces on display, corner the featured artist for comment on his/her work, soak in the music of the strolling

musicians, and strike up a conversation with the person next to you who is eyeing that same piece of art with the same respect and admiration. It's a party. People dress up, but don't be afraid to come casually. Take your time and immerse yourself in the immense variety and high quality of art on display in Lahaina 6-10 p.m.

Halloween

This is one of the big nonofficial events of the year. It seems that everyone dresses in costume, strolls Front Street, parties around town, and gets into the spirit of the evening. It is a party in the street with lots of people, dancing, music, color, and activities. In fact, it's becoming so popular with some that they fly in from Honolulu just for the night.

Nightspots and Dancing

All of the evening musical entertainment in Lahaina is in restaurants and lounges, except for the acclaimed Old Lahaina Luau, now at its new venue near Mala Wharf.

There's piano music with the sound of water falling in the background at the **Blue Lagoon** in the lower courtyard of the Wharf Cinema Center. You, too, can be a disco king or queen on **Longhi's** black-and-white chessboard dance floor every weekend. Longhi's has live music on Friday and Saturday nights featuring island groups. **Moose McGillycuddy's** (just listen for the loud music on Front Street) is still a happening place with nightly music, though it's becoming more of a cruise joint for post-adolescents. Those who have been around Lahaina for a while usually give it a miss, but if you want to feast your eyes on prime American two-legged beef on the hoof, this place is for you.

The open-air **Cheeseburger in Paradise** rocks with live music nightly until 11 p.m. There's no cover charge, and you can sit upstairs or down listening to the tunes. Similarly, you can hear live rock music at **Il Bucaniere** at the Wharf Cinema Center across from the banyan tree, and at the **Pioneer Inn Grill and Bar** at the Pioneer Inn. Other restaurants also offer live music, particularly on the weekends.

Cinemas

Lahaina Cinemas, once the only multiplex theater on West Maui, is located on the third floor of the Wharf Cinema Center. Showing only first-run features, movies start at about noon and run throughout the day. Adults $7, kids 2-11 $3.50, seniors $3.75; all seats $4 until 5 p.m. Call (808) 661-3347 for what's showing. Lahaina's second cinema is **Front Street Theaters** at the Lahaina Center.

The Hawaii Experience Domed Theater, 824 Front St., tel. (808) 661-8314, has continuous showings on the hour daily 10 a.m.-10 p.m. (45-minute duration), for adults $6.95, children 4-12 $3.95. The idea is to give you a total sensory experience by means of the giant, specially designed concave screen. You sit surrounded by it. You will tour the islands as if you were sitting in a helicopter or diving below the waves. And you'll be amazed at how well the illusion works. You'll soar over Kauai's Waimea Canyon, dip low to frolic with humpbacks, and rise over Hawaii's active volcanoes. If you can't afford the real thing, this is about as close as you can get. The lobby of the theater doubles as a gift shop where you can pick up souvenirs like carved whales, T-shirts, and a variety of inexpensive mementos, including Maui chips.

Hula and Polynesian Shows

For a different type of entertainment, stop to see the free grown-up hula show, Wednesday and Friday at 2 p.m., or the *keiki* hula show, same days at 6 p.m., at Hale Kahiko in the parking lot of the Lahaina Shopping Center. Hale Kahiko is a reproduction Hawaiian village displaying implements and items of everyday use; open 9 a.m.-6 p.m. Various weekly shows are also offered at center stage at the Lahaina Cannery Mall. Tuesday and Thursday at 7 p.m. there's a free Polynesian show, and a *keiki* hula show is presented Saturday and Sunday 1-2 p.m.

SHOPPING

Once learned, everybody loves to do the "Lahaina Stroll." It's easy. Just act cool, nonchalant, and give it your best strut as you walk the gauntlet of Front Street's exclusive shops and boutiques. The fun is just in being here. If you begin in the evening, go to the south end of town and park down by Prison Street; it's much easier to find a spot and you walk uptown, catching the sunset.

The Lahaina Stroll

On Prison Street, check out **Dan's Green House,** tel. (808) 661-8412, open daily 9 a.m.-5 p.m., specializing in *fuku-bonsai,* miniature plants originated by David Fukumoto. They're mailable (except to Australia and Japan), and when you get them home, just plop them in water and presto . . . a great little plant (from $25). Dan's also specializes in exotic birds like African gray parrots, macaws from Australia, common cockatoos, and various cheeky parrots, and has a few other miniature animals. Dan's is a great place to browse, especially for families.

As you head up Front Street, the first group of shops includes **Sea Level Trading Company** with mostly women's alohawear and men's aloha shirts, and **Camellia** with a treasure chest laden with gifts and jewelry made from gold, silver, and ivory. Here as well is **Original Maui Divers,** which has some fancy jewelry including its specialty, black tree coral. Check out the jewelry design center on the second floor of the Wharf Cinema Center a few steps away. Visit the "pin and ink" artist upstairs at **Skin Deep Tattooing,** 626 Front St., tel. (808) 661-8531, open daily 10 a.m.-10 p.m., until 5 p.m. Sunday, where you can get a permanent memento of your trip to Maui. Skin Deep features "new age primal, tribal tattoos," Japanese-style intricate beauties, with women artists available for shy women clientele. The walls are hung with sample tattoos that you can choose from. A sobriety test is necessary to get tattooed. No wimps allowed! This is a legitimate place where the artists know what they're doing; they've been in business now for over 20 years.

Moving down the Line

The following shops are all located along Front Street. By no means exhaustive, this list just gives you an idea of some of the unique shops here.

Between the Pioneer Inn and the seawall, walk onto the sandy floor of the Polynesian-style **Gecko Store,** where all the items including shorts, T-shirts, bathing suits, and sweatshirts bear the bug-eyed sucker-footed logo of Hawaii's famous clicking geckos. Nearby is the **Lahaina Hat Co.,** where you can find the perfect chapeau to shield your head from the "merciless" Lahaina sun.

Noah himself would have been impressed with the **Endangered Species Store,** open daily 9 a.m.-10:30 p.m., where a life-sized mountain gorilla, coiled python, flitting butterflies, and fluttering birds bid you welcome to this lovely jam-packed menagerie. The shelves hold world globes, maps, cuddly panda bears, posters of trumpeting elephants, sculptures of soaring eagles, parlor games, postcards, and memento flora- and fauna-inspired T-shirts of 100% cotton designed by local artists. A percentage of the profits from every purchase is set aside to advance environmental issues of all kinds. Moreover, the store tries to deal with vendors who also contribute to the well-being of endangered species and the environment.

Golden Reef, 695 Front St., is open daily 10 a.m.-10 p.m. Inside is all manner of jewelry from heirloom quality to costume baubles made from black, gold, red, and pink coral, malachite, lapis, and mother of pearl. All designs are created on the premises. Everyone will be happy shopping here because prices range from $1 to $1,000 and more. Golden Reef is also very happy to create an individual one-of-a-kind work for you and you alone.

Back on the mountain side of the street, **Tropical Blues,** 754 Front, presents the T-shirt art of Mark and Irene Ciaburri, who create all the designs for their cotton shirts. A display case holds the shimmering rhinestones and twinkling gold of costume jewelry. Next door at 752 Front, one of the three **Serendipity** shops on the island offers a unique collection of casual island wear, furniture, woodcarvings, and accouterments of an Asian and Hawaiian nature.

The **Whaler's Locker,** 780 Front St., open 9 a.m.-10 p.m., is a sea chest filled with hand-engraved scrimshaw on fossilized walrus and mammoth ivory. Lahaina, historically a premier whaling port, has long been known for this sailor's art etched on everything from pocketknives to whale-tooth pendants. Display cases also hold gold and amber jewelry, Niihau shellwork, Japanese netsuke, and even some coral necklaces. If you are looking for a distinctive folk-art gift that truly says Maui, the Whaler's Locker is an excellent store from which to make your choice.

Sharing the same address is **The South Seas Trading Post.** Open daily 8:30 a.m.-10 p.m., it is the second oldest shop in modern Lahaina, dating back to 1871. It indeed has artifacts from the South Pacific, like tapa cloth from Tonga, but also colorful rugs from India, primitive carvings from Papua New Guinea, and Burmese *kalaga* wall hangings with their beautiful and intricate stitching for $30-300. You can pick up a one-of-a-kind bead necklace for only a few dollars, or a real treasure that would adorn any home, for a decent price. Sold are antiques and reproductions; the bona fide antiques have authenticating dates on the back or bottom sides.

In the courtyard just off Front Street and Lahainaluna Rd. is **The Lahaina Market Place,** a collection of semi-open-air stalls and a handful of storefronts, open daily 9 a.m.-9 p.m. Some vendors have roll-up stands and sell trinkets and baubles. Some is junk, but it's neat junk. Four little gift shops here compete for your business as do **Captain Dave's,** which sells fish and chips and other snacks, and a **Häagen-Dazs Dessert Shop,** which has that cooling ice cream you've been looking for. **Maui Crystal Creations** has fine examples of Austrian crystal and pewterware and seems a mainstay of this alleyway market. Three art galleries, all facing Lahainaluna Road, back up against this courtyard.

The Far End

On both sides of Front Street beyond Lahainaluna Road the shops continue. The "sexually incorrect" will love **David's of Hawaii,** at 815 Front St., where you can find all kinds of lewd postcards, T-shirts, and souvenirs. If T-shirts bearing sexually implicit puns offend you, keep strolling—it's nasty in there. Funky and audacious. Open daily 9 a.m.-10:30 p.m.

In the **Old Poi Factory** at 819 Front St. is **Pacific Visions,** selling hand-painted local garments done at Haiku, art-deco items from Los Angeles, San Francisco, and New York, and lots of artifacts from Bali. Open daily. One of the oldest shops at the Poi Factory is **Valley Isle Promotions,** opened in 1974, which specializes in children's and women's clothing, along with 14-karat gold jewelry designed in Indonesia by Jeanette, the store's owner.

Lahaina Scrimshaw, 845 Front St. (across from Wo Hing temple), tel. (808) 661-8820, open daily 9 a.m.-10 p.m., boasts its own master scrimshander, John Lee, who works in the window every day from about 7:30 a.m.-noon, and

who is friendly and willing to answer questions about this seaman's art. Most of the scrimshaw is done on antique whale's teeth from the whaling era or on fossilized walrus and mastodon tusks. The scrimshaw offered is authentic, and made by about 40 artists, most of whom are from Hawaii.

Luana's features contemporary resortwear, hand-painted accessories, and jewelry. **Seabreeze Ltd.** is a souvenir store with fake lei and generic muumuu that are no better or worse than others you'll find along Front Street, but the prices are good, especially for film.

Crazy Shirts also has a great assortment of T-shirts and other clothes. Also in this store at 865 Front St. is the tiny but intriguing **Lahaina Whaling Museum** (free), displaying antiques, nautical instruments, scrimshaw, harpoons, and other whaling artifacts. Open Mon. Sat. 9 a.m.-10 p.m., Sunday until 9 p.m.

Off the Main Drag

Fox Photo at 139 Lahainaluna Rd., tel. (808) 667-6255, open daily, is a full-service, one-hour-developing camera store. It's good in West Maui for any specialized photo needs. A second one-hour lab is down the street and around the corner at 820 Front Street.

Take Home Maui, at 121 Dickenson St., mail order tel. (800) 545-MAUI, is a food store and delicatessen that specializes in packaging "agriculturally inspected" Maui produce such as pineapples, papayas, Maui onions, protea, potato chips, macadamia nut products, and even Kona coffee that they will deliver to you at the airport before your departing flight.

Even if you haven't been out on a whale-watching tour, stop in at the **Pacific Whale Foundation** shop at 143 Dickenson St. for a look at all the clothing, posters, jewelry, and gift items relating to the whale and other sea creatures. It's almost an education having a look here, and the proceeds help support this worthy organization.

Up the street at Dickenson Square is a **Whalers General Store,** for sundries.

The **Salvation Army Thrift Shop** on Shaw Street just up from Front Street has the usual collection of inexpensive used goods but occasionally some great buys on older aloha shirts. Open Mon.-Sat., regular business hours.

505 Front Street Mall

The 505 Front Street Mall, with most shops open daily 9 a.m.-9 p.m., offers a barrel full of shops and restaurants at the south end of Front Street, away from the heavier foot traffic. The mall is like a New England village, and the shopping is good and unhurried with free underground parking for customers. Some shops include a **Whalers General Store; KPOA FM Music Shop,** where you can find the latest in cassettes and CDs, with an emphasis on local Hawaiian sounds; and **Mad About Art,** which handles mostly nostalgic alohawear, jewelry, and Hawaiian-made gifts, photos, and postcards. Several other art and clothing shops inhabit this mall, as do half a dozen restaurants.

The Wharf Cinema Center

The Wharf Cinema Center at 658 Front offers three floors of eateries, shops, and a movie theater. Playing first-run movies, the triplex **Lahaina Cinemas** occupies much of the third floor. Browse **Crazy Shirts** with its excellent selection of quality T-shirts, or **Gigi's Leather Boutique,** for everything from jackets to purses. **Hawaiian Styles and Creations** offers tropical sportswear, and **Island Swimwear** carries bathing suits for men and women. There's a coffee bar where you can relax and read. **Island Coins and Stamps** on the second floor is a shop as frayed as an old photo album. It specializes in philatelic supplies. For postal needs and gifts, stop by the **Lahaina Mail Depot** on the lower level at the rear; open weekdays 10 a.m.-4 p.m., Saturday until 1 p.m. Across the walk is a free exhibit about the lighthouses of Hawaii, a project of the Lahaina Restoration Foundation. The Fresnel lens on display was once in the lighthouse at Kalaupapa on Molokai. Next door to this display is **Island Sandals,** tel. (808) 661-5110, a small shop run in the honest old-style way that produces fully adjustable tie sandals, styled from the days of Solomon. As the gregarious sandalmaker says, he creates the right sandal for $135 ($115 women's) and gives you the left as a gift. Stop in and have him trace your feet for an order. As he works, he'll readily talk about political, social, or local island issues. Out front is an **ABC Discount Store.** For those coming from Kaanapali, both the West Maui Shopping Express and the free Lahaina Express shuttles stop at the Wharf Cinema Center.

Pioneer Inn Shops

Below Pioneer Inn is a clutch of shops that includes **Aloha Magnets** for a zillion of these colorful items to stick on your refrigerator, **Fox One-hour Photo, Products of Hawaii Too** for gift and craft items, **Watch-N-See** for timepieces and sunglasses, a **Lifestyle** alohawear clothing shop, and a **Whalers General Store.** Several other clothing stores are here as are **Waterfront Gallery** for jewelry, gifts, and artwork, **Häagen-Dazs** for ice cream treats, and an **Atlantis submarine** booth where you can arrange a memorable underwater Maui adventure. Most shops are open 9 a.m.-9 p.m.

The Lahaina Shopping Center

The Lahaina Shopping Center, just behind Longhi's, has a few inexpensive shops, **Ace Hardware,** and **Nagasako's Market,** known for its good selection of local and Oriental food. Here as well are the midtown **post office,** a **Bank of Hawaii,** and an **American Savings Bank.** In the back portion, you'll find **Nagasako General Store, Nagasako Variety,** and the **Lahaina Pharmacy,** along with several inexpensive restaurants.

Across Wainee Street is the **Lahaina Square Shopping Center,** with a big **Foodland** grocery store and more cheap eateries. Next door at **Anchor Square** is an activities center.

The Lahaina Center

Lahaina's newest shopping center, at the corner of Front and Papalaua Streets at the north edge of downtown, had the finishing touches put on it in early 1993. The signature establishments of this mall are the **Hard Rock Café,** filled with memorabilia of rock 'n' roll greats and serving American standards and cold beer; the Hawaiian department store Liberty House; a Banana Republic for livable fashions; and **Hilo Hattie** for Hawaiian clothing and gifts. In the center you will also find **Local Motion Hawaii,** a hip clothing store selling tank tops, swimwear, and locally designed T-shirts that can be stenciled on the premises; **Wet Seal** for young women's clothing; several other fashion shops; an **ABC** store for sundries and inexpensive beach gear; a **Dive Maui** outlet for water activities and equipment; and a **Made in Hawaii** shop for a good selection of local products. With pool and foosball tables, the **World Cafe** is something of a sports bar and late-night entertainment spot that also serves food. Cool yourself down at the **Paniolo Coffee Company** with a shave ice or milk shake, or give yourself a pick-me-up with a steaming espresso. Lahaina's second cinema complex, the **Front Street Theaters**, occupies one of the center buildings. There is a pay parking lot here that's free with validation. The West Maui Shopping Express shuttle stops at the Hilo Hattie store more than 10 times a day on its route between Lahaina and Kaanapali; $1 per person each way.

After shopping, stop by **Hale Kahiko** and have a look at the traditional-style Hawaiian buildings and items of everyday use displayed as a cultural showcase in a landscaped enclosure to the side of the parking lot. Open daily 9 a.m.-6 p.m. While here enjoy the hula show at 2 p.m. on Wednesday and Friday or the *keiki* hula show at 6 p.m. on the same days.

Lahaina Cannery Mall

As practical looking as its name on the outside—it is a converted pineapple cannery, after all—the center's bright, well-appointed, and air-conditioned interior features some of the best and most convenient shopping on West Maui, open daily 9:30 a.m.-9 p.m. The mall is located at 1221 Honoapiilani Hwy., near Mala Wharf. If you'll be staying at a condo and doing your own cooking, the largest and generally least expensive supermarket on West Maui is **Safeway,** open daily 24 hours. To book any activities, from a whalewatch to a dinner cruise, you'll find the **Ocean Activities Center** kiosk offers the great activities on Maui for the right price. Sundries can be picked up at the **ABC Store,** and you can beat the sun's glare by stopping into **Shades of Hawaii.** Some of the clothing shops you'll find here are **Crazy Shirts, Maui Waterwear, Escape to Maui,** and **Reyn's.** Food is available at **Compadres Mexican Bar and Grill** and **Mango Cafe,** as well as other shops in the food court. Although the mall is relatively new, don't let that fool you because some of Lahaina's oldest and best shops, like **Lahaina Printsellers,** are here. **Waldenbooks** has one of its excellent, well-stocked stores in the mall. One of the most unusual shops is **The Kite Fantasy,** featuring kites, windsocks, and toys for kids of all ages. You can buy kites like a six-foot flexifoil for more than $100 or a simple triangular plastic kite for only a few bucks. Cloth kites are made from nylon with nice designs for a reasonable $15.95. If you're

into designer coffees and cigars come to **Sir Wilfred's.** It's one of the few places on this side of the island for such delicacies. If you're hungry, try the deli case for pastries and the like, or order up a cup of soup, quiche, lasagna, or a cool drink. A good assortment of gift items round out what's sold here. **Longs Drugs** is one of the cheapest places to buy and develop film. You can also find a selection of everything from aspirin to boogie boards. There's plenty of free parking at this mall, but the West Maui Shopping Express bus stops here a dozen times a day shuttling between Lahaina and Kaanapali; $1 per person each way.

Booths are set up in the mall Mon.-Fri. 10 a.m.-4 p.m., displaying and selling Hawaiian art and crafts. Also, a free **Polynesian Show** is presented every Tuesday and Thursday evening 7-8 p.m., and there's a **Keiki Hula Show** every Saturday and Sunday 1-2 p.m.

Arts

It's said that Lahaina is the world's third-largest art market. Who determined that to be so is a question unanswered, yet it is certain that you can view countless works of art here and spend a fortune acquiring it. Many artists on display at the galleries in Lahaina are local island artists and others from the state, although other Americans and numerous foreigners are also represented. Although not all, many of the galleries in town are open until 10 p.m.

Due to the renovation of the old Lahaina Courthouse in 1998, the **Lahaina Art Society Galleries** had to vacate its digs in the basement of the old jail. They've moved (at least temporarily) to a space in the Lahaina Center, where they still put on month-long exhibits and periodic individual exhibitions. fWhere its future home will be is still in question. For now stroll under the banyan tree every Saturday and Sunday 9 a.m.-5 p.m. to see these artists and craftspeople displaying their wares for sale at **Art in the Park.** The artists here are up and coming, and the prices for sometimes remarkable works are reasonable. These artists are trying to make a living by their skills, and most are not displayed at the well-known galleries in town.

The Village Galleries, with two locations at 120 Dickenson St., tel. (808) 661-4402 or (800) 346-0585, open daily 9 a.m.-9 p.m., and at 180 Dickenson St., tel. (808) 661-5559, were founded by Lynn Shue in 1970 and are among the oldest continuous galleries featuring original works of Maui artists. At the original gallery at 120 Dickenson, enter to find everything from raku pottery to hand-blown glass, and sculptures done in both wood and metal. Some of the accomplished painters on display are: George Allan, who works in oils; Joyce Clark, another oil painter noted for her seascapes; Betty Hay-Freeland, a landscape artist; Fred Kenknight, who uses watercolors to depict island scenes; Lowell Mapes, who also uses oil to render familiar landmarks like the Pioneer Inn. The galleries also have inexpensive items like postcards, posters, and limited edition prints, all perfect as mementos and souvenirs. The gallery at 180 Dickenson St. features more contemporary and abstract works that evoke a feeling more than an actual scene.

The Wyland Gallery, 711 Front St., tel. (808) 667-2285, showcases the works of Wyland, renowned worldwide for his "whaling wall" murals of cavorting whales. Wyland's visionary oil and watercolor paintings of marvelous aquatic scenes adorn the walls, while his compassionate bronze renderings of whales and dolphins sing their soul songs from white pedestals. Also displayed are the organic sculptures of Dale Joseph Evers, a pioneer in functional furnishings, who has turned bronze and acrylic into dolphin-shaped tables. Outside is a quiet lanai overlooking the harbor, where more aquatic-inspired glass sculptures are counterpointed against the actual living sea. At 697 Front St., a second Wyland Gallery, tel. (808) 661-7099, vibrates with fantastic colors and images created by Hawaii's premier artists. At 136 Dickenson is a third Wyland Gallery, tel. (808) 661-0590.

The two Galerie Lassen, at 700 and 844 Front St., tel. (808) 661-1101 and (808) 667-7707, showcase original and limited edition prints by Christian Reise Lassen, who boldly applies striking colors to bring to life his two-worlds perspective of sea and earth. Typical of his dynamic vision is a displayed painting entitled *Majestic Encounters,* which depicts a pond alive with whales and dolphins who are being observed by a fierce-eyed tiger, who in turn is espied by the fixed and ageless glare of a stony-eyed sphinx. Complementing the exaggerated hues of Lassen's works is the subtle patina of Richard Steirs' cast-iron sculptures of supple whales and dolphins. Mr. Steirs, an Upcountry resident, is among the most admired sculptors on Maui with his limited edition castings.

The Lahaina Galleries, 728 Front St., tel. (808) 667-2152 (a branch gallery at the Kapalua Shops), is one of the oldest galleries on the island. The gallery, with a central room and two in the rear, is hung with the works of Dario Campanile, Thomas Le Yung, Guy Buffet, and other widely acclaimed painters, and the mesmerizing acrylic sculptures of Fredrick Hart.

Robert Lynn Nelson Studio, 802 Front St. on the corner of Lahainaluna Rd., tel. (808) 667-9300, shows originals and prints only of Robert Lynn Nelson, the father of the modern marine art movement, which splits the canvas between land and undersea scenes.

Displaying idyllic home scenes, waterfalls, snowscapes, and the like by Thomas Kincade is the Thomas Kincade Gallery, 780 Front St., tel. (808) 667-7170.

Flowers, birds, and Chinese fans make up the majority of works displayed at the David Lee Galleries, 712 Front St., tel. (808) 667-7740. David Lee uses natural powder pigments to create his vivid colors and even grinds lapis, pearl, turquoise, and gold for their colors. Originals, lithographs, and posters.

Displaying works in the pop and contemporary vein is Madeline Michaels, 816 Front St., tel. (808) 661-3984. Showing more pop art with bright colors and other nontraditional works of art in many and various mediums is another gallery right on the corner of Front St. and Lahainaluna Road. Around the corner and up Lahainaluna Road are Island Art Collection and the well-established Sargents Fine Art gallery, both carrying more traditional works or art.

Lahaina Printsellers at the Lahaina Cannery Mall, open daily 9:30 a.m.-9 p.m., tel. (808) 667-7843 or (800) 669-7843, has walls festooned with beautiful prints of old Hawaii, including endangered birds and historical figures that featured prominently in Hawaii's past. Printsellers specializes in antique maps, especially those depicting the Pacific basin, and Captain Cook memorabilia. Original antique prints and maps, many from the beginning of last century, start at only $25 and can go all the way up to $100,000. Lahaina Printsellers also offers hand-rubbed koa frames and will be happy to send you a brochure of thitseir selections if you would like to choose your artwork at home. With its heavy use of dark wood, many tables, and frames everywhere, this shop has the feel of an old library just waiting to be explored.

Food/Liquor Stores

The following markets/supermarkets are in and around Lahaina. The larger ones also stock beer, wine, and liquor.

Safeway, at the Lahaina Cannery Mall, open 24 hours, is a large supermarket complete with deli, fish market, floral shop, and bakery.

Foodland, at the Lahaina Square Shopping Center, is also a well stocked supermarket.

Nagasako Supermarket, at the Lahaina Shopping Center, open daily 7 a.m.-9 p.m., Sunday until 7 p.m., is a local supermarket with plenty of ethnic Hawaiian, Japanese, Chinese, and Korean foods, along with liquor selections. The market is also known for its fresh fish and produce.

Mr. Wine, tel. (808) 661-5551, on the corner of Lahainaluna and Wainee St., not only has a huge selection of wines, and some beer, liquors, and liqueurs, but keeps the better wines and champagnes under cellar conditions in a climatically controlled room at 55° F and 70% humidity. Beat the hot Lahaina sun and stop in for a perfect bottle for the evening. Open Mon.-Sat. 11 a.m.-7 p.m.

For bulk foods, health food items, vitamins, minerals, and supplements, and hot and cold prepared foods, try the full-service **Westside Natural Foods and Deli,** tel. (808) 667-2855, at

the corner of Lahainaluna and Wainee Street. Open daily, with shorter hours on Sunday.

The Olowalu General Store, tel. (808) 661-3774, located five miles east of Lahaina along Rt. 30, open Mon.-Fri. 6 a.m.-6:30 p.m., Saturday 7 a.m.-6:30 p.m., Sunday 7 a.m.-5 p.m., is fairly well stocked and the only place to pick up supplies in this area. It also has light snacks including sandwiches and hot dogs, a perfect stop if you are snorkeling or swimming on the nearby beaches.

Sports, Excursions, and Equipment

The **Maui Dive Shop,** at the Lahaina Cannery Mall, tel. (808) 661-5388, and a second store at the Lahaina Center are full-service dive shops offering tours, snorkel and scuba rentals, lessons, and equipment and clothing sales. **Lahaina Divers,** tel. (808) 667-7496, next to the Pacific Whale Foundation store at 143 Dickenson St., also rents snorkel equipment, offers scuba lessons, and arranges tours on its fleet of boats. Everyone gives this company a thumbs-up. **Capt. Nemo's Scuba Shack,** 150 Dickenson, tel. (808) 661-5555, has been around for many years and offers similar service and equipment, sales, rentals, and lessons.

Snorkel Bob's, at 161 Lahainaluna Rd., tel. (808) 661-4421, rents snorkel gear for $15 per week (daily rental also), which you can take to a neighboring island and return there for a small extra fee. Boogie boards are available at $13 per day or $26 per week, and Snorkel Bob's advice, whether you need it or not, is plentiful and free.

Lahaina Harbor

ROBERT NILSEN

West Maui Cycles, 193 Lahainaluna Rd., tel. (808) 661-9005, rents snorkel gear, surfboards, and boogie boards, but its big thing is the sale, service, and rental of road and mountain bicycles. Stop here for all your cycling needs.

Companies that can set you up with most any activity offered on the island include **Barefoot's Cashback Tours,** tel. (808) 661-8889, 834 Front St.; **Ocean Activities Center,** tel. (808) 661-5309, at the Lahaina Cannery Mall; **Activity Warehouse,** tel. (808) 667-4000, across from Kamehameha III School along Front St.; and **Activity Information Center,** with two locations, one at the Anchor Square Center, tel. (808) 667-7777, and the other at the Wharf Cinema Center, tel. (808) 662-3100.

SERVICES AND INFORMATION

Emergency: For fire, police, or ambulance, dial 911 throughout the Lahaina area. The police station, fire station, and Lahaina civic center are located above Wahikuli State Wayside Park between Lahaina and Kaanapali. **Banks:** In Lahaina during normal banking hours try the **Bank of Hawaii,** tel. (808) 661-8781, or the **American Savings Bank,** tel. (808) 667-9561, in the Lahaina Shopping Center; or **First Hawaiian Bank,** 215 Papalaua St., tel. (808) 661-3655.

Post Office

The post office is on the very northwest edge of town where Kaanapali begins, tel. (808) 667-6611. The in-town postal branch, tel. (808) 661-0550, is located at the Lahaina Shopping Center.

Lahaina Mail Depot is a post office contract station located at The Wharf Cinema Center, 658 Front St., tel. (808) 667-2000. It's open weekdays 10 a.m.-4 p.m. (Saturday until 1 p.m.), and along with the normal stamps, etc., it specializes in sending packages home. Mailing boxes, tape, and packaging materials are all available, as are souvenir packs of coffee, nuts, candies, and teas, which might serve as a last-minute purchase, but are expensive. In the Lahaina Shopping Center

you'll find **The Mail Room,** tel. (808) 661-5788, for shipping and packaging services and supplies. Hours are Mon.-Fri. 9:30 a.m.-6 p.m., Saturday until 3:30 p.m.; closed for lunch.

Medical Treatment

A concentration of all types of specialists is found at the **Maui Medical Group,** 130 Prison St., tel. (808) 661-0051. Open Mon.-Fri. 8 a.m.-5 p.m. and Saturday 8 a.m.-noon; call for emergency hours. Professional medical care can also be found at the **Kaiser Permanente** clinic, 910 Wainee St., tel. (808) 661-7400. Alternatively, the **Lahaina Health Center,** 180 Dickenson St. at Dickenson Square, Suite 205, tel. (808) 667-6268, offers acupuncture, chiropractic, therapeutic massage, and podiatry.

Pharmacies in Lahaina include: **Lahaina Pharmacy** at the Lahaina Shopping Center, tel. (808) 661-3119; **Longs Drugs** at the Lahaina Cannery Mall, tel. (808) 667-4384; and **Valley Isle Pharmacy,** 130 Prison St., tel. (808) 661-4747.

Laundromat

For a self-service laundromat try **Kwik N Kleen,** tel. (808) 661-7949, at the Lahaina Shopping Center.

Information

The following groups and organizations should prove helpful: **Lahaina Restoration Foundation,** P.O. Box 338, Lahaina, HI 96761, tel. (808) 661-3262, or in the Master's Reading Room next to the Baldwin Home along Front Street. The foundation is a storehouse of information about historical Maui; be sure to pick up the brochure *Lahaina, A Walking Tour of Historic and Cultural Sites.* The **Lahaina Art Society,** tel. (808) 661-3228, has information about the art scene and art events in town.

For popular events and activities happening in Lahaina, contact the Lahaina Visitors Center events line at (808) 667-9194.

The **Lahaina Public Library** is at 680 Wharf St., tel. (808) 662-3066, open Mon.-Fri., various hours.

KAANAPALI

Five lush valleys, nourished by streams from the West Maui Mountains, stretch luxuriously for 10 miles from Kaanapali north to Kapalua. All along the connecting **Honoapiilani Highway** (Rt. 30), the dazzle and glimmer of beaches is offset by black volcanic rock. Two sensitively planned and beautifully executed resorts are at each end of this drive. Kaanapali Resort is 500 acres of fun and relaxation at the south end. It houses six luxury hotels, a handful of beautifully appointed condos, a shopping mall and museum, 36 holes of world-class golf, tennis courts galore, and epicurean dining in a chef's salad of cuisines. Two of the hotels, the **Hyatt Regency** and **Sheraton,** are inspired architectural showcases that blend harmoniously with Maui's most beautiful seashore surroundings. At the northern end is another gem, the **Kapalua Resort,** 1,650 of Maui's most beautifully sculpted acres with its own showcases, the **Kapalua Bay Hotel** and the **Ritz-Carlton.** Here, too, is prime golf, Kapalua and Fleming Beaches, plus exclusive shopping, horseback riding, and tennis aplenty.

Kaanapali with its four miles of glorious beach is Maui's westernmost point. It begins where Lahaina ends and continues north along Route 30 until a mile or so before the village of Honokowai. From here to Kapalua are the villages of Honokowai, Kahana, and Napili, which service the condos tucked away here and there along the coast. All are practical stops where you can buy food, gas, and all necessary supplies to keep your vacation rolling. The accommodations are not as grand, but the beaches and vistas are. Along this entire shore, Maui flashes its most captivating pearly white smile. The sights here are either natural or manmade, but not historical. This is where you come to gaze from mountain to sea and bathe yourself in natural beauty. Then, after a day of surf and sunshine, you repair to one of the gorgeous hotels or restaurants for a drink or dining, or just to promenade around the grounds.

History

Western Maui was a mixture of scrub and precious *lo'i,* land, reserved for taro, the highest life-sustaining plant given by the gods. The farms stretched to Kapalua, skirting the numerous bays all along the way. The area was important enough for a "royal highway" to be built by Chief Piilani, and it still bears his name. Westerners used the lands surrounding Kaanapali to grow sugarcane, and **The Lahaina, Kaanapali, and Pacific Railroad,** known today as the "Sugar Cane Train," chugged to Kaanapali Beach to unburden itself onto barges that carried the cane to waiting ships. Kaanapali, until the 1960s, was a blemished beauty where the Pioneer Sugar Mill dumped its rubbish. Then Amfac, one of the "Big Five," decided to put the land to better use. In creating Hawaii's first planned resort, it outdid itself. Robert Trent Jones was hired to mold the golf course along this spectacular coast, while the Hyatt Regency and its grounds became an architectural marvel. The Sheraton-Maui was built atop, and integrated with, Puu Kekaa, "Black Rock." This area is a wave-eroded cinder cone, and the Sheraton architects used its sea cliffs as part of the walls of the resort. Here, on a deep underwater shelf, daring divers descend to harvest Maui's famous black coral trees. The Hawaiians believed that Puu Kekaa was a very holy place where the spirits of the dead left this earth and migrated into the spirit world. Kahekili, Maui's most famous 18th-century chief, often came here to leap into the sea below. This old-time daredevil was fond of the heart-stopping activity, and made famous "Kahekili's Leap," an even more treacherous sea cliff on nearby Lanai. Today, the Sheraton puts on a sunset show where this "leap" is reenacted.

Unfortunately, developers picked up on Amfac's great idea and built condos up the road starting in Honokowai. Interested in profit, not beauty, they earned that area the dubious title of "condo ghetto." Fortunately, the Maui Land and Pineapple Co. owned the land surrounding the idyllic Kapalua Bay. Colin Cameron, one of the heirs to this holding, had visions of developing 750 acres of the plantation's 23,000 into the extraordinary Kapalua Bay Resort. He teamed up with Laurence Rockefeller, and the complex was opened in 1979, later expanding to 1,650 acres.

Black Rock

One of the most easily accessible and visually engaging snorkeling spots on Maui is located at

KAANAPALI

To Napili Kapulua ↗

KAHEKILI BEACH PARK

KAI ALIA DR.

30

PUUKOLII STATION

PUUKOLII RD.

INTERNATIONAL COUNTRY CLUB

KAANAPALI PLANTATION

MAUI KAANAPALI VILLAS

ROYAL LAHAINA RESORT

DR.

MAUI ELDORADO

KEKAA

KAANAPALI STATION

PUU KEKAA

SHERATON MAUI

KAANAPALI BEACH HOTEL

THE WHALER

WHALERS VILLAGE MALL AND MUSEUM

KAANAPALI ROYAL

KAANAPALI GOLF COURSE

HONOAPIILANI HWY.

WESTIN MAUI

KAANAPALI ALII

CLUBHOUSE

KAANAPALI PARKWAY

LUIGI'S

MAUI MARRIOT

NOHEA KAI DR.

30

HYATT REGENCY

0   0.25 mi
0   0.25 km

HANAKAOO BEACH PARK

To Lahaina ↓

the Sheraton's Black Rock. Follow the main road past the Sheraton until it climbs the hill around back. Walk up the hill and through the hotel grounds until you come to a white metal fence. Follow the fence down toward the sea. You'll come to a spur of rock jutting out, and that's it. The entire area is like an underwater marine park. Enter at the beach area and snorkel west around the rock, staying close to the cinder cone. There are schools of reef fish, rays, and even a lonely turtle. There is limited free public parking in Kaanapali, so you may have to park in one of the few pay lots. Alternately, park at Kahekili Beach Park at the far north end of Kaanapali near the Maui Kaanapali Villas, from where it's only a 10-minute walk.

Whaling Museum

The free **Whalers Village Museum** at Whaler's Village shopping mall has a few outside displays, but most items are inside on the upper level of the mall. The most dramatic outside display is the skeleton of a 40-foot sperm whale. This big boy greets you at the entrance to the mall as you come up the steps. The compact display area upstairs on the mezzanine level is full of whaling history, photographs, drawings, artifacts from whaling ships, a reconstructed forecastle, a video on whaling, and many informative descriptions and stories about the whaling industry, whaling life, and the whalers themselves. After a walk through the museum, pick up a memento at the museum gift shop.

Across the walkway, **Hale Kohola** is set up to explain the evolution of the whale, describe the various species, display specimens of whale parts, and show a video on whales and dolphins. Engross yourself in these exhibit halls. They are a learning experience.

Sports

For a full listing of the sporting facilities and possibilities in the Kaanapali area, contact the information booth at Whalers Village or any of the activity desks at the hotels on the strip. **Golf** courses at the Kaanapali Golf Courses, tel. (808) 661-3691, are each par 71. Both the north and south courses share a clubhouse that sits at the entrance to Kaanapali along the Honoapiilani Highway. For **tennis**, the most famous is the Royal Lahaina Tennis Ranch with 10 courts, tennis clinics, and tournaments. The Hyatt and Marriott have five courts each, the Sheraton three, and five are located at The Whaler. For **water sports,** catamarans are available from the Hyatt, Sheraton, and Westin Maui. Other water sport activities and equipment are available from each hotel. Contact any major hotel beach activities desk, or Beach Activities of Maui at the Whalers Village, tel. (000) 001-5552.

Kaanapali Extras

Two situations in and around Kaanapali mar its outstanding beauty—you might refer to them as "Kaanapali Perfumes." There are still plenty of sugarcane fields in the area, and when they're being burned off, the smoke is heavy in the air; the soot falling at this time is called "black snow" by locals. Also, the sewage treatment plant is inadequate, and even the constantly blowing trade winds are insufficient to push this stench out to sea.

Transportation

Kaanapali is serviced by the free **Kaanapali Trolley** within the resort area. The **West Maui Shopping Express** runs between Kaanapali and Lahaina, and the **Whalers Village Shuttle** runs to South Maui. Going as far as Maalaea is the **Maui Ocean Center Shuttle,** and the **TransHawaiian** airporter shuttles make runs to the airport in Kahului. The **Sugar Cane Train** offers fun for the entire family on its route between Kaanapali and Lahaina. The Kapalua-West Maui Airport is the most convenient for air travel to this end of the island, but few airlines operate in

and out of this airstrip. Most air traffic to Maui still goes via Kahului. For transportation details, see "Getting There" and "Getting Around" in the Out and About chapter.

BEACHES

The four-mile stretch of pristine sand at Kaanapali is what people come to experience in Maui, and they are never disappointed.

Hanakaoo Beach Park

Just as you leave Lahaina and enter Kaanapali you'll find this beach park. It's a good swimming and sailboarding spot, with lifeguards, showers, and parking; and while so close, it's away from the hotel crowds of Kaanapali. The Kahana Canoe Club is based here and you can often see rowers out on the water practicing their strokes. Between the beach and the road is an old cemetery with mostly Chinese characters written on the headstones.

Hanakaoo Beach is an uninterrupted stretch of sand running from the park, past the Hyatt Regency to the Sheraton. Although these are some of the most exclusive hotels on the island, public access to the beach is guaranteed in the state's constitution. There are "rights of way," but parking your car is definitely a hassle. A good idea is to park at either Hanakaoo or Wahikuli park and walk northward along the beach. You can park (10 cars)

Burning cane fields create "Kaanapali incense."

J.D. BISIGNANI

in the Hyatt's lower lot and enter along a right of way. There's access between the Hyatt and the Marriott (pay parking ramp), between the Marriott and the Kaanapali Ali'i, which also has limited parking, and between the Kaanapali Ali'i and the Westin Maui. There is also some parking near the Sheraton and at the Whalers Shopping Center parking ramp, but you must pass through the gauntlet of shops.

Kahekili Park

A short stroll down the beach from Black Rock, this park is dedicated to Maui's King Kahekili. The newest beach park in the area, it's a commodious place with a broad lawn, palm trees, a pavilion for cooking, and tables for a picnic. The large shaded parking area can accommodate many cars, and you can count on always finding someone here. The beach, sometimes used for scuba lessons, runs uninterrupted to Black Rock.

Beach Walk

As in Wailea, a beach walkway has been created in Kaanapali that runs along the sand from the Hyatt Regency in the south to the Sheraton in the north. This walkway is a convenient way to pass from one property to another: peruse your neighbor hotel, try one of the restaurants down the line, or walk to shop. During the cool hours of the day and at sunset, this walkway is also used by joggers out for exercise and those who want the perfect location to watch the sun go down.

HOTELS

The Kaanapali Resort offers hotels and condos ranging from "moderate deluxe" to "luxury." There are no budget accommodations here. As usual, condos are more of a bargain the longer you stay, especially if you can share costs with a few people by renting a larger unit. And as always, you'll save money on food costs. The following should give you an idea of what's available.

Hyatt Regency Maui

The moment you enter the main lobby of this luxury hotel the magic begins. A multitiered architectural extravaganza opens to the sky, birds fly freely, and magnificent potted plants and full-sized courtyard palm trees create the atmosphere of a modern Polynesian palace located at Kaanapali's southern extremity, at 200 Nohea Kai Drive, Lahaina, HI 96761, tel. (808) 661-1234 or (800) 233-1234, fax (808) 667-4498. Nooks and crannies abound where you can lounge in kingly wicker thrones. Peacocks strut their regal stuff amid impeccable Japanese gardens, and ducks and swans are floating alabaster on landscaped ponds. The swimming pools are inspired by the islands: grottoes, caves, waterfalls, and a huge slide are all built in. A swinging wooden bridge connects the sections, and you can have an island drink at a sunken poolside bar. There are four fine restaurants on property, half a dozen lounges, and the Drums of the Pacific Luau. The "Elephant Walk" is a covey of specialty shops and boutiques. The little kids will love it here too. Camp Hyatt for children ages 3-12 runs daily 9 a.m.-3 p.m. for $50 a child and includes activities and excursions that change daily, arts and crafts, lunch, and snacks. An evening camp 6-10 p.m. is also available, so put those little kiddies in the care of professionals and have a romantic night out. All beach activities, equipment rentals, and lessons, including a sail/snorkel ride on the *Kiele V* catamaran, can be arranged through the beach activities center at oceanside, or expend some energy at the health club and tennis center. For those with less physical activity in mind, check out the daily Hawaiian demonstrations in the lobby, the hotel wildlife tour, the art and garden tour, or the nightly astronomy show on the hotel roof. Rates are $275 for terrace rooms, $345 for golf/mountain rooms, $375 for ocean-view rooms, and $415 for oceanfront rooms. Rates are higher for the special Regency floors. Suites run $600-3,000. If you visit, valet parking is in front of the hotel, complimentary if you validate your ticket by dining at Spats or the Palm Court, or spend $25 in one of the shops. Or you can self-park out front or around in the back. From here, both the north end of Lahaina, pretty at night with its colored lights reflecting on the water, and Lanai, floating across the Lahaina Roads, are easily visible.

Sheraton Maui

The 510 rooms of the Sheraton Maui, 2605 Kaanapali Pkwy., Lahaina, HI 96761, tel. (808) 661-0031 or (800) 325-3535, fax (808) 661-0458, Web site: www.sheraton-maui.com, are built around Kaanapali's most conspicuous natural phenomenon, Puu Kekaa, "Black Rock." Originally opened in 1963, the Sheraton reopened in 1997 after a two-year complete renovation. Open, bright, and breezy, the lobby looks out over the finely landscaped gardens and an enticing meandering pool with a water slide. Three classy restaurants grace the hotel, and a bar is situated at poolside. The guest activities desk can arrange almost any activity that the island offers, and you can rent water equipment and have lessons from the beach activity booth. The snorkeling around Black Rock is the best in the area, and every evening there is a torch-lighting ceremony and cliff dives from the rock. As a guest, you can avail yourself of several daily catamaran rides aboard the *Teralani* or head for some sporting competition at the resort's tennis club. The north end of the Kaanapali beach walk ends at the Sheraton, so you can walk all the way to the Hyatt at the south end without leaving the oceanside. Most rooms at the Sheraton face the ocean, and all are air conditioned and have full amenities. Rates are $290-330 for garden and mountain views, $360-365 for ocean-view and oceanfront rooms, $575 for an Ohana family suite, and other suites from $750.

The Westin Maui

The newest in luxury hotels to spring up along Kaanapali, at 2365 Kaanapali Pkwy., Lahaina, HI 96761, tel. (808) 667-2525 or (800) 228-3000, fax (808) 661-5764, Web site: www.westin-maui.com, is actually a phoenix, risen from the old Maui Surf Hotel. True to the second life of that mythical bird, it is a beauty. Westin is known for its fabulous entranceways, lobbies, and quiet nooks. You won't be disappointed here. A series of strolling paths takes you through resplendent manicured grounds that surround an extensive multi-pool area. Waterfalls, water slides, and natural rock formations all blend to create civilized paradise. To the left of the main lobby is a collection of exclusive boutiques. You'll find just what you want to eat or drink at any time of day at one of the hotel's eight restaurants and lounges. The ocean activity center can set you up with all sorts of rentals on the beach, or a ride on *Gemini*, the hotel's catamaran. A business center is set up for the traveling businessperson, and kids are taken care of at the supervised daily Keiki Kamp. The daily kids' program runs 9 a.m.-3 p.m. at $45 a child, with evening programs also available.

For the experience of all, each Friday 8:30 a.m.-5 p.m. brings Ho'olauna, a Hawaiian culture and arts program, which is put on at various spots around the hotel. If you just want to soak in some beauty, have a tour of the hotel's $2 million art collection. The Westin Maui has over 750 guest rooms. Standard terrace rooms run $265, a garden-view room $295, golf/mountain-view $345, ocean-view $375-420, oceanfront $445-495, and suites go upward from there.

Royal Lahaina Resort

Twenty-seven idyllic acres surround 542 luxurious rooms of the Royal Lahaina Resort, the largest complex in Kaanapali, 2780 Kekaa Dr., Lahaina, HI 96761, tel. (808) 661-3611 or (800) 447-6925, fax (808) 661-6150, Web site: 2maui.com. Here the tropical landscaping leads directly to the sun-soaked beach. The Royal Lahaina, one of the first properties to be developed, is divided into cottages and towers. Rates range from a standard room at $215 to an oceanfront room at $335. Cottages rent for $295 and $385, suites $600-1,500; condo/car packages are available. The renovated rooms are decorated in a comfortable Hawaiian style with all amenities and private lanai; some of the cottages have kitchens. There are no less than three restaurants, a nightly luau, and three swimming pools on the well-maintained grounds. A score of shops are located in the main hotel for your convenience. The beach activities booth rents snorkel equipment, windsurfing boards, and kayaks, and arranges scuba lessons. The resort is also home to the **Royal Lahaina Tennis Ranch**, boasting 10 courts and a 3,500-seat stadium along with special tennis packages for those inclined.

Maui Marriott

The fifth of the big five hotels on Kaanapali Beach is the Maui Marriott, 100 Nohea Kai Dr., Lahaina, 96761, tel. (808) 667-1200, (800) 228-9290, or (800) 542-6821 in Hawaii. With over 700 rooms, two swimming pools, a beach recreation center, five tennis courts, two dozen shops, a half dozen restaurants and lounges, and indoor and outdoor parking, the Marriott is one of the largest properties on West Maui, but not as elegant as some others in Kaanapali. Open to the beach and facing the setting sun, the hotel is graced with cooling breezes that waft across its manicured courtyard and through the open atriums of both its buildings. Indoors, the many flowers and potted plants bring the outdoors inside. On the premises are Lokelani, an excellent seafood restaurant, Nikko Japanese Steak House, one of the best spots for Japanese cuisine on the island, the Makai Bar for excellent *pu pu* and evening entertainment, and the Marriott Luau. The hospitable staff orchestrates the numerous daily handicraft and recreational activities, and a kids' program is scheduled three times a week. There's plenty to keep every family busy. Snorkel sets, boogie boards, and kayaks can be rented at the beach activities center, and kayak tours are led from here. Room rates range from $280 for a standard room to $328 for a deluxe ocean view; $399 for suites. Special honeymoon, tennis, golf, and family plans are available, as well as optional meal plans.

Kaanapali Beach Hotel

Not as luxurious as its famous neighbors, but an excellent hotel nonetheless, the Kaanapali Beach Hotel is a bargain. Located at 2525 Kaanapali Pkwy., tel. (808) 661-0011, (800) 262-8450, or (800) 233-1014, Web site: www.kaanapalibeachhotel.com, e-mail: mauikbh@aloha.net, this is perhaps the most "Hawaiian" of the hotels in Kaanapali. There is no glitz here, just warm and friendly service, reasonably priced restaurants, and nearly as many activities and amenities as the big boys down the line. Guest service provides many activities and demonstrations including lei-making, hula lessons, *lau hala* weaving, and a free sunset hula show nightly; the tour desk can always hook you up with any activity on the island. Have a swim in the distinctive whale-shaped pool or check with the beach center for water equipment for rent. Standard rooms range from $160 to $250 for an ocean view, with suites priced $210-585; many special packages available.

CONDOS

Generally less expensive than the hotels, most condos offer full kitchens, TVs, some maid service, swimming pools, tennis courts, and often convenience stores and laundry facilities. Combinations of the above are too numerous to mention, so it's best to ask all pertinent questions when booking. Off-season rates and discounts for longer stays are usually offered. Not all con-

dos accept credit cards, and a deposit is the norm when making reservations.

Located right on the strip along the water are the fancy high-rise Kaanapali Ali'i and The Whaler condos. Set amidst the golf links and following the lay of the land are the low-rise Kaanapali Royal and El Dorado. The International Colony Club is located in a more residential area up above the highway and are farther away from the water and golf courses. A short way north up the beach and off on a road by itself is Maui Kaanapali Villas.

Kaanapali Ali'i

The Kaanapali Ali'i sits in a finely landscaped yard right on the ocean. The four high-rise towers are aesthetically pleasing and are set off by flowers and greenery hanging from many of the balconies. If you need space, try here as each of the large units runs 1,600-1,900 square feet. All have full kitchens, separate living and dining rooms, two full baths, and air conditioning. Free parking, a beach activity center, complimentary tennis, and room service from the Maui Marriott next door are extras. Many area activities and restaurant bills can be put on your room charge as a service. Room rates are $240-650, slightly higher during high season. For information and reservations, contact Kaanapali Ali'i, 50 Nohea Kai Dr., Lahaina, HI 96761, tel. (808) 667-1400 or (800) 642-6284, fax (808) 661-1025, Web site: kaanapali-alii.com, e-mail: info@classicresorts.com.

The Whaler

The Whaler comprises two high-rise buildings set right on the beach next to Whalers Village shopping mall. Outwardly, it has less character than the Kaanapali Ali'i but offers numerous amenities. On property are a pool and spa, exercise room, and tennis courts. These units run from a 640-square-foot studio to a 1,950-square-foot two-bedroom two-bath suite. Rates are $195-470, slightly higher for some units during high season. There is a two-night minimum stay and several car/condo, honeymoon, and senior packages are available. The Whaler is located at 2481 Kaanapali Pkwy., Lahaina, HI 96761, tel. (808) 661-4861 or (800) 367-7052, Web site: ten-io.com/vri.

Outrigger Properties

Both the Kaanapali Royal and Maui Eldorado Resort are managed by Outrigger Hotels and Resorts. **Kaanapali Royal,** 2560 Keka'a Dr., tel. (808) 879-2205, fax 874-3497, a golfer's dream right on the course, has rooms for $195-250, with low-season and long-term discounts. Each suite has a full kitchen and a lanai that faces the fairway. Take advantage of the guest-only swimming pool, lighted tennis courts, and barbecue pit. The **Maui Eldorado Resort,** 2661 Keka'a Drive, tel. (808) 661 0021, fax 667 7030, Wob oito: www.outrig ger.com, slides down the hill alongside a fairway culminating in beachfront cabanas. There are also three swimming pools and a sundries store on property. These studios and suites run $175-325 during the winter season but are discounted the rest of the year. For toll-free reservations and information, call Outrigger at (800) 688-7444.

Some units here are also offered for rent directly by their owners or through independent agents like Whaler's Realty, tel. (800) 367-5632.

Aston Maui Kaanapali Villas

Enjoy the surroundings of 11 sculpted acres at this affordable condo at 45 Kai Ala Dr., tel. (808) 667-7791 or (800) 922-7866, fax (808) 667-0366. The extensive grounds of cool swaying palms harbor three pools, a beach service booth, the Castaway Restaurant, and a sundries shop. Rates begin at $160 for a hotel room with refrigerator. Studios with kitchens run $200-230, and it's $245-280 for a one-bedroom suite with a/c, cable TV, full kitchen, plus maid service. This property, located at the far north end of the Kaanapali development, has an added bonus of peace and quiet along with the best of the Kaanapali beach, although you remain just minutes from the action and a short stroll from Black Rock, a superb snorkeling area. These units are very large with spacious bedrooms; even the studios are capable of handling four people.

International Colony Club

This condo, near the Sugar Cane Train rail line, is on the *mauka* side of Route 30 at 2759 Kalapu Dr., tel. (808) 661-4070. This hillside property with two pools and walkways connecting all units offers fully furnished one- and two-bedroom cottages that sleep from two to six people. One-bedroom units run $105, two-bedroom units $125; three-night minimum. For rental information, contact Maui Diversified Real Estate, tel. (800) 642-6098.

FOOD

Every hotel in Kaanapali has at least one restaurant, with several others scattered throughout the area. Some of the most expensive and exquisite restaurants on Maui are found in these hotels, but surprisingly, at others you can dine very reasonably. The only cheap eats in the area are the few fast food restaurants at Whalers Village shopping mall

Reilley's Steak House

This Irish restaurant and bar is located upstairs in the clubhouse at Kaanapali Golf Courses, tel. (808) 667-7477. Open for breakfast, lunch, and dinner, Reilley's is known for its Tuesday all-you-can-eat prime rib dinner for $16.95 and its Sunday full lobster dinner for $19.95. Other meat and seafood entrees are generally in the $20-25 range. Reilley's has a full bar, so come and have a drink after a round of golf or just to watch the sun set over the fairway.

Luigi's

This is one of two locations for Luigi's, located just off Honoapiilani Highway at the entrance to Kaanapali Resort. Pizza prices start at $10.99 for a regular cheese-only item to $27.99 for a large House Special, super combination pizza smothered with toppings, or you can nibble a salad for only $3.99. Pasta ranges from $10.99 for a marinara sauce to $15.99 for manicotti. Full-course meals include scallops Luigi for $16.99 and top sirloin Luigi-style for $19.99. Early bird specials on pasta 5:30-6:30 p.m. run $9.95. This is a pleasant, family-oriented restaurant. Don't expect food like mama used to make, but it's not bad for adopted Italians. For reservations call (808) 661-4500. Downstairs is **Kaanapali Pizza,** which also runs a bar.

Westin Maui

Cook's At The Beach is known especially for its nightly all-you-can-eat prime rib buffet for $27.95 ($19.95 before 6:30 p.m.). Regular menu selections are also available and include barbecued spare ribs, fresh island catch, and the chef's famous stir-fry. From 7:30 p.m., a hula show accompanies dinner. Starting at 6:30 a.m., a breakfast buffet is offered, with American and Japanese selections, along with an à la carte menu. Lunch is lighter fare with salads, sandwiches, and burgers.

Finer dining at the hotel is at **The Villa.** Set over the lagoon like floating islands, this restaurant serves the best of island fish and seafood. Open for dinner only 6-10 p.m., reservations are recommended and resort attire is expected. Appetizers include paper rice prawn spring rolls. Fish might be a ginger marinated snapper, and sake glazed salmon is one of the specialties; most entrees are priced $22-26. The chef's special prix-fixe menu runs $28. To enjoy the flavors but save a little cash, have the early bird special 6-6:30 p.m. for $19.95.

Perhaps the most well-known dining at the Westin is the champagne Sunday brunch, $24.95, served 9 a.m.-1 p.m. at the **Sound of the Falls** restaurant. Here, you'll be treated to scrumptious delicacies, the waterfall will fill your ears, and your eyes will feast on pink flamingos with the blue ocean as a backdrop.

Royal Lahaina Resort

You have no less than three establishments from which to choose, plus a luau. Follow your nose nightly at 4:45 p.m. to the **Luau Gardens** for the banquet and show, where the biggest problem after the Polynesian Revue is standing up after eating mountains of traditional food. Reservations needed, tel. (808) 661-3611; adults $64, children under 12 $28. The **Royal Ocean Terrace,** the resort's best dining, is open daily for breakfast, lunch, and dinner, offering a breakfast buffet and better-than-average salad bar. Most evening entrees are in the $17-22 range. Sunday brunch 9 a.m.-2 p.m. is a winner. **Beachcombers** is a bit more casual with nightly specials and the flavors of Hawaii.

Located at the entrance to the Royal Lahaina Resort is **Basil Tomatoes,** tel. (808) 662-3210, an Italian grill that's open 5:30 p.m.-midnight—food served until 10 p.m.; reservations suggested. Start with an antipasto like fried green tomatoes at $7.95 or seafood-stuffed mushrooms at $8.95 and move on to a Caesar salad for $9.95 or another fine bowl of greens. The entrees cover the whole range of pastas, meats, poultry, and fish, and are generally in the $16-24 range. To complement any dinner selection, choose from a variety of beers, wine, or aperitifs, and round out your meal with cup of coffee and a sweet dessert.

Hyatt Regency

The **Swan Court** is the Hyatt's signature restaurant. Save this one for a very special evening. You don't come here to eat, you come here to dine, peasant! Anyone who has been enraptured by those old movies where couples regally glide down a central staircase to make their grand entrance will have his or her fantasies come true. Although expensive, with entrees $19-30, you get your money's worth not only with the many wonderful tastes but also with the attention to detail; prosciutto is served with papaya, ginger butter with the fresh catch-of-the-day, and pineapple chutney with the oysters. The wine list is a connoisseur's delight. The Swan Court offers a sumptuous breakfast buffet daily. Dinner, 6-10 p.m., is grand; reservations are recommended, and resort attire is required. For reservations, call (808) 667-4727. The cocktail lounge is open 11 a.m.-11 p.m.

Also at the Hyatt, **Spats Trattoria** is open for dinner only. This restaurant is downstairs and decorated in heavy dark wood and carpets, premodern artwork, and low light. Spats specializes in "country homestyle" Italian food, with the average entree around $25. Casual attire, reservations recommended. Music at Spats piano bar entertains 7:30-11:30 p.m. nightly.

Sheraton

The **Coral Reef Restaurant** is the hotel's finest restaurant. Open for dinner only, the Coral Reef presents Pacific Rim cuisine and is reasonably priced with most entrees $14-26. Reservations are needed, tel. (808) 661-0031. Reservations are also necessary at the dinner-only **Teppan Yaki Dan,** where the Japanese food is prepared with a flourish at your table. Entrees here are a bit more expensive. Less expensive and less formal is the **Keka'a Terrace** restaurant where you can order all day long while surveying the gardens, pool, and Black Rock.

Maui Marriott

The signature restaurant at the Maui Marriott, the **Lokelani,** tel. (808) 667-1200, serves dinner only Wed.-Sun. 6-9 p.m. Seafood is the focus of this award-winning restaurant, but the menu changes monthly. Starters might include Maui onion soup and Big Island shrimp cocktail, and entrees could be seared jumbo tiger prawns, pepper-crusted grilled ahi steak, or *opakapaka* and rack of lamb.

Expect to pay $20-25 per person. A special Hukilau Feast is offered nightly 6-6:45 for $20.

The **Nikko Japanese Steak House** is open for dinner nightly 6-9 p.m. No cheap imports here; prices are high, but the Japanese chef works right at your table slicing meats and vegetables quicker than you can say "samurai." Aside from *teppan yaki*, Nikko is known for its tempura and sushi. Western entrees are also available. An expensive but fun meal. The less expensive Samurai Sunset menu is offered 6-6:30 p.m. Serving breakfast, lunch, and dinner by the gardens is **The Moana Terrace**. This family-style restaurant is known for its buffets and is reasonably priced.

Kaanapali Beach Hotel

The restaurants here are down-to-earth, reasonably priced, and offer a native Hawaiian diet unlike any other restaurants in the area. The **Tiki Terrace** is the main food venue of the Kaanapali Beach Hotel and offers casual dining in an open-air setting. Breakfast can be à la carte or buffet style and consists mostly of American standards. It runs 7-11 a.m. daily, except for Sunday when it gives way to a Champagne Sunday Brunch that runs 9 a.m.-2 p.m. More Hawaiian-inspired dishes are on the table for this brunch, $20.95, and the whole affair is accompanied by Hawaiian music. Dinner in the Tiki Terrace runs 6-8 p.m. and reservations are recommended, tel. (808) 661-0011. Expect your meal to run around $20. Many Hawaiian dishes are on the menu, and on Friday the Tiki Terrace does a *huli huli* barbecue of whole pig. Aside from the eats, a free hula show is given nightly at 6:30 p.m.

Open daily 6 a.m.-9 p.m., the **Kaanapali Mixed Plate** restaurant serves all-you-can-eat meals and deli sandwiches 2-4 p.m. In the courtyard next to the whale-shaped pool, have a salad, sandwich, or burger from the **Tiki Bar and Grill**, 11:30 a.m.-6 p.m., or just stop for a drink when the *pu pu* are put out 3-6 p.m.

At Whalers Village

This shopping mall has a half dozen or so dining establishments. You can find everything from pizza and frozen yogurt to lobster tails. Prices range from bargain to moderate.

The well-established **Leilani's**, tel. (808) 661-4495, has a downstairs Beachside Grill open 11 a.m.-11 p.m., and the upstairs fine-dining section is open for dinner 5-10 p.m. A daily dinner special is featured 5-6:30 p.m. The Beachside Grill offers plate lunches of barbecued ribs, *paniolo* steak, or stir-fry chicken all priced around $10, along with appetizers like sashimi at a daily quote, and creamy seafood chowder for $3.50. The burgers range $5.95-7.95. Dinner from the upstairs broiler can be fresh fish of the day, filet mignon for $19.95 from the lava rock broiler, baby back pork ribs at $15.95 from the kiawe-wood smoker, or spinach, mushroom, and cheese raviolis for $10.95. A children's menu helps keep prices down, and cocktails are served until midnight.

Another favorite here is the partially indoors but mostly outdoors **Hula Grill and Barefoot Bar,** tel. (808) 667-6636. Open 11 a.m.-midnight, with dinner served 5-9:30 p.m. You can eat either in the casual Barefoot Bar under a thatch umbrella or in the more formal dining area. No matter where you sit, however, the sunsets are always great. At the Barefoot Bar, try burgers, salads, pizza, and fish. The dining room features seafood and steak in a style known as Hawaiian regional cuisine. Expect to pay about $25 for your meal. Music and hula dancing nightly.

The **Rusty Harpoon,** tel. (808) 661-3123, offers a completely new menu and pleasing atmosphere. It also has a bar that claims to serve the best daiquiris on Maui, along with a happy hour 2-6 p.m. Breakfast served 8-11 a.m. gets you started for the day with three-egg-create-your-own omelettes for $8.95, a homestyle breakfast with potatoes, eggs, and sausage links for $7.95, continental breakfast at $7.95, and a Belgian waffle bar with your choice of various fruit toppings and garnishes for $7.95. Lunch, 11 a.m.- 4:30 p.m., is an extensive menu starting with appetizers like a house salad for $4.95, or crab-stuffed mushrooms for $9.95. Sandwiches are priced $8.95-9.95, burgers around the same. Dinner 5-10 p.m. offers entrees priced $16.95-24.95 including linguine Mediterranean, pineapple teriyaki chicken, and rack of lamb; only the Pacific lobster tail at $39.95 is pricier. Don't forget about the sushi and seafood bar, or the luscious desserts. To save money the Rusty Harpoon has a senior special 5-6 p.m. and a children's menu.

Castaway Cafe

The Maui Kaanapali Villas resort is the only Kaanapali condo that has a restaurant. The casual Castaway Cafe is located only steps from the beach and is open for breakfast, lunch, and dinner. Breakfast items include omelettes, items from the griddle, and fruit, all for under $7. Burgers, sandwiches, and salads are served for lunch, and for dinner, a variety of seafood, pasta, chicken, and steaks go for $13-18. Every day there are specials and the full bar can set you up with a drink any time of the day.

ENTERTAINMENT

The dinner shows accompanying the luau at the Hyatt Regency feature pure island entertainment. "Drums of the Pacific" is a musical extravaganza that you would expect from the Hyatt. There are torch-lit processions and excitingly choreographed production numbers, with all the hula-skirted *wahines* and *malo*-clad *kanes* that you could imagine. Flames add drama to the setting and the grand finale is a fire dance. Similarly, the luau at the Royal Lahaina Resort and Maui Marriott entertain you with music and dance while you stuff yourself on fine island cuisine. The Kaanapali Beach Hotel presents a free hula and music show nightly in its courtyard.

Spats at the Hyatt has a quiet piano bar, but if you are into livelier music try the **Hula Grill** or the **Makai Bar** at the Marriott. For Hawaiian music and song, check with the Kaanapali Beach Hotel.

SHOPPING

Kaanapali provides a varied shopping scene: the **Whalers Village** shopping complex, which is affordable; the **Maui Marriott** and **Royal Lahaina Resort** for some distinctive purchases; and the **Hyatt Regency, Westin Maui,** and **Sheraton** where most people get financial jitters even window-shopping.

Whalers Village
You can easily find anything at this shopping complex that you might need. Some of the shops are: **Reyn's,** for upscale tropical clothing; **Giorgiou** and others for expensive women's fashions; the exclusive **Louis Vuitton** for designer luggage; **Blue Ginger Designs,** for women's and children's re-

sortwear and alohawear; **Dolphin Gallery,** with beautiful creations in glass, sculptures, paintings, and jewelry; **Lahaina Scrimshaw,** for fine scrimshaw pieces and other art objects ranging from affordable to expensive; **Endangered Species Store,** where you are greeted by a stuffed python and proceeds go to help endangered species; **Eyecatcher Sunglasses,** where you can take care of your eyes with shades from $150 Revos to $5 cheapies; **Jessica's Gems,** featuring the work of designer David Welty, along with coral jewelry and black Tahitian pearl rings; **Fox Photo** for film developing; **Whalers Fine Wine and Spirits,** a full-service bottle shop; and an **ABC Discount Store** for sundries. There are many other shops tucked away here and there. They come and go with regularity.

A fascinating shop is **Lahaina Printsellers,** featuring original engravings, drawings, maps, charts, and naturalist sketches ranging in age from 150 to 400 years, each with an authenticity label. The collection comes from all over the world, but the Hawaiiana collection is amazing in its depth, with many works featuring a nautical theme reminiscent of the amazing explorers who opened the Pacific. The Lahaina Printsellers have been collecting for over 20 years and are the largest purveyor of material relating to Captain Cook in the entire Pacific Basin. Prices range from $25 for the smallest antique print up to $15,000 for rare museum-quality work.

The Whalers Village also has plenty of fast-food shops, three restaurants, West Maui Healthcare Center, a whaling museum, and a tourist information booth in the lower courtyard. The Kaanapali Shuttle, West Maui Shopping Express, and the Whalers Village Shuttle all stop at the mall.

Be sure to catch the free **hula show** at 7 p.m. Monday, Wednesday, and Sunday, and the periodic sand sculpture demonstration in front of the stage on the lower level. Contemporary Hawaiian music is also performed at the center on the last Sunday of every month.

SERVICES AND INFORMATION

Banks
There are no banks in Kaanapali; the closest are in Lahaina. Most larger hotels can help with

some banking needs, especially with the cashing of traveler's checks. An ATM machine is located on the lower level of the Whalers Village mall.

Medical

The **West Maui Healthcare Center** maintains an office at the Whalers Village shopping mall, tel. (808) 667-9721; open 8 a.m.-10 p.m. daily. **Doctors On Call,** tel. (808) 667-7676, operates daily

out of the Hyatt Regency and Westin Maui but makes house calls.

Information

Stop by the tourist information booth at Whalers Village mall. For a complete source of information on all aspects of the Kaanapali area, contact Kaanapali Beach Resort Association, tel. (808) 661-3271.

HONOKOWAI, KAHANA, AND NAPILI

You head for Honokowai, Kahana, and Napili if you want to enjoy Maui's west coast and not spend a bundle of money. They're not quite as pretty as Kaanapali or Kapalua, but proportionate to the money you'll save, you come out ahead. These areas are not clearly distinct from one another so you may have some trouble determining where one ends and the next begins, but generally they are separated by some stretch of residential neighborhood. Napili is at the far north end of this strip. It adjoins and in some ways is connected to Kapalua. However, because of the distinct difference between the condo setting and the manicured resort, Napili is included in this section. To get to this area, travel along Honoapiilani Highway past Kaanapali and then take Lower Honoapiilani Road through Honokowai, and continue on it to Kahana and Napili. Three short connector roads link the new highway with the old road.

Beaches

The whole strip here is rather rocky and full of coral, so not particularly good for swimming. However, there are two spots that might do and one that's a winner.

Honokowai Beach Park is right in Honokowai just across from the Food Pantry. Here you have a large lawn with palm trees and picnic tables, but a small beach. The water is shallow and tame—good for tots. The swimming is not as nice as at Kaanapali, but take a dip after shopping. Snorkeling is fair, and you can get through a break in the reef at the north end.

Kahana Beach is near the Kahana Beach Resort; park across the street. Nothing spectacular, but the protected small beach is good for catching some rays. There's a great view of Molokai and the beach is never crowded. Just

south of there is **Ponakii Park.** It's a narrow strip with only a few parking stalls but is often used for picnics or by surfers.

By far the best beach in this area, and one of the best on the island, is that at **Napili Bay.** This gentle crescent slopes easily into the water, and its sandy bottom gives way to coral so snorkeling is good here as well. There are rights of way to this perfect, but condo-lined, beach. Look for beach access signs along Napili Place and on Hui Drive. They're difficult to spot, but once on the beach there's better-than-average swimming, snorkeling, and a good place for beginning surfers and boogie boarders.

ACCOMMODATIONS

At last count there were well over three dozen condos and apartment complexes in the four miles encompassing Honokowai, Kahana, and Napili. There are plenty of private homes out here as well, which gives you a good cross-section of Hawaiian society. A multimillion-dollar spread may occupy a beach, while out in the bay is a local fisherman with his beat-up old boat trying to make a few bucks for the day. And his house may be up the street. Many of the condos built out here were controversial. Locals refused to work on some because they were on holy ground, and a few actually experienced bad luck jinxes as they were being built. The smarter owners called in *kahuna* to bless the ground and the disturbances ceased.

As usual, condos are more of a bargain the longer you stay, especially if you can share costs with a few people by renting a larger unit. And as always, you'll save money on food costs. The following should give you an idea of what's avail-

To Kahakuloa and Kahului

Honolua Bay
MARINE LIFE CONSERVATION DISTRICT — 30 — WESTSIDE SPORTING CLAYS
Makuleia Bay

Honokahua Bay

Makaluapuna Point — D.T. FLEMING BEACH PARK — PLANTATION COURSE CLUBHOUSE AND PLANTATION RESTAURANT

Oneloa Bay — RITZ-CARLTON — VILLAGE TENNIS CENTER

Hawea Point — VILLAGE COURSE CLUBHOUSE
HONOLUA STORE

KAPALUA BAY HOTEL — BAY COURSE CLUBHOUSE
Kapalua Bay — TENNIS GARDEN

Napili Bay — KAPALUA GOLF COURSE

Napili

Haukoe Point — IRONWOOD STABLES
NAPILIHAU ST.
NAPILI PLAZA

30

KAHANA GATEWAY SHOPPING CENTER
HOOHUI RD.
Kahana — ALA
HOKU PL.
Kahana Beach
POHAKU PARK — KAPALUA WEST MAUI AIRPORT

HONOKOWAI TO KAPALUA

0   1 mi
0   1 km

HONOKOWAI BEACH PARK
Honokowai

Honokowai Point
KAANAPALI SHORES PL.
30

To Lahaina

able in this area, starting from the south end moving north.

Mahana at Kaanapali

Aston's Mahana at Kaanapali is billed as an "all oceanfront resort," and in fact all apartments have an ocean view at no extra cost. The second that you walk into these reasonably priced condos and look through a large floor-to-ceiling window framing a swimming pool and the wide blue sea, your cares immediately begin to slip away. The condo sits on a point of beach at 110 Kaanapali Shore Place, tel. (808) 661-8751 or (800) 922-7866, fax (808) 661-5510, and is one in the first group of condos north of Kaanapali. Enjoy a complete kitchen plus pool, sauna, tennis, maid service, activities desk, and a money-saving family plan. Rates begin with studios at $105-135 to one-bedroom suites at $265-300 and huge two-bedroom suites (up to six people) for $400-455.

Embassy Vacation Resort

Open, airy, and with an atrium courtyard, this pink pyramid occupies a sliver of beach between the Mahana and Kaanapali Shores. Each suite has a kitchen, separate living area, large-screen TV, and lanai. Daily maid service is offered, as are a children's program, two restaurants, an ocean activities desk, and laundry facilities. Rates run $270-410 for a one-bedroom suite and $560 for a two-bedroom suite that sleeps six. A Marc Resort, the Embassy is located at 104 Kaanapali Shores Place, tel. (808) 661-2000 or (800) 669-3155.

Aston Kaanapali Shores

The green tranquillity of this created oasis at 3445 Lower Honoapiilani Road., tel. (808) 667-2211 or (800) 922-7866, fax (808) 661-0836, offers an unsurpassed view of sun-baked Lanai and Molokai just across the channel. You enter a spacious and airy open lobby, framing a living sculpture of palms and ferns. The grounds are a trimmed garden in large proportions dappled with sunlight and flowers. Soak away your cares in two whirlpools, one tucked away in a quiet corner of the central garden area for midnight romance, the other near the pool. Make use of the gift shop, fitness center, lighted tennis courts, and activities desk, or enroll the little ones in Camp Kaanapali, a program for children ages 3-8. Enjoy a romantic dinner at The Beach Club restaurant, which serves meals all day and offers entertainment in the evening. All studios and suites have been refurbished and include full kitchens, sweeping lanai, TV, a/c, and daily maid service. Prices range from an affordable studio at $195 to a two-bedroom oceanfront suite for $465. Several hotel rooms with refrigerators are also available at $165. The Aston Kaanapali Shores offers good value for the money.

Paki Maui Resort

At 3615 Lower Honoapiilani Rd., tel. (808) 669-8235 or (800) 535-0085, this excellent-value condo presents airy and bright rooms with sweeping panoramas of the Lahaina Roads. Well-appointed studios for two begin at $179, to $299 for a two-bedroom oceanfront apartment for up to six people; additional guests $15. Amenities include maid service, a/c, cable TV, complete kitchens, pool with spa, and coin laundry facilities. Every unit has a private lanai overlooking a gem of a courtyard or the ocean. You can save money by getting a garden-view unit without sacrificing that delightful feeling that you are in the tropics. A complimentary mai tai party is held weekly for all guests. Although the Paki Maui is in town, it feels secluded the moment you walk onto this property, which forms a little oasis of tranquillity. There is no sand beach fronting the condo, but the snorkeling along the reef is excellent. A Marc Resort.

Maui Park

On the *mauka* side of the road at 3626 Lower Honoapiilani Rd., tel. (808) 669-6622 or (800) 367-5004, this condo is a regular kind of place that offers excellent value. Rooms start at $99 for a hotel room with a refrigerator. Studios run $109-115, and suites $125-169. All studios and suites have full kitchens, and every room has a/c and a lanai. There is a large swimming pool on property, as well as a spa and barbecue area.

Honokowai Palms

At 3666 Lower Honoapiilani Rd., tel. (808) 669-6130 or (800) 669-6284, this condo is an old standby for budget travelers. A basic two-story cinder block affair, originally used as housing for workers constructing the Sheraton down the road, it's basically a long-term place now with a few rental units. The Palms is older, but not run-down; no tinsel and glitter, but neat, clean, and ade-

quate. There is no view. Fully furnished with kitchens, TV, full baths, and queen- or king-size beds. A swimming pool and coin laundry are on the premises. A one-bedroom unit runs $65, $75 for two bedrooms; three nights minimum. Contact the Klahani Resort for details and reservations, tel. (808) 667-2712 or (800) 628-6731.

Hale Maui

This very reasonably priced apartment hotel, P.O. Box 516 Lahaina, HI, 96767, tel. (808) 669-6312, fax 669-1302, owned and operated by Hans Zimmerman, offers one-bedroom apartments that can accommodate up to five people. All have a full kitchen, private lanai, color TV, and limited maid service, with washers and dryers and barbecue grills available to guests. Rates are $65-95, extra person $10, weekly and monthly discount rates available; three nights minimum. All units are bright, tasteful, and clean. The Hale Maui is an excellent choice for budget travelers who would rather spend money on having fun than on a luxurious hotel room.

Hale Ono Loa

Four floors high with a pool in the garden, this place will give you a basic condo experience. Amenities include complete kitchens, separate living and dining areas, TV, lanai, partial maid service, and laundry facility. Hale Ono Loa, 3823 Lower Honoapiilani Rd., tel. (808) 669-0525 or (800) 300-5399, fax (808) 669-0631, has peak- and low-season rates with a $20 difference. High-season one-bedroom, ocean-view is $95, a two-bedroom ocean-view runs $185; three nights minimum, discounts for stays over 28 days.

Noelani

This AAA-approved condo located at 4095 Lower Honoapiilani Rd., tel. (808) 669-8374 or (800) 367-6030, fax (808) 669-7904, Web site: www.noelani-condo-resort.com, e-mail: noelani@maui.net, rents studios from $97, one bedrooms for $120, two and three bedrooms for $167 and $197; 10% discount offered after 28 days. Car/condo, senior, AAA, and honeymoon discounts are given. All units are oceanfront, with fully equipped kitchens, ceiling fans, color TVs, VCRs (video rental available), washer/dryers in the nonstudio units, and midweek maid service. On the grounds are two heated pools, a jacuzzi spa, and a barbecue area.

You're welcomed on the first morning with a complimentary continental breakfast served poolside, where you are given an island orientation by the concierge. You'll find peace and quiet here; you can't go wrong.

Blue Horizons B&B

True to its name, the Blue Horizons has good views of the blue Pacific looking to the west over Honokowai and Kahana. Set in a residential neighborhood below the Kapalua-West Maui Airport, this modern-style bed and breakfast offers three rooms. All have private bathrooms, one has a kitchenette, and two have refrigerators. The living room, kitchen, screened lanai, lap pool, barbecue grill, and washer/dryer are for everyone's use. Breakfast is included Mon.-Saturday. Room rates run $79-99 for two, $15 an additional person; two nights minimum. The Blue Horizon is located at 3894 Mahinahina St., perhaps the only B&B north of Lahaina on the west coast. Write or call: P.O. Box 10578, Lahaina, HI 96761, tel./fax (808) 669-1965, tel. (800) 669-1948, Web site: www.maui.net /~chips, e-mail: chips@maui.net.

Sands of Kahana

You know you're in Kahana when you pass Pohaku Park and spot the distinctive blue tile roofs of this gracious complex, which forms a central courtyard area at 4299 Lower Honoapiilani Rd., tel. (808) 669-0400 or (888) 669-0400, Web site: www.sandsofkahana.com, e-mail: info@sands-of-kahana.com. The condo boasts the poolside Kahana Terrace Restaurant, which serves breakfast, lunch, and dinner. The sandy-bottomed beach fronting the property is very safe and perfect for swimming and sunbathing. The Sands of Kahana gives you extraordinarily large units for the money, with lots of glass for great views, and to sweeten the pot, they're beautiful and well appointed, mostly in earth tones and colors of the islands. One-bedroom units from $185, two-bedroom units from $250, and three-bedroom units from $320 are massive with two lanai, two baths with a tub built for two, walk-in closets, and great ocean views. Each unit offers a gourmet kitchen, cable TV (free HBO), daily maid service, and washer/dryer units. The property, with pool, three tennis courts, putting green, barbecue area, fitness center, and spa, exudes a sense of peace and quiet, and although there are plenty of guests,

you never feel crowded. This is where you come when you want to get away from it all, but still be within reach of the *action.*

Kahana Villa Maui

Across the street from the Sands of Kahana, at 4242 Lower Honoapiilani Rd., tel. (808) 669-5613 or (800) 535-0085, fax (808) 669-0397, this modern, five-story condo steps up the hillside and looks out over the channel to Lanai and Molokai. Pleasantly and casually attractive with contemporary designs and Hawaiian artwork, each of the large units features a complete kitchen, color TV, video equipment in some rooms, washer/dryer, and daily maid service. This is a suite-only condo. On the property are a pool, jacuzzi, barbecue grills, tennis and volleyball courts, an activities desk, and a sundries store. An added special feature is highly acclaimed Erik's Seafood Grotto restaurant, privately operated but located on the property. High-season rates start at $159 for a one-bedroom garden-view unit that sleeps four to $259 for a deluxe ocean-view two-bedroom suite that sleeps six. A Marc Resort.

Kahana Village

Up the road at 4531 Lower Honoapiilani Rd., tel. (808) 669-5111 or (800) 824-3065, fax (808) 669-0974, Web site: www.maui.net/~village/kahana.html, this graceful vacation condominium is a group of low beach houses surrounded by well-manicured lawns on three acres. Each of the pleasantly comfortable units is individually owned, so all have a slightly different character. All are light and breezy, appointed in earth tones, and each has a complete kitchen, color TV, VCR, and large lanai. Ground-level apartments are large at 1,700 square feet and feature three bedrooms and two baths. The upper-level units are a bit smaller but still spacious at 1,200 square feet and have two bedrooms (one as a loft), two baths, and high open-beam ceilings. There is a narrow pebble beach out front, and the property has a swimming pool, jacuzzi, and barbecue grills. Rates are $195-235 for second-floor units and $255-320 for ground-level units, one to four persons, and $20 per night for each extra person; five nights minimum. Low season rates are abut 20% less; 10% discount for stays longer than 14 days.

Kahana Sunset

This property has a superb spot on a wonderful little beach. Set alone on the small and protected Keoninue Bay, the finely sculpted gardens and trellised lanai set off the attractive and privately owned condo units that step down to the water. All units have full kitchens, private lanai, color TVs, washers and dryers, and daily maid service. Ceiling fans are used in each unit and louvered windows catch the cooling sea breezes Rates are $160-180 for a one-bedroom unit, and two bedrooms run $165-265, with substantial off season and monthly discounts. Some packages available. There is a two-night minimum, except during the year-end holidays when there's a 14-day minimum. Some credit cards accepted. At 4909 Lower Honoapiilani Road. Contact P.O. Box 10219, Lahaina, HI 96761, tel. (808) 669-8011 or (800) 669-1488, fax (808) 669-9170, Web site: www.kahanasunset.com.

Napili Point Resort

Napili Point is one of the most beautifully situated complexes on Maui. This low-rise property sits on its own promontory of black lava separating Kahana and Napili, located at 5295 Honoapiilani Rd., tel. (808) 669-9222 or (800) 669-6252, fax (808) 669-7984, Web site: www.napilipointresort.com, e-mail: napilipt@compuserve. The reef fronting the condo is home to a colorful display of reef fish and coral, providing some of the best snorkeling on the west end. Not graced with a sand beach (it's 100 yards north along a path), nature, however, was generous in another way. Each room commands an unimpeded panorama with a breathtaking sunset view of Lanai and Molokai. You get a deluxe room for a standard price. Because of the unique setting, little development has occurred in the area, and the condo is very secluded though convenient to shops and stores. The two-story buildings offer fully furnished one- and two-bedroom units from a very affordable $184 to $279, less during regular season, with full kitchens, washers and dryers, walk-in closets, and large dressing and bath areas. Up to four people, rollaway $10, and this includes maid service, two pools, barbecue grills, and a family plan. Two-bedroom units on the second floor include a loft with its own sitting area. Floor-to-ceiling windows frame the living still life of sea and surf so you can enjoy the view from every part of the apartment.

Napili Shores

Next door to Napili Point and overlooking Napili Bay from the lava-rock shoreline is the two-story Napili Shores condominium, 5315 Lower Honoapiilani Rd., tel. (808) 669-8061 or (800) 688-7444, fax (808) 669-5407. All units surround a tropical garden, fishpond, manicured lawn, jacuzzi, and swimming pool. Although not large nor ostentatious, each unit is comfortable and contains a full kitchen, color TV, and large lanai. Rates run $150-200 for studios, $210-245 for one-bedroom units, with an additional $15 for extra persons. Many packages available. There are three restaurants on the premises, including the Orient Express Thai Restaurant, Harry's Sushi and Pupu Bar, and the Gazebo; da Store for food items, gifts, and sundries; an activity desk; and a guest laundry.

Napili Surf Beach Resort

Located at 50 Napili Pl., tel. (808) 669-8002 or (800) 541-0638, fax (808) 669-8004, Web site: www.napilisurf.com, these are reasonably priced full condo units at the south end of Napili Beach that attract mostly an older crowd with some younger families. Both the buildings and grounds have been upgraded recently. The grounds are not luxurious but nicely manicured, and have two pools and three shuffleboard lanes. Very clean rooms with full kitchens have ceiling fans, TVs, and their own lanai. Daily maid service is provided, and there's a laundry facility on premises. Garden-view studio units run $89 during regular season and $104 during high season. Ocean-view studio and one-bedroom units run $130-180, respectively, during low season and $142-199 during high season. Minimum stay is five nights, 10 during the Christmas holiday season; 10% discount for 30 days or longer. Car/condo packages and other special deals are offered.

Napili Sunset

At 46 Hui Dr., this newer AAA-approved condo has two buildings on the beach and one away from the water. All units have fully equipped kitchens, ceiling fans, color TVs, and daily maid service, and share the pool, the beachfront barbecue grill, and a laundry area. Studio apartments in the building away from the beach go for $95, one bedrooms $185, and two bedrooms $265; all have reduced rates during the low season. For additional information and reservations contact

Napili Sunset at (808) 669-8083 or (800) 447-9229, fax (808) 669-2730, Web site: www.napilisunset.com.

The Mauian

Opened in 1959, this property is the oldest on the bay and it couldn't have a better location. Don't let the age fool you, however, as all 44 units have been recently and attentively renovated with new kitchens and bathrooms, pleasing period-style reproduction bamboo and hardwood furniture, and Hawaiian artwork that helps conjure up the feeling of a slower, more hospitable Hawaii. And you'll find hospitality here. Lots of it. This is a gem. The '50s-era buildings blend well with the garden, in which you'll find not only tropical flowers and bushes, but also taro and medicinal plants. The open central lawn holds a pool and shuffleboard courts (join a tournament), and every unit has a lanai with a view of the beach and ocean. It's the kind of place where you might expect to hear slack-key guitar wafting across the garden, and you'll certainly hear the water lapping at the shore, lulling you to sleep at night. Ceiling fans and louvered windows create air flow; there is no air conditioning. There also are no TVs or phones in the studios, but there is a TV and a phone as well as video and book libraries in the community Ohana Room, where a complimentary continental breakfast is served daily. Because of the hospitality and sense of *ohana* (family), many guests return year after year. Based on double occupancy, rates for low and high seasons are: $155/$175 for a beachfront unit, $140/$160 for beach-view units, and $125/$145 for garden units; $10 each extra person. The Mauian is located at 5441 Lower Honoapiilani Road. For information and reservations call (808) 669-6205 or (800) 367-5034, fax (808) 669-0129, Web site: www.mauian.com, e-mail: info@mauian.com.

Napili Kai Beach Club

At 5900 Honoapiilani Rd., tel. (808) 669-6271 or (800) 367-5030, fax (808) 669-5740, Web site: www.napilikai.com, e-mail: nkbc@maui.net, this accommodation is the last in Napili before you enter the landscaped expanse of Kapalua. The Napili Kai Beach Club, the dream-come-true of now deceased Jack Millar, was built before regulations forced properties back from the water. Jack Millar's ashes are buried near the restaurant under a flagpole bearing the U.S. and Canadian flags.

The setting is idyllic, with the beach a crescent moon with gentle wave action. The bay itself is a swim-only area with no pleasure craft allowed. It's expensive at $170 for a garden-view hotel room to $550 for an oceanfront luxury two-bedroom suite, but amenities include a kitchenette, private lanai, air-conditioning in most units, complimentary snorkel gear, daily tea party, activities desk, and all the comforts of home. Several special packages are available. There are four pools, "Hawaii's largest whirlpool," an exercise room, a croquet lawn, putting greens, and tennis courts on property, and the Kapalua Bay Golf Course is just a nine-iron away. All rooms have Japanese touches complete with shoji screens. There's fine dining, dancing, and entertainment at the Sea House Restaurant overlooking the beach.

FOOD AND ENTERTAINMENT

The Beach Club

Whether you're a guest or not, a quiet and lovely restaurant in which to dine is The Beach Club at the Aston Kaanapali Shores. One of Honokowai's best-kept secrets, the restaurant is centered in the condo's garden area and opens directly onto the sea. Request a table on the terrace overlooking the pool for an especially romantic setting. The restaurant changes throughout the day from a casual cafe in the morning to a more formal candlelit room in the evening, but always the service is friendly. Breakfast, served 7-11:30 a.m., with early bird specials until 9 a.m., can be *paniolo* French toast, scrambled eggs and bacon, or a variety of gourmet omelettes. Lunch, served 11:30 a.m.-3 p.m., offers sandwiches and lighter fare. The evening dinner menu, served 5:30-9:30 p.m., whets your appetite with sautéed mushrooms or Cajun *ahi* served with *wasabi* and *shoyu*. The soup of the day and salads lead to main entrees like chicken marsala, grilled scallops, or clams pesto with linguine, with most in the $15-20 range. A children's menu is also offered, and entertainment is provided several nights a week.

Lourdes Kitchenette

At Da Rose Mall, 3481 Lower Honoapiilani Rd., tel. (808) 669-5725, just as you enter Honokowai proper, Lourdes offers takeout or delivery service along with a few red picnic tables out front where you can eat. Open daily until 4 p.m. They prepare plate lunches and simple Filipino food with everything under $6.50. Lourdes is small, simple, clean, and adequate.

Pizza and Deli

Pizza Hut, in 5-A Rent a Space at 3600 Lower Honoapiilani Rd., tel. (808) 669-6996, open Sun.-Thurs. 11 a.m.-11 p.m., weekends until midnight, offers carryout and delivery pizza. For a quick bite, **Honokowai Ōkuzuya Deli** is available for an amazing selection of Chinese, Japanese, Italian, Mexican, and vegetarian foods.

breadfruit

(sidebar, rotated) DIANA LASICH-IAFPER

Erik's Seafood Grotto

At 4242 Lower Honoapiilani Road, second floor of Kahana Villa, tel. (808) 669-4806, Erik's is open daily for lunch 11:30 a.m.-2 p.m. and dinner 5-10 p.m. It is decorated in an appropriately nautical theme, with fish tanks, divers' helmets, and mounted trophy fish. The early bird specials run 5-6 p.m. and cost $12-14. Bouillabaisse, cioppino, and baked stuffed prawns are among the chef's specialties. Shellfish, lobster, steak, and poultry are on the menu, but the real focus is the wide variety of fish that can be prepared in numerous ways. Most dinners run $17-25 with a good selection of appetizers. Erik's is known to have the *best* selection of fresh fish on Maui—up to nine selections nightly. This is a quality restaurant with excellent service. The food is delicious but the prices are not cheap.

Kahana Terrace Restaurant

Under the blue roof by the pool at the Sands of Kahana Resort, 4299 Lower Honoapiilani Road, tel. (808) 669-5399, this open-air and moderately priced restaurant is good for sunsets. Breakfast offerings feature omelettes and items from the griddle; lunch is mostly sandwiches and burgers. Appetizers like coconut shrimp and crab quesadilla and various salads precede entrees that can be fresh catch of the day at $16.95, New York steak for $17.95, or shrimp fettuccine at $14.95. A couple of early bird specials run $9.95. This is not fine cuisine, but is nutritious and satisfying. Live music nightly 5-7 p.m.

Dollie's

Located at 4310 Honoapiilani Hwy. in the Kahana Manor Shops, tel. (808) 669-0266, Dollie's is open daily 11 a.m.- midnight, with happy hour 4-6 p.m. Dollie's features several TVs with satellite hook-up for sporting events, cappuccino, and weekend entertainment. The good food and fair prices on Dollie's menu feature 20 sandwiches from which to choose, all priced around $7.50; plates of lasagna, fettuccine Alfredo, or linguine marinara for $8.95-10.95; pizza by the tray for $7.95-20 or by the slice during happy hour for $1.25; and plenty of finger foods. The sandwiches and other entrees are good, but the pizza is the best. The bar has a wide selection of domestic and imported beers, wines, and a daily exotic drink special. Dollie's, one of the few eateries in the area, is usually a laid-back pub/pizzeria but can get hopping on the weekend and is perhaps the most happening place for late night get-togethers in Kahana.

China Boat

The China Boat restaurant at 4474 Lower Honoapiilani Hwy. in Kahana, tel. (808) 669-5089, is open daily for lunch 11:30 a.m.-2 p.m. and dinner 5-10 p.m. It's almost elegant with its highly polished, black lacquer furniture, pink tablecloths, scroll paintings, and island-inspired prints, but the food quality is variable. A typically large MSG-free Chinese menu offers seafood, beef, chicken, vegetables, pork, and noodle dishes at a reasonable price.

Roy's Kahana Bar and Grill

Finally McDonald's has a culinary purpose—to landmark Roy's Kahana Bar and Grill, located at the new Kahana Gateway Mall, 4405 Honoapiilani Hwy., Kahana, tel. (808) 669-6999, open daily for dinner 5:30-10 p.m., where Roy Yamaguchi, the restaurant's founder and inspirational chef, and the executive chef work kitchen magic preparing the best in Pacific Rim cuisine. Roy has a penchant for locating his restaurants in pragmatic shopping malls. At Roy's Kahana, the surroundings are strictly casual, like a very upscale cafeteria. The enormous room, reverberating with the clatter of plates and the low hum of dinner conversations, has 40-foot vaulted ceilings, a huge copper-clad preparation area, heavy koa tables and booths, track lighting, and windows all around. Roy's philosophy is to serve truly superb dishes post haste, but impeccably, focusing on the *food* as the dining experience, not the surroundings. Although part of the menu changes every night, you could start your culinary extravaganza with island-style pot stickers with a spicy almond sate peanut sauce for $5.75, wood-roasted Sichuan baby back pork ribs for $7.50, or treat yourself to penne pasta with grilled shrimp, or pesto and tomato sauce for $8.95. There are also individual *imu* pizzas for less than $7.50. Fresh salads include a crispy Upcountry romaine salad with a creamy parmesan garlic dressing for only $6.75, and savory fresh mahimahi with cilantro vinaigrette for $7.95. Move on to the entrees like hibachi-style chicken at $15.95, grilled filet mignon $24.95, or seared Tex-Mex grilled marlin with smoked scallops and risotto for $21.95. Desserts feature the chocolate macadamia tart or a fluffy dark chocolate soufflé at $6.50 (allow 20 minutes to prepare). The full bar serves beer, mixed drinks, and personally selected wine by the bottle or glass. Eating at Roy's "elegant cafeteria" is no place to linger over a romantic cocktail. It's more like sipping the world's finest champagne from a beer mug. But the best by any other name is still the best!

Roy's Nicolina Restaurant

Nicole Yamaguchi has a restaurant named in her honor, just next door to her dad's place at the Kahana Gateway, open daily from 5:30 p.m., tel. (808) 669-5000. The restaurant features Euro-Asian cuisine heavily spiced with California and Southwestern dishes. For example, try a gourmet pizza-like flatbread covered in red onions, tomatoes, and pesto; or Cajun shrimp and handmade sausage for under $6. Appetizers can be pan-fried calamari with anchovy mayonnaise, or seared goat cheese and eggplant with cilantro pesto and red pepper vinaigrette for under $9. Entrees are delicious and fascinating, offerings like roasted orange-ginger plum duck at $19.50, or Yankee pot roast with mashed potatoes and garlic spinach for only $11.95. While much of the menu at Nicolina's is the same across the hall at Roy's, about half is created only for this restaurant and it too changes nightly. If dad's place is filled up, you'll love the quieter Nicolina's, a "Sichuan-spiced taco chip off the old block."

Napili Plaza Restaurants

The following restaurants are all located at Napili Plaza, easily spotted just off the highway. **Koho's Grill and Bar,** an American standard comfortably appointed with booths and tables, ceiling fans, and wide-screen TVs with satellite feed, also has a full-service bar. The menu offers chili cheese fries for $5.95, soups and dinner salads for $2.45, and fish and chips for $6.25. A sandwich board offers everything from BLTs to a club sandwich, all for under $6.25, while full-dress burgers are priced around $6. Plate lunches, all around $6.50, include teriyaki beef or chicken and mahimahi, and some standard fajitas run about $8.50 More substantial entrees include rib plate at $11.95 and a strip steak for $14.95. Open 11 a.m.-11 p.m. daily, with early bird specials from 4-7 p.m.

Maui Taco has reasonably priced, health-conscious fast food and a variety of drinks. Try a chimichanga for up to $5.95, a tostada for under $5, tacos for about $2, or a two-fisted burrito that will keep you full all day for $6.95. The salsa and guacamole are made fresh daily. No MSG or lard is used.

Subway Submarine, open daily 7 a.m.-10 p.m., Friday and Saturday to midnight, serves double-fisted fatso sandwiches.

Napili Shores Resort

Three restaurants are located at this resort, 5315 Honoapiilani Hwy., about one mile before Kapalua town. The **Orient Express,** tel. (808) 669-8077, is open daily for dinner only 5:30-10 p.m. The restaurant serves Thai and Chinese food with a flair for spices; duck salad and stuffed chicken wings are a specialty. The early bird special, served before 6:30 p.m., is a five-course dinner for $11.95. The full but not extensive menu of finely spiced foods includes Orient Express's well-known curry dishes; takeout available. Most entrees are in the $10-13 range. Overlooking the koi pond at the resort, this restaurant is a good choice. Sharing the same space with the Orient Express is **Harry's Sushi and Pupu Bar,** where everything is prepared before you at the counter. Nigiri sushi orders run $4-6, sashimi $9-15, with a few other items on the menu. Both Harry's and the Orient Express are associated with the fine dining restaurants

Chez Paul in Olowalu and the Lobster Cove Restaurant in Wailea.

The **Gazebo**, tel. (808) 669-5621, open 7:30 a.m.-2 p.m., one of the best-kept secrets in the area, is a little brown gazebo with louvered windows next to the resort pool. Be prepared for a line. Locals in the know come here for a breakfast of the Gazebo's famous banana, pineapple, and especially the macadamia nut pancakes for $5.25 There are also eggs and omelettes of all sorts under $6.95. The lunch menu features a range of sandwiches from $4.75 to $6.95, along with burgers and lunch plates under $7.95. You can enjoy a world-class view sitting inside or outside the Gazebo for down-home prices.

The Sea House

At the Napili Kai Beach Club, tel. (808) 669-1500, the Sea House is open daily for breakfast 8-11 a.m., lunch 12-2 p.m., and dinner 5:30-9 p.m.; reservations suggested. Inside the semi-open-air restaurant, appetizers like lemongrass-crusted prawns range $8-12, and soups and salads are equally reasonable. Dinner choices, all served with almond flatbread, vegetables, and rice pilaf or potato, include fresh catch (priced daily); seared pork loin medallions for $17; seasoned and broiled rack of lamb for $24; and a special "lite" fare. Besides the normal menu, every night brings a special dinner menu, but the best is the lobster tail dinner on Thursday for $17.95. A full wine list includes selections from California and France. There is Hawaiian music nightly and a wonderful Friday night Napili Kai Foundation children's Polynesian show (dinner seating at 6 p.m., show at 7:30 p.m.; $35 adults, $20 children) put on by local children who have studied their heritage under the guidance of the foundation. If you just want to soak up the rays and gorgeous view of Napili Bay, you can wear your swimwear and have a cool drink or light fare on the **Whale Watcher's Bar.**

SHOPPING AND SERVICES

Da Rose Mall

Look for this tiny mall located at the south end of town at 3481 Lower Honoapiilani Rd., where you'll find **A & B Rentals and Sportswear**, tel. (808) 669-0027, open daily 9 a.m.-5 p.m., specializing in mopeds, bicycles, snorkel gear, boogie boards, and surfboards. Prices are: mopeds $13 for two hours or $150 per week; bicycles $15 for 24 hours, $60 per week; snorkeling gear $2.50 per day and $9 per week. Boogie boards, surfboards, and even fishing poles are rented by the day or week. The sportswear includes lycra mini dresses, tie-dyed dresses, sundresses, sarongs, T-shirts, and men's printed shirts. In front is **Lourdes Kitchenette,** and around the side are **One Hour Wiki Wiki Photo,** whose name says it all, **Blooming Rose Boutique** studio for women's fashions, and the **Macadamia Nut Shop,** selling gifts and souvenirs. Next door is **ABC Store,** hours 6:30 a.m.-11 p.m., a minimarket selling everything from resortwear to wine.

Every Monday and Thursday morning 6:30-11:30 a.m. a **farmers' market** is held in the parking lot of Da Rose Mall, with vendors selling mostly food items and some clothing and crafts.

5-A Rent a Space Mall

At 3600 Lower Honoapiilani Hwy., this mall is usually located by reference to the Pizza Hut here. Honokowai Okozuya Deli is the other eatery in this strip of shops. Here you'll find **Snorkels N' More,** tel. (808) 665-0804, open daily 8 a.m.-5 p.m., which has reasonable rates for sales and rental of snorkel gear, boogie boards, surfboards, and other water equipment. There are a usually a few billed for rent as well, and same-day film processing. If you're staying at one of the condos in the area, **Kelly's Video,** tel. (808) 669-6004, can provide the evening's entertainment.

Honokowai Food Pantry

Aside from the Napili Supermarket in Napili Plaza, the only real place north of Lahaina that has a full selection of groceries, fruits, vegetables, meats, and sundries is the Food Pantry located at 3636 Lower Honoapiilani Rd., tel. (808) 669-6208, open daily 6:30 a.m.-11 p.m. The prices are just about right at this supermarket. Condo convenience stores in the area are good in a pinch but charge way too much. Stock up here; it's worth the drive.

The **Honokowai post office** is inside the Honokowai Food Pantry. Never busy, this full-service post office accepts packages.

Kahana Manor Shops

Aside from **Dollie's,** in the Kahana Manor Shops there is the **Kahana Manor Groceries,** a one-stop sundries and liquor store open Mon.-Sat. 7

a.m.-11 p.m.; the **Women Who Run With Wolves** boutique for beach and athletic wear and accessories for active women; and the **Wiki Wiki Photo II** for all your camera needs. **West Maui Cycles,** tel. (808) 669-1169, rents bikes by the day or week, so stop in for some good exercise and inexpensive fun. The sundry store at **The Kahana Villa** has most everything from beer to sunglasses, plus fresh fruits and vegetables.

Kahana Gateway Shopping Center
At this newest shopping addition to the Kahana area, easily spotted along Rt. 30 by **McDonald's** golden arches, you'll find a **gas station**, a **Whalers General Store, Bank of Hawaii,** and the **Koin-Op Laundromat.** However, the premier stop is **Roy's Kahana Bar and Grill,** one of the finest gourmet restaurants on Maui, and **Roy's Nicolina Restaurant** next door. Also at the center is the **Maui Dive Shop,** tel. (808) 669-3800, a full-service water activities store where you can rent snorkel equipment, scuba gear, and beach accessories; **O'Rourke's Tourist Trap,** for a 99-cent beach mat, artificial lei, or postcards; **Gallerie Hawaii** for contemporary artwork; and **Kafe Kahana,** tel. (808)

669-6699, which not only has the sweetest buns in town, but also sandwiches and salads.

Napili Plaza
Napili's newest shopping center offers the full service **First Hawaiian Bank; Napili Supermarket,** open daily 6:30 a.m.-11 p.m., featuring fresh fish; **Mail Services Plus,** open daily 9 a.m.-6 p.m., Saturday until 1 p.m., closed Sunday, for all your postal and shipping needs; and several inexpensive eateries.

Napili Village Shopping Center
At 5425 Lower Honoapiilani Rd., the **Napili Village General Store,** tel. (808) 669-6773, is a well-stocked little store and known landmark, good for last-minute items, with fairly good prices for where it is. You can pick up picnic items and sandwiches, groceries, sundries, and liquor. Next door is **Snorkel Bob's,** tel. (808) 669-9603, where you can rent snorkel equipment (prescription masks available) and boogie boards for only $15 per week; **da Store** at Napili Shores is mainly a gift shop and convenience store, open 8 a.m.-9 p.m. daily

KAPALUA

Kapalua sits like a crown atop Maui's head. One of the newest areas on Maui to be developed, it's been nicely done. Out here are the Kapalua Bay and Ritz-Carlton luxury hotels, upscale condominium communities, exclusive shops, three championship golf courses, two tennis centers, horseback riding at the Ironwood Ranch stables, a sporting clays shooting range, sweeping vistas, and terrific beaches (Web site: Kapaluamaui.com). All of this has been carved out of the 23,000 acre Honolua Ranch.

The complimentary **Kapalua Shuttle** runs throughout the resort for resort guests. While there is no regular schedule, it does make a continuous round of stops at the hotels and villas, tennis courts, golf courses, and the Kapalua-West Maui Airport.

BEACHES AND BAYS

Kapalua Beach
Just past Napili Bay is the equally as nice Ka-

palua Bay with its fine crescent beach that's popular though usually not overcrowded. Look for access just past the Napili Kai Beach Club. Park in the public lot and follow the path through the tunnel below the Bay Club restaurant to the beach. The well-formed reef has plenty of fish for snorkeling. Also here are restrooms, showers, and a hotel beach concession.

Oneloa Beach
Located around the point from Kapalua Beach, Oneloa is a small sandy beach down a steep path, where swimming is good and locals come to surf. Seldom visited and private; parking available.

D.T. Fleming Beach Park
One of Maui's best—a long wide beach backed by wonderful shade trees. This beach park is on Honoapiilani Highway just past the Ritz-Carlton where the road dips back down to the coast. Here you'll find parking, showers, barbecue grills, and excellent swimming except in winter, when

there's a pounding surf. There's fair snorkeling here and good surfing and body boarding. This has become the beach for the Ritz-Carlton so the south end of the beach closest to the hotel has become a bit exclusive while the rest maintains its very local flavor.

Mokuleia Bay

Also known as "Slaughterhouse," Mokuleia Bay is about 200-300 yards after mile marker 32; walk down to the water through a stand of trees. This beach has great bodysurfing, but terribly dangerous currents in the winter when the surf is rough. Be careful. Follow the trail to the left for the beach. The path straight ahead takes you to a rocky lava flow. This entire area, plus all of adjacent Honolua Bay, is a Marine Life Conservation District and the underwater life is fabulous. Some of the best snorkeling in the area.

Honolua Bay

Just past Mokuleia Bay heading north, look for a dirt road, then park. The bay is good for swimming, snorkeling, and especially surfing. Many people stay the night without much problem. For good views of the surfers, drive a little farther along the road and park along the cliff just as the road reaches the top, or drive down the dirt road at the edge of the pineapple field for a spot - there will be lots of cars on a good wave day.

ACCOMMODATIONS

Ritz-Carlton Kapalua

The green sweep of tended lawns fading into the distant sea foaming azure heralds your entrance into an enchanted realm as you wind your way down the serpentine roadway leading to the Ritz-Carlton Kapalua, One Ritz-Carlton Dr., Kapalua, HI 96761, tel. (808) 669-6200, (800) 262-8440, or (800) 241-3333, fax (808) 665-0026, Web site: ritzcarlton.com, e-mail: mauiritz@maui.net. At the porte cochere a waiting bellman will park your car. Enter the main hall and relax in the formal parlor of overstuffed chairs, marble-topped tables, and enormous flower arrangements. Evenings in the hall bring mellow entertainment softly illuminated by emerald-green chandeliers. Register, then peer through a huge set of double doors that look straight out into the central courtyard. Walk ahead to the terrace built from Chinese slate and peer into the floral heart of the hotel grounds. Below are seashell-shaped swimming pools and fluttering palms. The roof line of the great hotel, borrowed from the Orient, covers the two wings that descend the hill toward the sea, creating an enormous central area between. Stroll the halls hung with the fine works by prominent island artists and last-century reproductions. Sit in a tiny alcove and let the music of sea and wind lull you into deep relaxation and contemplation. All this, coupled with the dark and rich woodwork, thick patterned carpets, floral drapery, and pineapple-pattern wallpaper, define the Ritz as the epitome of elegance and luxury.

On the beach, a sweeping crescent of white sand is embraced by two sinewy arms of jet-black lava. It becomes immediately obvious why the diminutive promontory was called Kapalua, "Arms Embracing the Sea," by the ancient Hawaiians who lived here. Notice on the rise above the sea a rounded shoulder of banked earth separated from the main hotel grounds by a low hedge: the spirits of the ancient ali'i linger here in this ancient burial ground. The original construction plans were altered and the hotel was moved away from the area in an attempt to protect it. A *kahuna* was asked to perform the ancient *mele* to appease the spirits, and to reconsecrate the land, passing the *kahu* (caretaking) of it to the Ritz. Although the small parcel was deeded to the state, the hotel management and staff alike take their responsibility very seriously.

The hotel's Village Tennis Center, combined with the Kapalua Tennis Garden a few minutes away, represent the largest private tennis facility in the state. The Village Tennis Center has 10 courts, five lighted for evening play, and a full-service pro shop. A few minutes away by shuttle, in different directions, are three championship golf courses: the Plantation Course, the Village Course, and the Bay Course. Both golf and tennis packages are available. The hotel also has a fitness center complete with stairmasters, massage therapists, beauty salon, sauna, and steam rooms. Other hotel offerings include the Ritz Kids children's program, the Aloha Fridays program of activities, a croquet lawn, putting green, business center, the Art School at Kapalua, and ecotours.

Located in two wings off the main reception hall, the luxury rooms, all with their own private lanai and sensational view, are a mixture of kings, doubles, and suites. Done in muted neutral tones, the rooms feature handcrafted quilts, twice-daily room attendance, turndown service complete with complimentary orchid and rich chocolates, remote control color TV, 24-hour room service, fully stocked honor bar, and an in-room safe. Wardrobes, hung with plush terry robes and plump satin hangers, feature automatic lights, steam irons, and ironing boards. The spacious bathrooms, regal with calcatta fabricatta Italian marble, offer wide, deep tubs, separate commodes, and shower stalls along with dressing and vanity mirrors, double sinks, hair dryers, and name-brand grooming products. Rates begin at $260 for a garden view to $375 for a deluxe oceanfront view. The Ritz-Carlton Club, an exclusive floor with its own concierge, and featuring continental breakfast, light lunch, cocktails, cordials, and a full spread of evening hors d'oeuvres, is $450. Suites from an executive one-bedroom to the magnificent Ritz-Carlton Suite run $495-2,700. Many special packages are offered.

Kapalua Bay Hotel

This, like other grand hotels, is more than a place to stay; it's an experience. The hotel steps down the hillside from its 6th-level entrance. The main lobby is partially open and accented with an enormous skylight. Plants trail from the tall ceiling, and the walls are hung with paintings by Peggy Hopper. All colors are soothing and subdued. A tiny brook splits the Gardenia Court restaurant and Lehua Lounge on the lower level of the lobby, and the view over the garden lawns and out to sea is spectacular. The clean lines of the hotel, its sparse decoration, and contemporary elegance let the view speak for itself without distraction. The ocean view vies for your attention here, while the pool pulls you down to the garden, and the beach lures you to the water. Not overly ornamented, guest rooms are done in muted colors—off whites, tans, and tropical greens. Each spacious room is neatly laid out with an entertainment center, three telephones, electronic safe, a soft couch and easy chairs, and louvered doors to the lanai. The well-lit bathrooms have his and her sinks at each end of the room, separate dressing closets, and individual areas for the tub, shower, and commode. Marble, tile, and chrome are used throughout. Concierge service and twice-daily maid service are additional amenities for guests. There are three restaurants and a lounge in the complex, a fitness room,

a small arcade with plenty of shops, a multitude of daily activities including Kamp Kapalua for kids, magnificent golf and tennis nearby, and a resort shuttle to get you to whereever you need to go in the resort. The least expensive room in the hotel is one with a garden view at $275. An ocean view runs $375, oceanfront prime $525, and the suites are $800-1,600; $50 each additional person 18 and older. Available for a reasonable sum, the American plan consists of breakfast and dinner with your room. The Kapalua Bay Hotel is associated with the Halekulani and Waikiki Parc hotels in Honolulu. Contact the Kapalua Bay Hotel at One Bay Dr., Kapalua, HI 96761, tel. (808) 669-5656 or (800) 367-8000, fax (808) 669-4690, Web site: www.kapaluabayhotel.com.

Kapalua Bay Villas

Several groups of vacation rentals dot this spacious resort. They range from one-bedroom villas to five-bedroom luxury homes. Each is individually owned so all are decorated differently, but all are equipped with full kitchens, a/c and fans, washers and dryers, telephone, and TV, and each has twice-weekly maid service. All groups of villas also have swimming pools, barbecue grills, and maintained gardens. One-bedroom villas with a fairway view start at $185 and climb rapidly to the two-bedroom oceanfront villas for $400. Daily rates for the luxury homes run $995 for three-bedroom to $4,000-5,000 for five-bedroom ones. Some golf packages and car/condo deals are also offered. The Kapalua Villa Reception Center is located at 550 Office Rd., Kapalua, HI 96761. Write or call for information and reservations, tel. (808) 669-8088 or (800) 545-0018, fax (808) 669-5234, Web site: www.kapaluavillas.com.

FOOD

Jameson's Grill and Bar

Don't underestimate this excellent restaurant just because it's located at a golf course. The Kapalua Bay Golf Course provides the backdrop and the restaurant provides the filling delicious food. The main room with its flagstone floor and open beam ceiling is richly appointed with koa wood, and large windows frame a sweeping view of the super-green fairways of the golf course. Sit inside or out on the patio. From the lunch menu select a calamari strip appetizer for $7.95 or a sandwich and salad for under $15. Lunch is served 11 a.m.-3 p.m., dinner 5-10 p.m. The dinner menu is more substantial. Start with an appetizer like Thai summer rolls for $8.95 or seared sashimi for $12.95, and move on to a soup or one of the many fine salads. Entrees include fish of the day for $17.95-23.95, herbed half chicken for $17.95, and rack of lamb at $24.95. To relax and soak up the scenery you can order dessert or sip wine selected from an extensive list. All items can be ordered takeout. An excellent restaurant with a lovely setting at 200 Kapalua Drive. Call (808) 669-5653 for reservations.

Ritz Carlton Restaurants

Dining at the Ritz-Carlton is a wonderful gastronomic experience with three main restaurants from which to choose, plus a lobby and sunset lounge and a beachside cafe, all under the skillful management of executive chef, Patrick Callarec. **The Terrace Restaurant,** open daily for breakfast 6:30-11:30 a.m. (buffet to 10:30) and for dinner 5:30-10 p.m., informal and relaxed, overlooks the central courtyard with the dramatic sea vista beyond. Tastefully appointed in green and burgundy, the restaurant features Pacific Rim and Asian food, with an emphasis on Japanese cuisine. Although there is an extensive à la carte breakfast menu, the house specialty is a breakfast buffet for $16.50 or $12 for a lighter selection. Apple blintzes, eggs royal and Benedict, Molokai French toast, plump sausages, grilled potatoes, and sizzling strips of bacon are surrounded by fruits, fresh juices, and jams. For dinner, Chef Steve Falsetti starts you with chilled oysters in chili-pepper water mignonette for $12.50, fried tofu and shiitake mushrooms in ginger broth for $8.50, or island clam chowder at $7.50. Main courses include lamb osso bucco for $21; grilled chow mein noodles with clams, shrimp, and scallops in a ginger sauce for $19; or seared salmon with asparagus and fennel $27. Monday evening brings an Asian buffet, Wednesday it's Italian, Friday the buffet is seafood, and Saturday it's a *paniolo* buffet inspired by the cowboys of Hawaii.

The Anuenue Room, serving dinner Tues.-Sat. 6-9:30 p.m. and Sunday Champagne brunch 10:30 a.m.-2:30 p.m. ($29 including champagne), is the hotel's most elegant restaurant. Reserva-

tions are recommended and resort attire is required. Formal yet intimate, the restaurant offers Hawaiian provincial cuisine prepared by master chef Craig Connole. Appetizers, salads, and soups fit for the *ali'i* include seared duck foie gras and potato risotto for $18, roasted eggplant and Kula tomato soup $12, and grilled quail with lettuce salad with red onion marmalade and balsamic vinegar $14. The finest entrees include herb-crusted onaga for $38, a wonderful sesame-seed rack of lamb with poha berries and pineapple chutney for $39, and grilled marinated chicken breast with basil garlic just $27. Desserts are mango tarto, banana crème brulée, or a fluffy soufflé of the day prepared just for you. The food is wonderful but the view over the lawns, sea, and Molokai in the distance is an added pleasure.

The Banyan Tree, an informal poolside restaurant open for lunch and appetizers 11:30 a.m.-4 p.m., is a good stop on your way to or from the beach. Fashioned like a Mediterranean court with stone floor and copper-and-green tiled bar, the restaurant offers seating in high-backed chairs at teakwood tables, with mood lighting reminiscent of old oil lamps. Dine alfresco on the redwood deck and watch cavorting whales just offshore. Selections start with beefsteak tomatoes salad with Upcountry greens and buffalo mozzarella for $15; mahimahi sandwich for $14; or panini pasta smothered in a sauce of roma tomatoes, fried capers, roasted peppers, and garlic for $12.50. Families will enjoy a selection of gourmet pizzas and calzones for $12-16.50, all from a wood-burning oven.

At the **lobby lounge** you'll find appetizers, salads, sandwiches, fruit, and coffee to have while you sit and gaze out over the courtyard from the patio. Down by the beach, on a patio surrounded by a manicured coconut grove, is the **Beachhouse,** serving tropical libations, healthy fruit smoothies, burgers, and sandwiches for under $12.

Kapalua Bay Resort Restaurants

The resort has three dining spots. The elegant **Bay Club,** tel. (808) 669-8008, offers fine dining for lunch 11 a.m.-1:30 p.m. and dinner 6-9:30 p.m. on a promontory overlooking the beach and Molokai in the distance. Traditionally elegant, there is a dress code; expect to spend at least $25 for a superbly prepared Mediterranean entree with overtones of flavors from the Pacific and Asia. Piano music nightly. The open-air and contemporary **Gardenia Court** restaurant on the lower lobby level of the main building serves breakfast and dinner. Best known for its Friday evening seafood buffet and Sunday brunch, Gardenia Court always offers Hawaiian music in the evening. Resortwear required. The casual **Plumeria Terrace** restaurant is located at poolside in the garden below the main building. Stop here for burgers, sandwiches, and light meals, or for a refreshing beer or tropical drink 11 a.m.-5 p.m. Aside from these fine restaurants, the **Lehua Lounge** in the entrance lobby serves *pu pu* and drinks in the evening, always with relaxing music to help let the cares of the day slip away.

Located in the Kapalua Bay Shops is **Sansei** seafood restaurant and sushi bar, which serves more than just Japanese sushi—a whole variety of Pacific Rim food and drinks from the bar. An early bird special is offered 5:30-6 p.m. Open 5:30-11 p.m. Sun.-Wed., until 1 a.m. Thursday and Friday when there is laser karaoke.

The Plantation House

Above Kapalua on the road leading to the Plantation Golf Course Club House, you'll find the lovely Plantation House Restaurant, open daily 8-11 a.m. for breakfast, 11 a.m.-3 p.m. for lunch, and 5:30-9 p.m. for dinner, tel. (808) 669-6299. Inside, the split-level floor, gabled roof, natural wood, and carpeted and marbled floor add elegance, but the real beauty is the natural still life that pours through the floor-to-ceiling French doors. Kapalua lies at your feet, Molokai floats upon the still blue sea, and the West Maui Mountains rise behind in a paisley of emerald green, indigo, and cloud-dappled grays. For breakfast, the extensive menu offers light fare like home-baked muffins for $2; a hearty rancher's breakfast of two eggs, toast, two scoops of rice or breakfast potatoes, grilled ham, bacon, or Portuguese sausage all for $8; or smoked salmon Benedict to $10. For lunch, start with pan-fried crab cakes served with roasted pepper aioli for $7, an oriental chicken salad for $8, or blackened chicken Caesar for $8. A half-pound double-fisted Plantation House burger is available for $6.50 and a grilled chicken breast sandwich for $8.50. The dinner menu tempts your palate with scallop skewers wrapped in apple-smoked

bacon for $8, hot and spicy seared sashimi at a daily quote, and warm goat cheese on a bed of fresh, mixed local greens with passion fruit vinaigrette for $7. The chef prepares *pasta al giorno* for $16, or tops it with scallops or shrimp for $21. Sautéed jumbo prawns with garlic mashed potatoes costs $21, and broiled double-cut lamb chops, shallots, and rosemary au jus runs $22. To complement your Mediterranean-style dinner, the mostly Californian wine list also offers a smattering of French and Italian wines, and the full bar can prepare any drink that you may desire.

Honolua Store

Just on the right before the Ritz-Carlton, this small general store also serves reasonably priced light meals and sandwiches during the week. The breakfast menu, served 6-10 a.m. offers "The Hobo"—eggs, sausage, and rice for $3.50—or two pancakes for $2.75. Plate lunches, sandwiches, grilled items, and salads all run under $7 and are served 10 a.m.-3 p.m. Sit at a table on the front porch and overlook the broad lawns and tall pine trees of the exclusive planned community of Kapalua. This is by far the cheapest place in the area to eat.

Village Cafe

This cafe at the Kapalua Village Golf Course clubhouse serves light meals, better than you would expect from a small snack shop with outdoor seating. Burgers, sandwiches, salads, and sides are all available, but the cafe is especially famous for its hot dogs, a steamed Vienna all-beef quarter pounder with all the trimmings on a French roll, and supposedly the best on the island. All are reasonably priced.

SHOPPING

Kapalua Shops

A cluster of exclusive shops service the resort, including **McInerny** with fine women's apparel; **Kapalua Kids** for the younger set; and **Kapalua Logo Shop** if you want to show off that you've at least been to the Kapalua Resort, since all items of clothing sport the butterfly logo. **Mandalay Imports** has a potpourri of silks and cottons from the East, especially Thailand. Visit **La Perle** for pearls, diamonds, and other jewels, and **South Seas** for antiques, art, and jewelry. **Lahaina Gallery** has a wonderful collection of island artists on display. When you get hungry from all the shopping, stop into the **Sansei** sushi shop and bar for a taste of Japan.

If you're here on Thursday, be sure to stop and see the free ancient hula show 10-11 a.m. On Tuesday 10 a.m.-noon come and listen to slack-key guitar and stories. These shops are connect-ed to those in Kaanapali and Lahaina by the West Maui Shopping Express shuttle.

Honolua Store

This well-stocked, reasonably priced store, open daily 6 a.m.-8 p.m., is a rare find in this expensive neck of the woods. The shelves hold beer, wine, and liquors, basic food items from bananas to sweets, books, and gifts, and even a smattering of sunglasses, shorts, hats, and aloha shirts

KEITH PERKINS

SOUTH MAUI

MAALAEA

Maalaea is a small community located in the southwestern corner of the Maui isthmus that is home to a handful of houses, a row of condos, two fine restaurants, a small harbor, and the new Maui Ocean Center.

Maalaea Harbor is a bite-sized working harbor, one of two on the island where tourist boats dock (the other being Lahaina Harbor). With the comings and goings of all types of craft, the harbor is colorful, picturesque, and always busy. Until the advent of plane travel to and between the islands, Maalaea was a busy port for inter-island steamer traffic, principally serving the Maalaea and Kihei area. Maalaea Harbor has the dubious distinction of being the second windiest harbor in the world, with sustained winds averaging 25 knots. Upon entering the village, you are greeted by a small U.S. Coast Guard installation at the east end, and Buzz's Wharf, a well-known restaurant, at the other. Between, you will find restrooms, the Maalaea Activity Center booth at harborside, and the Shinto fishing shrine

Ebisuku Kotohira Jinsha, which was constructed in 1914. The condominiums line Hauoli St., which culminates in Haycraft Park, the western end of Maalaea Beach.

SIGHTS

Maalaea Beach
Consisting of three miles of windswept sand partially backed by Kealia Pond National Wildlife Refuge, Maalaea Beach has many points of access between Maalaea and Kihei along Route 31. The strong winds make the beach undesirable for sunning and bathing, but it's a windsurfer's dream. The hard-packed sand is a natural track for joggers, profuse in the morning and afternoon. The beachcombing and strolling are quiet and productive. From the Maalaea end, you can access the beach from Haycraft Park. If you're up by 6 a.m. you can see the Kihei canoe club practice at the Kihei end; they put their ca-

noes in the water near the Kihei wharf just across the road from Suda's Store.

Maui Ocean Center

The newest addition to Maalaea, and the most radical change for the community in years, has been the opening of the Maui Ocean Center. The Ocean Center is a large aquarium and marine park with several dozen indoor and outdoor displays and hands-on exhibits. Explore the realm of the reef in the Living Reef building, handle tide pool creatures at the Touch Pool, and learn about the fascinating turtles, stingrays, and whales in their separate exhibits. As an added benefit during winter months, whales can be seen cavorting and breaching in the bay beyond the harbor. Perhaps the most unique feature at the center is the Underwater Journey, where you walk through a transparent acrylic tunnel in the "open ocean" tank, Hawaii's largest aquarium, which offers a 240-degree view of the waterlife. There are no trained animal shows here, only periodic feedings. No matter what your focus, this will be an educational experience as you'll learn about Hawaii's unique marine culture; all animals are indigenous or endemic. A stop here could easily be a half-day affair, so when you get hungry, have a quick bite at the Reef Cafe snack bar or try the Seascape Restaurant for a more substantial meal. Before leaving, pick up a memento of your day's visit at the gift shop. The Maui Ocean Center, tel. (808) 270-7000, Web site: www.coralworld.com/moc, is open daily 9 a.m.-5 p.m.; $17.50 adults, $12.50 children 3-12. If you're without transportation, ride the Maui Ocean Center trolley, $7 roundtrip, from Kaanapali or Kihei/Wailea.

Kealia Pond National Wildlife Refuge

This refuge stretches between Maalaea and Kihei, mostly on the inland side of Rt. 31. Now set aside for stilts, coots, and other wildlife, this pond was once two productive fishponds used by Hawaiians living around the bay. As with most such refuges, this shore environment lies in a delicate balance and changes according to the season. Aside from the stilt and coot, other birds and fowl that inhabit the pond are Hawaiian duck, black-crowned night heron, golden plover, and ruddy turnstone. Migratory waterfowl such as the pintail and shoveller visit the refuge, and

hawksbill turtles come to shore to lay eggs. There are no facilities.

PRACTICALITIES

Accommodations

There are no hotels in Maalaea. Condominiums stand one after another along the water east of the harbor. For rooms, check with the Maalaea Bay Rentals agency, tel. (808) 244-7012 or (800) 367-6084, fax (808) 242-7476. It has an office at the Hono Kai Resort, 280 Hauoli St., Maalaea, HI 96793, and handles over 100 units in a majority of the condos along this road. All units are fully furnished, and each property has a pool and laundry facility. Rates run $85-175 during high season, with substantial discounts for summer and fall and a 10% discount for monthly stays. Minimum stay is five nights.

Food

The award-winning **Waterfront Restaurant** at the Milowai Condo, tel. (808) 244-9028, has a well-deserved reputation and a great view of the harbor and bay. It's owned and operated by the Smith brothers, who work both the front and the kitchen. The Waterfront is open for lunch 10 a.m.-1:00 p.m. daily except Saturday and from 5 p.m. for dinner. Choose a horseshoe-shaped booth tucked around the room's perimeter or a table out on the deck with sea breezes and the setting sun, and order a bottle of wine from the extensive international list. For starters, consider the Caesar salad for $7.75, Pacific oysters on the half shell at $9.25, or exotic Indonesian escargot for $6.75. Definitely order the Maine lobster chowder, a famous specialty, for $6.95. The entree scampi is $23.95, baked prawns Wellington is $23.95, while rack of lamb in a Sichuan peppercorn sauce is priced at $27.95. However, the best choice is the fresh island fish, priced daily, which is prepared in a variety of ways: Sicilian; à la meuniere in a white wine sauce with lemon; Bastille, which is imprisoned in angelhair potato and sautéed and topped with fresh scallions; Southwestern; sautéed; broiled; baked; or poached. Save room for one of the prize-winning desserts—white chocolate and cream cheese cake, upside-down apple pie, chocolate mousse, or chocolate-dipped strawberries. The Waterfront provides an excellent

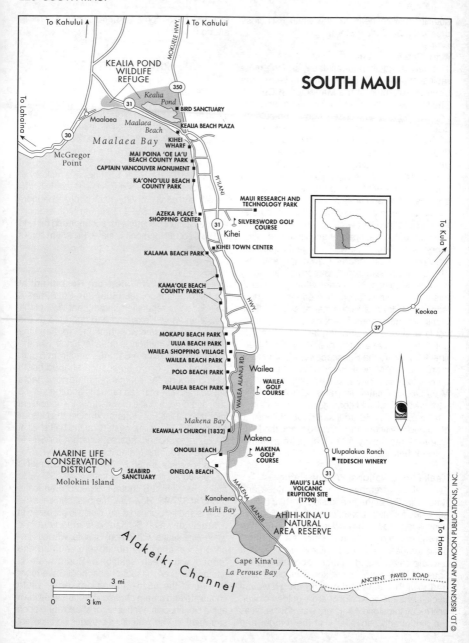

SOUTH MAUI

To Kahului
MOKUELE HWY
To Kahului

KEALIA POND
WILDLIFE
REFUGE

350
31
Kealia Pond

BIRD SANCTUARY

To Lahaina

Maalaea
Maalaea Beach
30
KEALIA BEACH PLAZA

Maalaea Bay
KIHEI WHARF

McGregor Point

MAI POINA 'OE LA'U BEACH COUNTY PARK

CAPTAIN VANCOUVER MONUMENT

KA'ONO'ULU BEACH COUNTY PARK

PI'ILANI HWY

MAUI RESEARCH AND TECHNOLOGY PARK

AZEKA PLACE SHOPPING CENTER

31
SILVERSWORD GOLF COURSE

Kihei

KIHEI TOWN CENTER

KALAMA BEACH PARK

KAMA'OLE BEACH COUNTY PARKS

To Kula
37
Keokea

MOKAPU BEACH PARK
ULUA BEACH PARK
WAILEA SHOPPING VILLAGE
WAILEA BEACH PARK
POLO BEACH PARK
PALAUEA BEACH PARK

WAILEA ALANUI RD.

Wailea

WAILEA GOLF COURSE

MOON

Makena Bay
KEAWALA'I CHURCH (1832)

Makena

MAKENA GOLF COURSE

ONOULI BEACH

MAKENA ALANUI

ONELOA BEACH

Ulupalakua Ranch
TEDESCHI WINERY
31

MARINE LIFE CONSERVATION DISTRICT

SEABIRD SANCTUARY

Molokini Island

MAUI'S LAST VOLCANIC ERUPTION SITE (1790)

Kanahena
Ahihi Bay

AHIHI-KINA'U NATURAL AREA RESERVE

To Hana

Alakeiki Channel

Cape Kina'u
La Perouse Bay

ANCIENT PAVED ROAD

0   3 mi
0   3 km

© J.D. BISIGNANI AND MOON PUBLICATIONS, INC.

dining experience, from the fine service to the wonderful food, and is well worth the price.

Buzz's Wharf restaurant, tel. (808) 244-5426, open daily 11 a.m.-11 p.m., specializes in seafood. The waterfront atmosphere and second-story views are unbeatable. It's a favorite spot and often busy. *Pu pu* selections include steamed clams for $12.95, escargot on the shell for $7.95, Buzz's salmon for $6.95, and fresh Pacific oysters on the half shell for $11.95. The lunch menu offers a tossed salad with shrimp for $11.95, an assortment of burgers and fries for under $10, and a Cajun open-faced chicken sandwich for $9.95. For dinner, try prawns Tahitian, the captain's

seafood platter, or a mouthwatering cut of prime rib au jus, for $15-30. Enjoy a liter of house wine for $12 or cocktail for $6. End your meal with dessert followed by a stroll around the moonlit harbor.

The **Tradewinds Deli and Mart,** located at the Maalaea Mermaid, carries groceries, drinks, and alcohol, creates deli sandwiches, and also rents snorkel equipment and boogie boards.

At Maalaea Harbor look for the **Maalaea General Store,** open daily except Monday 8 a.m.-5 p.m., where you have a much better chance of buying fishing tackle than you do a loaf of bread. It does have some very limited groceries and sundries

KIHEI

Kihei ("Shoulder Cloak") takes it on the chin whenever anti-development groups need an example at which to wag their fingers. For the last two decades, construction along both sides of Kihei Road, which runs the length of town, has continued unabated. Since there was no central planning for the development, mostly high-rise condos and a few hotels were built wherever they could be squeezed in: some lovely, some are crass. There's hardly a spot left where you can get an unobstructed view of the beach as you drive along. That's the "slam" in a nutshell. The good news is that Kihei has so much to recommend it that if you refrain from fixating on this one regrettable feature, you'll thoroughly enjoy yourself, and save money, too.

The developers went "hyper" here because it's perfect as a tourist area. The weather can be counted on to be the best on all of Maui. Haleakala, looming just behind the town, catches rainclouds before they drench Kihei. Days of blue skies and sunshine are taken for granted. On the other side of the condos and hotels are gorgeous beaches, every one open to the public. Once on the beachside, the condos don't matter anymore. The views out to sea are unobstructed vistas of Lanai, Kahoolawe, Molokini, and West Maui, which gives the illusion of being a separate island. The buildings are even a buffer to the traffic noise! Many islanders make Kihei their home, so there is a feeling of real community here. It's quieter than Lahaina, with fewer restaurants and not as much action; but for sun and surf activities, this place has it all.

The six-mile stretch bordered by beach and mountain that makes up Kihei has always been an important landing spot on Maui. Hawaiian war canoes moored here many times during countless skirmishes over the years; later, Western navigators such as Capt. George Vancouver found this stretch of beach a congenial anchorage. A totem pole across from the Maui Lu Hotel marks the spot where Vancouver landed. During WW II, when a Japanese invasion was feared, Kihei was considered a likely spot for an amphibious attack. Overgrown pillboxes and rusting tank traps are still found along the beaches. Many look like cement porcupines with iron quills. Kihei is a natural site with mountain and ocean vistas. It's also great for beachcombing up toward Maalaea, but try to get there by morning because the afternoon wind is notorious for creating minor sandstorms.

Kihei's commercial sections are separated by residential areas. There is no one town center as such, although the highest concentration and greatest number of businesses are near the post office and the Azeka Place shopping centers. From the north, the first commercial area is that around Suda's Store and the Gateway Mall. Following that down the way are business centers around the post office, across from Kalama Beach Park, and fronting the Kamaole beaches.

The new Maui Research and Technology Park has been established above the Silversword Golf Course in Kihei, sprucing up the image of the area a little and bringing in some high-tech white collar jobs at the same time. While only a handful of shiny new office buildings have been built so far, land has been set aside for many more.

BEACHES

Mai Poina Oe Lau Beach Park
On Kihei's northern fringe, fronting Maui Lu Hotel, this beach offers only limited paved parking, otherwise just along the road. Showers, tables, and restrooms front the long and narrow white-sand beach, which has good safe swimming but is still plagued by strong winds by early afternoon. A windsurfer's delight, here you can see upwards of 100 sporting enthusiasts out trying the wind when conditions are optimal.

Kalepolepo Beach Park
Next to the Whale Sanctuary office, this beach is small and good for kiddies. Centuries ago, the thriving community of Kalepolepo occupied this area of Kihei and farmed the six-acre **Koieie Fishpond** here. Remnants of its rock wall can still be seen arcing through the water. Now much reduced in size, the walls once stood higher than high tide. It's estimated that more than 2,000 pounds of fish a year were harvested from these waters when it was a functioning fishpond in the late 1500s.

Kalama Park
This park, located in the middle of town, is more suited to family outings and enjoying the vista than it is for beach activities. Kalama has a large lawn ending in a breakwater, a small beach in summer, and none in winter. However, there are 36 acres of pavilions; tables; barbecue pits; volleyball, basketball, and tennis courts; a baseball diamond; a soccer field; and plenty of expanse to throw a frisbee. With its great views of Molokini and Haleakala, it is considered the best family park in the area. At its extreme southern end, just across the highway bridge, is an area called Cove Park, where locals put small boats in the water.

Kamaole I, II, and III
These beach parks, often referred to as Kam 1, 2, and 3, are at the south end of town near Kihei Town Center. All three have beautiful white sand,

picnic tables, lifeguards, and all the amenities. The swimming and bodysurfing are good. Snorkeling is good for beginners on the reef between II and III, where much coral and many colorful reef fish abound. Kamaole III has a kids' playground. Shopping and dining are nearby.

Kihei Boat Ramp
Just south of Kamaole III Beach is the Kihei Boat Ramp, used by many ocean activity companies in the area to launch boats and rafts.

ACCOMMODATIONS

The emphasis in Kihei is on condos. With keen competition among them, you can save some money while having a more homey vacation. Close to 100 condos, plus a smattering of vacation apartments, cottages, and even a few hotel resorts, are all strung along Kihei Road. As always, you pay more for ocean views. Don't shy away from accommodations on the *mauka* side of Kihei Road. You have total access to the beach, some superior views of Haleakala, and you usually pay less money. The accommodations below are listed north to south.

Hotels
The Kihei area offers three small hotels that are reasonably priced and well appointed. **Maui Lu Resort,** 575 S. Kihei Rd., Kihei, HI 96753, tel. (808) 879-5881, (800) 922-7866, or (800) 321-2558 in Hawaii, attempts to preserve the feeling of old Hawaii with its emphasis on *ohana*. Amenities here include an activities desk, tennis, a Maui-shaped pool, and tiny private beaches strung along its 28 acres. Rooms, located mostly in the new wing that is mountainside and quieter, are priced $99-185, $18 per extra person, and include refrigerators and air-conditioning. This full-service hotel pampers you in the old Hawaiian style. This is an Aston property.

The Maui Coast Hotel, 2259 S. Kihei Rd., Kihei, HI 96753, tel. (808) 874-6284 or (800) 895-6284, fax (808) 875-4731, Web site: www.maui.net /~mch, e-mail: mch@maui.net, is Kihei's newest hotel, completed in 1993. The rooms and suites are bright and cheerful, blending Southwestern pastels and Hawaiian-style furniture. Adding to your comfort are standard amenities like remote-control color TV, a/c and ceiling fans, complimentary in-wall safes, coffee makers, refrigerators, slippers to pad around in, full bathrooms that include a jacuzzi bathtub and a "who asked for one" bathroom scale. A wet bar is in all the larger suites. Guests are also treated to morning coffee, and washers and dryers are on every other floor. This seven-story hotel offers two spas with whirlpools, a swimming pool, lighted guests-only tennis courts, a restaurant, poolside bar with nightly entertainment, sundries shop, and free parking. Rates are $129-139 for a standard room, $149-300 for a suite, $10 each additional person, with discounted off-season and weekly rates. Rental car packages are also available. The Maui Coast Hotel, set back from busy Kihei Road, offers a small oasis of peace and tranquillity with excellent rates for the standard of rooms and amenities offered.

Maui Oceanfront Inn is at 2980 S. Kihei Rd., Kihei, HI 96753, tel. (808) 879-7744, 874-0145, or (800) 367-5004. This is a very affordable and well-maintained hotel recently given a complete makeover including buildings, furnishings, and grounds. The hotel is fronting a long sandy beach, located just before you get to Wailea at the south end of town. Rates are $95 standard, $100 superior, $110 deluxe, and a one-bedroom family unit is $170; $15 extra person, off-season $10-20 lower. The hotel amenities include air-conditioning, room refrigerators, free morning coffee and donuts, and a garden. You can't go wrong at this terrific little hotel!

Condos and Cottages

One of the several condos at the far north end of Kihei at the eastern end of Maalaea Beach is **Sugar Beach Resort**, 145 N. Kihei Rd., tel. (808) 879-7765. All one- and two-bedroom units have full kitchens, ceiling fans and a/c, TV, and lanai, with guest-only tennis courts, swimming pool, spa, sauna, barbecue grills, sundries shop, sandwich shop, and activities desk on property. All are individually owned and decorated. Rates run about $100-150 for one-bedroom and $175-225 for two-bedroom units. Most rooms here are rented by rental agencies. Contact the following for rooms here and at other condos at this extreme northern end of Kihei: Condominium

Rentals Hawaii, tel. (800) 367-5242 or (800) 663-2101 in Canada; Rainbow Rentals, tel. (800) 451-5366; Maui Condominium and Home Realty, tel. (800) 822-4409.

Nani Kai Hale, 73 N. Kihei Rd., tel. (808) 875-0630 or (800) 367-6032, is very affordable at $99 for one-bedroom standard for seven days or longer, $105 for fewer than seven days. One-bedroom ocean views run $115/$125, oceanfronts $135/$145; two-bedroom standards are $135/$145. The two-bedroom oceanfront units go for a $185 nightly rate only. Substantial savings offered during off-season, four day minimum stay required, monthly rates available. There's a good beach plus sheltered parking, pool, laundry facilities, private lanai, and barbecues on premises. Good views.

The Polynesian-style roofs and dark wooden siding might draw you to the **Maalaea Surf Resort,** 12 S. Kihei Rd., tel. (808) 879-1267 or (800) 423-7953, fax (808) 874-2884, but the fully furnished bright interiors, well-tended lawns, tennis courts, swimming pools, and white-sand beach will captivate you. Each unit has a/c and daily maid service. One-bedroom suites run $186 during high season and $165 for low season. Two-bedroom units are $252 and $217, respectively.

The first place south of Cuda's Store is **Nona Lani Cottages,** 455 S. Kihei Rd., tel. (808) 879-2497 or (800) 733-2688, owned and operated by Dave and Nona Kong. These clean and neat units on the *mauka* side of the road have full kitchens and baths, queen beds, and daybeds. Laundry facilities, public phones, hammocks, chaise lounges, and barbecues are on the premises, and each unit has a raised lanai with tables. Rates are $68 a night or $455 a week during low season, four-night minimum, $7 additional person. There is a seven-night minimum and slightly higher rates in high season, but call to find out if anything's available on a shorter basis or for off-season weekly rates. These individual plantation-style units are about as down-home Hawaiian as you can get, a good place to come if you're looking for relaxation.

Menehune Shores, 760 S. Kihei Rd., mailing address P.O. Box 1327, Kihei, HI 96753, tel. (808) 879-3428 or (800) 558-9117, fax (808) 897-5218, is a huge, family-oriented and moderately priced high-rise condo on the beach overlooking an an-

KIHEI

To Maalaea, Lahaina

Mokuleke Hwy.
To Kahului

KEALIA
BEACH PLAZA

SUDA'S
STORE

KIHEI WHARF

KENOLIO RD.

31

MAI POINA OE
LAU BEACH PARK

KIHEI
GATEWAY
PLAZA

NONA LAI
COTTAGES

KENOLIO ST.

MAUI LU HOTEL

KALEPOLEPO
PARK

S. KIHEI RD.

MENEHUNE
SHORES

PIILANI HWY.

WAIPULANI
PARK

MAUI SUNSET

LONG'S CENTER

POST OFFICE

AZEKA II

AZEKA PLACE SHOPPING CENTER

KIHEI PROFESSIONAL
PLAZA

HALE KAI O KIHEI

ST. TERESA'S
CATHOLIC CHURCH

E. LIPOA ST.

SILVERSWORD
GOLF COURSE

HALAMA ST.

WELAKAHAO RD.

KUKUI MALL

KIHEI TOWN CENTER

KALAMA
BEACH PARK

KALAMA VILLAGE
MARKET PLACE

LIHI KAI
APT. HOTEL

31

KAMAOLE
BEACH PARK
#1

DOLPHIN
PLAZA

RAINBOW MALL

KAMAOLE
SHOPPING CENTER

KAMAOLE
BEACH PARK
#2

KEONEKAI
RD.

KAMAOLE
BEACH PARK
#3

KAMAOLE
SANDS

MAUI
HILL

PIILANI HWY.

0   0.5 mi

0   0.5 km

KIHEI BOAT
RAMP

MANA KAI
RESORT

To Wailea,
Makena

cient fishpond. The building is highlighted with replicas of Hawaiian petroglyphs. On the first floor is Hamilton's Beach Cafe, outside of which is a new swimming pool. The Menehune is used mostly by seniors, except during Christmas when families come. All units have an ocean view and rates are $100-175 for one- to three-bedroom condos in high season, three-day minimum. Low-season rates are a little less, discounts are given for month stays, and special car/room packages can be arranged. Full kitchens with dishwasher, washer and dryer, and disposals are in each unit, which are individually owned, so furnishings vary.

Kauhale Makai, 938 S. Kihei Rd., write Maui Condominium and Home Realty, P.O. Box 1840 Kihei, HI 96753, or call (808) 879-5445 or (800) 822-4409. Rates from $70 studio, $80 one-bedroom, $100 two-bedroom, four-night minimum; weekly and monthly discounts given. Fully furnished, individually decorated rooms are a mixture of garden, mountain, and ocean view. A swimming pool, kiddie pool, barbecues, putting green, and sauna are available.

The boxy **Leinaala** condos, 998 S. Kihei Rd., tel. (808) 879-2235 or (800) 334-3305, may not attract everyone, but don't let the appearance fool you. Each of the 24 fully appointed units faces the beach. Splash in the condo pool or stroll across the huge lawn to the shore. This lawn and the tennis courts here are part of a county park. Winter rates are $95 and $115 for one- and two-bedroom units during high season. The best time for space is during the summer when rates are $15-20 less; four nights minimum. Reduced rates for AARP and AAA.

Just down the back street at 1310 Uluniu Rd., Kihei, HI 96753, tel. (808) 879-2757 or (800) 457-7014, fax (808) 875-8242, is **Hale Kai O Kihei.** This apartment-like cinder block affair, simple and utilitarian, is clean, well-kept, and cute for what it is. Each furnished unit has a direct ocean view with a lanai that looks over the pool, garden, and beach. There is also parking, shuffleboard, barbecue grills, and coin laundry, with maid service on request. Reasonable rates are $110 for a one-bedroom unit ($75 for low season) and $135 for two bedrooms ($100 low season); three nights minimum—15% discount for stays of one month or greater. Cash only, no credit cards.

Just south of Kalama Park is **Lihi Kai Cottages,** 2121 Ili'ili Rd., Kihei, HI 96753, tel. (808) 879-2335 or (800) 544-4524. These nine cottages are such a bargain they're often booked by returning guests, particularly during winter months. They're not plush, there's no pool, but they're homey and clean, with little touches like banana trees growing on the property. Rates are $69 daily for three to seven nights, $64 for seven or more nights; three nights minimum. Monthly rates are available on request, no credit cards accepted. For reservations, call or write well in advance c/o Manager, at the above address.

Maui Vista, 2191 S. Kihei Rd., tel. (808) 879-7966 or (800) 535-0085, fax (808) 874-5612, is a pleasing 10-acre condo complex that has 38 units managed by Marc Resorts. Three pools, six tennis courts, barbecue grills, and an activities desk are available to all guests. All studios and suites have kitchens, are modern in their appointments, spacious in layout, and have maid service. Studios run $139, one-bedroom suites $149-169, and two-bedroom suites $189-199, $20 less during "value" periods, $15 each extra person.

At **Kamaole Sands,** 2695 S. Kihei Rd., tel. (808) 874-8700 or (800) 367-5004, all apartments come completely furnished with a full bath and kitchen, roomy living area, and lanai. Prices are: $130 studio, $160-190 one-bedroom, $215-265 two-bedroom, $320-340 three-bedroom, fifth night free; off-season discounts and rental car packages available. Stepping down the hillside, the Kamaole Sands is a full-service, family-oriented condo geared toward making the entire family comfortable. The Sandpiper Grill, situated poolside and for guests only, serves inexpensive breakfasts, lunches, and dinners featuring fresh island fish and pasta. One of the main features of the Kamaole Sands is its wonderful tennis courts, free to guests, with a tennis instructor to help you work on the fine points of your game. The Kamaole Sands is bright, cheerful, and gives you a lot for your money.

Maui Hill is located at 2881 S. Kihei Rd., tel. (808) 879-6321, (800) 922-7866, or (800) 321-2558 Hawaii. If you want to rise above it all in Kihei come to this upbeat condo with a Spanish motif. This condo resort sits high on a hill and commands a sweeping view of the entire area. The one-, two-, or three-bedroom suites are spacious, bright,

and airy; all have ceiling fans and a/c, cable TV, daily maid service, and gourmet kitchens. A concierge service helps with your every need, and all sun and surf activities can be arranged at the ocean activity desk. The grounds are secluded, beautifully maintained, and offer a pool with whale mosaic on the bottom, tennis courts, and spa. Rates are: one-bedroom from $175 (up to four people), two-bedroom from $205 (up to six people), three-bedroom from $260 (up to seven people); $35 less during off-season times. A weekly complimentary mai tai party complete with games, singing, and door prizes is held for guests, along with a continental breakfast at 8 a.m. that offers an orientation on island activities. Guests can also enjoy a weekly afternoon lei-making class and a poolside scuba orientation several days per week.

At the south end of Kihei is **Mana Kai Maui** oceanfront resort, 2960 S. Kihei Rd., tel. (808) 879-1561, (800) 367-5242 Mainland, or (800) 663-2101. Hotel features include front desk check-in, an activities desk, daily maid service, a sundries store, swimming pool, and a fine restaurant and bar on premises. Condo units have full kitchens, TV, private lanai, and ceiling fans. All hotel rooms, with outdoor access, air-conditioning, and refrigerators, are on the garden level. Winter rates run $100 for the hotel rooms, $180-210 for a one-bedroom and $190-220 for a two-bedroom suite. Summer rates are about 20% cheaper, and there is a 10% discount for stays of one month or more.

Aside from the above-listed properties, there are many rental agencies that handle condo units and rental homes. Several of these agencies are: **Condo Rentals Hawaii,** 362 Huku Li'i Place, #204, Kihei, HI 96753, tel. (800) 367-5242 U.S. or (800) 663-2101 Canada, Web site: www.maui.net/~crh, e-mail: crh@maui.net; **Kihei Maui Vacations,** P.O. Box 1055, Kihei, HI 96753, tel. (808) 879-7581 or (800) 541-6284, Web site: www.kmv-maui.com/home.html; **Maui Condominium and Home Realty,** P.O. Box 1840, Kihei, HI 96753, tel. (808) 879-5445 or (800) 822-4409, Web site: www.mauicondo.com; and **Unique Island Homes,** tel. (808) 875-8808 or (800) 961-9196.

Bed and Breakfasts

Owned and operated by Cheryl and Dan Olson, **By The Sea B&B** is tucked under tall palm trees down a side street near Ohukai windsurfing beach at the north end of Kihei. This private home has three units all with separate entrances that look over the back garden and pond. Rooms include a small kitchenette, large bathroom, ceiling fan, TV, and phone, plus daily breakfast; the second floor unit has a deck. Rates run $75-95 a night single, $85-110 double, three nights minimum—no charge for the friendly advice on island activities and places to eat, or for the time you spend lounging in the hammock out back! Weekly discounts are offered and rental cars can be arranged. By The Sea B&B is located at 20 Wailana Place, Kihei, HI 96753, tel. (808) 891-0348 or (888) 879-2700, fax (808) 879-5540, Web site: www.bythesea.net, e-mail: bythesea@maui.net.

Babson's Vacation Rentals, 3371 Keha Dr., Kihei, HI 96753, tel. (808) 874-1166 or (800) 824-6409, fax (808) 879-7906, offers a combination of B&B rooms, separate studio apartment, and private cottage in the quiet residential area of Maui Meadows perched on the hillside between Kihei and Wailea. From this vantage point, you can watch the sun set over the Lahaina Roads with Kahoolawe, Molikini, Lanai, and even Molokai floating on the horizon, or pay closer attention to the finely landscaped gardens that surround the house. All rentals include cable TV, telephone, and laundry facilities. Ann and Bob are happy to recommend their favorite scenic spots, activities, and restaurants, and will provide you with towels and a cooler for a day at the beach. Rates on the main home's B&B rooms, the Bougainvillea and Molokini suite, are $70-85 and include all-you-can-eat continental breakfast. The Hibiscus Hideaway, a first-floor studio priced at $85, has its own bath, kitchen, separate bedroom, and garden. The two-bedroom Sunset Cottage, which can sleep six comfortably, offers a sweeping ocean view, cathedral ceilings, two private baths, and full kitchen, rents for $105. All prices are for double occupancy; $10 for each extra person. Ann and Bob go out of their way to make your stay enjoyable, having mastered the art of allowing you to enjoy it yourself.

FOOD

Inexpensive

Azeka's Snacks, Azeka Place, is open daily except Sunday 7:30 a.m.-5 p.m. Basically takeout, the menu features $1.50-1.90 hamburgers and a variety of plate lunches, saimin, and sushi for under $5. Azeka's is popular with locals and terrific for picnics.

International House of Pancakes is toward the rear of Azeka Place. Open daily 6 a.m.-midnight, Friday and Saturday until 2 a.m. Same American standards as on the Mainland with most sandwiches and plate lunches under $8, dinners under $12, and breakfasts anytime around $6. Not exotic, but basic and filling with a good reputation in the area for inexpensive but passable fresh fish and daily specials.

Let the rich aroma of 40 different types of roasting coffee lure you to **The Coffee Store,** Azeka Place II, tel. (808) 875-4244, open Sun.-Thurs. 6 a.m.-9 p.m., Friday and Saturday until 11 p.m. Breakfast fare, served all day, features quiche for $3.75 or a breakfast quesadilla for $5.95. Lunch selections, always served with crusty homemade bread, include a Caesar salad at $4.95—or $6.95 for the large size that can easily feed two—and sandwiches like tuna or turkey for $5.50. The vegetarian sandwiches cost $6.50. Pizza, on a six-inch Boboli crust, ranges $6.50-10. Daily homemade soup for $3.95 including bread and coffee, and stuffed quesadillas of all sorts for $4-6, complete the menu. Enjoy coffee drinks that range in price $1-2.50, along with hot and iced herbal teas, hot chocolate, and Italian cream sodas. A deli case is filled with luscious desserts sure to satisfy any sweet tooth. You can purchase bulk coffee, espresso machines, distinctive aprons, kitchen gadgets, and T-shirts as well. You can dine inside, or sit outside, especially in the evening to hob-nob with local residents who come here to chat and enjoy a rich cup of coffee and snack.

The fountain bar, jukebox, Formica tabletops, leatherette booths, distinctive color scheme, and period decorations and music peg **Peggy Sue** as a classic, theme hamburger joint—with a modern twist. You can order your Big Bopper burger for $7.25 or the Earth Angel garden burger for $6.25, or sample one of the salads, sandwiches, or plate lunches, most for under $9. No '50s joint worth its name would be without that cool summer favorite, so Peggy Sue serves up ice cream, shakes, and fountain drinks. Stop in for the nostalgia rush. At Azeka Place II.

Tie-dyed Deadheads or heat-flushed tourists hoping to chill out should head for **Stella Blue's Cafe and Deli,** located at Longs Shopping Center, tel. (808) 874-3779, open daily 8 a.m.-9 p.m. Inside, the full coffee bar serves up the standards from a cup of house blend to a mocha, along with fresh hot bagels for $2.50, a tuna salad plate for $7.25, or a tossed green salad for $2.25. Sandwiches, everything from roast beef to veggie, average about $7.50. From the grill you can have a tuna melt, veggie burger, or pastrami melt for under $7.75. Breakfast, served 8-11 a.m., features a continental breakfast for $4.05 to homestyle waffles for $6.25. Dinner includes spinach lasagna for $12.95 and chicken parmesan at $13.95. Also, Stella pours frothy mugs of ice-cold beer, perfect to help cool you down before returning to the beach. A few racks hold a small selection of *pareo,* alohawear, and psychedelic T-shirts, tie-dyed fashions, and stickers.

Kalbi House, in a corner of Longs Shopping Center, open daily except Sunday 9 a.m.-9:30 p.m., offers a full range of Korean standards like barbecued short ribs, fried squid, chicken teriyaki, noodles, stews, and small intestine soup, as well as plate lunches and combination plates. Most everything is under $10; takeout available. The restaurant is basic but clean

If you've been having too much fun and need a reviving cup of espresso, stop in at the **Kihei Caffe,** at Kalama Village Marketplace, tel. (808) 878-2230, open daily at 5 a.m., Sunday at 6 a.m., and enjoy your coffee along with an excellent assortment of sandwiches and baked goods. This full coffee bar serves up coffee drinks costing $1-2.50. Order a complete breakfast of eggs, bacon, home fries, and biscuits with gravy for $5.50, or a giant raisin muffin for $2.50. Sandwiches, all under $6.25, are served on your choice of homemade bread. Lighter fare includes couscous salad for $6.25, or honey cashew chicken salad for $6.25. Only cold sandwiches after 2 p.m. The cafe provides a few tables and stools inside, and more outside where you can watch the action on Kihei Road, or across the road through Kamaole Beach Park to the ocean.

A few steps away is **Alexander's Fish and Fowl,** tel. (808) 874-0788, open 11 a.m.-9 p.m. This local long-term establishment is definitely a cut above most fast-food restaurants, and has taken a few steps along the upscale, yuppie, health-conscious road. The menu offers fresh fish, shrimp, and chicken sandwiches for $6.25-7.50. Plate lunches, sides, salads, and drinks, as well as larger baskets for $15.75-19.95, are also on the menu. Full meals are served with cole slaw and french fries or rice. All deep frying is done in Canola oil but you can request broiling instead. There's not much decor or atmosphere, but the food is delicious and makes a perfect takeout meal that can be enjoyed at the beach.

Sports Page Bar and Grill, at the Kamaole Beach Center, tel. (808) 879-0602, open 11 a.m.-midnight for cocktails and 11:30 a.m.-10 p.m. for food service, scores big with a full bar and a large-screen TV. Order a mug of beer and a light snack like oyster shooters for $1 or teriyaki chicken breast strips for $6.95. The burger and sandwich menu goes all the way with a San Francisco '49er burger topped with bacon and cheese, a Chicago Cubs hot dog, or a Boston Celtics turkey sandwich, all for under $8.50. There's music on Wednesday evenings 8-10:30 p.m. and comedy from 8-10 p.m. on Saturday nights when a $10 cover is charged. Families and even the athletically challenged will be comfortable here and more than welcome. Also in Kamaole Beach Center is **Hawaiian Moon's Deli and Natural Foods,** open Mon.-Sat. 8 a.m.-9 p.m., Sunday until 6 p.m. Stop for a healthy deli sandwich and drink, or shop for groceries, vitamins, and bulk foods.

Denny's at the Kamaole Shopping Center is more than a usual mainland Denny's. Along with the large and varied selection of food, you have pool tables, games, and the "Good Times" bar.

For plate lunches from $4.25-6.25, salads, sandwiches, noodles and burgers, try **Sub Tropix** at the Rainbow Shopping Mall. Open 10 a.m.-9 p.m.

Kay's Cafe and Deli at Kai Nani Village Plaza serves smoothies, juices, coffees, and a variety of quick snack deli items.

Moderate

Margarita's Beach Cantina, at 101 N. Kihei Rd in the Kealia Beach Plaza, tel. (808) 879-5275, open daily 11:30 a.m.-midnight, has a well-deserved reputation for good food at fair prices. Formerly vegetarian, it now serves a variety of meat and chicken dishes but still uses the finest ingredients, cold-pressed oils, and no lard or bacon in the bean dishes. The decor is classical Mexican with white stucco walls and tiled floors. There's an outdoor deck affording a great sunset view and sea breezes, or stop by for live music and dancing Friday 5-7 p.m. and Sunday 2:30-5 p.m. The *carta* offers taco salads for $7.95, combination plates for $8.95-12.95, and money-saving daily lunch specials like *carnitas burrito* for under $7. Most entrees are in the $10-12 range, with nothing over $17. Well drinks are $3, imported beers $3.50; during happy hour 2:30-5:30 p.m., margaritas are only 96 cents or $3 by the pitcher.

Restaurant Isana, located at 515 S. Kihei Rd., tel. (808) 874-5700, is open daily for the best Korean food in the area, and also has Japanese sushi at night. You can either sit at the sushi bar or have dinner cooked at your table. Upstairs is the bar, which has a karaoke singalong after 10 p.m. Most dinners are in the $15-20 range.

Although you can get appetizers, salads, burgers, shrimp, and chicken at **Tony Roma's,** tel. (808) 875-1104, at the Kukui Mall, Tony's is a place for ribs, ribs, and more ribs. Prepared in several different ways, rib entrees run about $14, with most other entrees less. For a very hungry couple, or a family perhaps, try one of the jumbo orders like honey ribs (40 pieces) for $40.50, or shrimp and ribs for $49.95.

Chuck's Steak House at the Kihei Town Center, tel. (808) 879-4489, open Mon.-Sat. for lunch 11:30 a.m.-2:30 p.m., dinner nightly 5:30-10 p.m., is a family restaurant featuring American standards with an island twist. With a gray-on-gray interior, the restaurant provides a pleasant atmosphere, and although they do not take reservations, they will tell you how busy they are if you call ahead. The lunch menu is affordable with selections like a Reuben sandwich for $5.95 and plate lunches for under $6. The early bird special, priced at a reasonable $10.95, is normally fresh fish or barbecued chicken, and includes the salad bar, homemade bread, and a choice of white rice or French fries. The dinner menu includes teriyaki steaks for $13.95 and a petite top sirloin priced at $12.95. Chuck's seafood selections include fresh fish or lobster

tail for $19.95, and prime rib and lobster tail for $29.95.

In the Rainbow Plaza, **The Thai Chef Restaurant,** tel. (808) 874-5605, offers you a full menu of tasty Thai food at reasonable prices. Like its sister restaurant in Lahaina, you can get appetizers like spring rolls for $7.50 or green papaya salad at $6.50, and various soups for around $10. Entrees include red, green, or yellow curries from $9-11, with noodle, rice, and seafood dishes up to $14. There's a hefty selection for vegetarians, and desserts run $2-3. Well maintained, the decor is casual.

KKO Kai Ku Ono, tel. (808) 875-1007, a semisports bar casual dining place, below the more upscale Kihei Prime Rib and Seafood House at Kai Nani Village Plaza, is open 7:30 a.m.-midnight. Grab a pizza and beer and cool off after a day at the beach with a game of pool or darts. Pizzas from their wood-fired oven range $13.95-21.95, and they're also sold by the slice. A variety of sandwiches, ribs, and side dishes are also available, with most items under $15.95. The full bar will set you up drinks, happy hour 3-7 p.m., while you kick back and catch your favorite sporting event on one of the six TVs. For special events, the big screen is turned on.

Tucked into the rear of Kai Nani Village Plaza is the **Greek Bistro,** tel. (808) 879-9330, a wonderful addition to the restaurant scene, where the flavors and textures of the Mediterranean dishes served by the Arabatzi family will excite your palate. Dinner is served 5-10 p.m. and includes souvlakia, spanakopita, moussaka, and lamb kabob, all ranging from $14.95 to $21.95. Other items are stuffed grape leaves for $6.95, Grecian village salad at $7.95, and several family-style platters for around $25. If you're in doubt as to what would be tasty, try the Greek Gods Platter, a sampling of several homemade entrees on the menu. Sit inside or out.

Expensive

The large open pavilion at the Maui Lu Hotel now houses **Ukulele** restaurant, tel. (808) 875-1188. Open for breakfast and dinner, there is Hawaiian entertainment nightly to accompany your evening meal. Available are pancakes, Belgian waffles, eggs Benedict, and such unusual items as a breakfast pizza for under $10. Dinner brings finer but casual dining with a full range of soups, salads, and entrees for $18-25. Prime rib is the specialty, but Ukulele is also known for fish and seafood dishes. Catering to the local populace as well as the tourist, it's a fine place for families.

Expanding from a very successful operation on Kauai, Chef Jean-Marie Josselin has opened **A Pacific Cafe,** tel. (808) 879-0069, at Azeka Place II. Open for dinner nightly 5:30-9:30, this restaurant presents the same kind of fine Hawaiian regional cuisine as at the original. Open, large, and masculine, the simply elegant decor of the dining areas, set off by modernistic touches, surround the exhibition kitchen with its wood fired pizza oven. Start with a tiger eye ahi sushi tempura with tomato and Chinese mustard sauce for $12 or a Caesar salad for $8.95. Soups might be a red Thai curry and coconut with fresh island fish and calamari for $6.75. Entrees average about $25, including grilled Pacific snapper with Indonesian sticky rice roll, Chinese style roasted duck with garlic mashed potatoes, or penne pasta with shrimp, scallop, wild mushrooms, mussels, and purple asparagus. No matter what your choice, the ingredients will be the freshest, the service prompt, and the result memorable.

Upstairs at the Kai Nani Village Plaza at 2511 S. Kihei Rd. is **Kihei Prime Rib and Seafood House,** open from 5 p.m., tel. (808) 879-1954, offering most entrees for $20-32, including a well-stocked salad bar. Sashimi, lobster, and stuffed mushroom appetizers are under $10, and the early bird specials, 5-6 p.m. are $12.95, salad bar included. One of the best choices is rack of lamb for $23.95. An island ambiance is created with carvings by Bruce Turnbull and paintings by Sigrid, both well-known local artists.

Overlooking the beach, the casual **Five Palms** restaurant, tel. (808) 879-2607, located at the Mana Kai Maui Resort at the south end of Kihei, is open for breakfast Mon.-Fri. 9-11:30 a.m. and a weekend champagne brunch 8 a.m.-2 p.m. Breakfast includes the usuals like eggs, sausages, pancakes, and the like, while the brunch also gives you the wider options of burgers, soups, salads, sandwiches, and some pastas. For lunch, try sandwiches, soup, pizza, or other entrees for $9-15. Dinner is served 5-9 p.m. (until 10 on Friday and Saturday), with ahi sashimi for $11.95, Kula green salad at $7, roasted rack of lamb for

$23.95, broiled lobster for $29.95, and many other delectable items on the menu, but the specialty is fish. Set so close to the water, the location and scenery are an integral part of the dining experience here.

Only steps from Wailea is the fine dining Italian restaurant called **Carrelli's On the Beach,** tel. (808) 875-0001. Open for dinner only 6-10 p.m., bar until 11 p.m., all parking is complimentary valet only because of limited space. If you don't want to deal with parking, take a limo, $15 each way, from along this coast. The excellent reputation and proximity draw many guests from the resorts and condos of Wailea. The seating couldn't be better, with the restaurant set right on the beach, and it's the water and sparkling light off the waves rather than the interior decoration that draws your attention most. Start with an antipasti or calamari friette for $12 and move on to a green salad, Caesar, or soup for $8-18. Pastas include ravioli for $22 and risotto con pettini prosciutto for $28. A bit pricier are the scampi and veal dishes for up to $36. For a bit more casual treat, try a homemade pizza from the wood-fired oven. Although rich and expensive, one of the fine desserts, like tiramisu or tartufo (a gelato ball rolled in chocolate and served with mango puree), might make a fine finish to your meal.

Former Kea Lani chef, Steve Amaral, has opened the new **Cucina Pacifica** restaurant, tel. (808) 875-7831, in the Rainbow Mall. Head upstairs. Food here, tasty, plentiful, and well-presented, is done with a Pacific Rim emphasis; lots of fish and seafood, with an Italian twist. Expect entrees in the $14-27 range. The restaurant has a round bar in the center of the room, a good place for conversation. Entertainment on the weekends. Open for dinner only.

ENTERTAINMENT

Kihei isn't exactly a hot spot when it comes to evening entertainment. Hawaiian music is offered on Friday and Saturday at the Ukulele Restaurant at the Maui Lu Hotel, and you can dance at **Margarita's Beach Cantina** now and again. Try the Maui Coast Hotel **Oasis** poolside bar for nightly music in a relaxed setting. **Kahale Beach Club,** a local bar for people who work in the area, is a place that offers music and dancing on an occasional basis. To its front is the fun little bar **Life's a Beach,** which serves up evening entertainment along with burgers, sandwiches, salads, and *pu pu.* **Hapas,** at 41 E. Lipoa St., is gaining a great reputation with its locally brewed beer, games, entertainment, and dancing nightly. Many of the restaurants offer entertainment on a hit-and-miss basis, usually one artist with a guitar, a small dinner combo, or some Hawaiian music. These are usually listed in the free tourist brochures.

For a different type of entertainment, stop for a movie at the **Kukui Mall Theater** in the Kihei Town Center, which has shows starting at about noon. It's a four-screen theater and admission is $6.50 for adults and $3.75 for seniors.

SHOPPING

While driving the length of Kihei, you will find shopping centers, both large and small, strung along the entire coastal area like shells on a dime store lei. At many you can buy food, clothing, sporting goods, camping and picnic supplies, sundries, photo equipment, cosmetics, resortwear, ice cream, pizza, dinner, and liquor. You can also book activities, order a custom bikini, or just relax with an ice-cold beer while your partner satisfies his or her shopping addiction. In Kihei, you have more than ample opportunity to spend your hard-earned vacation money that would be a sin to take back home. Aloha!

North End Shopping

At the very north end of Kihei as you approach from Kahului or Lahaina is the **Sugar Beach General Store,** with a small clutch of shops selling resortwear, snacks, gifts, and jewelry. The activities company here can set you up for a fun afternoon or rent you a bicycle. Nearby at **Kealia Beach Plaza** is the **Kealia General Store,** and upstairs are the **Pacific Whale Foundation** office and shop, open 9 a.m.-5 p.m. daily, and **Margarita's Beach Cantina.**

Suda's Store is a basic little market with limited food items, but with cold beer, fresh fish, and deli items. Open Mon.-Sat. 7:30 a.m.-5 p.m. and 8 a.m.-3 p.m. on Sunday, it sits along the *mauka* side at 61 S. Kihei Road. A few minutes

down the road from Suda's heading for Kihei, look for the **Nona Lana Cottages** where you can pick up a fresh flower lei for a reasonable price.

One of Kihei's newest shopping center, **Kihei Gateway Plaza,** has opened along Piilani Highway (Rt. 31), the main thoroughfare above Kihei that parallels Kihei Road. The entrance to this small group of shops is marked by a gas station and minimart.

Azeka Place

At the Azeka Place Shopping Center, along S. Kihei Rd. in what might be considered the center of town, you'll find numerous small shops and fast-food eating establishments. There's also a great community bulletin board listing apartments, yard sales, and odds and ends. Most shops are open daily 9 a.m.-9 p.m. with shorter Sunday hours. **Rainbow Connection** features personalized and Polynesian gifts. **Island Memories** is stocked with carved koa boxes, shells, earrings, woven basketry, a good selection of pottery, and hula instruments, all made in Hawaii. **Tropical Tantrum** specializes in hand-painted clothing by local artists, mostly for women but with a few selections for men as well. In case you need a toggle bolt, try **Kihei Ace Hardware.**

Here as well is the Kihei **post office** at 1254 S. Kihei Rd., a gas station, and a county Department of Motor Vehicles office. Just down the street is a **Star Market** for all your grocery needs.

Azeka Place II

Located just across the street from the original Azeka's, this new and larger shopping center features a **Maui Dive Shop,** a full-service dive shop and activity center; **The Coffee Store,** a great place for a cup of coffee (40 kinds), a light lunch, or even a late-night snack; **In's Eelskin** for bags, belts, and accouterments made from eel; **Liberty House,** a department store with tasteful island fashions; **Bank of Hawaii,** a full-service bank with ATM machines; **Roland's Shoes** for everything from slippers to hiking boots; **Elephant Walk** filled with gifts and boutique items; and **Postal Connection of Kihei,** open Mon.-Fri. 8:30 a.m.-6 p.m. and Saturday 9 a.m.-5 p.m., for all your boxing, shipping, and copying needs. Also in this center is **General Nutrition Center** for vitamins, minerals, and supplements; and **Kaiser Permanente Kihei Clinic** for your health concerns.

Longs Shopping Center

Located at 1215 S. Kihei Rd., just up from Azeka Place II, this shopping center is dominated by a huge **Longs Drugs,** stocked with electronics, photo equipment, sundries, cosmetics, stationery, and even sporting goods. Around the center you will find the **T-Shirt Factory** featuring all kinds of discounted wearable take-home gifts; **Mavrik Motorcycles,** which rents the big hogs; and you can do everything from faxing to packing and shipping at **Mail Boxes Etc.** Sports enthusiasts should try **Maui Sporting Goods,** which carries everything from inline skates to spear fishing equipment, or **Maui Sports and Cycle,** for rental and sale of sports equipment. **American Savings Bank** is conveniently located here for all the shopping that you may be doing in this center and along the Kihei strip.

Kukui Mall

At the Kukui Mall, 1819 S. Kihei Rd., are **Waldenbooks, Kihei Kukui Laundromat, J.R.'s Music Store, Whalers General Store** for sundries, and several apparel stores including **Local Motion.** Tired of the beach, or just need to beat the heat? Stop at the multiscreen **Kukui Mall Theater,** the only cinema on this side of the island.

Kihei Town Center

This small shopping center just south of the Kukui Mall offers a 24-hour **Foodland, Hawaii Products Too** for gifts, **Rainbow Attic** consignment shop, and several eateries. Across the street at the corner is the **Aloha Marketplace** covered by awnings and trees, where you can shop for jewelry, clothing, carvings, and other touristy gifts.

Kihei Kalama Village Market Place

Look for this bargain-filled, semi-open-air collection of stalls at 1945 S. Kihei Rd., offering everything from tourist trinkets to fine art; clothes, crafts, and jewelry predominate. Around the periphery are other shops. Among them you will find **Serendipity,** a small, well-appointed boutique that displays imported items mainly from Malaysia and Brazil; **Gallery and Gifts** with Hawaiian-made items; and the **Treasure Cove** next door with its arts, crafts, crystals, gifts, jewelry, and sculpture. Out front at the corner, **Maui Discount Activity World** will set you with your day's activity, and around back is **Snorkel Bob's** for snorkel and boogie board rentals.

Dolphin Shopping Plaza

This small, two-story plaza at 2395 S. Kihei Rd. includes **Pro Photo Lab,** featuring 40-minute processing, and **Tropical Disk** music store. If you have a craving for pizza try **Pizza Hut.** In a condo and want to cook your own pizza? Try **Pizza Fresh:** "we make it, you bake it." If you need to work off some of those pizza pounds, stop at **Barefoot's Cashback Tours,** where he can set you up with virtually any kind of activity on the island at a 10% discount to you. Or see about some equipment at **Maui Sports and Cycles.** Upstairs, you'll find **Kihei Medical Services** and **Kihei Chiropractic.**

Kamaole Beach Center

A small group of shops between Dolphin and Rainbow plazas, offering several places to eat, **Hawaiian Moon's Deli and Natural Food Store,** and the **Honolulu Surf Company** clothing store.

Rainbow Mall

Yet another small mall just up the road at 2439 S. Kihei Rd. features **South Pacific Kayaks and Outfitters** and **Auntie Snorkel** for the sales and rental of snorkel gear, boogie boards, kayaks, and camping and hiking gear for very reasonable prices. Other shops in the mall are the **Awesome Tees; Maui Custom Beach Wear,** where you can buy off the rack or have a bikini made especially for you; **Premiere Video,** for evening entertainment if you're staying in a condo; **Topaz,** a fine jewelry and watch store; and the **Topaz Gallery** upstairs. **Rainbow Discount Liquor** is located at the back of the mall.

Kamaole Shopping Center

Last in this quick succession of small malls is the slightly larger Kamaole Shopping Center at 2463 S. Kihei Rd. This mall has several inexpensive eateries and various clothing, souvenir, and sundries stores. From its two floors of shops you can buy baubles, beads, some nicer pieces at **Unique Jewels;** and groceries, liquor, and souvenirs at **Whalers General Store. Lappert's Ice Cream** sells island-made delights and fat-free yogurt.

Also in the center is a **Maui Dive Shop,** a complete diving and water sports store offering rentals, swimwear, snorkels, cruises, and windsurfing lessons, and an **Ocean Activities Center** booth for booking water sports.

Kai Nani Village Plaza

This small cluster of shops sits at the south end of Kihei. Aside from the Greek Bistro, Kihei Prime Rib and Seafood House, KKO, and Annie's Deli eateries, you'll find the **International Gift Shop,** and **Sunshine Mart** for sundries and food items.

Swap Meet and Farmers' Market

If you're looking for a bargain on clothes, gifts, craft items, and odds and ends, try the **Kihei swap meet** every Saturday 7 a.m.-4 p.m. across the road from Kalama Beach Park.

A small **farmers' market** is held in the parking lot in front of Suda's Store at 61 S. Kihei Rd., every Tuesday and Friday 1-5:30 p.m. Besides fresh produce, stalls sell shells, T-shirts, and knickknacks of all kinds. There is also a farmers' market in the Longs Shopping Center every Saturday 8 a.m.-noon.

Food/Liquor Stores

Foodland, at Kihei Town Center (open 24 hours), and **Star Market,** at 1310 S. Kihei Rd., are full-service supermarkets with a complete liquor, wine, and beer section. **Rainbow Discount Liquor** has a good selection of liquor, imported beers, and wine at the Rainbow Mall. At the very south end of Kihei at Mana Kai Maui Resort, try **Keawakapu General Store** for groceries, sundries, snacks, and spirits. Open daily 7 a.m.-9 p.m.

Aloha Moon's Natural Foods at the Kamaole Beach Center is a small but full service natural health food store. Stop in for bulk foods, groceries, herbs, organic fruits and vegetables, vitamins, minerals and supplements, juices, bottled water, soy drinks, and beer. There's even a freezer case for ice cream and a deli case for takeout sandwiches.

Kihei Wine and Spirits, located at 300 Ohukai Rd., open daily 10 a.m.-6 p.m., Saturday until 5 p.m., has a fantastic selection of wine and beer and a great little gourmet food section. Along with your liquor, pick up some imported pasta, sun-dried zucchini or tomatoes, olives, and fancy cheese. Even the most discriminating yuppie will find all necessary items for a first-class picnic at Kihei Wine and Spirits.

The **Pikake Bakery,** open daily 7:30 a.m.-6 p.m. except Sunday, also at 300 Ohukai Rd., bakes some of the best breads and pastries in Kihei. Choose a bread flavored with red onions and olives or red potatoes and rosemary. Order a cup of cappuccino and choose a cinnamon roll with macadamia nuts; a walnut muffin; cheese, custard, or chocolate bear claw; or a passion fruit poppyseed muffin. All breads and pastries are made fresh with the finest ingredients.

The **Kalama Village Bakery,** 1913 S. Kihei Rd. behind Alexander's, also offers the community the best in baked goods. Stop in for a freshly baked loaf of homestyle bread to take home or sit out back on the patio deck and eat your pastry there. With so many selections, your only problem might be what to choose. Whole cakes and tortes are available, and birthday and wedding cakes can be ordered.

DIVE SHOPS AND MARINE RENTALS

The **Maui Dive Shop** has a main store and office at 1455 S. Kihei Rd. near the Star Market in Kihei, and offers a full range of equipment, lessons, and rentals. Open daily 7:30 a.m.-9 p.m., it is one of the oldest and most respected companies in the business. Other locations along this coast are those at the Kamaole Shopping Center, tel. (808) 879-1533, and at the Wailea Shopping Village, tel. (808) 879-3166, with several others around the island.

The **Dive and Sea Center,** 1975 S. Kihei Rd., tel. (808) 874-1952, open Mon.-Sat. 7 a.m.-5 p.m., is a full-service dive shop offering scuba dives, four-day certification classes for $250, air refills, equipment rentals (scuba gear $19.95 per day, snorkel gear $5 per day), and dive/snorkel trips to Molokini Crater (snorkelers pay $65; a one-tank beginner dive costs $85) on a six-passenger Farallon boat so that you are given individual attention and full value for the money.

Snorkel Bob's, tel. (808) 879-8225, is easy to spot at 1913 S. Kihei Road. The weekly prices can't be beat at $15 for snorkel gear or boogie boards (day rentals available too). You also get snorkel tips, a fish I.D. card, and the semi-soggy underwater humor of Snorkel Bob.

Auntie Snorkel, tel. (808) 879-6263, located at the Rainbow Mall and operated by Melissa and Mike McCoy, rents snorkel gear, along with boogie boards, beach chairs, and even ice chests. These are among the lowest prices in the area.

Also at the Rainbow Mall, **South Pacific Kayaks and Outfitters**, tel. (808) 875-4848, open daily 8 a.m.-5 p.m., offers a half-day introductory kayak trip for $65, or an advanced explorer trip along the remote coastline of East Maui for $89. Both tours include lunch along with plenty of snorkeling opportunities as you glide in and out of tiny bays fashioned from jutting lava rock fingers. South Pacific Kayaks offers rentals of single kayaks at $30 and double kayaks at $50, per day.

SeaEscape U-Drive Boat Rental, 1979 S. Kihei Rd., tel. (808) 879-3721, offers seagoing motorized rafts and Boston Whalers that you can pilot yourself to all the snorkel, dive, and picturesque spots of the Lahaina Roads. Rates run $75-95 per hour, two-hour minimum.

Ocean Activities Center, tel. (808) 879-4465, is at the Kamaole Shopping Center. You can book every fun activity on Maui and purchase anything you'll need for sun and surf at this excellent one-stop store.

SERVICES AND INFORMATION

Medical

For medical emergencies try: **Kihei Physicians**, tel. (808) 879-7781, at 1325 S. Kihei Rd., Suite 103, open 8 a.m.-10 p.m. daily; **Kihei-Wailea Medical Center**, tel. (808) 874-8100, 41 E. Lipoa St., with physicians, a pharmacy, physical therapy, and a clinical laboratory, open Mon.-Fri. 8 a.m.-8 p.m., Saturday and Sunday until 5 p.m.; **Kihei Clinic and Wailea Medical Service**, 2349 S. Kihei Rd., tel. (808) 879-1440, open Mon.-Fri. 8 a.m.-7 p.m., Saturday until 6 p.m., and Sunday

and holidays 9 a.m.-2 p.m.; or the walk-in **Kaiser Permanente Kihei Clinic**, tel. (808) 891-3000, in Azeka Place II, open Mon.-Fri. 8 a.m.-5 p.m., closed noon-1 p.m., weekends, and holidays. Chiropractic services are available at the **Chiropractic Clinic of Kihei**, tel. (808) 879-7246, 1847 S. Kihei Rd., which specializes in non-force techniques, and **Kihei Chiropractic Center**, tel. (808) 879-0638, at the Dolphin Plaza. There's also **Kihei Acupuncture Clinic**, tel. (808) 874-0544, run by Dr. Nancy Macauley, specializing in gentle needling techniques and offering a full selection of Chinese herbs.

Postal

The main **post office** in Kihei is located at Azeka Place, 1254 S. Kihei Rd., tel. (808) 879-2403.

Mail Boxes Etc. at Longs Shopping Center, open weekdays 8 a.m.-6 p.m., Saturday 9 a.m.-5 p.m., Sunday 10 a.m.-3 p.m., offers fax services, copies, notary, and packing and shipping. With basically the same services, you'll find **Postal Connection of Kihei** at Azeka Place II, open Mon.-Fri. 8:30 a.m.-6 p.m. and Saturday 9 a.m.-5 p.m.

Information

The member organization **Kihei Destination Association** has a great deal of information about South Maui: hotels, B&Bs, restaurants, activities, shopping, services, real estate, and more. Contact the association at: 101 N. Kihei Rd., #4, Kihei, HI 96753, tel. (808) 874-9400 or 891-0770, fax 879-1283, Web site: www.maui.net/~kda.

Laundry

At the Kukui Mall is the **Kukui Laundromat**, tel. (808) 879-7211, open daily 7:30 a.m.-8 p.m., featuring self- or full-service washing. **Lipoa Laundry Center**, 41 E. Lipoa, tel. (808) 875-9266, is also a full-service laundry and dry cleaning establishment. Open 8 a.m.-8 p.m. with shorter hours on Sunday.

Reading

The Kihei Public library, tel. (808) 875-6833, is across the street from the Kihei Town Center. It has variable daily hours.

For a full-service bookstore browse at **Waldenbooks** at the Kukui Mall, tel. (808) 874-3688, open Mon.-Sat. 9 a.m.-9 p.m., Sunday 10 a.m.-5:30 p.m. You will find shelves stocked with all kinds of books and titles from fiction to travel guidebooks.

Transportation
From Kihei, shuttles run to various places on the island. **SpeediShuttle** makes numerous daily trips to the airport in Kahului. The old-style trolley-like bus, **"Da Mall" Trolley,** connects Wailea and Kihei to Kaahumanu Center, the Maui Mall, and Maui Marketplace in Kahului for your shopping pleasure. If the malls in Kahului aren't enough to satisfy you shopping needs, the Whalers Village shuttle **Maui Shopping Express** runs from South Maui to the Whalers Village mall in Kaanapali. To reach Maalaea, take the **Maui Ocean Center Shuttle.** For details, see "Alternative Transportation" in the "Getting Around" section of the Out and About chapter.

WAILEA

Wailea ("Waters of Lea" or "Joyful Waters") isn't for the hoi polloi. It's a deluxe resort area custom-tailored to fit the egos of the upper class like a pair of silk pajamas. This section of southeastern Maui was barren and bleak until Alexander and Baldwin Co. decided to landscape it into an emerald 1,450-acre oasis of world-class golf courses and destination resorts. Every street light, palm tree, and potted plant is a deliberate accessory to the decor so that the overall feeling is soothing, pleasant, and in good taste. To dispel any notions of snootiness, the five sparkling beaches that front the resorts were left open to the public and even improved with better access, parking areas, showers, and picnic tables—a gracious gesture even if state law does require open access! You'll know when you leave Kihei and enter Wailea. The green, quiet, and wide tree-lined avenues give the impression of an upper-class residential area. Wailea is where you come when quality is the most important aspect of your vacation. The brilliant five-star resorts are first-rate architecturally, and the grounds are exquisite botanical jewel boxes.

Aside from the beaches, the two main attractions in Wailea are the fantastic golf and tennis opportunities. Three magnificent golf courses have been laid out on Haleakala's lower slopes, all open to the public. Tennis is great at the Wailea Tennis Center and many of the hotels and condos have their own championship courts.

Running along the water from one end of Wailea to the other is a 1.5-mile long beach walk. This walkway cuts across all properties in the area from the Renaissance Wailea Beach Resort to the Kai Lani Hotel, and like the beaches is open to the public. Used often in the early morning or late afternoon for exercise by walkers and joggers, it's a convenient way to get to the next beach or to the next resort for lunch or dinner. Even if you're not staying in the area, take a stroll down the path and have a look at the wonderfully landscaped gardens and resort properties here.

You can get to Wailea by coming straight down South Kihei Road through the strip of condos and shopping centers. To miss this area and make better time, take Piilani Hwy., Rt. 31. This route takes you up on the hillside, where you have some nice views out over the water and can watch Kihei slip by in a blur below.

Onward and Backward
If you turn your back to the sea and look toward Haleakala, you'll see its cool, green forests and peak wreathed in mysterious clouds. You'll want to run right over, but you can't get there from here! Outrageous as it may sound, you have to double back 18 miles to Kahului and then head down Route 37 for another 20 miles just to get to the exact same spot on Route 37 that you can easily see. On the map there's a neat little private road that connects the Wailea/Makena area with Upcountry in a mere three-mile stretch, but it's always closed as it traverses ranchland! An ongoing fight over who's responsible for its maintenance keeps it that way. If this appalling situation is ever rectified, you'll be able to travel easily to the Tedeschi Winery and continue on the "wrong way" to Hana, or go left to Kula and Upcountry. For now, however, happy motoring!

BEACHES

If you're not fortunate enough to be staying in Wailea, the best reason for coming here is its beaches. These little beauties are crescent moons

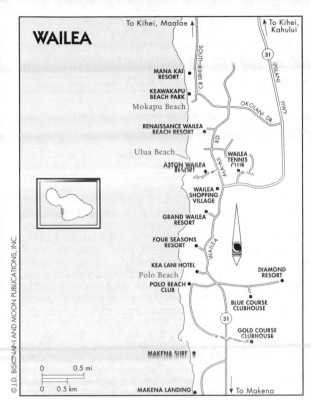

WAILEA

To Kihei, Maalae
To Kihei, Kahului
SOUTH KIHEI RD.
PIILANI HWY.
MANA KAI RESORT
KEAWAKAPU BEACH PARK
Mokapu Beach
OKOLANI DR.
RENAISSANCE WAILEA BEACH RESORT
Ulua Beach
WAILEA TENNIS CLUB
ASTON WAILEA RESORT
WAILEA SHOPPING VILLAGE
GRAND WAILEA RESORT
FOUR SEASONS RESORT
KEA LANI HOTEL
Polo Beach
POLO BEACH CLUB
DIAMOND RESORT
BLUE COURSE CLUBHOUSE
GOLD COURSE CLUBHOUSE
MAKENA SURF
MAKENA LANDING
To Makena

0   0.5 mi
0   0.5 km

© J.D. BISIGNANI AND MOON PUBLICATIONS, INC.

Mokapu and Ulua

These two beaches are shoulder to shoulder, separated only by a rock outcropping. Turn right off Wailea Alanui at the first turn past the Aston Wailea Resort. The beach is clearly marked, and there's a parking area, showers, and restrooms. Being resort beaches, they're both particularly well-kept. Beautiful white sand and protected waters are perfect for swimming. There's good snorkeling at the outcropping separating the beaches, or swim out to the first reef just in front of the rocks for excellent snorkeling.

Wailea Beach

The Aston, Grand Wailea, and Four Seasons resorts front this beach. One-half mile past the Wailea town center, turn right onto a clearly marked access road; at the beach there's good parking, as well as showers and toilets. A short but wide beach of white sand, Wailea offers good swimming and bodysurfing, but the snorkeling is only fair.

of white sand that usually end in lava outcroppings on both ends. This makes for sheltered swimmable waters and good snorkeling and scuba. Many of the hotel guests in Wailea seem to hang around the hotel pools, maybe peacocking or just trying to get their money's worth, so the beaches are surprisingly uncrowded. The following beaches are listed from north to south, toward Makena.

Keawakapu

The first Wailea beach, almost a buffer between Kihei and Wailea, is just past the Mana Kai Resort. Turn left onto Kamala Place, or proceed straight on S. Kihei Road until it dead-ends. Plenty of parking at both accesses, but no amenities. Keawakapu is a lovely white-sand beach with a sandy bottom. Good swimming and fair snorkeling. There's also a beginner's dive spot offshore where an underwater junkyard of a few hundred cars forms an artificial reef.

Polo Beach

Follow Wailea Alanui toward Makena. Turn right on Kaukahi St. just past the Kea Lani Resort and right again at the clearly marked sign near Polo Beach condo. Here also are paved parking, showers, and toilets. Polo Beach is good for swimming and sunbathing, with few tourists. There's excellent snorkeling in front of the rocks separating Polo from Wailea Beach—tremendous amounts of fish, and one of the easiest spots to get to.

ACCOMMODATIONS

Renaissance Wailea Beach Resort

Always a beauty, the Renaissance Wailea, 3550 Wailea Alanui, Wailea, HI 96753, tel. (808) 879-4900 or (800) 992-4532, fax (808) 879-6128, is like a rich red cabernet that has aged superbly. The Renaissance is a superbly appointed resort with attention given to the most minute detail of comfort and luxury. When you enter the main lobby, you're actually on the fifth floor; the ones below terrace down the mountainside to the golden-sand beach. The lobby has original artworks on the walls and a sweeping marble staircase leading down to the Palm Court Restaurant. A bubbling spa fashioned from lava rock is surrounded by vines and flowering trees; another spa contains three little pools and a gurgling fountain, so that while the therapeutic water soothes your muscles, the music of the fountain soothes your nerves. The hotel boasts the best beach in the area, long known as an excellent vantage point from which to view humpback whales in season. The impeccable grounds have grown into an actual botanical garden. And everywhere there is water, cascading over tiny waterfalls, tumbling in brooks, and reflecting the amazing green canopy in tranquil lagoons.

The white-on-tan rooms are appointed with koa and rattan furniture. Beds are brightened with quilted pillows, and each room is accented with standing lamps, paintings of Hawaiian flora, an entertainment center with VCR and remote-control TV, wall safe, a glass-topped writing desk, even matching *yukata* for an evening of lounging. Sliding doors lead to a lanai where you can relax or enjoy a quiet in-room meal. The bathrooms are small but adequate, with double marble-topped sinks, a queen-size tub, pulsing shower head, vanity mirror, hair dryer, and quality lotions, soaps, and creams.

The hotel features the very private **Mokapu Beach Club,** a detached low-rise wing complete with its own pool and daily continental breakfast, where the hotel's impeccable service rises yet higher with valet service and 24-hour concierge. Room rates are $320 for a standard, $350 for a garden view, $380-435 for an ocean view, $550 for a room in the Makapu Beach Club, and $650 for a one-bedroom suite; $25 additional person. Varying rates include a family plan, where children under 18 stay free if they're in their parents' room, and also a variety of golf and tennis packages.

Renaissance Wailea Beach Resort has been acclaimed as a five-diamond resort by the AAA Motor Club for 10 consecutive years. You will enjoy the Palm Court, Hana Goin Japanese, and poolside Maui Onion restaurants; a cocktail lounge; and the Wailea Sunset Luau that is held three times weekly. For large groups, the Raffles serves as the fine dining restaurant. Renaissance offers valet parking, 24-hour room service, a fit-ness center, therapeutic massage and body care, a children's program, free daily newspaper, a small shopping arcade, and an activities desk to book you into every kind of outdoor Maui activity. The most amazing feature about the resort is its feeling of peace and tranquillity. Now part of the Marriott family of hotels.

Aston Wailea Resort

The Aston Wailea Resort, 3700 Wailea Alanui, Wailea, Maui, HI 96753, tel. (808) 879-1922 or (800) 367-2960, fax (808) 875-4878, is a class act. Even the Wrong Way signs politely state "*Please,* Do Not Enter." The main lobby, supported by gigantic wooden beams, is inviting with overstuffed chairs in an informal setting and frames a wide panorama of the sea and Lanai floating on the horizon. Walk out onto a stone-tiled portico and below, in a central courtyard ringed by palms, is a series of quiet lily ponds highlighted with red torch ginger and alive with serenading bullfrogs in the evening. Stroll the 22 meticulously landscaped acres and dip into one of the three pools: two for relaxing, the third a lap pool designed to give the illusion that the pool stretches to the sea.

The Aston Wailea Resort was the first large hotel property in Wailea. It has roots here. Not only that, but it makes the claim of being the "most Hawaiian hotel in Wailea." From the little touches to the large efforts, many would say that it is so. The hotel has established a position of Director of Hawaiian Activities and runs a Hawaiian cultural program called Ho'olokahi that not only educates the staff about its own Hawaiian heritage but also shares the Hawaiian culture with guests and brings the community to the hotel for cultural exchanges. The Hawaiian cultural program has a varied schedule of activities and workshops presented by knowledgeable Hawaiian elders and teachers. All you need to do to attend is sign up. Some activities are hula demonstrations and contests, a lei festival, an evening torchlight ceremony, and a Friday art and craft display and sale in the hotel lobby. Aston also hosts a Hawaiian sailing canoe regatta, which is accompanied by numerous cultural activities and events. In addition, the restaurant Hula Moons is dedicated to Don Blanding, an early enthusiast of Hawaii and Hawaiian culture from the early 20th century, and it proudly displays some of Blanding's personal belongings and mementos of the times.

At least 70% of Aston's rooms have ocean views, which in most cases are actually oceanfront. Rooms are coordinated with light pastel tones of green-on-tan and beige, appointed with marble-topped writing desks and incidental tables. All have a large entertainment center with remote-control TV, a small refrigerator, coffeemaker, and a double closet with full-length mirror. Marble bathrooms are well-proportioned with a full bath and shower, double sinks, and separate dressing area. Doors open to a terra-cotta floored lanai, flushed with sunshine and sea breezes, from where you have a private view of the Lahaina Roads. More amenities include room service, a self-service laundry, complimentary valet parking, a beauty salon, and fitness center. For the kids, Keiki Club Gecko fills the day with supervised activities for a nominal fee. Hotel restaurants are Lea's, Hula Moons, and the Lanai Terrace, and they'll certainly please, or pop into the Pa'ani game bar for a friendly little game of foosball and a beer. While you're here, you won't want to miss the award-winning luau and Polynesian show, "Wailea's Finest Luau." Room rates run $219 for a standard garden room to $399 for a deluxe oceanfront room; suites are available for $499-899, $30 per extra person. Special family plans, room and car, honeymoon, and golf packages are available.

Grand Wailea Resort and Spa

A sublime interplay of cascading water, light diffused and brilliant, and the music of natural sound have been entwined with fine art, sculpted landscaping, and brilliant architecture to create the intangible quality of grandeur so apparent at the astounding Grand Wailea Resort and Spa, 3850 Wailea Alanui, Wailea, HI 96753, tel. (808) 875-1234, fax 874-2442, Web site: grandwailea.com. On arrival the spume of a thunderous waterfall, misting a heroic sculpture of the warrior king, Kamehameha, is the tangible spirit of the grand hotel. Inside the towering reception atrium, alive with the essence of over 10,000 plants, flowers, and ferns, the water and sculpture interplay continues. Hula dancers both male and female, some with arms outstretched to the sun, others in repose or in a stance of power, are the visual *mele* singing of the ancient times. A mermaid, bronzed, bare-breasted, offers a triton shell of sweet water, and behind, sleek canoes float on a pond of blue. Alcoves and arches frame dramatic scenes in every direction. Ahead the glimmering sea, foaming surf, and wind-tossed palms dance to their immortal tune. Left and right, Fernando Botero's sculpted women—enormous, buxom, and pleasant—lie in alluring repose. Bellmen, in starched white livery, lead you to your room over marble floors embossed with mosaic tiles and laid over with rich carpets.

Rooms, the least of which has an ocean view, feature private lanai that look out over the water and flower gardens below, while inside they are sanctuaries of pure luxury. All are appointed in soothing earth tones with comfortable puffed-pillowed chairs, a complete entertainment center with remote color TV, VCR, mini-fridge and bar, in-room safes, multiple phones, twice daily maid service, and turndown service. Rates are $380-445 for standard rooms, and $1,100-2,000 for suites. Guests of the Napua Tower have concierge service and many special amenities. Rooms here run $580, suites $1,400-3,000.

If Nero had the health and relaxation resources found at the hotel's Spa Grande, his fiddle playing would have vastly improved and Rome never would have burned. You enter the facility and the magic begins as soon as you shed your clothing and don a fluffy terry cloth robe. Walk the marble floors and choose a loofah scrub or dip first into a Japanese *ofuro* that unjangles nerves and soothes muscles. From there, a cold dip to revitalize and then into the Terme Circuit, a series of baths, one more intriguing than the other. Choose from a jello green papaya bath, a dark green *limu* bath, a mud bath, or the crystal waters of an aroma bath. Special to the facility are the Hawaiian rejuvenating bath, made from Hawaiian alae salt and a number of spices, and the tropical enzyme bath, especially good for the skin. From there a cascading waterfall massages you with watery fingers, or a jet bath sends 50 penetrating streams of water in varying temperatures that let you know that you are indeed alive. Awaiting you are private massage rooms where you can choose seven different types of massage and five different types of facials. Each room opens to the sea whose eternal rhythm helps to create complete relaxation.

The pool area surrounds a "volcano" and fronts Wailea beach. Here, a formal fountain, surrounded by royal palms, is reflected in a rectangular pool inlaid with white and gold tile forming a giant hibiscus. A canyon river, complete with gentle current, glides you through a series of pools and past small grottoes where you can stop to enjoy a jacuzzi, swing like Tom Sawyer on a suspended rope, swim up to a bar for your favorite drink, or just slip along until you are deposited in the main pool. Waiting is the world's only water elevator, to lift you to the top again and again.

To make a family visit perfect, there is **Camp Wailea**, $40 half day or $65 per day, for children ages 4-12. The day camp, run by professionals, features movies, a preschool playroom, arts and crafts, a computer learning center, video game room, and a kids' restaurant with their own dance floor and soda fountain. Scuba diving lessons, a catamaran sail, and other water activities and rentals are arranged by an outside concession on hotel property near the beach. Periodic tours of the grounds and hotel art are offered. The grounds tour is free and given Thursday at 10 a.m.; the art tour is Tuesday and Friday at 10 a.m., and is free to hotel guests but $6.25 for nonguests. And finally, there is a nondenominational **chapel,** a miniature cathedral with floor-to-ceiling stained-glass windows by renowned Indonesian artist Yvonne Cheng, as well as a number of exclusive shops and boutiques for your shopping pleasure.

Four Seasons Resort Wailea
AAA five-diamond award winner the Four Seasons, 3900 Wailea Alanui, Wailea, Maui, HI 96753, tel. (808) 874-8000 or (800) 334-6284, fax (808) 874-6449, situated on 15 acres at the south end of Wailea Beach, is oriented to the setting sun and opens itself up to the sweet sea breezes. Casually elegant, the open-air lobby is full of cushy chairs and couches, fountains, flowers, fans, and a grand staircase that glides down to the huge pool at beach level. On the way down, say "hello" to Ricky and Lucy, the hotel parakeets who make their home below the staircase. The pool and the colonnade of lobby pillars above it hint at a Romanesque architectural influence, yet the ambiance and colors of the hotel say island natural. Original artwork and reproductions hang throughout the lobby and hallways, while huge fossilized sea anemones are displayed on lobby tables, and birds and plants bring the outdoors inside. Countless little details make this resort pleasant and special.

The Four Seasons is a study of cream-on-cream, and this color scheme runs throughout the resort, offset by coral, almond, muted greens, and other pastels. Each large room has a bedroom and sitting area, an exceptionally large bath with separate shower and deep tub, a well-stocked wet bar, TV, room safe, and private lanai; 85% of the rooms have an ocean view and all have twice-daily room service. While air-conditioning is standard, rooms also have sliding screen doors or louvered French doors and overhead fans. Double rooms and suites are even more spacious, with the addition of a second bathroom and/or a dining area. Rates for the standard rooms run $295 for a mountain view to $550 for a prime ocean view, $80 extra person. Depending upon the number of bedrooms and location, suites run $545-5,200. Rates on the Club Floor, which includes on-floor check-in, complimentary continental breakfast, afternoon tea, sunset cocktails and hors d'oeuvres, and a personal concierge, run $625-5,700 a day, $140 extra person. The club lounge on this floor also provides books, newspapers, magazines, and board games; golf, family, room and car, and romance packages are also available.

Other amenities include three top-notch restaurants, a lobby lounge, a game room with a fine collection of surfing memorabilia, meeting rooms for conventions, complimentary valet parking, 24-hour room service, and an early arrival-late departure lounge where you can relax and enjoy the hotel services, store a small bag, or shower off the grit of travel. In addition, the supervised "Kids for all Seasons" program can keep your little ones ages 5-12 busy for all or part of the day, 9 a.m.-5 p.m., with games and activities. On site are two tennis courts and lawn croquet (for guests only); an expanded health club with exercise machines and a steam room that offers massage and personal training; and organized beach activities. Five shops are also here, among them Viewpoint, for alohawear; Hildgund Jewelers; and Lamonts, a gift and sundries shop. Down by the beach, all beach chairs, cabanas, snorkel equipment (free rental for one hour), boogie boards, and the like are complimentary—added value for guests. These and most hotel amenities are included in the room charge. Although not cheap, you get a lot for your money and great service.

Kea Lani Hotel
While Aladdin napped and dreamed of high adventure, his genie was at work building a pleasure dome more splendid than the great Khan's Xanadu. The Kea Lani Hotel, 4100 Wailea Alanui, Wailea, HI 96753, tel. (808) 875-4100 or (800) 882-4100, fax (808) 875-1200, Web site: www

.kealani.com, is an alabaster fantasy bazaar where turrets and cupolas cover vaulted and coved ceilings suspended above towering pillars. Enter the central lobby, an open-air court with a bubbling fountain, completely sculpted and gilded; sultan's slippers would be appropriate here to pad around on the mosaic floors. A staircase leads to a tranquil pool area fronting a wide sweep of grass and perpetual blue sea. On the second level is a parlor, formal but comfortable, with giant shoji-like mirrors and sculpted harps and lyres embedded in the walls.

Lodging at the Koa Lani is in one-bedroom luxury suites priced $295-595, or in opulent one-, two- and three-bedroom villas priced $900-1,400 that include a car and private pool. Several room/car and room/meal packages are available. Enter the suites, very roomy at just under 900 square feet, to find the rich embossed weave of a Berber carpet contrasting with white-on-white walls. Double doors open to the master bedroom with its own entertainment center, minibar, large dresser/vanity, and brass valet. The parlor, formal but comfy, is appointed with puff-pillowed chairs, a queen-size sleeper sofa, entertainment center, marble-topped tables, and a full bar with microwave and coffeemaker. All rooms are air conditioned, but there are also cooling fans. The bathroom, marble from floor to ceiling, features an oversized tub, two pedestal sinks, a huge stall shower, bath products, full-length mirror, a hair dryer, a vanity mirror, and cotton *yukata* for a day of lounging. A steam iron and board are available for last minute touch-ups.

The villas are magnificent. Outside is a private courtyard complete with table, cotton-clad chaise lounges, and a plunge pool, slightly heated and perfect for two. Inside, the bilevel villa includes a completely tiled living room, furnished with an Oriental rug, glass-topped tables, couches and chairs, and a complete entertainment center. The kitchen includes a fridge, stove, microwave, trash compactor, dishwasher, and laundry room. Two downstairs bedrooms, each with full baths, pamper you with queen-size beds. Upstairs, an alcove leads to the master bedroom self-contained with entertainment center; minibar; two pedestal sinks; a deep, almost two-person tub; and a huge shower area. The walk-in closet, as large as many hotel rooms, features a wall safe.

The hotel's pool area is grand, just right for frolicking or for savoring an afternoon siesta. A free-form upper pool, boasting a swim-to bar, and serviced by the Polo Beach Grill, is connected to the lower pool by a 140-foot water slide. The lower area is family oriented with a football-shaped children's pool, but escape is at hand at the casbah pool, inlaid with multi-hued tiles forming an entwined moon and sun around it; adults can shelter in Camelot-like tents providing shade and privacy.

Other amenities include an activities desk, in-house doctor's office, video library, complimentary fitness center, spa, a clutch of swank boutiques, jewelry store, and a hair salon. The children have their own Keiki Lani children's program, open daily 9 a.m.-3 p.m., where children ages 5-12 are entertained with a mixture of fun and educational activities, and even given lunch.

Destination Resorts Hawaii

Located at 3750 Wailea Alanui, Wailea, HI 96753, tel. (808) 879-1595 or (800) 367-5246, fax (808) 874-3554, Web site: www.destinationresortshi.com, this complex is made up of six separate villages that are scattered along the coast or up around the golf course. Located near the Blue Course, **Ekolu** has one- and two-bedroom condo units for $140-230. Also on the golf links and next to Wailea Tennis Club is **Grand Champions,** with one- and two-bedroom units for $150-240. **Ekahi,** located at the entrance to Wailea and the least expensive of the oceanfront properties, has studio, one- and two-bedroom condos for $149-349. Tucked between two ritzy hotels, **Elua** fronts Ulua Beach and has condominiums ranging $240-600. Right on Polo Beach is **Polo Beach Club,** the only highrise condo building in the bunch. Rates here are $275-425 for one- or two-bedroom units. The newest and perhaps the most exclusive is **Makena Surf,** on a private section of coast a short way down the road toward Makena. Here one-, two-, and three-bedroom units run $305-600.

Special golf, tennis, car, and romance packages are available. There is a three- to five-night minimum stay, 10-14 nights during the Christmas-New Year's season; $20 extra person. The fifth or seventh night is free depending upon the village. All units are plush and fully furnished, with daily housekeeping service, concierge service, a swimming pool or pools, barbecue grills, and some with tennis courts on the premises.

The beach, two golf courses, and additional tennis courts are nearby.

Diamond Resort

Formerly a member-only resort, this condo property is now open to all but gets mostly Japanese visitors. The Diamond Resort, 555 Kaukahi St., Wailea, HI 96753, tel. (808) 874-0500 or (800) 800-0720, fax (808) 874-8778, sits high above the Wailea Blue Golf Course and has a wonderful view over the ocean. The slate roof and stone exterior on the round portion of the main building make a wonderful first impression, and the pools and stream that cascade down between the buildings create a restful feeling. Let the resort's two restaurants fill your belly and the spa soothe your muscles. The spa features Japanese *ofuro,* Scandinavian saunas, and jacuzzis. The 72 large air-conditioned guest suites have ocean or partial-ocean views and come with kitchenettes, TV and VCRs, and lanai. Rates run $170-240 a night.

FOOD

At the Renaissance

The **Palm Court** is the main dining room at the Renaissance. Walk though the lobby and look over the rail to the partially open-air restaurant below, open for breakfast 6-11 a.m. and for dinner nightly from 6 p.m. The menu offers a different buffet every night featuring cuisines ranging from Italian to the Southwestern. The Palm Court is a first-rate restaurant with very reasonable prices, a good choice.

The **Sunset Terrace** just off the lobby is a delightful perch on which to have a drink and survey the grounds and beach below. Every evening brings a dramatic torch-lighting ceremony. The drums reverberate and the liquid melancholy of the conch trumpet sends a call for meditation at day's end. Drinks include the full complement of island specialties, and you can order wonderful gourmet-quality *pu pu.*

The **Maui Onion** is a convenient snack-type restaurant at poolside. Burgers, sandwiches, salads, smoothies, and Maui onion rings, the specialty, are on the limited menu. Prices are reasonable, especially if you don't want to budge from your lounge chair. On Wednesday and Friday evenings 5:30-8:30 p.m., relax here and dine under the stars on a limited choice of entrees.

Aston

Lea's, the new fine dining restaurant at Aston Wailea, is sure to please. Sit inside in the sumptuous booths or out on the balcony overlooking the pool and garden. A breakfast buffet is served for $17, along with a full à la carte menu. In the evening you can hear the poolside music at Hula Moons waft up from downstairs. While there is much more on the menu, Lea's specializes in fresh fish and seafood. Start with a tiger shrimp lumpia for $8.95 and baked Maui onion soup at $4.95. Move on to seafood "Black Thai" risotto, a sautéed combination of lobster, shrimp, and scallops braised with black Thai rice in a spicy Sichuan broth, for $24.95, or stick with a market price fresh catch of the day, charbroiled, steamed, seared, or sautéed. One of the wonderfully rich desserts is certainly an appropriate way to round off your meal. Great care is taken at Lea's to use only the best ingredients; portions are filling, the presentation is pleasing, and there is something on the wine list to accompany any meal. Aston's fine dining establishment, Lea's is a class act.

Hula Moons, open daily for lunch and dinner, is a casual indoor/outdoor restaurant draped with awnings for shade and privacy. The name Hula Moons derives from the writings of Don Blanding, Hawaii's poet laureate, who arrived by steamship in 1924, dead broke, and remained for over 40 years, all the while singing the island's praises. At the restaurant's entrance are opened drawers from Don Blanding's desk filled with memories—Lucky Strike cigarettes, round sunglasses, a box camera, matchboxes, and playing cards—all whispering of the time when Hawaii was a distant land where only the rich and famous came to escape. Nice nostalgic touch. Choose a table or horseshoe booth and for lunch dine on everything from a juicy foot-long hot dog for $7 to mahimahi tempura for $10.50. The poolside menu also offers sandwiches, salads, and appetizers. For dinner, the menu begins with kalua pork spring rolls for $7 and crisp lobster and crab fritters for $9. Entrees include lilikoi roast duckling for $21, a whole Maine lobster at $37, medallions of beef tenderloin at $24, and stir-fried Maui vegetables for $14. New to the restaurant, and for the chocoholics in all of us, is the "all-you-care-to-eat" chocolate dessert bar, featuring more than a dozen chocolate concoctions nightly. Hula Moons has an extensive wine list, with selections from France to Australia, and a full bar serving exotic drinks. There's entertainment nightly, with—what else—a hula show for part of the evening.

A special Sunday Champagne Brunch is offered in the Makani Room 10 a.m.-1 p.m. for $28. Let the piano accompaniment soothe your soul as you satiate your body with made-to-order omelettes, fresh fruits and pastries, or mouthwatering entrees of fish, poultry, and meat.

Grand Wailea

The resort has an eclectic mix of restaurants, all landscaped around the central theme of water, art, and flowers, offering a variety of cuisines catering to all tastes and appetites. **The Grand Dining Room Maui** is French with an Oriental twist. Start with wonderful appetizers like lobster noodle soufflé, a Maui Onion broth with Gruyère, or a Mandarin chicken salad for $8-12. Entrees beginning at about $27 range from grilled ahi Nicoise, to Hoisin encrusted lamb loin. A fun and informal restaurant more reasonably priced is **Bistro Molokini.** Come for antipasti, pasta smothered in everything from shrimp to pancetta, pizza with fresh tomato, cheeses, and Italian meats, and main dishes like piccata Milanese, veal dipped in Parmesan and served with risotto.

Humuhumu is a thatched-roof Polynesian restaurant afloat on its own lagoon complete with 2,000 varieties of tropical fish in a huge aquarium. The specialties prepared at the Humuhumu come from throughout the Pacific. *Pu pu* like fried coconut shrimp or a dim sum basket are great to nibble on while enjoying a special exotic drink like a Humu Heaven. Entrees are delightful with offerings like wok-seared scallops Sichuan or an enormous porterhouse steak. Delectable but not cheap.

The **Cafe Kula** specializes in "Spa Cuisine," dishes especially prepared with dynamic health in mind. Here the freshest fruits, organic vegetables, and whole grains provide the foundation for most dishes. For breakfast enjoy fresh carrot juice for $5, homemade granola at $7, or apple-stuffed crepes with fresh brandied currants for $10. Healthful entree choices are Basmati rice torte or grilled salmon.

Perhaps the most elegant restaurant is **Kincha,** serving superb Japanese cuisine. Enter over stepping stones past a replica of a golden tea kettle used by Toyotomi Hideyoshi, revered as both a great warrior and a master of the *chanoyu*, the tea ceremony. Follow the stones past stone

lanterns that light your way over a humpbacked bridge, a symbol of life, that crosses a tiny stream brimming with orange and white *koi*. Inside a raised *tatami* area awaits with sushi chefs ready to perform their magic. Private rooms, comfortable with *zabuton* backrests, are perfect for a very refined full meal. For a treat order the sashimi moriawase, a sampler of the best sashimi, or start with a hot appetizer like *kani shumai*, deep-fried croquette of crab. Soups and salads are *wafu* salad, *miso wan*, or *cha soba*, tea-flavored buckwheat noodles. Entrees are Japanese favorites like hamachi teriyaki, broiled yellowtail tuna, or tempura, regular or deluxe, with prices from $35 on up.

Four Seasons

Located at the Four Seasons Resort, the elegant **Seasons** restaurant is an experience in fine dining. With table linen, crystal, classical music, and jackets required for men, the Seasons is elegant, but not stuffy. The decor is teal and weathered bamboo, the windows open to let in sea breezes and moonlight, and the island cuisine is offered in a "homelike" presentation. It is here that the freshest of Hawaiian ingredients with a French technique, give this regional cuisine a French soul. Emphasis is on fresh island seafood. Open for dinner only Tues.-Sat. 6-9:30 p.m.; live music and dancing until 10.00. Reservations are recommended, and proper dress required.

The casual **Pacific Grill** restaurant combines a large selection of foods from the Orient and the West. The breakfast buffet is a long-established special, but an à la carte menu is also available. For dinner, entrees are from Asia and the Pacific, some cooked in view of the guests. Pacific edge entree specialties include steamed ehu Oriental style at $28.50 and charred duck breast with a citrus glaze for $27.50; some home-style cooking entrees are roasted half chicken for $21.50 and grilled and herb marinated porterhouse at $32.50. At the Pacific Grill, alohawear and activewear are the norm.

Ferraro's at Seaside serves as two distinct restaurants. For lunch, 11:30 a.m.-3 p.m., dine on healthy light fare, mostly seafood and grilled items. *Pu pu* and drinks are served 3-5 p.m. As Italian as Italian can be, Ferraro's opens at 6 p.m. and serves up with Hawaiian entertainment. Start with an antipasti like deep-fried mozzarella and olives in tomato sauce for $9, and move on to pepper-crusted seared ahi at $27, chicken breast wrapped with prosciutto for $22.50, or pasta with tomato, eggplant, and caper sauce for $21.50. Set almost on the water, Ferraro's is a great place to watch the sunset.

Kea Lani

For casual dining any time of the day visit **Cafe Ciao,** rich with the smell of espresso, where the shelves hold homemade jellies, jams, chutney, peppercorn ketchup, and Italian olives. Choose fresh-baked bread, pastries, a spicy focaccia, pesto salad, even ready-to microwave Italian rigatoni and chicken Parmesan. For lunch and dinner try the poolside **Polo Beach Grill and Bar** for a light salad, sandwich, or kiawe-grilled burger.

Towering glass and wooden doors open into **Kea Lani** restaurant, where elegant dining is assured in this sanctuary hung with huge chandeliers and capped with a molded ceiling. Ocean breezes flow freely through louvered windows into the white-on-gray great hall furnished with marble-topped tables. For a romantic evening, choose a table in a more intimate area, where a lowered ceiling and massive sideboard filled with wine and set with pottery create a warmer, candle-lit atmosphere. At the entrance to the restaurant is a lounge area with a hand-rubbed wooden bar that offers evening entertainment, usually a jazz or Hawaiian ensemble. Dinners are a combination of Pacific Rim and European in flavor, with fish as a specialty. Expect entrees from $25, and quality to match.

Diamond Resort

The two restaurants here are the **Taiko** and the **Le Gunji.** Taiko serves breakfast, lunch, and dinner and is open 7 a.m.-9 p.m. The day starts with a Japanese- or Western-style breakfast for $13; lunch includes sandwiches and burgers, or Japanese *soba, udon,* or other traditional dishes. Dinner entrees, like teriyaki chicken and lobster daiyaki, run $18-27; a whole range of sushi is also available. Le Gunji has limited seating at 6 p.m. and 7:30 p.m. only; reservations are a necessity and a dress code is enforced. Choose from five set menus, ranging $45-75. Here, French food is prepared, unusually, on a *teppan yaki* grill.

Sandcastle Restaurant

Located at Wailea Shopping Village, tel. (808) 879-0606, this moderate restaurant is far enough out of the way that you can count on getting a table, but reservations are recommended anyway. The restaurant, overlooking a small courtyard, has wraparound glass and mirrors, vaulted ceilings, and latticework partitions allowing for some privacy. Lunch served daily 11:30 a.m.-3 p.m. offers a full range of sandwiches from $6.95 to $12.95. Lighter appetites will enjoy a full salad selection for $3.95-8.95, which you can combine with a pizza for a full yet inexpensive meal. Dinner runs 5-9 p.m. Early bird specials, offered 5-6 p.m., are complete dinners for $9.95-14.95, otherwise the dinner menu offers entrees like roasted rack of lamb for $21.95, filet mignon for $19.95, fresh catch at the daily quote, and prime rib of beef au jus for $17.95. The Sandcastle also has a full bar with an excellent wine list. This restaurant is slated to be torn down when the Wailea Shopping Village is demolished for rebuilding.

Golf Ball Soup

The following restaurants are located at the golf links in the area. **The Chart House,** on the 14th fairway of Wailea Blue Course up from the Wailea Shopping Center, 100 Wailea Ike Dr., tel. (808) 879-2875, open daily for dinner from 5:30 p.m., is part of a small chain that deserves its reputation for consistently well-prepared and reasonably priced food. The menu has starters like artichoke salad for $5.25 or a Caesar salad for $8.95. Entrees include the specialty, prime rib, for $22.95 or $26.95 depending on cut, steaks costing $19.95-25.95, grilled teriyaki chicken breast for $16.50, or shrimp Santa Fe at $19.95. There's a children's menu with most dinners priced under $6.95. Aside from the regular menu, there's a daily menu with other tasty choices. Don't forget about the enticing desserts, like chocolate mousse pie for $4.95 to key lime pie at $4.75 or mud pie for $6.25. The dining area is done in stout sturdy chairs and tables, and the green of the ferns and bamboo inside reflect the fairway green captured in the full glass wall. Also on the premises is the **Sunset Lounge,** an open-air bar, open from 5 p.m. until closing, where you can enjoy an evening cocktail.

The **Lobster Cove Restaurant,** tel. (808) 879-6677, across from the Chart House and open daily 5:30-10 p.m., is a seafood restaurant that shares space with **Harry's Sushi Bar** (as a second Harry's shares space with the Orient Express in Napili). Appetizers include garlic clams for $9.50, sweet and sour crispy shrimp at $11, and lobster cakes for $11.50. These would go well with the rock shrimp Caesar salad at $7.50. Entrees, limited but wonderful, might be seafood ravioli and spiny lobster and shrimp for $22, fresh island fish at market price, or a filet mignon at $24. Choose from an adequate wine list for a bottle to accompany your meal. You can order *pu pu* or make a meal from the offerings at Harry's. The choices of sushi are numerous and run $3.50-6 apiece, and are double that for a plate of sashimi. Also consider such items as California rolls for $5.25 or deep-fried soft-shell crabs at $7.

A little up the hill and across the road at the Wailea Tennis Club is **Joe's Bar and Grill,** tel. (808) 875-7767. Open for lunch 11 a.m.-2 p.m. and again for dinner 5:30-10 p.m., Joe's serves large and tasty portions of honest American, home-style comfort food in a relaxing atmosphere. Joe's is set directly above the tennis courts in a wood-floored open-beamed room, and cool breezes waft through the sliding glass partitions. Owner, operator, and chief schmoozer Joe Gannon is the other half to Haliimaile General Store restaurant's chef Beverly Gannon. Lunch is basically soup, salad, and sandwiches, while dinner offers heartier fare. Entrees range from Joe's famous meatloaf at $17 to filet mignon and grilled prawns for $30. The full bar has a full range of beers and can make any mixed drink that you desire.

At the Wailea Blue Golf Course clubhouse is the **Fairway Restaurant,** tel. (808) 879-4060. Open from 7:30 a.m. for breakfast, Fairway offers everything from eggs Benedict for $5.95 to a simple omelette for $4.75 or buttermilk pancakes, all you can eat, for $3.50. Lunch includes burgers and sandwiches costing $5-7. Dinner selections for $15-20 include filet mignon, New York pepper steak, veal parmigiana, or the salad bar for $11.95. Although the dining room isn't ultra fancy, there's a terrace, and the ambiance is peaceful and unhurried. A good place to eat in an area not known for budget restaurants.

More recently, the **SeaWatch** restaurant, tel. (808) 875-8080, has opened at the Emerald Golf Course clubhouse, serving Hawaiian regional cuisine breakfast and lunch both 8 a.m.-3 p.m. Start with fruit for breakfast, or an egg or omelette concoction for $7-12. Salads, sandwiches, and

noodle dishes run mostly $6.50-8, while main courses, like linguine, New York steak, and porcini-crusted veal chop range $18-28.

ENTERTAINMENT, SHOPPING, AND SERVICES

Entertainment
If you haven't had enough fun on the Wailea beaches during the day, you can show off your best dance steps at the **Tsunami** nightclub at the Grand Wailea. Easy listening music is performed every evening at the Sunset Terrace lounge on the lobby level of the Renaissance Resort overlooking the gardens, and for hula and local music try **Hula Moons** at the Aston Wailea.

Wailea Shopping Village
The only shopping in this area is at **Wailea Shopping Village,** open daily 9 a.m.-7 p.m., Sunday 10 a.m.-6 p.m., just east past the Aston Wailea Resort off Wailea Alanui. It has the usual collection of boutiques and shops. **Superwhale** offers alohawear for children. **Weber Goldsmith Galleries** sells fine jewelry, while **Miki's** has racks of alohawear at very competitive prices. More exclusive shops are: **Maui's Best** with a range of gifts from the islands; **Isle Style,** a fine-arts gallery with works by local artists; the **Elephant Walk,** a shopping gallery of fine crafts; and **For Your Eyes Only,** which sells sunglasses for every eye and lifestyle. Money needs are handled by the **First Hawaiian Bank; Island Camera** offers accessories and processing; **Whalers General Store** sells food and liquor; **Fox 1-Hour Lab** takes care of your photo needs; and **Sub-Tropix** sells fast food, sandwiches, ice cream, beverages, and gift-food items. The **Maui Dive Shop** is a full-service dive shop with snorkel and scuba rentals, sales, and diving excursions.

The major hotels have an arcade of shops for quick and easy purchases. One of note is the **Coast Gallery, Maui** at the Aston Wailea Resort, which displays a wide range of mostly island art, including some unique wood and pottery pieces not usually on display at art galleries.

Medical
For immediate care of a nonemergency nature see **Kihei Medical Services,** tel. (808) 879-

8828, at the Kea Lani Hotel, or contact the concierge at your hotel.

Transportation

The **Wailea Shuttle** is a complimentary jitney that stops at all major hotels and condos, the Wailea Shopping Village, and golf and tennis courts in Wailea about every 20-30 minutes. It operates 6:30 a.m.-8:30 p.m. Be sure to check with the driver about the last pickup times if you are out in the evening. With a little walking, this is a great way to hop from one beach to the next. For information on the schedule and stops, call (808) 879-2828.

MAKENA

Just a skip south down the road is Makena Beach, but it's a world away from Wailea. This was a hippie enclave during the '60s and early '70s, and the freewheeling spirit of the times is still partially evident in the area even though Makena is becoming more refined, sophisticated, and available to visitors. For one thing, "Little Makena" is a famous clothing-optional (unofficial) beach, but so what? You can skinny-dip in Connecticut. What's really important is that Makena is *the last* pristine coastal stretch in this part of Maui that hasn't succumbed to undue development . . . yet. Wailea Point, a promontory of land between Wailea and Makena, is the site of one new development, and others will be following in coming years on both sides of the road.

Aside from the sundries shop at the Maui Prince Hotel, there's nothing in the way of amenities past Wailea, so make sure to stock up on all supplies. In fact, there's nowhere to get *anything* past the hotel except for the lunch wagon that's usually parked across from the state park entrance. The police come in and sweep the area now and again, but mostly it's mellow. They do arrest the nudists on Little Makena to make the point that Makena "ain't free no more." Rip-offs can be a problem, so lock your car, hide your camera, and don't leave anything of value. Be careful of the *kiawe* thorns when you park; they'll puncture a tire like a nail. The road south of the Maui Prince Hotel to La Perouse Bay is by and large fairly good with a decent surface. It does, however, narrow down to almost a single lane in spots, particularly where it slides past small coves. Drive carefully and defensively.

Makena is magnificent for bodysurfing and swimming. Whales frequent the area and come quite close to shore during the season. Turtles waddled on to Makena to lay their eggs in the warm sand until early in this century, but too many people gathered the eggs and the turtles scrambled away forever. The sunsets from **Red Hill** (Puu Olai), the cinder cone separating Makena from Little Makena, are among the best on Maui; you can watch the sun sink down between Lanai, Kahoolawe, and West Maui. The silhouettes of pastel and gleaming colors are awe-inspiring. Oranges, russets, and every shade of purple reflect off the clouds that are caught here. Makena attracts all kinds: gawkers, burn-outs, adventurers, tourists, free spirits, and a lot of locals. It won't last long, so go and have a look now!

The Naked Truth

Some years ago in an extremely controversial episode, the Maui police came down hard on the nudists. They arrested nine top-free women from various parts of the U.S. and from foreign countries. The police acted in defiance of a then-recent Hawaii Supreme Court ruling that a woman's breasts when uncovered in appropriate circumstances (i.e., isolated beaches) do not violate the state's "open lewdness" statute. The women, defended by attorney Anthony Ranken, sought compensation for malicious prosecution. Some point directly at former mayor Hannibal Tavares for running a personal crusade against the au naturel sun-worshippers. To show the extent of the conflict, one harebrained scheme actually proposed was to pave a walkway to Red Hill so that Little Makena would no longer be an "isolated beach." The justification was to provide "wheelchair access" to Little Makena although a wheelchair would have to negotiate hundreds of yards of deep sand to get there. Imagine the consternation if the first wheelchair-bound sunbather just happened to be a nudist!

Recreation

As the Maui Prince Hotel is a destination resort, on-site recreation possibilities include the beach and the swimming pool. Golf at **Makena Golf Course** and tennis at **Makena Tennis Club** are just across the road and offer world-class courts and links. **Makena Stables** offers trail rides at its location at the end of the road at La Perouse Bay. They also have kayaks and run tours along the coast here.

Keawalai Church

In Makena, you'll pass this Congregational Church, established in 1832. It was restored in 1952, and services are held every Sunday at 9:30 a.m. Many of the hymns and part of the sermon are still delivered in Hawaiian. Notice the three-foot thick walls and the gravestones, many with a ceramic picture of the deceased. A parking lot, restrooms, and showers are across the road for the beach access, which is just down the road. Take Honoiki Rd., passing Makena Boat Landing on the way.

Small Beaches

You'll pass by these local beaches, via the Old Makena Road, as you head toward Makena. There are usually few people and no amenities. **Palauea** and **Poolenalena** are about three-quarters of a mile past Polo Beach. Good swimming and white sloping sands. **Nahuna ("Five Graves") Point** is just over a mile past Polo. An old graveyard marks the entrance. Not good for swimming but great for scuba because of deep underwater caves. Snorkelers can enjoy this area, too. A

short distance farther on is the **Makena Boat Landing** (water, restrooms, showers), a launch site for boaters and scuba divers. **Papipi** is along the road 1.5 miles past Polo, but its small sand beach is too close to the road. **Oneuli** ("Black Sand Beach") on the north side of Red Crater actually has a salt-and-pepper beach. Turn down a rutted dirt road for a third of a mile. Not good for swimming, but good diving, unofficial camping, and shore fishing. No amenities.

Makena Beach State Park

A few minutes past the Maui Prince Hotel, look for a *kaukau* wagon on the left where you might pick up a snack before turning right onto the access road. Negotiate the excessive speed bumps for a few hundred yards to the parking lot and a few portable toilets; a second beach access is a few hundred yards farther on. This is **Oneloa Beach,** generally called **Makena Big Beach,** a nice long golden strand of sand. Right leads you to **Puu Olai** ("Red Hill"), a 360-foot cinder cone. When you cross over the point from Big Makena Beach you'll be on **Little Makena,** a favorite clothing-optional beach for locals and tourists alike. You'll know that you're on the right beach by the bare bums and the peace sign outlined in white-painted rocks on the lava outcrop that you just climbed over to get to where you are. Both beaches are excellent for swimming (beware of currents in winter), bodysurfing, and superb snorkeling in front of Red Hill. With families and

Keawalai Church, Makena

ROBERT NILSEN

MAKENA TO LA PEROUSE

To Wailua

POLO BEACH PARK

PALAUEA BEACH PARK

Po'olenalena Beach

WAILEA GOLF COURSE

WAILEA ALANUI RD.

Makena Bay

MAKENA BOAT LANDING

KEAWALA'I CHURCH (1832)

Makena

MAUI PRINCE HOTEL

ONOULI BEACH (LITTLE MAKENA)

MAKENA TENNIS CLUB

MAKENA GOLF COURSE

MOLOKINI ISLAND SEABIRD SANCTUARY

ONELOA BEACH (BIG MAKENA)

Pu'u Olai (360 ft.)

(ROUGH ROAD)

Kanahena

Ahihi Bay

AHIHI-KINA'U NATURAL AREA RESERVE

1790 LAVA FLOW

MAKENA STABLES

MAKENA RD.

Cape Kina'u

La Perouse Bay

To Kahului

37

TEDESCHI WINERY

Ulupalakua Ranch

SITE OF MAUI'S LAST VOLCANIC ERUPTION (1790)

31

To Hana

HOAPILI (KING'S) TRAIL   ANCIENT PAVED ROAD

Alakeiki Channel

0   3 mi

0   3 km

© J.D. BISIGNANI AND MOON PUBLICATIONS, INC.

clothed sunbathers moving in (especially on weekends), Little Makena is no longer so "remote" or isolated. The beginning of the end may be in sight, although there is a movement loosely organized to retain this small sanctuary as a place for those who still wish to swim in the buff.

Ahihi-Kinau Natural Reserve

Look for the sign four miles past Polo Beach. Even this far down toward the end of the road—or perhaps because of it—this stretch of the coast is becoming a bit more populated and fancy homes are popping up here and there. The jutting thumb of lava is **Cape Kinau,** part of Maui's last lava flow, which occurred in 1790. Here you'll find a narrow beach, the small community of Kanahena, and a desolate, tortured lava flow. Within the reserve, several walking trails start at pullouts along the road and lead to the water. Please stay on established paths and wear sturdy hiking shoes or boots. Dolphins often play off this point and whales can be seen near shore during winter months. Aside from the lava fields, Ahihi-Kinau is also an underwater reserve, so the scuba and snorkeling are first-

rate. The best way to proceed is along the reef toward the left, or along the reef to the right if you enter at La Perouse Bay. Beware not to step on the many spiny urchins in the shallow water. If you do, vinegar or urine will help with the stinging.

La Perouse Bay

On the far side of Cape Kinau is La Perouse Bay, named after the French navigator Jean de François La Pérouse, first Westerner to land on Maui in May 1786. The bay is good for snorkelers and divers, but beware of the urchins on entry. If you walk farther around to the south you'll come across a string of pocket-sized beaches. The currents can be tricky along here. Past the bay are remnants of the **Hoapili ("King's") Trail,** still hikable along some of its distance. The public road ends at the entrance to La Perouse Bay, but with a 4WD you can get a fair distance down the rough track from here for good shore fishing and unofficial camping. Right before the pavement ends you'll find Makena Stables, where you can arrange trail rides in this dry, remote region.

ACCOMMODATIONS

A gleaming wing-shaped building, understated and almost stark on the outside, the **Maui Prince Hotel,** 5400 Makena Alanui, Makena, HI 96753, tel. (808) 874-1111 or (800) 321-6284, fax (808) 879-8763, is a fabulous destination resort that opens into an enormous central courtyard, one of the most beautiful in Hawaii. Japanese in its architecture and its sense of beauty, the courtyard is a protected haven of cascading waters, black lava rock, stone lanterns, breeze-tossed palms, and raked Zen-like gardens. Lean over the hardwood rails of the balconies on each floor and soak in the visual pleasure of the landscape below, where from these balconies cascade flowers and ferns in sympathetic mimicry of Maui's waterfalls.

All rooms have an alcove door so that you can open your front door yet still have privacy and allow the breeze to pass through. Ocean-view and oceanfront rooms ranging $260-410 are beautifully accentuated in earth tones and light pastels. The bathrooms have a separate commode and a separate shower and tub. One-bedroom suites, priced $500-1,000, feature a giant living room, three lanai, a large-screen TV and VCR, and white terry cloth robes for lounging. The master bedroom has its own TV, listening center, and king-size bed. A nonsmoking wing is also available. The Prince also offers the very reasonable Prince Special that includes an ocean-view room, midsize rental car, and buffet breakfast for two priced only $235 per night per couple; other honeymoon, golf, tennis, and car packages are also available.

The Maui Prince faces fantastic, secluded Maluaka Beach, almost like a little bay, with two points of lava marking it as a safe spot for swimming and snorkeling. Seven sea turtles live on the south point and come up on the beach to nest and lay their eggs. To the left you can see Puu Olai, a red cinder cone that marks Makena. The boat *Kai Kanani* arrives each morning and will take you snorkeling to Molokini or arrange other activities throughout the island. The pool area is made up of two circular pools, one for adults, the other a wading pool for kids; two whirlpools; blue cabanas; and a poolside snack bar. There's volleyball, croquet, six plexi-pave tennis courts with a pro on the staff, and the 36 holes of the Makena Golf Course, designed by Robert Trent Jones Jr., the main attraction of the Maui Prince. The concierge desk offers a variety of complimentary activities including a snorkel and scuba introduction. Sign up here for Makena Adventures, an interpretive tour through the entire Makena area via a hotel minivan, or for the Legend of Makena Luau. For the little ones, the Prince Kid's Club children's program can be arranged for $20 for a half day or $40 for a full day of healthy supervised activities. For the big people, see what the complimentary fitness center can do for you.

FOOD

The Prince has three restaurants, and head chef Gregory Gaspar is building an island-wide reputation for exquisite dining. The fanciest restaurant is the **Prince Court,** featuring fine dining for dinner only, except for the truly exceptional Sunday champagne brunch. The evening fare is Hawaiian regional cuisine and then some. Start with appetizers like orange-cured smoked salmon with warm Maui onions for $11.50, or soups and salads that include saffron parsley mussels soup for $9. From the grill, entrees include roasted ginger Kona lobster with poi risotto and shiitake mushrooms for $21, Tahitian peppered ahi steak at $23, and grilled tenderloin of beef in a mushroom herb sauce for $30. The room is subdued and elegant, and highlighted with snow-white tablecloths and sparkling crystal. The view is serene facing the courtyard, or dramatic looking out to sea.

When chefs from the best restaurants on Maui want to impress visiting friends with a **brunch,** they come to the Maui Prince on Sunday. For only $34 you can surpass most of your dining fantasies. You start with a table laden with exotic fruits and fresh-squeezed juices. Nearby are plump and steaming rolls, croissants, and pastries rich in chocolates and creams. Then comes an omelette gauntlet, where you pick and choose your ingredients and an attendant chef creates it before your eyes. Hot entrees for the gastronomically timid are offered, from roast beef to fresh fish. But the real delights are the cornucopia of smoked seafood and shellfish. To the left pâté, to the right sushi, and sashimi straight ahead, or choose cracked crab to nibble while you decide. Fat yellow rounds of imported cheeses squat on huge tables. Waiters and waitresses attend with fresh plates, champagne by the glass, and pots of coffee. You couldn't possibly eat like this every day, but *sacrifice* yourself at least once like this while on Maui.

Hakone is a Japanese restaurant and sushi bar with all chefs from Japan. It serves complete dinners like sukiyaki, tempura, and shabu shabu for under $35, and it also serves sushi and sashimi, plus traditional seven- to nine-course *kaiseki* dinners. A special Monday night dinner buffet is offered at $38 where you have your choice from 25 delightful dishes. In keeping with the tradition of Japan, the room is subdued and simple, with white shoji screens counterpointed by dark open beams. The floor is black slate atop packed sand, a style from old Japan.

The main dining room is the more casual **Cafe Kiowai,** open for breakfast, lunch, and dinner, located on the ground level, opening to the courtyard and fishponds. For now, food and accommodations in Makena mean the Maui Prince. The only exceptions are the **Makena Club House Restaurant,** which serves only soups, salads, sandwiches, and grilled items for lunch for under $15.

For nightly entertainment in Makena, the only option is the **Molokini Lounge** at the Maui Prince.

heleconia

DIANA LASICH HARPER

UPCOUNTRY

Upcountry is much more than a geographical area to the people who live there: it's a way of life, a frame of mind. You can see Upcountry from anywhere on Maui by lifting your gaze to the slopes of Haleakala. There are no actual boundaries, but this area is usually considered as running from Makawao in the north all the way around to Kahikinui Ranch in the south, and from below the cloud cover down to about the 1,500-foot level. It swathes the western slope of Haleakala like a large green floral bib patterned by pasturelands and festooned with wild and cultivated flowers. In this rich soil and cool-to-moderate temperatures, cattle ranching and truck farming thrive. Up here, *paniolo* ride herd on the range of the enormous 35,000-acre Haleakala Ranch, spread mostly around Makawao, and the smaller but still sizable 23,000 acres of the Ulupalakua Ranch, which *is* the hills above Wailea. Pukalani, the largest town and expanding residential area, is a way station for gas and supplies, and is pineapple country. While

Makawao retains some of its real cowboy town image with saddleries, rodeos, and hitching posts. It has become more sophisticated, with some exclusive shops, fine dining restaurants, art galleries, and alternative healing practitioners.

Kula is Maui's flower basket. This area is one enormous garden producing brilliant blooms and hearty vegetables. Polipoli Spring State Recreation Area is a forgotten wonderland of tall forests, a homogenized stand of trees from around the world. Tedeschi Winery in the south adds a classy touch to Upcountry; a place where you can taste wine and view the winemaking process. There are plenty of commercial greenhouses and flower farms to visit all over Upcountry, but the best activity is a free Sunday drive along the mountain roads and farm lanes, just soaking in the scenery. The purple mists of mountain jacaranda and the heady fragrance of eucalyptus encircling a mountain pasture manicured by herds of cattle portray the soul of Upcountry.

UPCOUNTRY

To Kahului

36

Paia

HANA HWY.

Haiku

HANA HWY.

360

390

UNION CHURCH

398

365

Ulumalu

HOLY ROSARY CHURCH

RAINBOW COUNTY PARK

BALDWIN AVE.

To Hana Hwy.

37

Pu'unene

HALEAKALA HWY.

Hali'imaile

Kokomo

HUI NO'EAU

KEAHUA RD.

Makawao

RODEO

365

POLO FIELD

OLINDA RD.

Pukalani

37

PUKALANI COUNTRY CLUB

OMAOPIO RD.

LOWER KULA RD.

To Kahului

PULEHU RD.

377

KIMO RD.

UPCOUNTRY PROTEA FARM

HALEAKALA HWY.

Kihei

Pulehu

KULA LODGE

SUNRISE PROTEA FARM

HOSMER GROVE CAMPGROUND

HOLY GHOST CHURCH

HALEAKALA CRATER RD.

378

UNIV. OF HA. AGR. STA.

Waiakoa

KEKAULIKE AVE.

NATIONAL PARK HEADQUARTERS

LELEWILI OVERLOOK

RICE PARK

Kula

Ka'akaulua Gulch

KULA BOTANICAL GARDENS

WAIPOLI RD.

HALEAKALA CRATER

Waiohuli Gulch

Kaipotoi Gulch

WAIAKOA LOOP TRAIL

VISITOR CENTER

Waiohuli

Pu'u Ula Ula (Red Hill) (10,023 ft.)

Keokea

UPPER WAIAKOA TRAIL

KULA HWY.

THOMPSON RD.

SKYLINE TRAIL

0   2 mi

Waimea

POLIPOLI SPRINGS STATE RECREATION AREA

KAHUA RD.

0   2 km

31

Pu'u Keokea

Makena

Polipoli (6,472 ft.)

Pu'u Makua (5,276 ft.)

MAKEE SUGAR MILL (1878)

Ulupalakua Ranch

TEDESCHI WINERY

Pu'u Mahoe (2,660 ft.)

31

PIILANI HWY.

Kahikinui Ranch

Manawainui

To Hana

MOON

© J.D. BISIGNANI AND MOON PUBLICATIONS, INC.

PUKALANI

This way station town, at the intersection of routes 37 and 365, is a good place to get gas and supplies for a walking or driving trek through Kula. It's a rapidly growing community with many new housing developments around its periphery. There are no outstanding cultural or historical sights in Pukalani, but a fine golf course graces its southern edge.

There's a shopping mall and several minimalls where you can pick up just about anything. **Bullock's** restaurant, just past the T intersection with Makawao Ave., serves a wide assortment of good-value sandwiches. The Moonburger is a tradition, but a full breakfast here for under $6 will give you all the energy you'll need for the day ahead. Bullock's also has plate lunches and some tropical fruit-flavored shakes.

Also at this intersection is the **Pukalani Superette**, a well-stocked grocery store, especially for this neck of the woods, and next door is a tiny **post office** that can take care of basic mailing needs. Here, too, you'll find two **gas stations** and the famous golden arches heralding a **McDonald's.**

The **Upcountry Cafe**, in the pink and gray building on Aewa Place, tel. (808) 572-0055, open daily except Tuesday 6:30 a.m.-3 p.m., Sunday until 1 p.m., and again for dinner Wednesday and Thursday 5:30-8:30 p.m., Friday and Saturday until 9 p.m., has brought upscale yet unpretentious dining to Upcountry. Inside, wooden tables, bent-back chairs, a tiled counter, and a black-on-white Holstein motif set the ambiance in this American/island standard restaurant. The breakfast menu has a cholesterol bomb for $5.95, a Belgian waffle for $4.50, or a vegetarian frittata for $4.75. Lunch brings a traditional Reuben for $4.95, or a Crab Supreme on Boboli bread for $7.50. You can also order entrees like sautéed mahimahi for $5.95, or vegetarian lasagna for $6.25. The Upcountry Cafe is a perfect breakfast or lunch stop while touring Kula. Behind the cafe is **Frenchy's Bakery**, tel. (808) 572-9778, open Mon.-Sat. 6:30 a.m.-6 p.m., where everything is baked fresh daily. Here you can choose from mouthwatering breads and a variety of pastries and cakes, plus soups, salads, and sandwiches.

In the Pukalani Terrace Center are an **Ace Hardware, Upcountry Laundry and Dry Cleaning, Foodland** grocery store, and both a **Bank of Hawaii** and **American Savings Bank,** both of which have teller machines. There is a wide variety of economical eateries here, including a **Subway** sandwich shop, **Royal King's Garden** Chinese restaurant (no MSG), **Mama Son's Barbecue** Korean restaurant, and **Ono Loco Food** mixed-plate shop. Across the street from this shopping center is a large community park with ball fields, basketball courts, and a great swimming center.

One of the best restaurants in the area is the **Pukalani Country Club Restaurant,** open daily 7:30 a.m.-2 p.m. and 5-9 p.m., tel. (808) 572-1325, at the Pukalani Country Club. It has a salad bar and sandwiches, but specializes in "local" and Hawaiian foods such as kalua pig and lau lau at reasonable prices. Most patrons are local people, so you know that they're doing something right. The only Upcountry golf course on Maui, **Pukalani Country Club,** offers 18 holes of inexpensive golf. In the bargain come spectacular views over the isthmus and up toward Haleakala. Turn south at the Pukalani Terrace Center and follow the road for four or five blocks to reach the golf course.

On Makawao Ave., going toward Makawao, is a second smaller shopping center, **Pukalani Square.** Here you'll find several medical offices, plus a pharmacy, **The Grill** eatery, and **Upcountry Cycles** for two-wheel transportation.

MAKAWAO

Makawao is proud of itself; it's not *like* a cowboy town, it *is* a cowboy town. Depending on the translation that you consult, Makawao means "Eye of the Dawn" or "Forest Beginning." Both are appropriate. Surrounding lowland fields of cane and pineapples give way to upland pastures rimmed with tall forests, as Haleakala's morning sun shoots lasers of light through the town. Makawao was settled late last century by Portuguese immigrants who started raising cattle on the upland slopes. It loped along as a *paniolo* town until WW II, when it received an infusion of life from a nearby military base in Kokomo. After the war it settled back down and became a sleepy village again, where as many horses were tethered on the main street as cars were parked. The majority of its false-front, one-story buildings are a half-century old, but their prototype is strictly "Dodge City, 1850." During the 1950s and '60s, Makawao started to decline into a bunch of worn-out old buildings. It earned a reputation for drinking, fighting, and cavorting cowboys, and for a period was derisively called "Macho-wao."

In the 1970s it began to revive. It had plenty to be proud of and a good history to fall back on. Makawao is *the* last real *paniolo* town on Maui and, with Kamuela on the Big Island, is one of the last two in the entire state. At the Oskie Rice Arena, it hosts the largest and most successful rodeo in Hawaii. Its Fourth of July parade is a marvel of homespun humor, *aloha,* and an old-fashioned good time. Many people ride their horses to town, leaving them to graze in a public corral. They do business at stores operated by the same families for 50 years. Though much of the dry goods are country-oriented, a new breed of merchant has come to town. You can buy a sack of feed, a rifle, designer jeans, and an imported silk blouse all on one street. At its eateries you can have lobster, vegetarian or Mexican food, or a steamy bowl of saimin, reputed to be the best on Maui. Artists of all mediums have found Makawao and the surrounding area fertile ground for their work, and the town has become a hotbed of alternative healing practitioners. Look on any bulletin board in town and you'll see a dozen fliers advertising formulas for better life, better health,

reawakening of the spirit, Oriental health therapies, and new-age, new-health concepts.

Everyone, old-timers and newcomers alike, agrees that Makawao must be preserved, and they work together. They know that tourism is a financial lifeline, but shudder at the thought of Makawao becoming an Upcountry Lahaina. It shouldn't. It's far enough off the track to keep the average tourist away, but easy enough to reach and definitely interesting enough to make the side trip absolutely worthwhile.

The main artery to Makawao is through Paia as you travel Route 36 (Hana Hwy.). In Paia turn right onto Baldwin Avenue. From there it's about six miles to Makawao. You can also branch off Route 37 (Haleakala Hwy.) in Pukalani, onto Route 365 (some maps show it as Rt. 40), which will lead you to the town.

SIGHTS

En route on Baldwin Avenue, Route 390, you pass the Paia **sugar mill,** a real-life Carl Sandburg poem. A smaller sister mill to that at Puunene, it's a green monster trimmed in bare lightbulbs at night, dripping with sounds of turning gears, cranes, and linkbelts, all surrounded by packed, rutted, oil-stained soil. Farther along Baldwin Avenue sits **Holy Rosary Church** and its sculpture of Father Damien. The rendering of Damien is idealized, but the leper, who resembles a Calcutta beggar, has a face that conveys helplessness while at the same time faith and hope. It's worth a few minutes' stop. Coming next is **Makawao Union Church,** and it's a beauty. Like a Tudor mansion made completely of stone with lovely stained-glass windows, the entrance is framed by two tall and stately royal palms. Farther up is **Rainbow County Park,** one of the few non-coastal parks on Maui.

At mile marker 5 along Baldwin Avenue, Haliimaile Road turns to the south and leads to the small pineapple town of **Haliimaile.** This tiny community, a combination of old plantation town and new development, offers a wonderful restaurant, the Haliimaile General Store—well worth driving the distance for—and a well-shaded

ROBERT NILSEN

sculpture of Father Damien at Holy Rosary Church

county park that features picnic tables, ball fields, and lighted tennis courts.

Farther up Baldwin Avenue is the **Hui No'eau** ("Club of Skills") Visual Arts Center, a local organization that features traditional and modern arts housed at Kaluanui, a mansion built in 1917 by the Baldwin family on their 10-acre estate. The member artisans and craftspeople produce everything from ceramics to *lau hala* weaving. The old house is home to the center office, gift gallery, and periodic shows, while the former stable and carriage house have become studios. Throughout the year classes, lectures, and exhibits are offered, along with an annual Christmas Fair featuring their creations. One of the best features of visiting Hui No'eau is the resplendent mansion itself. Built in a neo-Spanish motif with red-tiled roof and light pink stucco exterior, Kaluanui sits amongst the manicured grounds that feature a reflection pond just in front of the portico. At 2841 Baldwin Ave., the gift shop and gallery are open Mon.-Sat. 10 a.m.-4 p.m., and

you'll often find someone around working in the studios. For information, contact the center at (808) 572-6560, Web site: www.maui.net/~hui, e-mail: hui@maui.net.

The back way reaches Makawao by branching off Route 36 through Ulumalu and Kokomo. Just where Route 36 turns into Route 360, there's a road to the right. This is Kaupakalua Road, or Route 365. Take it through backcountry Maui, where horses graze around neat little houses, Haleakala looms on the horizon; guavas, mangos, and bananas grow wild. At the first Y intersection, bear left to Kaupakalua. Pass a large junkyard and continue to Kokomo. There's a general store here. Notice the mixture of old and new houses—Maui's past and future in microcosm. Here, the neat little banana plantation on the outskirts of the diminutive town says it all. Pass St. Joseph's Church and you've arrived through Makawao's back door. This is an excellent off-track route to take on your way to or from Hana. You can also come up Kokomo Road, Route 398, skirting Haiku, or come over Route 365 through Pukalani, incorporating Makawao into your Haleakala trip.

Nearby Attractions

Take Olinda Road out of town. All along it custom-designed houses have been built. **Seabury Hall**, a private boarding school for grades 6-12, sits amongst trees above Makawao. In May, it hosts an arts and crafts fair, with entertainment, food, and games. Look for **Pookela Church,** a coral-block structure built in 1843. In four miles you pass **Rainbow Acres,** tel. (808) 572-8020. Open Friday and Saturday 10 a.m.-4 p.m., it specializes in cactus and succulents. At the top of Olinda turn left onto Piiholo Road, which loops back down. Along it is **Aloha O Ka Aina,** tel. (808) 572-9440, a nursery specializing in ferns. Open Wednesday and Sunday 10 a.m.-4 p.m.

PRACTICALITIES

Accommodations

Olinda Country Cottages and Inn, tel. (808) 572-1453 or (800) 932-3435, Web site: www.mauibn-bcottages.com, e-mail: olinda@mauibnbcottages .com, is up above Makawao past mile marker 11, at 536 Olinda Road. Located on a protea farm and surrounded by the Haleakala Ranch, this B&B is spacious and comfy. The main house has rooms and there are three separate cottages down below. The two bedrooms in the house have a private entrance and share a sitting room, and each has a private bath. Guests can also use the living room on the first floor, which is filled with antiques and collectibles. Breakfast is provided each morning. The individual cottages are more like small homes, with all the amenities. As each has a kitchen, breakfast is served only the first morning. The County Cottage and Hidden Cottage are older; the Pineapple Sweet Cottage is new. The bedrooms run $95 a night, the cottages $110-140. The rooms have a two-night minimum, the cottages three. Highly recommended for quiet and seclusion yet close enough to get to a fine restaurant in town. Gregarious hosts, good value. The only drawback for some folks might be the windy road leading up to the B&B.

Built in 1924, the plantation house **Hale Ho'okipa Inn,** 32 Pakani Place, tel. (808) 572-6698, fax 573-2580, Web site: www.maui.net /~mauibnb, e-mail: mauibnb@maui.net, has recently been turned into a lovely B&B. Not a modern rendition, this well-loved place has real world, lived-in charm, and is filled with comfortable period-style and antique furniture and furnishings, and artwork by Hawaiian artists. Three rooms have their own private baths, while the two-bedroom suite shares a bath and has use of the big country kitchen. A continental breakfast is served each morning for guests in the rooms. Rates run $60-80 a night for the rooms and $135 for the suite. The inn is within walking distance from town, up above the Eddie Tam Center.

Food

All the following establishments are on Makawao or Baldwin Avenue. An excellent place to eat is **Polli's Mexican Restaurant,** tel. (808) 572-7808, open daily 7 a.m.-10 p.m. The sign, "come in and eat or we'll both starve," greets you at the front. The meals are authentic Mexican, using the finest ingredients. Formerly vegetarian—they still will prepare any menu item in a vegetarian manner— they still use no lard or animal fat in their bean dishes. You can have breakfast entrees for $6-8, a full lunch for $8-10, or dinner for $12-16. Margaritas are large and tasty for $4, and the champagne Sunday brunch is particularly good. Monday night is barbecue night, Tuesday is kid's

night. Still down home, still wholesome meals, still a happening place.

A surprising and delicious dining experience is found at **Casanova Italian Restaurant and Deli,** tel. (808) 572-0220, located across from Polli's at the main intersection of town. The deli is open daily for breakfast, lunch, and dinner. The interior is utilitarian—a refrigerated case loaded with cold cuts, shelves stocked with Italian delectables and designer chocolates, and a counter for eating. Specials are offered nightly, but the best dishes are the fresh-made lasagna, ravioli, and spaghetti, all smothered in different sauces. Many of the best restaurants on Maui order their pasta from Casanova's. Order at the counter. The best place to sit is on the front porch where you can perch above the street and watch Makawao life go by. Upcountry-yuppie-elegant, Casanova's restaurant occupies the adjoining section of the building, open daily except Sunday, for lunch 11:30 a.m.-2 p.m., and for dinner 5:30-11 p.m., featuring pizza, pasta, and other fine Italian cuisine. Of course, pasta is the staple, but meat, fish, and poultry entrees are also popular. Expect entrees in the $15-25 range. While the food is as good as the deli fare next door, many come for the music and dancing. Having a nightclub atmosphere, and featuring live bands on the weekends, a large dance floor, and a first-class sound system, it draws people not only from Upcountry but also from Central and West Maui. Casual attire is fine, but remember, Upcountry gets cool at night, so long pants would be in order.

Makawao Steak House, tel. (808) 572-8711, is open daily for dinner from 5 p.m., with early bird specials until 6:30, Sunday brunch 9:30 a.m.-2 p.m. Casual, with wooden tables, salad bar, and good fish selections, dinners run upward to around $25. The steak dishes, especially the prime rib, are the best. The lunch menu is more limited. The Makawao Steak House has been around a long time and maintains a good, solid reputation, although it has recently changed hands. The lounge is open from 5 p.m. until closing.

Kitada's, tel. (808) 572-7241, makes the best saimin on Maui, according to all the locals. It's across from the Makawao Steak House; open Mon.-Sat. 6 a.m.-1:30 p.m. Walk in, pour yourself a glass of water, and take a hardboard-topped table. The saimin is delicious and inexpensive. There are plate lunches, too. The walls have paintings of Upcountry by local artists; most show more heart than talent. Bus your own table while the owner, Kitada-*san,* calculates your bill on an abacus. His birthday, May 26, has become a town event.

Komoda's is a corner general store that has been in business for over 50 years. It sells everything, but the bakery is renowned far and wide. It's open 7 a.m.-5 p.m. except Wednesday and Sunday, and until 2 on Saturday. People line up outside to buy their cream buns and homemade cookies—all gone by 9 a.m.

If you want a break from sightseeing in Makawao, come to **Abbey's Place** in the Court yard of Makawao, open Mon.-Fri. 7 a.m.-5 p.m., until 3 on Saturday. People come just for the coffee, but you can also get an egg or waffle breakfast, or hot or cold sandwich. Hot meals, including sandwiches and grilled fish and chicken, are available only until 2 p.m.

The **Haliimaile General Store Restaurant,** tel. (808) 572-2666, open Mon.-Fri. 11 a.m.-2:30 p.m., and again 5:30-9:30 p.m., with a Sunday brunch 10 a.m.-2:30 p.m., serves elegant gourmet food to anyone lucky enough to find this Upcountry roadhouse. Located in Haliimaile village along Haliimaile Rd. between Baldwin Ave. and the Haleakala Highway, the restaurant is housed in what was this pineapple town's general store. Climb the steps to a wide veranda and enter to find the vintage utilitarian wood floored interior transformed into an airy room with tropical fish hung from the ceiling, primitive ceramics and sculptures placed here and there, and paintings of brilliant colors. Choose a table in the casual front room; perch on a canvas chair at the classic wooden bar in front of the open kitchen; or ask for a table in the back room, more formal with dark wood paneling, ceiling fans, track lighting, and floral displays. Master chef Beverly Gannon presents magnificent "Hawaiian regional cuisine with an American and international twist," while her Irish husband, master schmoozer Joe Gannon, presents an equally magnificent Blarney Stone atmosphere! The lunch menu starts with soup of the day for $3.50. Salads are the famous house salad for $5, a Caesar at $7, and a Nicoise salad, which is the catch of the day grilled and served with olives, tomatoes, mixed greens, and cucumbers, for $12. Sandwiches, priced under $10, are special and include the grilled catch of the day

as well as the Haliimaile BOLT (bacon, Maui onion, lettuce, and tomato), and entrees may be ravioli or baby back ribs, all under $14. Dinner at Haliimaile opens with appetizers like the sashimi Napoleon for $14, or an Asian pear and duck taco for $9. Entrees include *paniolo* ribs for $17, coconut seafood curry for $23, or aged Midwest beef rib eye for $24. The restaurant is also part contemporary boutique and art gallery, with the walls hung with original works and the old grocery shelves filled with distinctive gift items like porcelain plates, dishes, and teapots. The dining is fine but the setting is casual. Alohawear is okay, but because of the elevation long sleeves and pants might be in order. The Haliimaile General Store has been reborn, and its spirit lives on in this great restaurant.

Food Markets and Liquor

Down to Earth Natural Foods, 1169 Makawao Ave., tel. (808) 572-1488, open daily 8 a.m.-8 p.m., is a first-rate health food store that originated in Wailuku and later opened a branch here in Makawao. Inside you'll find shelves packed with minerals, vitamins, herbs, spices, and mostly organic fruits and vegetables. Bins hold bulk grains, pastas, honey, and nut butters, while a deli case holds sandwiches and drinks. You can even mix up a salad from the salad bar to take out. Down to Earth has a philosophy by which it operates, "to promote the living of a healthy lifestyle by eating a natural vegetarian diet; respect for all forms of life; and concern for the environment."

Nature's Nectar, 3647 Baldwin Ave., tel. (808) 572-9122, open 10 a.m.-4 p.m. daily, is a juice bar that specializes in herbs and natural elixirs. Inside are tinctures, bulk herbs, supplements, and plenty of literature on alternative health. Sterling jewelry, amber, red coral, and crystals are also for sale. From the juice bar order carrot juice, wheatgrass juice, organic salads, or homemade vegetarian soup with whole grain bread. Having expanded, you can now also get simple entrees like vegan lasagna or a nut rice burger for about $6, or choose something from the deli case. Here you can find something for your mind, body, and spirit.

Liquor Shack and Deli, 1143 Makawao Ave., tel. (808) 572-7775, can provide all the fixings for a lunch, or a full range of liquid refreshments.

Rodeo General Store, 3661 Baldwin Ave., is a one-stop shop with a wide selection of natural foods, pastries, produce, fresh fish, wines, spirits, and cigars. Open 6:30 a.m.-10 p.m. daily.

Shopping
Makawao is changing quickly, and nowhere is this more noticeable than in its local shops. The population is now made up of old-guard *paniolo*, yuppies, and alternative people. What a combo! You can buy a bullwhip, a Gucci purse, a cold Bud, or sushi all within 100 feet of each other. Some unique and fascinating shops here can provide you with distinctive purchases.

When Mimi Merrill opened **Miracles Bookery**, at 3682 Baldwin Ave., tel. (808) 572-2317, hours Mon.-Sat. 9 a.m.-9 p.m., Sunday 9 a.m.-8 p.m., she put her heart, soul, and all of her resources into the place, running out of funds before she could finish the floor. Her friends, building off the "miracles do happen" theme of the store, got together and painted it. Every evening for a week they came, and with regular house paint created a mosaic of stones, bricks, and flowers, fashioning what the local people call "the stained-glass floor." Miracles Bookery specializes in books on new-age spirituality, astrology, Tarot, children's classics, Hawaiiana, general novels and poetry, "pre-loved" books, and even travel guidebooks! A different astrologer, palmist, or Tarot reader is "in residence" every day, and on the third Saturday of every month there's an open house with $5 readings all day long. Miracles also has unique gift items: angels and more angels, petroglyph reproductions, Native American jewelry, bumper stickers with an attitude, T-shirts with a message, posters, and music of all kinds from spiritual to rock.

The Courtyard of Makawao is a consortium of shops at 3620 Baldwin Ave. where you can dine, buy fine art, or watch as glassblowers pursue alchemical art. In the reconstructed Makawao Theater building, **Maui Hands**, tel. (808) 572-5194, is open daily except Sunday 10 a.m.-6 p.m., specializing in Maui-made art and crafts like semiprecious stone necklaces, sterling and gold jewelry, prints, bamboo work, raku pottery, primitive basketry, and even some T-shirts. **Viewpoints Gallery**, tel. (808) 572-5979, open daily 10 a.m.-6 p.m., is an artists' cooperative specializing in locally created paintings, sculptures, handicrafts, and jewelry. Some of the art displayed includes: oil paintings by Kathleen MacDonald;

impressionistic oils by George Allen; the mixed-media art of Joelle Chichebortiche; and the combination pastel and oils by Diana Dorenzo. Most of the artists live in the area, and with enough notice will come to meet you if time permits. The shop is perfectly suited as a gallery with track lighting and movable partitions, so even the room itself is quite artistic with a feeling of brightness. It is a perfect place to spend an afternoon perusing the contemporary art scene so vibrant in Upcountry. Outside is a pleasant courtyard, around which are several more shops. Here you will find Bill and Sally Worcester making magic at **Hot Island Glass**, open daily 10 a.m.-5 p.m., tel. (808) 572-4527. These very talented glassblowers, assisted by their son Michael, turn molten glass into everything from simple paperweights to gorgeous vases. Just line up at their window and watch the artists work. Between the three of them they have won almost every meaningful art award on Maui and in their former Oregon home. This includes the Art Maui Award that they have brought home every year since 1985. Incidental pieces run as cheap as $10, but the masterpieces go for several thousand. Don't worry about shipping or packing glass; they're also masters at packing so things don't break on the way home.

Upcountry Legends, tel. (808) 572-3523, open daily 10 a.m.-6 p.m., Sunday 11 a.m.-5 p.m., sells handpainted silk shirts, ladies apparel, sterling silver jewelry, huggable teddy bears and other stuffed animals, greeting cards, candles, and baskets.

Collections Boutique, tel. (808) 572-0781, open daily till 6 p.m., Saturday until 4, imports items from throughout Asia: batik from Bali, clothes from India, silk Hawaiian shirts, jewelry, lotions, cosmetics, accessories, sunglasses, and handicrafts from various countries. Operated by Pam Winans.

Hi Hearth and Leisure, tel. (808) 572-4569, has the largest line of wood-burning and gas stoves in Hawaii. That's right, stoves! Nights in the high country can get chilly, and on top of Haleakala downright cold. Also here are fireplaces, chimneys, and accessories, a good selection of cutlery, and a few residuals left over from when it was a great hardware and tack store.

For fine art, check out **David Warren's Studio**, tel. (808) 572-1864, across from the Courtyard. David is one of the featured artists at the prestigious Maui Crafts Guild in Paia, but he chose Upcountry for his studio. His medium is oil, his canvas might be just that or another material like a pottery vase. Farther up Baldwin Ave. is the **S. Reeve Gallery**. Along Makawao Ave. are **Gallery Maui** and **Ola's Makawao**, for contemporary American art, and the newer **Élan Vital's** gallery of contemporary art and sculpture.

Another shop along Baldwin Avenue is **Gecko Trading Co.**, tel. (808) 572-0249, open daily 10 a.m. 5:00 p.m., Sunday 11 a.m.-4 p.m., bright with fashions for men, women, and children; Gecko also sells sterling silver and amber jewelry, handbags, teddy bears, straw hats, old bottles, and imported clothing from Asia and around the world. Listen for tinkling wind chimes to locate **Goodies**, tel. (808) 572-0288, open daily 9.30 a.m.-5:30 p.m., Sunday 10 a.m.-5 p.m., a boutique that looks like a spilled treasure chest. Crystals, silk and cotton casual and elegant clothing, dolls, children's wear, stuffed animals, locally crafted trays, and magic wands fill this shop.

About the only shop in town for men's clothing is **Tropo**, tel. (808) 573-0356, where you can find shorts, polo shirts, aloha shirts, and even hats and ties. Owner Avi Kiriaty helps to design the clothing on sale here. Open Mon.-Sat. 10 a.m.-6 p.m., Sunday 11 a.m.-4 p.m.

Down a narrow alley a few steps from the intersection of Baldwin and Makawao Avenues is **The Dragon's Den Healing Center**, tel. (808) 572-2731, a shop stuffed full of Chinese herbs and medicines, minerals, crystals, teas, gifts, and books on Eastern healing arts. Also in the alley are two new features to the ever-changing face of this Upcountry community: **Healing Hui** health and resource center, tel. (808) 572-6091 for therapeutic massage and colonic therapy, and **Grace Health Clinic**, tel. (808) 572-6091, which specializes in chiropractic, massage, traditional Oriental medicine.

Events

Makawao has a tremendous rodeo season every year. Most meets are sponsored by the Maui Roping Club. They start in the spring and culminate in a massive rodeo on or around July 4th, with substantial prize money. These events attract the best cowboys from around the state. Both males and females try their luck in separate groupings. The numerous competitions include barrel racing, breakaway roping, team roping, and calf roping. The organization of the event is headed by long-time resident Brendan Balthazar, who welcomes everyone to participate with only one rule, "Have fun, but maintain safety."

KULA

Kula could easily provide all of the ingredients for a full-course meal fit for a king. Its bounty is staggering: vegetables to make a splendid chef's salad, beef for the entree, flowers to brighten the spirits, and wine to set the mood. Up here, soil, sun, and moisture create a garden symphony. Sweet Maui onions, cabbages, potatoes, grapes, apples, pineapples, lettuce, and artichokes grow with abandon. Herefords and Black Angus graze in knee-deep fields of sweet green grass. Flowers are everywhere: beds of proteas, camellias, carnations, roses, hydrangeas, and blooming peach and tangerine trees dot the countryside like daubs from van Gogh's brush. As you gain the heights along Kula's lanes, you look back on West Maui and a perfect view of the isthmus. You'll also enjoy wide-open spaces and rolling green hills fringed with trees like a lion's mane. Above, the sky changes from brooding gray to blazing blue, then

back again. During light rainy afternoons, when the sun streams in from the west, you could easily spot a rainbow form on the hillside, as if sprouting from the rich green pastureland. Kula is a different Maui—quiet and serene.

Getting There

The fastest way is the same route to Haleakala Crater. Take Route 37 through Pukalani, turn onto Route 377, and when you see Kimo Road on your left and right, you're in Kula country. If you have the time, take the following scenic route. Back in Kahului start on Route 36 (Hana Hwy.), but as soon as you cross Dairy Road look for a sign pointing to Pulehu-Omaopio Road on your right. Take it! You'll wade through acres of sugarcane, and in six miles these two roads will split. You can take either, but Omaopio to the left is better because, at the top, it deposits you in the middle of things to see. Once the roads fork, you'll pass some excellent examples of flower and truck farms. You'll also go by the cooperative **Vacuum Cooling Plant** where many farmers store their produce. Then Omaopio Road comes again to Route 37 (Kula Hwy.). Don't take it yet. Cross and continue until Omaopio dead-ends, in a few hundred yards. Turn right onto Lower Kula Road and watch for Kimo (Lower) Drive on your left, and take it straight uphill. This brings you through some absolutely beautiful countryside and in a few miles crosses Route 377, where a right will take you to Haleakala Crater Road.

SIGHTS

Curtis Wilson Cost Gallery

In the basement of the Kula Lodge is the Curtis Wilson Cost Gallery, tel. (808) 878-6544 or (800) 508-2278, Web site: www.costgallery.com. One of Maui's premier artists, Cost captures scenes reflecting the essence of Upcountry Maui; handles color, light, and shadow to perfection; and portrays the true pastoral nature of the area. This is traditional realism with a touch of imagination. Stop in and browse daily 8:30 a.m.-4:30 p.m.

Upcountry Harvest

This little flower shop sits next door to the Kula Lodge and is open daily 8 a.m.-5:30 p.m., tel. (808) 878-2824 or (800) 575-6470. Don't miss seeing the amazing fresh and dried flowers and arrangements. Here you can purchase a wide range of protea and other tropical flowers that can be shipped back home. Live or dried, these flowers are fantastic. Gift boxes starting at $38 are well worth the price. The salespeople are friendly and informative, and it's educational just to visit.

Upper Kimo Road

If you want to be intoxicated by some of the finest examples of Upcountry flower and vegetable farms, come up here. First, head back down Route 377 past the Kula Lodge and turn on Upper Kimo Road on your right. One mile up, at the very end, is **Cloud's Rest Protea Farm,** open daily 8 a.m.-4:30 p.m.; for phone orders call (800) 332-8233. The farm has over 50 varieties of protea and other flowers. You can walk the grounds or visit the gift shop, where they offer gift packs and mail orders. Although harvested year-round since something is always blooming, the ultimate time for viewing and sending protea as gifts is from September through January.

Sunrise Protea Farm

This farm and gift shop is less than half a mile up Haleakala Crater Road. The shop sells gift items, local Maui produce, homemade sweets, sandwiches, and fruit juices. In the flower shop you'll find fresh and dried flowers and arrangements that can be sent anywhere in the country; fresh bouquets from $40, dried arrangements from $30. An easy stop on the way back from Haleakala Crater.

protea

ROBERT NILSEN

Open weekdays 8 a.m.-4 p.m., weekends 7 a.m.-5 p.m., tel. (808) 876-0200 or (800) 222-2797 for phone orders.

Kula Botanical Gardens

Follow Route 377 south (it turns into Kekaulike Ave.) and look for the gardens on your left just before the road meets again with Route 37. These privately owned gardens, tel. (808) 878-1715, are open daily 9 a.m.-4 p.m.; be sure to start by 3 p.m. to give yourself enough time for a thorough walk-around. Admission is $4, children 6-12 are $1. Here are nearly six acres of identified tropical and semitropical plants on a self-guided tour. There is a stream that runs through the property, a koi pond, and small aviary. Some of the 2,000 different varieties of plants include protea, orchid, fuchsia, native koa, *kukui,* and sandalwood, as well ferns and many introduced species. First opened to the public in 1971, the gardens are educational and will give names to many flowers and plants that you've observed around the island. It makes for a relaxing afternoon, with picnic tables provided. Enter through the gift shop.

Enchanting Floral Gardens

Located across from mile marker 10 on the Kula Highway, this privately owned flower garden is newer and more commercial than Kula Botanical Garden, yet worthy of a look. Its eight acres are neatly laid out, with many of the 1,500 varieties of flowers and plants identified. Stroll down the path and be captivated by the abundance. Plan on about a hour to see the entire lot. Open 9 a.m.-5 p.m., entrance $4; tel. (808) 878-2531.

Polipoli Spring State Recreation Area

If you want quietude and mountain walks, come here, because few others do. Just past the Kula Botanical Gardens look for the park sign on your left leading up Waipoli Road. This 10-mile stretch is only partially paved; the first half zigzags steeply up the hill, and the second half, although fairly flat, is dirt and can be very rutted, rocky, or muddy. Hang gliders use this area, jumping off farther up and landing on the open grassy fields along the lower portion of this road. Hunting is also done in the forests here, and a number of trails lead off this road to prescribed hunting areas. As always, the trip to the end is worth it. Polipoli is an established forest of imported trees from around the world:

eucalyptus, redwoods, cypress, ash, cedar, and *sugi* pines. Much of the area was planted in the '20s by the state and in the '30s by the CCC. These trees do well here as the park lies right in that band where moisture laden clouds seem to hang around the mountain. There is a great network of trails in the immediate area, and even one that leads up to the top of the mountain. One of the most popular is the **Redwood Trail,** which you can take to a shelter at the end. These trails are for hiking and mountain biking only—no motorcycles or horses. At 6,200 feet, the camping area can be brisk at night. Camping is free but permits are required and are available from the Division of State Parks, 54 S. High St., Wailuku, HI 96793, tel. (808) 984-8109. Water, picnic tables, and outhouses are provided at the camping spot, which is a small grassy area surrounded by tall eucalyptus trees. The cabin here is a spacious three-bedroom affair with bunks for up to 10 people. It starts at $45 a night for one to four people and goes up $5 per additional person. It's rustic, but all camping and cooking essentials are provided, including a wood-burning stove. If you want to get away from it all, this is your spot.

Others

The University of Hawaii maintains an agriculture experimental station of 20 acres of flowers and other tropical and agricultural plants that change with the seasons. Located on Mauna Place above Route 37, open Mon.-Thurs. 7:30 a.m.-3:30 p.m. Check in with the station manager at the office, which is closed during the lunch hour. A self-guided tour map may be available there.

The nursery and flower shop **Proteas of Hawaii,** tel. (808) 878-2533 or (800) 367-7768, Web site: www.hawaii-exotics.com, is located across the road; hours are 8 a.m.-4:30 p.m. Fresh protea baskets, tropical bouquets, and individual flowers can be purchased and shipped anywhere. Prices start at about $20.

Holy Ghost Church, on Lower Kula Road in Waiakoa, is an octagonal building raised in 1897 by the many Portuguese who worked the farms and ranches of Upcountry. Recently restored, it has many fine statues and an elaborate altar that was sent by the king and queen of Portugal when the church was built.There's a gas station here, as well as **Morihara Store,** spacious but spartan; **Cafe 808,** which serves down-home local food with nothing on the menu over $8.95; the **Hawaii Institute of Astronomy;** and a post office.

Near the intersection of Highways 37 and 377 is **Rice Park,** a grassy wayside rest area that has a few picnic tables, bathrooms, and a public phone. From here, you get a good view over the lower mountain slope and the coast at Kihei and Wailea.

CONTINUING SOUTH

Keokea

Continue south on Route 37 through the town of Keokea, where you'll find gas, Henry Fong's and Ching's general stores, and an excellent park for a picnic. At the far end of the village are two new establishments. **Keokea Gallery** displays works by Maui artists, and next door is **Grandma's Maui Coffee.** Grandma's is open every day, 7:30 a.m.-5 p.m. You can enjoy fresh pastries for breakfast until 10 a.m., and sandwiches, saimin, and pies for lunch. The real treat, however, is the coffee, grown on the slope below and roasted in an old-fashioned coffee machine in the shop. Stop in for a sip or take a package to go. At the end of Thompson Road south of town are Thompson Ranch Riding Stables and Silvercloud guest ranch.

Tedeschi Winery

Past Keokea you'll know you're in ranch country. The road narrows and herds of cattle graze in pastures that seem like manicured gardens highlighting *panini* (prickly pear) cactus. You'll pass Ulupalakua Ranch and then come to the Tedeschi Winery tasting room on the left, tel. (808) 878-6058. Open for tasting daily 9 a.m.-5 p.m., the winery sells bottles of all its wines and cushioned boxes for transporting it. Free, 15-minute tours of the winery are offered as well, every hour on the half hour 9:30 a.m.-2:30 p.m. Here, Emil Tedeschi and his partner Pardee Erdman, who also owns the 23,000-acre Ulupalakua Ranch, offer samples of their wines. This is one of two wineries in Hawaii. When Erdman moved here in 1963 from California and noticed climatic similarities to the Napa Valley, he knew that this country could grow decent wine grapes. Tedeschi comes from California, where his family has a small vineyard near Calistoga. The partners have worked on making their dream of Maui wine a reality since 1974.

It takes time and patience to grow grapes and turn out a vintage wine. While they waited for their carnelian grapes (a cabernet hybrid) to mature and be made into a sparkling wine, they fermented pineapple juice, which they call Maui Blanc. If you're expecting this to be a sickeningly sweet syrup, forget it. Maui Blanc is surprisingly dry and palatable. In 1984 the first scheduled release of the winery's carnelian champagne, Maui Brut, celebrated the patience and craftsmanship of the vintners. Maui Blush, a zinfandel-like light dinner wine, and Maui Nouveau, a young red wine, were then added to the list. Most recently, Plantation Red, a very dry, oaky, red wine; Maui Splash, a sweet dessert wine which is a combination of pineapple and passion fruit; the fruity Pineapple Sparkling Wine; the mellow Ulupalakua Red table wine; and the dry salmon-colored Rose Ranch Cuvee Champagne have made their debut. You can taste these wines at the white ranch house set amongst the tall proud trees just off the highway, once visited by King Kalakaua in 1874. From here, the tour takes you to the working winery buildings just a few steps away. Hugging the ground closer to the road is a 100-year-old plaster and coral building that used to be the winery's tasting room. Formerly, it served as the jailhouse of the old Rose Ranch owned by James Makee, a Maui pioneer sugarcane planter. Look for the 22-acre vineyard one mile before the tasting room on the ocean side of the highway. Tedeschi wines are available in restaurants and stores around the island.

Across the street are remains of the old **Makee Sugar Mill** and down the road, the Ulupalakua Ranch office and the ranch store and deli. Hanging around the store like old plantation workers after a hard day's work are several carved and painted lifelike figures, representing various groups of people who've contributed to Maui's past. Sit down and have a chat.

ACCOMMODATIONS AND FOOD

Kula Lodge

The Kula Lodge, RR 1, Box 475, Kula, HI 96790, tel. (808) 878-1535 or (800) 233-1535, fax (808) 878-2518, is on Route 377 just past Kimo Road and just before Haleakala Crater Road. Lodging here is in five detached chalets ranging $100-165; check-in is at the restaurant. Two have fireplaces with wood provided, four have lofts for extra guests, and all have lanai and excellent views of lower Maui. With their dark wood, carpets, and cathedral ceilings, they are almost contemporary in appearance. The Kula Lodge is a fine establishment with a wonderful location. Elevation 3,200 feet.

The lobby and dining area of the **Kula Lodge Restaurant,** tel. (808) 878-1535, are impressively rustic, with open beamwork and framing, dark wood, and stone. This building started as a private residence some 50 years ago. The walls are covered with high-quality photos of Maui: windsurfers, silverswords, sunsets, cowboys, and horses. The surprisingly large main dining room has a giant bay window with a superlative view. Breakfast is served daily 6:30-11:45 a.m., lunch 11:45 a.m.-4:45 p.m., dinner 4:45-9 p.m. The menus are surprisingly large. Try Hawaiian buttermilk griddle cakes or vegetarian Benedict for breakfast, or a sandwich or grilled chicken breast for lunch. Start dinner with wild mushroom risotto or Maui greens salad, and move on to a salmon filet, pepper steak, or pasta. The assortment of gourmet desserts includes a tasty mango pie, and one of these should round out your meal. There may be entertainment in the evenings. Before or after dinner, sit at the bar for a drink or warm yourself on the couches that front the stone fireplace. Perhaps the only drawback is the clamor created when riders on the Haleakala downhill bike trips arrive in a large group for breakfast. Be up early so as not to be disturbed.

The **Terrace Garden Restaurant** below at the garden level is only open for lunch, and everything is cooked in a wood-fired stove near the gazebos. While you wait for your meal, have a short stroll through the very lovely but diminutive flower gardens there.

Kula Sandalwoods Restaurant

This restaurant is just up the road from the Kula Lodge, set on the uphill side of the road, tel. (808) 878-3523. Breakfast, lunch, and a Sunday brunch are served. Here you can get breakfast for under $9 and lunch for about $12. Some bike groups stop here on their way down the mountain so you may have competition for service at certain times of the morning. The scenery from here isn't bad if you can ignore the power lines that drape across the view.

Kula Hula Inn

Located at 112 Ho'opalua Dr. in the lower Kula area not far out of Pukalani, this B&B has a room in the main house and two separate cottages. The room has its own bath, entrance, and lanai It rents for $85. For $100 you can get the three-room Suite Plumeria. The larger and more private two-bedroom Hula Moon Cottage with full bath and kitchen goes for $115. Breakfast is included for all except the cottage, where it's optional for an additional charge. A large lawn surrounds this property. For information, contact the inn at (808) 572-9351 or (888) 485-2466, Web site: www.maui.net/~kulahula, e-mail: kulahula@maui.net.

Silvercloud Upcountry Guest Ranch

A good place for groups, the Silvercloud, RR 2, Box 201, Kula, HI 96790, tel. (808) 878-6101 or (800) 532-1111, fax (808) 878-2132, Web site: www.maui.net/~slvrcld, e-mail: slvrcld@maui.net, has six rooms and five studios in two separate buildings and a cottage up behind. All are surrounded by pastureland and have unobstructed views down on the green lower slopes of the mountain. Rooms in the large well-appointed main house run $85-125. Everyone has access to the kitchen, living room, and dining room, and each bedroom has a private bath. The studios run $105 and $145, and come with a bath, kitchen, and private lanai. The cottage is the most private and is a fully furnished unit, $150. The guest ranch is located at the end of Thompson Road, just out of Keokea.

HALEAKALA NATIONAL PARK

Haleakala ("House of the Sun") is spellbinding. Like seeing Niagara Falls or the Grand Canyon for the first time, it makes no difference how many people have come before you; it's still an undiminished, powerful, personal experience. The mountain is a power spot, a natural conductor of cosmic energy. *Kahuna* brought their novitiates here to perform final rites of initiation. During their heyday, intense power struggles took place atop the mountain between the healing practitioners, the *kahuna lapa'au,* and their rivals the *kahuna ana'ana,* the "black magic" sorcerers of old Hawaii. **Kawilinau,** the "Bottomless Pit," a natural feature on the crater floor, was the site of an ancient battle between Pele and one of her siblings, and thus held tremendous significance for both schools of *kahuna.* Average Hawaiians did not live on Haleakala, but came now and again to quarry tool-stones. Only *kahuna* and their apprentices lived here for any length of time, as a sort of spiritual preparation and testing ground. Today, students of higher consciousness from around the world are attracted to this natural cosmic empire because of the rarefied energy. They claim that it accelerates personal growth, and compare it to remote mountain and desert areas in the Holy Lands. Even the U.S. Air Force has a facility here, and their research indicates Haleakala is *the* strongest natural power point in America. Not only is there an energy configuration coming from the earth itself, but there is also a high focus of radiation coming from outside the atmosphere. No one is guaranteed a spiritual experience on Haleakala, but if you're at all sensitive, this is fertile ground.

Natural Features

Haleakala is the world's largest dormant volcano, composed of amazingly dense volcanic rock, almost like poured cement. Counting the 20,000 feet or so of it lying under the sea makes it one of the tallest mountains on earth. Perhaps this mass accounts for the strange power of Haleakala as it sits like a mighty magnetic pyramid in the center of the North Pacific. The park's boundaries encompass 28,655 variable acres, which stretch from Hosmer Grove to Kipahulu and include dry forests, rainforests, desert, and subtropical beaches. The most impressive feature is the crater itself. It's 3,000 feet deep, 7.5 miles east to west, and 2.5 miles north to south, accounting for 19 square miles, with a circumference of 21 miles. A mini-mountain range of nine cinder cones marches across the crater floor. They look deceptively tiny from the observation area, but the smallest is 600 feet, and the tallest, Puu O Maui, is 1,000 feet high. Haleakala was designated as a national park in 1961. Before that it was part of the Big Island's Volcanoes National Park. The entire park is a nature preserve dedicated to Hawaii's quickly vanishing indigenous plants and animals, and it was recognized as an International Biosphere Reserve by the United Nations in 1980. Only Volcanoes and Haleakala are home to the **nene,** the Hawaiian wild goose, and the **silversword,** a fantastically adapted plant.

Weather

As high as it is, Haleakala helps to create its own weather. Sunshine warms air that rises up the mountainside. When this moisture-laden air pushes into a cooler strata, it creates a band of clouds that moisten the forest and create what is known as the cloud forest. Often, these clouds will push up into the crater itself, gushing up through the Koolau and Kaupo gaps, sometimes obscuring the crater from view. In the cool of the evening, these clouds retreat back down the mountainside, leaving the crater clear once again. As air temperature drops about three degrees for every 1,000 feet, the top may be over 30° cooler than the sunny beaches along the Kihei coast below. Haleakala also traps moisture from the trade winds, so the high mountain slopes above Hana get about 400 inches of rain a year, creating thick forest cover, while the slopes above Kihei, mostly dry and scrubby, get only a dozen inches yearly.

The Experience

If you're after *the* experience, you must see the sunrise or sunset. Both are magnificent, but both perform their stupendous light show with astonishing speed. Also, the weather must be cooperative. Misty, damp clouds can surround the crater, blocking out the sun, or pour into the basin, ob-

HALEAKALA NATIONAL PARK

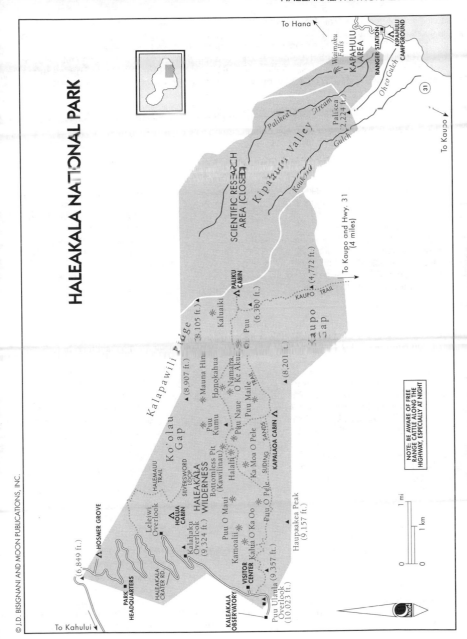

© J.D. BISIGNANI AND MOON PUBLICATIONS, INC.

To Kahului

PARK HEADQUARTERS ▲ (6,849 ft.)

▲ HOSMER GROVE

Leleiwi Overlook

HALEAKALA CRATER RD.

Kalahaku Overlook

▲ HOLUA CABIN

Silversword Loop

HALEMAUU TRAIL

HALEAKALA WILDERNESS

Kalahaku Overlook (9,324 ft.)

Bottomless Pit (Kawilinau)

Puu O Maui ✽

Kamoali ✽

Kaluta O Ka Oo ✽

VISITOR CENTER

KALEAKALA OBSERVATORY

Puu Ulaula Overlook (10,023 ft.)

Puu Ulaula (9,357 ft.)

Ko'olau Gap

✽ Puu Kumu

✽ Halalii

Puu O Pele ✽

Ka Moa O Pele ✽

SLIDING SANDS

KAPALAOA CABIN ▲

Haupaakea Peak (9,157 ft.)

Kalapawili Ridge

▲ (8,907 ft.)

✽ Mauna Him

Honokahua ✽

✽ Namana O Ke Akua

Pau Naue TRAIL

Puu Maile ✽

▲ (8,201 ft.)

Kaupo Gap

(8,105 ft.) ▶

Kaluaiki

▲ PALIKU CABIN

Ch. Puu (6,300 ft.) ✽

KAUPO TRAIL

▲ (4,772 ft.)

To Kaupo and Hwy. 31 (4 miles)

SCIENTIFIC RESEARCH AREA (CLOSED)

Kipahulu Valley

Palikea Stream

Palikea 2,224 ft.)

Kaulana Gulch

Ohea Gulch

To Hana

Waimoku Falls

KAPAHULU AREA

RANGER STATION

KIPAHULU CAMPGROUND

(31)

To Kaupo

NOTE: BE AWARE OF FREE RANGE CATTLE ALONG THE HIGHWAY, ESPECIALLY AT NIGHT

0   1 mi

0   1 km

scuring even it from view. The *Maui News* prints the hours of sunrise and sunset (on a daily basis) as they vary with the season, so make sure to check. The National Weather Service provides a daily weather recording at (808) 871-5054. For more specific information, you can call the ranger station at (808) 572-7749 for a recorded message, or call (808) 572-9306 for a ranger. Plan on taking a minimum of 90 minutes to arrive from Kahului, and to be safe, arrive at least 30 minutes before dawn or dusk, because even one minute is critical. The sun, as it rises or sets, infuses the clouds with streaks, puffs, and bursts of dazzling pastels, at the same time backlighting and edging the crater in glorious golds and reds. Prepare for an emotional crescendo that will brim your eyes with tears at the majesty of it all. Engulfed by this magnificence, no one can remain unmoved.

Note: If you want to avoid downhill bikers and tourists you can also get a great view from the Kalahaku Overlook. When you drive back down the mountain, shift into a low gear to control your speed to prevent riding the brakes.

Crater Facts

Haleakala was formed primarily from pa'hoe-hoe lava. This lava is the hottest natural substance on earth, and it flows like swift fiery rivers. Because of its high viscosity, it forms classic shield volcanoes. Plenty of a'a is also found in the mountain's composition. This rock comes out partially solidified and filled with gases, then breaks apart and forms clinkers. You'll be hiking over both, but be especially careful on a'a, because its jagged edges will cut you as quickly as coral. The crater is primarily formed from erosion, not from caving in on itself. The erosion on Hawaii is quite accelerated due to carbonic acid build-up, a by-product of the quick decomposition of abundant plant life. The rocks break down into smaller particles of soil which are then washed off the mountain by rain, or blown off by wind. Natural drainage patterns form, and canyons begin to develop and slowly eat their way to the center. The two largest are **Keanae Valley** in the north and **Kaupo Gap** in the south. These canyons, over time, moved their heads past each other to the center of the mountain, where they took several thousand feet off the summit and formed a huge amphitheater-like crater.

Some stones that you encounter while hiking will be very light in weight. They once held water and gases that evaporated. If you knock two together, they'll sound like crystal. Also, be observant for **Maui diamonds.** They are garnet stones, a type of pyroxene or crystal.

The cinder cones in the crater are fascinating. They're volcanic vents with a high iron content and may form electromagnetic lines from the earth's center. Climbing them violates park rules made to protect endangered plants and threatened insects that pollinate them. On top, they are like funnels, transmitters and receivers of energy, natural pyramids. Notice the color of the compacted earth on the trails. It's obvious why you should remain on them. All the plants (silverswords, too) are shallow-rooted and live by condensing moisture on their leaves. Don't walk too close to them because you'll compact the earth around them and damage the roots. The ecosystem on Haleakala is very delicate, so please keep this in mind to better preserve its beauty for future generations.

SIGHTS

You'll start enjoying Haleakala long before you reach the top. Don't make the mistake of simply bolting up the mountain without taking time to enjoy what you're passing. Route 37 from Kahului takes you through Pukalani, the last big place to buy supplies. There it branches to clearly marked Route 377; in six miles it becomes the zigzag of Route 378 or **Haleakala Crater Road.** Along the way are forests of indigenous and introduced trees, including eucalyptus, beautifully flowering jacaranda, and stands of cactus. The vistas change rapidly from one vantage point to the next. Sometimes it's the green rolling hills of Ireland, and then instantly it's the tall, yellow grass of the plains. This is also cattle country, so don't be surprised to see all breeds, from Holsteins to Brahmans.

Headquarters

After paying your entrance fee, the first stopping point in the park is **Hosmer Grove Campground** (see "Camping" below) a short way down a secondary park road on your left. Proceed past here a few minutes and you'll arrive at **park headquarters,** elev. 7,000 feet, open daily 7:30 a.m.-4

The Hawaiians were the finest stone adze makers in Polynesia. One of the best quarries was atop Haleakala.

LOUISE FOOTE

p.m. Campers can get their permits here and others will be happy to stop for all manner of brochures and information concerning the park, for water, or to use the toilet or pay phone. There are some silverswords outside, and a few *nene* can occasionally be seen wandering the area. After you pass the park headquarters, zig and zag a couple more times, there's parking for Halemauu Trail on your left (see "Hikes" below). Following are two overlooks, **Leleiwi** and **Kalahaku.** Both offer tremendous views and different perspectives on the crater. They shouldn't be missed—especially Kalahaku, where there are silverswords and the remnants of a travelers' lodge from the days when an expedition to Haleakala took two days.

Visitors Center

Near road's end is the visitors center, elev. 9,740 feet, approximately 10 miles up the mountain from headquarters, and a half-hour drive. You get one of the best views into the crater from here. It's open from sunrise to 3 p.m. and contains a clear and concise display featuring the geology of Haleakala. Maps and books are available, and periodic ranger talks are particularly informative, delving into geology and the legends surrounding the great mountain. Various ranger-led hikes are also given, including the hike down Sliding Sands Trail, daily interpretive talks at the summit, and the Hosmer Grove forest walk. Additional interpretive talks and ranger-led hikes are conducted at the Kipahulu ranger station. Check with the park headquarters or the visitors center for times and days of programs. All mule and horse rides into the crater and bike trips down the mountainside through the park start from the parking lot to the front of the visitors center. By 10 a.m., there will be lots of people at the top, so enjoy the time between when the bikers leave and the buses arrive.

Bikes going down the mountain travel about 20-25 miles an hour, sometimes faster. If you're caught behind a string of bikes on your way down, just slow down and wait for them to pull over and let you pass.

HIKING AND CAMPING

Walks

One of the outside paths leads to **Pakaoao** ("White Hill"). An easy quarter-mile hike will take you to the summit, and along the way you'll pass stone shelters and sleeping platforms from the days when Hawaiians came here to quarry the special toolstone. It's a type of whitish slate that easily flakes but is so hard that when you strike two pieces together it rings almost like iron. Next comes **Pu-u'ulaula** ("Red Hill"), the highest point on Maui, at 10,023 feet. Atop is a glass-enclosed observation area (open 24 hours). This is where many people come to view the sunrise and sunset. From here, if the day is crystal clear, you can see all of the main Hawaiian Islands except Kauai. To add some perspective to size and distance, it's 100 miles from the top of Haleakala to the volcanic peak Mauna Kea on the Big Island to the southeast. Behind you on the slope below is **Maui Space Surveillance Complex,** tel. (808) 243-1313, a research facility with eight telescopes that's manned by the University of Hawaii and the Department of Defense. Open to the public one day a month; tours are booked months in advance.

The easy **Hosmer Grove Nature Trail** leads you through a stand of introduced temperate zone trees that was planted in 1910 to see if any would be good for commercial lumber use. There are perhaps a dozen different species of trees here, and the walk should take a half hour or so over mostly level ground. Originally planted in separate areas, these trees and others have intermingled now. Here you will see Jeffrey pine, ponderosa pine, lodgepole pine, incense cedar, eucalyptus, Norway spruce, eastern red cedar, Douglas fir, and Japanese *sugi.* Several signs are posted along the trail to explain what the trees are and how the forest developed.

Various **ranger-led walks** are given during the week, leaving either from the visitors center or from Hosmer Grove campground. On Monday and Thursday at 9 a.m. and noon, a naturalist leads a hike down into the Waikamoi cloud forest from Hosmer Grove, and on this hike you'll learn about trees, birds, and natural features of the area. Three hours, three miles, moderately strenuous. A ranger-led hike also goes down the Sliding Sands trail on a Cinder Desert Hike on Tuesday and Friday at 10 a.m. and noon from the trail-head at the visitors center parking lot. Two hours, two miles, moderately strenuous.

Hikes

There are three trails in Haleakala Wilderness Area: Halemauu, Sliding Sands, and Kaupo. **Halemauu Trail** starts at the 8,000-foot level along the road about three miles past the park headquarters. It descends quickly to the 6,600-foot level on the crater floor. En route you'll pass Holua Cabin, Silversword Loop, the Bottomless Pit (a mere 65 feet deep), then a portion of Sliding Sands Trail and back to the visitors center. You shouldn't have any trouble hitching back to your car from here.

Sliding Sands begins at the summit of Haleakala near the visitors center. This is the main crater trail and gives you the best overall hike. It joins the Kaupo Trail at Paliku Cabin; alternatively, at Kapaloa Cabin you can turn left to the Bottomless Pit and exit via Halemauu Trail. This last choice is one of the best, but you'll have to hitch back to your car at the visitors center, which shouldn't be left for the dwindling late-evening traffic going up the mountain.

The **Kaupo Trail** is long and tough. It follows the Kaupo Gap to the park boundary at 3,880 feet. It then crosses private land, which is no problem, and after a steep and rocky downhill grade deposits you in the semi-ghost town of Kaupo. This is the rugged part of the Hana loop. You'll have to hitch west just to get to the scant traffic of Route 31, or head nine miles east to Kipahulu and its campground, and from there back along the Hana Road.

For those inclined, there are also horse and mule tours of the crater. Hikers should also consider a day with the professional guide service **Hike Maui**. The guide's in-depth knowledge and commentary will make your trip not only more fulfilling, but enjoyably informative as well. (See "Sports and Recreation" in the Out and About chapter.)

Trekkers

Serious hikers or campers must have sturdy shoes, good warm clothes, rain gear, canteens, down bags, and a serviceable tent. Hats and sunglasses are needed. Compasses are useless because of the high magnetism in the rock,

but binoculars are particularly rewarding. No cook-fires are allowed in the crater, so you'll need a stove. Don't burn any dead wood—the soil needs all the decomposing nutrients it can get. Drinking water is available at all of the cabins within the crater, but the supply is limited so bring what you will need. This environment is particularly delicate. Stay on the established trails so that you don't cause undue erosion. Leave rocks and especially plants alone. Don't walk too close to silverswords or any other plants because you'll compact the soil. Leave your pets at home; ground-nesting birds here are easily disturbed. If nature "calls," dig a very shallow hole, off the trail, and pack out your used toilet paper since the very dry conditions are not conducive to it biodegrading.

Camping

Admission to the park is $10 per car, $5 for bikers, hikers, and motorcycles, and is good for seven days (national park discount passes are honored), but camping is free with a necessary camping permit from park headquarters. The Hosmer Grove campground is at the 6,800-foot level, just before park headquarters; the free camping here is limited to three nights and to 25 people, but there's generally room for all. There's water, pit toilets, picnic tables, grills, and a pavilion. It was named after Ralph Hosmer. While here take a stroll along the half-mile forest loop that threads its way through the grove of trees that Hosmer planted.

Kipahulu Campground is a primitive camping area over near Oheo Stream. It's part of the park, but unless you're an intrepid hiker and descend all the way down the Kaupo Trail, you'll come to it via Hana.

There are campsites in the crater at **Holua, Paliku**, and **Kapalaoa**. All three offer cabins, and tent camping is allowed at the first two. Camping at any of these is extremely popular, and reservations for the cabins must be made at least 90 days in advance by mail using only a special cabin reservation request form. Each cabin is reserved for one group of up to 12 people only. A lottery of the applicants chosen for sites keeps it fair for all. Environmental impact studies limit the number of campers to 25 per area per day. Camping is limited to a total of three days per month, with no more than two consecutive days at each spot. Rates for cabin use are $40 for up to six persons and $80 to a maximum of 12 people. For complete details and reservation form contact: Haleakala National Park, P.O. Box 369, Makawao, HI 96768, tel. (808) 572-9306, Web site: www.nps.gov/hale.

Making Do

If you've come to Hawaii for sun and surf and you aren't prepared for alpine temperatures, you can still enjoy Haleakala. For a day trip, wear your jogging suit or a sweater, if you've brought one. Make sure to wear socks, and even bring an extra pair as makeshift mittens. Use your dry beach towel to wrap around inside your sweater as extra insulation, and even consider taking your hotel blanket, which you can use Indian fashion. Make rain gear from a large plastic garbage bag with holes cut for head and arms; this is also a good windbreak-er. Take your beach hat, too. Don't worry about looking ridiculous in this get-up—you will! But you'll also keep warm! Remember that for every thousand feet you climb, the temperature drops three degrees Fahrenheit, so the summit is about 32 degress cooler than at sea level. As the sun reaches its zenith, if there are no rain clouds, the crater floor will go from about 50 to 80 degrees. It can flip-flop from blazing hot to dismal and rainy a number of times in the same day. The nights may drop below freezing, with the coldest recorded temperature a bone-chilling 14 degrees. Dawn and dusk are notorious for being bitter. Because of the altitude, be aware that the oxygen level will drop, and those with any impairing conditions should take precautions. The sun is ultrastrong atop the mountain, and even those with deep tans are subject to burning. Noses are particularly susceptible.

In a sennit casket rested the bones of the dead.

LOUISE FOOTE

EAST MAUI

THE HANA ROAD

On the long and winding road to Hana's door, most people's daydreams of "paradise" come true. A trip to Maui without a visit to Hana is like ordering a sundae without a cherry on top. The 50 miles that it takes to get there from Kahului are some of the most remarkable in the world. The Hana Highway (Route 36) starts out innocently enough, passing Paia. The inspiration for Paia's gaily painted storefronts looks like it came from a jar of jelly beans. Next come some north-shore surfing beaches where windsurfers fly, doing amazing aquabatics. Soon there is a string of "rooster towns," so named because that's about all that seems to be stirring. Then Route 36 becomes Route 360 and at mile marker 3 the *real* Hana Road begins.

The semi-official count tallies over 600 rollicking turns and 57 one-lane bridges, inducing everyone to slow down and soak up the sights of this glorious road. It's like passing through a tunnel cut from trees. The ocean winks with azure blue through sudden openings on your left. To the right, streams, waterfalls, and pools sit wreathed with jungle and wildflowers. Coconuts, guavas, mangos, and bananas grow everywhere on the moun-tainside. Fruit stands pop up regularly as you creep along. Then comes Keanae with its arboretum and taro farms indicating that many ethnic Hawaiians still live along the road. There are places to camp, picnic, and swim, both in the ocean and in freshwater streams.

Then you reach Hana itself, a remarkable town. The great Queen Kaahumanu was born here, and many celebrities live in the surrounding hills seeking peace and solitude. Past Hana, the road becomes even more rugged and besieged by jungle. It opens up again around Oheo Gulch. Here waterfalls cascade over stupendous cataracts, forming a series of pools until they reach the sea. Beyond is a rental car's no-man's land, where the passable road toughens and Haleakala shows its barren volcanic face scarred by lava flows.

PAIA

Paia ("Noisy") was a bustling sugar town that took a nap. When it awoke, it had a set of whiskers and its vitality had flown away. At the beginning of the 19th century, many groups of ethnic field workers lived here, segregated in housing clusters called "camps" that stretched up Baldwin Avenue. Paia was the main gateway for sugar on East Maui, and even a railroad functioned here until about 30 years ago. During the 1930s, its population, at over 10,000, was the largest on the island. Then fortunes shifted toward Kahului, and Paia lost its dynamism, until recently. Paia was resuscitated in the 1970s by an influx of paradise-seeking hippies, and then again in the '80s came another shot in the arm from windsurfers. These two groups have metamorphosed into townsfolk and have pumped new life into Paia's old mucoloo. The practical shops catering to the pragmatic needs of a "plantation town" were replaced. The storefronts were painted and spruced up. A new breed of merchants with their eye on passing tourists has taken over. Now Paia focuses on boutiques, crafts, artwork, and food. Since you've got to pass through on your way to Hana, it serves as a great place not only to top off your gas tank, but also to stop for a bite and a browse. The prices are good for just about everything, and it boasts one of the island's best fish restaurants and art shops. Paia, under its heavy makeup, is still a vintage example of what it always was—a homey, serviceable, working town.

Sights

A mile or so before you enter Paia on the left is **Rinzai Buddhist Temple** located on Alawai Road—reached by going through H.P. Baldwin Park. The grounds are pleasant and worth a look. **Mantokuji Buddhist Temple** on the eastern outskirts of Paia heralds the sun's rising and setting by ringing its huge gong 18 times at dawn and dusk.

H.P. Baldwin Beach County Park is on your left about seven miles past Kahului on Route 36, just past Maui Country Club and the well-

PAIA AND ENVIRONS

© J.D. BISIGNANI AND MOON PUBLICATIONS, INC.

to-do community of Sprecklesville; this spacious park is good for swimming, shell-collecting, and decent winter surfing. It has full amenities. Unfortunately, Baldwin has a bad reputation. It's one of those places that locals have staked out with the attitude of "us against them." Hassles and robberies have been known to occur. Be nice, calm, and respectful. For the timid, to be on the safe side, be gone.

Hookipa Beach Park is about 10 minutes past Paia. There's a high grassy sand dune along the road and the park is down below, where you'll enjoy full amenities—unofficial camping occurs. Swimming is advisable only on calm days, as there are wicked currents. Primarily a surfing beach that is now regarded as one of the best sailboarding areas in Hawaii, this is home to the Aloha Classic, held yearly in October or November. The world's best sailboarders come here, trying to win the $5,000-10,000 prize. Bring binoculars.

Accommodations

One of the few place to lodge in Paia is at the **Nalu Kai Lodge,** located just behind the Wine Corner where Baldwin Avenue meets the Hana Highway, tel. (808) 579-8009; ask for Myrna. This plain and simple two-story cement building offers clean, quiet, adequate rooms. Don't expect anything fancy, just the necessities. Rates vary—Myrna bargains—but expect to spend about $40 for one night, or $350 for a month. There are seven units, one double and six singles. Most people stay long-term.

About a mile away in Ku'au next to Mama's Fish House is the **Kuau Plaza Condo,** tel. (808) 579-8080, fax 579-8533. Rooms have private baths and color televisions. Laundry facilities are located on premises. Rooms run $30 a night on a weekly rate and $20 a night on a monthly rate; suites are $55 and $40 a night, respectively.

Food

Picnic's, 30 Baldwin Ave., tel. (808) 579-8021, is open daily 7 a.m.-7 p.m. Breakfast and lunch offer everything from roast beef to vegetarian sandwiches like a scrumptious spinach nut burger or tofu burger, all under $5. The best options are boxed picnic lunches that add a special touch if you're heading to Hana. They start from the basic Upcountry Picnic, which includes sandwiches and sides at $7.95 per person, to the Executive with sandwiches, *kiawe*-broiled chicken, sides, nut bread, condiments, cheeses, and even a tablecloth all in a Styrofoam ice chest for $42.50. (Supposedly feeds two, but with extra buns will feed four!) Numerous others are available. Picnic's is one of the best stops along the Hana Road even for a quick espresso, cappuccino, or frozen yogurt. Or treat yourself with the fresh-baked pastries like macadamia nut sticky buns and the apple and papaya turnovers: worth the guilt!

Another place for boxed picnic lunches is **Peach's Bakery and Delicatessen,** 2 Baldwin Ave., tel. (808) 579-8612, open 6:30 a.m.-6 p.m., Thursday and Friday to 7:30 p.m., where you can enjoy a scone, the famous peach crumble

Montokuji Buddhist Temple, Paia

ROBERT NILSEN

and Hawaiian coconut cake, and a cup of cappuccino. For a boxed lunch try the Hana Bay box at $6.95. Peach's also serves sandwiches made from homemade breads, great spinach lasagna, and fresh pastries of all sorts.

At the corner is **Pala Fish Market Restaurant,** tel. (808) 579-8030, a casual sit-down restaurant with picnic tables inside. Specializing in charbroiled fish, the menu also includes over a dozen types of fish, all at market price, that can be prepared in one of four different manners. You can also have charbroiled chicken, blackened sashimi, seafood salad, or fresh fish to take home and prepare yourself. The lunch and dinner menus include burgers, pasta, and fajitas. Across the street on the corner, a great place to people-watch or be watched is **Milagros Bar and Restaurant,** tel. (808) 579-8755, for burgers, sandwiches, and fish; eat inside or outside.

Jacques Bistro and bar, 89 Hana Hwy., is a relative newcomer. Seating is inside at tables with white linen or on the patio out back under shade trees. The lunch menu includes mostly sandwiches, salads, and fish, and might be a mahi sandwich for $6.95 or tomato mozzarella salad for $7.95. For dinner, try grilled chicken, *paniolo* cut steak, or seafood linguine. All entrees are under $19.95, except for the seafood bowl at $24.50.

Kihata Restaurant, tel. (808) 579-9035, open Tues.-Sat. 11 a.m.-1:30 p.m. for lunch, and 5-9 p.m. for dinner, is a small Japanese restaurant and sushi bar that you can easily pass by. Don't! It's just where Baldwin Avenue meets Route 36 along the main road. The traditional Japanese menu offers *bento* and sushi, with all entrees under $10, mostly $6-8, like *don buri, soba,* and *udon.* The sushi bar opens about 5:30 p.m.

Visit **Raw Experience,** 42 Baldwin Ave., for uncooked, organic, vegan foods. Here you'll find many items, albeit in a different form, that you'd find elsewhere, but with a big twist—no heat is used in preparation. Try a sprouted hummus appetizer, or angel hair pasta that's made from threads spun from carrots and beets with a sun-dried tomato marinara and vegetables. How about a pizza in the raw, regular or marinated salad, desserts, smoothies, juices, and other drinks. It may sound strange, but it's healthy, wholesome, well-presented food. Friendly, smoke-free environment. Open Mon.-Sat. 10:08 a.m.-8:01 p.m., Sunday 11:30 a.m.-3:30 p.m.

The **Bangkok** Thai cuisine restaurant, tel. (808) 579-8979, an indoor/outdoor cafe with a courtyard area surrounded by palm trees, is open for lunch 11 a.m.-3 p.m. and then again for dinner 5-9:30 p.m. Appetizers ranging $5.50-7.95 include Thai crispy noodles and sateh chicken. Try a green papaya salad or a spicy seafood coconut soup before your entree, which might be the Evil Prince shrimp or fish for $9.95, or seafood combo with broccoli at $11.95. In addition, there are many curry, noodle, fish, and vegetarian dishes. Desserts include tapioca and warm coconut milk at $2.95. Food here is good value, decently presented, and authentic. Soft drinks and bar drinks available.

For a quick bite you have **Charley's,** tel. (808) 579-9453, a saloon with pool tables and restaurant specializing in pizza, pasta, and sandwiches, open 7 a.m. for breakfast, from 11:30 for lunch, and 5 p.m. for dinner. Charley's is also known for its breakfasts. Breakfast choices include Charley's Eggs Benedict, $8, and huevos rancheros, $7.25; for lunch select a fish sandwich, $9.50, or pasta for around $9. Some specials, like shrimp scampi or chicken marsala at about $15, are more pricey. Soups, salads, and appetizers are priced equally well. This is a big rambling amiable place where tourists and locals alike come for a pleasant time.

The **Vegan Restaurant,** located at 115 Baldwin Ave., tel. (808) 579-9144, open daily 11 a.m.-8:30 p.m. except Monday, is an extraordinary health-conscious restaurant, a "hippie" hangout that others into healthy food frequent. People don't come for the decor—brightly colored wall hangings on no-nonsense walls—they come for the large portions of incredibly delicious food. The Vegan serves only vegetarian food made with organic products and uses no dairy, honey, or animal products of any kind; the food is mostly cholesterol-free. Standard menu items include hummus salad at $4.95, the Vegan burger for $4.75, and veggie lasagna for $8.95; specials nightly. Luscious smoothies are priced at $2.95. There's a great bulletin board, a few tables at which you can eat, or you can call ahead for orders to go.

A short way up Baldwin Ave., the **Paia Coffee Company,** tel. (808) 579-9296, offers more than coffee. Of course, you can get your morning jolt of espresso, caffe latte, or straight black cup of joe, but you might also like to try a crepe. On Friday nights, it's an all-you-can-eat pasta night for $5. You can't beat it.

Perhaps the most upscale restaurant in Paia itself is **Impromptu,** 71 Baldwin Ave., tel. (808) 579-8477. Open for breakfast, lunch, and dinner, evening entrees are in the $17.95-22.95 range.

Mama's Fish House, reservations highly recommended, tel. (808) 579-8488, is just past Paia on the left heading toward Hana. Look for the turnoffs near the blinking yellow light; you'll see a vintage car with a sign for Mama's, a ship's flagpole, and a fishing boat marking the entranceway. There's plenty of off-road complimentary valet parking. Mama's, serving lunch 11 a.m.-2:30 p.m., cocktails and *pu pu* until dinner at 5 p.m., has earned the best reputation possible—it gets thumbs up from local people even though it is expensive. It's perhaps the best upscale beach shack on the island, set right on the beach surrounded by coconut trees and tiki torches with outrigger canoes drawn on the lawn out front. The fish is fresh daily, with some broiled over *kiawe,* while the vegetables come from local gardens and the herbs are Mama's own. Fish entrees run $30-35, others $25-45. Special Hawaiian touches, wonderful food, friendly professional service, and a great view of Maui's north shore, add to the enjoyment of every meal. A terrific idea is to make reservations here for the evening's return trip from Hana.

Mana Natural Foods, 49 Baldwin Ave., tel. (808) 579-8078, open daily 8 a.m.-8 p.m., is a well-stocked health-food store, maybe the best on Maui. Inside the old building you'll find local organic produce, vitamins, grains, juices, bulk foods, and more. For takeout, try the salad bar or look for picnic items in the cooler. Outside, check out the great community bulletin board for what's selling and happening around Paia.

For boxed and canned goods, picnic items, meats, vegetables, and fresh-cut flowers, try the old-time shop **Horiuchi Market.** Just before Baldwin Ave. along the Hana Hwy. is **Nagata Store,** a general grocery store, open Mon.-Fri. 6 a.m.-7 p.m., Saturday 6 a.m.-6 p.m., Sunday 6 a.m.-1 p.m.

The **Wine Corner,** appropriately located at the corner of Baldwin Avenue and the Hana Highway, is a well-stocked bottle shop with wines, liquor, and ice-cold beer. Microbreweries are well represented. Open Monday noon-10 p.m., Tues.-Sun. 9 a.m.-10:30 p.m.

Shopping

Maui Crafts Guild is on the left just as you enter Paia, at 43 Hana Hwy., P.O. Box 609, Paia, HI 96779, tel. (808) 579-9697. Open daily 9 a.m.-6 p.m., the Crafts Guild is one of the best art outlets in Hawaii. It's owned and operated by the artists themselves, now numbering over two dozen, all of whom must pass a thorough jurying by present members. All artists must be islanders, and they must use natural materials found in Hawaii to create their work except for some specialized clay, fabrics, and printmaking paper. Items are tastefully displayed and you'll find a wide variety of artwork and crafts including pottery, prints, woodwork, bamboowork, stained glass, batik, and jewelry. Different artists staff the shop on different days, but business cards and phone numbers are available if you want to see more of something you like. Prices are reasonable and this is an excellent place to make that one "big" purchase. Upstairs is the gallery of wood sculptor Arthur Dennis Williams.

In town is **Paia Trading Co.,** a discovery shop open Mon.-Fri. 9 a.m.-5 p.m. with collectibles like glass, telephones, aloha shirts, lanterns, jewelry, license plates, oil lamps, flotation balls, old bottles, and a smattering of pottery and antique furniture. Next door is **Boutique II,** open daily 10 a.m.-6 p.m., Sunday to 4 p.m., filled with ladies' apparel and alohawear. **Nuage Bleu,** a boutique open daily 10 a.m.-5 p.m., features distinctive fashions and gift items, mostly for women. **Jaggers,** open daily 9 a.m.-5 p.m., carries alohawear, fancy dresses, replicas of vintage aloha shirts for men, and some umbrellas. Across the street is the **Maui Gecko Factory** for T-shirts; a shaved ice shop; **Sand and Sea,** primarily a sculpture gallery featuring dolphins; and **Paia Bay Gallery** for unique island art.

Walk along Baldwin Avenue for a half block and you'll find a drawerful of boutiques and fashion shops, including **Moon Bow Tropics** carrying women's sun dresses, men's aloha shirts, short, T-shirts, and jewelry; fine batik dresses and shirts made in Indonesia at **Batonga;** and **Alpha and Omega** for ladies' clothing, artwork, glass, and crystal.

Also along Baldwin Avenue are the **Bank of Hawaii,** the **post office,** and a washerette.

For the windsurfer, look for boards and gear at **Hi-Tech Surf Sports,** or **Sailboards Maui.** At these and other places in town, you can dress yourself for the beach and get a board to ride over those waves.

Paia has two gas stations: **Unocal,** which has made-to-order sandwiches at its minimart, and **Chevron,** open 24 hours. These gas stations are the last places to fill your tank before reaching Hana. Next door is **Paia General Store** for groceries, supplies, and sundries, with a takeout snack window called the **Paia Drive Inn** where most items are under $7. Next to that, in what was at one time the Lower Paia Theater, are a gift shop, antique shop, and combination clothing and sailboard shop. Across the street is the Paia Mercantile Shopping Complex, a collection of shops ranging from surfing equipment to **Mandala** for clothing, craft items, and gifts from Asia.

Heading down the road to Hana you'll see the **Maui Community Center** on your right, the Mantokuji Buddhist temple on your left, and a little farther on the **Ku'au Market,** a convenience store to get snacks for the road. Just around the bend is **Mama's Fish House,** and shortly after Hookipa Beach. Near mile marker 14 on the mountain side of the highway you'll come across **Maui Grown Market and Deli.** Housed in a vintage corrugated roof plantation-style building with a porch out front, it carries mostly sandwiches, salads, smoothies and packaged food items, with a limited supply of fresh produce. Lunch boxes are a specialty. This is the last place before you really start to wind your way down the Hana Highway. A public phone is out front. Open daily 6:30 a.m.-7 p.m. (until 6 p.m. on Sunday). Aside from side trips to Haiku, Pauwela, and Ulumalu, you'll have clear sailing down the road to Hana.

HAIKU

Around mile marker 11, Haiku Road heads up the hill to the little community of Haiku. From Upcountry, follow Kauhikoa Road down the hill after turning off of Route 365 below Kokomo and Makawao. Haiku is an old cannery town, canning, boxing, and sending millions of pineapples and guavas to the world over the decades. After the cannery companies stopped production, their industrial buildings were renovated and turned into shops and studios, and have become, along with the Pauwela Cannery down the road, a center for artists and craftsmen. In the largest of the old cannery buildings, the pineapple cannery, you'll find among the many shops here a **True Value Hardware** store, the **Haleakala Bike Company** shop, **Haiku Video, Haiku Pizza and Subs.** To the side of the huge parking lot in a separate building is **Trattoria Haiku,** a wonderful Italian place to eat. Open daily except Monday for dinner only, this restaurant serves honest family food and is especially full on Tuesday when it offers a two-for-one special.

At the main intersection in this little community is **Haiku Grocery,** open seven days a week and a good place to pick up supplies. Across the street are the **post office** and the **Haiku Mart Liquor and Deli.** There's a community bulletin board in front of the grocery store and a few more around town, so you can stop and check out what's happening in the community.

Tucked behind Haiku Mart is **Haiku Town Center,** the second of the big remodeled cannery buildings that's slowly been turned into space for other use. This was the guava cannery. Among other shops that will fill the space you'll find **Sativa,** a store dealing almost entirely with the numerous and various products made from the hemp plant.

Haiku Road runs east, wending its way along the mountain, in and out of gulches, over bridges, and through thickly vegetated forests to Kuiaha. It's a great way to see the back roads of lower mountain Maui. There are lots of roads in this area, and many people have settled here, carving out their little bit of paradise. An alternate road to Kuiaha from the Hana Hwy. starts just past mile marker 12. Look for W. Kuiaha Road and make a right heading for the old **Pauwela Cannery,** which is less than five minutes up the road. This huge tin can of a building has been divided into a honeycomb of studios and workshops housing fine artists, woodworkers, potters, and sailboard makers. These artists and craftspeople come and go, so you're never sure just who will be occupying the studios. However, all welcome guests to come and browse, and buy. While here, be sure to stop at the **Pauwela Cafe** for a cold drink, hot coffee, salad, sandwich, or pastry. Sit inside or out. Open Mon.-

Sat. 7 a.m.-3 p.m., Sunday 8 a.m.-2 p.m. Have a peek at the art and crafts displayed next door at **Makani Hau.** For other needs, try **Okashiro General Store** across the street.

THE ROAD BEGINS

The road to Hana holds many spectacles and surprises, but one of the best is the road itself . . . it's a marvel! The road was hacked out from the coastline and completed in 1927, every inch by hand using pick and shovel. Crushed volcanic rock was the first surface material. Rebuilt and partially paved in 1962, only in 1982 was the road fully paved. Mother nature and man's machines have taken their toll on the road, and in the early '90s, the Hana Highway was widened and again resurfaced. Today it's smooth sailing. An ancient Hawaiian trail followed the same route for part of the way, but mostly people moved up and down this coastline by boat. What makes the scenery so special is that the road snakes along Maui's windward side. There's abundant vegetation and countless streams flowing from Haleakala, carving gorgeous valleys. There are a few scattered villages with a house or two that you hardly notice, and the beaches, although few, are empty. Mostly, however, it's the "feeling" that you get along this road. Nature is close and accessible, and it's so incredibly "South Sea island" that it almost seems artificial. But it isn't.

Hana Road Tips

You've got 30 miles of turns ahead when Route 36 (mile marker 22) becomes Route 360 (mile marker 0) and the fun begins. The Hana Road has the reputation of being a "bad road," but this isn't true. It's narrow, with plenty of hairpin turns, but it's well banked, has clearly marked bridges, and there's always maintenance going on (which can slow you up). Years back, it was a harrowing experience. When mudslides blocked the road, drivers were known to swap their cars with those on the opposite side and carry on to where they were going. The road's reputation sets people up to expect an ordeal, so they make it one, and unfortunately, drive accordingly. Sometimes it seems as though tourists demand the road to be rugged, so that they can tell the folks back home that they, too, "survived the road to Hana."

This popular slogan appears on T-shirts, copyrighted and sold by Hasegawa's famous store in Hana, and perpetuates this belief. You'll have no problem, and you'll see much more if you just take it easy.

Your speed will often drop below 10 miles per hour and will rarely exceed 25. Standard-shift cars are better for the turns. Cloudbursts occur at any time so be ready for slick roads. A heavy fall of fruit from roadside mango trees can also coat the road with slippery slime. Look as far up the road as possible and don't allow yourself to be mesmerized by the 10 feet in front of your hood. If your tire dips off a rough shoulder, don't risk losing control by jerking the wheels back on immediately. Ride it for a while and either stop or wait for an even shoulder to come back on. Local people trying to make time will often ride your rear bumper, but generally they won't honk. Pull over and let them by when possible. Pull-offs on this road are not overabundant, so be sure to choose your spot carefully. As a safety measure and courtesy to others, yield to all oncoming traffic at each bridge.

Driving from Kahului to Hana will take three hours, not counting some recommended stops. The greatest traffic flow is from 10 a.m. to noon; returning "car trains" start by 3 p.m. and are heaviest around 5 p.m. Many white-knuckled drivers head for Hana as if it were a prized goal, without stopping along the way. This is ridiculous. The best sights are before and after Hana; the town itself is hardly worth the effort. Expect to spend a long day exploring the Hana Road. To go all the way to Oheo Stream and take in some sights, you'll have to leave your hotel at sunup and won't get back until sundown. If your budget can afford it, plan on staying the night in Hana (reservations definitely) and return the next day. This is a particularly good plan if you have an afternoon departing flight from Kahului Airport. Also, most tourists seem terrified of driving the road at night. Actually it's easier. There is far less traffic, road reflectors mark the center and sides like a runway, and you're warned of oncoming cars by their headlights. Those in the know make much better time after dark! In case of **emergency,** a roadside telephone is located *makai* between mile markers 5 and 6. Only 3,000 people live along the entire north coast of East Maui leading to and including Hana.

SIGHTS

Twin Falls

A favorite of locals, the trail to Twin Falls should take about an hour. It's one of the first places to stop and enjoy along the road. Park near mile marker 2 just before the Hoolawa Bridge. A new metal gate marks the jeep trail. This is private property, but everyone seems to use it as if it were open to all. Walk the trail up to the irrigation ditch. On the way, a couple of side trails go off to the left and down to the steam. Guavas grow in this area and you might find ripe fruit at the right time of the year—there used to be a guava cannery in Haiku not far away. Follow the irrigation ditch until you reach the first falls. Alternately, follow the stream. The first pool is feed by two falls that give the area its name. A trail to the right goes up to the top of the falls and on to a second falls a short distance above. There you'll have more privacy. Some people come here to skinny-dip.

Huelo

A few miles past the new bridge and pulloff for Twin Falls is Huelo. Huelo means "Famous Owl," a name given for the birds that used to inhabit trees in the area. In the 1840s, Huelo was bustling sugar town surrounded by bono fields and even sustained a mill. Later, the area grew pineapple, but it's now just a quiet "rooster town" famous for **Kaulanapueo Church,** built in 1853. The structure is made from coral that was hauled up block by block from Waipio Bay below and is reminiscent of New England architecture. It's still used on the second and fourth Sundays of each month at 10 a.m., and a peek through the door will reveal a stark interior with straight-backed benches and a platform. The pit on the ocean side of the church building was used to make the lime and mortar mix. Few bother to stop, so it's quiet and offers good panoramas of the village and sea below. At the broad turnoff to Huelo between mile markers 3 and 4 there's a public telephone, in case of emergency, and a row of mailboxes.

Kailua

The next tiny town is Kailua. Plenty of mountain apple trees flourish along this stretch. The multi-colored trees are rainbow eucalyptus, introduced late last century from Australia and some of the most beautiful trees in Hawaii. Close by is a cousin, *Eucalyptus robusta,* which produces great timber, especially flooring, from its reddish-brown heartwood. This tree, due to its resins, gets extremely hard once it dries, so it must be milled immediately or you can do nothing with it. A few minutes beyond Kailua, notice a sudden difference in the humidity and in the phenomenal jungle growth that becomes even more pronounced.

Waikamoi Ridge

This nature walk (mosquitoes!) is a good place to stretch your legs and learn about native and introduced trees and vegetation. The turnout, good for about half a dozen vehicles, is not clearly marked along the highway past mile marker 9, but look for a metal gate at roadside and picnic tables in a clearing above the road. The well-defined, gradual trail leads through tall stands of trees. It's about one mile long and takes less than an hour. On the way, you will get glimpses of the highway and stream below. For those never before exposed to a bamboo forest, it's most interesting when the wind rustles the trees so that they knock together like natural percussion instruments. Picnic tables are available at the start and end of the trail. Tall mango trees tower over the upper picnic area. Return via the same trail or walk down the jeep path. Back on the road, and at the next bridge, is excellent drinking water. There's a stone barrel with a pipe coming out, and local people come to fill jugs with what they call "living water." It doesn't always run in summer but most times can be counted upon.

Garden of Eden

A new stop along this road is the landscaped Garden of Eden, a private arboretum and botanical garden. Entrance $3; open daily 9 a.m.-2 p.m. Have a stroll here among the tropical trees and flowering bushes, some of which are labeled for easy identification, or walk out to the Puohokamoa Falls overlook where you have a fine view down onto this graceful waterfall.

Puohokamoa Falls

Following is Puohokamoa Falls, where you'll find a nice pool and picnic table. A short trail will take you to the pool and its 30-foot cliff, from which local kids jump off. You'll also find a trail near the falls, and if you go upstream about 100

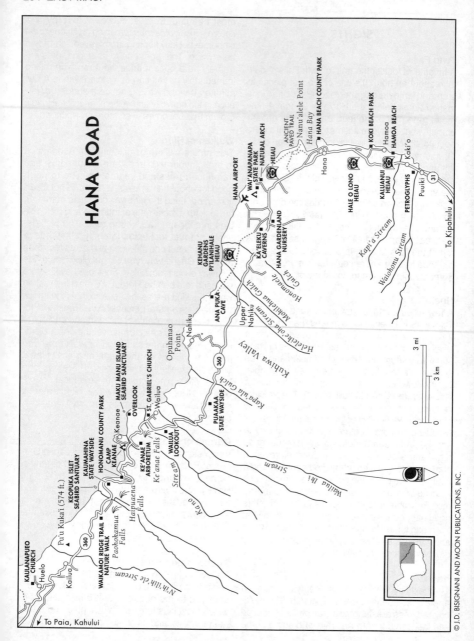

HANA ROAD

KAULANAPUEO
CHURCH

Huelo

To Paia, Kahului

Pu'u Kuka'i (574 ft.)

360

Kailua

WAIKAMOI RIDGE TRAIL
NATURE WALK

N'ih'ili'ili'ch'i Stream

Paohokamua
Falls

Ka no

Stream

Haipuaena
Falls

KEOPUKA ISLET
SEABIRD SANCTUARY

KAUMAHINA
STATE WAYSIDE

HONOMANU COUNTY PARK

CAMP
KEANAE

Keanae

MAKU MANU ISLAND
SEABIRD SANCTUARY

OVERLOOK

ST. GABRIEL'S CHURCH

Wailua

KE'ANAE
ARBORETUM

Ke'anae Falls

WAILUA
LOOKOUT

Wailua Iki Stream

Kapa 'ula Gulch

PUAAKAA
STATE WAYSIDE

360

Opuhanao
Point

Nahiku

ANA PUKA
CAVE

Upper
Nahiku

Helelcike'oha Stream

Mokulehua Gulch

Honomaele
Gulch

Kuhiwa Valley

KEHANU
GARDENS
PI'ILANIHALE
HEIAU

HANA GARDENLAND
NURSERY

KA'ELEKU
CAVERNS

HANA AIRPORT

WAI'ANAPANAPA
STATE PARK

NATURAL ARCH

HEIAU

ANCIENT
PAVED TRAIL

Nanu'alele Point

Hana Bay

HANA BEACH COUNTY PARK

Hana

HALE O LONO
HEIAU

Kapi'a Stream

KAIUANUI
HEIAU

Waiohonu Stream

PETROGLYPHS

Koki'o

Puiiki

31

To Kipahulu

KOKI BEACH PARK

Hamoa

HAMOA BEACH

3 mi

3 km

0

0

MOON

© J.D. BISIGNANI AND MOON PUBLICATIONS, INC.

yards you'll discover another invigorating pool with yet another waterfall. Swimming is great here, and the small crowd is gone. If you hike downstream about one-half mile *through* the stream (no trail), you come to the top of a 200-foot falls from where you can peer over the edge. Be very conscious of water conditions and the dangers of being near the cliff edge.

Wayside Rest and Park

Less than two miles past Waikamoi Ridge are **Kaumahina State Wayside,** along the road, and **Honomanu County Park,** down at Honomanu Bay. Permits are required for camping at the county park. Camping here is in a rainforest with splendid views out to sea overlooking the rugged coastline and the black-sand beach of Honomanu Bay. Honomanu is not good for swimming because of strong currents, but is good for surfing. There are no amenities at Honomanu, but Kaumahina has picnic tables and restrooms. From Kaumahina, you're rewarded with splendid views down the coast to the Keanae Peninsula. Puohokamoa Falls is just a short walk back down the road.

At Nua'ailua Bay, one bay farther on, two roads lead down to the water on either side of the stream. This spot is one where locals come to fish or surf and to spend a leisurely day by the ocean.

Keanae

Going back about five miles toward the center of the mountain, Keanae Valley is the largest valley on the north side of Haleakala. Most of the big valleys that once existed, especially on East Maui, were filled in by lava flows, greatly reducing their original size. Also going deep into the heart of the mountain is Hoomanu Valley, located just before Keanae Valley. Hoomanu Valley has 3,000-foot cliffs and 1,000-foot waterfalls. Unfortunately, the trails here are quite difficult both to find and to negotiate.

Clearly marked on the right side of the highway will be the six-acre **Keanae Arboretum,** established in 1971. A hike through this facility will exemplify Hawaiian plant life in microcosm. There are two sections, one of ornamental tropical plants (identified) and the other of Hawaiian domestic plants. Toward the upper end of the arboretum are taro fields, and the hillsides above are covered with the natural rainforest vegetation. You can picnic along Piinaau Stream. Although the trail is hard to pick out, hardier hikers can continue for another mile or so through the rainforest; at the end of the trail is a pool and waterfall. As there is a gate across the entrance to the arboretum (located at a sharp curve in the road), pull well off the road to park your car and walk in.

Camp Keanae YMCA is just before the arboretum. It looks exactly as its name implies, set in a gorgeous natural pasture. There are three bunkhouses (you must provide your own bedding), two bathrooms with showers, a gymnasium, and a dining room and kitchen for large group events. Camping is allowed on the lawn. Cooking grills

ROBERT NILSEN

cane fields

are available from the camp caretaker. Arrival time is between 3 and 6 p.m., three-day maximum stay, $10 per person. All accommodations are by reservation only. For more information call the camp at (808) 248-8355; for reservations contact the Maui Family YMCA office in Kahului at (808) 242-9007.

Keanae Peninsula is a thumb-like appendage of land formed by a lava flow that came down the hollowed-out valley from Haleakala Crater. A fantastic lookout is here—look for a telephone pole with a tsunami loudspeaker atop at mile marker 17, and pull off just there. Below you'll see neat little farms, mostly raising taro. Shortly before this lookout, and about 200 yards past the arboretum, a public road heads down into the peninsula to a turnaround by the church. If you walk, park well off the roadway just as you get down the hill. The road makes an arc around to the parking lot by the church, and a trail continues on to the stream. About a mile, this stroll should take less than half an hour, but you may want to stop to chat. Most people living here are native Hawaiians. They still make poi the old-fashioned way: listen for the distinctive thud of poi-pounding in the background. Though *kapu* signs abound, the majority of people are friendly. If you visit, be aware that this is one of the last patches of ground owned by Hawaiians and tended in the old way. Be respectful, please. Notice the lava-rock missionary church. Built in 1860, **Lanikili Ihi Ihi O Lehowa O na Kaua Church** was rebuilt in 1969. Neat and clean, it has straight-back, hardwood pews and a pleasant altar inside. Services are held twice a month. The cemetery to the side is groomed with tropical flowers while the grounds are rimmed by tall coconut trees.

Fruit Stands

Past Keanae between mile markers 17 and 18 is the **Halfway to Hana** roadside refreshment stand, where you can buy hot dogs, shave ice, ice cream, sandwiches, and some fruit. Notice the picture-perfect, idyllic watercress farm on your left.

Do yourself a favor and look for **Uncle Harry's Fruit Stand,** clearly marked on the left past the Keanae Peninsula just beyond the Keanae school. Unfortunately, this *kahuna,* who knew a great deal of the natural pharmacology of old Hawaii and was a living encyclopedia on herbs and all their healing properties, has passed away, but his spirit lives on. Past mile marker 18 on the right is a fruit stand operated by a fellow named Joseph. He not only has coconuts, pineapples, and papayas, but also little-tasted exotic fruits like mountain apples, star fruit, strawberry guavas, and Tahitian lemons. An authentic fruit stand worth a stop. Another one, operated by a Hawaiian woman, is only 50 yards farther on the left. If you have a hankering for fruit, this is the spot. Other fruit stands pop up now and again on this road. It's just a down-home cottage industry. No definite times necessarily, just open when they are. Look for them as you pass, stop to refresh yourself, and leave a little for the local economy.

Wailua

At mile marker 18, you come to Wailua. Similar to Keanae, it too is covered in taro but not to as great an extent, and is a picturesque spot. Turn left here on Wailua Road, following signs for **Coral Miracle Church.** You'll find the **Miracle of Fatima Shrine** here as well, so named because a freak storm in the 1860s washed up enough coral onto Wailua Beach that the church could be constructed by the Hawaiian congregation. Here also are St. Gabriel's Church and St. Augustine's Shrine. There is a lovely and relatively easy-access waterfall nearby. Pass the church, turn right, and park by the large field. Look for a worn path (may be private, but no signs or hassle) that leads down to the falls. Look inland up the valley and you'll see a long sliver of a falls just below the roadway that clings to the *pali.* You can look down on this village and valley from several pulloffs along the highway and from the Wailua Wayside Park, all past the Wailua Road turnoff.

Wailua Wayside Park

Cut into the ridge directly along the roadway is the small parking lot of this tiny wayside park. Drive slowly and keep your eyes peeled as the sign comes up quickly and you have little time to signal your turn to get off the road. A short series of steps leads up under a canopy of overhanging *hao* tree branches to a flat grassy area about 20 feet above the road. From here you have an expansive view down onto Wailua and up along the face of the *pali.* From the rear of the parking area, you can peer into the adjoining *mauka* valley. No facilities.

Puaa Kaa State Wayside

This lovely spot is about 14 miles before Hana.

There's no camping, but there are picnic tables, grills, and restrooms. Nearby are Kopiliula and Waikani Falls. A stream provides some smaller falls and pools suitable for swimming.

Nahiku

The village, named after the Hawaiian version of the Pleiades, is reached by a steep but now paved three-mile road and has the dubious distinction of being one of the wettest spots along the coast. The well-preserved and tiny village church near the bottom of the road was constructed in 1867 (renovated in 1993) and is just big enough for a handful of pews. You may see school kids playing ball in the yard next to the church, the only place in the community open and large enough. The turnaround at oceanside is where many locals come to shore-fish. Every evening during the summer months, beginning around 3 p.m., an extended family pod of dolphins enters Nahiku Bay to put on an impromptu performance of water acrobatics just for the joy of it. At one time Nahiku was a thriving Hawaiian village with thousands of inhabitants. Today it's home to only about 70 people, the best-known being former Beatle George Harrison. A few inhabitants are Hawaiian families, but mostly the people are wealthy Mainlanders seeking isolation. After a few large and attractive homes went up, the real estate agents changed the description from "desolate" to "secluded." What's the difference? About $500,000 per house! At the turn of the century it was the site of the Nahiku Rubber Co., the only commercial rubber plantation in the United States. Many rubber trees still line the road, although the venture collapsed in 1912 because the rubber was poor due to the overabundance of rainfall. Some people have augmented their incomes by growing *pakalolo* in the rainforest of this area. However, the alternative-lifestyle people who first came here and have settled in have discovered that there is just as much money to be made raising ornamental tropical flowers ($5,000-10,000 per acre), and have become real "flower children." Many have roadside stands along the Hana Highway where payment for the flowers displayed is on the honor system. Leave what is requested—prices will be marked.

Near mile marker 29 in Upper Nahiku, you'll come upon Nahiku Hawaiian Ti Gallery for gifts and crafts, a pastry and refreshment shop, and a little stand selling baked breadfruit bread.

ACCOMMODATIONS

A number of bed and breakfast establishments and similar accommodations lie along the road to Hana, many in or near Huelo. Only a few are listed below.

Hono Huako Tropical Plantation B&B, down behind Kaulanapueo Church on a 300-foot cliff above Waipio Bay, is a peaceful 38-acre retreat and alternative working plantation farm that retains a connection to the past in the guise of a *heiau* while it looks toward the peace and tranquility of the future. The property is dotted with tropical permaculture orchards and gardens, and the stream was blocked to form a natural heart-shaped pond. Set amidst bamboo, a globe-like kiva meditation hall sits about the main house and office, below which is a heated swimming pool and spa. The two suites on the garden level of the house rent for $80 and $85 a night, or together for $135. The gazebo suite at poolside below the nine-sided office is often used by newlyweds; it runs $125. Overlooking much of the farm and surrounding forested hillsides, the bamboo hexa-hale goes for $100, while the smaller bamboo house set near the heart pond in the orchard is $65. The cliff house, set on the precipice of the 300 foot *pali* next to a waterfall with a commanding view of the bay, is yours for $250 with a three-night minimum. Breakfast of organic fruits from the property, home-baked muffins and croissants, juice, and tea arrives every morning at your doorstep and is included in the price of the room, even though each unit is equipped with a kitchenette. Come, relax, refresh, and reinvigorate. Write or call for additional information and reservations: P.O. Box 600, Haiku, 96708, tel. (808) 573-1391, fax 573-0141, Web site: www.maui.net/~bnb/BB.html.

Also in the community of Huelo, with a spectacular view up the coast toward Hana, is **Huelo Point Lookout B&B.** Here, the main house and three cottages are scattered around the acreage, which is finely landscaped with tropical trees and bushes. The rock-wall swimming pool is inviting and a soak in the hot tub under a cloudless night sky befits a day on the island. Wake up to the sound of birds singing in the trees, have your breakfast on the lanai, and spend your day leisurely hanging out here or venture out to see the island sights. Once a fisherman's cottage, surrounded by banana trees and heliconia, the remodeled Star Cottage has an indoor/outdoor bathroom, a solarium, and a queen bed and double futon, $125-160. Although smaller, Haleakala Cottage studio has a full kitchen and king bed in one room, $95-125. Outside is an enclosed shower and a covered lanai. The Rainbow Cottage is a newer building, renting for $200-275. Downstairs are the living room and kitchen; a 22-foot tall wall of glass offers the best views of the coast from either floor. Make your way up the handmade wooden spiral staircase to the upstairs bedroom where a king bed lies under a large skylight. Outside is your own private hot tub. The main house also can be rented for families or groups of four for $1,850-2,150 a week. For additional information: P.O. Box 117, Paia, HI 96779, tel. (808) 573-0914 or (800) 871-8645, fax (808) 573-0227, Web site: www.maui.net/~dreamers, e-mail: dreamers@maui.net.

About one mile down a dirt road near Twin Falls is **Maluhia Hale B&B,** tel. (808) 572-2959, P.O. Box 687 Haiku, HI 96708, Web site: www.maui.net/~djg/index.html, e-mail: djg@maui.net. Off the main route, this 2.5-acre quiet and relaxing spot is enveloped by greenery yet has the wide ocean vista spreading at your feet. A detached open-beam plantation-style cottage with screened porch and a sitting room has a king bed, a nearly full kitchen, and a detached bathing room that has a clawfoot tub and shower; very commodious. A bit more refined, the suite in the house is decorated with Chinese antiques in a style that says blue and white porcelain. The suite sleeps two, the cottage can accommodate three. Light, open, and airy, both rent for $95 a night with breakfast, two nights minimum.

Down at the end of the road is the **Tea House Cottage.** This B&B is "off the grid," generating its own power by photovoltaic cells and collecting its own water. Quiet, with no distractions, from here you have broad views of the ocean. The one cottage has a Japanese "feel," with a living room, kitchen, bedroom, and screened lanai; a few steps away is the redwood bathhouse. Art on the walls is by the owner/artist, and it complements the rattan furniture and oriental rugs. The room rate is $95 a night, two nights minimum; a daily breakfast is provided. A tunnel through the trees leads you to the house, and walkways run throughout the property, one to a small stupa built some 20 years ago by a Tibetan monk. For more information: P.O. Box 335, Haiku, HI 96708, tel. (808) 572-5610, Web site: www.maui.net/~teahouse, e-mail: teahouse@maui.net.

Nearby is **Half Way to Hana House.** Surrounded by trees, bamboo, and wild flowers, this B&B has one studio apartment on the lower level of the house. Its private entrance leads into a comfortable room with double bed and mini kitchen. In a separate room is another bed and bath. Breakfast of pastries and fruit from the property is waiting every morning. Room rates are $55 single and $60 double; add $5 per person for a simple continental breakfast. Three nights minimum, 10% discount for a week or more. A kayak and scuba enthusiast, the owner can tell you about good ocean spots to visit. Contact: P.O. Box 675, Haiku, HI 96708, tel. (808) 572-1176, fax 572-3609, Web site: www.maui.net/~gailp, e-mail: gailp@mauilnet.

Not situated along the coast but in the rangeland above Ulumalu is **Lanikai Farm,** P.O. Box 797, Haiku, HI 06708, tel. (808) 572-1111, or fax (808) 572-3498. This "Victorian-European style" newer home lies next to the Koolau forest preserve and is surrounded by tropical fruit trees. The guest rooms have private entrances, TV, small refrigerators, and lanai, and there is use of the washer/dryer and barbecue grill. A scrumptious breakfast of European-style breads and fresh fruit is served every morning. Rates are $65 single, $70 double, or $100 for two rooms; two nights minimum. A studio rental without breakfast runs $80, two rooms is $105. The athletically inclined might want to have a turn on the squash court on property. Web site: www.maui.net/~lanibb, e-mail: lanibb@maui.net.

HANA

Hana is about as pretty a town as you'll find anywhere in Hawaii, but if you're expecting anything stupendous you'll be sadly disappointed. For most it will only be a quick stopover at a store or beach en route to Oheo Stream: the townsfolk refer to these people as "rent-a-car tourists." The lucky who stay in Hana, or those not worried about time, will find plenty to explore throughout the area. The town is built on rolling hills that descend to Hana Bay; much of the surrounding lands are given over to pasture, while trim cottages wearing flower corsages line the town's little lanes. Before the white man arrived, Hana was a stronghold that was conquered and reconquered by the kings of Maui and those of the north coast of the Big Island. The most strategic and historically laden spot is Kauiki Hill, the remnant of a cinder cone that dominates Hana Bay. This area is steeped in Hawaiian leg-

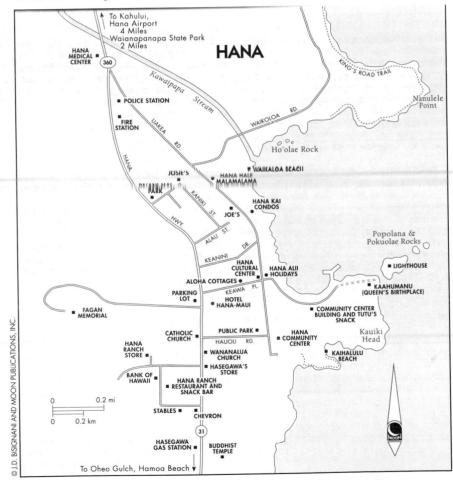

HANA

To Kahului,
Hana Airport
4 Miles
Waianapanapa State Park
2 Miles

HANA MEDICAL CENTER · 360

KING'S ROAD TRAIL

Nanulele Point

Kawaipapa Stream

■ POLICE STATION

WAIKOLOA RD.

■ FIRE STATION

UAKEA RD.

Ho'olae Rock

HANA HWY

JOSIE'S ■

PARK

■ WAIKALOA BEACH

HANA HALE MALAMALAMA

KANIKI ST.

JOE'S ■

HANA KAI CONDOS

Popolana & Pokuolae Rocks

ALAU ST.

KEANINI DR.

HANA CULTURAL CENTER ●

HANA ALII ● HOLIDAYS

■ LIGHTHOUSE

ALOHA COTTAGES ●

PARKING LOT ■

KEAWA PL.

HOTEL HANA-MAUI ●

■ KAAHUMANU (QUEEN'S BIRTHPLACE)

■ FAGAN MEMORIAL

PUBLIC PARK ■

● COMMUNITY CENTER BUILDING AND TUTU'S SNACK

CATHOLIC CHURCH ■

HAUOLI RD.

HANA ■ COMMUNITY CENTER

Kauiki Head

HANA RANCH STORE ■

■ WANANALUA CHURCH

■ KAIHALULU BEACH

BANK OF HAWAII ■

■ HASEGAWA'S STORE

HANA RANCH ■ RESTAURANT AND SNACK BAR

0   0.2 mi

0   0.2 km

STABLES ■

■ CHEVRON

31

HASEGAWA GAS STATION ■

■ BUDDHIST TEMPLE

MOON

To Oheo Gulch, Hamoa Beach ↓

© J.D. BISIGNANI AND MOON PUBLICATIONS, INC.

end, and old stories relate that it was the demigod Maui's favorite spot. It's said that he transformed his daughter's lover into Kauiki Hill and turned her into the gentle rains that bathe it to this day.

Changing History

Hana was already a plantation town in the mid-1800s when a hard-boiled sea captain named George Wilfong started producing sugar on his 60 acres there. Over the years the laborers came from the standard mixture of Hawaiian, Japanese, Chinese, Portuguese, Filipino, and even Puerto Rican stock. The *luna* were Scottish, German, or American. All have combined to become the people of Hana. Sugar production faded out by the 1940s and Hana began to die, its population dipping below 500. Just then, San Francisco industrialist Paul Fagan purchased 14,000 acres of what was to become the **Hana Ranch.** Realizing that sugar was *pau,* he replanted his lands in *pangola* range grass and imported 300 Hereford cattle from another holding on Molokai. Their white faces staring back at you as you drive past are now a standard part of Hana's scenery. Today, Hana Ranch has about 3,000 acres and raises over 2,000 head of cattle. Hana's population, at 1,900, is about 48% Hawaiian.

Fagan loved Hana and felt an obligation to and affection for its people. He also decided to retire here, and with enough money to materialize just about anything, he decided that Hana could best survive through limited tourism. He built the Hotel Hana-Maui, which catered to millionaires, mostly his friends, and began operation in 1946. Fagan owned a baseball team, the San Francisco Seals, and brought them to Hana in 1946 for spring training. The community baseball field behind the hotel was made for them. This was a brilliant publicity move because sportswriters came along; becoming enchanted with Hana, they gave it a great deal of copy and were probably the first to publicize the phrase "Heavenly Hana." It wasn't long before tourists began arriving.

Unfortunately, the greatest heartbreak in modern Hana history occurred at just about the same time, on April 1, 1946. An earthquake in Alaska's Aleutian Islands sent huge tidal waves that raked the Hana coast. These destroyed hundreds of homes, wiping out entire villages and tragically sweeping away many people. Hana recovered, but never forgot. Life went on, and the menfolk

began working as *paniolo* on Fagan's spread and during round-up would drive the cattle through town and down to Hana Bay where they were forced to swim to waiting barges. Other entire families went to work at the resort, and so Hana lived again. It's this legacy of quietude and old-fashioned *aloha* that attracted people to Hana over the years. Everyone knows that Hana's future lies in its uniqueness and remoteness, and no one wants it to change. The people as well as the tourists know what they have here. What really makes Hana "heavenly" is similar to what's preached in Sunday school: everyone wants to go there, but not everyone makes it.

Hana Festivals

As is the case in most Hawaiian towns, Hana has many local festivals and events. First in the year is the fireworks on New Year's Eve over Fagan's cross. In late March, the weekend **Taro Festival,** Web site: hookele.com/tarofest, with its traditional ceremonies, games, music, authentic foods and a food market, arts and crafts exhibitions, and hula demonstrations thrills everyone. People come from all over the state to watch and participate; make plans well in advance. Later in June or early July, the children of town get treated to the **Makeke,** a children's festival, when all sorts of games and celebrations are held. For decades, Hana has had a tie with the great American sport. To honor this connection, a softball tournament is held over the Labor Day weekend, pitting families and friends against one another in friendly but serious competition. As with all of the state, the **Aloha Festival** is celebrated with gusto. Parades, luau, a fishing tournament, and many other activities are organized.

SIGHTS

Hana Bay

Dominating the bay is the red-faced **Kauiki Hill.** Fierce battles raged here, especially between Maui chief Kahekili and Kalaniopuu of Hawaii, just before the islands were united under Kamehameha. Kalaniopuu held the natural fortress until Kahekili forced a capitulation by cutting off the water supply. It's believed that Kamehameha himself boarded Capt. James Cook's ship after a lookout spotted it from this hill. More importantly,

Queen Kaahumanu, Kamehameha's favorite and the Hawaiian *ali'i* most responsible for ending the old *kapu* system and leading Hawaii into the "new age," was born in a cave here in 1768. Until very recent times fish-spotters sat atop the hill looking for telltale signs of large schools of fish.

To get there, simply follow Uakea Road when it splits from the Hana Road at the police station, and follow the signs to the bay. Take it right down to the pier and **Hana Beach County Park,** open 6 a.m.-10 p.m. Hana Beach has full amenities and the swimming is good. It's been a surfing spot for centuries, although the best breakers occur in the middle of the bay. Until the '40s, cane trains rode tracks from the fields above town out onto the pier, where the cut stalks were loaded onto boats to be taken to the mill for processing. To explore Kauiki look for a pathway on your right and follow it. Hana disappears immediately; few tourists come out this way. Walk for a few minutes until the lighthouse comes clearly into view. The footing is slightly difficult but there are plenty of ironwoods to hang onto as the path hugs the mountainside. A few pockets of red-sand beach eroded from the cinder cone are below. A copper plaque erected in 1928 commemorates the spot of Kaahumanu's birth. This entire area is a great spot for a secluded picnic only minutes from town. Proceed straight ahead to the lighthouse sitting on a small island. To arrive, you'll have to leap from one jagged rock to another. If this doesn't suit you, take your

bathing suit and wade across a narrow sandy-bottomed channel. Stop for a few moments and check the wave action to avoid being hurled against the rocks. When you've got it timed, go for it! The view from up top is great.

Fagan Memorial

Across from the Hotel Hana-Maui, atop Lyon's hill, is a lava-stone cross erected to the memory of Paul I. Fagan, who died in 1960. The land is privately owned, but it's okay to walk or drive up there if there are no cattle in the pasture. If you drive, you must exchange your license for a gate key to get entry. Whether you walk or drive, always inquire at the hotel if it's all right to go up. The road to the top starts at the hotel guest parking lot. From atop the hill you get the most panoramic view of the entire Hana area. After a rain, magic mushrooms have been known to pop up in the "cow pies" in the pasture surrounding the cross.

Wananalua Church

Near the hotel is the Wananalua Congregational Church, built from coral blocks in 1838 and placed on the National Register of Historic Places in 1988. Sunday service is at 10 a.m. The missionaries deliberately and symbolically built it on top of an old *heiau,* where the pagan gods had been worshipped for centuries. It was the custom of chiefs to build *heiau* before entering battle. Since Hana was always contested ground,

J.D. BISIGNANI

Wananalua Church

dozens of minor *heiau* can be found throughout the region.

Across the street is the newer and lovely St. Mary's Catholic Church. Its wood construction and decorative detail contrast vividly with the plain, sturdy, rather unornamented Wananalua Church. Mass Sunday 9 a.m., weekdays 7 a.m., and Friday 5 p.m. Visitors welcome.

Hana Cultural Center

Located along Uakea Road on the right, kitty-corner from the Hana Bay entrance road, this center is open daily 10 a.m.-4 p.m.; donations gladly accepted. Founded in 1971 by Babes Hanchett, the Hana Cultural Center, tel. (808) 248-8622, Web site: www.planet-hawaii.com/hana, e-mail: hccm @aloha.net, occupies an unpretentious building (notice the beautifully carved koa doors, however) on the grounds of the old courthouse and jail. The center houses fine examples of quiltwork: one, entitled "Aloha Kuuhae," was done by Rosaline Kelinoi, a Hana resident and the first woman voted into the State Legislature. There are precontact stone implements, tapa cloth, and an extensive shell collection. Your donation entitles you to visit the courthouse and jail next door. Simple but functional, with bench and witness stand, it makes "Andy of Mayberry" look like big-time. This tiny courthouse was used regularly from 1871 to 1978, and is still used monthly for the same purpose. The jail, "Hana Lockup," was also built in 1871 and finally renovated in 1997. The townsfolk knew whenever it held an inmate because he became the groundskeeper and the grass would suddenly be mowed.

In the ancient Hawaiian style, using traditional materials, a sleeping house, cook house, meeting house, and canoe shed have been constructed to the side and below the center to give you an idea of what types of buildings were used in Hawaii in the past. On the terrace below these structures is a small **ethnobotanical garden** of medicinal and agricultural native plants. Pick up a brochure about the plants inside the museum. Be sure to stop at the cultural center while in Hana to learn a bit about local history and culture.

Hana Gardenland Nursery

On the Hana Hwy., you pass several sights east of Nahiku before you actually reach town. The first is Hana Gardenland Nursery, open daily 8:30 a.m.-5 p.m., where you're free to browse. The nursery sells fresh-cut flowers, and the prices are some of the best on Maui. This certified nursery, which can ship plants or cut flowers to the Mainland, sits on more than five acres, over which you can wander at your leisure, and acquaint yourself with the spectacular plantlife that you will encounter throughout the Hana area. Many of the plants are labeled, so it's a bit like a botanical garden, and there are over 200 varieties of rare palms—a specialty. On the premises is the Jungle Cafe, a "semi-gourmet window restaurant." Inside the main building is a gift gallery featuring crafts mostly by local artisans.

Ka'eleku Caverns

The newest adventure in Hana is spelunking. There are 50 known caves on Maui and 150 on the Big Island. Only a short section of the Thurston Lava Tube on the Big Island can be entered. Some 30,000 years old, Ka'eleku ("Standing in the Dark") Cave near Kahanu Gardens in Hana is the only cave on Maui that's open to the public, and it's a beauty. There is no evidence that Ka'eleku Caverns was ever used for burials like so many on the islands. This cave, like all others in Hawaii, is actually a lava tube 30-40 feet below the surface, so the cave follows the lay of the land up the mountainside. No matter what the temperature is outside, it's always a moderate 64-67° inside. You enter through a skylight and make your way down the steps to the floor of the cave, which once flowed with molten lava. Here you must let your eyes adjust to the darkness before proceeding. As liquid lava surged through this tube it scored the walls, leaving striations. Here and there, you will also see benches and ledges along the sides where lava cooled faster on the periphery than the middle. Some rubble has fallen from the ceiling or off the walls creating mounds that you'll have to climb around or over. Although walkable upright most of the way, there are a few sections where you must kneel or even get down on all fours to squeeze through. This is not for the claustrophobic. Still at other spots the tube opens up to form large chambers, at one point with an unusually tall 50-foot ceiling. Other natural features that occur in this cave are lava stalactites and stalagmites, drip columns, a bowling alley-like channeling with gutters down both sides, ropy pahoehoe lava levees, clinkers of rough a'a, side loops, convergent channels, and over tubes. A very unusual feature and one that may be peculiar only to this cave is the delicate, filigreed grape-like botryoid clusters. And the colors, who would have thought? There is gray, blue, brown, gold, and copper—quite astounding. One of the mysteries of this cave is that the air flows in two different directions. Through the lower portion, the flow is downward and out a series of skylights; in the upper section, the air flows uphill, exiting at a yet undiscovered spot. As this cave has only recently been open to visitors, it is still in very pristine condition. Care must be taken not to touch delicate formations or accidentally crush or break anything fragile. "Cave softly and carry a big light" is the owner's motto. Maui Cave Adventures is run by Chuck Thorne and his wife Deborah, and they can set you up with a tour. All tours are guided and are very informative. Chuck is happy to share with you what he knows about this cave as well as other caves in the state. A hard hat, light, and drinks are provided. Wear long pants, closed-toe shoes, and a T-shirt—something that you don't mind getting a little dirty. If you have any interest in caving, you'll be glad you had a look at this one. A two-hour tour costs $50 per person, and adventurers must be at least nine years old. The four-hour tour is $100 per person, with an age requirement of 18 years old. The six-hour tour is $150 per person; you must be 18 and in very good physical condition, and jeans and hiking boots are necessary. Two-person minimum for tours to run. For information and advanced reservations, call or write: tel. (808) 248-7308 (8 a.m.-8 p.m. daily), fax 248-7074, Maui Cave Adventures, P.O. Box 40, Hana, HI 96713, Web site: www.maui.net /~hanacave, e-mail: hanacave@maui.net.

Kahanu Gardens

Turn off Hana Highway onto Ulaino Road and proceed toward the ocean. Here, the pavement soon gives way to a dirt track and leads about a mile and a half to Kahanu Gardens, located just past a shallow stream. The gardens are open by appointment only, and may be closed at any time if, because of heavy rains, the stream (no bridge) is too high or moving too swiftly to cross. This 120-acre tropical garden runs down to the tortured lava coastline. Part of the Pacific Tropical Botanical Garden, the Kahanu Gardens contain a huge variety of domestic and imported tropical plants, including a native pandanus forest and large and varied collections of breadfruit and coconut trees. Also within the gardens is **Piilanihale Heiau,** Hawaii's largest, with massive walls that rise over 50 feet. Two-hour guided walking tours are given daily at 1 p.m. for $10 per person (schedule open to change); meet at the gate. Half-hour van tours are also given for $5 at the same time. Call (808) 248-8912 for information and reservations.

Pool at Ulaino

Past Kahanu Gardens, Ulaino Road continues to roughen, crosses two more streams, passes several homesites being carved out of the bush, and ends after more than a mile at a parking area near the ocean. This may not be drivable during heavy rains. Walk across the boulders that form the beach at the mouth of the stream and stay along the *pali* for 100 yards or so until you come upon what some people call Blue Pond tucked behind some larger rocks. This hideaway is an old local favorite, a clothing-optional swimming spot where a waterfall drops fresh water into an oceanside pool. Not always blue, it's sometimes murky when water brings large amounts of sediment down from the hillside above. As always at pools, be aware of stones and branches that might come over the top and give you a limit on your noggin as a souvenir of your time in paradise.

Hana Airport

Less than a mile in toward town from Ulaino Road, on Alalele Road, a sign points left to Hana Airport, where **Island Air,** tel. (800) 323-3345, or (808) 248-8328 in Hana, operates two daily flights to Kahului, and **Pacific Wings,** tel. (808) 873-0877, schedules some charter flights. All flights to Hana go through Kahului, from where you can get connecting flights to other Hawaiian cities and the Mainland. Hotel Hana-Maui operates a shuttle between the airport and the hotel for its guests, and can make rental car arrangements for its guests. There is no public transportation in Hana, and only **Dollar Rent A Car,** tel. (808) 248-8237, can provide wheels for you—make reservations *before* arriving in Hana. Aside from the airline counters, there is only a public telephone and restrooms here at this tiny terminal.

Blue Hawaiian helicopters makes one run up the Hana coast that stops at the Hana Airport.

Here, it connects with ground transportation by **Temptation Tours,** so you can go one way by air and the other by land, a fly-drive offering. Neither company has an office at the Hana Airport.

Waianapanapa State Park

Only three miles outside Hana, and down a road that's clearly marked along the highway near mile marker 32, this state park offers not only tent camping but houskeeping cabins sleeping up to six. Set some distance from the beach and tenting area, the cabins offer hot water, electricity, a full kitchen, bathroom, bedrooms, and bedding, and rent for $45 a night for up to four people and $5 for each additional person. A deposit is required. They're very popular so book far in advance by writing Division of State Parks or visiting its office at 54 S. High St., Wailuku, HI 96793, tel. (808) 984-8109. The grassy camping area has picnic tables, water, showers, and restrooms. Even for those not camping, Waianapanapa is a "must stop." Pass the office to get to the beach park and its black-sand beach. The swimming is dangerous during heavy surf because the bottom drops off quickly, but on calm days it's mellow. The snorkeling is excellent, and it should be, as Wainapanapa means "Glistening Waters." Just offshore is a clearly visible natural stone bridge.

A short, well-marked trail leads to **Waianapanapa Caves.** The tunnel-like trail passes through a thicket of vines and *hao,* a bush used by the Hawaiians to mark an area as *kapu.* The two small caves are formed from lava. The water trapped inside is clear. These caves mark the site of a Hawaiian legend, in which a lovely princess named Popoalaea fled from her cruel husband Kakae. He found her hiding here and killed her. During certain times of the year millions of tiny red shrimp invade the caves, turning the waters red, which the Hawaiians say is a reminder of the poor slain princess.

Along the coastline here are remnants of the ancient Hawaiian **paved trail** that you can follow for a short distance. To get to the section running north toward the airport, cross the black sand beach and head up the trail on the far side. Most of the way, the trail stays on or near the cliffs; this walk takes about two hours. A section of the trail also runs south along the coast toward Hana. This trail should take about three hours, and along the way you'll pass lava cliffs, blow holes, an old *heiau,* and graves.

BEACHES

Red Sand Beach

Named Kaihalulu ("Roaring Waters"), this is a fascinating and secluded beach area, but unfortunately the steep walk down is treacherous. The path, after a while, skirts the side of a cliff, and the footing is made tough because of unstable and crumbly cinders. Grave accidents have occurred, and even locals won't make the trip. Follow Uakea Road past the turnoff to Hana Bay. Proceed ahead until you pass the public tennis courts on your right and the community center on your left. The road dead-ends a short way later. Head through the open lot between the community center and hotel property, where you pick up a worn path. Ahead is a Japanese cemetery with its distinctive headstones, some now being lost to wave erosion and a degrading shoreline. Below are pockets of red sand amidst fingers of black lava washed by sky-blue water. There are many tide pools here. Keep walking around Kauiki Head until you are obviously in the hollowed-out amphitheater of the red cinder cone. Pat the walls to feel how crumbly they are—the red "sand" is eroded cinder. The water in the cove is fantastically blue against the redness.

Across the mouth of the bay are little pillars of stone, like castle parapets from a fairy kingdom, that keep the water safe for swimming. This is a favorite fishing spot for local people and the snorkeling is good, too. The beach is best in the morning before 11 a.m.; afterward it can get hot if there's no wind and rough if the wind is from the north—remember the beach's name. The coarse red sand massages your feet, and there's a natural jacuzzi area in foamy pools of water along the shore.

Koki Beach

The beach is a mile or so out of town heading toward Oheo. Look for Haneoo Road on your left with a sign directing you to Koki and Hamoa Beaches. Koki is only a few hundred yards on the left, at the first set of pullouts by the water. The riptides are fierce in here so don't swim unless it's absolutely calm. The winds can whip along here, too, even though at Hamoa Beach, less than a mile away, it can be dead calm. Koki is excellent for beachcombing and for a one-night unofficial bivouac.

A very special person named Smitty lived in a cave on the north side of the beach. A distinguished older man, he "dropped out" a few years back and came here to live a simple monk's existence. He kept the beach clean and saved a number of people from the riptide. He was a long-distance runner who would tack up a "thought for the day" on Hana's public bulletin board. People loved him and he loved them in return. In 1984 the roof of his cave collapsed and he was killed. When his body was recovered, he was in a kneeling position. At his funeral, all felt a loss, but there was no sadness because all were sure that Smitty had gone home.

Hamoa Beach

Follow Hamoa Road a few minutes past Koki Beach to the other side of this small thumb of a peninsula to Hamoa Beach. Between Hamoa and Koki are the remnants of an extensive Hawaiian fishpond, part of which is still discernible. This entire area is an eroding cinder cone known as **Kaiwi O Pele** ("The Bones of Pele"). This is the spot where the swinish pig god, Kama pua'a, ravished her. Pele also fought a bitter battle with her sister here, who dashed Pele on the rocks, giving them their anatomical name. Out to sea is the diminutive Alau Island, a remnant left over by Maui after he finished up the Hawaiian Islands.

You can tell that Hamoa is no ordinary beach the minute you start walking down the paved, torch-lined walkway. This is the semiprivate beach of the Hotel Hana-Maui. But don't be intimidated, because no one can own the beach in Hawaii. Hamoa is terrific for swimming and snorkeling on calm days or bodysurfing or surfing on days when the wind is up a little. The hotel guests are shuttled here by buses throughout the day that leave from the hotel on the hour, so if you want this lovely beach to yourself arrive before midmorning and stay after late afternoon. There is a pavilion that the hotel uses for its Tuesday night luau and its lunch buffets, as well as restrooms and showers.

ACCOMMODATIONS

Hotel Hana-Maui

The legacy of Paul Fagan, who built it in the late '40s, this is as close to a family-run hotel as you can get; HI 96713, tel. (800) 321-4262 or (808) 248-8211 on Maui. Most personnel have either been there from the beginning, or their jobs have passed to their family members. Guests love it that way, proven by an astonishing 80% in repeat visitors, most of whom feel like they're staying with old friends. The hotel has had only eight managers in the last 50 years. The public areas in the hotel are done in muted tans and browns. It's open and airy with flagstone floors and easy furniture of hardwood and bamboo. All guest rooms have been extensively renovated and the hotel can now proudly take its place among the truly luxury hotels of Hawaii. Rooms, all with their own lanai, surround the beautifully appointed grounds where flowers add a splash of color to the green-on-green blanket of ferns and

a bed & breakfast in Hana

ROBERT NILSEN

gently sloping lawn. Inside the colors are subdued shades of white and tan. Morning light, with the sun filtering through the louvered windows, is especially tranquil. All suites have a wet bar and large comfortable lounge area with rattan furniture covered in billowy white pillows. A glass-topped table is resplendent with a floral display, and homemade banana bread greets all guests. There's even fresh Kona coffee that you grind and brew yourself. The floors are a deep rich natural wood counterpointed by a light reed mat in the central area. The beds, all king-size or two twins, are covered with handmade Hawaiian quilts, while Casablanca fans provide all the cooling necessary. The guest-cottage rooms have large free-standing pine armoires; all rooms have two walk-ins. The bathrooms, as large as most sitting rooms, are tiled with earthtone ceramic. You climb a step to immerse yourself in the huge tub, then open eye-level windows that frame a private mini-garden like an expressionist's still life.

The hotel staff adds an intangible quality of friendliness and *aloha* that sets the hotel apart from all others. Upon arrival, you are greeted with a shell lei and a chilled glass of juice. Housekeepers visit twice a day, leaving beige terrycloth robes, and, if you have turndown service, fresh flowers on every pillow. There is a library for use by guests, and a few shops for clothes, necessities, and gifts. The hotel restaurant is open for breakfast, lunch, and dinner, and the Paniolo Bar serves drinks from the late morning until 10:30 p.m. Other facilities and activities include a wellness center, two heated swimming pools, tennis courts, superb horseback riding, a three-hole practice golf course, free bicycle use by guests, hikes to archaeological sites, and a famous luau held every Tuesday, 6 p.m., at the hotel's facilities on Hamoa Beach. Also held at Hamoa Beach, 11:30 a.m.-1:30 p.m. Tuesday, Thursday, Saturday, and Sunday, is a barbecue lunch cookout. All activities are easily arranged by visiting the activities desk that can be counted on to keep family and children happy with Hawaiian language lessons, lei-making, or swaying hula lessons. Free shuttle service is provided by the hotel throughout the area in its vintage vehicles.

Rates start at $395 for a garden-view room and progress up to $795 for the sea ranch cottage suites. An option, for an additional $95, includes three meals under the full American plan, or $75 for breakfast and dinner. Otherwise you can pay as you eat. The entire scene isn't stiff or fancy, but it is a memorable first-class experience!

Heavenly Hana Inn

The second most famous Hana accommodation, the Heavenly Hana Inn, resembles a Japanese *ryokan*. Walk through the formal garden and remove your shoes on entering the open-beamed main dining hall. The inn is homey and delightful. Skylights brighten this central area, set around a central hearth. Having undergone renovations, the inn is more beautiful than ever in its simplicity. A variety of woods give warmth to the living areas, *soji* screens hide what need not always be present, and the decoration is perfectly authentic. The three suites seem like little apartments broken up into sections by shoji screens. Each has a sleeping room, bathroom with soaking tub, and a sitting room with television. There are no telephones, and no smoking is allowed. Guests stay just three nights only—no exceptions—a Monday arrival with departure on Thursday. Rates are $2000 for a single or couple, $1000 for an additional person; most (gourmet) meals are included. An application for reservation, which includes references from people who have stayed at the inn previously, must be filled out by each guest. Write P.O. Box 790, Hana, HI 96713, tel. (808) 248-8442, or e-mail: hanainn@maui.net.

Hamoa Bay Bungalow

Run by Jody Baldwin, this captivating rental sits in a copse of trees and bamboo just off the Hana Highway above Hamoa Beach. Inspired by the architecture of Bali, two stone lions holding umbrellas greet you at the driveway. There is only one second-story unit here but it has all the amenities: living room/bedroom with king-size bed, full kitchen, bath, jacuzzi/shower on the screened porch, and ceiling fans. Cute little place, a fine romantic getaway. Laundry facilities are available. Rates are on a sliding scale: $175 for one night, $165 for each of two nights, $145 for three to six nights, and $135 for seven through 13 nights; monthly rates can be arranged. A continental breakfast is served on the first morning only. Call, fax, or write: P.O. Box 773, Hana, HI 96713, tel. (808) 248-7884, fax 248-8642.

Ekena

Set high above the west end of town is a luxurious vacation rental owned and operated by Robin and Gaylord Gaffney. The upper and lower floors are separate, but only one level is rented at a time—unless the entire building is desired—so you won't be disturbed by anyone. So spacious are these that each floor could be rented by two couples, one on each end, who want to share the cost and enjoy each others' company. Both floors have large living rooms, fully equipped kitchens, two master bedrooms and spacious bathrooms. Ekena is a wonderful pole building with a huge deck and spectacular views both down to the coast and up the mountainside. As it sits high up the hill, it almost always is graced with trade winds, so even if it's dead calm in town it may be breezy up there. At the upper end of the vacation rental bracket, it's not cheap but it's good value for the money. The Jasmine level with one bedroom goes for $150 a night, two bedrooms $190. The Sea Breeze level is $275. Both together run $450 a night. Three nights minimum, no kids younger than 14. For information and reservations, contact: T. Isetorp, P.O. Box 728, Hana HI 96713, tel. (808) 248-7047, Web site: www.maui.net/~ekena, e-mail: ekena@maui.net.

Hana Hale Malamalama

A magnificent place on the lower road into town, Hale Malamalama sits on a steep hillside overlooking an ancient fishpond that's been rebuilt. This is a culturally significant site and numerous artifacts have been found here. Great care has been taken to aesthetically landscape the property so that the buildings seem to fit in as if they have been here for years. Three units make up the compound: set next to the pond, the Royal Suite occupies a two-floor, 1,800-square-foot house made in the Philippines, transported here, and reconstructed; the Garden Suite in set in a rock garden on the hillside; and the Tree House Cottage sits up top over a carport. The Royal suite runs $175, the Garden suite $110, and the Tree House Cottage is $150. This is a perfect place for a honeymoon or for a couple who just wants a little luxury and class without spending an arm and a leg. Call John Romain for reservations, tel. (808) 248-7718, fax 248-7429, or write: Hana Hale Malamalama, P.O. Box 374, Hana, HI 96713, e-mail: hanahale@maui.net.

Hana Plantation Houses

Hana Plantation Houses offers a unique service whereby you can rent a private house on the lush, tropical Hana coast. You have 11 homes to choose from ranging from a deluxe cedar one-bedroom, slooping four and complete with lanai, full kitchen, barbecue, and your own private mini-garden for $150, to the Lanai Makaalae Studio, a Japanese-style studio for two at $70. Several other newly remodeled homes are available around town, like the two-story Hale Kipa plantation house ($100 downstairs and $135 upstairs), which has full amenities as well as an outdoor jacuzzi, and the two-story two bedroom The Palms, which can accommodate up to six people for $150 per night. Contact Blair's Original Hana Plantation Houses at P.O. Box 249, Hana, HI 96713, tel. (808) 248-7868, fax 248-8240, or (800) 228-1962 for reservations, Web site: www.kestrok.com/~hana, e-mail: hana@kestrok.com. Check-in is at Hana Gardenland, open daily 9 a.m.-5 p.m., just past mile marker 30, *mauka* side before entering Hana. Late check-ins should call for instructions.

Hana Ali'i Holidays

A second agency in Hana renting everything from a seaside cottage to large plantation homes scattered throughout the Hana area, Hana Ali'i Holidays offers over a dozen homes to choose from. Rates vary, $75-200 a night; weekly and monthly rentals are also available. Contact Duke; he will set you up: P.O. Box 536, Hana, HI 96713, tel. (808) 248-7742 or (800) 548-0478, fax (808) 248-8595, Web site: www.hanaalii.com, e-mail: info@hanaalii.com.

Hana Kai Maui Resort

These resort condos, the only condo rentals in town at 1533 Uakea Rd., are all well maintained and offer a lot for the money. Rates are: studios $125-145, deluxe one-bedrooms $145-195; fifth night free, and weekly and monthly rates available. All have private lanai with exemplary views of the bay, maid service, laundry facilities, and barbecues. The views couldn't be better as the grounds, laid out in a lovely garden highlighting the interplay of black lava rock and multihued blooms, step down the mountainside to Popolana Beach on Hana Bay. For additional information, contact: P.O. Box 38, Hana, HI 96713, tel. (808) 248-8426 or (800) 346-2772, fax (808) 248-7482, Web site: www.hanakai.com.

Aloha Cottages

Adjacent to the Hana Cultural Center, these units are owned and operated by Zenzo and Fusae Nakamura and are the best bargain in town. The cottages are meticulously clean, well built, and well appointed. For $60-90 double, $10-20 per additional guest, you get two bedrooms, a full kitchen, living room, deck, and outdoor grills. Mrs. Nakamura is very friendly and provides daily maid service. In season, fruit trees on the property provide free fruit to guests. For reservations, contact: P.O. Box 205, Hana, HI 96713, tel. (808) 248-8420.

Josie's Hana Hideaway

Josie offers two spartan rooms in the rear of her house and one up at the front. Each large and comfy unit (the front unit is smaller than the ones behind) has a bedroom/sitting room with a kitchenette in the corner, color TV by the queen bed, a full bathroom, and a separate entrance. If you want, you can prepare your meal in the kitchenette on the upper lanai. Daily room rates are $55 single, $65 double, and up to two kids $10 each; five-day, seven-day, and monthly rates also available. Josie also rents the three-bedroom, two-bath house next door for $85 a night, and a cabin behind it for $75 a night. To find Josie's turn off the Hana Highway onto Kauiki Street, near Pa'ani Mai Park, and go down to the bend in the road, where you will find Josie's Hana Hideaway. For information, call Josie Diego at (808) 248-8418, or write P.O. Box 265, Hana HI, 96713.

Joe's Place

Down the road from Hana Kai Maui Resort is Joe's Place, tel. (808) 248-7033. A very modest but clean self-serve guesthouse, this is a home that's been split into eight guest rooms. A Maui-style sign reads, "If our office is closed, check key rack at left, and you may use a room and either pay in the morning or lock payment and key in the room before leaving, two persons to a room." Rooms for singles or doubles cost $45, $55 with a private bath. Also available is a cottage for $100 that can sleep three. Cash or traveler's checks only. Checkout time is at 10 a.m. and check-in is at 3 p.m. "or as soon as room is available." Reservations are held until 6 p.m. There's kitchen access, a communal TV room, daily towel change, and maid service on request at an extra charge.

Hana Maui Vacation Rental

Across from the Heavenly Hana Inn, this is a small place with three new units. Neat and tidy, one has a kitchen while the other two have only microwaves. All have bedrooms separate from the cooking area, bathrooms with showers, and separate entrances. While not large, it's certainly adequate, and the price is right. The room with a kitchen runs $65 a night, with the microwave $55; maximum three per room. Monthly and *kama'aina* rates available. Call or write for reservations: P.O. Box 455, Hana HI, 96713, tel./fax (808) 248-8087.

Flower Farm Rentals

Two tropical flower farms on the outskirts of town that rent rooms or bungalows on their property are Tradewinds Cottages and Heavenly Flora. **Tradewinds Cottages** has two detached houses set in the garden that have full kitchens and bathrooms, queen beds and sleeper sofas, color TV, and ceiling fans. The Tradewinds Cottage runs $115 a night, maximum of six, while the Hana Cabana is $95 a night, maximum of four; $10 each additional person after the first couple. Information: Tradewinds Tropicals Vacation Rentals, P.O. Box 385, Hana, HI 96713, tel. (808) 248-8980 or (800) 327-8097, Web site: www.maui.net/~twt/cottage.html, e-mail: twt@maui.net.

Heavenly Flora rents two rooms in the main house. Both are tastefully decorated, one with a king bed, the other with a queen bed. Guests have use of the full kitchen, laundry facilities, and swimming pool. The king room is $100 and the queen room runs $80 a night. For information and reservations write or call: P.O. Box 748, Hana, HI 96713, tel. (808) 248-8680.

FOOD

Hotel Hana-Maui

As far as dining out goes, there's little to choose from in Hana. The Hotel Hana-Maui main dining room offers breakfast, lunch, and dinner. Prices vary according to your choice of options, but expect to spend up to $14 for breakfast, $25 for lunch, and $50 for dinner. Reservations recommended.

Hotel guests have first preference, but the hotel will try its hardest to seat. Afternoon snacks are also served at the Paniolo Bar 2:30-5 p.m.

Meals become a long-remembered sumptuous event. Follow the hostesses to your table in the dining room. Here, breakfasts, served 7:30-10 a.m., are all manner of fresh exotic fruits and juices, hot pastries, banana macadamia-nut waffles, eggs poached or herbed into omelettes accompanied by petite steaks, fresh fish, or Hana Ranch sausages. Lunches, 11:30 a.m.-2 p.m., which upon request are prepared as very civilized picnics in wicker baskets, include chilled seafood chowder, Oriental sesame chicken salad, smoked turkey and bacon sandwich, *kiawe*-grilled chicken breast, and a potpourri of vegetables. Special dinner menus are prepared daily, but you can begin with a sashimi plate, sautéed chicken with peanut sauce, and then move on to an assortment of grilled and roasted fowl, seafood, wild boar, or locally grown beef and lamb, all basted in a variety of gourmet sauces. Vietnamese whole fish for two is especially tantalizing. Desserts are too tempting to resist, and if you can somehow save the room try lime or macadamia nut pie, banana cream cake, coconut mousse, or a rainbow of rich and creamy ice creams and sherbets. Dinner is served 6-9 p.m.

The hotel luau, held every Tuesday at 6 p.m. at Hamoa Beach, and a barbecue lunch cookout at the same site, offered 11:30 a.m.-1:30 p.m. Tuesday, Thursday, Saturday, and Sunday, are other alternatives. Make reservations at the activities desk in the hotel lobby.

Entertainment at the hotel—and that, quite frankly, is it for the whole town—is two informal hula and Hawaiian music shows put on by local families on during the Sunday evening buffet. Aside from that, nightly music is performed at the bar, usually by one or two local musicians on ukulele and/or guitar, who fill the entire building with good cheer and melodious song. The Paniolo Bar is open daily 11:30 a.m.-10:30 p.m. For alternate entertainment, try the frequent evening baseball games at the ballpark behind the hotel.

Hana Ranch Restaurant

The Hana Ranch Restaurant, tel. (808) 248-8255, serves very tasty family-style meals, but it can be stampeded by ravenous tourists heading up or down the Hana Road. Reservations recommended. It's a sturdy place with wood floors, rattan furniture, and heavy slabs of wood as tables. Seating is inside or outside under a timber framework. Breakfast, daily 6:30-10 a.m., is served from an adjoining service window only, but a shaded area with picnic tables is provided. Lunch, also served from the service window daily 11 a.m.-2:30 p.m., is an assortment of sandwiches, saimin, or plate lunches. An inside buffet, served daily 11 a.m.-3 p.m. for adults $12.95, children $6.50, salad only $7.95, includes barbecue beef ribs, teriyaki chicken, baked beans, assorted vegetables, and baked potato. Dinner is served inside Friday and Saturday evenings 6-8 p.m., and Wednesday is pizza night. The dinner menu includes appetizers like fried calamari for $5.50 and crispy onion rings for $3.50, various pizzas range $12.50-18.50, salad, and pasta entrees for around $10. A short wine list is available, or you can choose some other drink from the bar. Not gourmet by any means, it is tasty, filling, and decently priced. The outside window is open daily 4-7 p.m. for plate lunches, burgers, and sandwiches. Besides the Hotel Hana-Maui, this is the only place to have an evening meal in Hana.

Jungle Cafe

Sit surrounded by the blooms and ferns of the Hana Gardenland Nursery and enjoy the delicious food prepared by the Jungle Cafe, tel. (808) 248-8975, a bamboo- and rattan-fronted "window restaurant" open daily 8:30 a.m.-5 p.m. Start your day with the Hana sunrise wrap for $5.50, *ono* steamed eggs and salsa $5, homemade banana bread for $2.95, waffles at $5.75, or a bowl of health-conscious granola for $3.75. Lunchtime brings mostly sandwiches, soups, and wraps that you can choose your own filling for. Try the smoked turkey sandwich for $6.95, garden island salad for $6.95, wraps at about $6, or lasagna for $8.95. Soups change daily. Refreshing beverages include espresso, cappuccino, fresh-squeezed orange or carrot juice, fruit smoothies, and tropical fruit iced tea for $1.50-3.50. Organic foods and local produce are used as much as possible. The cafe will be happy to prepare your food to go.

Tu Tu's

Tu Tu's Snack Shop, open daily 8 a.m.-4 p.m., is at the community center building at Hana Bay, offering window service with tables available. Eggs, loco molo, French toast, and other breakfast items all under $4.50, sandwiches to $3.75, and plate lunches under $6. Other items include salads, saimin, hamburgers, drinks, and ice cream. This building was donated by Mrs. Fagan, the wife of Paul Fagan, the original owner of the Hotel Hana-Maui, to the community.

SHOPPING

Hasegawa's General Store
In the ranks of general stores, Hasegawa's would be commander-in-chief. This institution, run by Harry Hasegawa, had been in the family for 75 years before it burned to the ground in the fall of 1990. While your gas tank was being filled, you could buy anything from a cane knife to a computer disk. There were rows of food items, dry goods, and a hardware and parts store out back. Cold beer, film, blue jeans, and picnic supplies—somehow it was all crammed in there. Everybody went to Hasegawa's, and it was a treat just to browse and people-watch.

Now housed in the old movie theater in downtown Hana, this store still serves the community and visitors that for so long sustained it. It's just as packed as ever, and it now also has a Bankoh bank machine. The only one-day film processing in town is handled by Hasegawa Gas Station just down the road. Open Mon.-Sat. 8 a.m.-5:30 p.m., Sunday 9 a.m.-4:30 p.m.; tel. (808) 248-8231.

Hana Store
From the Hana Road, make the first right past St. Mary's Catholic Church and go up to the top of the hill to find the Hana Store, open daily 7 a.m.-7 p.m., tel. (808) 248-8261, a general store with an emphasis on foodstuffs. It carries a supply of imported beers, a wide selection of food items, film, videos, and some gifts. The bulletin board here gives you a good idea of what's currently happening in town.

Hana Treasures
In the small complex across from the Hana Ranch Restaurant, look for Hana Treasures, open Mon.-Fri. 10 a.m.-4 p.m., Saturday until 3 p.m., and Sunday 10:30 a.m.-2:30 p.m., operated by Cheryl, a Hana resident who is friendly and willing to offer local information. The small shop features airbrushed T-shirts by Hana artists, an assortment of Hawaiian gifts, particularly those made in the Hana area, and two display cases of silver necklaces, bracelets, and rings.

Hana Coast Gallery
Located at Hotel Hana-Maui, this gallery displays many fine works of art by Hawaiian residents. The gallery, tel. (808) 248-8636, is open daily 9 a.m.-5 p.m.

Hana Gardenland Gift Shop
Inside the main building at the Hana Gardenland Nursery is a gift gallery featuring crafts, mostly by local artisans. The shelves hold a smattering of books on Hawaii, postcards, handmade jewelry, baskets and other woven items, koa wood boxes, some prints, photos, and posters, and T-shirts, of course. Its a nice little collection with quality items to choose from. While here, enjoy a walk through the gardens or stop and have a bite to eat at the Jungle Cafe window.

ACTIVITIES

Hana Bay Kayak
Arranged through the Hotel Hana-Maui activities desk, tel. (808) 248-8811, this adventure heads to Hana Bay for a two-hour session and can take as many as eight people. Kayak and snorkel tours are given at 9:30 a.m. and 2 p.m.; $59 per person, half price under age 12. They'll even videotape underwater for you as you snorkel.

Horseback Riding
Horseback rides are given at the Hana Ranch Stables. The one-hour trail rides, either along the coast or in the upper pastures, leave at 8:30 and 10 a.m. and again at 1:30 p.m. Rides cost $35 per person, and riders must be seven years old. Private rides can be arranged 3-5 p.m. for $70 per person.

Jogging Trail
A walking/jogging trail is maintained on Hana Ranch property, on what was the narrow-gauge sugarcane railbed. The trail runs for a bit over two miles and starts near the Fagan Memorial. Walk south.

SERVICES

Hana Medical Center
Along the Hana Road at the Y intersection, clearly marked on the right just as you enter town, is Hana Medical Center, tel. (808) 248-8294. Open weekdays 8 a.m.-6 p.m. (until 8 p.m. on Tuesday and Thursday) and Saturday 8 a.m.-noon; closed Sunday. Walk-in, nonemergency treatment. For emergencies, use the phone at the hospital entrance.

Police Station
The police station is at the Y intersection between Hana and Uakea Roads, just as you enter town. For emergencies call 911; otherwise, tel. (808) 248-8311.

Money, Mail, and Books
The Bank of Hawaii, tel. (808) 248-8015, is open Mon.-Thurs. 3-4:30 p.m., Friday 3-6 p.m.; cash advances on Visa and Mastercard can be made there. For an ATM bank machine go to Hasegawa's store. The **post office** is open weekdays 8 a.m.-4:30 p.m. Both are next door to the Hana Ranch Restaurant. The excellent Hana school/public **library,** tel. (808) 248-7714, is located at the new Hana School on the western edge of town; open weekdays 8 a.m.-5 p.m. (until 8 p.m. on Monday and from 9 a.m. on Tuesday).

Gas
There are two gas stations in town. The Chevron station next to the horse stables is open daily 7:30 a.m.-6 p.m. Hasagawa's gas station and visitor information center is about a hundred yards farther along the highway. Gas in Hana is expensive, about 20-25 cents per gallon higher than elsewhere on the island. Be sure to fill up before leaving town as the nearest gas station west is in Paia; going south around the bottom, the closest is in Keokea.

Rental Cars
Dollar Rent A Car, tel. (808) 248-8237, is the only show in town. It's best to call in advance to ensure a reservation. Cars may be available on short notice during low season, but don't count on it.

BEYOND HANA

About a half mile south of Hana is mile marker 51. From there, the mile markers decrease in number as you continue around the south coast back to Kahului. Now you're getting into adventure. The first sign is that the road becomes narrower, then the twists and turns begin again. After Oheo Gulch, there are a few miles that are still unpaved, and this is followed by a long stretch that's nothing more than a patchwork quilt of potholes. You know you're in a rural area with not much traffic when you come across the sign "Caution: baby pig crossing." There are no phones, no gas, only a fruit or flower stand or two, one *kaukau* wagon, and one store until you reach Ulupalakua Ranch. Although the road is good for most of the year, during heavy rains sections do still wash out and become impassable. The fainthearted should turn back, but those with gumption are in for a treat. There are roadside waterfalls, thick luscious forests, cascading streams filling a series of pools, a hero's grave, tiny plantation communities, some forgotten towns, isolated homesteads, and desolate scrubby ranchland. If you persevere all the way, you pop out at the Tedeschi Winery, where you can reward yourself with a glass of bubbly before returning to civilization.

Waioka Pool
Also referred to by some as Venus Pool, a myth-legend says Waioka Pool was once used exclusively by Hawaiian royalty. At the Waiohonu bridge just past mile marker 48, cross over the fence and hike (public access trail) through the fields above the river to its mouth. There you'll find a spring-fed, freshwater pool scoured out of the solid rock walls of this water course. Used by Hawaiian royalty during centuries past, it's now a refreshing, usually solitary, place for a swim or to sunbathe on the smooth rocks. Be safe and stay out of the ocean—the surf, which is just over the narrow sandbar, is strong. At certain times of the year you may see giant turtles just off the rocks a short way farther down the coast. They are best seen from the road a quarter mile past the river at

a sharp turn in the highway. In the fields above and to the north of Waioka Pool are the remains of an old sugar mill and part of the King's Highway, a paved pathway that once ran along the coast.

Wailua Falls

About seven miles after leaving Hana, Wailua and Kanahualui Falls tumble over steep lava *pali*, filling the air with a watery mist and filling their pools below. They're just outside your car door, and a minute's effort will take you to the mossy grotto at the base. There's room to park. If not for Oheo up ahead, this would be a great picnic spot, but wait! Sometimes roadside artists park here, and basket makers plying their trade. Check out the taro fields that have been created on the ocean side of the road. In a few minutes you pass a little shrine cut into the mountain. This is the **Virgin by the Roadside.** It's usually draped with a fresh lei.

KIPAHULU:
THE COASTAL BOUNDARY
OF HALEAKALA NATIONAL PARK

This is where the enormous **Kipahulu Valley** meets the sea. The majority of this valley, more than a third of the national park area, is off limits to the public, set aside as a scientific research preserve. Palikea Stream starts way up on Haleakala and steps its way through the valley, leaving footprints of waterfalls and pools until it spends itself in the sea. The area was named the Seven Sacred Pools by a publicity person in the late '40s. The area should have been held sacred, but it wasn't. Everything was right here. You can feel the tremendous power of nature: bubbling waters, Haleakala red and regal in the background, and the sea pounding away. Hawaiians lived here but the *heiau* that you would surely expect are missing. Besides that there aren't seven pools; there are more like 24! The name "Seven Sacred Pools" is falling into disfavor because it is inaccurate, with local people and the National Park Service preferring the proper name Kipahulu, or Oheo Gulch, instead. It's about 10 miles out of Hana.

Visitors Center

As you progress along the road, you'll come to a large cement arched bridge (excellent view) and then a parking area to your left with a ranger's station/visitors center, restrooms, and public telephone. The visitors center is relatively new. Information on the Kipahulu district of the national park, area trails and their conditions, the native Hawaiian people who lived in the area and their lifestyle, and the natural resource of the district are all well explained. Check out the koa canoe. It was cracked when the tidal wave struck the area in the 1940s. The center also stocks a selection of books about the area. A small bulletin board outside displays other information. The center is open 9 a.m.-5 p.m. daily. The rangers are friendly and informative, so before doing any exploring stop in and ask about trail conditions. They know a tremendous amount of natural history concerning the area and can inform you about the few dangers in the area, such as the flash flooding that occurs in the pools. Interpretive talks are given at the ranger station daily at 12:30, 1:30, 2:30, and 3:30 every afternoon, and occasional cultural programs are offered. Call the ranger station, tel. (808) 248-7375, for information. You can hike the trail by yourself but ranger-led hikes are also given. A short one-mile hike goes to the Bamboo Forest daily at 9 a.m. On Saturday at 9:30 a.m., they lead a group all the way to Waikamoi Falls, four miles there and back. Those intending to hike or camp should bring their own water. The vast majority of the people go to the easily accessible lower pools, but a stiff hike up the mountain takes you to the upper pools, a bamboo forest, and a fantastic waterfall; 99% of park visitors are gone by sundown. From the parking lot, a short dirt trail leads down to the large grassy camping area.

The Lower Pools

Head along the clearly marked path from the parking area to the flat, grass-covered peninsula. The winds are heavy here as they enter the mouth of the valley from the sea. A series of pools to choose from is off to your left. It's delightful to lie in the last one and look out to the sea crunching the shore just a few yards away. Move upstream for the best swimming in the largest of the lower pools. Be careful, because you'll have to do some fairly difficult rock climbing. The best route is along the right-hand side as you face up the valley. Once you're satiated, head back up to the road along the path on the left-hand side. This will take you up to the bridge that you crossed when arriving, one of the best vantage points from which to look up and down this amazing valley.

The Upper Pools

Few people head for the upper pools. However, those who do will be delighted. The trail is called **Waimoku Falls Trail,** and it begins at the ranger station. The falls at Makahiku are a half mile uphill and Waimoku Falls is two miles distant. The toughest part is at the beginning as you huff-puff your way straight uphill. The trail leads to a fenced overlook from where you can see the lace like falls at Makahiku as they plummet 181 feet to the rugged valley floor below. Behind you a few paces and to the left will be a waterworn, trench-like path. Follow it to the very lip of the falls and a gorgeous little pool. You can swim safely to the very edge of the falls. The current is gentle here, and if you stay to the right you can peer over the edge and remain safe behind encircling boulders. Be extremely conscious of the water rising, and get out immediately if it does!

After refreshing yourself, continue on the path through a grassy area. Here you'll cross the creek where there's a wading pool, and then zigzag up the opposite bank. After some enormous mango trees, you start going through a high jungle area. Suddenly you're in an extremely dense bamboo forest—an incredible experience in itself. The trail is well cut as you pass through the green darkness of this stand. If the wind is blowing, the bamboo will sing a mournful song for you. Emerge into more mangos and thimbleberries and there's the creek again. Turn left and follow the creek, without crossing yet, and the trail will become distinct again. There's a wooden walkway, and then, eureka! . . . Waimoku Falls. It cascades over the *pali* and is so high that you have to strain your neck back as far as it will go. It's more than a waterfall; it's silver filigree. You can stand in the shallow pool below surrounded by a sheer rock amphitheater. The sunlight dances in this area and tiny rainbows appear and disappear.

One word of warning. As at all such waterfalls on the islands, where the pool beckons to slack the heat and the surrounding scenery is so captivating, rocks and boulders periodically dislodge from the *pali* above and tumble into the pool below. How else have the boulders in the pool gotten to where they are? Usually, although not always, these falling rocks are accompanied by sounds of rock

striking rock. Always keep an ear out for danger and an eye upward. At popular and oft-visited waterfalls, warning signs are posted to warn you of such dangers and to keep you out of harm's way. Know the dangers and heed the warnings.

Camping

Kipahulu is part of Haleakala National Park, and camping is free (obtain permit at the visitors center) in designated sites only for a three-day limit. No backcountry camping or camping along the streams. Groups of more than 12 should obtain permits from the park superintendent at Park Headquarters, P.O. Box 369, Makawao, HI 96768, tel. (808) 572-9306. The campgrounds are primitive and mostly empty, except for holiday weekends when they can be packed. From the parking lot follow the camping sign and continue down the hill on the rutted dirt track. Bear right to a large grassy area overlooking the sea, where signs warn not to disturb an archaeological area. Notice how spongy the grass is here. Move to the trees to escape the wind. Here are clean outhouses, picnic tables, and barbecue grills, but no potable water, so make sure to bring your own.

BEYOND OHEO GULCH

Some of Route 31 beyond Oheo is genuinely rugged and makes the car companies cry. But it can be driven, and even the tourist vans make it part of their regular route. Be aware, however, that rough weather can bring landslides; the road may be closed by a locked gate with access available only for official business and local residents. Check the bulletin board at the ranger station for road conditions or ask one of the rangers! In 1.5 miles you come to the well-kept clapboard **St. Paul's Church,** which sits right next to the highway. Services are conducted here twice a month. A little farther along and down a side road is **Palapala Hoomau Church** (founded 1864) and its tiny cemetery, where Charles Lindbergh is buried. People, especially those who are old enough to remember the "Lone Eagle's" historic flight, are drawn here like pilgrims. The public is not really encouraged to visit, but the human tide cannot be stopped. If you go, please follow all of the directions posted. Right next to the church cemetery is the tiny

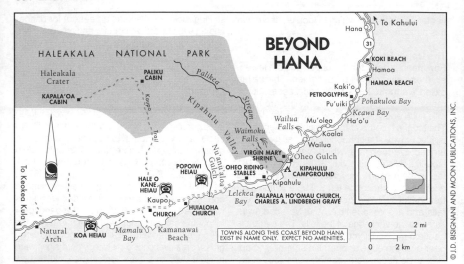

BEYOND
HANA

© J.D. BISIGNANI AND MOON PUBLICATIONS, INC.

TOWNS ALONG THIS COAST BEYOND HANA
EXIST IN NAME ONLY. EXPECT NO AMENITIES.

Kipahulu Lighthouse Point County Park,
which sits on the edge of the cliff overlooking
the frothy ocean below. Several trees and picnic
tables provide a quiet and shaded place for a
bite to eat and a rest. Up the road is Samuel F.
Pryor's Kipahulu Ranch. Mr. Pryor was a vice
president of Pan Am and a close chum of Lindbergh's. It was he who encouraged Lindbergh to
spend his last years in Hana.

Kipahulu Ranch has seen other amazing men.
Last century a Japanese samurai named Sen-
taro Ishii lived here. He was enormous, especially for a Japanese of that day, over six feet tall.
He came in search of work, and at the age of 61
married Kehele, a local girl. He lived in Kipahulu
until he died at the age of 102.

Past Sam Pryor's place is **Oheo Riding Stables.** From here two rides a day are taken
through the lush vegetation to spots overlooking
Makahiku and Waimoku Falls, both in the national park. About three hours are spent in the
saddle. Past here the road really begins to get
rugged and narrow, but only about four miles
remains unpaved.

Kaupo
Once you get to the Kaupo Gap, the tropical
vegetation suddenly stops and the landscape
is barren and dry. Here Haleakala's rain shadow
creates an environment of yellow grassland dot-

ted with volcanic rock. Everywhere are *ahu,* usually three stacked stones, that people have left as
personal prayers and wishes to the gods. Just
after Kaupo, the dirt road becomes a beat-up
pothole patchwork that wheels along with the
ocean far below. Around mile markers 28 and 29,
notice an ancient lava flow that spilled into the
sea and created a huge arch. Beyond that, you
can look down on Maui's last lava flow and La
Perouse Bay. Also, be aware of free-range cattle, which can be in the middle of the road around
any turn. Enjoy the road, because in a few minutes the pavement will improve and you'll be
back in the civilized world.

Kaupo Store
The vistas open up at the beginning of the Kaupo
Gap just when you pass **Hui Aloha Church.**
Built in 1859, this church sits on a level grassy
spot below the road near the sea; the road down
may be very rough and impassable except with
a 4WD vehicle. The village of Kaupo and the
Kaupo Store follow Hui Aloha Church. After so
many years of erratic hours and unpredictable
closures, Kaupo Store now has regular hours,
Mon.-Sat. 10:30 a.m.-5:30 p.m. A real anachro-
nism, the store serves double duty as unofficial
dusty museum and convenience store. Along
with the antiques hanging on the walls and filling
the shelves (not for sale), the store stocks cold

juices and beer, ice cream and chips—mostly snacks and traveling food.

Only a few families live in Kaupo, old ones and new ones trying to live independently. During decades past, Kaupo Store was the center of this community. If only the walls could talk, what stories they would tell. Kaupo is the last of a chain of stores that once stretched all the way from Keanae and were owned by the Soon Family. Nick Soon was kind of a modern-day wizard. He lived in Kaupo, and among his exploits he assembled a car and truck brought piecemeal on a barge, built the first electric generator in the area, and even made from scratch a model airplane that flew. He was the son of an indentured Chinese laborer.

A short distance past Kaupo is **St. Joseph's Church.** Built in 1862, it has recently been remodeled, and services are held here periodically.

Auntie Jane's

Wonders never cease! About 100 yards east of the Kaupo Store is a *kaukau* wagon, owned and operated by Auntie Jane Aki, who, along with her *paniolo* husband Charles, owns and operates a small cattle ranch. Their organic beef is made into the large juicy burgers offered on the limited menu. Definitely stop by if only just to "talk story" with Auntie Jane, a lifelong Hawaii resident, who came to the Kaupo area 35 years ago. Open from "about 11 a.m. to about when the sun goes down, everyday except Thursday" (when she goes for supplies), Auntie Jane offers big juicy regular burgers for $5, along with local ice cream, $5 large and $3 small, and $1 sodas. These huge burgers are loaded with all the trimmings and a meal in themselves. Auntie Jane says, "Everything is made my way, not McDonald's way." When she first opened, Auntie Jane had no sign to advertise her business. To remedy that, the island artist Piero Resta created one for her. What a blessing. Have a look. Also along with her husband, Jane owns and operates **Charley's Trailrides,** which offers guided overnighters from Kaupo to Haleakala Crater. Auntie Jane has "plenty aloha," which is as nourishing to the soul as her burgers are to the belly. Fill up!

KAHOOLAWE

OVERVIEW

The island of Kahoolawe ("The Taking Away") is clearly visible from many points along Maui's south shore. From Lahaina and Maalaea, the outline of Kahoolawe on the horizon resembles the back and dorsal fin of a whale half out of the water, ready to dive. In fact, many whales and dolphins do congregate around the island in summer to calve their young and mate for the coming year. Until recently Kahoolawe was a target island, uninhabited except for a band of wild goats that refused to be killed off.

Kahoolawe was a sacred island born to Wakea and Papa, the two great mythical progenitors of Hawaii. The birth went badly and almost killed Papa, and it hasn't been any easier for her ill-omened child ever since. Kahoolawe became synonymous with Kanaloa, the mangod. Kanaloa was especially revered by the *kahuna ana'ana,* the "black sorcerers" of old Hawaii. Kanaloa, much like Lucifer, was driven from heaven by Kane, the god of light. Kanaloa held dominion over all poisonous things and

ruled in the land of the dead from his power spot here on Kahoolawe. Kanaloa was also revered as the god of voyaging by early Polynesians and as such held an important place in their cast of deities.

For years, a long, bitter feud raged between the U.S. Navy, which wanted to keep the island as a bombing range, and Protect Kahoolawe Ohana, a Hawaiian native-rights organization, which wants the sacred island returned to the people. The Navy has finally agreed to stop bombing and return the island to the state of Hawaii, bringing the Ohana one step closer to its goal.

The Land

Kahoolawe is 11 miles long and six miles wide, with 29 miles of coastline. Its 45 square miles make it the seventh largest of the main Hawaiian islands, larger only than Niihau, and its mean elevation of about 600 feet is lower than all the other islands except for that small private enclave. The tallest hill, Moaulanui, is in the eastern section at 1,477 feet. Across the shallow Luamakika Crater is the nearly-as-tall hill Moaulani-ki, at 1,444 feet. There are no natural lakes or

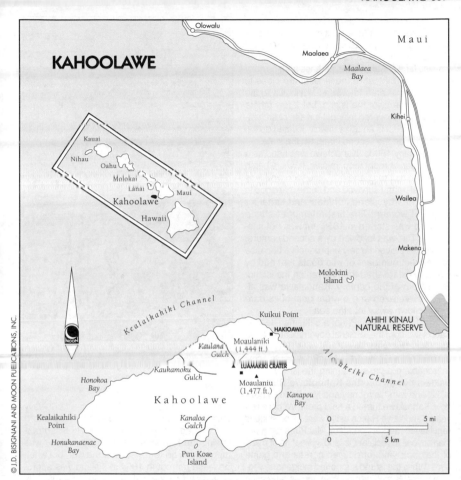

ponds on the island, and all streams except for one or two are seasonal. As Kahoolawe lies in Maui's rain shadow (it's six miles across to South Maui), it receives only about 25 inches of rain a year.

The land is covered by sparse vegetation and is cut by ravines and gulches. Much of the island, particularly the south and east coasts, is ringed by steep *pali,* but the land slides off more gradually to the north and west. There are few beaches on the island, but the best are at the west end between Honokoa Bay and Honukanaenae Bay. Also

known as Smuggler Cove, Honukanaenae Bay is said to be the site of a treasure buried on the beach in 1880 and as yet unclaimed. Kealaikahiki Point is the island's western tip, and this rock was used as a beacon during centuries past for canoe travelers to and from the island to the south.

HISTORY

It's perfectly clear that small families of Hawaiians lived on Kahoolawe for countless generations and that religious rites were carried out by many visiting *kahuna* over the centuries, but mostly Kahoolawe was left alone. There are scores of archaeological sites and remnants of *heiau* all over the bomb-cratered face of Kahoolawe, perhaps from as early as A.D. 1150. Most of these sites are close to water near the area known as Hakioawa in the northeast corner of the island, but a few others have been discovered inland. One site of archaeological interest is an adze quarry, located up top and said to be the second largest in the state.

In the early 1800s, Kahoolawe was used as a place of banishment for criminals. It was a harsh sentence, as the island had little food and less water. Yet, many survived and some managed to raid the nearby islands of Maui and Lanai for food and women! The first attempt at sheep ranching was started in 1858 but was not successful. This was followed by a second venture, which also proved largely unproductive because of the great numbers of wild goats that had by that time established themselves on the island. By the turn of the century, Kahoolawe was already overgrazed and a great deal of its bare topsoil blown away into the sea.

In 1917 Angus MacPhee, a cattleman, leased Kahoolawe from the territorial government for $200 per year. The lease would run until 1954 with a renewal option, if by 1921 MacPhee could show reasonable progress in taming the island. Harry Baldwin bought into the **Kahoolawe Ranch** in 1922, and with his money and MacPhee's know-how, Kahoolawe turned a neat profit. Within a few years Kahoolawe Ranch cattle were being shipped regularly to markets on Maui. MacPhee did more than anyone to reclaim the land. He got rid of many of the goats and introduced horses and game birds. While the island supported indigenous vegetation such as ohia, mountain apples, and even Hawaiian cotton and tobacco, MacPhee planted eucalyptus and range grass from Australia, which caught on well and stopped much of the erosion. Gardens were planted around the homestead and the soil proved to be clean and fertile.

The Navy Arrives

In 1939, with the threat of war on the horizon, MacPhee and Baldwin, stimulated by patriotism, offered a small tip of Kahoolawe's southern shore to the U.S. Army as an artillery range. One day

J.D. BISIGNANI

The Protect Kahoolawe Ohana resolutely builds a longhouse, pitting traditional Hawaiian beliefs against naval artillery.

after the attack on Pearl Harbor, the U.S. Navy seized all of Kahoolawe to further the "war effort" and evicted MacPhee, immediately disenfranchising the Kahoolawe Ranch. The island was supposed to be returned after the war, but when the lease ran out in 1954 the island was appropriated by Presidential decree for use solely by the military. No compensation was ever given to MacPhee or his family. Kahoolawe has since become the most bombarded piece of real estate on the face of the earth. During WW II the Navy praised Kahoolawe as being *the* most important factor in winning the Pacific War, and it held Kahoolawe until the fall of 1990.

The Protect Kahoolawe Ohana

Founded in 1976, the Protect Kahoolawe Ohana (PKO) is an extended group favoring traditional values based on *aloha aina* (love of the land), which is the primary binding force for all Hawaiians. They would like the island to return to Hawaiian Lands inventory with the *kahu* (stewardship) in the hands of native Hawaiians. The point driven home by the Ohana is that the military has totally ignored and belittled native Hawaiian values, which are now beginning to be asserted. They maintain that Kahoolawe is not a barren wasteland, but a vibrant part of their history and religion. Indeed, Kahoolawe was placed on the National Register of Historic Sites in 1981.

In a formal agreement with the PKO and the state of Hawaii in 1980, the U.S. Navy granted legal access to the island for four days per month. The PKO has built a *halau* (longhouse), and members use the time on Kahoolawe to dedicate themselves to religious, cultural, and social pursuits. The Ohana look to Kahoolawe as their *pu'uhonua* (refuge), where they gain strength and knowledge from each other and the *aina*. Hopefully Kahoolawe's future as a sacred island is now secure.

Changing Hands
In 1990, then-president George Bush issued an order to immediately halt the bombing of Kahoolawe, and at the same time established a congressional commission to create the terms and conditions for returning the island to the state. At that time, Ka Lahui Hawaii, the Native Nation of Hawaii, founded in Hilo in 1987, demanded that the island, as "totally ceded lands," be given to them as part of their sovereign nation. The Protect Kahoolawe Ohana, in a more moderate stance, suggested "land banking" the island under the control of the state or federal government until the United States recognizes the sovereignty of the Ka Lahui Hawaii. In the meantime, the PKO continues to lobby for exclusive rights to the stewardship of Kahoolawe. Finally, on May 7, 1994, Kahoolawe was returned to the state of Hawaii.

Transition
With the transfer of the island back to state protection, Kahoolawe has become an "island reserve." Congress has dedicated $400 million over a 10-year period (the Navy will be gone in 2003) toward cleaning the island of scrap and unexploded ordnance, and for the rejuvenation of the environment. What appears to be a huge amount of money is already being used at a rapid pace and appears to be only enough to start the process of making the island safe and healthy. The Kahoolawe Island Reserve Commission (KIRC) was established by state law to oversee and manage this effort until the Navy leaves. The reserve includes the island of Kahoolawe plus the waters surrounding the it to a distance of two miles. This total area is one of restricted access.

Now that the goats are gone and some of the ordnance cleaned up, the greatest problem seems to be erosion. While vegetation has a hold in some valleys and clings to spots where goats could not feed, much of the soil covering the island's plateau and gentle slopes has been blown off, exposing red, hardpan earth. Much work has been done; various approaches tried to establish grasses and other plants, and dams of grasses have been placed to prevent dirt from washing down gullies to the sea. Still, much more needs to be done. Introduced species are overtaking the dwindling native plants, and field mice are swiftly eating native seeds. Two other serious problems that must be overcome are the remaining unexploded ordnance, which is both expensive and risky to dispose of, and the perpetual lack of water. While the ordnance clean-up effort continues by the military, Mother Nature must be coaxed to help out with water. With similar natural conditions to South Maui, the island gets only minimal rain each year. Freshwater comes from rain catchment, and few streams ever run.

The only habitation sites on Kahoolawe are the traditional structures put up by the PKO near Hakioawa and the military installation on the west end of the island. There is currently virtually no infrastructure on the island except for a few rutted dirt roads. Over the years, about 5,000 people have visited the island, mostly to help with the cleanup efforts or to participate in religious and cultural activities. Kahoolawe might be a great cultural resource, a place where Hawaiians could go to practice age-old traditions in a sympathetic environment. But it probably will never be a place for any large-scale habitation, at least not in the foreseeable future.

While the exact plans for the future are still up in the air, it seems most likely that the island will be kept out of the hands of developers and open to visitors if the risk factor finally drops low enough. How the island will be managed and what status it will eventually attain is still undecided.

The Book on Kahoolawe

Inez MacPhee Ashdown lived on the island with her father and was a driving force in establishing the homestead. She has written a book, *Recollections of Kahoolawe,* that chronicles the events from 1917 until the military takeover and is rife with myths, legends, and historical facts about Kahoolawe.

Information

Unless you are one of the lucky few, you must be content to view Kahoolawe from across the water. For information about current happenings relating to this tortured island, log on to the PKO's Web site: www.kahoolawe.org. Alternately, try that of the KIRC at www.state.hi.us/kirc, or a Navy information site at www.efdpac.navfac.navy.mil/news /kaho/hp1.htm. To contact the PKO, write: P.O. Box 152, Honolulu, HI 96810. For the KIRC: 33 S. King St., Room 501, Honolulu, HI 96813, tel. (808) 586-0761 or (800) 468-4644 from the Neighbor Islands, e-mail: kirc@lava.net.

LANAI

INTRODUCTION

Lanai, in the long dark past of Hawaiian legend-history, was a sad and desolate place inhabited by man-eating spirits and fiendish bloodcurdling ghouls. It was redeemed by spoiled but tough Prince Kaululaau, exiled there by his kingly father, Kakaalaneo of Maui. Kaululaau proved to be not only brave, but wily too; he cleared Lanai of its spirits through trickery and opened the way for human habitation. Lanai was for many generations a burial ground for the *ali'i* and therefore filled with sacred mana and *kapu* to commoners. Later, reports of its inhospitable shores filled the logs of old sailing vessels. In foul weather, captains navigated desperately to avoid its infamously treacherous waters, whose melancholy whitecaps still outline Shipwreck Beach and give credence to its name.

The vast majority of people visiting the Hawaiian Islands view Lanai from Lahaina on West Maui but never actually set foot upon this lovely quiet island. For two centuries, first hunters and then lovers of the humpback whale have come to peer across the waters of the Auau Channel, better known as the "Lahaina Roads," in search of these magnificent giants. Lanai in Hawaiian means "Hump," and it's as if nature built its own island-shrine to the whale in the exact spot where they are most plentiful. Lanai is a victim of its own reputation. Most visitors were informed by even long-time residents that Lanai, nicknamed "The Pineapple Island," was a dull place covered in one large pineapple plantation: endless rows of the porcupine plants, sliced and organized by a labyrinth of roads, contoured and planted by improbable-looking machines, and tended by mostly Filipino workers in wide-brimmed hats and goggles. Although changing somewhat, this image still persists. It's true that Lanai had the largest pineapple plantation in the world, 15,000 cultivated acres, which accounted for about 90% of U.S. production. The remnants of these fields are still obvious in the swirls of green grasses as you approach the island by air. Now only about 100 acres remain in cultivation out by the airport—as a testimony to a by-

the south coast
of Lanai

ROBERT NILSEN

gone era—and these fruits are raised for local consumption only. All other pineapples on the island are raised by local gardeners. But the island has 74,000 acres that remain untouched and perfect for exceptional outdoor experiences, ranging from golf to mountain biking to snorkeling.

Because of its past reputation as a place where almost no one went and recent shift from pineapple production to tourism that caters to the well-to-do who want their peace and quiet, Lanai is once again becoming known as the "Secluded Island."

AN OVERVIEW

The people of Lanai live in one of the most fortuitously chosen spots for a working village in the world: Lanai City. All but about two dozen of the island's 2,800 permanent residents make their homes here. Nestled near the ridge of mountains in the northeast corner of the Palawai Basin, **Lanai City** (elevation 1,600 feet) is sheltered, cooled, and characterized by a mature and extensive grove of Cook pines planted in the early 1900s by the practical New Zealand naturalist George Munro. This evergreen canopy creates a parklike atmosphere about town while reaching tall green fingers to the clouds. A mountainous spine tickles drizzle from the water-bloated bellies of passing clouds for the thirsty, red, sunburned plains of Lanai below. The trees, like the bristled hair of an annoyed cat, line the **Munro Trail** as it climbs Lanaihale, the highest spot on the island (3,370 feet). The Munro Trail's magnificent panoramas encompass sweeping views of no less than five of the eight major islands as it snakes along the mountain ridge, narrowing at times to less than 30 yards across.

Maunalei Gulch, a vast precipitous valley, visible from "The Trail," was the site of a last-ditch effort of Lanai warriors to repel an invasion by the warrior king of the Big Island at the turn of the 18th century. Now its craggy arms provide refuge to mouflon sheep as they execute death-defying leaps from one rocky ripple to the next. On the valley floors roam axis deer, and, until recently, on the northwest grasslands were the remnants of an experimental herd of pronghorn antelope brought from Montana in 1959. After saturating yourself with the glories of Lanai from the heights, descend and follow a well-paved road from Lanai City to the southern tip of the island. Here, **Manele** and **Hulopoe** bays sit side by side. Manele is a favorite spot of small sailing craft that have braved the channel from Lahaina. Hulopoe Bay, just next door, is as salubrious a spot as you can hope to find. It offers camping and all that's expected of a warm, sandy, palm-lined beach. With its virtually untouched underwater marine park, Hulopoe is regarded as one of the premier snorkeling spots in the entire island chain.

You can hike or 4WD to **Kaunolu Bay,** one of the best-preserved ancient Hawaiian village sites.

Kamehameha the Great came to this ruggedly masculine shore to fish and frolic his summers away with his favorite cronies. Here, a retainer named Kahekili leaped from a sea cliff to the ice-blue waters below, and challenged all other warriors to prove their loyalty to Kamehameha by following his example and hurtling themselves off what today is known as **Kahekili's Leap.**

You can quickly span a century by heading for the southeast corner of Lanai and its three abandoned villages of **Lopa, Naha,** and **Keomuku.** Here legends abound. *Kahuna* curses still guard a grove of coconut trees, which are purported to refuse to let you down if you climb for their nuts without offering the proper prayers. Here also are the remnants of a sugar train believed to have caused its cane enterprise to fail because the rocks of a nearby *heiau* were disturbed and used in its track bed. A decaying abandoned Hawaiian church in Keomuku insists on being photographed.

You can head north along the east shore to **Shipwreck Beach,** where the rusting hulk of a liberty ship, along with timbers and planks from the great wooden square-riggers of days gone by, lie along the beach, attesting to the authenticity of its name. Shipwreck Beach is a shore stroller's paradise, a real beachcomber's boutique. Also along here are some thought provoking petroglyphs. Other petroglyphs are found on a hillside overlooking the former "pine" fields of the Palawai Basin.

If you hunger for a totally private beach, head north for the Polihua Trail. En route, you'll pass through a fantastic area of ancient cataclysm aptly called **The Garden of The Gods.** This raw, baked area of monolithic rocks and tortured earth turns incredible shades of purple, red, magenta, and yellow as the sun plays upon it from different angles. You have a junction of trails here. You can bear left to lonely **Kaena Point,** where you'll find Lanai's largest *heiau,* a brooding setting full of weird power vibrations. If you're hot and dusty and aching for a dip, continue due north to trail's end where the desolation of the garden suddenly gives way to the gleaming brightness of virtually unvisited **Polihua Beach.**

After these daily excursions, return to the green serenity of Lanai City. Even if you're only spending a few days, you'll be made to feel like you're staying with old friends. You won't have to worry about bringing your dancing shoes, but if you've had enough hustle and bustle and yearn to stroll in quietude, sit by a crackling fire, and look up at a crystal-clear sky, head for Lanai. Your jangled nerves and ruffled spirit will be glad you did.

THE LAND

The sunburned face of Lanai seems parched but relaxed as it rises in a gentle, steady arc from sea level. When viewed from the air it looks like an irregularly shaped kidney bean. The sixth largest of the eight main islands, Lanai is roughly 140 square miles, measuring 18 miles north to south and 13 miles east to west at its longest points, with 47 miles of coastline. A classic single-shield volcano, at one time Lanai was probably connected to Maui, Molokai, and Kahoolawe as a single huge island. Marine fossils found at the 1,000-foot mark and even higher in the mountains indicate its

LANAI CITY AVERAGE HIGH/LOW TEMPERATURE AND RAINFALL

	JAN.	MARCH	MAY	JUNE	SEPT.	NOV.
High	70	71	75	80	80	72
Low	60	60	62	65	65	62
Rainfall	3	3	2	0	2	4

Note: Rainfall in inches; temperature in °F

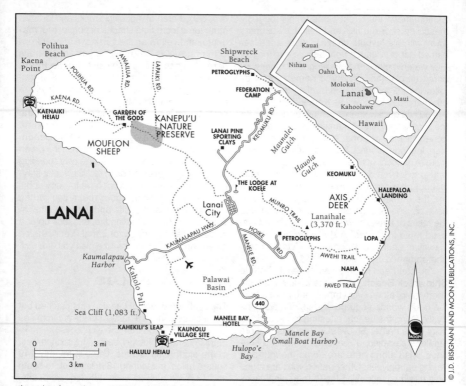

slow rise from the sea. Its rounded features appear more benign than the violent creases of its closest island neighbors; this characteristic earned it the unflattering Hawaiian name of "Hump." More lyrical scholars, however, have refuted this translation and claim the real meaning has been lost to the ages, but Lanai does look like a hump when viewed from a distance at sea.

Its topography is simple. A rugged mountain ridge runs northwest to southeast through the eastern half of the island, and its entire length is traversed by the Munro Trail. The highest peak is Lanaihale (3,370 feet). This area is creased by precipitous gulches: the two deepest are Maunalei and Hauola at more than 2,000 feet. The topography tapers off steadily as it reaches the sea to the east. Beaches stretch from the white sands of Polihua in the north, along the salt-and-pepper sands of Naha on the east, and end with the beautiful rainbow arches of Manele and Hulopoe in the

south. Until 1993, Palawai, Lanai's central basin, was completely cultivated in manicured, whorled fields of pineapple. Early this century, Palawai was covered in cactus; now cattle graze across sections of the plain and some wheat is grown. The southwest and west coasts have phenomenal sea cliffs accessible only by boat. Some of the most majestic are the **Kaholo Pali,** which run south from Kaumalapau Harbor, reaching their most amazing ruggedness at Kaunolu Bay. At many spots along this stretch the sea lies more than 1,500 feet below. Starting at Lanai City in the center, a half hour of driving in any direction presents a choice of this varied and fascinating geography.

Climate

The daily temperatures are quite balmy, especially at sea level, but it can get blisteringly hot in the basin and on the leeward side, so be sure to carry plenty of water when hiking or four-wheel driving. Lanai City gets refreshingly cool in the evenings and early mornings, but a light jacket or sweater is adequate, although thin-blooded residents bundle up.

Water

Lying in the rain shadow of the West Maui Mountains, even Lanai's windward side receives only 40 inches of rainfall a year. The central basins and leeward shores taper off to a scant 12 inches, not bad for pineapples and sun worshippers. Lanai has always been short of water, but wells now help satisfy the needs of the residents. Its scruffy vegetation and red baked earth are responsible for its inhospitable reputation. There are no real rivers, and the few streams, found mostly in the gulches of the windward mountains, carry water only when the rains come and are otherwise dry. Most ventures at colonizing Lanai, both in ancient and modern times, were kept to a minimum because of this water shortage. The famous Cook pines of Lanai City, along with other introduced greenery, greatly helped the barrenness of the landscape and provided a watershed. They tickle the underside of and drink water from the clouds that graze the highland ridge. But the rust-red earth remains unchanged, and if you get it onto your clothes, it'll remain there as a permanent souvenir.

FLORA AND FAUNA

Most of Lanai's flora and fauna have been introduced. In fact, the Cook pine and the regal mouflon sheep were a manmade attempt to improve the natural, often barren habitat. These species have adapted so well that they now symbolize Lanai, as the ubiquitous pineapple once did. Besides the mouflon, Lanai boasts axis deer and a few feral goats. A wide variety of introduced game birds include the Rio Grande turkey, ring-necked pheasant, and an assortment of quail, francolins, and doves. Like the other Hawaiian islands, Lanai, unfortunately, is home to native birds that are headed for extinction. Along the Munro Trail and on the windward coast you pass through forests of Cook pines, tall eucalyptus stands, shaggy ironwoods, native koa, and silver oaks. Everywhere, dazzling colors and fragrances are provided by Lanai's flowers.

Flowers

Although Lanai's official flower is the *kaunaoa,* it's not really a flower, but an airplant that grows wild. It's easily found along the beach at Keomuku. It grows in conjunction with *pohuehue,* a pinkish-red, perennial seashore morning glory. Native to Hawaii, the *pohuehue* grows in large numbers along Lanai's seashore. It's easy to spot, and when you see a yellow-orange airplant growing with it, you've found Lanai's *kaunaoa,* which is traditionally fashioned into lei. The medicinal *ilima,* used to help asthma sufferers, is found in large numbers in Lanai's open fields. Its flat, open yellow flower is about one inch in diameter and grows on a waist-high shrub. Two other flowers considered by some to be pests are the purple *koali* morning glory and the miniature red and yellow flowering lantana, known for its unpleasant odor. Both are abundant on the trail to the Garden of the Gods.

Cook Pines

These pines were discovered by Captain Cook. Imported in great numbers by George Munro, they adapted well to Lanai and helped considerably to attract moisture and provide a firm watershed. Exquisitely ornamental, they can also be grown in containers. Their perfect cone shape makes them a natural Christmas tree, used as such in Hawaii; some are even shipped to the Mainland for this purpose.

Endemic Birds

The list of native birds still found on Lanai gets smaller every year, and those still on the list are rarely seen. The *amakahi* is about five inches long with yellowish-green plumage. The males deliver a high-sounding tweet and a trilling call. Vegetarians, these birds live mostly on grasses and lichen, building their nests in the uppermost branches of tall trees. Some people believe that the *amakahi* is already extinct on Lanai.

The *ua'u* or Hawaiian petrel is a large bird with a 36-inch wingspan. Its head and back are shades of black with a white underbelly. This "fisherbird" lives on squid and crustaceans that it regurgitates to its chicks. Unfortunately, the Hawaiian petrel nests on the ground, sometimes laying its eggs under rocks or in burrows, which makes it an easy prey for predators. Its call is reported to sound like a small yapping dog.

The *apapane* is abundant on the other main islands, but dwindling rapidly on Lanai. It's a chubby red-bodied bird about five inches long with a black bill, legs, wingtips, and tail feathers. It's quick, flitty, and has a wide variety of calls and songs from beautiful warbles to mechanical buzzes. Its feathers were sought by Hawaiians to produce distinctive ornate featherwork.

Axis Deer

This shy and beautiful creature came to Lanai via Molokai, where the first specimens arrived in 1868 as a gift from the Hawaiian consul in Hong Kong. Its native home is the parkland forests of India and Sri Lanka. The coats of most axis deer are golden tan with rows of round lifetime spots, along with a black stripe down the back and a white belly. They stand three to four feet at the shoulder, with bucks weighing an average of 160 pounds and does about 110. The bucks have an exquisite set of symmetrical antlers that always form a perfect three points. The antlers can stand 30 inches high and more than 20 inches across, making them coveted trophies. Does are antlerless and give birth to one fawn, usually between November and February, but Hawaii's congenial weather makes for good fawn survival anytime of year. Axis deer on Lanai can be spotted anywhere from the lowland *kiawe* forests to the higher rainforests along the Munro Trail. Careful and proper hunting management should keep the population stable for many generations. The meat from axis deer is reported to have a unique flavor, different from Mainland venison—one of the finest tasting of all wild game.

Mouflon Sheep

Another name for these wild mountain sheep is Mediterranean or European bighorn. One of only six species of wild sheep in the world, mouflon are native to the islands of Sardinia and Corsica, whose climates are quite similar to Hawaii's. They have been introduced throughout Europe, Africa, and North America. Although genetically similar to domestic sheep, they are much more shy, lack a woolly coat, and only infrequently give birth to twins. Both rams and ewes are a similar tannish brown, with a snow-white rump, which is all that most people get to see of these always-alert creatures as they quickly and expertly head for cover. Rams weigh about 125 pounds (ewes a bit less) and produce a spectacular set of recurved horns. They need little water to survive, going for long periods on only the moisture in green plants. On Lanai they are found along the northwest coast in the grasslands and in the dry *kiawe* forests.

HISTORY

Kakaalaneo peered across the mist-shrouded channel between West Maui and Lanai and couldn't believe his eyes. Night after night, the campfire of his son Kaululaau burned, sending its faint but miraculous signal. Could it be that the boy was still alive? Kaululaau had been given every advantage of his noble birth, but still the prince had proved to be unmanageable. King Kakaalaneo had even ordered all children born on the same day as his son to be sent to Lahaina, where they would grow up as his son's friends and playmates. Spoiled rotten, young Kaululaau had terrorized Lahaina with his pranks and one day went too far: he destroyed a new planting of breadfruit. Even the chief's son could not trample the social order and endanger the livelihood of the people. So finally the old *kahuna* had to step in. Justice was hard and swift: Kaululaau must be banished to the terrible island of Lanai, where the man-eating spirits dwelled. There he would meet his fate, and no one expected him to live. But weeks had passed and Kaululaau's nightly fires still burned. Could it be some ghoulish trick?

axis deer

Kakaalanoo oont a canoe of men to investigate. They returned with incredible news. The boy was fine! All the spirits were banished! Kaululaau had cleansed the island of its evil fiends and opened it up for the people to come and settle.

Oral History

In fact, it's recorded in the Hawaiian oral genealogical tradition that a young Kaululaau did open Lanai to significant numbers of inhabitants in approximately A.D. 1400. Lanai passed through the next few hundred years as a satellite of Maui, accepting the larger island's social, religious, and political dictates. During this period, Lanai supported about 3,000 people who lived by growing taro and fishing. Most inhabited the eastern shore facing Maui, but old home sites show that the population became established well enough to homestead the entire island. Lanai was caught up in the Hawaiian wars that raged in the last two decades of the 1700s, and was ravaged and pillaged in 1778 by the warriors of Kalaniopuu, aging king of the Big Island. These hard times marked a decline in Lanai's population; accounts by Western sea captains who passed even a few years later noted that the island looked desolate, with no large villages evident. Lanai began to recover and saw a small boost in population when Kamehameha the Great established his summer residence at Kaunolu on the southern shore. This kept Lanai vibrant for a few years at the beginning of the 19th century but it began to fade soon thereafter. The decline continued until only a handful of Hawaiians remained by the 20th century. The old order ended completely when one of the last traditional *kanaka*, a man named Ohua, hid the traditional fish god, Hunihi, and died shortly thereafter in his grass hut in the year 1900.

Early Foreign Influences

No one knows his name, but all historians agree that a Chinese man tried his luck at raising sugarcane on Lanai in 1802. He brought boiling pots and rollers to Naha on the east coast, but after a few years of hard luck gave up and moved on. About 100 years later a large commercial sugar enterprise was attempted in the same area. This time the sugar company even built a narrow-gauge railroad to carry the cane. A story goes that after disrupting a local *heiau* to make ballast for the rail line, the water in the area, never in great abun-

dance to begin with, went brackish. Again sugar was foiled.

In 1854 a small band of Mormon elders tried to colonize Lanai by starting a "City of Joseph" at Palawai Basin. This began the career of one of Hawaii's strangest, most unfathomable yet charismatic early leaders. Walter Murray Gibson came to Palawai to start an idyllic settlement for the Latter-day Saints. He energetically set to work improving the land with funds from Utah and hard work of the other Mormon settlers. The only fly in Gibson's grand ointment occurred when the Mormon Church discovered that the acres of Palawai were not registered to the church at all but to Walter Murray Gibson himself! He was excommunicated and the bilked settlers relocated. Gibson went on to have one of the strangest political careers in Hawaiian history, including championing native rights and enjoying unbelievable influence at the royal Hawaiian court. His land at Palawai passed on to his daughter who became possessed by the one evil spirit Kaululaau failed to eradicate: she tried to raise sugarcane, but was fated, like the rest, to fail.

A few other attempts proved uneconomical, and Lanai languished. The last big attempt at cattle raising produced The Ranch, part of whose lands make up the Cavendish Golf Course in Lanai City. This enterprise did have one bright note. A New Zealander named George Munro was hired as the manager. He imported all manner of seeds and cuttings in his attempt to foliate the island and create a watershed. The Ranch failed, but Munro's legacy of Cook pines stands as a proud testament to this amateur horticulturist.

The Coming of Pineapples

The purchase of Lanai in 1922 was one of the niftiest real estate deals in modern history. James D. Dole, the most enterprising of the pineapple pioneers, bought the island—lock, stock, and barrel—from the Baldwins, an old missionary family, for $1.1 million. That comes to only $12 per acre, though many of those acres were fairly scruffy, not to mention Lanai's bad economical track record. Dole had come from Boston at the turn of the century to figure out how to can pineapple profitably. Dole did such a remarkable job of marketing the "golden fruit" on the Mainland that in a few short years, Midwestern Americans who'd never even heard of pineapples before were buying cans of it regularly from the shelves of country grocery stores. In 1922, Jim Dole needed more land for his expanding pineapple fields, and the arid basin of Palawai seemed perfect.

Lanai Plantation was an oligarchy during the early years, with the plantation manager as king. One of the most famous of these characters was H. Broomfield Brown, who ran Lanai Plantation in the '30s. He kept watch over the fields from his house through a telescope. If anyone loafed, he'd ride out into the fields to confront the offender. Mr. Brown personally "eyeballed" every new visitor to Lanai: all prostitutes, gamblers, and deadbeats were turned back at the pier. An anti-litter fanatic, he'd even reprimand anyone who trashed the streets of Lanai City. During the labor strikes of the 1960s, workers' grievances were voiced and Lanai began to function as a more fair enterprise. With pineapple well established on the world market, Lanai finally had a firm economic base. From a few thousand fruits in the early days, the flow at its peak reached a million fruits per day during the height of the season. They were shipped from the manmade port at Kaumalapau, which was specially built to accommodate Lanai's "pines."

Crushed Pineapples

At its height, Lanai had 18,000 acres of pineapples under production (15,000 acres for most of its heyday). These acres made up the largest single pineapple plantation in the world. Virtually the entire island was operated by The Dole Co., whose name had become synonymous with pineapples. In one way or another, everyone on Lanai owed their livelihood to pineapples, from the worker who twisted his ankle in a pine field to the technician at the community hospital who X-rayed it. Now, all has changed and only a few plots remain, mostly for use by the hotels.

Foreign production, especially in the Philippines, has greatly increased, and the Lanai pineapple industry has virtually folded. As acreage was taken out of pineapple production, and as the population of the island and number of visitors have increased, the company has experimented with raising various organic vegetables, grains, and cattle to diversify the island's economy. This seems to be a pet project of David Murdoch, and the hope is to make the economy of Lanai more locally sustainable and less dependent on imports from the other islands and the Mainland.

Changing Lanai

Most are amazed that George Munro's pines still shelter a tight-knit community that has remained untouched for so long. But all that's changing, and changing quickly. Two new hideaway luxury hotels have risen, and they're beauties. The coming of these resorts has brought the most profound changes to Lanai since James Dole arrived at the turn of the century. Castle and Cooke, practically speaking, owns the island (98%). David Murdoch is the CEO of Castle and Cooke, and the hotels are his babies. He developed them and the two golf courses, and continues to develop residential lots (up to 700 in the next 10 years) through a permutation of companies that is now called the Lanai Company. This company employs a staff of about 1,200 or so, more than all the workers needed to tend the pineapple fields, which was just over 500 people. The hotels have brought an alternative job market, new life to the downtown area, and a housing spurt. One fact was undeniable concerning Lanai: if you wanted to make a living you either had to work the pineapple fields or leave. Now that has changed. To stop the disenfranchisement of the local people, which was generally the case with rapid development, the Lanai Company has built several new housing projects, which have come with a promise. Local people, according to seniority with the company and length of residence on Lanai, have first choice. One group of houses is multiple-family, geared to the entry-level buyer, and the second is single-family homes. Million-dollar homes are also starting to pop up above town and now begin to line the fairways of the new golf courses. This isn't all *heart* on the part of the Lanai Company. It wants to ensure that the hotels will have a steady and contented workforce to keep them running without a hitch and to make the whole venture economically viable.

Downtown Lanai is inadequate. It couldn't possibly handle the hotel guests and all the new workers and their families who have moved to the island. Old buildings have been refurbished, some torn down and replaced, with more upscale businesses taking their place. The tired little shops in town are on Lanai Company property, most with month-to-month leases. The Lanai Company again promises to be fair, but like the rest of Lanai, they'll have a choice: progress or perish. Most islanders are optimistic, keeping an open mind and adopting a "wait and see" attitude concerning the inevitable changes and the promises that have been made for a better life.

THE PEOPLE

Lanai is characterized by the incredible mix of racial strains so common in Hawaii—Filipino, Japanese, Hawaiian, Chinese, and Caucasian. It is unique, however, in that 60% of its people are Filipino. The Filipinos, many recent immigrants, were solicited by Castle and Cooke to work as laborers on the pineapple plantation. Mostly young men, the majority speak Ilocano and may have come to join relatives already on Lanai. Most arrive on their own; they learn English and from Lanai they spread out. As workers they were perfect: industrious and quiet. At night you wonder where they all are. Due to the tremendous shortage of eligible women, most workers stay home or fish or have a beer in the back yard with buddies. And on Sundays, there is the illegal (officially nonexistent) cockfight. For high living, everyone heads for Maui or Oahu.

The next largest racial groups are Japanese (14%), Hawaiian (12%), and whites (11%). The Japanese started as the field workers before the Filipinos but now, along with the whites, are Lanai's professionals and middle management. The races coexist, but there are still unseen social strata. There's even a small Chinese population (1%), who continue their traditional role as shopkeepers. Finally, about 2% fall into the "mixed" category, with many of these Filipino-Hawaiian.

Community
Lanai has a strong sense of community and uniqueness that keeps the people close. For example, during a bitter three-month strike in 1964, the entire community rallied and all suffered equally: laborers, shopkeepers, and management. All who remember say that it brought out the best in the island tradition of *aloha*. If you really want to meet Lanaians just sit in the park in the center of Lanai City for an hour or two. You'll notice a lot of old-timers, who seem to be very healthy. You could easily strike up a conversation with some of them.

Other Faces
It once might have struck you that most of the people you saw around Lanai were men. That in itself was a social comment about Lanai, where men worked the fields and women stayed at home in their traditional roles, nurturing and trying to add the pleasantries of life. Now you will see more and more women about, many who work at the hotels. You might notice that there are no famous crafts of Lanai and few artists working commercially. This is not to say there is no art on Lanai, but the visitor rarely sees it. One reason that Lanai produces so little commercial art is that it's a workers' island with virtually no unemployment, so everyone is busy making a living. Old-timers are known to make superb fishing poles, nets, and even their own horseshoes. The island ladies are excellent seamstresses and, with the rising interest in hula, make lovely lei from the beautiful *kaunaoa,* Lanai's flower. If you turn your attention to the young people of Lanai, you'll see the statewide problem of babies having babies. Although the situation is getting better, teenage parents are still not uncommon. Young guys customize their 4WDs although there's no place to go. If as a young person you wish to remain on Lanai, then in almost every case your future will be tied to the Lanai Company. If you have other aspirations, it's "goodbai to Lanai." These islanders are some of the most easygoing and relaxed people you'll encounter in Hawaii, but with the electronic age extending its long arms of communication, even

LANAI ETHNICITY

FILIPINO
60%

JAPANESE
14%

HAWAIIAN
12%

CAUCASIAN
11%

OTHER
2 %

CHINESE
1%

© MOON PUBLICATIONS, INC.

here they're not nearly as "backwater" as you might think.

GETTING THERE

By Air
Hawaiian Airlines, tel. (800) 367-5320 Mainland and Canada, on Lanai (800) 565-7281, flies to Lanai. It currently has morning flights from Honolulu that run Friday, Saturday, and Sunday, and return via Molokai; daily afternoon flights through Molokai return directly to Honolulu. Morning and afternoon flights to Kahului go via Molokai or Honolulu.

Daily flights are available to and from Lanai by **Island Air,** tel. (808) 565-6744, (800) 652-6541 Neighbor Islands, or (800) 323-3345 Mainland. Using some jets and some turbo-props, Island Air flies to and from Honolulu 11 times daily, with three flights daily to/from Kahului, and once daily to Kona on the Big Island.

Lanai Airport is a practical little strip about four miles southwest of Lanai City, out near the remaining pineapple fields. The pleasing new terminal offers a departure lounge, gift shop, bathrooms, and public phones. If you are staying at any of the three hotels, a free shuttle will transport you into town and drop you at the appropriate place. Complimentary airport pickup can also be arranged with either of the two vehicle rental companies if you rent from them. Otherwise **Lanai City Service,** tel. (808) 565-7227, can taxi you into town for $5 per person.

By Boat
Expeditions, a passenger ferry, now plies daily between Lahaina and Manele Bay. No luxury transportation, this shuttle offers speedy and convenient alternative transportation to the island. The crossing takes less than one hour and the ferry leaves Manele Bay at 8 a.m., 10:30 a.m., 2 p.m., 4:30 p.m., and 6:45 p.m. From Lahaina's public loading pier, ferries leave at 6:45 a.m., 9:15 a.m., 12:45 p.m., 3:15 p.m., and 5:45 p.m. The adult fare is $25 one-way while children under 2-11 pay $20; *kama'aina* rates available. Luggage is taken free of charge, except for a $10 fee for bicycles. It's best to reserve a place. For information and reservations call (808) 661-3756 or (800) 695-2624, or write P.O. Box 10, Lahaina, HI 96767.

One other possibility for getting to Lanai is going by pleasure boat from Maui. These are basically tour boats specializing in snorkeling, dinner cruising, whalewatching, and the like, but they may be willing to drop you off and pick you up at a later date. It's an enjoyable way of going. As there are no fixed rates for this service, you'll have to make your own arrangements with the boat captains, most berthed at Lahaina Harbor. Remember that, in effect, you're going standby with these companies, but there is generally room for one more. This alternative is particularly attractive to campers, as they anchor on Lanai at Manele Bay, just a five-minute walk from the campsites at Hulopoe. One company to try is Trilogy, tel. (808) 661-4743 or 565-2387 on Lanai. Another outfit is Club Lanai, tel. (808) 871-1144, but it anchors at its own private beach on very remote east Lanai, with no way of getting anywhere except by a long and dusty hike.

GETTING AROUND

Taxi and Shuttle Transportation
No public bus transportation operates on Lanai, but **Lanai City Service,** tel. (808) 565-7227, or 565-9553 after hours, operates a free airport limousine service if you're renting a car/jeep from them. Otherwise the service to/from the airport to anywhere in Lanai City is $5 per person, and to Manele Bay, $12.50. The company also runs throughout the day from Lanai City to Manele Bay for $10, and from the bay to the Manele Bay Hotel for $2.50. You can also call 7 a.m.-7 p.m. for service anywhere on Lanai.

Lanai Resort Shuttle
A free shuttle service is offered for guests of the two big resorts and Hotel Lanai. This bus runs daily 7 a.m.-11 p.m. every 30 minutes on the hour and half hour, and picks up passengers at the front of each hotel.

Car, 4WD, and Moped Rental
For a car, or better yet, a jeep, try **Lanai City Service, Dollar Rent A Car,** Lanai City, HI 96763, tel. (808) 565-7227 or (800) 533-7808. You'll be outfitted with wheels and given a drive guide with information about road conditions and where to go. Pay heed! Make sure to tell them your plans, especially if you're heading for a remote area.

That way, if you have problems and don't return, they'll know where to send the rescue party! Lanai City Service is a subsidiary of Trilogy Excursions and has a franchise with Dollar Rent A Car. It rents compacts for $59 per day, midsize cars for $79, 4WDs (mostly Jeep Wranglers) for $119 per day, eight-passenger minivans for $129, and 15-passenger maxivans for $175 per day. They also may have a 2WD "hunter's truck" pickup for $145, but check before arrival on the island. Ask about the weekly, monthly, and *kama'aina* rates. No insurance is available for vehicles rented on Lanai. In case of trouble, cellular phones can be rented for $5 a day and the use charge is $1.50 a minute; arrange one at the counter when renting your vehicle. Lanai City Service offers free shuttle service to and from the airport if you rent with them.

For those who just need to zip around town for the day or a set of wheels to get to Hulopoe Beach, mopeds are also available from Lanai City Service at $30 a day, including a helmet.

Red Rover rents four different types of Defender 90 Land Rovers for your off-road pleasure, from four-seater open cabs to a nine-passenger safari van. Rates run $119-159 per vehicle per day. Most have manual transmission, some have hard tops, luggage racks, and/or air conditioning. Each also comes with a tool kit, a winch, and a two-way radio and cell phone (rates apply) that you can use to contact others in your party or call for help if you really get stuck. They'll send out a rescue party. Music tapes, snorkel gear, body boards, and surfboards are also offered free for the use, as is the advice about where to go to use them. The company will pick you up and drop you off at the airport or harbor, or deliver the vehicle to anywhere on the island. For more information, contact Red Rover, Inc., P.O. Box 464, Lanai City, HI 96763, tel. (808) 565-7722, fax 565-7377, or cell phone 565-1155.

Using a 4WD Rental

With only 30 miles of paved road on Lanai and rental cars firmly restricted to these, there is no real reason to rent one. The *real* adventure spots of Lanai require a 4WD vehicle, which on Lanai is actually useful and not just a yuppie showpiece, since mind-boggling spots on Lanai are reachable only on foot or by 4WD. Unfortunately, even the inveterate hiker will have a tough time because the best trailheads are quite a distance from town, and you'll spend as much time getting to them as hiking the actual trails.

Many people who have little or no experience driving 4WDs are under the slap-happy belief that they are unstoppable. Oh, that it were true! They do indeed get stuck, and it's usually miserable getting them unstuck. The rental agencies will give you up-to-the-minute info on the road conditions and a fairly accurate map for navigation. They tend to be a bit conservative on where they advise you to take "their" vehicles, but they also live on the island and are accustomed to driving off-road, which balances out their conservative estimates. Also, remember that road conditions change rapidly: a hard rain on the Munro Trail can change it from a flower-lined path to a nasty quagmire, or wind might lay a tree across a beach road. Keep your eye on the weather, and if in doubt don't push your luck. If you get stuck, you'll not only ruin your outing and have to hike back to town, but you'll also be charged for a service call, which can be astronomical, especially if it's deemed to be due to your negligence. Most of your off-road driving will be in *compound* 4WD: first gear, low range.

Sightseeing Tours

Personalized escorted van tours to various spots on the island can be arranged by Lanai City Service, tel. (808) 565-7227. Since the tours are changeable, it's best to call in advance to get the rates and times. One of the best is the **4X4 Van Tour.** Departing weekdays around 7:45 a.m., it returns at 1:30 p.m. and shows you around town and many of the sights of the island including the Munro Trail, Shipwreck Beach, and Garden of the Gods. The rate is $79 per person, including a continental breakfast, lunch, and snacks as you go. If you are unsure about driving off-road or may not want to rent a jeep for the out-of-the-way places, leave the driving to the professionals. It can be a good deal.

Uncle Sam Shin also does a personalized tour, arranged through Lanai City Service, which can be adjusted to your liking. These usually last about four hours and run $80 per person.

Hitchhiking

Like everywhere else in Hawaii, hitching is technically illegal, but the islanders are friendly and quite good about giving you a lift. Lanai, however, is a workers' island, and the traffic is really skimpy during the day. You can only reasonably expect to get a ride from Lanai City to the airport or to Manele Bay since both are on paved roads and frequented by normal island traffic, or to Shipwreck Beach on the weekends. There is only a very slim chance of picking up a ride farther afield, toward the Garden of the Gods or Kaunolu, for example, so definitely don't count on it.

ACCOMMODATIONS

The Manele Bay Hotel

Glass doors curved in a traditional Roman arch sympathize with the surging Pacific as you enter the seaside 250-room Manele Bay Hotel, P.O. Box 310, Lanai City, HI 96763, tel. (808) 565-3800 or 565-7700, (800) 321-4666, Lanai's newest luxury resort fashioned in a fusion of Mediterranean, Oriental, and Hawaiian architecture. The open reception area, all marble and glass, holds two massive murals of Lanai and the wide Pacific dotted with islands. Heroic paintings depict pioneering Polynesians in a double-hulled canoe sighting the Hawaiian Islands and the rascal Prince Kaululaau, redeemer of Lanai, standing triumphantly on a windswept beach after banishing the vexatious specters of Lanai. Underfoot, a fern and pineapple motif is woven into the rich carpet, and chandeliers hang overhead from coved and molded ceilings. The lower lobby in contrast has a decidedly Oriental feel, with hints of Hawaii and the Southwest. High on the upper walls are painted huge murals depicting Chinese scenes. Below, salubrious chairs and cushions invite you to relax, Asian-style adornments please the eye, and a huge Hawaiian-theme chandelier provides light. Throughout the hotel are sitting areas and niches where you will find velvet-covered chairs and marble-topped or lacquer tables. Mythical dragons fashioned from mirrors and gold filigree, lamps of Chinese flute players, carved elephant tusks, and billowy curtains add a touch of style. For an elegant evening, order a drink and have it in the hotel **Library,** a salubrious room filled with leather-bound tomes, globes, and models of sailing ships. Overhead, the recessed wooden ceiling has been painted with various emblems of Hawaii; the floor is the intricate paisley of tasseled Persian carpets. Sit in a highbacked chair just near the Library's balcony and enjoy the vantage point overlooking Hulopo'e Court below.

From the main reception area, descend a grand staircase and pass a formidable lava rock wall draped with the purples and pinks of living bougainvillea. Here is the grand cloverleaf pool encircled by a marble apron where you can relax upon white chaise lounges softened with billowy pillows and shaded by white canvas umbrellas. Near the pool is the hotel spa and fitness center, complete with steam rooms, saunas, fitness machines, free weights, and professional staff. The formal gardens, two on the east and three on the west, are tranquil oases where rivulets drop into koi ponds surrounded by patches of broad-leafed taro and swaying stands of bamboo. It's a marvelous setting, but perhaps the best outdoor feature of all is the unobstructed natural beauty of Hulopoe Bay

The hotel rooms and suites are mainly in two wings, east and west. East rooms bear marine names derived from the sea; the west rooms are named after flowers. These oversized guest rooms ranging in price $275-525, designed with Mediterranean and Oriental themes, offer woolen carpets, four-poster mahogany beds covered with thick quilts, double-wide louvered closets, wicker lounge chairs, wet bars, and user-friendly entertainment centers. The tiled bathroom, a study in relaxation with thick white carpets on marble floors, features extra-deep soaking tubs, double sinks and vanity, separate commodes, glass-enclosed shower stalls big enough for two, name-brand bath products, hair dryers, and slippers and robes for lounging. Each room has its own private lanai that either overlooks one of the gorgeous gardens or offers an ocean panorama. The hotel also offers 12 suites that range in price $525-2,000. A typical midrange suite offers a formal parlor and separate master bedroom with a dressing room attached. Butlers will pack and unpack clothing, make dinner reservations, and act as your personal liaison at the hotel. They will draw hot baths, pour cold champagne, and tuck you and your teddy bear in for the night.

The hotel also offers valet parking, tennis courts, a children's program, three restaurants, and a cocktail lounge. At the Manele Bay Hotel Gift Shop you can get a windbreaker, polo shirt, sweatshirt, children's alohawear, stuffed animals, incidental bags, jewelry, or light reading material. Saturdays and Sundays are special with *keiki* hula dancers who come to perform their special magic in the Hulopo'e Court. Complimentary afternoon tea is also served here daily as well. Another treat is to walk a few minutes to the hotel's **Lanai Conference Center,** where the antechamber holds museum-quality artifacts. In glass cases, you will find stone implements ranging from *ulu maika,* Hawaiian bowling stones similar to Italian boccie, to *poho kukui* (*kukui* nut oil lamps). Most of these implements, including a petroglyph stone, have been gathered from Lanai. There is also a very impressive replica of a Hawaiian double-hulled canoe. If you care to explore a bit farther, try a section of the old king's trail that runs from the beach and up along the coast by the golf course.

The Lodge at Koele

A stately row of Cook pines bids welcome as they line the red brick driveway leading to this grand manor house perched in genteel quietude just a 10-minute walk from downtown Lanai City. An upland country hotel befitting this area of trees and cool summers, it's gracefully done in neo-Victorian style. Here, a huge pineapple mural painted above the front entrance greets everyone upon arrival. "Koele" is variously interpreted as black sugarcane, the banging together of hula sticks, or the summoning of a commoner to do tithe work for an *ali'i.* The Lodge at Koele, P.O. Box 310, Lanai City, HI 96763, tel. (808) 565-3800 or 565-7300, (800) 321-4666, with its encircling veranda and swoop of broad lawn, includes gracious relaxation. You enter into the Great Hall where the back ceiling is a translucent skylight through which the sun casts diffused beams onto the formal Victorian parlors below. Encircled by a rich koa balcony, the Great Hall holds two immense fireplaces, the largest in Hawaii. Parlor settings of green velvet chairs, lace doilies, pink couches, with wicker lounges, credenzas covered in flowers and ferns, and lustrous end tables are perfect for a lazy afternoon of perusing the newspapers and magazines of the world. At each corner of the spacious Great Hall is a hexagonal room of beveled windows: one for dining; one for music; one a library; and the last a game room with backgammon, chess, and dominoes.

An unexpected favorite for many guests is the hotel's Visiting Artist Program. Started in 1992, this ongoing cultural event brings writers, musicians, chefs, poets, filmmakers, and a whole host of other creative people to the hotel for informal gatherings and presentations.

Out front is a croquet lawn, to the side a bowling green. Out back through glass French doors are the swimming pool and spa, gazebo and reservoir, Japanese strolling garden, orchid house, palm and fruit gardens, and an executive putting green—a professionally designed "miniature" but real golf course. Here, with putter and a glass of chilled champagne and chocolate-dipped strawberries, you can test your skill against tiny sand traps, puddle-sized water traps, and challenging Chihuahua-inspired doglegs both left and right.

Walk along the wide covered veranda past a row of rocking chairs to the two wings off the Great Hall, where you will find the 102 guest rooms, which range in price from $325 for a garden view to $1,500 for the best suite. Once inside, you can

ROBERT NILSEN

the Lodge at Koele

take the brass-doored elevator but climb instead the sweeping wooden staircases bearing carved pineapples, the symbol of hospitality, and walk the broad hardwood hall hung with the works of island artists (ask the concierge for an art list for the hotel), letting period wall lamps light your way. Rooms are furnished in a combination of wicker and heavy knotty pine, with a four-poster bed—each topped with a carved pineapple—covered by a downy quilt, while billowy printed curtains flutter past a window seat. Along with this turn-of-the-century charm comes a full entertainment center with remote-control color TV, video viewer, in-room safe, and wet bar. Each room has its own lanai with tile floor and wooden furniture. The bathroom, perhaps blue- or black-on-white marble, features a pedestal sink and deep soaking tub with old-fashioned brass knobs, a full assortment of name-brand bath care products, huge towels, and separate commode. Each room also has multiple phones, ceiling fans, even walking sticks for an afternoon foray into the surrounding hills.

Two in-house restaurants are here to serve the guests. You can find sundries at the hotel shop, open 8 a.m.-9 p.m., and all hotel and island activities, including croquet, tennis, golf, hunting, horseback riding, jeep tours, sporting clays, and beach and boating activities, can be arranged by the concierge. There is free shuttle service to meet all arriving and departing planes, to and from Lanai City, and to Manele and Hulopoe Bays.

Hotel Lanai

Being the only hotel on the island until 1990, you'd think the lack of competition would have made Hotel Lanai, P.O. Box 520, Lanai City, HI 96763, tel. (808) 565-7211 or (800) 795-7211 (7 a.m.-7 p.m. local time), arrogant, indifferent, and expensive. On the contrary: It is delightful. The hotel has gone through a few cosmetic changes since it was built in 1923 as a guest lodge, then called "The Clubhouse," primarily for visiting executives of Dole Pineapple Co., the progeny of which still owns it. Its architecture is simple plantation-style Hawaiiana, and its setting among the tall Cook pines fronted by a large lawn is refreshingly rustic. With a corrugated iron roof, board and batten walls inside and out, wooden floors, and two wings connected by a long enclosed veranda, it looks like the main building at a Boy Scout camp. But don't be fooled. The 10 remodeled rooms may not be plush,

but they are cozy as can be. All have been painted in lively colors, and are immaculate with refurbished private baths. All have pine dressers and tables, floor lamps, area rugs, and ceiling fans, and patchwork quilts like grandma used to make cover each comfortable bed. A newly renovated cottage behind the main building, at one time the manager's house, has its own private yard and bath. Room rates are $95-135; checkout is 11 a.m.

The hotel has the only in-town bar, where guests and at times a few islanders have a quiet beer and twilight chat. The dining room, which occupies the center of the hotel, is paneled in knotty pine boards and lined with hunting trophies. So if you're lured by the quiet simplicity of Lanai and wish to avail yourself of one of the last family-style inns of Hawaii, stay at the lovely little Hotel Lanai.

B&Bs and Vacation Rentals

For a more homey stay on the Pineapple Island, try one of the few bed and breakfast inns or vacation rentals on Lanai, all of which are in Lanai City. These places offer a substantially cheaper alternative to staying on Lanai than the resorts and they get you into the community.

Dreams Come True, tel. (808) 565-6961, fax 565-7056, or (800) 566-6961, Web site: www.go-native.com/inns/0117.html, a true B&B in the oldest part of town at 12th and Olapa St., is surrounded by lots of trees and flowers. Three rooms in this plantation house are rented to guests, each with its own bathroom and use of the common room. Not large or luxurious by any means, but decent size for the island, one room has a queen bed and a single while the others have queen beds. A continental breakfast is served each morning. Rates are $82.50 double or $67.50 single; $10 extra for a child in the same room as parents. The owners, Michael and Susan Hunter, also have two vacation rental houses, Web site: www.10kvacationrentals.com/dreamscometrue/index.pht, one original plantation house and one new, a two-bedroom, two-bath unit and a three-bedroom, two-bath unit.

Hale Moe, tel. (808) 565-9520, on the south side of town at 502 Akolu St., P.O. Box 196, Lanai City, HI 96763, rents three rooms, each with a bathroom. Usually no breakfast is served, but guests can make use of the kitchen. Two rooms go for $60, and the third, at $70, has a deck off the room.

Hale O Lanai, tel. (808) 247-3637, fax 235-2644, Web site: www.hotspots.hawaii.com /beachrent1.html, e-mail: hibeach@lava.net, is a newer two-bedroom, two-bath house on 4th and Lanai Ave. that has all the amenities for a fine vacation stay. It rents for $95 a night, two nights minimum; weekly rates available.

Aside from these, try Dolores Fabrao, tel. (808) 565-6134, who rents rooms in the family house for $55 double or $45 single and also has a larger room that's often used by hunting groups.

For additional information, contact any of the bed and breakfast associations listed in the Out and About chapter.

Okamoto Realty

This is Lanai's first house rental agency. Although the number of houses in its listing varies, there are always a handful available from two-bedroom affairs at $150 a night to a four-bedroom, three-bath cedar house for $395 a night. All houses are completely furnished including linens and kitchen utensils, and most have washer/dryer and TV. Houses are rented by the day, week, or month. Write Okamoto Realty, 730 Lanai Ave., P.O. Box 552, Lanai City, HI 96763, tel. (808) 565-7519, fax 565-6106, for current information.

Camping

The only official camping permitted to nonresidents is located at Hulopoe Bay, administered by the Lanai Company. Reservations for one of the six official campsites on the grass here are a must, although unbelievably there's usually a good chance of getting a space. Lanai Company officials state that they try to accommodate any "overflow" unreserved visitors, but don't count on it. Since Lanai is by and large privately owned by Castle and Cooke Inc., the parent company of the Lanai Company, you really have no recourse but to play by their rules. It seems they want to hold visitors to a minimum and keep strict tabs on the ones that do arrive.

Nonetheless, the campsites at Hulopoe Bay are great. Lining the idyllic beach, they're far enough apart to afford some privacy. The showers are designed so that the pipes, just below the surface, are solar heated. This means a good hot shower during daylight and early evening. Campsite use is limited to seven nights. The fee includes a one-time $5 group registration and is $5 per person per night. For reservations write to the Lanai Land Co., P.O. Box 310, Lanai City, Lanai, HI 96763, or call (808) 565-3978. Permits, if not mailed in advance, are picked up at the Lanai Company office. If visiting on the spur of the moment from a neighboring island, it's advisable to call ahead.

Note: While hiking or four-wheel driving the back roads of Lanai, especially along Naha, Shipwreck, and Polihua beaches, a multitude of picture-perfect camping spots will present themselves, but they can be used only by Lanai residents, although there's little supervision. A one-night bivouac would probably go undetected. No other island allows unofficial camping, and unless it can be statistically shown that potential visitors are being turned away, it seems unlikely that the Lanai Company will change its policies. If you're one of the unlucky ones who have been turned down, write your letter of protest to parent company Castle and Cooke, 650 Iwilei Rd., Honolulu, HI 96817, tel. (808) 548-4811.

RESTAURANTS

Aside from the new hotels, Lanai City is the only place on the island where you can dine, shop, and take care of business. Until recently, the food situation on Lanai was discouraging. Most everything had to be brought in by barge, and the fresh produce, fish, and meat was at a premium. People surely ate differently at home, but in the two tiny restaurants open to the traveler, the fare was restricted to the "two-scoop rice and teri beef" variety, with fried noodles and Spam as the pièce de résistance. But, "the times they are a-changin'!" Now, there are more options from which to choose, and more culinary variety.

By far the best restaurant in town is **Henry Clay's Rotisserie** at the Hotel Lanai, tel. (808) 565-7211; open for dinner. Henry Clay has worked under Gerard Reversade of Gerard's in Lahaina, so he's had good training. Evening appetizers run the gamut from oyster shooters at $1.35 apiece to Cajun shrimp for $10.95. A soup or salad prepares the way for an entree, be it eggplant creole and angel hair pasta at $16.95, baby back ribs at $16.95, or hunter-style rabbit at $24.95. Gourmet pizzas are also served and don't forget dessert. Order a variety of beers from around the world or a glass of wine with your meal or simply stop by the bar for a drink.

The banging screen doors announce your presence as you enter the plantation-era wainscoted **Blue Ginger Cafe,** tel. (808) 565-6363, open daily 6 a.m.-2 p.m. and 3-9 p.m., which could actually be called chic for Lanai. Upon entering, baked goods in a case let you know that not long ago it was Dahang's Bakery, a Lanai institution whose motto, "Mo betta grind ova hea" has also survived. It offers a full breakfast menu with choices like two eggs with sausage for $4.75, along with plenty of side orders, and fresh pastries. Plate lunches are $6 or so, while a bowl of saimin goes for $2.95. Burgers, sandwiches, pizza, and Dave's Ice Cream are also on the menu at comparable prices. Varying nightly, dinner specials, served with rice "toss" salad or macaroni salad, run $8-16. Eat inside or on the veranda, where you can see everything there is to see in Lanai City.

An authentic workers' restaurant and sundries store, **Tanigawa's** (formerly S.T. Property), open daily except Wednesday for breakfast and lunch 6:30 a.m.-1 p.m., is one of those places that you must visit at least for morning coffee. Totally downhome, but a pure cultural experience. Arrive before 7 a.m. when many of the older people come to "talk story." Just one look around at the crinkled faces will reveal the tough but sweet spirit of Lanai.

For a healthy, quick, light meal, try **Pele's Other Garden,** tel. (808) 565-9628. This juice bar, pizzeria, and deli is open daily 11 a.m.-7 p.m. (until 9 p.m. on Friday and Saturday). Eat in or take out. Try a turkey, veggie, or other sandwich for $4.45-4.99, or a hot entree for less than $6. Pizzas run $13-26, or choose something else from the deli case. A picnic basket might be a good choice if you're going to be away from town all day. Be sure to check the special board, as you never know what scrumptious delicacy will be offered each day.

Hotel Restaurants

The master chef, aided by a hand-picked staff at the Manele Bay Hotel's formal **Ihilani Dining Room** (jackets required) offers two fixed menus nightly, along with a complete menu of à la carte suggestions. Expect entrees in the $35-45 range. Begin with ravioli of Hawaiian goat cheese in a sauce of parsley and sun-dried tomatoes, or Maine lobster with Hayden mango and arugula salad. Second courses can be a delicately roasted squab breast in a marmalade of onions and a

Molokai sweet potato puree. Entrees are roasted Chinese duck with Hawaiian seasoning, Oriental rice, and pickled ginger plum sauce, or an array of curries from Thai shrimp red curry and pan-fried *onaga* in a North Indian style. Grill selections include catch of the day, or Colorado lamb chops with polenta topped by a roasted garlic sauce. All of this, with a superb view of the bay and beach—magnifique!

The less formal but still extremely elegant **Hulopo'e Court** offers breakfast and dinner of contemporary Hawaiian regional cuisine, with prices similar to the Ihilani. This is perhaps the best breakfast spot on the island. Begin the day with a continental breakfast of assorted pastries, sliced fruits, a selection of cereals, chilled juices, and rich Kona coffee, or choose all manner of traditional favorites from the breakfast buffet (à la carte selections available as well). Lunch and dinner begin with appetizers like Chinese spring rolls, seared *ahi* in a spicy crust, or a fresh dim sum basket. Soups and salads include Maui onion soup, Caesar salad with croutons, or Lanai field greens in a lilikoi vinaigrette. Entrees are fresh pasta, Chinese noodles with duck covered in a chili oyster sauce, or penne pasta primavera. You can also have a gourmet pizza of Tandoori chicken or Peking duck. An excellent selection of domestic and imported beer and wine completes the meal.

The least formal dining setting is poolside at **The Pool Grill,** an alfresco restaurant serving appetizers like chicken quesadilla or cocktail of Pacific shrimp. Lighter appetites will enjoy main course salads including marinated grilled vegetables, Cobb salad, or seafood salad. The sandwich board features a good old-fashioned club, a grilled beef burger, or hot dog. Special offerings are Hawaiian favorites like grilled fresh catch, or a steamy bowl of savory saimin.

One must not forget the **Clubhouse Restaurant** at the Challenge at Manele golf course, which has superb underwater scene murals painted on its walls by John Wulbrandt. The view from here is perhaps the best on the property, overlooking both the hotel and bay, with Haleakala in the background, particularly on a night when the full moon is rising early. Food is served all day, dinner nightly except Sunday. Small plates are the theme here. Some selections are shrimp satay, spiced lamb, and grilled ahi with white bean cassoulet, all for under $15 a plate.

In harmony with the rest of the Lodge at Koele, the dining rooms are impeccably furnished. **The Terrace,** set in a section off the Great Hall and the more casual of the two restaurants, looks out over the exotic gardens, while the separate dinner only **Formal Dining Room** lends itself to evening attire—jackets required. Breakfast selections include continental breakfast, eggs Benedict, and sweet rice waffles with lilikoi-coconut chutney. At midday satisfy your hunger with jumbo shrimp with papaya relish, pan-fried Kona crab cakes with a spicy remoulade, grilled pastrami of striped marlin on a tomato fennel salad, spinach pasta with grilled scallops, or smoked salmon and herbed goat cheese on a salad of field greens and vegetables with cilantro dressing. Simple tastes might also enjoy a barbecued pork sandwich with cabbage slaw, or ask for a picnic basket for two and find a shady tree where you can enjoy an alfresco lunch. Dinner, like the other daily fare, is made from the freshest island ingredients. Choose standards like rack of lamb, prime rib, a superbly prepared catch of the day, or, for a special treat, the Lanai mixed pheasant, quail, and axis deer sausage with Pinot Noir sauce.

In the Formal Dining Room you'll have a grand dining experience. It always gets rave reviews form diners who are into serious eating. Once again, the freshest island ingredients are used to prepare each meal that leaves the kitchen. Not only are they sumptuous but they are presented in a pleasing manner. All this elegance doesn't come cheap, however. Expect prices in the $40-50 range for an entree.

The **Clubhouse** at the **Experience at Koele** golf course sells excellent soups, sandwiches, and salads at very reasonable prices. Everyone is welcome, and the standing room only lets you know that the food is very good. Try a roasted eggplant sandwich with mozzarella cheese, Caesar salad, or one of the many pasta dishes for $6-21. Dinner is now served as well on Friday and Saturday 5:30-8:30 p.m. Indoor or outdoor seating, with a great view of the 18th green.

SHOPPING

Except for the clutch of shops at the Lodge at Koele and Manele Bay Hotel, and the gift shop at the airport, shopping on Lanai means shopping in Lanai City. Be aware that all but a few are closed on Sunday, and remember that some shops in town may close their doors for an hour or longer at midday for a siesta.

The two grocery stores in town are fairly well stocked with basics. The markets are almost next door to each other. **Pine Isle Market,** tel. (808) 565-6488, run by Kerry Honda and open 8 a.m.-7 p.m. every day except Sunday, is Lanai's closest equivalent to a supermarket. **Richards Shopping Center,** tel. (808) 565-6047, is open Mon.-Sat. 8:30 a.m.-6:30 p.m. A small grocery and sundries store, it supplies all your basic camping, fishing, and general merchandise needs, including clothing and medicines, some groceries, liquor, and odds and ends.

Lying between these two is **Akamai Trading Company,** tel. (808) 565-6587, which sells furniture and gifts, hardware and books, T-shirts and party supplies, espresso and other types of coffee, and also does film processing. Open daily 9 a.m.-5:30 p.m. (until 5 p.m. on Sunday). Around the corner is **International Food and Clothing Center,** tel. (808) 565-6433, where you can pick up not only things to eat and wear, but also hardware and hunting supplies. This is an old-fashioned general store, definitely a local place; open weekdays 8 a.m.-6 p.m., until 1:30 on Sunday, closed Saturday. Across the park is the **Lanai Family Store,** tel. (808) 565-6485, for video rentals and furniture. Next door at **Maria M's Boutique,** tel. (808) 565-9577, you can find clothing items.

Wonders never cease. A health food store has come to Lanai. Opened in 1995, this was the first new store in town in years. **Pele's Garden,** tel. (808) 565-9629, stocks a limited but generous range of packaged items, herbs, juices, vitamins and minerals, and even a few books. It's a full-service health food store in miniature. She'll have most of what you might desire, and you may get a whole nutrition lesson at no extra cost. Owned by Ms. Beverly Zigmond, this fine store is open Mon.-Sat. 9:30 a.m.-6:30 p.m. Out front and connected to her store is **Pele's Other Garden,** opened in 1997, a deli and juice bar that offers cool refreshment and healthy quick food, run by her brother and his wife.

Between these two is **Gifts With Aloha,** tel. (808) 565-6589, a small shop that carries art and craft items from local and other Hawaii residents. Some items include cloth and clothing, jewelry, quilts, and candles. You should be able to find something for that special occasion here. **Heart of Lanai Art Gallery,** tel. (808) 565-6678, housed in a vintage plantation-era building in downtown Lanai, open Mon.-Sat. 10 a.m.-5 p.m., is bright with the paintings, sculptures, and handicrafts of its contributing artists, all island and many Lanai residents. The artwork displayed is constantly changing, but some of the regulars include: Margaret Leach, whose watercolors capture the simple spirit of Lanai life; Steve Lance, a longtime resident who moved away but whose surrealistic paintings are filled with the vibrant colors of the islands (Steve is also a very talented wood sculptor and some of his pieces are displayed as well); Sandy Phillips, who creates primitive basketry and paintbrushes made from Lanai bamboo and axis deer hair; Sherry Menze, current Lanai harbormaster and former fisherwoman and boat captain, who has captured her love of the sea in the Japanese technique of *gyotaku,* or fish printing; Ruth Puchek, who arrived on Lanai in 1972 and has captured the mysterious moods of the islands in her paintings. She also sells postcards of her original works. Also exhibited are the works of Rony Doty, a watercolorist who paints the flowers and fauna of Lanai.

Two doors down is the **Lanai Art Program,** tel. (808) 565-7503, open weekdays 9 a.m.-4 p.m. (closed for lunch) and a few irregular hours on the weekend, which has taken the spirit of the Zimbabwe saying "If you can walk, you can dance," and changed it into "If you've got life, you've got art." This co-op of local Lanai citizens has created a nonprofit organization dedicated to developing the artistic talents of its members. Classes, chaired by guest artists, are periodically offered in photography, woodworking, Japanese doll-making, fabric-making, drama, and pen and ink drawing. The showroom offers purchases like hand-dyed silk scarves, stenciled T-shirts, naturally dyed incidental bags, notecards, lovely *pareau* for women, and even homemade jams and jellies. Pottery and silk painting seem to predominate. The work is always changing, but you are sure to find a distinctive island memento that couldn't be more genuine. All are welcomed, resident or not, so you can drop in on a workshop, pay for your supplies, and create your own art.

For snacks and sundries, you can also try the shop at Lanai City Service. For last-minute souvenirs, have a look at the **airport gift shop** in the terminal building.

SPORTS AND RECREATION

No question that Lanai's forte is its natural unspoiled setting and great outdoors. Traffic jams, neon lights, blaring discos, shopping boutiques, and all that jazz just don't exist here. The action is swimming, hiking, snorkeling, fishing, horseback riding, and some hunting. Tennis and golf round off the activities. Lanai is the place to revitalize your spirits—you want to get up with the birds, greet the sun, stretch, and soak up the good life.

Snorkeling and Scuba

Lanai, especially around Manele/Hulopoe Bay, has some of the best snorkeling and scuba in Hawaii. If you don't have your own equipment, and you're not a guest at one of the hotels, your only choice is to buy it from Pine Isle or Richards stores, but their prices are quite high. If you're the adventurous sort, you can dive for spiny lobsters off Shipwreck or Polihua, but make absolutely sure to check the surf conditions as it can be super treacherous. It would be best to go with a local person.

Trilogy Ocean Sports, tel. (808) 565-2387 or (888) 628-4800, Web site: www.sailtrilogy.com, operates the new *Trilogy III* catamaran and a rigid-bottom inflatable raft from Manele Boat Harbor for a number of sailing options. The four-hour snorkel/sail ($95) leaves daily at 8:45 a.m. Two scuba adventures, both for around $140, leave around the same time, but not every day. A circle-island rafting tour is also offered ($130), as are an afternoon marine mammal tour ($75) and a two-hour Saturday only champagne sunset sail ($65). Book directly or through the concierge desk at the Manele Bay Hotel or at the Lodge at Koele. Trilogy, in the business for years, has worked out all the kinks, and their boat, crew, and services are truly state-of-the-art. No matter how many times they make the trip, they never seem to forget that it's a new and exciting adventure for you, and they go out of their way to be helpful, upbeat, and caring without being intrusive. *Trilogy III's* aft is set up for easy entry and exit, with steps going down to the water level. Just make like a seal and slither in and out! If the winds are up, the captain will be happy to set sail as they head toward Kahekili's Leap and other famous Lanai landmarks. The experience is not just underwater, but also in the magnificent views of this pristine island that hasn't changed since the days of the Polynesian explorers. On morning sails, you return in the early afternoon with plenty of time left for more sightseeing or just relaxing.

Spinning Dolphin Charters, owned and operated by Capt. Jeff Menze, a long-time Lanai resident, P.O. Box 491, Lanai City, 96763, tel. (808) 565-6613, will take you fishing (children welcome), snorkeling, and whalewatching in season. Captain Jeff is a commercial fisherman and master diver who knows all of the best spots in Lanai's waters. Offered are whole-day and half-day adventures, special off-the-beaten-path dives, and private boat charters.

Swimming
Lanai City has a new swimming pool. Located in town near the high school, it's open to the public daily during summer, and on a limited schedule during other seasons. Each of the two resorts has its own swimming pool and spa. By far the best swimming beach on Lanai is at Hulopoe Bay, but a few other spots for a dip can be found along the coast from Shipwreck Beach to Naha.

Hiking, Biking, and Kayaking
An independent company that caters largely to hotel guests, **Lanai EcoAdventure Centre** can take you along the sheer sea cliffs of west Lanai on a kayak, walking into the Kaiholena Valley, biking down to Shipwreck Beach, or on several other outings on the island. Guided tours and introduction are provided, and rentals can be accommodated. Half-day outings cost $69 per person. Private tours can be arranged. See your hotel concierge or arrange directly: P.O. Box 1394, Lanai City, HI 96763, tel. (808) 565-7737, e-mail: treklanaimaui.net.

Tennis and Golf
You can play tennis at two lighted courts at the Lanai School. They have rubberized surfaces called royal duck and are fairly well maintained—definitely okay for a fun game. The Lodge at Koele and the Manele Bay Hotel have plexipave courts that are free to hotel guests and $9 per hour to nonguests. The courts at Manele Bay are newer and in better condition. Equipment rental (rackets and ball machines) and court times are arranged by the concierge. Private lessons and clinics are available.

Golfers will be delighted to follow their balls around Cavendish Golf Course on the outskirts of Lanai City. This nine-hole, 3,071-yard, par 36 course is set among Cook pines. It's free to all, but visitors are requested to leave a donation for maintenance. Unless you're familiar with the course, it's hard to find the first tee. The course is located at the end of Nani Street.

eighth hole at Experience at Koele

ROBERT NILSEN

LANAI GOLF AND TENNIS

GOLF COURSE	PAR	YARDS	FEES	CART	CLUBS
Cavendish Golf Course tel. (808) 565-9993	36	3,071	Free (Donation)	None	None
Challenge at Manele tel. (808) 565-2222	72	7,039	$175 nonguest $125 hotel guest	Incl.	$35
Experience at Koele tel. (808) 565-4653	72	7,014	$140 nonguest $125 hotel guest	Incl.	$35

TENNIS COURTS		
LOCATION	NO. OF COURTS	LIGHTED
The Lodge at Koele	3	Yes
Manele Bay Hotel	6	No
Near Lanai School (Lanai City)	2	Yes

The **Experience at Koele,** a Greg Norman-designed course, won the *Fortune Magazine* Best New Golf Course of 1991 award. This magnificent course, set in the mountains above the Lodge, not only offers challenging links, but a fantastic series of views of Molokai and Maui on a shimmering canvas of sea. With four sets of tees ranging from forward to tournament, the course yardage varies accordingly from 5,425 yards to 7,014 yards. The course also boasts the only bent-grass greens in the state. Two of the finest holes are the number 8, 444-yard par-four, which cascades 250 feet from mountaintop to glen below, and the short but maximum water-challenged number 9, a 180-yard par-three. For information and tee times, call (808) 565-4653.

The **Challenge at Manele,** designed by the legendary Jack Nicklaus, officially opened on Christmas Day, 1993. Employing the five-tee concept, the par-72 course ranges in length 5,024-7,039 yards. Three of the main holes, including the signature number 12 par-three hole, demand a tee shot over the greatest water hazard in the world, the wide Pacific. Call (808) 565-2222 for tee times.

Horseback Riding

The Stables at Koele, tel. (808) 565-4424, open daily, just a few minutes from the Lodge at Koele (contact the concierge at either hotel), offers a variety of mounted excursions. The beginners' Plantation Trail Ride lasts one hour and costs $25, while the Paniolo Lunch Ride lasts three hours, includes lunch, and costs $90. Other rides are available, including a children's pony ride and carriage rides. Lanai enjoys a ranching heritage that goes back to the 1870s. Many of the trails that you'll be following date from those early days. Riders must be in good health, weigh less than 250 pounds, and wear long pants and shoes. Safety helmets will be provided for all riders.

Hiking and Jogging

All the paved roads and many of the gravel roads on the plateau and in the basin are decent for walking and jogging. Although the traffic is not heavy, be careful if you're on the roadway.

One trail on the island has been marked, the trail to Koloiki Ridge. Start at the rear of the Lodge at Koele and head up through the golf course into a tall stand of pine trees. Cross under the power lines and into Hulopoe Valley, where an abandoned road heads down to the Munro Trail. Once there, turn right and head south, walking into and out of Kukui Gulch, until you round a very eroded "moonscape" on your right. A short way farther, turn left and head through a tunnel in the bushes on the trail to the Koloiki lookout.

Shorter and easier is Fisherman's Trail, a 1.5 mile shoreline trail that runs from Hoopole Bay to the west, below the Manele Bay Hotel. A project of the State Na Ala Hele trail system, this was once part of an ancient trail that circled the island.

Hunting

The first cliché you hear about Lanai is that it's one big pineapple plantation. The second is that it's a hunter's paradise. The first was true, the second still is. Both private and public hunting are allowed. As virtually all of Lanai is privately owned, about two-thirds of the island is set aside as a private reserve, and one-third is leased to the state for public hunting and is cooperatively managed.

The big game action for public hunting is provided by mouflon sheep and axis deer. Various days are open for the hunting of game birds, which include ring-necked and green pheasant; Gambel's, Japanese, and California quail, wild turkey; and a variety of doves, francolins, and partridges. The public hunting area is restricted to the northwest corner of the island. Brochures detailing all necessary information can be obtained free of charge by writing to Dept. of Land and Natural Resources, 1151 Punchbowl St., Honolulu, HI 96813. Contact Derwin Kwon at the Lanai regional office, P.O. Box 732, 911 Fraser Ave., Lanai City, HI 96763, tel. (808) 565-6688. Licenses are required ($15 resident, $100 nonresident) and can be purchased by mail from Dept. of Land and Natural Resources or picked up in person at the office on Lanai.

Public archery hunting of mouflon sheep is restricted to the last Saturday in July and first Saturday in August. The muzzleloader rifle season occurs on the second and third Saturday in August, and for rifles, shotguns, and bows and arrows for the nine following Saturdays. Tags are required and hunters are restricted by public drawing. Axis deer regular season (rifle, shotgun, and bows) opens on the nine consecutive Saturdays starting from the last Saturday in March; it's also restricted by public drawing. Muzzleloader season is the two Saturdays before that, and archery season for axis deer is the two Saturdays preceding the muzzleloader season. Bag limits are one mouflon ram and one buck.

On the private land, axis deer only are hunted. Hunting is done year-round, although the best trophy season is May-November. Hunting dates must be mutually agreed upon by the hunter and the rangers, as there are a limited number of rangers and this is a three-day process, although the hunt itself is only one long day affair. Write three to six months in advance for best results. The rate is $275 per day for a regular hunting permit, or $50 for an archery hunting permit that is good until the Hawaiian hunting license expires. Guide service is not officially mandatory, but you must prove that you have hunted Lanai before and are intimately knowledgeable about its terrain, hunting areas, and procedures. If not, you *must* acquire the services of a guide. Guide service is $750 a day, and this includes a permit and all necessities, except lodging and meals, from airport pickup to shipping the trophy. For all hunters, a Hawaii state hunting license and a hunter safety card are required. For full details write to Gary Onuma, Chief Ranger, The Lanai Co., Game Management, P.O. Box 310, Lanai City, HI 96763, tel. (808) 565-3981, fax 565-3984.

Sporting Clays

An outgrowth of hunting, sporting clays is a sport that helps develop and maintain your hand-eye coordination. Shooting is done from different stations around a course, and the object is to hit a small round clay disk. Different than trap or skeet shooting, sporting clays relies upon moving targets that mimic different animals and birds, hopping along the ground as a rabbit, springing off the ground like a quail, or flying high like a pheasant. Here you can have all the enjoyment of hitting a target without the guilt of killing a living animal. Lanai Pine Sporting Clays, tel. (808) 565-3800 or (800) 321-4666, fax (808) 565-3868, is a high-tech operation that services both beginners and the advanced shooter. To satisfy everyone's needs, there are skeet and trap ranges here as well.

Register at the pro shop and pick up your needed supplies and accessories there. A paved path connects each of the 14 stations; take a golf cart or walk the course. The basic package, including 100 targets, gun rental, cartridges, eye and ear protection, and safety vest runs $125 per person; $65 for 50 targets. For experienced shooters, guns, cartridges, targets, and carts can be rented separately, and you may use your own gun. Instruction is also given for beginners at $55; private lessons are available. Pull!

Fishing

Only the Spinning Dolphin Charters fishing boat operates out of Lanai, but that's not to say there are no fish. On the contrary, one of the island's greatest pastimes is this relaxing sport. Any day in Lanai City Park, you'll find plenty of old-timers to ask where the fish are biting. If you have the right approach and use the right smile, they just might tell you. Generally, the best fishing and easiest access on the island is at Shipwreck Beach running west toward Polihua. Near the lighthouse ruins is good for *papio* and *ulua,* the latter running to 50 pounds. Many of the local fishermen use throw-nets to catch the smaller fish such as *manini,* preferred especially by Lanai's elders. Throw-netting takes skill usually learned from childhood, but don't be afraid to try even if you throw what the locals call a "banana" or one that looks like Maui (a little head and a big body). They might snicker, but if you laugh too, you'll make a friend.

Mostly you'll fish with rod and reel using frozen squid or crab, available at Lanai's general stores. Bring a net bag or suitable container. This is the best beachcombing on the island and it's also excellent diving for spiny lobster. There is good shore fishing (especially for *awa*) and easy accessibility at Kaumalapau Harbor, from where the pineapples used to be shipped and where the supplies for the island now come. There is also superb offshore fishing at Kaunolu, Kamehameha's favorite angling spot on the south shore. You can catch *aku* and *kawakawa,* but to be really successful you'll need a boat. Finally, Manele Hulopoe Marine Life Conservation Park has limited fishing, but as the name implies, it's a conservation district so be sure to follow the rules prominently posted at Manele Bay.

PRACTICALITIES

Information

For general information about Lanai, and activities and services on the island, contact **Destination Lana'i,** P.O. Box 700, Lanai City, HI 96763, tel. (808) 565-7600 or (800) 947-4774, fax 565-9316, e-mail: dlanai@aloha.net. Additionally, maps, brochures, and pamphlets on all aspects of staying on Lanai are available free from **The Lanai Company,** P.O. Box 310, Lanai City, HI 96763, tel. (808) 565-3000.

For an upclose look at local news and what's happening in the community, have a look at the monthly *Lanai Times.*

Money

Try full-service **First Hawaiian Bank,** tel. (808) 565-6969, in Lanai City for your banking needs. It has the only ATM machine on the island. **First Federal Savings,** tel. (808) 565-6426, also has a branch here. All major businesses accept traveler's checks. Banks are open Mon.-Thurs., 8:30 a.m.-3 p.m. (First Federal to 4:30 p.m.), until 6 p.m. on Friday.

Post Office

The Lanai post office, tel. (808) 565-6517, on the edge of Dole Park, is across the street from the Lanai Company offices on Lanai Avenue. Open daily 8 a.m.-4:30 p.m., it's full service, but it does not sell boxes or padded mailers in which to send home beachcombing treasures; you can get those at the two general stores in town.

Lanai Playhouse

On the corner of Lanai Ave. and 7th., Lanai Playhouse, tel. (808) 565-7500 is the only theater on the island; it runs current movies.

Laundromat

The laundromat, located next to the art gallery, is open every day from "morning until nighttime": 6 a.m.-9 p.m. Bring coins.

Useful Phone Numbers

Lanai City Service gas station, tel. (808) 565-7227; Dept. of Land and Natural Resources, tel. (808) 565-6688; Lanai Airport, tel. (808) 565-6757; Lanai Community Library (open weekdays), tel. (808) 565-6996; police, tel. (808) 565-6428; weather and surf conditions, tel. (808) 565-6033; Lanai Community Hospital, tel. (808) 565-6411; Lanai Family Health Center, tel. (808) 565-6423; Dr. Nick's Family Dentistry, tel. (808) 565-7801.

EXPLORING LANAI

LANAI CITY

Lanai City (pop. 2,800) would be more aptly described and sound more appealing if it were called Lanai Village. A utilitarian town, it was built in the 1920s by Dole Pineapple Company. The architecture, field-worker plain, has definitely gained "character" in the last 70 years. It's an excellent spot for a town, sitting at 1,600 feet in the shadow of Lanaihale, the island's tallest peak. George Munro's Cook pines have matured and now give the entire town a green, shaded, park-like atmosphere. It's cool and breezy—a great place to launch off from in the morning and a welcome spot to return to at night. Most visitors head out of town to the more spectacular sights and never take the chance to explore the back streets.

Houses

As you'd expect, most houses are square boxes with corrugated roofs, but each has its own personality. Painted every color of the rainbow, they'd be garish in any other place, but here they break the monotony and seem to work. The people of Lanai used to make their living from the land and can still work wonders with it. Around many homes are colorful flowerbeds, green gardens bursting with vegetables, fruit trees, and flowering shrubs. When you look down the half-dirt, broken-pavement roads at a line of these houses, you can't help feeling that a certain nobility exists here. The houses are mud-spattered where the rain splashes red earth against them, but inside you know they're sparkling clean. Some modern suburban homes sprawl on the south end of town. Most of these belong to Lanai's miniature middle class and would fit unnoticed in any up-and-coming neighborhood on another island. On the north edge of town are few new apartments and multi-family buildings, and on the slope above town are the townhouses and luxury homes that will over the years become more predominant if development goes as planned.

Around Town

Lanai City streets running east-west are numerical starting with 3rd Street and running to 13th Street; the streets running north-south have alphabetical first letters and include Fraser, Gay, Houston, Ilima, Jackaranda, Koele, and Lanai Avenues, with a few more streets beyond this central grid, mostly new residential areas. If you manage to get lost in Lanai City you should seriously consider never leaving home.

Downtown

If you sit on the steps of Hotel Lanai and peer across its huge front yard, you can scrutinize the heart of downtown Lanai City. Off to your right are the offices of the Lanai Company sitting squat and solid. In front of them, forming a type of town square, is Dole Park where old-timers come to sit and young mothers bring their kids for some fresh air. No one in Lanai City rushes to do anything. Look around and you'll discover a real fountain of youth: the many octogenarians walk with a spring in their step. Years of hard work without being hyper or anxious is why they say they're still around. The park is surrounded by commercial Lanai. There's nowhere to go except over to the schoolyard to play some tennis or to Cavendish Golf Course for a round of nine holes. Lanai City has a movie theater, and its now showing pictures once again. You can plop yourself at the Blue Ginger Cafe or Tanigawa's for coffee, or stay in the park if you're in the mood to strike up a conversation—it won't take long.

Meander down Lanai Avenue past a complex of former agricultural buildings and shops. Once full of heavy equipment, this is where Lanai showed its raw plantation muscle. It has now been tamed and is the site of a new senior citizen's housing complex. Beyond the commercial buildings on both sides of the downtown park are the rows of plantation houses, now with newer subdivisions farther to each end. Do yourself a favor—get out of your rental car and walk around town for at least 30 minutes. You'll experience one of the most unique villages in America.

TENNIS COURTS

To Shipwreck Beach

STABLES

440

THE LODGE AT
KOELE BANK

THE
EXPERIENCE AT
KOELE GOLF
COURSE

KEOMUKU RD.

CAVENDISH
GOLF COURSE

LANAI CITY

3RD ST.
HOUSTON GAY
IIMA AVE.
JACARANDA AVE.
KOELE AVE.
LANAI ST.
MAHANA AVE.
NANI AVE.
FRASER
4TH AVE.
5TH
6TH ST.

BANK

THEATER

TANIGAWA'S

HEART OF LANAI

LANAI ART PROGRAM

LAUNDROMAT

BLUE GINGER

LANAI CO.

CLINIC

DESTINATION LANAI

POST
OFFICE

HOTEL LANAI

DOLE PARK

GYM

BANK

RICHARD'S SHOPPING CENTER

AKAMAI TRADING

PINE ISLE MARKET

POOL

TENNIS
COURTS

POLICE

8TH ST.

PELE'S
GARDEN

INTERNATIONAL FOOD
AND CLOTHING

9TH

LANAI CITY
SERVICE

DLNR

10TH

RED
ROVER

PUUPALI DR.

11TH

12TH

13TH

AHA
MANA
OLAPA
PALAWAI
GUEENS

AKOLU

0   0.25 mi
0   0.25 km

FIRE
STATION

440

To Airport

KAUMALAPAU HWY.

MANELE RD.

To Manele Bay

MUNRO TRAIL

The highlight of visiting Lanai is climbing the Munro Trail to its highest point, Lanaihale (3,370 feet), locally called **The Hale**. As soon as you set foot on Lanai the silhouette of this razorback ridge with its bristling coat of Cook pines demands your attention. Set off for The Hale and you're soon engulfed in its cool stands of pines, eucalyptus, and ironwoods, all colored with ferns and wildflowers. George Munro, a New Zealander hired as the manager of the Lanai Ranch a short time before Jim Dole's arrival, is responsible. With a pouch full of seeds and clippings from his native New Zealand, he trudged all over Lanai planting, in an attempt to foliate the island and create a permanent watershed. Driven by that basic and primordial human desire to see things grow, he climbed The Hale time and again to renew and nurture his leafy progeny. Now, all benefit from his labors.

Getting There

There are two basic ways to go to The Hale, by foot or 4WD. Some local people go on horseback. Head out of town on Route 440 toward Shipwreck Beach. Make sure to start before 8 a.m.; cloud cover is common by early afternoon. After less than two miles, still in the Lanai City side of the mountains, take the first major gravel road to the right. In about one-quarter mile the road comes to a Y intersection—go left. You immediately start climbing and pass through a forested area past a series of gulches. Continue and the road forks; again bear left. Always stay on the more obviously traveled road. The side roads look muddy and overgrown and it's obvious which is the main one. Robert Frost would be disappointed.

The Trail

As you climb, you pass a profusion of gulches, great red wounds cut into Lanai's windward side. First comes deep and brooding **Maunalei ("Mountain Lei") Gulch**, from where Lanai draws its water through a series of tunnels bored through the mountains. It's flanked by **Kuolanai Trail**, a rugged and dangerous footpath leading all the way to the coast. Next is **Hookio Gulch**, a battleground where Lanai's warriors were vanquished in 1778 by Kalaniopuu and his ferocious fighters from the Big Island. All that remains are a few

room-sized notches cut into the walls where the warriors slept and piled stones to be hurled at the invaders. After Hookio Gulch, a trail bears left, bringing you to the gaping mouth of **Hauola Gulch**, over 2,000 feet deep. Keep your eyes peeled for axis deer, which seem to defy gravity and manage to cling and forage along the most unlikely and precipitous cliffs. Be very careful of your footing—even skilled Lanai hunters have fallen to their deaths in this area.

The jeep trail narrows on the ridge to little more than 100 feet across. On one side are the wild gulches, on the other the bucolic green, whorling fingerprints of the former pineapple fields. Along the trail you can munch strawberries, common guavas, and as many thimbleberries as you can handle. At the crest of The Hale, let your eyes pan the horizon to see all the main islands of Hawaii (except for Kauai). Rising from the height-caused mirage of a still sea is the hazy specter of Oahu to the north, with Molokai and Maui clearly visible just 10 miles distant. Haleakala, Maui's magical mountain, has a dominant presence viewed from The Hale. Sweep right to see Kahoolawe, bleak and barren, its body shattered by the bombs of the U.S. Navy, a victim of controversial war games. Eighty miles south of Kahoolawe is the Big Island, its mammoth peaks, Mauna Loa and Mauna Kea, looming like ethereal islands floating in the clouds.

Just past the final lookout is a sign for **Awehi Trail**, which leads left to Naha on the beach. It's extremely rough and you'll definitely need a 4WD in compound-low to get down. Follow the main road down past several more lookouts. Take either Hoike Road, which flattens out and joins with Route 44 just south of Lanai City, or head straight ahead and join the highway near where it heads down the hill to Manele Bay. If you have time for only one outing on Lanai or funds budgeted for only one day of 4WD rental, make sure to treat yourself to the unforgettable Munro Trail.

HEADING SOUTH

Joseph Kaliihananui was the last of the free Hawaiian farmers to work the land of Lanai. His great-grandson, Lloyd Cockett, still lives in Lanai City. Joseph made his home in the arid but fertile Palawai Basin, which was later bought by Jim

Dole and turned into the heart of the pineapple plantation. Just south of Lanai City on Route 440 (Manele Road), the Palawai Basin is the crater of the extinct single volcano of which Lanai is formed. Joseph farmed sweet potatoes, which he traded for fish. He gathered his water in barrels from the dew that formed on his roof and from a trickling spring. His lands supported a few cattle among its now-extinct heavy stands of cactus. Here, too, Walter Murray Gibson attempted to begin a Mormon colony, which he later aborted, supposedly because of his outrage over the idea of polygamy. Nothing noteworthy remains of this colony, but high on a hillside overlooking Palawai are the Luahiwa Petroglyphs, considered to be some of the best-preserved rock hieroglyphics in Hawaii.

Luahiwa Petroglyphs

The route through the fields that leads to the petroglyphs is tough to follow, but the best recipe for success is being pointed in the right direction and adding a large dollop of perseverance. Heading south on Manele Road, look to your left for the back side of a triangular yield sign at Hoike Road. Hoike Road was once paved but has now disintegrated into gravel. After turning left onto Hoike, head straight toward a large water tank on the hill. You pass two round-bottomed irrigation ditches, easily spotted as they're always green with grass due to the water they carry. At the second ditch turn left and follow the road, keeping the ditch on your right. Proceed until you come to a silver water pipe about 12 inches in diameter. Follow this pipe as it runs along a hedgerow until you reach the third power pole. At the No Trespassing sign, bear left.

Follow this overgrown trail up the hill to the boulders on which appear the petroglyphs. The boulders are brownish-black and covered in lichen. Their natural arrangement resembles an oversized Japanese rock garden. Dotted on the hillside are sisal plants that look like bouquets of giant green swords. As you climb to the rocks be very careful of your footing—the ground is crumbly and the vegetation slippery. The boulders cover a three-acre area; most of the petroglyphs are found on the south faces of the rocks. Some are hieroglyphics of symbolic circles, others are picture stories complete with canoes gliding under unfurled sails. Dogs snarl with their jaws agape, while enigmatic triangular stickmen try to tell their stories from the

past. Equestrians gallop, showing that these stone picture-books were done even after the coming of the white man. The Luahiwa Petroglyphs are a very special spot where the ancient Hawaiians still sing their tales across the gulf of time.

Hulopoe and Manele Bays

Proceed south on Route 440 to Lanai's most salubrious spots, the twin bays of Manele and Hulopoe. At the crest of the hill, just past the milepost, you can look down on the white, inviting sands of Hulopoe to the right, and the rockier small boat harbor of Manele on the left. The island straight ahead is Kahoolawe, and on very clear days you might be able to glimpse the peaks of Hawaii's Mauna Loa and Mauna Kea. Manele Bay is a picture-perfect anchorage where a dozen or so small boats and yachts are tied up on any given day. Ferries from Maui drop off passengers here, and tour boats also tie up here. In the trees overlooking the harbor are a few picnic tables and a public bathroom. Manele and Hulopoe are a Marine Life Conservation District with the rules for fishing and diving prominently displayed on a large bulletin board at the entrance to Manele. Because of this, the area is superb for snorkeling, and you can often see a pod of spinner dolphins playing in the water. No boats are allowed within Hulopoe Bay except for Hawaiian outrigger canoes.

Hulopoe Bay offers very gentle waves and soothing, crystal-clear water. The beach is a beautiful expanse of white sand fringed by palms with a mingling of large boulders that really set it off. This is Lanai's official camping area, and six sites are available. All are well spaced, each with a picnic table and fire pit. A series of shower stalls made of brown plywood provides solar-heated water and just enough privacy, allowing your head and legs to protrude. After refreshing yourself you can fish from the rock promontories on both sides of the bay, or explore the tide pools on the left side of the bay out near the point. It's difficult to find a more wholesome and gentle spot anywhere in Hawaii.

Kaumalapau Harbor

A side trip to Kaumalapau Harbor might be in order. This manmade facility, which used to ship more than a million pineapples a day during peak harvest, was the only one of its kind in the world. Activity is now way down, with only one ferry a week on Thursday to deliver supplies. As you've probably already rented a vehicle, you might as well cover these few paved miles from Lanai City on Route 440 just to have a quick look. En route you pass Lanai's odoriferous garbage dump, which is a real eyesore. Hold your nose and try not to notice. The harbor facility itself is no-nonsense commercial, but the coastline is reasonably spectacular, with a glimpse of the island's dramatic sea cliffs. Also, this area has super-easy access to some decent fishing, right off the pier. An added bonus for making the trek to this lonely area is that it is one of the best places on Lanai from which to view the sunset, and you usually have it all to yourself.

KAUNOLU: KAMEHAMEHA'S GETAWAY

At the southwestern tip of Lanai is Kaunolu Bay. At one time, this vibrant fishing village surrounded Halulu Heiau, a sacred refuge where the downtrodden were protected by the temple priests who could intercede with the benevolent gods. Kamehameha the Great would escape Lahaina's blistering summers and come to these very fertile fishing waters with his loyal warriors. Some proved their valor to their great chief by diving from Kahekili's Leap, a manmade opening in the rocks 60 feet above the sea. The remains of over 80 house sites and a smattering of petroglyphs dot the area. The last inhabitant was Ohua, elder brother of Joseph Kaliihananui, who lived in a grass hut just east of Kaunolu in Mamaki Bay. Ohua was entrusted by Kamehameha V to hide the *heiau* fish-god, Kuniki; old accounts by the area's natives say that he died because of mishandling this stone god. The natural power still emanating from Kaunolu is obvious, and you can't help feeling the energy that drew the Hawaiians to this sacred spot.

Getting There

Proceed south on Manele Road from Lanai City through Palawai Basin until it makes a hard bend to the left. Here, a sign points you to Manele Bay. Do not go left to Manele, but proceed straight and stay on the once-paved pineapple road. At a dip by a huge silver water pipe, go straight through the pineapple fields until another obvious dip at two orange pipes (like fire hydrants) on the left and right. Turn left here onto a rather small road. Follow the road left to a weatherworn sign that actually says "Kaunolu Road." This dirt track starts off innocently enough as it begins its plunge toward the sea. Only two miles long, the local folks consider it the roughest road on the island. It *is* a bone-cruncher, so take it super slow. Plot your progress against the lighthouse on the coast. This road is not maintained. Because of natural erosion, it may be too rugged for any vehicle to pass. Ask in town about its condition before attempting to proceed down. This area is excellent for spotting axis deer. The deer are nourished by *haole koa,* a green bush with a brown seed pod that you see growing along the road. This natural feed also supports cattle, but is not good for horses, causing the hair on their tails to fall out.

Kaunolu

The village site lies at the end of a long dry gulch that terminates at a rocky beach, suitable for times past as a canoe anchorage. This entire area is a mecca for archaeologists and anthropologists. The most famous was the eminent Dr. Kenneth Emory of the Bishop Museum; he filed an extensive research report on the area. At its terminus, the road splits left and right. Go right to reach a large *kiawe* tree with a rudimentary picnic table under it. Just in front of you is a large pile of nondescript rocks purported to be the ruined foundation of Kamehameha's house. Unbelievably, this sacred area has been trashed out by disrespectful and ignorant picnickers. Hurricane Iwa also had a hand in changing the face of Kaunolu, as its tremendous force hit this area head on and even drove large boulders from the sea onto the land. As you look around, the ones that have a whitish appearance were washed up on the shore by the fury of Iwa.

The villagers of Kaunolu lived mostly on the east bank and had to keep an ever-watchful eye on nature because the bone-dry gulch could suddenly be engulfed by flash floods. In the center of the gulch, about 100 yards inland, was **Paao,** the area's freshwater well. Paao was *kapu* to menstruating women, and it was believed that if the *kapu* was broken, the well would dry up. It served the village for centuries. It's totally obliterated now; in 1895 a Mr. Hayselden tried to erect a windmill over it, destroying the native caulking and causing the well to turn brackish—an example of Lanai's precious water being tampered with by outsiders, causing disastrous results.

The Sites

Climb down the east bank and cross the rocky beach. The first well-laid wall close to the beach on the west bank is the remains of a canoe shed. Proceed inland and climb the rocky bank to the remains of Halulu Heiau. Just below in the undergrowth is where the well was located. The *heiau* site has a commanding view of the area, best described by the words of Dr. Emory himself: "The point on which it is located is surrounded on three sides by cliffs and on the north rises the magnificent cliff of Palikaholo, terminating in Kahilikalani crag, a thousand feet above the sea. The ocean swell entering Kolokolo Cave causes a rumbling like thunder, as if under the *heiau*. From every point in the village the *heiau* dominates the landscape." As you climb the west bank, notice that the mortarless walls are laid up for over 30 feet. If you have a keen eye you'll notice a perfectly square fire pit right in the center of the *heiau*.

This area still has treasures that have never been catalogued. For example, you might chance upon a Hawaiian lamp, as big and perfectly round as a basketball, with an orange-sized hole in the middle where *kukui* nut oil was burned. Old records indicate that Kuniki, the temple idol itself, is still lying here face down no more than a few hundred yards away. If you happen to discover an artifact, do not remove it under any circumstance. Follow the advice of the late Lloyd Cockett, a *kapuna* of Lanai, who said, "I wouldn't take the rock because we Hawaiians don't steal from the land. Special rocks you don't touch."

Kahekili's Leap

Once you've explored the *heiau,* you'll be drawn toward the sea cliff. **Kaneapua Rock,** a giant tower-like chunk, sits perhaps 100 feet offshore. Below in the tide pool are basin-like depressions in the rock-salt evaporation pools, the bottoms still showing some white residue. Follow the cliff face along the natural wall obstructing your view to the south. You'll see a break in the wall about 15 feet wide with a very flat rock platform. From here, **Shark Island,** which closely resembles a sharkfin, is perfectly framed. This opening is **Kahekili's Leap,**

named after a Lanai chief, not the famous chief of Maui. Here, Kamehameha's warriors proved their courage by executing death-defying leaps into only 12 feet of water, and clearing a 15-foot protruding rock shelf. Scholars also believe that Kamehameha punished his warriors for petty offenses by sentencing them to make the jump. Kahekili's Leap is a perfect background for a photo. Below, the sea surges in unreal aquamarine colors. Off to the right is Kolokolo Cave, above which is another, even more daring leap at 90 feet. Evidence suggests that Kolokolo is linked to Kaunolu Gulch by a lava tube that has been sealed and lost. On the beach below Kahekili's Leap the vacationing chiefs played *konane,* and many stone boards can still be found from this game of Hawaiian checkers.

Petroglyphs

To find the petroglyphs, walk directly inland from Kaneapua Rock, using it as your point of reference. On a large pile of rocks are stick figures, mostly with a bird-head motif. Some heads even look like a mason's hammer. This entire area has a masculine feeling to it. There aren't the usual swaying palms and gentle sandy beaches. With the stones and rugged sea cliffs, you get the feeling that a warrior king would enjoy this spot. Throughout the area is *pili* grass, used by the Hawaiians to thatch their homes. Children would pick one blade and hold it in their fingers while reciting *"E pili e, e pili e, au hea kuu hale."* The *pili* grass would then spin around in their fingers and point in the direction of home. Pick some *pili* and try it yourself before leaving this wondrous, powerful area.

THE EAST COAST: KEOMUKU AND NAHA

Until the turn of this century, most of Lanai's inhabitants lived in the villages of the now-deserted east coast. Before the coming of Westerners, 2,000 or so Hawaiians lived along these shores, fishing and raising taro. It was as if they wanted to keep Maui in sight so that they didn't feel so isolated. Numerous *heiau* from this period still mark the ancient sites. The first white men also tried to make a go of Lanai along this stretch. The Maunalei Sugar Co. tried to raise sugarcane on the flat plains of Naha but failed and pulled up stakes in 1901— the last time that this entire coastline was populated to any extent. Today, the ancient *heiau* and a de-caying church in Keomuku are the last vestiges of habitation, holding out against the ever-en-croaching jungle. You can follow a jeep trail along this coast and get a fleeting glimpse of times past.

The shallow coastline that wraps around the north and east coast of Lanai opposes the shal-low south coast of Molokai. Although many fewer than on that coast of Molokai, the majority of ancient fishponds of Lanai were located here and their remnants can still be seen. Because of the shallow nature of the water and its rocky bottom, swimming is not particularly good along most of this coast except for a few isolated sandy spots. In fact, the water cannot be seen well from the road most of the way to Naha because of the growth of trees and bushes along the beach. Numerous pullouts and shore access roads have been created, however, so you can get to the water. Unfortunately, inconsiderate visitors have left these pullouts a bit trashy with junk tossed to the ground rather than taken out.

Getting There

Approach Keomuku and Naha from one of two di-rections. The most straightforward is from north to south. Follow Route 440 (Keomuku Road) from Lanai City until it turns to dirt and branches right (south) at the coast about a half hour. This road meanders for about 12 miles all the way to Naha, another one-half to one hour. Though the road is partial gravel and packed sand and not that rugged, you will need a 4WD in spots. Watch for washouts and fallen trees. It's paralleled by a much smoother route that runs along the beach part way down the coast, but it can only be used at low tide. Many small roads connect the two, so you can hop back and forth between them every 200-300 yards. Consider three tips: First, if you take the beach road, you can make good time and have a smooth ride, but could sail past most of the sights since you won't know when to hop back on the inland road; second, dry sand can easily bog down even a 4WD vehicle, making an expensive rescue mis-sion for a tow truck, so be wise and only drive where sand is hard-packed; third, be careful of the *kiawe* trees—the tough, inch-long thorns can puncture tires as easily as nails.

The other alternative is to take Awehi Trail, a rugged jeep track, about halfway between Lopa and Naha. This trail leads up the mountain to the Munro Trail, but because of its ruggedness it's best to take it down from The Hale instead of up. A good long day of rattling in a jeep would take you along the Munro Trail, down Awehi Trail, then north along the coast back to Route 440. If you came south along the coast from Route 440, it would be better to retrace your steps instead of heading up Awehi. When you think you've suf-fered enough and have been bounced into sub-mission by your jeep, remember that many of these trails were carved out by Juan Torqueza. He trailblazed alone on his bulldozer, unsupervised, and without benefit of survey. Now well into his 70s, he can be found in Dole Park in Lanai City, except when he's out here fishing.

Keomuku Village

There isn't much to see in Keomuku ("Stretch of White") Village other than an abandoned Hawaiian church. This was the site of the Mau-nalei Sugar Co. The town was pretty much aban-doned after 1901 when the sugar company ceased operations, and most all the decaying buildings were razed in the early 1970s. A few hundred yards north and south of the town site are examples of some original fishponds. They're tough to see (overgrown with mangrove), but a close observation gives you an idea of how ex-tensive they once were. The **Hawaiian church** is worth a stop—it almost pleads to be pho-tographed. From outside, you can see how frail it is, so if you go in, tread lightly. The altar area, a podium with a little bench, remains. A banner on the fading blue-green walls reads *"Ualanaano Jehova Kalanakila Malamalama,* October 4, 1903." Only the soft wind sounds where once strong voices sang vibrant hymns of praise.

A few hundred yards south of the church is a walking trail. Follow it inland to **Kahea Heiau** and a smattering of petroglyphs. This is the *heiau* disturbed by the sugarcane train; its desecra-tion was believed to have caused the sweet water of Keomuku to turn brackish. The people of Keomuku learned to survive on the brackish water and kept a special jug of fresh water for vis-itors.

Heading South

Farther south a Japanese cemetery and monu-ment were erected for the deceased workers who built **Halepaloa Landing,** from where the cane was shipped. Today, only rotting timbers and stonework remain, but the pier offers an excellent vantage point for viewing Maui, and it's a good spot to fish.

An island venture based on Maui called **Club Lanai,** tel. (808) 871-1144 or (800) 531-5262, has opened the remote east coast of Lanai to visitors. Its six acres of manicured beachfront property sit on one of the nicest stretches of sand, about halfway down the coast. Basically Club Lanai transports tourists from Maui aboard its boats to their its facility for a day of fun, games, and feasting.

The road continues past **Lopa,** ending at **Naha.** On the way, you'll pass several roads heading inland that lead to hunting areas. You also pass a few coconut groves. Legend says that one of these was cursed by a *kahuna*—if you climb a tree to get a coconut you will not be able to come down. Luckily, most tourists have already been cursed by "midriff bulge" and can't climb the tree in the first place. When you get to Naha check out the remnants of the paved Hawaiian walking trail before slowly heading back from this decaying historical area.

SHIPWRECK BEACH

Heading over the mountains from Lanai City to Shipwreck Beach offers you a rewarding scenario: an intriguing destination point with fantastic scenery and splendid panoramas on the way. Head north from Lanai City on Route 440 (Keomuku Road). In less than 10 minutes you crest the mountains, and if you're lucky the sky will be clear and you'll be able to see the phenomenon that guided ancient navigators to land: the halo of dark brooding clouds over Maui and Molokai, a sure sign of landfall. Shorten your gaze and look at the terrain in the immediate vicinity. Here are the famous precipitous gulches of Lanai. The wounded earth bleeds red while offering patches of swaying grass and wildflowers. It looks like the canyons of Arizona have been dragged to the rim of the sea. As you wiggle your way down Keomuku Road, look left to see the rusting hull of a WW II Liberty Ship sitting on the shallow reef almost completely out of the water. For most, this derelict is the destination point on Shipwreck Beach.

The Beach

As you continue down the road, little piles of stones, usually three, sit atop a boulder. Although most are from modern times, these are called *ahu,* a traditional Hawaiian offering to ensure good fortune while traveling. Under no circumstances disturb them. Farther down, the lush grasses of the mountain slope disappear, and the scrub bush takes over. The pavement ends and the dirt road forks left (west) to Shipwreck Beach, or straight ahead (south) toward the abandoned town of Naha. If you turn left you'll be on an adequate sandy road, flanked on both sides by thorny, tire-puncturing *kiawe* trees. In less than a mile is a large open area to your right. If you're into unofficial camping, this isn't a bad spot for a one-night bivouac—the trees here provide privacy and an excellent windbreak against the constant strong ocean breezes. About two miles down the road is Federation Camp, actually a tiny village of unpretentious beach shacks built by Lanai's workers as "getaways" and fishing cabins. Charming in their humbleness and simplicity, they're made mostly from recycled timbers and boards that have washed ashore. Some have been worked on quite diligently and skillfully and are actual little homes, but somehow the rougher ones are more attractive. You can drive past the cabins for a few hundred yards, but to be on the safe side, park just past them and begin your walk.

Petroglyphs

At the very end of the road is a cabin that a local comedian has named the "Lanai Hilton." Just off to your left *(mauka)* are the ruins of a lighthouse. Look for a cement slab where two graffiti artists of bygone days carved their names: John Kupau and Kam Chee, Nov. 28, 1929. Behind the lighthouse ruins an arrow points you to "The Bird Man of Lanai Petroglyphs." Of all the petroglyphs on Lanai these are the easiest to find; trail-marking rocks have been painted white by Lanai's Boy Scouts. Follow them to a large rock bearing the admonition "Do Not Deface." Climb down the path with a keen eye—the rock carvings are small, most only about 10 inches tall. Little childlike stick figures, they have intriguing bird heads whose symbolic meaning has been lost.

Hiking Trail

The trail along the beach goes for eight long hot

miles to Polihua Beach. That trip should be done separately, but at least walk as far as the Liberty Ship, about a mile from the cabins. The area has some of the best beachcombing in Hawaii; no telling what you might find. The most sought-after treasures are glass floats that have bobbed for thousands of miles across the Pacific, strays from Japanese fishnets. You might even see a modern ship washed onto the reef, like the Canadian yacht that went aground in the spring of 1984. Navigational equipment has improved, but Shipwreck Beach can *still* be a nightmare to any captain caught in its turbulent waters and long ragged coral fingers. This area is particularly good for lobsters and shore fishing. And you can swim in shallow sandy-bottom pools to refresh yourself as you hike.

Try to time your return car trip over the mountain for sundown. The tortuous terrain, stark in black and white shadows, is awe-inspiring. The larger rocks are giant sentinels: it's easy to feel the power and attraction they held for the ancient Hawaiians. As you climb the road on the windward side with its barren and beaten terrain, the feelings of mystery and mystique attributed to spiritual Lanai are obvious. You come over the top and suddenly see the valley—manicured, rolling, soft, and verdant with pineapples and the few lights of Lanai City beckoning.

THE GARDEN OF THE GODS AND POLIHUA

The most ruggedly beautiful, barren, and inhospitable section of Lanai is out at the north end. After passing through a broad stretch of former pineapple fields, you come to Kanepu'u Preserve, the island's only nature reserve and best example of dryland forest. Just as you pop out the far side of the preserve, you reach the appropriately named Garden of the Gods. Waiting is a fantasia of otherworldly landscapes— barren red earth, convulsed ancient lava flows, tortured pinnacles of stone, and psychedelic striations of vibrating colors, especially moving at sunrise and sunset. Little-traveled trails lead to Kaena Point, a wasteland dominated by sea cliffs where adulterous Hawaiian wives were sent into exile for a short time in 1837. Close by is Lanai's largest *heiau,* dubbed Kaenaiki, so

isolated and forgotten that its real name and function were lost even to Hawaiian natives by the middle of the 19th century. After a blistering, sun-baked, 4WD drubbing you emerge at the coast on Polihua, a totally secluded, pure-white beach where sea turtles once came to bury their eggs in the natural incubator of its soft warm sands.

Getting There

Lanai doesn't hand over its treasures easily, but they're worth pursuing. To get to the Garden of the Gods you have to traverse the former pineapple field roads. Head for the Lodge at Koele, and turn right onto the road that runs between the tennis courts and the riding stable. After about one minute, the road turns right. Follow it, keeping the prominent ridge on your right. Proceed for about a half hour until you pass through the Kanepu'u dryland forest preserve. Along the way, you'll come to a sign pointing to Kaena Point; in a minute or so, a sign points to Kuamo'o. Shortly, a marker points you off to the right on Lapaiki Road. Proceed straight ahead to another marker pointing you down Awalua Trail to the right and Polihua straight ahead. Once out the back side of the preserve, you soon begin to see large boulders sitting atop packed red earth, the signal that you're entering the Garden of the Gods. It's about another half hour down to Polihua Beach, and on the way you'll find another marker for Kaena Road, which leads to magnificent sea cliffs and Kaenaiki Heiau.

Note: These roads are very confusing, and oftentimes the signs, due to heavy weather and vandalism, are missing. Check at the jeep rental office for up-to-the-minute road conditions and instructions. Definitely do not attempt the lower reaches of this road without 4WD.

Hiking

Anyone wishing to hike this area should drive to the end of the former pineapple fields. It's close to half the distance and the scenery is quite ordinary. Make sure to bring plenty of water and a windbreaker because the heavy winds blow almost continuously. Sturdy shoes and a sun hat are also needed. There is no official camping at Polihua Beach, but again, anyone doing so overnight probably wouldn't meet with any hassles.

Kanepu'u Preserve

Straddling the road leading to the Garden of the Gods, this 590-acre preserve is the best remaining example of dryland forest on Lanai and a sampling of what covered much of the lower leeward slopes of the Hawaiian Islands before the coming of man. In this forest you'll find *olopua,* a native olive tree, *lama,* a native ebony, *na'u,* Hawaiian gardenia, the *iliahi* sandalwood tree, and numerous other plant varieties, 49 species of which are found only in Hawaii, as well as many species of birds. Over the centuries, these dryland forests were reduced in size by fire, introduced animals, and the spread of nonnative weeds and trees. Under the care of the Nature Conservancy and local conservation groups, this forest and others like it are being protected.

As you pass through this preserve, stop at the self-guided loop trail to get a close-up look at some of the trees in the forest. It's about a 15-minute walk over level ground, if you stop and read the posted signs. Overlooking this trail and set on a nearby rise is Kanepu'u ("Kane in Hill Form") Heiau.

Every month, guided hikes are offered through the preserve. Call (808) 565-7430 for more information about these hikes or general information about the preserve.

The Garden of the Gods

There, a shocking assault on your senses, is the bleak, red, burnt earth, devoid of vegetation, heralding the beginning of the garden—a Hawaiian Badlands. The flowers here are made of rock, the shrubs are the twisted crusts of lava, and trees are baked minarets of stone, all subtle shades of orange, purple, and sulfurous yellow. While most is obviously created by natural erosion, some piles of stone are just as obviously erected by man. The jeep trail has been sucked down by erosion and the garden surrounds you. While the beginning seems most dramatic, much more spreads out before you as you proceed down the hill. Stop many times to climb a likely outcropping and get a sweeping view. While you can't see Lanai's coastline from here, you do have a nice view of Molokai across the channel. The wind rakes these badlands and the silence penetrates to your soul. Although eons have passed, you can feel the cataclysmic violence that created this haunting and

lei on rocks, Garden of the Gods

delicate beauty. The Garden of the Gods is perhaps best in the late afternoon when slanting sunlight enriches colors and casts shadows that create depth and mood.

Polihua Beach

Abruptly the road becomes smooth and flat. Straight ahead, like a mirage too bright for your eyes, an arch is cut into the green jungle, framing white sand and moving blue ocean. As you face the beach, to the right it's flat, expansive, and the sands are white, but the winds are heavy; if you hiked eight miles, you'd reach Shipwreck Beach. More interesting is the view to the left, which has a series of lonely little coves. The sand is brown and coarse and large black lava boulders are marbled with purplish-gray rock embedded in long, faulted seams. Polihua is not just a destination point where you come for a quick look. It takes so much effort coming and going that you should plan on having a picnic and a relaxing afternoon before heading back through the Garden of the Gods and its perfectly scheduled sunset light show.

MOLOKAI

INTRODUCTION

Molokai is a sanctuary, a human time capsule where the pendulum swings inexorably forward, but more slowly than in the rest of Hawaii. It has always been so. In ancient times, Molokai was known as Pule-oo, "Powerful Prayer," where its supreme chiefs protected their small underpopulated refuge, not through legions of warriors but through the chants of their *kahuna*. This powerful, ancient mysticism, handed down directly from the goddess Pahulu, was known and respected throughout the archipelago. Its mana was the oldest and strongest in Hawaii, and its practitioners were venerated by nobility and commoners alike—they had the ability to "pray you to death." The entire island was a haven, a refuge for the vanquished and *kapu*-breakers of all the islands. It's still so today, beckoning to determined escapees from the rat race!

The blazing lights of supermodern Honolulu can easily be seen from western Molokai, while Molokai as viewed from Oahu is fleeting and ephemeral, appearing and disappearing on the horizon. The island is home to the largest number of Hawaiians. In effect it is a tribal homeland: over 6,000 of the island's 6,700 inhabitants have more than 50% Hawaiian blood and, except for Niihau, it's the only island where they are the majority. The 1920s Hawaiian Homes Act allowed *kuleana* of 40 acres to anyone with more than 50% Hawaiian ancestry. *Kuleana* owners form the grassroots organizations that fight for Hawaiian rights and battle the colossal forces of rabid developers who have threatened Molokai for decades.

AN OVERVIEW

Kaunakakai and West
Kaunakakai, the island's main town, once looked like a Hollywood sound stage where Jesse James or Wyatt Earp would feel right at home. The town is flat, with few trees, and three blocks long. Ala Malama, its main shopping street, is lined with false-front stores; pickup trucks are parked in front where horses and buggies ought to be. To the west are the prairie-like plains of Molokai, some sections irrigated and now plant-

MOLOKAI

Molokai Forest Reserve

Moomomi Beach

Kaluakoi Resort

Keonelele Desert

Kalaupapa Peninsula
Kauhako Crater
Kalawao
Kalaupapa
Kalae
Palau State Park
Kualapuu
Hawaiian Homelands Office
Hoolehua
Hoolehua Airport

Wailau Valley
Pelekunu Valley
Waikolu Valley
Sandalwood Pit
Kamakou (4970 ft)

Halawa
Halawa Beach Park
Puu O Hoku Ranch
Moaula Falls
Halawa Valley
Waialua
Pauwalu
Pukoo
Wavecrest Resort
Ualapue
Kamalo
Kakahia National Wildlife Refuge
Kawela
Kamehameha V Hwy
One Alii Beach Park
Kaunakakai

Maunaloa
Halena
Kolo Wharf
Kaunala Bay
Hale O Lono Harbor
Llau Point
Ilio Point
Kawakiu Iki Bay
Papohaku Beach
Kaluakoi Rd

Kauai
Niihau
Oahu
Molokai
Lanai
Kahoolawe
Maui
Hawaii

0 5 mi
0 5 km

© J.D. BISIGNANI AND MOON PUBLICATIONS, INC.

ed in profitable crops. The northern section of the island contains **Palaau State Park,** where a campsite is always easily found, and **Phallic Rock,** a natural shrine where island women came to pray for fertility. Most of the west end is owned by the mammoth 54,000-acre **Molokai Ranch.** Part of its lands supports several thousand head of cattle and herds of axis deer imported from India in 1867.

The 40-acre *kuleana* are here, as well as abandoned Dole and Del Monte pineapple fields. The once-thriving pineapple company towns of **Maunaloa** and **Kualapuu** are now semi-ghost towns since the pineapple companies pulled up stakes in 1975. Undergoing a massive face-lift, Maunaloa is holding on as the ranch is expanding its operations to include more tourism-related activities. The Kualapuu area now produces coffee and attracts its scattered Filipino workers mostly on weekends, when they come to unofficially test their best cocks in the pit. Look for the small A-frame shelters in yards here that house these creatures.

On the western shore is the Kaluakoi Resort and a handful of condos perched above the island's best beaches. Here, 6,700 acres sold by the Molokai Ranch to the Louisiana Land and Exploration Company and later sold to another concern are slowly being developed as homesites. Already there are houses scattered here and there. This area, rich with the finest archaeological sites on the island, is a hotbed of contention between developers and preservationists. The Kaluakoi Resort with its hotel, condominiums, and golf course, however, is often pointed to as a well-planned development, a kind of model compromise between the factions. Its low Polynesian-style architecture blends well with the surroundings and is not a high-rise blight on the horizon.

The East Coastal Road

Highway 450 is a magnificent coastal road running east from Kaunakakai to Halawa Valley. A slow drive along this writhing country thoroughfare rewards you with easily accessible beach parks, glimpses of fishponds, *heiau,* wildlife sanctuaries, and small one-room churches strung along the road like rosary beads. Almost every mile has a historical site, like the **Smith and Bronte Landing Site** where two pioneers of trans-Pacific flight ignominiously alighted in a mangrove swamp,

and **Paikalani Taro Patch,** the only one from which Kamehameha V would eat poi.

On Molokai's eastern tip is **Halawa Valley,** a real gem accessible by car. This pristine gorge has a series of waterfalls and their pools, and a beach park where the valley meets the sea. The majority of the population of Halawa moved out in 1946 when a 30-foot tsunami washed their homes away and mangled their taro fields, leaving a thick salty residue. Today only a handful of mostly alternative lifestylers live in the valley among the overgrown stone walls that once marked the boundaries of manicured and prosperous family gardens. Just south on the grounds of Puu O Hoku Ranch is **Kalanikaula,** the sacred *kukui* grove of Lanikaula, Molokai's most powerful *kahuna* of the classic period. This grove was planted at his death and became the most sacred spot on Molokai. Today the trees are dying.

The Windward Coast

Kalaupapa ("Flat Leaf") is a lonely peninsula formed by lava flow from the 400-foot-high Kauhako Crater, the highest spot on this relatively flat nub of land. Kalaupapa leper colony, completely separated from the world by a hostile pounding surf and a precipitous 1,600-foot *pali,* is a modern story of human dignity. Kalaupapa was a howling charnel house where the unfortunate victims of leprosy were banished to die. Here humanity reached its lowest ebb of hopelessness, violence, and depravity, until one tiny flicker of light arrived in 1873—Joseph de Veuster, a Belgian priest known throughout Hawaii as Father Damien. In the greatest example of pure *aloha* yet established on Hawaii, he became his brothers' keeper. Tours of Kalaupapa operated by well-informed former patients are enlightening and educational.

East of Kalaupapa along the windward (northeast) coast is a series of amazingly steep and isolated valleys. The inhabitants moved out at the beginning of this century except for one pioneering family that returned a few years ago to carve out a home. Well beyond the farthest reaches of the last road, this emerald-green primeval world awaits. The *pali* here mark the tallest sea cliffs in the world (although some dispute this designation), with an "average incline of more than 55 degrees." Many spots are far steeper. About halfway down the coast near Umilehi Point, the cliffs are at their highest at 3,300 feet. Farther to the east and diving headfirst out of a hanging valley is **Kahiwa ("Sacred One") Falls,** the highest in Hawaii at 1,750 feet. You get here only by helicopter excursion, by boat in the calmer summer months, or by foot over dangerous and unkempt mountain trails. For now, Molokai remains a sanctuary, reminiscent of the Hawaii of simpler times. Around it the storm of modernity rages, but still the "Friendly Island" awaits those willing to venture off the beaten track.

THE LAND

With 260 square miles, Molokai is the fifth largest Hawaiian island. Its western tip, at Ilio Point, is a mere 22 miles from Oahu's eastern tip, Makapuu Point. Resembling a jogging shoe, Molokai is about 38 miles from heel to toe and 10 miles from laces to sole, totaling 166,425 acres, with just over 88 miles of coastline. Most of the arable land on the island is owned by the 54,000-acre Molokai Ranch, primarily on the western end, and the 14,000-acre Puu O Hoku Ranch on the eastern end. Molokai was formed by three distinct shield volcanoes. Two linked together to form Molokai proper, and a later eruption formed the flat Kalaupapa Peninsula.

Physical Features
Although Molokai is rather small, it has a great deal of geographical diversity. Western Molokai is dry with rolling hills, natural pastures, and a maximum elevation of only 1,381 feet. The eastern sector of the island has heavy rainfall, the tallest sea cliffs in the world, and craggy narrow valleys perpetually covered in a velvet cloak of green mosses. Viewed from the sea it looks like a 2,000-foot vertical wall from surf to clouds, with tortuously deep chasms along the coastline. Mount Kamakou is the highest peak on Molokai, at 4,961 feet. The south-central area is relatively swampy, while the west and especially northwest coasts around Moomomi have rolling sand dunes. Papohaku Beach, just below the Kaluakoi Resort on western Molokai, is one of the most massive white-sand beaches in Hawaii. A controversy was raised when it was discovered that huge amounts of sand were dredged from this area and hauled to Oahu; the Molokai Ranch was pressured and the dredging ceased. A hefty section of land in the north-central area is a state forest where new species of trees are planted on an experimental basis. The 240-acre Palaau State Park is in this cool upland forested area.

Manmade Marvels
Two manmade features on Molokai are engineering marvels. One is the series of ancient fishponds strung along the south shore like pearls on a string—best seen from the air as you approach the island by plane. Dozens still exist, but

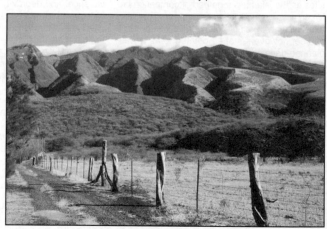

East Molokai
Mountains

ROBERT NILSEN

KAUNAKAKAI, MOLOKAI, AVERAGE HIGH/LOW TEMPERATURE AND RAINFALL

	JAN.	MARCH	MAY	JUNE	SEPT.	NOV.
High	79	79	81	82	82	80
Low	61	63	68	70	68	63
Rain	4	3	0	0	0	2

Note: Rainfall in inches; temperature in °F

the most amazing is the enormous **Keawanui Pond,** covering 54 acres and surrounded by a three-foot-tall, 2,000-foot-long wall. The other is the modern **Kualapuu Reservoir** completed in 1969. The world's largest rubber-lined reservoir, it can hold 1.4 billion gallons of water. Part of its engineering dramatics is the Molokai Tunnel, which feeds it with water from the eastern valleys. The tunnel is eight feet tall, eight feet wide, and almost 27,000 feet (five miles) long.

Climate
The average island temperature is 75-85° F (24° C). The yearly average rainfall is 30 inches; the east receives a much greater percentage than the west.

FLORA AND FAUNA

Land animals on Molokai were brought by man: pigs, goats, axis deer, and cattle. The earliest arrival still extant in the wild is the *pua'a* (pig). Molokai's pigs live in the upper wetland forests of the northeast, but they can actually thrive anywhere. Hunters say the meat from pigs that have lived in the lower dry forest is superior to those that acquire the muddy taste of ferns from the wetter upland areas. Pigs on Molokai are hunted mostly with the use of dogs who pin them by the ears and snout while the hunter approaches on foot and skewers them with a long knife.

Offspring from a pair of **goats** left by Captain Cook on the island of Niihau spread to all the islands; they were very well adapted to life on Molokai. Originally from the arid Mediterranean, goats could live well without any surface water,

a condition quite prevalent over most of Molokai. They're found primarily in the mountainous area of the northeast.

The last free-roaming arrivals to Molokai were **axis deer.** Molokai's deer came from the upper reaches of the Ganges River, sent to Kamehameha V by Dr. William Hillebrand while on a botanical trip to India in 1867. Kamehameha V sent some of the first specimens to Molokai, where they prospered. Today they are found mostly on western Molokai, though some travel the south coast to the east.

The island is unique in that it harbors a wildlife park on the grounds of the Molokai Ranch. This park has several hundred animals mostly imported from the savannas of Africa. Who knows? Perhaps in a few thousand years after some specimens have escaped there might be such a thing as a "Molokai giraffe" that will look like any other giraffe except that its markings resemble flowers. This sanctuary is now closed to the public, but the ranch still takes seriously its responsibility for the health and well-being of these animals.

Birdlife
A few of Hawaii's endemic birds can be spotted by a determined observer at various locales around Molokai. They include: the Hawaiian petrel *(ua'u);* Hawaiian coot *(alae ke'oke'o),* prominent in Hawaiian mythology; Hawaiian stilt *(ae'o),* a wading bird with ridiculous stick legs that protects its young by feigning wing injury and luring predators away from the nest; and the Hawaiian owl *(pueo),* a bird that helps in its own demise by being easily approached. Molokai has a substantial number of introduced game birds that attract hunters throughout the year.

The nonprofit organization **Nene O Molokai** operates a facility that breeds, releases, and monitors the state bird, the *nene*. Located about four miles east of Kaunakakai, they offer free tours but you must make an appointment to visit. To learn more about these friendly geese, call (808) Sincerely, 553-5992 or visit their website at www.aloha.net/~nene.

Flora

The *kukui* or candlenut tree is common to all the Hawaiian Islands; along with being the official state tree, its tiny white blossom is Molokai's flower. The *kukui,* introduced centuries ago by the early Polynesians, grows on lower mountain slopes and can easily be distinguished by its pale green leaves.

Conservation Controversy

It has long been established and regretted that introduced animals and plants have destroyed Hawaii's delicate natural balance leading to the extinction of many of its rare native species. A number of well-meaning groups and organizations are doing their best to preserve Hawaii habitat, but they don't always agree on the methods employed. Feral pigs, indiscriminate in their relentless hunt for food, are ecological nightmares that virtually bulldoze the rainforest floor into fetid pools and gouged earth where mosquitoes and other introduced species thrive while driving out the natives. Molokai's magnificent Kamakou Preserve, Upper Pelekunu, and Central Molokai Ridges are the last remaining pockets of natural habitat on the island. The Kamakou Preserve, 2,774 pristine acres, is covered, like the others, in ohia forest, prime habitat for the almost-extinct *oloma'o* (Molokai thrush), *kakawahie* (creeper), and the hearty but beleaguered *apapane* and *amakihi.* No one disagrees that the wild boar must be managed to protect these areas, but they do not agree on *how* they should be managed. The Nature Conservancy in its dedication to preserving the rainforest backed a policy to snare the wild boar, maintaining that this was the best possible way of eliminating these pests while placing the forest under the least amount of stress. In opposition to the practice of snaring is Pono, a local organization of native Molokai hunters that maintains snaring pigs is inhumane, causing the animals to starve to death or to die slowly from strangulation. Pono also abhors the wasting of the meat, and the indiscriminate killing of sows, the future of pigs on Molokai.

Aside from the **Kamakou Preserve,** the Nature Conservancy also maintains 5,714 acres of the Pelekunu Valley on the remote north coast of the island, where there is no public access. There is periodic access, however, to the **Moomomi Preserve,** a 921-acre area of sand dunes west of Moomomi Beach that is safe harbor for several species of endangered plants, seabirds, and green sea turtles.

Another grassroots group, **Na Ala Hele,** with branches on all islands, is dedicated to opening the ancient and extensive Hawaiian trail and access system. As part of its lobbying to open these trails, many of which now cross private property, it is trying to free landowners from any liability for those walking over the trails. So far the progress has been very slow.

HISTORY

The oral chant *"Molokai nui a Hina . . ."* ("Great Molokai, child of Hina") refers to Molokai as the island-child of the goddess Hina and the god Wakea, male progenitor of all the islands; Papa, Wakea's first wife, left him in anger as a result of this unfaithfulness. Hina's cave, just above Kaluaaha on the southeast coast, can still be visited and has been revered as a sacred spot for countless centuries. Another ancient spot, Halawa Valley, on the eastern tip of Molokai, is considered one of the oldest settlements in Hawaii. As research continues, settlement dates are pushed farther back, but for now scholars agree that early wayfarers from the Marquesas Islands settled Halawa in the mid-seventh century.

Molokai, from earliest times, was revered and feared as a center for mysticism and sorcery. **Ili'ili'opae Heiau** was renowned for its powerful priests whose incantations were mingled with the screams of human sacrifice. Commoners avoided Ili'ili'opae, and even powerful *kahuna* could not escape its terrible power. One, Kamalo, lost his sons as sacrifices at the *heiau* for their desecration of the temple drum. Kamalo sought revenge by invoking the help of his personal god, the terrible shark deity Kauhuhu. After the proper prayers and offerings, Kauhuhu sent a flash flood to wipe out Mapulehu Valley where Ili'ili'opae was located. All perished except for Kamalo and his family, who were protected by a sacred fence around their home.

This tradition of mysticism reached its apex with the famous Lanikaula, "Prophet of Molokai." During the 16th century, Lanikaula lived near Halawa Valley and practiced his arts, handed down by the goddess Pahulu, who predated even Pele. Pahulu was the goddess responsible for the "old ocean highway," which passed between Molokai and Lanai and led to Kahiki, lost homeland of all the islanders. Lanikaula practiced his sorcery in the utmost secrecy and even buried his excrement on an offshore island so that a rival kahuna could not find and burn it, which would surely cause his death. Hawaiian oral history does not say why Kawelo, a sorcerer from Lanai and a friend of Lanikaula, came to spy on Lanikaula and observed him hiding his excrement. Kawelo burned it in the sacred fires, and Lanikaula knew that his end was near. Lanikaula ordered his sons to bury him in a hidden grave so that his enemies could not find his bones and use their mana to control his spirit. To further hide his remains, he had a kukui grove planted over his body. **Kalanikaula** ("Sacred Grove of Lanikaula") is still visible today, though most of the trees appear to be dying.

Western Contacts

Captain James Cook first spotted Molokai on November 26, 1778, but because it looked bleak and uninhabited he decided to bypass it. It wasn't until eight years later that Capt. George Dixon sighted the island and decided to land. Very little was recorded in his ship's log about this first encounter, and Molokai slipped from the attention of the Western world until Protestant missionaries arrived at Kaluaaha in 1832 and reported the native population at approximately 6,000.

In 1790 Kamehameha the Great came from the Big Island as a suitor seeking the hand of Keopuolani, a chieftess of Molokai. Within five years he returned again, but this time there was no merrymaking: he came as a conquering emperor on his thrust westward to Oahu. His war canoes landed at Pakuhiwa Battleground, a bay just a few miles east of Kaunakakai; it's said that warriors lined the shores for more than four

miles. The grossly outnumbered warriors of Molokai fought desperately, but even the incantations of their kahuna were no match for Kamehameha and his warriors. Inflamed with recent victory and infused with the power of their horrible war-god Ku ("of the Maggot-dripping Mouth"), they slaughtered the Molokai warriors and threw their broken bodies into a sea so filled with sharks that their feeding frenzy made the waters appear to boil. Thus subdued, Molokai slipped into obscurity once again as its people turned to a quiet life of farming and fishing.

Molokai Ranch

Molokai remained almost unchanged until the 1850s. The Great Mahele of 1848 provided for private ownership of land, and giant tracts were formed into the Molokai Ranch. About 1850, German immigrant Rudolph Meyer came to Molokai and married a high chieftess named Dorcas Kalama Waha. Together they had 11 children, with whose aid he turned the vast lands of the Molokai Ranch into productive pastureland. A man of indomitable spirit, Meyer held public office on Molokai and became the island's unofficial patriarch. He managed Molokai Ranch for the original owner, Kamehameha V, and remained manager until his death in 1897, by which time the ranch was owned by the Bishop Estate. In 1875, Charles Bishop had bought half of the 70,000 acres of Molokai Ranch, and his wife, Bernice, a Kamehameha descendant, inherited the remainder. In 1898, the Molokai Ranch was sold to businessmen in Honolulu for $251,000. This consortium formed the American Sugar Co., but after a few plantings the available water on Molokai turned brackish and once again Molokai Ranch was sold. Charles Cooke bought controlling interest from the other businessmen in 1908 and remained in control of the ranch until 1988 when it was sold to Brierly Investments, a business concern from New Zealand.

Changing Times

Very little happened for a decade after Charles Cooke bought the Molokai Ranch from his partners. Molokai did become famous for its honey production, supplying a huge amount to the world up until WW I. During the 1920s, political and economic forces greatly changed Molokai. In

1921, Congress passed the **Hawaiian Homes Act,** which set aside 43,000 acres on the island for people who had at least 50% Hawaiian blood. By this time, however, all agriculturally productive land in Hawaii had already been claimed. The land given to the Hawaiians was very poor and lacked adequate water. Many Hawaiians had long since left the land and were raised in towns and cities. Now out of touch with the simple life of the taro patch, they found it very difficult to readjust. To prevent the Hawaiians from selling their claims and losing the land forever, the Hawaiian Homes Act provided that the land be leased to them for 99 years. Making a go of these 40-acre parcels *(kuleana)* was so difficult that successful homesteaders were called "Molokai Miracles."

In 1923 Libby Corporation leased land from Molokai Ranch at Kaluakoi and went into pineapple production; Del Monte followed suit in 1927 at Kualapuu. Both built company towns and imported Japanese and Filipino field laborers, swelling Molokai's population and stabilizing the economy. Many of the native Hawaiians subleased their tracts to the pineapple growers, and the Hawaiian Homes Act seemed to backfire. Instead of the homesteaders working their own farms, they were given monthly checks and lured into a life of complacency. Those who grew little more than family plots became, in effect, permanent tenants on their own property. Much more importantly, they lost the psychological advantage of controlling their own future and regaining their pride as envisioned in the Hawaiian Homes Act.

Modern Times

For the next 50 years life was quiet. The pineapples grew, providing security. Another large ranch, **Puu O Hoku** ("Hill of Stars") was formed on the eastern tip of the island. It was originally owned by Paul Fagan, the amazing San Francisco entrepreneur who also developed Hana on Maui. In 1955, Fagan sold Puu O Hoku to George Murphy, a Canadian industrialist, for a meager $300,000. The ranch, under Murphy, became famous for beautiful white Charolais cattle, a breed originating in France.

In the late 1960s "things" started quietly happening on Molokai. The Molokai Ranch sold 6,700 acres to the Kaluakoi Corp., which they controlled along with the Louisiana Land and Exploration Company. In 1969 the long-awaited Molokai reser-

voir was completed at Kualapuu; finally west Molokai had plenty of water. Shortly after Molokai's water problem appeared to be finally under control, Dole Corp. bought out Libby in 1972, lost millions in the next few years, and shut down its pineapple production at Maunaloa in 1975. By 1977 the acreage sold to the Kaluakoi Corp. started to be developed, and the Molokai Sheraton (now the Kaluakoi Hotel) opened along with low-rise condominiums and 270 fee-simple home sites ranging 5-43 acres selling for a minimum of $150,000 ($350,000 for oceanfront sites). Future plans for this area include two more resorts, additional condominiums, shopping facilities, bridle paths, and an airstrip (it's only 20 minutes to Honolulu). Lo and behold, sleepy old Molokai with the tiny Hawaiian Homes farms was now prime real estate and worth a fortune.

To complicate the picture even further, Del Monte shut down its operations in 1982, throwing more people out of work. In 1986 it did resume planting 250-acre tracts, but now all the pineapple is gone. Recently, coffee has been put into production near the old pineapple town of Kualapuu, some experimental plots of fruits and vegetables have been planted, and the Molokai Ranch has brought in sheep and cattle. After Brierly Investments bought the Molokai Ranch, bigger changes have started to take place, including a total facelift for the town of Maunaloa and greater emphasis on tourism for a slice of the ranch's income. These new avenues of diversification are still in their infant stages but might possibly lead to greater economic strength and stability. Today Molokai is in a period of flux in other ways. There is great tension between developers, who are viewed as "carpetbaggers" interested only in a fast buck, and those who consider themselves the last remnants of a lost race holding on desperately to what little they have left.

ECONOMY

If it weren't for a pitifully bad economy, Molokai would have no economy at all. At one time the workers on the pineapple plantations had good steady incomes and the high hopes of the working class. With all the pineapple jobs gone, Molokai was transformed from an island with virtually no unemployment to a hard-luck community with a high rate of the people on welfare. With the start of the coffee plantation and the slowly growing tourism industry, this bleak economic situation has lessened somewhat. Inexplicably, Molokai also has the highest utility rates in Hawaii. Some say this is due to the fact that the utility company built a modern biomass plant and didn't have enough biomass to keep it operating—the people were stuck with the fuel tab. The present situation is even more ludicrous when you consider that politically Molokai is part of Maui County. It is lumped together with Kaanapali on Maui's western coast, one of Hawaii's poshest and wealthiest areas, where the vast majority of people are recent arrivals from the Mainland. This amounts to almost no political/economic voice for grassroots Molokai.

Agriculture

The word that is now bandied about is "diversified" agriculture. What this means is not pinning all hope to one crop like the ill-fated pineapple, but planting a potpourri of crops. Attempts at diversification are evident as you travel around Molokai. Fields of corn, wheat, fruits, nuts, and coffee are just west of Kaunakakai; many small farmers are trying truck farming by raising a variety of garden vegetables that they hope to sell to the massive hotel food industry in Honolulu. Watermelon, bell pepper, onions, and herbs are perhaps the most well known. The problem is not in production, but transportation. Molokai

raises excellent crops, but little established transport exists for the perishable vegetables. A barge service, running on a loose twice-weekly schedule, is the only link to the market. The lack of storage facilities on Molokai makes it tough to compete in the hotel food business, which requires the freshest produce. Unfortunately, vegetables don't wait well for late barges.

Development

A debate rages between those in favor of tourist development, which they say will save Molokai, and grassroots organizations championed by OHA (Office of Hawaiian Affairs), which insist unchecked tourism development will despoil Molokai and give no real benefit to the people. A main character in the debate is the Kaluakoi Corp., which wants to build condos and sell more home lots. It claims that this, coupled with a few more resorts, will bring in jobs. The people know that they will be relegated to service jobs (maids and waiters), while all the management jobs go to outsiders. Most islanders feel that only rich people from the Mainland can afford million-dollar condos, and that eventually they will become disenfranchised on their own island. Claims are that outsiders have no feeling for the *aina* (land) and will destroy important cultural sites whenever growth dictates.

A few years back the Kaluakoi Corp. hired an "independent" research team to investigate Kawakiu Iki Bay, known to be an ancient adze quarry. After weeks of study, this Maui-based

Meyer Sugar Mill

ROBERT NILSEN

research team reported that Kawakiu was of "minor importance." Hawaii's academic sector went wild. The Society of Hawaiian Archaeology dispatched its own team under Dr. Patrick Kirch, who stated that Kawakiu was one of the richest archaeological areas in Hawaii. In one day they discovered six sites missed by the "independent" research team, and stated that a rank amateur could find artifacts by merely scraping away some of the surface. Reasonable voices call for moderation. Both sides agree Molokai must grow, but the growth must be controlled, and the people of Molokai must be represented and included as beneficiaries.

THE PEOPLE

Aside from the tiny island of Niihau, Molokai has the largest percentage of Hawaiian population, and this is perhaps due in part to relatively small commercial development on the island throughout its history, which did not bring in large numbers of ethnic workers. While sugar was tried early on with some success, it never grew to vast size, and the pineapple production on the island was also limited. Only ranching has really persevered and this doesn't require any large number of laborers. More recently, with the slow development of tourism, white collar workers have filtered into the workforce and there has been some increase in tourism-related jobs, but mostly local Hawaiians make up 48% of Molokai's population; 21% are Filipino, 18% Caucasian, 9% Japanese, 1% Chinese, and 3% various other groups.

Molokai is obviously experiencing a class struggle. The social problems hinge on the economy—the collapse of pineapple cultivation and the move toward tourism. The average income on Molokai is quite low and the people are not consumer-oriented. Tourism, especially "getaway condos," brings in the affluent. This creates friction; the "have-nots" don't know their situation until the "haves" come in and remind them. Today, most people hunt a little, fish, and have small gardens. Some are small-time *pakalolo* growers who get over the hard spots by making a few dollars from some backyard plants. There is no organized crime on Molokai. The worst you might run into is a group of local kids drinking on a weekend in one of their favorite spots. It's a territorial thing. If you come into their vicinity they might feel their turf

is being invaded, and you could be in for some hassles. All this could add up to a bitter situation except that the true nature of most of the people is to be helpful and friendly. Just be sensitive to smiles and frowns and give people their space.

Ethnic Identity

An underground link exists between Molokai and other Hawaiian communities such as Waianae on Oahu. Molokai is unusual in that it is still Hawaiian in population and influence, with continuing culturally based outlooks that remain unacceptable to Western views. Ethnic Hawaiians are again becoming proud of their culture and heritage, as well as politically aware and sophisticated, and are just now entering the political arena. Few are lawyers, doctors, politicians, or executives; with ethnic identity returning, there is beginning to be a majority backlash against these professions. Among non-Hawaiian residents, it's put down or unacknowledged as a real occurrence.

Social problems on Molokai relate directly to teenage boredom and hostility in the schools, fueled by a heavy drinking scene. A disproportionate rate of teen pregnancy is a direct by-product. Teachers unofficially admit that they prefer a student who has smoked *pakalolo* to one who's been drinking. It mellows them out. The traditional educational approach is failing.

Ho'opono'opono is a fascinating family problem-solving technique still very much employed on Molokai. The process is like "peeling the onion," where a mediator, usually a respected *kapuna,* tries to get to the heart of a problem. Similar to group therapy, it's a closed family ordeal, never open to outsiders, and lasts until all emotions are out in the open and all concerned feel "clean."

BEACHES

Eastern Beaches

The beaches of Molokai have their own temperament, ranging from moody and rebellious to sweet and docile. Heading east from Kaunakakai along Route 450 takes you past a string of beaches that vary from poor to excellent. Much of this underbelly of Molokai is fringed by a protective coral reef that keeps the water flat, shallow, and at some spots murky. This area was ideal for fishponds but leaves a lot to be desired as far as beaches are concerned. The farther east you go,

No. 20 Beach, Molokai

the better the beaches become. The first one you come to is at **One Ali'i Park,** about four miles east of Kaunakakai. Here you'll find a picnic area, campsites, good fishing, and family-class swimming where the kids can frolic with no danger from the sea. Next you pass **Kakahaia Beach Park** and **Kumimi Beach,** one of a series of lovely sandy crescents where the swimming is fine. Just before you reach Pukoo, a small dirt road on your right goes to a hidden beach perfect for a secluded swim.

Halawa Bay, on Molokai's far east end, is the best all-around beach on the island. It's swimmable year-round, but be extra careful during the winter months. The bay protects the beach for a good distance; beyond its reach the breakers are excellent for surfing. The snorkeling and fishing are good to very good.

West End Beaches
The people of Molokai favor the beaches on the northwest section of the island. **Moomomi Beach** is one of the best and features good swimming, fair surfing, and pleasurable snorkeling along its sandy, rocky bottom. You have to drive over a very rutted dirt road to get there. Although car rental agencies are against it, you can make it, but only in dry weather. From Moomomi you can walk west along the beach and find your own secluded spot.

Very few visitors go south from Maunaloa town, but it is possible and rewarding for those seeking a secluded area. As you enter Maunaloa town a dirt track goes off to your right. Follow it through the Molokai Ranch and down the hill to **Hale O Lono Harbor,** start of an Outrigger Canoe Race. The swimming is only fair but the fantasy-feeling of a deserted island is pervasive.

Papohaku and **Kepuhi Beaches** just below the Kaluakoi Resort are excellent, renowned for their vast expanses of sand. Unfortunately, they're treacherous in the winter with giant swells and heavy rips, which make them a favorite for surfers. Anyone not accustomed to strong sea conditions should limit themselves to sunning and wading only to the ankles. During the rest of the year this area is great for swimming, becoming like a lake in the summer months. North of Kepuhi Bay is an ideal beach named **Kawakiu.** Although it's less than a mile up the coast, it's more than 15 miles away by road. You have to branch off Route 460 and follow the seven-mile dirt track north well before it forks toward the Kaluakoi. This area is well established as an archaeological site, and access to the beach was a hard-fought controversy between the people of Molokai and the Molokai Ranch. Good swimming, depending upon tide conditions, and free camping on weekends.

SPORTS AND RECREATION

Since Molokai is a great place to get away from it all, you would expect an outdoor extravaganza. In fact, Molokai is a "good news, bad news" island when it comes to recreation, especially in the water. Molokai has few excellent beaches with the two best, Halawa and Papohaku, on opposite ends of the island; **Papohaku Beach** on the west end is treacherous during the winter months. Surfers and windsurfers will be disappointed with Molokai except at a few locales at the right time of year, while bathers, sun worshippers, and families will love the small secluded beaches with gentle waves located around the island.

Molokai has a small population and plenty of undeveloped "outback" land. This *should* add up to great trekking and camping, but the land is mostly privately owned and the tough trails are poorly maintained. However, permission is usually granted to trek across private land, and those bold enough to venture into the outback will virtually have it to themselves. Day-hiking trails and lightly used camping areas with good facilities are no problem. Molokai has tame, family-oriented beach parks along its southern shores, superb hunting and fishing, two excellent golf courses, and a handful of fine tennis courts. Couple this with clean air, no industrial pollution, no city noise, and a deliciously casual atmosphere, and you wind up with the epitome of relaxation.

Snorkeling and Scuba

Some charter fishing boats arrange scuba and snorkeling excursions, but scuba and snorkeling on Molokai are just offshore and you don't need a boat to get to it. Beginners will feel safe at **One Ali'i Park,** where the sea conditions are mild, though the snorkeling is mediocre. The best underwater area is the string of beaches heading east past mile marker 18 on Route 450, and especially at mile marker 20. You'll wind up at Halawa Bay, which is tops. Moomomi Beach on the northwest shore is very good, and Kawakiu Beach out on the west end is good around the rocks, but stay away during winter. For those staying at Molokai Ranch, Halena and Kolo Beaches along the south coast also offer descent snorkeling.

Molokai Fish and Dive in Kaunakakai, tel. (808) 553-5926, is a full-service snorkel shop. It has very good rental rates ($9 a set), can give you directions to the best spots, and arranges excursions.

Bill Kapuni's Snorkel and Dive Adventure, tel. (808) 553-9867, P.O. Box 1962, Kaunakakai, HI 96748, is an excellent way to enjoy Molokai's underwater spectacle, with Bill Kapuni, a native Hawaiian, who is intimately familiar with both the marinelife that you will encounter and the Hawaiian myths and legends of his heritage. Bill's trips, 7:30 a.m., 10:30 a.m., and 1 p.m., including complimentary snacks, are $45 for snorkeling and $85 for a one-tank dive. Bill offers professional PADI instruction and has a compressor to fill tanks for certified divers.

Ma'a Hawaii, Molokai Action Adventures

Walter Naki knows Molokai—its mountains, seas, shores, trails, flowers, trees, and birds. His one-man action-adventure company, Ma'a Hawaii, P.O. Box 1269, Kaunakakai, HI 96748, tel. (808) 558-8184, loosely translates as "used to, accustomed to, familiar with Hawaii." As a native Hawaiian raised on the island and versed in its myths and mysteries, his spirit is strengthened and revitalized by the *aina* to which he is so closely attached. Walter has won the Hawaiian decathlon five times—a 10-event competition that includes sprinting, spear throwing, heaving a 28-pound stone, and swimming. He has also proven to be one of Hawaii's most renowned athletes in statewide spearfishing and free diving contests, training himself to stay underwater for over two minutes while descending to depths of 85 feet. Walter's modest but lovingly tended home, which he shares with his two children, is lined with his trophies. Outside a pet deer, Pua ("Flower"), which he has raised since she was a tiny fawn, comes when he calls, loves sweets, and follows his truck like a puppy whenever he leaves. If it has to do with the outdoors Walter does it. Hunting of axis deer, wild boar, or goats on private land costs $200 per day for bow hunters and $300 per day for rifle hunts (two hunters per day only). Hiking and "camera safaris" over many of the same hunting trails cost $50 for a half day (up to six people only), while snorkeling, skin-diving, spear fishing, and reef fishing are $50 per half day; kayak trips are available on request. Walter is extremely ecologically minded, employing practical knowledge that he has learned from years of living *with* the land and sea. The wild game that he hunts is used for food, not just trophies, and by taking pig, goats, and deer, he helps to manage the forest, balancing the destruction caused by these introduced animals so that native species can survive.

Walter is a great guide, but he is definitely "fo real," absolutely genuine with no glitz or glamour. He transports his gear, much of which is homemade and which he pulls from a shed in his back yard, in a used but not abused old truck, and he takes you to sea in a very seaworthy 21-foot Boston Whaler with twin 90s on the back, capable of going around to the north coast. Walter will do everything that he can to make your day safe and enjoyable, even stopping at his friend's taro patch to give you a glimpse of preserved island life. Remember, however, that it is up to you to be completely honest about your physical abilities, especially underwater, because with Walter's great skills and enthusiasm, it is easy for him to push you to your limit while he is just taking a stroll in the park. Whether it's snorkeling, diving, reef fishing, hiking, or camping in a north coast valley, Walter can do it all. If you seek a unique experience where you can touch the spirit of Molokai, travel for a day with Walter Naki. It will make all the difference.

Kayaking

Whether its to the calm south shore with its reef and many fishponds, or the rugged north shore and its isolated valleys, **Lani's Kayak Tours and Rentals,** tel. (808) 558-8563, can get you there. Destinations may depend upon the season and water conditions. South shore trips are $45 and north shore trips $65, $10 extra for snorkeling gear.

Sailing

Molokai is nearly devoid of charter sailboats. However, for those who like to feel the salty sea breeze in their hair, hear the snap of a full-furled sail, or enjoy the sunset from the deck of a sailing ship, try an excursion with **Molokai Charters,** tel. (808) 553-5852, P.O. Box 1207, Kaunakakai, HI 96748. The only charter sailing ship on the island is its 42-foot sloop *Satan's Doll,* berthed at the Kaunakakai wharf. Tours offered are a two-hour sunset sail for $40 and a full day sail to Lanai for swimming and snorkeling for $90. In season, whalewatching tours are also run for $50. Four-person minimum.

Surfing

The best surfing is out on the east end past mile marker 20. Pohakuloa Point has excellent breaks, which continue eastward to Halawa Bay. Moomomi Beach has decent breaks as does Kepuhi Beach in front of Kaluakoi Resort; Kawakiu's huge waves during the winter months are suitable only for experts.

Horseback Riding

For riding options on Molokai, there's slim pickin's. The **Molokai Ranch,** tel. (808) 552-2767, which offers a variety of rides over its ranch lands as part of the all-inclusive accommodation/activity packages, will also take nonguests. The **Molokai Horse and Wagon Ride,** tel. (808) 558-8380 or 588-8132, near Pukoo also does rides along with the wagon ride through the Mapulehu mango grove and up to the Ili'ili'opae Heiau, largest on the island.

Molokai Ranch

While daily activities are included in the cost of staying at the Molokai Ranch, other guests may also sign up for these outings. Activities include horseback riding, mountain biking, and hiking. Sign up at the Molokai Ranch Outfitters Center in Maunaloa, or call (808) 552-2791.

Golf

Molokai's two golf courses are as different as custom-made and rental clubs. The **Kaluakoi Golf Course,** tel. (808) 552-2739, is a picture-perfect beauty that would challenge any top pro. Laid out by master links designer Ted Robinson, it's located out at the Kaluakoi Resort. The 6,564-yard, par-72 course winds through an absolutely beautiful setting including five holes strung right along the beach. There's a complete pro shop, driving range, and practice greens. Golf lessons by the hour are also available. Greens fees for 18 holes are $45 for resort guests and $65 for nonguests; twilight specials available.

Molokai's other golf course is the homey **Ironwood Hills Golf Club,** tel. (808) 567-6000. Open 7 a.m.-5 p.m. daily, this rarely used but well-maintained mountain course is nine holes, par 34, and 3,086 yards long. Pay the affordable greens fee, $10 for nine holes and $14 if you want to loop the course twice, to the office manager or to a groundskeeper who will come around as you play. Twilight rates, club rental, riding cart, and hand cart are also available. The course is located up in the hills in Kalae at 1,200 in elevation, just before the Meyer Sugar Mill—look for the sign. Ironwood Hills is turning from a frog to a prince. Recent work has concentrated on improving the grounds. Even today there is no pro shop or snack shop available—all these will come in time—and only a small mobile building as an office.

MOLOKAI GOLF AND TENNIS

GOLF COURSE	PAR	YARDS	FEES	CART	CLUBS
Ironwood Hills Golf Club tel. (808) 567-6000	34	3,086	$10/9 holes $14/18 holes	$7	$7
Kaluakoi Golf Course tel. (808) 552-2739	72	6,564	$45 guest $75 nonguest	$15 $15	$22

TENNIS COURTS

LOCATION	NAME OF COURT	NO. OF COURTS	LIGHTED
Kaunakakai	Community Center	2	Yes
Molokai High	Hoolehua	2	Yes

Tennis

Two courts are available at the **Ke Nani Kai Condos,** near the Kaluakoi Resort, which are free to guests. Two courts at the **Wavecrest Condo** east of Kaunakakai on Route 450 are also free to guests. Public courts are available at Molokai High School in Hoolehua and at the Community Center in Kaunakakai, but you may have to reserve a spot with the office in the Mitchell Pauole Center next door for the courts in town.

Fishing

The Penguin Banks of Molokai are some of the most fertile waters in Hawaii. Private boats as well as the commercial fishing fleets out of Oahu come here to try their luck. Trolling produces excellent game fish such as marlin, mahimahi, *ahi* (a favorite with sashimi lovers), and *ono,* with its reputation of being the best-tasting fish in Hawaii. Bottom fishing, usually with live bait, yields *onaga* and *uku,* a gray snapper favored by local people. Molokai's shoreline, especially along the south and west, offers great bait-casting for *ulua* and *ama ama. Ulua* is an excellent eating fish, and with a variance in weight from 15 to 110 pounds, can be a real whopper to catch from shore. Squidding, *limu* gathering, and torch-fishing are all quite popular and productive along the south shore, especially around the old fishpond sites. These remnants of Hawaii's one-time vibrant aquaculture still produce mullet, the *ali'i's* favorite; an occasional Samoan crab; the less desirable, introduced tilapia; and the better-left-alone barracuda.

The **Alyce C.,** tel. (808) 558-8377, is a 31-foot, fully equipped diesel-powered fishing boat, owned and operated by Capt. Joe Reich, who can take you for full- or half-day charters and offers whale-watching tours in season.

The **Molokai Fish and Dive Co.,** tel. (808) 553-5926, also arranges deep-sea charters as well as excursions and shoreline sailing.

Hunting

Some of the best hunting on Molokai is on the private lands of the 54,000-acre **Molokai Ranch,** tel. (808) 552-2741, open to hunting year-round. However, the enormous fees charged by the Ranch have effectively stopped hunting on their lands to all but the very determined or very wealthy. Ecological conditions may also affect hunting at certain times of the year. A permit to hunt game animals including black buck, aoudad sheep, eland antelope, and axis deer costs $400 per day for a guided hunt with an additional fee of $250 per person (up to three). Game fees are $1000 for each of the animals, except that the trophy fee (certain animals of a certain size) is $1,500! Game bird hunting is also offered during regular state hunting season, following state rules and regulations, at $150 per day.

Public hunting lands on Molokai are open to anyone with a valid state hunting license. Wild goats and pigs can be hunted in various hunting units year-round on weekends and state holidays except when bird hunting is in effect. Bag limits are two animals per day. Hunting game birds (ring-necked pheasants, various quails and doves, wild turkeys, partridges, and francolins) is open on public lands from the first Saturday in November to the third Sunday in January. A special dove season runs late January through March. For full information, license, and fees (as well as State Park and Forest Service camping permits) contact the Division of Forestry and Wildlife, P.O. Box 347, Kaunakakai, HI 96748, tel. (808) 533-5019.

Camping
The best camping on Molokai is at **Pala'au State Park** at the end of Route 470, in the cool mountains overlooking Kalaupapa Peninsula. It's also the site of Molokai's famous Phallic Rock. Here you'll find pavilions, grills, picnic tables, and freshwater. What you won't find are crowds; in fact, most likely you'll have the entire area to yourself. The camping here is free, but you need a permit, good for seven days, from the camp headquarters office in Kalae or from the Division of State Parks in Wailuku on Maui. Camping is permitted for up to a week at **Waikolu Lookout** in the Molokai Forest Reserve, but you'll have to follow a tough dirt road (Main Forest Road) for 10 miles to get to it. A free permit must be obtained from the Division of Forestry and Wildlife, Olu Ave., about one mile west of Kaunakakai, tel. (808) 553-5019.

Seaside camping is allowed at **One Ali'i Park,** just east of Kaunakakai, and at **Papohaku Beach**

Park, west of Kaunakakai. These parks have full facilities but due to their beach location and easy access just off the highway they are often crowded, noisy, and bustling. Also, you are a target here for any rip off artists. A county permit ($3 per day) is required and available from County Parks and Recreation at the Mitchell Pauole Center in Kaunakakai, tel. (808) 553-3204.

Hawaiian Homelands, P.O. Box 198, Hoolehua, HI 96729, tel. (808) 567-6104 or 567-6296, fax 567-6665, offers camping at **Kioea Park,** one mile west of Kaunakakai. The permit to this historical coconut grove costs $5 a day. Be sure to reserve well ahead of time; graduation, summer, and December are usually booked. One of the most amazing royal coconut groves in Hawaii, it's a treat to visit, but camping here, though quiet, can be hazardous. Make sure to pitch your tent away from any coconut-laden trees if possible, and vacate if the winds come up.

You may be able to camp free (unofficially) at Moomomi Beach on the island's northwest shore on a grassy plot near the pavilion, or at isolated Kawakiu Iki Bay farther to the west. You can't officially camp at Halawa Bay Beach Park either, but if you continue along the north side of the bay you'll come to a well-used but unofficial campground fringed by ironwoods and recognizable by old fire pits. This area does attract down-and-outers so don't leave your gear unattended.

Tentalow, Molokai Ranch

ROBERT NILSEN

Hiking

Molokai should be a hiker's paradise and there are exciting, well-maintained, easily accessible trails, but others cross private land, skirt guarded *pakalolo* patches, are poorly maintained, and tough to follow. This section provides a general overview of the trekking possibilities available on Molokai. Full info is given in the respective "Sights" sections.

One of the most exciting hassle-free trails descends the *pali* to the **Kalaupapa Peninsula.** You follow the well-maintained mule trail down, and except for some "road apples" left by the mules, it's a totally enjoyable experience suitable for an in-shape family. You *must* have a reservation with the guide company to tour the former leper colony, however (see "The Kalaupapa Experience" under "Middle Molokai and Kalaupapa," below).

Another excellent trail is at **Halawa Valley,** following Halawa Stream to cascading Moaula Falls, where you can take a refreshing dip if the famous *moo,* a mythical lizard said to live in the pool, is in the right mood. This trail is strenuous enough to be worthwhile and thrilling enough to be memorable. In years past anyone could walk up into Halawa Valley; however, due to abuse, disrespect, and degradation of the land, it was closed to the public for two years. It has been opened again, but entrance is restricted to those who go in with **Pilipo's Halawa Valley Hike.** Tour leader Pilipo Solitorio was born and bred in the valley, so a walk with him is like having a private historical and cultural lesson. For reservations, call (808) 553-4355 in the early evening.

Molokai Forest Reserve, which you can reach by driving about 10 miles over the rugged Main Forest Road (passable by 4WD only in the dry season), has fine hiking. At road's end you'll find the Sandalwood Measuring Pit. The hale and hearty who push on will find themselves overlooking Waikolu and Pelekunu, two fabulous and enchanted valleys of the north coast.

The most formidable trail on Molokai is the one that completely crosses the island from south to north and leads into **Wailau Valley.** It starts innocently enough at Ili'ili'opae Heiau about 15 miles east of Kaunakakai, but as you gain elevation it gets increasingly tougher to follow. After you've trekked all day, the trail comes to an abrupt halt over Wailau. From here you have to pick your way down an unmarked, slippery, and treacherous 3,000-foot *pali.* Don't attempt this trail alone. It's best to go with the Sierra Club, which organizes periodic hikes, or with a local person who knows the terrain. Wailau Valley is one of the last untouched valleys of bygone days. Here are bananas, papayas, and guavas left over from the last major inhabitants, who left early in this century. The local people who summer here, and the one family who lives here year-round, are generous and friendly, but also very aware and rightfully protective of the last of old Hawaii in which they live. If you hike into Wailau Valley remember that in effect you are a guest. Be courteous and respectful and you'll come away with a unique and meaningful island experience.

SHOPPING

Coming to Molokai in order to shop is like going to Waikiki and hoping to find a grass shack on a deserted beach. Molokai has only a handful of shops where you can buy locally produced crafts and Hawaiiana. Far and away, most of Molokai's shopping is centered along Ala Malama Street in downtown Kaunakakai. All three blocks of it! Here you'll find the island's only health food store, three very good food markets, a drugstore that sells just about everything, and a clutch of souvenir shops. Away from Kaunakakai the pickin's get mighty slim. Heading west you'll find the **Kualapuu General Store** off Route 470 on the way to Kalaupapa, and a sundries store along with a Liberty House at the Kaluakoi Resort on the far west end. The Maunaloa Road (Rt. 460) basically ends in Maunaloa town. Go there! The best and most interesting shop, **The Big Wind Kite Factory,** is in town and is worth a visit in its own right. Also, in Maunaloa you'll find a market and a restaurant. Heading east from Kaunakakai is another shoppers' wasteland with only the sundries store at the Molokai Shores condo and the store and lunch window at Pukoo Neighborhood Store for anything to buy.

GETTING THERE

Hawaiian Airlines, tel. (800) 367-5320 or (808) 533-3644 on Molokai, has two regularly scheduled flights each way connecting Molokai and Honolulu. The morning flight from Honolulu and the afternoon flight to Honolulu go through Lanai.

The second morning flight to Honolulu continues on to Kahului.

Island Air, tel. (808) 567-6115 or (800) 323-3345 Mainland, offers flights connecting Molokai with Oahu and Maui. There are 11 daily flights to Honolulu 6:35 a.m.-6:25 p.m. The two daily flights from Hana go through Kahului, from where there are an additional three daily flights.

Molokai Air Shuttle, tel. (808) 567-6847 Molokai or (808) 545-4988 Oahu, flies a Piper Aztec to/from Honolulu and Molokai for $50 roundtrip. This is not a scheduled route: you call and let them know when you want to fly and they will tell you what's available that day. Aside from this flight, Molokai Air Shuttle runs roundtrip charter service from Honolulu and Molokai to Lanai for $275 from Molokai. A 20-minute air tour of the north coast of Molokai is offered for $52, and they can fly you down to Kalaupapa, connect you with a tour of the settlement there, and fly you back for around $80. Always call to ask what's available on the day you want to go.

Paragon Air, tel. (808) 244-3356 or (800) 428-1231, does island-wide air charters in small aircraft, including from Molokai to Honolulu.

Pacific Wings, tel. (888) 575-4546, flies out of Kahului for Molokai (four a day), Hana (three a day), and Kamuela on the Big Island (one a day), as well as from Honolulu to those three destinations, no more than twice daily, using eight-seat, twin engine Cessna 402C aircraft.

Molokai Airport

The **Hoolehua Airport** has a small terminal with an open-air baggage claim area to the far right, check-in counters next to that, and the waiting lounge on the left side. In the baggage claim area, Dollar and Budget have rental car booths, and each has a base yard a few steps away across the free public parking lot out front. Ground transportation waits at the front but doesn't hang around long after a plane arrival. Also at the airport you'll find a lounge and lunch counter with not-too-bad prices, toilets, and public telephones. Pick up a loaf of excellent Molokai bread, the best souvenir available, or a lei from the small gift shop. Tourist brochures are available from a rack in the arrival area.

By Sea

Currently there is no scheduled sea connection to Molokai. The *Maui Princess* used to sail daily from Kaunakakai wharf to Lahaina, but for eco-nomic reasons the service was stopped in 1997, affecting many businesses on Molokai. Hopefully, it will be restarted at some point in the future, as it provides a fun and economical way to reach the island. The *Maui Princess* does, however, offer several day and overnight tour packages to Molokai. For information and reservations call (808) 661-8397 or (800) 833-5800.

GETTING AROUND

Public Transportation

No public bus transportation services Molokai. The following are taxi and limousine services that also provide some limited tours. **Kukui Tours and Limousines,** tel. (808) 553-5133, is a 24-hour taxi service, taking reservations 8 a.m.-5 p.m. **Molokai Off-road Tours and Taxi,** tel. (808) 553-3369, is another option. **Friendly Isle Tours and Transportation,** tel. (808) 553-9046, does transfers from the airport 8 a.m.-6 p.m. for $7 per person ($8 after hours), minimum of three.

Rental Cars

Molokai offers a limited choice of car rental agencies—make reservations to avoid being disappointed. Rental car booths close after the last flight of the day has arrived. Rental car companies on Molokai dislike their cars being used on dirt roads (there are plenty) and strongly warn against it. No jeeps are available on Molokai at this time, but it's always in the air that one of the car companies will make them available sometime in the future. **Dollar Rent A Car,** tel. (808) 567-6156, provides professional and friendly service, also offering some of the best rates on the island; **Budget Rent A Car,** tel. (808) 567-6877, is another option. These companies have booths and base yards at the airport. Pick up a copy of the *Molokai Drive Guide* magazine for maps and useful information on sights and activities.

The new guy in the market is a local company called **Island Kine Auto Rental.** Its slant is to rent the kind of vehicle that the big companies don't. It has a handful of cars, pickups, and vans, all used but well-maintained, that start at $30 a day. For further information and reservations, contact the company at: 51 Ilio Road, P.O. Box 1018, Kaunakakai, HI 96748, tel. (808) 553-5242, fax 553-3880, Web site: www.molokai-aloha.com/cars, e-mail: cars@molokai-aloha.

A few unofficial rental car dealers exist on the island that "lend" vehicles and accept only "donations." Their vehicles are usually used and "local." Unless you personally know someone who runs this sort of business, be cautious.

Hitchhiking

The old thumb gives fair to good results on Molokai. Most islanders say they prefer to pick up hitchers who are making an effort by walking along, instead of lounging by the side of the road. It shows that you don't have a car but do have some pride. Getting a ride to or from Kaunakakai and the airport is usually easy.

GUIDED TOURS

Only a few limited tours are offered on Molokai. Mostly, it's you and your rental car. **Friendly Isle Tours and Transportation,** tel. (808) 553-9046, runs a four-hour van tour for $49 from the Kaluakoi Resort or the airport that hits many of the highlights of the island. Also offered is a two-hour tour of the upcountry area around Kalae for $36.

For a similar tour of the highlights of the island contact **Kukui Tours and Limousines,** tel. (808) 553-5133.

Molokai Off-road Tours and Taxi, tel. (808) 553-3369, offers half- and full-day narrated tours by van or 4WD Mon.-Sat., reservations required. The "Rainforest Adventure" for $53 takes you up into the forest preserve (minimum four people). Bring lunch.

One of the most fun-filled cultural experiences that you can have is to spend an afternoon on the **Molokai Horse and Wagon Ride,** tel. (808) 558-8380, 588-8132, or (800) 670-6965, Web site: www.visitmolokai.com/wgnride, e-mail: wgnride@aloha.net. Rides are given Mon.-Sat. 10:30 a.m. until finished. Call at least a day in advance. Rates are $35 for the wagon ride ($17.50 for kids under 12), $40 if you would like to go along on horseback, and lunch is provided. The experience starts and ends from a hidden beach just past mile marker 15 on the east end of the island along Route 450. As you drive, look to the right for a sign to Mapulehu Mango Grove; you'll follow the road to a small white house and a picnic area prepared on the beach. The wonderful aspect of this venture is that it is a totally local operation com-

pletely devoid of glitz, glamour, and hype. It's run by Junior Rawlins, wagonmaster, and his wife, Nani.

After loading, the wagon leaves the beach and rolls through the **Mapulehu Mango Grove,** one of the largest in the world, with over 2,000 trees and 32 varieties. Planted by the Hawaiian Sugar Co. in the 1930s in an attempt to diversify, trees came from all over the world, including Brazil, India, and Formosa. Unfortunately, most of the U.S. was not educated about eating exotic fruits, so the mangos rotted on the tree unpicked, and the grove became overgrown. The ride proceeds down a tree-shrouded lane with music, singing, and anecdotes along the way. In about 20 minutes you arrive at **Ili'ili'opae Heiau,** among the largest Hawaiian places of worship in the islands. You are told about the history of the *heiau,* pointed out exotic fruits and plants in the area, and led atop the *heiau* for a photo session. You then return to the beach for a barbecue lunch and a demonstration of coconut husking, throw-netting (one of the oldest and most fascinating ways of catching fish), and maybe even a hula lesson. You can also count on the Hawaiian tradition of hospitality. These guys know how to treat you well, but remember that this is a *real* experience, so don't expect anything fancy or pretentious.

Coupled with a tour of the Kalaupapa settlement, the **Molokai Mule Ride** runs tours from topside down to the peninsula. The well-trained mules will transport you roundtrip down and up the 1,600-foot *pali* face, expertly negotiating 26 hairpin switchbacks on the trail. The ride each way is about 90 minutes. Conducted 8 a.m.-3:30 p.m. daily except Sunday, this tour is $120 and includes the ground tour of the settlement and lunch. No riders over 240 pounds please; all must be at least 16 years old and in good physical shape. Molokai Mule Ride can also arrange the ground tour for you ($38) if you desire to hike down the hill, or a fly-in from Hoolehua Airport and ground tour for $88. An accommodation and tour package, as well as air transportation from Honolulu and tour, are also available. For information and reservations, call (808) 567-6088 or (800) 567-7550, Web site: www.muleride.com, e-mail: muleman@aloha.net.

The **Meyer Ranch** in Kalae has opened part of its 1,800 acres to guided mountain bike and 4WD tours. All tours leave from the Molokai Museum and Cultural Center, which is included as part of the tour. Call (808) 567-6624 or (800) 962-9989 for complete information and details.

Helicopter and Airplane Flights

An amazing way to see Molokai—particularly its north coast—is by helicopter. This method is admittedly expensive, but dollar for dollar it is *the* most exciting way of touring and can get you places that no other means can. A handful of companies operate mostly from Maui and include overflights of Molokai. Though helicopter trip will put a big hole in your budget, most agree they are among the most memorable experiences of their trip. Try **Sunshine Helicopters**, tel. (808) 871-0722 or (800) 544-2520; **Hawaii Helicopters**, tel. (808) 877-3900 or (800) 994-9099; **Air Maui**, tel. (808) 877-7005; and **Blue Hawaiian Helicopters**, tel. (808) 871-8844 or (800) 786-2583.

Molokai Air Shuttle, tel. (808) 567-6847 on Molokai, (808) 545-4988 on Oahu, does scenic flights around Molokai and down to Kalaupapa. If you are lucky, your regularly scheduled flight from Kahului to Hoolehua will also fly along the north coast and give you a glimpse, although not real close, of this spectacular line of *pali* and valley.

INFORMATION AND SERVICES

Telephone numbers for service agencies that you might find useful: emergency, 911; police, tel. (808) 553-5355; County Parks and Recreation, tel. (808) 553-3204; Division of Forestry, tel. (808) 553-5019; Hawaiian Homelands, tel. (808) 567-6104 or 567-6296; Molokai Public Library (1937), tel. (808) 553-5483; Office of Hawaiian Affairs (OHA), tel. (808) 553-3611; Kaunakakai post office, tel. (808) 553-5845; Bank of Hawaii, tel. (808) 553-3273; American Savings Bank, tel. (808) 553-3263.

Molokai Visitors Association

The MVA, tel. (808) 553-3876, (800) 553-0404 statewide, or (800) 800-6367 Mainland, Web site: www.molokai.com/mva, e-mail: mva@molokai.com, is an excellent organization that can help with every aspect of your trip to Molokai. Lawrence Aki and his friendly staff dispense up-to-the-minute information on hotels, car rentals, activities, and services. Molokai Visitors Association should be your first contact if you are contemplating a visit to Molokai. Open Mon.-Fri. regular business hours.

For general information about the island, try the Web sites www.molokaialoha.com and molokaihawaii.com.

Newspapers

For a local look at what's happening on the island of Molokai, check out either of the island's two newspapers. The larger and more mainstream is **The Dispatch**, published in Maunaloa, while the more humble **Molokai Advertiser-News** is published in Kaunakakai by solar power.

Medical

Molokai is a small place with a small population so there is not as much available here in the way of medical treatment as on Maui or the other larger islands. Yet Molokai has **Molokai General Hospital**, tel. (808) 553-5331, which is located at the end of Home Olu St. just above Ala Malama Ave. in Kaunakakai. There are half a dozen doctors on the island and half as many dentists. For alternative care, try the **Healing Touch Center**, tel. (808) 553-3595, for massage, acupuncture, and chiropractic. Try **Molikai Pharmacy**, tel. (808) 553-5790, in the new Kamo'i Professional Center, one block off the main drag, for prescription drugs, first aid items, potions, lotions, and sundries. It's open Mon.-Sat. 8:45 a.m.-5:45 p.m.

Laundry

Molokai Dry Cleaning, located next to the Pizza Cafe, is open Mon.-Fri. 9 a.m.-5 p.m., Saturday 9 a.m.-1 p.m., closed Sunday. There is also a laundromat behind Outpost Natural Foods.

KAUNAKAKAI

No matter where you're headed on the island you have to pass through Kaunakakai ("Beach Landing"), the tiny port town and economic and government center that is Molokai's hub. An hour spent walking the three blocks of Ala Malama Street, the main drag, gives you a good feeling for what's happening. As you walk along you might hear a mechanical whir and bump in the background—Molokai's generating plant almost in the middle of town! If you need to do any banking, mailing, or shopping for staples, Kaunakakai's the place. Hikers, campers, and even day-trippers should get all they need here since shops, both east and west, are few and far between, and mostly understocked. Evenings are quiet here, with no bars or nightspots, neon or glamour.

SIGHTS

Head toward the lagoon and you'll see Kaunakakai's wharf stretching out into the shallow harbor for over a half mile. Townsfolk like to drive their cars onto it, but it's much better to walk out. The fishing from the wharf isn't great but it's handy and you never can tell. If you decide to stroll out here, look for the remains of Lot Kamehameha's summer house (circa 1864), a raised platform surrounded by stone, near the canoe shed along the shore west of the road.

Kapuaiwa Coconut Grove
A three-minute drive or a 10-minute walk west brings you to this 11-acre royal coconut grove planted in the 1860s for Kamehameha V (Lot Kamehameha), or Kapuaiwa to his friends. Kapuaiwa Coconut Grove was originally built because there were seven pools here in which the *ali'i* would bathe, and the grove was planted to provide shade and seclusion. The grove also symbolically provided the king with food for the duration of his life. The grove has diminished from the 1,000 trees originally planted, but more than enough remain to give a sense of grandeur to the spot. Royal coconut palms are some of the tallest of the species, and besides providing nuts, they served as natural beacons pinpointing

the spot inhabited by royalty. These here are over 80 feet tall. Now the grove has a parklike atmosphere and mostly you'll have it to yourself. Pay heed to the signs warning of falling coconuts. An aerial bombardment of hefty five pounders will rudely customize the hood of your rental car. Definitely do not walk around under the palms if the wind is up. Just next to the grove is **Kioea Park,** where camping is permitted for $5 a day through the Hawaiian Homelands Department (see above).

Church Row
Sin has no chance against this formidable defensive line of churches standing altar-to-altar along the road across from Kapuaiwa Coconut Grove. A grant from Hawaiian Homelands provides that a church can be built on this stretch of land to any congregation that includes a minimum number of Hawaiian-blooded parishioners. The churches are basically one-room affairs that wait quietly until Sunday morning when worshippers come from all over the island. Let there be no doubt: old Satan would find no customers around here as all spiritual loopholes are covered by one denomination or another. Visitors are always welcome, so come join in. Be wary of this stretch of road—all services seem to let out at the same time on Sunday morning, causing a minuscule traffic jam.

Classic Fishponds
Molokai is known for its fishponds, which were a unique and highly advanced form of aquaculture prevalent from at least the early 13th century. Molokai, because of an abundance of shallow, flat waters along its southeastern shore, was able to support a network of these ponds numbering over five dozen during their heyday. Built and tended by the commoners for the royal *ali'i,* they provided succulent fish that could easily be rounded up at any time for a meal or impromptu feast. The ponds were formed in a likely spot by erecting a wall of stone or coral. It was necessary to choose an area that had just the right tides to keep the water circulating, but not so strong as to destroy the encircling walls. Openings were left in

small Molokai church

J.D. BISIGNANI

the wall for this purpose. **Kalokoeli Pond** is about two miles east of Kaunakakai along Route 450. Easily seen from the road, it's an excellent example of the classic fishpond. You can proceed a few more minutes east until you come to a coconut grove just a half mile before One Ali'i Beach Park. Stop here for a sweeping view of **Ali'i Fishpond,** another fine example.

ACCOMMODATIONS

Besides camping, Kaunakakai has only a handful of other places to stay. The other lodging options on the island are way out on the west end at the exclusive Kaluakoi Resort or the two condos that surround it, and at the Wavecrest Condo east of Kaunakakai along the south coast. A few bed and breakfasts are also available, many along the road to the east. Head for Kaunakakai and its limited but adequate accommodations if you want to save money.

Pau Hana Inn

For years the Pau Hana ("Work's Done") Inn had the reputation for being *the* budget place to stay on Molokai. Now all that's left is the reputation, although it's still not too expensive. It still has a strong "local" feel, just right for laid-back Molokai. The owner is Molokai Beach, Ltd., and many changes have been made in the last few years; rooms are refurbished, and the whole place is spiffed up. Special touches still remain,

though, like leaving the windows of the dining room open so that birds can fly in to peck crumbs off the floor. A fireplace is lit in the morning to take the chill off the place; hanging over it is a noble stag with wide, perfect antlers and tearful eyes. Breakfast and lunch are served daily, with dinner only on Friday and Saturday evenings. Outside, in the courtyard bar, a magnificent Bengalese banyan provides the perfect setting in which to sit back and relax. The waitresses are friendly and go out of their way to make you feel welcome and comfortable. The Pau Hana Bar is a favorite with local people. Friday and Saturday nights feature live music and dancing under the banyan tree. Room rates are: Long House, a barracks-type building, clean with carpeted floors $47.50, cottages $55, studio with kitchenette $97.50, poolside unit $78.50, oceanfront $97.50, suite $125; extra person $10. For reservations contact Pau Hana Inn, P.O. Box 860, Kaunakakai, HI 96748, tel. (808) 553-5342.

Molokai Shores Suites

This is a relatively new condo a few minutes east of the Pau Hana with full kitchens, large living rooms, and separate bedrooms. The white walls contrasting with the dark brown floors are hung with tasteful prints. Plenty of lounge furniture is provided along with a table for outside dining and barbecues. The upper floor of the three-story building offers an open-beam ceiling including a full loft. Some units have an extra bedroom built into the loft. The grounds are very

KAUNAKAKAI

well kept, quiet, and restful. The swimming pool fronts the gentle but unswimmable beach, and nearby is a classic fishpond. The only drawback is the architecture: it's pragmatic and neat, but not beautiful. Rates are $144 one-bedroom oceanfront, $189 two-bedroom oceanfront; $15 for each additional person. For information, call (808) 553-5954 direct or call central reservations, tel. (800) 535-0085, fax (800) 633-5085. A Marc Resorts Hawaii property.

Hotel Molokai

This hotel was built in 1966 by an architect (Mr. Roberts) enamored with the South Seas, who wanted to give his hotel a Polynesian village atmosphere. He succeeded. The buildings are two-story, semi-A-frames with sway-backed roofs covered with split wood shingles. Outside staircases lead to the large, airy studios that feature a lanai with swing. This hotel had its heyday before the big resort and the big money came to the island. After a change of ownership, Hotel Molokai was closed for extensive renovation and anticipates to be entertaining guests again by the beginning of 1999. The hotel was known for good dining, weekend entertainment, a well-appointed gift shop, a swimming pool, and a poolside lounge. With luck, all will again be open and better than ever. In the meantime, the lounge is open daily noon-10 p.m. For current information and status on dining and room availability, contact Hotel Molokai, tel. (808) 553-5347.

FOOD

Like the hotel scene, Molokai has only a handful of places to eat, but among these are veritable institutions that if missed make your trip to Molokai incomplete. The following are all located on Kaunakakai's main street, or just a minute away. Just ask anyone where they are.

The 50-year-old **Mid-Nite Inn** in "downtown" Kaunakakai was started as a saimin stand by Mrs. Kikukawa, the present owner's mother. People would come here to slurp noodles while waiting for the midnight interisland steamer to take them to Honolulu. The Mid-Nite was well known for its large, tasty, island-inspired meals, and very friendly service. The steamers are gone but the restaurant remains, sort of. The Mid-Nite Inn was gutted by fire some years ago, and while townsfolk hope that someone will reopen a restaurant on the same spot, nothing has yet taken place.

The **Kanemitsu Bakery,** tel. (808) 553-5855, has been in business for more than 70 years and is still run by the same family. The bakery is renowned for its Molokai breads, boasting cheese and onion among the best of its 19 varieties. Mrs. Kanemitsu's cookies are scrumptious, and anyone contemplating a picnic or a day hike should load up. The bakery is open 5:30 a.m.-6:00 p.m., closed Tuesday. There's a lunch counter in the back where you can get eggs, pancakes, and omelettes for breakfast, and local Hawaiian foods for lunch, open 5:30 a.m.-1 p.m.

Oviedo's Filipino Restaurant is the last building on the left along Ala Malama, where every item on the menu is about $5. Choose from ethnic selections like pork *adobo,* chicken papaya, tripe stew, sweet and sour ribs, pig's feet, mongo beans, and a good selection of ice cream for dessert. Oviedo's is small, run-down, but clean. The decor is worn linoleum floors and Formica tables, and the cooling is provided by breezes that readily pass through large cracks in the walls.

Kamo'i Snack-N-Go is in the new Kamo'i Professional Center. Stop here for Dave's ice cream, candies, cold drinks, and other snacks. Open daily until 0 p.m.

The **Molokai Drive In,** open daily 0 a.m. 10 p.m., is along Kamehameha Highway in a bluish-gray, flat-roofed building that has the look of the '60s. You order from the window and then take your meal to eat under an awning, or step into the air-conditioned inside to find a few tables. Breakfast offers omelettes, eggs, spam, bacon, or ham along with sides of rice, hash browns, or toast for under $5. Lunch is chili dogs, nachos, subs, fish, shrimp, and chicken burgers, with a special featured every day. The drive-in is actually tasteful, bright, and clean. It's a local place with decent food and very affordable prices. It would make a great stop for a picnic lunch to go, especially if you're heading to Halawa and points east.

Don't let the name **Molokai Pizza Cafe,** tel. (808) 553-3288, fool you! Although this bright and cheery restaurant makes designer pizza, the emphasis is on *cafe.* Owned by Julie and Sean Connolly, and located wharfside of the junction of Routes 450 and 460, this eatery is open daily 11 a.m.-10 p.m. (until 11 p.m. on Friday and Satur-

day). Molokai's answer to upscale dining, the cafe is fast food with a flare. Pizzas come in three sizes and range in price from a Molokai small for $7.80 up to their giant Big Island with everything including green peppers, onions, sausage, beef, and bacon for $21.95. Sandwiches can be an Italian sub laden with turkey, ham, and roast beef, or a plump fresh-baked pocket sandwich. Hearty appetites will enjoy meals like pasta in marinara sauce, barbecued spareribs (great!), or the fresh catch. Order it! Caught in these waters, the fish comes in the back door, is filleted, cooked, and served to you as fresh as it can be. For dessert, you can be repentant and go for a low-fat frozen yogurt, or be brazen and order the strawberry shortcake, or let the devil take the hindmost and order the Chocolate Suicide. The Molokai Pizza Cafe delivers, perfect for anyone staying in a condo. Takeout available.

Outpost Natural Foods, tel. (808) 553-3377, serves wholesome, healthy, nutritious quick foods from its inside window, Sun.-Fri. 10 a.m.-3 p.m. Here you can find various sandwiches for less than $5, burritos for up to $4.25, salads, veggie and tempeh burger around $5, and the daily lunch specials for under $6. In addition, there is an assortment of fresh juices and smoothies. While there, pick up any groceries that you'll need for your time on the island.

The restaurant at the **Pau Hana Inn** serves breakfast and lunch daily and dinner on Friday and Saturday evenings; American and Hawaiian fare. The Pau Hana Bar has a daily happy hour with *pu pu* 4-6 p.m. Here you can relax under the famous banyan tree for an early evening cocktail. On Friday and Saturday evenings there is live music and dancing, but there may be an annoying cover charge, even for hotel guests who only want a quiet drink.

SHOPPING

Molokai Fish and Dive in downtown Kaunakakai, tel. (808) 553-5926, sounds very practical, and it is, but it has a good selection of souvenirs, T-shirts and fashions, books (including a couple written by shop owner James Brocker), maps of Molokai, island music, jewelry, and a good assortment of film along with its fishing equipment. They can give you detailed information about fishing and water sports on Molokai, and they rent some water gear like snorkel sets, boogie boards, or a rod and reel for $9 a day.

Molokai Island Creations, connected to Molokai Fish and Dive and also open daily 9:30 a.m.-4:30 p.m., features authentic Molokai designs on ladies' blouses, tank tops, and men's T-shirts. It also has original Molokai glassware, china, and porcelain, along with Hawaiian cards and notebooks. Fashions also include *pareo,* children's alohawear, shorts, hats, aloha shirts, muumuu, swimwear, a good selection of jewelry, and a rack of cosmetics and perfumes in island scents.

Imamura's, open daily except Sunday 8:45 a.m.-5:45 p.m., is a very friendly down-home shop that sells everything from flip-flops to fishnets. It also specializes in lei-making needles and has a great selection of inexpensive luggage. The shelves hold beach mats and hats, T-shirts, pots and pans, and kitchen utensils. The sales staff are all friendly and slow-paced; when you return, they'll smile a welcome.

Lourdes Shoes Clothing and Jewelry is a basic local shop offering a smattering of alohawear, handbags, jogging shoes, baby clothes, towels, and women's clothing. **Mango Video,** tel. (808) 553-3600, is a place to find entertainment for the evening. It rents camcorders and even sells a smattering of snorkel gear. There is no theater in Kaunakakai, but since 1998 there has been one in Maunaloa. People who want to watch a big screen show must now travel to the west end for it—and they do.

Molokai Surf, open daily except Sunday 9 a.m.-6 p.m., has bathing suits, sandals, T-shirts, shorts, and alohawear.

Dudoit Imports, which used to be on the main drag but has moved to the little row of shops by Molokai Pizza Cafe, features wicker baskets, rattan furniture, handcrafted items made on Molokai, arts and collectibles, and, what else, lots of imports.

For those into wholesome health food, **Outpost Natural Foods,** tel. (808) 553-3377, is at 70 Makaena Place across from the government buildings and near Kalama's Gas Station. It's the only store of its kind on Molokai, but it's excellent. It's open Sun.-Thurs. 9 a.m.-6 p.m., Friday 9 a.m.-3 p.m., closed Saturday. The fruits and vegetables are locally and organically grown as much

as possible. Along with the usual assortment of health foods you'll find bulk grains, granola, nuts, and dried fruits. The jam-packed shelves also hold rennetless cheese, fresh yogurt, nondairy ice cream, vitamins, minerals, supplements, and a good selection of herbs, oils, and spices. If you can't find what you need, ask Dennis, the owner, or the general manager on duty. The juice bar, open Sun.-Fri. 10 a.m.-3 p.m., is a great place for a healthy lunch and cold drink. Shaded picnic tables are provided out back.

For general shopping along Ala Malama Street, the **Friendly Market,** open Mon.-Fri. 8:30 a.m.-8:30 p.m., Saturday to 6:30 p.m., is by far the best-stocked grocery store on Molokai. There's a community bulletin board outside. It might list cars for sale, Hawaiian genealogies, or fund-raising sushi sales. Have a look!

Just down the street **Takes Variety Store** and **Misaki's Groceries and Dry Goods** a few steps farther along sell just about everything in food and general merchandise that you'll require. Across from the Mid-Nite Inn is the mini-mart **C. Paascua Store** for snack items and drinks.

The **Kaunakakai Market,** along the main drag, open 7 a.m.-10:30 p.m., is fairly well-stocked, with a selection of canned goods and some fresh veggies.

For that special evening, try **Molokai Wines and Spirits,** open Sun.-Thurs. 9 a.m.-10 p.m., until 10:30 p.m. Friday and Saturday, which has a small but good selection of vintage wines as well as beer and gourmet treats.

Molokai Drugstore, tel. (808) 553-5313, open daily 8:45 a.m.-5:45 p.m., closed Sunday, is the only full-service pharmacy and drugstore on the island. Don't let the name fool you because it sells much more than potions and drugs. You can buy anything from sunglasses to film, watches, toys, baby food, small appliances, and garden supplies. It has the best selection of film on Molokai, with a very good selection of books, especially on Hawaiiana. Film processing, including slides, takes 48 hours. It too has moved from its spot on the main street to the town's newest mall, the small Kamo'i Professional Center, one street back. Also in this center is **Kamo'i Snack-N-Go** for ice cream, candies, snacks, and cold drinks; open daily until 9 p.m.

EAST TO HALAWA VALLEY

The east end of Molokai, from Kaunakakai to Halawa Valley, was at one time the most densely populated area of the island. At almost every milepost is a historical site or point of interest, many dating from precontact times. A string of tiny churches attests to the coming of the missionaries in the mid-1800s, and a crash-landing site was an inauspicious harbinger of the deluge of Mainlanders bound for Hawaii in this century. This entire stretch of Route 450 is almost entirely undeveloped, and the classical sites such as *heiau*, listening stones, and old battlegrounds are difficult to find, although just a stone's throw from the road. The local people like it this way, as most would rather see the south shore of Molokai remain unchanged. A determined traveler might locate the sites, but unless you have local help, it will mean hours tramping around in marshes or on hillsides with no guarantee of satisfaction. Some sites such as **Ili'ili'opae Heiau** are on private land and require permission to visit. It's as if the spirits of the ancient *kahuna* protect this area.

CITIES

It's a toss-up whether the best part about heading out to the east end is the road itself or the reward of Halawa Valley at the end. Only 30 miles long, it takes 90 minutes to drive. The road slips and slides around corners, bends around huge boulders, and dips down here and there into coves and inlets. The cliff face and protruding stones have been painted white so that you can avoid an accident, especially at night. Sometimes the ocean and road are so close that spray splatters your windshield. Suddenly you'll round a bend to see an idyllic house surrounded by palm trees with a gaily painted boat gently rocking in a protected miniature cove. Behind is a valley of verdant hills with colors so vibrant they shimmer. You negotiate a hairpin curve and there are Lanai and Maui, black on the horizon, contrasted against the waves as they come crashing in foamy white and blue. Down the road chugs a pickup truck full of local people. They wave you a "hang loose" as their sincere smiles light up your already glorious day. Out in one of the innumerable bays are snorkelers, while beyond the reef, surfers glide in exhilarating solitude.

The local people think of the road as "their road." Why not? They use it as a sidewalk, playground, and extension of their back yards. Dogs snooze on it, while the rumps of grazing stock are only inches away from your fender. The speed limit is 35, but go slower and enjoy it more. The

a scenic coconut grove and fishpond typical of east Molokai

J.D. B.SIGNANI

EAST MOLOKAI

Kahiu Point
Kalaupapa Peninsula
Kalaupapa
Kalawao
Haupa Bay
Pelekunu Bay
Wailau
Kahiwa Falls (1,750 ft.)
Halawa
HEIAU MANA
HALAWA BEACH PARK
Cape Halawa
SACRED KUKUI GROVE
PUU O HOKU RANCH
Waikolu Valley
Pelekunu Valley
Hipuapua Falls (500 ft.)
Moaula Falls (250 ft.)
Halawa Valley
Wailau Valley
Kahana Rock
Mokuhooniki Island
Kamehameha Hwy.
To Kaunakakai
Kamakou (4,970 ft.)
Wailau Trail
Waialua
MURPHY'S BEACH PARK
ILI'ILI'OPAE
OCTOPUS STONE
BELLSTONE
PAIKALANI TARO PATCH
Pukoo
ONE ALI'I BEACH PARK
Kawela
PAKUHIWA BATTLEGROUND (1736)
SMITH-BRONTE LANDING (1927)
ST. JOSEPH CHURCH (1876)
KAKAHAIA NATIONAL WILDLIFE REFUGE AND COUNTY BEACH PARK
Kamalo
UALAPUE WAVECREST RESORT
Paialoa Fishpond
Kalae Loa Harbor
Pailolo Channel
0   2 mi
0   2 km

© J.D. BISIGNANI AND MOON PUBLICATIONS, INC.

mile markers stop at mile 17, then four miles farther you come to the best part. Here, the well-tended two-lane highway with the yellow stripe plays out. The road gets old and bumpy, but the scenery gets much more spectacular. It's about nine miles from where the bumpy part begins until you reach the overlook at Halawa Valley. Come with a full tank of gas, plenty of drinking water, a picnic lunch, and your sense of wonder.

One Ali'i Beach Park

A few minutes east of Kaunakakai the road brings you to a stand of perhaps 80 coconut palms. Here is a little-used, unnamed beach park with an excellent view of one of the string of fishponds that are famous in this area. One Ali'i Beach Park, only a few minutes farther along, is open for camping. It's too close to the road, not well shaded, and a bit too overused to be comfortable. The swimming here is only fair for those who like a challenging surf, but excellent for families with little children who want calm waters. Clean restrooms and showers are available and the grounds are generally in good shape. Those not camping here would find it pleasant enough for a day excursion, but it's nothing compared with what's farther east along the road.

About two minutes past One Ali'i, Makanui Road leads up the hillside on the *mauka* side of the road. A two-minute ride up this road exposes the beginnings of a condo development. As you gain height (one of the only roads that allows you to do so) you'll have an excellent view of the coastline with a panorama of the fishponds below and Lanai and Maui out to sea. Beyond this road is another just like it, leading into a future subdivision with much the same overview.

Kawela

The Kawela area was a scene of tragedy and triumph in Molokai's history. Here was Pakuhiwa, the battleground where Kamehameha I totally vanquished the warriors of Molokai on his way to conquering Oahu. In nearby Kawela Gulch was Pu'u Kaua, the fortress that Kamehameha overran. The fortress oddly doubled as a *pu'uhonua*, a temple of refuge, where the defeated could find sanctuary. Once the battle had been joined, and the outcome inevitable, the vanquished could find peace and solace in the very area that they had so recently defended.

Today the area offers refuge as **Kakahai'a County Beach Park and National Wildlife**

Refuge. The beach park is not used heavily: it, too, is close to the road. The fishpond here is still used though, and it's not uncommon to see people in it gathering *limu*. This is also an excellent area for coconut trees, with many nuts lying on the ground for the taking. The refuge is an area where birdwatchers can still be captivated by the sight of rare endemic birds.

Kamalo to Pukoo

This six-mile stretch is loaded with historical sites. Kamalo is one of Molokai's natural harbors and was used for centuries before most of the island commerce moved to Kaunakakai. In the late 1800s, **Kamalo Wharf** (turn right down the dirt road at mile marker 10) was the island's principal landing site. Tracks once ran out on the wood and stone "mall" to help unload ships.

Saint Joseph Church, next in line, was built in 1876 by Father Damien. It's small, no more than 16 by 30 feet, and very basic. Inside is a small wooden altar adorned with flowers in a canning jar. A picture of Father Damien and one of St. Joseph adorn the walls. Outside is a black metal sculpture of Damien.

ROBERT NILSEN

St. Joseph Church

One mile or so past St. Joseph's is the **Smith and Bronte Landing Site.** These two aviators safely crash-landed their plane here on July 14, 1927, completing the first trans-Pacific civilian flight in just over 25 hours. All you can see is a mangrove swamp, but it's not hard to imagine the relief of the men as they set foot even on soggy land after crossing the Pacific. They started a trend that would bring over six million people a year to the islands. The Wavecrest Resort Condominium is nearby at mile marker 13.

Before Pukoo are two noteworthy sites. **Kalua'aha Church** looks like a fortress with its tiny slit windows and three-foot-thick plastered walls and buttresses. It was the first Christian church on Molokai, built in 1844 by the Protestant missionaries Rev. and Mrs. Hitchcock, and is considered by some to be the most significant building on the island. Used for worship until the 1940s, it has since fallen into disuse. In 1967, the bell and steeple came down, the roof is caving in, and the rest is mostly in ruins. While parishioners had repair plans, it is doubtful that the structure can be saved without major rehabilitation.

Then comes **Ili'ili'opae Heiau,** one of Hawaii's most famous human-sacrifice temples, and a university of sorcery, as it were, where *kahuna* from other islands were tutored. (For a unique tour of this area, along with nearby Manulehu Mango Grove, see the description of the **Molokai Horse and Wagon Ride,** under "Guided Tours" in the "Introduction," above.) All of the wooden structures on the 267-foot stone platform have long since disappeared. Legend holds that all of the stone was carried across the island from Wailau Valley and perfectly fitted in one night of amazing work. Legend also holds that the sorcerers of Ili'ili'opae once sacrificed nine sons of a local *kahuna.* Outraged, he appealed to a powerful shark-god for justice. The god sent a flash flood to wipe out the evil sorcerers, washing them into the sea where the shark-god waited to devour them. The trailhead for Wailau Valley begins at Ili'ili'opae, but since the temple is now on private land it is necessary to receive permission to visit it.

Our Lady of Sorrows Church, another built by Father Damien in 1874 and rebuilt by the parishioners in 1966, is next. Inside are beautiful pen-and-ink drawings of the Stations of the Cross imported from Holland. Just past Our Lady of Sorrows are the **bell stones,** but they're almost impossible to locate.

Before Pukoo, near mile marker 16, is the **Manee Canoe Club** with its well-tended lawns and tiny inlets. There has recently been a controversy about public access to the beach on the bay across from the canoe club, which has been the norm for generations. The situation culminated in public protests and walks to the beach. There is, however, public access to the old wharf area directly west of the canoe club, but it's not good for swimming.

Just past Pukoo is the **octopus stone,** a large stone painted white next to the road. It is believed that this is the remainder of a cave inhabited by a mythical octopus, and that the stone still has magical powers.

More East End Beaches

Waialua Beach, almost at mile marker 19, is one of the best beaches on the island for swimming, snorkeling, and beginner surfing. A freshwater stream entering the ocean is very convenient for rinsing off.

Two minutes past mile marker 19 is a sand and coral beach where you can walk knee-deep out to the reef. At high tide, it's chest high.

Mile Marker 20 Beach, with its huge strand of white sand and protected lagoon, is the main beach on the east end. Pull off at a handy spot and enjoy the great snorkeling, although the swimming is only mediocre. It's very safe and perfect for a family outing.

Note: All of these beaches have sharp coral. Wear a pair of reef walkers or good old sneakers. You do not want to go out there barefoot!

On to Halawa Valley

Past Pukoo, the road gets very spectacular. Many blow-your-horn turns pop up as you wend around the cliff face following the natural roll of the coastline. Coming in rapid succession are incredibly beautiful bays and tiny one-blanket beaches, where solitude and sunbathing are perfect. Be careful of surf conditions! Some of the fruitful valleys behind them are still cultivated in taro, and traditional community life beckons young people from throughout the islands to come and learn the old ways. Offshore is the crescent of **Moku Ho'oniki Island,** and Kanaha Rock in front. The road swerves inland, climbing the hills to the 14,000 acres of **Puu O Hoku ("Hill of Stars") Ranch.** People often mistake

one of the ranch buildings along the road for a store. It's the ranch office, but the people inside can direct you to an overlook where you can see the famous and sacred *kukui* grove where Lanikaula, one of the most powerful sorcerers of Molokai, is buried. The different-looking cattle grazing these hilly pastures are French Charolais, imported by Puu O Hoku Ranch and now flourishing on these choice pasturelands. The road comes to a hairpin turn where it feels like you'll be airborne. Before you is the magnificent chasm of Halawa Valley with its famous waterfalls sparkling against the green of the valley's jungle walls. Hundreds of feet below, frothy aquamarine breakers roll into the bay.

Halawa Valley and Bay

This choice valley, rich in soil and watered by Halawa Stream, is believed to be the first permanent settlement on Molokai, dating from the early seventh century. Your first glimpse is from the road's overlook from which you get a spectacular panorama across the half-mile valley to Lamaloa Head forming its north wall, and eastward, deep into its four-mile cleft, where lies Moaula Falls. Many people are so overwhelmed when they gaze from the overlook into Halawa that they don't really look around. Turn to your right and walk only 15 yards directly away from Halawa. This view gives a totally different perspective of a deep-V valley and the pounding surf of its rugged beach—so different from the gently arcing haven of Halawa Bay. For centuries, Halawa's farmers carved geometric terraces for taro fields until a tidal wave of gigantic proportions inundated the valley in 1946 and left a plant-killing deposit of salt. Most people pulled out and left their homes and gardens to be reclaimed by the jungle.

Follow the paved road into the valley until you see a house that was obviously a church at one time. Cross Halawa Stream and follow the road as far as you can. Here you have a choice of bathing in the cool freshwater stream or in the surf of the protected bay. Don't go out past the mouth of the bay because the currents can be treacherous. This area is great for snorkeling and fishing, and is one of the only good surfing beaches on Molokai.

Halawa Bay is a beach park, but it's not well maintained. There are toilet facilities and a few dilapidated picnic tables, but no official overnight camping, and the water is not potable. You can bivouac for a night on Puu O Hoku Ranch land at the far north end of Halawa Bay under a canopy of ironwood trees, but be aware that this area attracts rip-offs and it's not safe to leave your gear unattended.

Moaula Falls

One of the best walks on Molokai, mosquitoes notwithstanding, is to the famous 250-foot Moaula ("Red Chicken") Falls. Halawa Stream can be a trickle or torrent, depending upon recent rains. If Moaula Falls is gushing, the stream too will be roaring. The entire area up toward the falls harbors the remains of countless taro patches and home sites. Groves of kemani trees mark the sites where ali'i were buried; their tall trunks at one time were used by Hawaiian fishermen and later by sailors as a landmark. Legend recalls that a female lizard, a moo, lives in the gorgeous pool at the bottom of the falls. Sometimes she craves a body and will drag a swimmer down to her watery lair. The only way to determine her mood is to place a ti leaf (abundant in the area) in the pool. If it floats you're safe, but if it sinks the lady lizard wants company—permanently! Minor gods who live in the rocks above Moaula Falls pool want to get into the act too. They'll drop tiny rocks on your head unless you make an offering (a penny under a ti leaf will do). Above Moaula Falls you can see **Upper Moaula Falls,** and beyond that the cascading brilliance of 500-foot **Hipuapua Falls.** For some years the trail to this waterfalls was closed; it goes across private property. You can once again gain access but only through a guided tour led by a man who was born and raised in the valley. (See "Hiking" under "Sports and Recreation" in the "Introduction," above, for details.)

Accommodations

First down the line is **Ka Hale Mala,** just less than five miles east of Kaunakakai on Kamakana Place. This vacation rental is the ground floor of a family house, set amidst a tropical garden. Here you have a large living room, full kitchen and bath, and a laundry room, plus use of a bicycle or snorkel gear. Rates are $60 without breakfast or $70 with. For more information, contact Cheryl Corbiell, P.O. Box 1582, Kaunakakai, HI 96748, tel./fax (808) 553-9009, Web site: www.molokai.com/kahale-mala, e-mail: 73124.1477@compuserve.com.

Depending on your point of view the **Wavecrest Resort** is either a secluded hideaway, or stuck out in the sticks away from all the action. It's east of Kaunakakai on Route 450 just at mile marker 13. You'll find no hustle, bustle, anxiety, nightlife, restaurants, or shopping. This condominium sits on five well-tended acres fronting a lovely-to-look-at lagoon that isn't good for swimming. It catches the morning sun and looks directly across the Pailolo Channel to Kaanapali on Maui. Enjoy a putting green, shuffleboard court, newly refurbished swimming pool, and two lighted tennis courts free to guests. Be aware that there are no phones in any of the units. For those who need to call, there are two pay phones at the front office. In each unit is a fully furnished kitchen, spacious living room, ceiling fan, television, and lanai. A laundry room is located on each floor for guest use. Even if you feel that you're too far from town, remember nothing is going on there anyway. Another attraction is that local fishermen may put in just next to the Wavecrest and sell their fish for unbeatable prices. Guests can barbecue on gas grills provided. Rates: one-bedroom ocean or garden view $119; one-bedroom oceanfront $149; two-bedroom oceanfront $189; $15 extra person. Car/condo packages are also available. Attractive monthly and low-season discounts available. Call the Wavecrest direct, tel. (808) 558-8103, or central reservations, tel. (800) 535-0085 or fax ((800) 535-0085 . A Marc Resorts Hawaii property.

Kamalo Plantation, HC 01, Box 300, Kaunakakai, HI 96748, tel./fax (808) 558-8236, e-mail: kamaloplantation@aloha.net, is a five-acre tropical fruit orchard, where Glenn and Akiko Foster welcome guests. About 10 miles east of Kaunakakai, and across from Father Damien's St. Joseph Church, Kamalo Plantation is surrounded by well-vegetated grounds and even has a heiau on the property. The Fosters can accommodate you in a fully contained private studio cottage with full kitchen, indoor and outdoor showers, and deck for $75, or as a B&B guest in a guest suite with private bath and private entry in the main house for $65. This large suite is secluded at one end of the house and has a sitting area, some cooking appliances, and an outside deck. A breakfast of fruit and baked breads and a tour of the grounds are part of the price. A fine place.

A short distance down the road is **Kumu'eli Farms B&B,** P.O. Box 1829, Kaunakakai, HI 96748, tel./fax (808) 558-8284, or 558-8281, Web site: www.visitmolokai.com/kumueli, e-mail: dcurtis@aloha.net. This lovely, contemporary-style wooden house has only one rental suite, which is set to the side of the main house. It has a private entrance off the connecting deck, and there is a lap pool off the back deck. The suite has a queen bed, ceiling fan, TV, and refrigerator, and runs $75 a night, two nights minimum. A homemade breakfast is served each morning. For more information, contact Dorothea or David Curtis, longtime Molokai residents.

At the far eastern end of the island, overlooking the lands of Puu O Hoku Ranch is **Puu O Hoku Country Cottage,** a vacation rental that was once a guest cottage at the ranch manager's residence. Check in at the ranch office along the highway near mile marker 25. If you're looking for a place to really be away, this is it. This cottage is a large two-bedroom house that has been renovated but is still charming in its simplicity. It has a living room with a wall of glass, dining room, and full kitchen. Each of the two bedrooms has a private bath. No television, radio, or telephone unless requested. Feel free to use the swimming pool up at the main house. The rental rate is $85 a night or $510 a week with the seventh night free. Contact: Puu O Hoku Ranch, HC 01 Box 900, Kaunakakai, HI 96748, tel. (808) 558-8109, fax 558-8100, e-mail: hoku@aloha.net.

The only place to find food on this end of the island is the **Neighborhood Store** in Pukoo. This convenience store carries basic necessities. Connected is a lunch window that serves breakfasts and lunches. Open 8 a.m.-6 p.m. daily.

MIDDLE MOLOKAI AND KALAUPAPA

As you head west from Kaunakakai on Route 460 toward Hoolehua Airport you pass fields planted in various crops. These are Molokai's attempt at diversified agriculture since the demise of pineapple a few years ago. Iowa-like cornfields make it obvious that the experiment is working well and has a chance, if the large corporations and the state government get behind it. The cultivated fields give way to hundreds of acres filled with skeletons of dead trees. It's as if some eerie specter stalked the land and devoured their spirits. Farther along and just before a bridge, the **Main Forest Road** intersects, posted for 4WD vehicles but navigable in a standard car during dry weather. This track leads to the Sandalwood Measuring Pit, a depression in the ground that is a permanent reminder of the furious and foolhardy trading of last century. Here too along little-used trails are spectacular views of the lost valleys of Molokai's inaccessible northeast shore.

West on Route 460 another branch road, Route 470, heads due north through Kualapuu, Del Monte's diminished pineapple town, to road's end at Palaau State Park, Molokai's best camping area and home to the famous Phallic Rock. Near the state park entrance is the lookout for Kalaupapa Peninsula and the beginning of the mule trail, which switchbacks down over 1,600 feet to the humbling and uplifting experience of Kalaupapa.

MAIN FOREST ROAD

Head west on Route 460 from Kaunakakai, and just before mile marker 4 turn right over a bridge (just past the Seventh-day Adventist Church). After a few hundred yards is a red dirt road called Main Forest or Maunahui Road, which heads into the mountains. Your car rental agency will tell you that this road is impassable except in a 4WD, and they're right—if it's raining! But, even if it isn't, this road is rough. Follow the rutted road up into the hills and you'll soon be in a deep forest of ohia, pine, eucalyptus, and giant ferns thriving since their planting early this century. The cool, pleasant air mixes with rich earthy smells of the forest. In just under six miles is a main intersection where you turn right. Proceed a few hundred yards and look for a sign pointing out a Boy Scout/Nature Conservancy Camp. Ignore many small roads branching off.

After 10 miles, look for the road sign, "Kamiloloa"; park 100 yards past in a turnout and walk five

CENTRAL MOLOKAI

Waikolu ("Three Waters") Overlook. From here you can peer down into the pristine valley 3,700 feet below. If rains have been recent, hundreds of waterfalls spread their lace as they fall to the green jungle. The water here seeps into the ground, which soaks it up like a huge dripping sponge. A water tunnel, bored into the valley, collects the water and conducts it for more than five miles until it reaches the 1.4 billion gallon Kualapuu Reservoir. Drive to this area only on a clear day, because the rain will not only get you stuck in mud, but also obscure your view with heavy cloud cover.

Hiking trails through this area are poorly marked, poorly maintained, and strenuous—great qualifications for those who crave solitude and adventure. Up-to-the-minute information and maps are available from the Division of Forestry and Wildlife, Olo Ave., about one mile west of Kaunakakai, tel. (808) 553-5019. **Hanalilolilo Trail** begins not far from Waikolu Lookout and winds through high mountain forests of ohia until it comes to a breathtaking view of **Pelekunu ("Foul Smelling, No Sunshine") Valley.** Don't let the name fool you. Hawaiians lived happily and well in this remote, north shore valley for centuries. Time, aided by wind and rain, has turned the 3,300-foot sea cliffs of Pelekunu into some of the tallest in the world. Today, Pelekunu is more remote and isolated than ever. There are no permanent residents, although islanders come sporadically to camp in the summer, when the waters are calm enough to land.

The Hanalilolilo Trail is in the 2,774-acre **Kamakou Preserve,** established by the Nature Conservancy of Hawaii in 1982. It seeks to preserve this unique forest area, home to five species of endangered Hawaiian birds, two of which are endemic only to Molokai. There are 250 species of Hawaiian plants and ferns, 219 of which grow nowhere else in the world. Even a few clusters of sandalwoods tenaciously try to make a comeback. The land was donated by the Molokai Ranch, which kept control of the water rights. Two officials of the ranch are on the conservancy board, which causes some people to look suspiciously at their motives. Most trails have been mapped, and hunting is encouraged throughout most of the area. If interested in obtaining a map, ask the preserve manager.

minutes to the **Sandalwood Measuring Pit** ("Lua Na Moku Iliahi"). It's not very spectacular, and this is a long way to go to see a shallow hole in the ground, but the Sandalwood Pit is a permanent reminder of the days of mindless exploitation in Hawaii when money and possessions were more important than the land or the people. Hawaiian chiefs had the pit dug to measure the amount of sandalwood necessary to fill the hold of a ship. They traded the aromatic wood to Yankee captains for baubles, whiskey, guns, manufactured goods, and tools. The traders carried the wood to China where they made huge profits. The trading was so lucrative that the men of entire villages were forced into the hills to collect it, even to the point where the taro fields were neglected and famine gnawed at the door. It only took a few years to denude the mountains of their copious stands of sandalwood, even more incredible when you consider that all the work was done by hand and all the wood was carried to the waiting ships on the coast using the *maka'ainana* as beasts of burden.

Travel past the Sandalwood Pit (beware the mud) for about one mile and you'll come to

KUALAPUU AND KALAE

Kualapuu was a vibrant town when pineapple was king and Del Monte was headquartered here. Now, coffee is king and some of the town's former vibrancy has resurfaced. It is the only town where you can find basic services on the way to Kalaupapa.

Right at the turnoff onto Farrington Ave. is the restored Plantation Store and lunch counter. Displayed in the store are many attractive island gifts, and the lunch counter has pastries, sandwiches, and various coffee and juice drinks. This is now coffee country, so pick up a bag of Mululani Estate or Muleskinner coffee at the store or try a cup at the lunch counter. Both are open daily 10 a.m.-3 p.m.

Weekday tours are given at the 500-acre **Coffees of Hawaii** coffee plantation. Pulled by Sherman and Goliath, the mule wagon takes you through the fields for an up-close look at the coffee plants, then heads to the mill and roasting room to see what happens to the beans once they are picked. The hour-long tours run at 10 a.m. and again at 1 p.m. Mon.-Fri., 10 a.m. only on Saturday, and cost $14 adult or $7 child; advance reservations required. For more information, call (808) 567-9270 or (800) 709-BEAN.

A minute down Farrington Avenue you'll come to the **Kualapuu Market,** open daily 8:30 a.m.-6 p.m. except Sunday. Here you'll find a selection of foodstuffs, fresh produce and beef, and general merchandise as well as the only gas pump in the area. The pumps are across the road.

Open 7:30-11:30 a.m. and 12:30-4:30 p.m., the Kualapuu post office is located to the side of the market.

Across the street is the **Kualapuu Cookhouse,** tel. (808) 567-6185, open daily except Sunday 7 a.m.-9 p.m., serving country-cooked foods of a local variety. Hearty breakfasts run $5-8, while the lunch menu has burgers, sandwiches, soups, and plate lunches for $7-9. The dinner menu is a notch or two fancier with items $8-18. It boasts about its homemade pies and cakes. The Kualapuu Cookhouse, headquarters of "The Slow Food Chain," is very friendly, meticulously clean, reasonably priced, and, well . . . slow! Takeouts available.

Notice also the world's largest rubber-lined reservoir across the highway from town. Holding 1.4 billion gallons, its water comes via a five-mile-long, eight-foot-round tunnel from the water-filled valleys to the east.

Purdy's Macadamia Nut Farm

A few miles west of Kualapuu, on Lihi Pali Ave, is **Purdy's Na Hua 'O Ka Aina Farm.** A former airline employee, Mr. Purdy grew up just down the road. When the airline pulled out of Molokai, he decided to stay home, become a farmer, and teach people about the exquisite macadamia nut. His farm has 50 trees that are about 70 years old. These trees still produce nuts prodigiously and continuously for 10 months of the year—Sept.-June—with nuts at all different stages of maturity on the tree at one time. When mature, nuts fall to the ground. Harvested from the ground, they are taken to be cracked and either kept raw or roasted and lightly salted. This one-acre grove of trees is farmed naturally, but Mr. Purdy has put in about 250 trees at another location on the island that are fertilized and treated with pesticides. Purdy's is the only mac nut farm on Molokai, and his yield is about 250-300 pounds of unshelled nuts per tree, as opposed to the 150-200 pounds on the thousand-acre farms of the Big Island. Visit the shop at the farm where Mr. Purdy tells everyone about the trees. Have a go at cracking one of the nuts, and have a taste of its rich fruit. Bags of nuts are sold here—a little treat to yourself for the road—and can be mailed anywhere in the country for you.

Molokai Museum and Cultural Center

Along Route 470, two miles past Kualapuu in the village of Kalae, you'll discover the old R.W. Meyer Sugar Mill, now part of the Molokai Museum and Cultural Center, tel. (808) 567-6436. Open Mon.-Sat. 10 a.m.-2 p.m., the mill tour is $2.50 adults, $1 students 5-18; entrance to the cultural center building with its few displays, gift and book shop, and historical video is free. Proceeds go into a fund to construct a new museum building. Built in 1878, the restored mill (1988) is on the National Register of Historic Places. It is in functioning order and clearly shows the stages of creating sugar from cane. As the smallest commercial mill in the state, it was used only until 1889, and it ground cane from 30 nearby upland acres. The museum and cultural center focus on preserving and demonstrating Hawaiian arts and handicrafts like quilting, *lau hala* weaving, woodcarving, plus demonstrations of lei-making and hula. The idea is to share and revive the arts of Hawaii, especially those of Molokai, in this interpretive center. As an outgrowth, the center is used as the Elderhostel campus for Molokai. In August, the annual Molokai music and dance festival takes place at the center. Hula is performed, local musicians play, and the whole community turns out.

Just beyond the center is the Meyer cemetery. You can enter, but be respectful. It is here that Rudolph Meyer, his wife, and children are buried. Up in amongst the trees above the mill is the Meyer home—not open to the public. Partially restored in 1979, it's now in disrepair. Perhaps one day it to will be restored again and preserved as another tangible link to the family that helped shape the history and economy of the island. The three acres that the cultural center sits on were graciously donated by the Meyer family. Aside from sugarcane, coffee, vegetables, fruits, and dairy cattle were raised on Meyer land, and the present Meyer Ranch still occupies a large tract of the surrounding upland area.

Kalae Cocks

A minute or two past the sugar mill is a surrealistic scene amidst the bucolic highland fields of knee-deep grass. Keep your eyes peeled for a tall cyclone fence topped with nasty looking barbed wire. Inside are row after row of tiny green A-frames, like the pup tents of a brigade of GIs on bivouac. Restrained by leashes just long enough to prevent mortal combat are hundreds of plumed, crowing roosters. Molokai's Filipino population has long been known for cockfighting, an illegal activity, but no law prevents the raising of the fighting birds. These glorious cocks, displaying their feathers while clawing the earth, challenge each other with quite a show of devil-may-care bravado. The spectacle is easily seen from the road.

Palaau State Park

A few minutes past Kalae are the stables for Molokai Mule Rides, which take you down to Kalaupapa. Even if you're not planning a mule ride, make sure to stop and check out the beauty of the countryside surrounding the mule stables. Follow the road until it ends at the parking lot for Palaau State Park.

In the lot, two signs direct you to the Phallic Rock and to the Kalaupapa Overlook (which is not the beginning of the trail down to the peninsula). Palaau State Park offers the best camping on Molokai although it's quite a distance from the beach. Follow the signs from the parking lot for about 200 yards to **Phallic Rock** ("Kauleomamahoa"). Nanahoa, the male fertility god inhabiting the anatomical rock, has been performing like a champ and hasn't had a "headache" in centuries! Legend says that Nanahoa lived nearby and one day sat to admire a beautiful young girl who was looking at her reflection in a pool. Kawahuna, Nanahoa's wife, became so jealous when she saw her husband leering that she attacked the young girl by yanking on her hair. Nanahoa became outraged in turn and struck his wife, who rolled over a nearby cliff and turned to stone. Nanahoa also turned to stone in the shape of an erect penis, and there he sits pointing skyward to this day. Barren women have come here to spend the night and pray for fertility. At the base of the rock is a tiny pool the size of a small bowl that collects rainwater. The women would sit here hoping to absorb the child-giving mana of the rock. You can still see offerings and of course graffiti. One says "Zap"—parents thankful for twins maybe.

Return to the parking lot and follow the signs to **Kalaupapa Overlook.** Jutting 1,600 feet below, almost like an afterthought, is the peninsula of Kalaupapa, which was the home of the lost lepers of Hawaii, picked for its remoteness and inaccessibility. The almost-vertical *pali* served as a natural barrier to the outside world. If you look to your right you'll see the mule trail switchbacking down the cliff. Look to the southeast sector of the peninsula to see the almost perfectly round **Kauhako Crater,** the remnant of the separate volcano that formed Kalaupapa.

THE KALAUPAPA EXPERIENCE

No one knew how the dreaded disease came to the Hawaiian Islands, but they did know that if you were contaminated by it your life would be misery. Leprosy has caused fear in the hearts of man since biblical times, and last century King Kamehameha V and his advisors were no exception. All they knew was that lepers had to be isolated. Kalawao Cove, on the southeast shore of Kalaupapa Peninsula, was regarded as the most isolated spot in the entire kingdom. So, starting in 1864, it was to Kalawao that the lepers of Hawaii were sent to die. Through crude diagnostic testing, anyone who had a suspicious skin discoloration, ulcer, or even bad sunburn was rounded up and sent to Kalawao. The islanders soon learned that once sent, there was no return. So the afflicted hid. Bounty hunters roamed the countryside. Babies, toddlers, teenagers, wives, grandfathers—none were immune to the bounty hunters. They hounded, captured, and sometimes killed anyone who had any sort of skin ailment. The captives were ripped from their villages and loaded on a ship. No one would come near the suspected lepers on board and they sat open to the elements in a cage. They were allowed only one small tin box of possessions. As the ship anchored in the always choppy bay at Kalawao, the cage was opened and the victims were tossed overboard. The contaminated cage was followed by a few sealed barrels of food and clothing that had been collected by merciful Christians. Those too weak or sick or young drowned; the unlucky made it to shore. The crew waited nervously with loaded muskets in case any of the howling, walking nightmares on shore attempted in their delirium to board the ship.

Hell on Earth

Waiting for the newcomers were the forsaken. Abandoned by king, country, family, friends, and apparently the Lord himself, they became animals—beasts of prey. Young girls with hardly a blemish were raped by reeking deformed men in rags. Old men were bludgeoned, their tin boxes ripped from their hands. Children and babies cried and begged for food, turning instinctively to the demented women who had lost all motherly feelings. Finally too weak even to whimper, they died of starvation. Those victims who could made rude dwellings of sticks and stones, while others lived in caves or on the beach open to the elements. Finally, the conscience of the kingdom was stirred in 1866: the old dumping ground of Kalawao was abandoned and the lepers were exiled to the more hospitable Kalaupapa side of the peninsula, just a few hundred yards to the west.

The Move to Kalaupapa

The people of the sleepy village of Kalaupapa couldn't believe their eyes when they saw the ravaged ones. But these lepers now sent to Kalaupapa were treated more mercifully. Missionary groups and kokua (helpers) provided food and rudimentary clothing. An end was put to the lawlessness and depravity. Still, the lepers were kept separate. For the most part they lived outdoors or in very rude huts. They never could come in direct contact with the kokua. If they met a healthy person walking along a path, they had to grovel at the side. Most fell to the ground, hiding their faces and attempting to crawl like beaten dogs under a bush. Many kokua, horrified by Kalaupapa, left on the next available boat. With no medical attention, death was still the only release from Kalaupapa.

Light in Hell

It was by accident or miracle that **Joseph de Veuster, Father Damien,** a Catholic priest, came from Belgium to Hawaii. His brother, also a priest, was supposed to come, but he became ill and Father Damien came in his place. Damien spent a few years in Hawaii, building churches and learning the language and ways of the people, before he came to Kalaupapa in 1873. What he saw touched his heart. He was different from the rest, having come with a sense of mission to help the lepers and bring them hope and dignity. The other missionaries saw Kalaupapa not as a place to live, but to die. Damien saw the lepers as children of God who had the right to live and be comforted. When they hid under a bush at his approach, he picked them up and stood them on their feet. He carried water all day long to the sick and dying. He bathed their wounds and built them shelters with his own two hands. When clothes or food or materials ran short, he walked topside and begged for more. Other church groups were against him, and the government gave him little aid, but he persevered. Damien scraped together some lumber and fashioned a flume pipe to carry water to his people, who were still dying mainly from pneumonia and tuberculosis brought on by neglect. Damien worked long days alone, until he dropped exhausted at night.

Father Damien modified **St. Philomena Church,** a structure that was originally built in Honolulu by Brother Bertrant in 1872, and shipped it to Molokai in segments. Father Damien invited his flock inside, but those grossly afflicted could not control their mouths, so spittle would drip to the floor. They were ashamed to soil the church, so Damien cut squares in the floor through which they could spit onto the ground. Slowly a light began to shine in the hearts of the lepers and the authorities began to take notice. Conditions began to improve, but there were those who resented Damien. Robert Louis Stevenson visited the settlement, and after meeting Damien wrote an open letter that ended ". . . he is my father." Damien contracted leprosy, but by the time he died in 1889 at age 49, he knew his people would be cared for. In 1936, Damien's native Belgium asked that his remains be returned. He was exhumed and his remains sent home, but a memorial still stands where he was interred at Kalaupapa. After lengthy squabbles with the Belgian government, Father Damien's right hand was returned to Kalaupapa in 1995 and has been reinterred as a religious relic. He has since been beatified by the Pope.

Father Damien just weeks before his death from Hansen's disease

pneumonia. Families could not visit members confined to Kalaupapa unless they were near death, and any children born to the patients—who were now starting to marry—were whisked away at birth and adopted, or given to family members on the outside. Even until the 1940s people were still sent to Kalaupapa because of skin ailments that were never really diagnosed as leprosy. Many of these indeed did show signs of the disease, but there is always the haunting thought that they may have contracted it after arrival at the colony. Jimmy, one of the guides for Damien Tours, was one of these. He had some white spots as a child that his Hawaiian grandmother would treat with herbs. As soon as she stopped applying the herbs, the spots would return. A public health nurse at school saw the spots, and Jimmy was sent to Kalaupapa. At the time he was given only 10 years to live.

In the mid-1940s sulfa drugs were found to arrest most cases of Hansen's disease, and the prognosis for a normal life improved. By the 1960s further breakthroughs made Hansen's disease noncontagious, and in 1969 the quarantine on patients was eliminated. Patients at Kalaupapa were then free to leave and return to their homes. No new patients were admitted, but most, already living in the only home they'd ever known, opted to stay. In total over the years, there have been about 8,000 unfortunate individuals who have been exiled to this forgotten spit of land. Almost as if it were an accident of fate designed to expunge evidence of the damning past, the community hospital along with all its records burned to the ground in the early '90s. No help was afforded by the local fire truck, which was unable to be started. Nonetheless, medical treatment continues and all needed care is still provided. The community of resident patients numbers less than 60 today—the average age is about 70—and state caretakers and federal employees in the community now out-

The Light Grows Brighter

Brother Dutton, who arrived in 1886, and Mother Marianne Cope, a Franciscan nun from Syracuse, New York, who came in 1888 with two other Sisters of Saint Francis, carried on Damien's work. In addition, many missionary groups sent volunteers to help at the colony. Thereafter the people of Kalaupapa were treated with dignity and given a sense of hope. In 1873, the same year that Damien arrived at Kalaupapa, Norwegian physician Gerhard Hansen isolated the bacteria that causes leprosy, and shortly thereafter the official name of the malady became Hansen's disease. By the turn of this century, adequate medical care and good living conditions were provided to the patients at Kalaupapa. Still, many died, mostly from complications such as TB or number patients. In all of Hawaii today, there are about 450 people registered with Hansen's disease; all but those at Kalaupapa live at home with their families. Each year on average, about 18 new cases are diagnosed in the state. Still the number of patients continues to drop as the old-timers die. Kalaupapa has been turned into a national historical park, jointly administered by the state Department of Health, but the residents are assured a lifetime occupancy and free care.

Getting There

It shouldn't be a matter of *if* you go to Kalaupapa, but *how* you go. You have choices. You can fly, walk, or ride a mule. No matter how you go, you *cannot* walk around Kalaupapa unescorted. You *must* take an official tour, and children under 16 are not allowed. If you're going by mule, arrangements are made for you by the company, but if you're walking down or flying in you have to call ahead to Richard Marks at **Damien Tours,** tel. (808) 567-6171, the only tour company now operating, and he will give you an exact place and time to meet once down on the peninsula. Damien Tours charges $32 for a fascinating, four-hour tour conducted by one of the residents. Definitely worth the money; the insight you get from the resident tour guide is priceless and unique. No food or beverages, except water, are available to visitors, so make sure to bring your own.

"I'd rather be riding a mule on Molokai" is an eye-catching bumper sticker sported by those lucky enough to have made the decent to Kalaupapa aboard sure-footed mules. After several years of closure for trail repair, the **Molokai Mule Ride** is now back in business. The well-trained mules will transport you down the 1,600-foot *pali* expertly negotiating 26 hairpin switchbacks on the trail to the bottom. After your tour of the settlement, these gutsy animals carry you right back up so you too can claim your bumper sticker and ride-completion certificate. You are on the mule about 90 minutes each way. This tour runs $120 and includes the ground tour of the settlement and lunch. No riders over 240 pounds please; you must be at least 16 years old and in good physical shape. For reservations, call (808) 567-6088 or (800) 567-7550.

If you're walking to Kalaupapa, follow the mule trail, cut by Manuel Farinha in 1886. Go about 200 yards past the stables and look for a road to the right. Follow this track down past pastureland to the trailhead, where there is a small metal building with an odd sign that reads "Advance Technology Center Hawaii USA" just near an overgrown observation point for the peninsula. The three-mile, 90-minute trail going down the steep north face of the *pali* is well maintained and only mildly strenuous. It will be rutted and muddy in spots, and you'll have to step around the road apples, so wear hiking boots if possible.

You can fly in and out, or out only, which is a good alternative and relatively cheap. **Molokai Air Shuttle** from Hoolehua offers roundtrip flights for $50. Flights are limited so call for schedules. When you fly in you must still arrange for the ground tour through Damien Tours before you will be sold a ticket. If you decide to fly, notice the breakers at the end of the runway sending spray 90 feet into the air. The pilots time their takeoff to miss the spray!

MOLOKAI'S WEST END

Long before contact with the Europeans, the west end of Molokai was famous throughout the Hawaiian Islands. The culture centered on Maunaloa, the ancient volcanic mountain that formed the land. On its slopes the goddess Laka learned the hula from her sister and spread its joyous undulations to all the other islands. Not far from the birthplace of the hula is Kaluakoi, one of the two most important adze quarries in old Hawaii. Without these stone tools, no canoes, bowls, or everyday items could have been fashioned. Voyagers came from every major island to trade for this perfect stone of Kaluakoi. With all this coming and going, the always-small population of Molokai needed godly protection. Not far away at Kalaipahoa, the "poison wood" sorcery gods of Molokai lived in a grove that supposedly sprouted to maturity in one night. With talismans made from this magical grove, Molokai kept invading warriors at bay for centuries.

Most of the island's arable land is out here. The thrust west began with the founding of the Molokai Ranch, whose 54,000 acres make up about 50% of the good farmland on the island, or about one-third of the island. The ranch was owned last century by Kamehameha V, and after his death it was sold to private interests who began the successful raising of Santa Gertrudis cattle imported from the famous Texas King Ranch. The ranch still employs *paniolo,* with the life of riding the range and rodeo still strong. Today, anywhere between 6,000-10,000 head of Brahmin and Brangus cattle roam ranch land with about 80 horses to do the work.

THE NORTHWEST

The northwest section of Molokai, centered at **Hoolehua,** is where the Hawaiian Homes parcels are located. The entire area has a feeling of heartland America, and if you ignore the coast-line in the background you could easily imag-ine yourself in the rolling hills of Missouri. Don't expect a town at Hoolehua. All that's there is a lit-tle post office and a government office.

Moomomi Beach
The real destination is Moomomi ("Jeweled Rep-tile") Beach. Follow Route 460 until it branches north at Route 480 a mile east of the airport. Fol-low Route 480 until it turns left onto Farrington Avenue in Hoolehua, and continue for about four miles until it turns into a red dirt road. This road can be extremely rutted, even tipping your car at a very precarious angle. Be advised! Continue for about 10 minutes until you come to a pavilion. Below you is Moomomi. This area is a favorite with local people who come here to swim, fish, and surf. The swells are good only in winter, but the beach becomes rocky at that time of year. The tides bring the sand in by April and the swim-ming until November is good. Unofficial camping is probably okay on this grassy area, and a toilet and water are available at the pavilion.

Moomomi Beach goes back in Hawaiian leg-end. Besides the mythical lizards that inhabited this area, a great shark-god was born here. The mother was a woman who became impregnated by the gods. Her husband was angry that her child would be from the spirit world, so he direct-ed her to come and sit on a large rock down by the beach. She went into labor and began to cry. A tear, holding a tiny fish, rolled down her cheek and fell into the sea and became the powerful shark-god. The rock upon which his mother sat is the large black one just to the right of the beach.

If you feel adventurous you can head west along the beach. Every 10 minutes or so you come to a tiny beach that you have entirely to yourself. Since this area is so isolated, be ex-tremely careful of surf conditions. About two miles west of Moomomi is **Keonelele,** a minia-ture desert of sand dunes. The wind whips through this region and carries the sand to the southwest shore. Geologists haunt this area try-ing to piece together Molokai's geological histo-ry. The Hawaiians used Keonelele as a burial site, and strange footprints found in the soft sandstone supposedly foretold the coming of white men. Today, Keonelele is totally deserted; although small, it gives the impression of a vast wasteland.

Kawakiu Beach
This secluded and pristine beach on the far north-western corner of Molokai was an item of contro-versy between the developers of the Kaluakoi Corp. and the grassroots activists of Molokai. For years access to the beach was restricted, and the Kaluakoi Corp. planned to develop the area. It was known that the area was very important dur-ing precontact times and rich in unexplored ar-chaeological sites. The Kaluakoi Corp. hired a supposed team of "experts" who studied the site for months and finally claimed that the area had no significant archaeological importance. Their find-ings were hooted at by local people and by schol-ars from various institutions who knew better. This controversy resulted in Kawakiu Beach being opened to the public with plans of turning it into a beach park; the archaeological sites will be pre-served.

The swimming at Kawakiu is excellent with the sandy bottom tapering off slowly. To get there go to the Paniolo Hale Condo at Kaluakoi Resort (see following) and park at the end of the dirt road that heads toward the sea, past the last paved parking lot of the condo. Walk across the golf course fairway of the 10th hole to the beach. Follow it north for three-quarters of a mile, dodg-ing the tide until you come to Kawakiu—definite-ly not recommended during periods of high surf, when swimming would be too dangerous any-way. If you have lots of time and energy, walk on farther to the ancient adze quarry and aban-

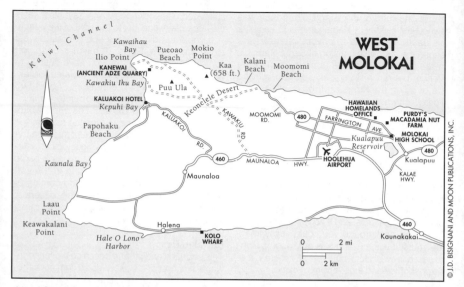

WEST MOLOKAI

© J.D. BISIGNANI AND MOON PUBLICATIONS, INC.

doned Coast Guard station on Lio Point. You can also drive there by following the dirt road past the condos until it branches inland. It eventually swings back and takes you to Kawakiu. The road is rough, and the hike mildly strenuous, but Kawakiu is definitely worth it.

Papohaku Beach

The best attraction in the area doesn't have a price tag. Papohaku Beach is the giant expanse of white sand running south from the Kaluakoi Resort. The sands here are so expansive that they were dredged and taken to Oahu in the 1950s. During the winter months a great deal of sand is stripped away and large lava boulders and outcroppings are exposed. Every spring and summer the tides carry the sand back and deposit it on the enormous beach. Camping is permitted at the **Papohaku County Beach Park** just past the resort. Pick up your permit at the Mitchell Pauole Center in Kaunakakai, tel. (808) 553-3204, before you come all the way out here. Here you'll find a large grassy play area, toilets, showers, picnic tables, grills for cooking, and a virtually empty beach. A sign on the road past the park tells you to watch out for deer. This road runs through a huge Papohaku Ranchlands home development area, with several beach ac-

cess roads and parking areas that lead to other spots along this huge expanse of beach.

The last beach access at the end of the paved road leads to a secluded and protected small bay and fine sand beach that is even safe during winter months when other beach areas are not. The Kaupoa Trail starts from the south end of this beach and runs into Molokai Ranch lands.

One of the attractions of Molokai is its remoteness. Here the sky is clear and at night the stars are brilliant. Yet, even here you know that you're not too far from the crush of humanity for directly across the Kaiwi Channel you can clearly see the glow of Honolulu, Wailua, and Kaneohe shimmering in the distance, and, closer at hand, the more muted lights of Maunaloa on the hill above.

Accommodations

Much of the west end of Molokai is the Kaluakoi Resort. The complex includes the Kaluakoi Hotel, two resort condominiums, world-famous Kaluakoi Golf Course, private home sites, and Papohaku, Hawaii's largest white-sand beach.

The **Kaluakoi Hotel and Golf Club**, P.O. Box 1977, Maunaloa, HI 96770, tel. (808) 552-2555, (800) 435-7208 statewide, or (800) 552-2550 Mainland, fax (808) 552-2821, Web site: www.kaluakoi.com, e-mail: Kaluakoi@juno.com, is the destination point for most of the people coming to Molokai. The low-rise buildings, made primarily of wood, blend with the surrounding countryside. The well-kept grounds are covered in manicured trees and shrubbery. All rooms have color TV, VCRs (video rental is at the front desk), and small refrigerators, and those on the second floor have open-beam construction. Some of the rooms have stove-tops, while the cottages have kitchens. Many rooms sit along the fairways of the golf course and most have at least a partial ocean view. Because of the constant cool breezes, no air-conditioning is necessary, but there are ceiling fans. A guest laundry is located on premises. At over 20 years old, this resort is beginning to show its age; it's becoming a little frayed around the edges. While not luxury, it is, nonetheless, quite adequate.

The rooms, many newly refurbished, are done in light pastels and earth colors. Dynamic color is provided by the large windows that open onto the fairways and the sea beyond. The least expensive hotel room is $105, the most expensive $275. Condo units go from $155 for a studio to $220 for a one-bedroom oceanfront cottage. Third person is $15. All guests of the Kaluakoi Hotel can golf free ($15 cart fee only) as part of their room charge.

Consult the activities desk for what's doing around the island. It can help you make all arrangements. On property you'll find a small Liberty House shop, along with the Kepuhi Sundries store, which sells snacks, magazines, and liquor, and the Laughing Gecko shop for antiques, art, jewelry, Hawaiiana, and locally designed T-shirts. Past the 10th hole, which would basically be the far north end of the property, you'll overlook a very private beach. Beyond that is one more. No rules or prying eyes here, so if you would like to swim au naturel, this is the place.

Some of the units at the resort complex, collectively called the **Kaluakoi Villas,** 1131 Kaluakoi Rd., Maunaloa, HI 96770, tel. (808) 552-2721 or (800) 367-5004 U.S. and Canada, (800) 272-5275 statewide, are managed by the Castle Group. Each studio, suite, and cottage has been tastefully decorated and includes a color TV, lanai, and refrigerator, and guests can use the resort's restaurants and all its recreational facilities. Rates range $125-150 for a studio, $150-180 for a suite, and $200 for the cottage; fourth night free.

Built in 1981, the **Ke Nani Kai Condos** are *mauka* of the road leading to the Kaluakoi Resort, and they cost $149-159 for one of the fully furnished one-bedroom apartments; two bedrooms rent at $179-199. All apartments are large and in excellent condition. Contact Ke Nani Kai, P.O. Box 289, Maunaloa, HI 96770, tel. (808) 552-2761 or (800) 535-0085, fax (808) 633-5085. A Marc Resort Hawaii property.

Newer yet, **Paniolo Hale** is another condo complex set in the trees surrounded by fairways. These buildings have more style than others on the area, and the whole complex a little more classy. The swimming pool, paddle tennis, and barbecue grill are for the use of all guests. Maid service is provided for stays of one week or longer, and each unit has a washer and dryer. Garden and ocean studios run $95 and $135, $115 and $160 for one bedroom, $145 and $195 for two bedrooms; $20 more in high season. Three nights minimum. Two-bedroom units have a hot tub and enclosed lanai. Contact Paniolo Hale, P.O. Box 190, Maunaloa, HI 96770, tel. (808) 552-2731 or (800) 367-2984, fax 552-2288, Web site: www.lava.net/paniolo, e-mail: paniolo@lava.net.

Food

The Kaluakoi Resort's **Ohia Lodge,** tel. (808) 552-2555, is an uninspired restaurant serving breakfast and dinner daily. It is the only restaurant at the resort and, aside from the Village Grill in Maunaloa, the only one on the west end of the island. Nice sunset views; reservations suggested. The garden-side snack bar is open daily 11 a.m.-4 p.m., selling sandwiches, burgers, and plate lunches, with most everything under $6. The **Ohia Lounge** is open all day and provides live local entertainment on Friday and Saturday.

MAUNALOA AND THE SOUTHWEST COAST

According to legend, the hilltop area of Maunaloa was the first place in the islands that the Hawaiians received hula instruction. Today, there are many *hula halau* on Molokai, and the yearly Molokai Hula Ka Piko festival is held down the hill at Papohaku State Park to honor this ancient music and dance form.

Most people heading east-west between Kaunakakai and the Kaluakoi Resort never make it into Maunaloa town. That's because Route 460 splits just east of Maunaloa, and Kaluakoi Road heads north toward the Kaluakoi Resort and away from the town. Until recently, with the pineapple gone and few visitors, the town barely hung on. Maunaloa was a wonderful example of a plantation town. It was a little patch of humble workers' houses carved into a field. In front you were likely to see a tethered horse, a boat, or glass fishing floats hanging from the lanai. Overhead you could see a kite flying—a sign that you had arrived in Maunaloa. The townsfolk were friendly and if you were looking for conversation or a taste of Hawaiian history, the old-timers hanging around under the shaded lean-to near the post office were just the ticket.

But the winds of change have started to blow in Maunaloa and the force increases. The Molokai Ranch, which owns the town, has begun to institute a new grand development scheme to completely "rejuvenate" the town. Most of the old homes, many falling apart and maybe uninsurable, have been torn down and have been replaced by new, similar-style homes. Bunched together away from the downtown area, these homes are set closer together than the old houses were. Starting at about $139,000, they are pricy yet affordable for many. Local people have been given first choice, and many have taken the deal. Additionally, streets have been paved and new ones laid out. A new sewer system and water reservoir have been installed. While several of the old standby commercial establishments have remained, others are being built. Already a movie theater, KFC, and ranch activities center are up and running. Future plans include a lodge, an old-town museum and cultural center, a city park, and new housing areas for custom homes. With all these changes there is certain to be some disagreement about their effect. While many take a wait-and-see attitude, others who live and/or work in town seem to think that the changes are for the better.

The only public access beach on this part of the island is **Hale O Lono**—follow the only road south of town and keep to the major track of crushed coral. A fine white-sand beach, Hale O Lono is the launch point for the annual Bankoh Molokai Outrigger Canoe Championship race to Waikiki. This is an old harbor that services the ranch, a few commercial boats related to the ranch, and the occasional passing ship. From here, the sand of Papohaku Beach was shipped to Oahu in the 1950s.

If you are staying at the Molokai Ranch, other spots along the coast might be of interest. About a mile east of Hale O Lono is **Halena Beach,** where there is an old Boy Scout camp and pavilion. East of there down the coastal dirt track is **Kolo Beach,** a fine long strand that sports the dilapidated **Kolo Wharf** at its far end. Kolo Wharf was where Molokai once shipped its pineapples. Now only naked pilings stand to mark the spot. On the far western end of the island is **Kaupoa Beach,** an old-time favorite of island residents.

Molokai Ranch

The only place to stay in Maunaloa in at the Molokai Ranch, but you don't just sleep there; activities are included. Accommodations are in three camps, placed in isolated yet picturesque spots. Paniolo Camp is set up near the rodeo arena, Kolo Camp overlooks the water near the old Kolo Wharf on the south shore, and Kaupoa Camp sits on a perfect white-sand crescent beach at the extreme west end. Paniolo and Kaupoa Camps have "tentalows," and Kolo has yurts. Wood-frame structures covered with heavy canvas, all are set up on wooden platforms that hold umbrella-covered patio tables, chairs, and benches. Inside are comfortable queen beds, a chest of drawers, and a chair. Set off to the side of the lanai is a composting toilet and no-roof shower that uses solar energy to heat the water. Electricity in each camp is powered by solar batteries. All this is done to impact the environment as little as possible. This is rustic simplicity—but luxurious for camping. Rates are on a sliding scale from $185-245 a night; children 4-12 are $75. These prices include morning and afternoon activities, three home-cooked meals a day, evening entertainment, and transportation to and from the airport and around the ranch property. For activities, you might choose horseback trail riding, *paniolo* roundup in the corral, mountain biking, hiking, kayaking, outrigger canoeing, sailing or whalewatching in season, or beach games; all equipment is provided. Multiday packages are available, and other island activities can be arranged at additional cost. For information and reservations contact Molokai Ranch, P.O. Box 259, Maunaloa, HI 96770, tel. (808) 552-2734 or (800) 254-8871, Web site: www.molokai-ranch.com; info@molokairanch.com.

Practicalities

A good reason to make the trek to Maunaloa is to visit the **Big Wind Kite Factory,** P.O. Box 10, Maunaloa, HI 96770, Web site: www.molokai.com /kites, e-mail: bigwind@aloha.net, tel. (808) 552-2364, open Mon.-Sat. 8:30 a.m.-5 p.m., Sunday 10 a.m.-2 p.m., owned and operated by Jonathan Sosher and his wife Daphane. The handcrafted kites and windsocks from this down-home cottage industry are the same ones that sell at Honolulu's oliok Ala Moana Mall, and at Kylo'o Kitoo at Tho Plantation on Kauai. All are made on the premises by Jonathan, Daphane, son Zachary, and a few workers who come up with designs like panda bears, rainbow stegosauruses, geckos with sunglasses, and hula girls in ti-leaf skirts—ask for a free factory tour. Jonathan will give you a lesson in the park next door on any of the kites, including the two-string-controllable ones. Prices range $10-200 for a rip-stop nylon kite; they make beautiful, easily transportable gifts that'll last for years.

The shop itself is ablaze with beautiful colors, as if you've walked into the heart of a flower. This is a happy store. Part of it, **The Plantation Gallery,** sells a variety of crafts by local artists—Hawaiian quilt pillowcases, Pacific isle shell jewelry, scrimshaw (on deerhorn), earrings, bracelets, boxes, bamboo xylophones, and other wood objects. Island cypress, Japanese *sugi* from a local tree, and *milo* have been carved by a local artist named Robin. Part of the boutique has batiks, Balinese masks, woodcarvings, quilts, and sarongs; especially nice are carved mirror frames of storks, birds, and flowers. And if you just can't live without a blowgun from Irian Jaya, this is the place. Here

too you'll find perhaps the island's best selections of books on Hawaii. After you've run through a million tourist shops and are sick of the shell lei, come here to find something truly unique. The Big Wind Kite Factory is *the* most interesting shop on Molokai.

Maunaloa General Store, tel. (808) 552-2868, is open Mon.-Sat. 9 a.m.-7 p.m., Sunday 10 a.m.-7 p.m. It's a well-stocked store where you can pick up anything that you'll need if you'll be staying in one of the condos at Kaluakoi. You can buy liquor, wine, beer, canned goods, meats, and vegetables.

The old Jojo's Cafe has been totally renovated and now operates with a new menu as **The Village Grill,** tel. (808) 552-0012. However, the bar that once did duty at the Pearl City Tavern in Oahu still occupies a spot in this new restaurant but has been retopped in bronze with cowboy designs added. Open 11 a.m.-2 p.m. for lunch, serving sandwiches, burgers, stir-fry, pasta, ribs, and pizza. For dinner, 6-9 p.m., the restaurant is more like a steakhouse with many meat and fish dishes, some pasta, and salads and dessert; entrees are in the $9-18 range.

To some people's delight and others' chagrin, there is now a KFC in town in the theater building. Usual fare, but limited; usual prices.

There was a theater is Maunaloa until the mid-1970s, after which the only one on the island was in Kaunakakai. When that closed, the island was without until the **Maunaloa Theater** was newly built in 1997. This triplex theater shows first movies and not only draws people from Maunaloa, but also from Kaluakoi and Kaunakakai as well.

SMILE
IT NO BROKE
YOUR FACE!

BOOKLIST

ASTRONOMY

Bryan, E.H. *Stars over Hawaii*. Hilo, HI: Petroglyph Press, 1977. Charts featuring the stars filling the night sky in Hawaii.

Rhoads, Samuel. *The Sky Tonight—A Guided Tour of the Stars over Hawaii*. Honolulu: Bishop Museum, 1993. Four pages per month of star charts—one each for the horizon in every cardinal direction. Exceptional!

COOKING

Alexander, Agnes. *How to Use Hawaiian Fruit*. Hilo, HI: Petroglyph Press, 1984. A full range of recipes using delicious and different Hawaiian fruits.

Beeman, Judy, and Martin Beeman. *Joys of Hawaiian Cooking*. Hilo, HI: Petroglyph Press, 1977. A collection of favorite recipes from Big Island chefs.

Choy, Sam. *Cooking From the Heart with Sam Choy*. Honolulu: Mutual Publishing, 1995. This beautiful, handbound cookbook contains many color photos by Douglas Peebles.

Fukuda, Sachi. *Pupus, An Island Tradition*. Honolulu: Bess Press, 1995.

Margah, Irish, and Elvira Monroe. *Hawaii, Cooking with Aloha*. San Carlos, CA: Wide World, 1984. Island recipes including *kalua* pig, *lomi* salmon, and hints on decor.

Rizzuto, Shirley. *Fish Dishes of the Pacific—from the Fishwife*. Honolulu: Hawaii Fishing News, 1986. Features recipes using all the fish commonly caught in Hawaiian waters (husband Jim Rizzuto is the author of *Fishing, Hawaiian Style*).

CULTURE

Hartwell, Jay. *Na Mamo: Hawaiian People Today*. Ai Pohaku Press, 1996. Profiles 12 people practicing Hawaiian traditions in the modern world.

Heyerdahl, Thor. *American Indians in the Pacific*. London: Allen and Unwin Ltd., 1952. Theoretical and anthropological accounts of the influence on Polynesia of the Indians along the Pacific coast of North and South America. Though no longer in print, this book is fascinating reading, presenting unsubstantiated yet intriguing theories.

Kirch, Patrick V. *Feathered Gods and Fishhooks: An Introduction to Hawaiian Archaeology and Prehistory*. Honolulu: University of Hawaii Press, 1985. This scholarly, lavishly illustrated, yet very readable book gives new insight into the development of precontact Hawaiian civilization. It focuses on the sites and major settlements of old Hawaii and chronicles the main cultural developments while weaving in the social climate that contributed to change. A very worthwhile read.

FAUNA

Boom, Robert. *Hawaiian Seashells*. Honolulu: Waikiki Aquarium, 1972. Photos by Jerry Kringle. A collection of 137 seashells found in Hawaiian waters, featuring many found nowhere else on earth. Broken into categories with accompanying text including common and scientific names, physical descriptions, and likely habitats. A must for shell collectors.

Carpenter, Blyth, and Russell Carpenter. *Fish Watching in Hawaii*. San Mateo, CA: Natural World Press, 1981. A color guide to many of the reef fish found in Hawaii and often spotted by snorkelers. If you're interested in the fish that you'll be looking at, this guide will be very helpful.

Fielding, Ann, and Ed Robinson. *An Underwater Guide to Hawaii.* Honolulu: University of Hawaii Press, 1987. If you've ever had a desire to snorkel/scuba the living reef waters of Hawaii and to be familiar with what you're seeing, get this small but fact-packed book. The amazing array of marinelife found throughout the archipelago is captured in glossy photos with accompanying informative text. Both the scientific and common names of specimens are given. This book will enrich your underwater experience and serve as an easily understood reference guide for many years

Goodson, Gar. *The Many-Splendored Fishes of Hawaii.* Stanford, CA: Stanford University Press, 1985. This small but thorough "fish-watchers" book includes entries on some deep-sea fish.

Hobson, Edmend, and E.H. Chave. *Hawaiian Reef Animals.* Honolulu: University of Hawaii Press, 1987. Colorful photos and descriptions of the fish, invertebrates, turtles, and seals that call Hawaiian reefs their home.

Hosaka, Edward. *Shore Fishing in Hawaii.* Hilo, HI: Petroglyph Press, 1984. Known as the best book on Hawaiian fishing since 1944. This book receives the highest praise because it has born and bred many Hawaiian fishermen.

Kay, Alison, and Olive Schoenberg-Dole. *Shells of Hawaii.* Honolulu: University of Hawaii Press, 1991. Color photos and tips on where to look for certain shells.

Mahaney, Casey. *Hawaiian Reef Fish, The Identification Book.* 1993. A spiral-bound reference work featuring many color photos and descriptions of common reef fish found in Hawaiian waters.

Nickerson, Roy. *Brother Whale, A Pacific Whalewatcher's Log.* San Francisco: Chronicle Books, 1977. Introduces the average person to the life of earth's greatest mammals. Provides historical accounts, photos, and tips on whalewatching. Well-written, descriptive, and the best "first time" book on whales.

Pratt, H.D., P.L. Bruner, and D.G. Berrett. *The Birds of Hawaii and the Tropical Pacific.* Princeton, N.J. Princeton University Press, 1987. Useful field guide for novice and expert birdwatchers, covering Hawaii as well as other Pacific Island groups.

van Riper, Charles, and Sandra van Riper. *A Field Guide to the Mammals of Hawaii.* Honolulu: Oriental Publishing. A guide to the surprising number of mammals introduced into Hawaii. Full-color pages document description, uses, tendencies, and habitat. Small and thin, this book makes a worthwhile addition to any serious trekker's backpack

FLORA

Kepler, Angela. *Exotic Tropicals of Hawaii.* Honolulu: Mutual Publishing, 1989. This small-format book features many color photos of exotic tropical flowers.

Kuck, Lorraine, and Richard Togg. *Hawaiian Flowers and Flowering Trees.* Rutland, VT: Tuttle, 1960. A classic, though no longer in print, field guide to tropical and subtropical flora illustrated in watercolor. A "to the point" description of Hawaiian plants and flowers with a brief history of their places of origin and their introduction to Hawaii.

Merrill, Elmer. *Plant Life of the Pacific World.* Rutland, VT: Tuttle, 1983. The definitive book for anyone planning a botanical tour to the entire Pacific Basin. Originally published in the 1930s, it remains a tremendous work, worth tracking down through the out-of-print book services.

Miyano, Leland. *Hawaii, A Floral Paradise.* Honolulu: Mutual Publishing, 1995. Photographed by Douglas Peebles, this large-format book is filled with informative text and beautiful color shots of tropical flowers commonly seen in Hawaii.

Sohmer, S.H., and R. Gustafson. *Plants and Flowers of Hawaii.* Honolulu: University of Hawaii Press, 1987. Sohmer and Gustafson cover the vegetation zones of Hawaii, from mountains to coast, introducing you to the wide and varied floral biology of the islands. They give a good introduction to the history and unique evolution of Hawaiian plantlife. Beautiful color plates are accompanied by clear and concise plant descriptions, with the scientific and common Hawaiian names listed.

Teho, Fortunato. *Plants of Hawaii—How to grow them.* Hilo, HI: Petroglyph Press, 1992. A small but useful book for those who want their backyards to bloom into tropical paradises.

HEALTH

McBride, L.R. *Practical Folk Medicine of Hawaii.* Hilo, HI: Petroglyph Press, 1975. An illustrated guide to Hawaii's medicinal plants as used by the *kahuna lapa'au* (medical healers). Includes a thorough section on ailments, diagnosis, and the proper folk remedy. Illustrated by the author, a renowned botanical researcher and former ranger at Volcanoes National Park.

Wilkerson, James A., M.D., ed. *Medicine for Mountaineering and Other Wilderness.* 4th ed. Seattle: The Mountaineers, 1992. Don't let the title fool you. Although the book focuses on specific health problems that may be encountered while mountaineering, it is the best first-aid and general health guide available today. Written by doctors for the layperson to use until help arrives, it is jam-packed with easily understandable techniques and procedures. For those intending extended treks, it is a must.

HISTORY

Apple, Russell A. *Trails: From Steppingstones to Kerbstones.* Honolulu: Bishop Museum Press, 1965. This "Special Publication #53" is a special-interest archaeological survey focusing on trails, roadways, footpaths, and highways and how they were designed and maintained throughout the years. Many "royal highways" from precontact Hawaii are cited.

Ashdown, Inez MacPhee. *Old Lahaina.* Honolulu: Hawaiian Service Inc., 1976. A small pamphlet-type book listing most of the historical attractions of Lahaina Town, past and present. Ash-

down is a life-long resident of Hawaii and gathered her information firsthand by listening to and recording stories told by ethnic Hawaiians and old *kama'aina* families.

—-*Ke Alaloa o Maui.* Wailuku, HI: Kama'aina Historians Inc., 1971. A compilation of the history and legends connected to sites on the island of Maui. Ashdown was at one time a "lady in waiting" for Queen Liliuokalani and has since been proclaimed Maui's "Historian Emeritus."

Cameron, Roderick. *The Golden Haze.* New York: World Publishing, 1964. An account of Capt. James Cook's voyages of discovery throughout the South Seas. Uses original diaries and journals for an "on the spot" reconstruction of this great seafaring adventure.

Daws, Gavan. *Shoal of Time, A History of the Hawaiian Islands.* Honolulu: University of Hawaii Press, 1974. A highly readable history of Hawaii dating from its "discovery" by the Western world down to its acceptance as the 50th state. Good insight into the psychological makeup of influential characters who helped form Hawaii's past.

Finney, Ben, and James D. Houston. *Surfing, A History of the Ancient Hawaiian Sport.* Los Angeles: Pomegranate, 1996. Features many early etchings and old photos of Hawaiian surfers practicing their native sport.

Free, David. *Vignettes of Old Hawaii.* Honolulu: Crossroads Press,1994. A collection of short essays on a variety of subjects.

Fuchs, Lawrence. *Hawaii Pono.* New York: Harcourt, Brace and World, 1961. A detailed, scholarly work presenting an overview of Hawaii's history, based upon psychological and sociological interpretations. Encompasses most socio-ethnological groups from native Hawaiians to modern entrepreneurs. A must for social historical background.

Fornander, Abraham. *An Account of the Polynesian Race; Its origins and Migrations, and the Ancient History of the Hawaiian People to the Times of Kamehameha I.* Rutland, VT: C.E. Tuttle Co., 1969. This is a reprint of a three-volume opus originally published 1878-85. It is still one of the best sources of information on Hawaiian myth and legend.

Handy, E.S., and Elizabeth Handy. *Native Planters in Old Hawaii.* Honolulu: Bishop Museum Press, 1972. A superbly written, easily understood scholarly work on the intimate relationship of precontact Hawaiians and the *aina* (land). Much more than its title implies, this book should be read by anyone seriously interested in Polynesian Hawaii.

II, John Papa. *Fragments of Hawaiian History.* Honolulu: Bishop Museum, 1959. Hawaii's history under Kamehameha I as told by a Hawaiian who actually experienced it.

Joesting, Edward. *Hawaii: An Uncommon History.* New York: W.W. Norton Co., 1978. A truly uncommon history told in a series of vignettes relating to the lives and personalities of the first white men in Hawaii, Hawaiian nobility, sea captains, writers, and adventurers. Brings history to life. Absolutely excellent!

Kurisu, Yasushi. *Sugar Town, Hawaiian Plantation Days Remembered.* Honolulu: Watermark Publishing, 1995. Reminiscences of life growing up on sugar plantations on the Hamakua Coast of the Big Island. Features many old photos.

Liliuokalani. *Hawaii's Story By Hawaii's Queen.* 1964. Reprint, Rutland, VT: Tuttle, 1991. A moving personal account of Hawaii's inevitable move from monarchy to U.S. Territory by its last queen, Liliuokalani. The facts can be found in other histories, but none provides the emotion or point of view expressed by Hawaii's deposed monarch. A "must-read" to get the whole picture.

McBride, Likeke. *Petroglyphs of Hawaii.* Hilo, HI: Petroglyph Press, 1996. A revised and updated guide to petroglyphs found in the Hawaiian Islands.

Nickerson, Roy. *Lahaina, Royal Capital of Hawaii.* Honolulu: Hawaiian Service, 1978. The story of Lahaina from whaling days to present, spiced with ample photographs.

INTRODUCTORY

Cohen, David, and Rick Smolan. *A Day in the Life of Hawaii.* New York. Workman, 1984. On December 2, 1983, 50 of the world's top photojournalists were invited to Hawaii to photograph the variety of daily life on the islands. The photos are excellently reproduced, and accompanied by a minimum of text.

Day, A.G., and C. Stroven. *A Hawaiian Reader.* 1959. Reprint, New York: Appleton, Century, Crofts, 1965. A poignant compilation of essays, diary entries, and fictitious writings that takes you from the death of Captain Cook through the "statehood services."

Department of Geography, University of Hawaii. *Atlas of Hawaii.* 2nd ed. Honolulu: University of Hawaii Press, 1983. Much more than an atlas filled with reference maps, this also contains commentary on the natural environment, culture, and sociology; a gazetteer; and statistical tables. Actually a mini-encyclopedia.

Michener, James A. *Hawaii.* New York: Random House, 1959. Michener's fictionalized historical novel has done more to inform and mis-inform readers about Hawaii than any other book ever written. A great tale with plenty of local color and information, but read it for pleasure, not facts.

Piercy, LaRue. *Hawaii This and That.* Honolulu: Mutual Publishing, 1994. Illustrated by Scot Ebanez. A 60-page book filled with one-sentence facts and oddities about all manner of things Hawaiian. Informative, amazing, and fun to read.

LANGUAGE

Elbert, Samuel, and Mary Pukui. *Hawaiian Dictionary.* Honolulu: University of Hawaii, 1986. The best dictionary available on the Hawaiian language. The *Pocket Hawaiian Dictionary* is a less expensive, condensed version of this dictionary, and adequate for most travelers with a general interest in the language.

Elbert, Samuel. *Spoken Hawaiian.* Honolulu: University of Hawaii Press, 1970. Progressive conversational lessons.

MYTHOLOGY AND LEGENDS

Beckwith, Martha. *Hawaiian Mythology.* 1970. Reprint, Honolulu: University of Hawaii Press, 1977. Nearly 60 years after its original printing in 1940, this work remains the definitive text on Hawaiian mythology. Beckwith compiled this book from many sources, giving exhaustive cross-references to genealogies and legends expressed in the oral tradition. If you are going to read one book on Hawaii's folklore, this should be it.

Colum, Padraic. *Legends of Hawaii.* New Haven: Yale University Press, 1937. Selected legends of old Hawaii, reinterpreted but closely based upon the originals.

Elbert, S., comp. *Hawaiian Antiquities and Folklore.* Honolulu: Univerity of Hawaii Press, 1959. Illustrated by Jean Charlot. A selection of the main legends from Abraham Fornander's great work, *An Account of the Polynesian Race.*

Kalakaua, His Hawaiian Majesty, King David. *The Legends and Myths of Hawaii.* Edited by R.M. Daggett, with a foreword by Glen Grant. Honolulu: Mutual Publishing, 1990. Originally published in 1888, Hawaii's own King Kalakaua draws upon his scholarly and formidable knowledge of the classic oral tradition to bring alive ancient tales from precontact Hawaii. A powerful yet somewhat Victorian voice from Hawaii's past speaks clearly and boldly, especially about the intimate role of pre-Christian religion in the lives of the Hawaiian people.

Melville, Leinanai. *Children of the Rainbow.* Wheaton, IL: Theosophical Publishing, 1969. A book on higher spiritual consciousness attuned to nature, which was the basic belief of pre-Christian Hawaii. The appendix contains illustrations of mystical symbols used by the *kahuna.* An enlightening book in many ways.

Thrum, Thomas. *Hawaiian Folk Tales.* 1907. Reprint, Chicago: McClurg and Co., 1950. A collection of Hawaiian tales from the oral tradition as told to the author from various sources.

Westervelt, W.D. *Hawaiian Legends of Volcanoes.* 1916. Reprint, Boston: Ellis Press, 1991. A small book concerning the volcanic legends of Hawaii and how they related to the fledgling field of volcanism at the turn of the century. The vintage photos alone are worth a look.

NATURAL SCIENCES

Abbott, Agatin, Gordon MacDonald, and Frank Peterson. *Volcanoes in the Sea.* Honolulu: University of Hawaii Press, 1983. A simplified yet comprehensive text covering the geology and volcanism of the Hawaiian Islands. Focuses upon the forces of nature (wind, rain, and surf) that shape the islands.

Carlquist, Sherwin. *Hawaii: A Natural History,* 2nd ed. National Tropical Botany, 1980. Definitive account of Hawaii's natural history.

Hazlett, Richard, and Donald Hyndman. *Roadside Geology of Hawaii.* Missoula, MT: Mountain Press Publishing, 1996. Begins with a general discussion of the geology of the Hawaiian Islands, followed by a road guide to the individual islands offering descriptions of easily seen features.

Hubbard, Douglass, and Gordon MacDonald. *Volcanoes of the National Parks of Hawaii.* 1982. Reprint, Volcanoes, HI: Hawaii Natural History Association, 1989. The volcanology of Hawaii, documenting the major lava flows and their geological effect on the state.

Kay, E. Alison, comp. *A Natural History of the Hawaiian Islands.* Honolulu: University of Hawaii Press, 1994. A selection of concise articles by experts in the fields of volcanism, oceanography, meteorology, and biology. An excellent reference source.

PERIODICALS

Aloha, The Magazine of Hawaii and the Pacific. Davick Publications, P.O. Box 49035, Escondido, CA 92046. This excellent bimonthly magazine is much more than glossy photography. Special features may focus on sports, the arts, history, flora and fauna, or just pure island adventure. *Aloha* is equally useful as a "dream book" for those who wish that they could visit Hawaii, and as a current resource for those actually going. One of the best for an overall view of Hawaii, and well worth the subscription price.

Hawaii Magazine. 1400 Kapiolani Blvd., Suite D, Honolulu, HI 96814. This magazine covers the Hawaiian Islands like a tropical breeze. Feature articles on all aspects of life in the islands, with special departments on travel, events, exhibits, and restaurant reviews. Up-to-the-minute information, and a fine read.

Naturist Society Magazine. P.O. Box 132, Oshkosh, WI 54920. This excellent magazine not only *uncovers* bathing-suit-optional beaches throughout the islands, giving tips for naturalists visiting Hawaii, but also reports on local politics, environment, and conservation measures from the health-conscious nudist point of view. A fine publication.

PICTORIALS

La Bruchene, Roger. *Hawaiian World, Hawaiian Heart.* Pine Valley, CA: Imagenes Press, 1989.

Grant, Glenn. *Hawaii The Big Island.* Honolulu: Mutual Publishing, 1988. Includes the historic, social, and nature photos of many photographers.

POLITICAL SCIENCE

Albertini, Jim, et al. *The Dark Side of Paradise, Hawaii in a Nuclear War.* Honolulu: cAtholic Action of Hawaii. Well-documented research outlining Hawaii's role and vulnerability in a nuclear world. This book presents the antinuclear and antimilitary side of the political issue in Hawaii.

Bell, Roger. *Last Among Equals: Hawaiian Statehood and American Politics.* Honolulu: University of Hawaii, 1984. Documents Hawaii's long and rocky road to statehood, tracing political partisanship, racism, and social change.

SPORTS AND RECREATION

Alford, John, D. *Mountain Biking the Hawaiian Islands.* Ohana Pub., 1997. Quite useful

Ambroso, Grog. *Surfer's Guide to Hawaii.* Honolulu: Bess Press, 1991. Island-by-island guide to surfing spots.

Ball, Stuart. *Hiker's Guide to Oahu.* Honolulu: University of Hawaii Press, 1993. Very excellent.

Cagala, George. *Hawaii: A Camping Guide.* Hunter Pub., 1994. Useful.

Chisholm, Craig. *Hawaiian Hiking Trails.* Lake Oswego, OR: Fernglen Press, 1989.

Lueras, Leonard. *Surfing, the Ultimate Pleasure.* Honolulu: Emphasis International, 1984. One of the most brilliant books ever written on surfing.

McMahon, Richard. *Camping Hawai'i: A Complete Guide.* Honolulu: University of Hawaii Press, 1997. A helpful handbook.

Morey, Kathy. *Oahu Trails.* Berkeley, CA: Wildorness Press, 1993. Morey's books are specialized, detailed trekker's guides to Hawaii's outdoors. Complete with useful maps, historical references, official procedures, and plants and animals encountered along the way. If you're focused on hiking, these are the best to take along. *Maui Trails, Kauai Trails,* and *Hawaii Trails* are also available.

Rosenberg, Steve. *Diving Hawaii.* Locust Valley, NY: Aqua Quest, 1990. Describes diving locations on the major islands as well as the marinelife divers are likely to see. Includes many color photos.

Smith, Robert. *Hawaii's Best Hiking Trails.* Huntington Beach, CA: Hawaiian Outdoor Adventures, 1991. Other guides by this author include *Hiking Oahu, Hiking Maui, Hiking Hawaii,* and *Hiking Kauai.*

Thorne, Chuck. *The Diver's Guide to Maui.* Hana, HI: Maui Dive Guide, 1994. A no-nonsense snorkeler's and diver's guide to Maui waters. Extensive maps, descriptions, and "straight from the shoulder" advice by one of Maui's best and most experienced divers. A must for all levels of divers and snorkelers.

Wallin, Doug. *Diving & Snorkeling Guide to the Hawaiian Islands,* 2nd ed. Pisces Books, 1991. A guide offering brief descriptions of diving locations on the four major islands.

TRAVEL

Clark, John. *Beaches of the Big Island.* Honolulu: University of Hawaii Press, 1985. Definitive guide to beaches, including many off the beaten path. Features maps and black-and-white photos.

Riegert, Ray. *Hidden Hawaii.* Berkeley, CA: And/Or Press, 1992. Ray offers a "user-friendly" guide to the islands.

Stanley, David. *South Pacific Handbook.* 6th ed. Chico, CA: Moon Publications, 1995. The model upon which all travel guides should be based. Simply the best book in the world for travel throughout the South Pacific.

Warner, Evie, and Al Davies. *Bed and Breakfast Goes Hawaiian.* Kapa'a, HI: Island Bed and Breakfast, 1990. A combination bed and breakfast directory and guide to sights, activities, events, and restaurants on the six major islands.

GLOSSARY

CAPSULE HAWAIIAN

The list on the following pages gives you a "taste" of Hawaiian and provides a basic vocabulary of words in common usage which you are likely to hear. Becoming familiar with them is not a strict necessity, but they will definitely enhance your experience and make talking with local people more congenial. You'll soon notice that many islanders spice their speech with certain words, especially when they're speaking pidgin, and you too can use them just as soon as you feel comfortable. You might even discover some Hawaiian words that are so perfectly expressive they'll become regular parts of your vocabulary. Many Hawaiian words have been absorbed into the English dictionary.

Also see the **Language** and **Food and Drink** sections in the Introduction for other applicable Hawaiian words and phrases. The definitions given are not exhaustive, but are generally considered the most common.

Words marked with an asterisk (*) are used commonly throughout the islands.

a'a*—rough clinker lava. A'a has become the correct geological term to describe this type of lava found anywhere in the world.

ae—yes

ahupua'a—pie-shaped land divisions running from mountain to sea that were governed by *konohiki,* local *ali'i* who owed their allegiance to a reigning chief

aikane—friend; pal; buddy

aina—land; the binding spirit to all Hawaiians. Love of the land is paramount in traditional Hawaiian beliefs.

akamai—smart; clever; wise

akua—a god, or simply "divine." You'll hear people speak of their family or personal *amakua* (ancestral spirit). Favorites are the shark or the *pueo* (Hawaiian owl).

ali'i*—a Hawaiian chief or noble

aloha*—the most common greeting in the islands; can mean both hello or goodbye, welcome or farewell. It can also mean romantic love, affection, or best wishes.

amakua—a personal or family spirit, usually an ancestral spirit

aole—no

auwe—alas; ouch! When a great chief or loved one died, it was a traditional wail of mourning.

awa, also known as *kava,* a mildly intoxicating traditional drink made from the juice of chewed awa root, spat into a bowl, and used in religious ceremonies

halakahiki—pineapple

hale*—house or building; often combined with other words to name a specific place, such as Haleakala ("House of the Sun"), or Hale Pa'I ("Printing House")

hana*—work; combined with *pau* means end of work or quitting time

hanai—literally "to feed." Part of the true *aloha* spirit. A *hanai* is a permanent guest, or an adopted family member, usually an old person or a child. This is an enduring cultural phenomenon in Hawaii, in which a child from one family (perhaps that of a brother or sister, and quite often one's grandchild) is raised as one's own without formal adoption.

haole*—a word that at one time meant foreigner, but which now means a white person or Caucasian. Many etymological definitions have been put forth, but none satisfies everyone. Some feel that it signified a person without a background, because the first white men could not chant their genealogies as was common to Hawaiians.

hapa*—half, as in a mixed-blooded person being referred to as *hapa haole*

hapai*—pregnant; used by all ethnic groups when a *keiki* is on the way

haupia*—a coconut custard dessert often served at a luau

heiau*—A platform made of skillfully fitted rocks, upon which temporary structures were built as temples and offerings made to the gods.

holomuu*—an ankle-length dress that is much more fitted than a muumuu, and which is often worn on formal occasions

hono—bay, as in Honolulu ("Sheltered Bay")

honu—green sea turtle (endangered)

ho'oilo—traditional Hawaiian winter that began in November

hoolaulea—any happy event, but especially a family outing or picnic

hoomalimali*—sweet talk; flattery

huhu*—angry; irritated

hui*—a group; meeting; society. Often used to refer to Chinese businesspeople or family members who pool their money to get businesses started.

hukilau—traditional shoreline fish-gathering in which everyone lends a hand to *huki* (pull) the huge net. Anyone taking part shares in the *lau* (food). It is much more like a party than hard work, and if you're lucky you'll be able to take part in one.

hula*—a native Hawaiian dance in which the rhythm of the islands is captured by swaying hips and stories told by lyrically moving hands. A *halau* is a group or school of hula.

huli huli—barbecue, as in *huli huli* chicken

i'a—fish in general. *I'a maka* is raw fish.

imu*—underground oven filled with hot rocks and used for baking. The main cooking method featured at a luau, used to steam-bake pork and other succulent dishes. The tending of the *imu* was traditionally for men only.

ipo—sweetheart; lover; girl- or boyfriend

kahili—a tall pole topped with feathers, resembling a huge feather duster. It was used by an *ali'i* to announce his or her presence.

kahuna*—priest; sorcerer; doctor; skillful person. In old Hawaii *kahuna* had tremendous power, which they used for both good and evil. The *kahuna ana'ana* was a feared individual because he practiced "black magic" and could pray a person to death, while the *kahuna lapa'au* was a medical practitioner bringing aid and comfort to the people.

kai—the sea. Many businesses and hotels employ *kai* as part of their name.

kalua—means roasted underground in an *imu*. A favorite island food is *kalua* pork.

kama'aina*—a child of the land; an old-timer; a longtime island resident of any ethnic background; a resident of Hawaii or native son or daughter. Hotels and airlines often offer discounts called *"kama'aina* rates" to anyone who can prove island residency.

kanaka—man or commoner; later used to distinguish a Hawaiian from other races. Tone of voice can make it a derisive expression.

kane*—means man, but actually used to signify a relationship such as husband or boyfriend. Written on a lavatory door it means "Men's Room."

kaola*—any food that has been broiled or barbecued

kapu*—forbidden; taboo; keep out; do not touch

kapuna—a grandparent or old-timer; usually means someone who has gained wisdom. The statewide school system now invites *kapuna* to talk to the children about the old ways and methods.

kaukau*—slang word meaning food or chow; grub. Some of the best food in Hawaii comes from the *"kaukau* wagons," trucks that sell plate lunches and other morsels.

kauwa—a landless, untouchable caste once confined to living on reservations. Members of this caste were often used as human sacrifices at *heiau*. Calling someone *kauwa* is still considered a grave insult.

kava—also known as *awa,* a mildly intoxicating traditional drink made from the juice of chewed awa root, spat into a bowl, and used in religious ceremonies

keiki*—child or children; used by all ethnic groups. "Have you hugged your *keiki* today?"

kiawe—an algaroba tree from South America commonly found in Hawaii along the shore. It grows a nasty long thorn that can easily puncture a tire. Legend has it that the trees were introduced to the islands by a misguided missionary who hoped the thorns would coerce natives into wearing shoes. Actually, they are good for fuel, as fodder for hogs and cattle, and for reforestation, none of which you'll appreciate if you step on one of their thorns or flatten a tire on your rental car!

kokua—help. As in "Your *kokua* is needed to keep Hawaii free from litter."

kona wind*—a muggy subtropical wind that blows from the south and hits the leeward side of the islands. It usually brings sticky hot weather and is one of the few times when air-conditioning will be appreciated.

konane—a traditional Hawaiian game, similar to checkers, played with pebbles on a large flat stone used as a board.

koolau—windward side of the island

kukui—a candlenut tree whose pods are polished and then strung together to make a beautiful *lei*. Traditionally the oil rich nuts were strung on the rib of a coconut leaf and used as a candle.

kuleana—homesite; the old homestead; small farms. Especially used to describe the small spreads on Hawaiian Homes Lands on Molokai.

Kumulipo*—ancient Hawaiian genealogical chant that records the pantheon of gods, creation, and the beginning of humankind

la—the sun. Often combined with other words to be more descriptive, such as Lahaina ("Merciless Sun") or Haleakala ("House of the Sun").

lanai*—veranda or porch. You'll pay more for a hotel room if it has a lanai with an ocean view

lani—sky or the heavens

lau hala—traditional Hawaiian weaving of mats, hats, etc., from the prepared fronds of the pandanus (screw pine)

lei*—a traditional garland of flowers or vines. One of Hawaii's most beautiful customs. Given at any auspicious occasion, but especially when arriving or leaving Hawaii.

lele—the stone altar at a *heiau*

limu—edible seaweed of various types. Gathered from the shoreline, it makes an excellent salad. It's used to garnish many island dishes and is a favorite at luau.

lomi lomi—traditional Hawaiian massage; also, raw salmon made into a vinegared salad with chopped onion and spices

lua*—the toilet; the head; the bathroom

luakini—a human-sacrifice temple. Introduced to Hawaii in the 13th century at Waha'ula Heiau on the Big Island.

luau*—a Hawaiian feast featuring poi, *imu*-baked pork, and other traditional foods. Good ones provide some of the best gastronomical delights in the world.

luna—foreman or overseer in the plantation fields. They were often mounted on horseback and were renowned for either their fairness or their cruelty. Representing the middle class , they served as a buffer between plantation workers and white plantation owners.

mahalo*—thank you. *Mahalo nui* means "big thanks" or "thank you very much."

mahele—division. The "Great Mahele" of 1848 changed Hawaii forever when the traditional common lands were broken up into privately owned plots.

mahimahi*—a favorite eating fish. It's often called a dolphin, but a mahimahi is a true fish, not a cetacean.

mahu—a homosexual; often used derisively like "fag" or "queer"

maile—a fragrant vine used in traditional lei. It looks ordinary but smells delightful.

maka'ainana—a commoner; a person "belonging" to the *aina* (land), who supported the *ali'i* by fishing and farming and as a warrior

makai*—toward the sea; used by most islanders when giving directions

make—dead; deceased

malihini*—what you are if you have just arrived: a newcomer; a tenderfoot; a recent arrival

malo—the native Hawaiian loincloth. Never worn anymore except at festivals or pageants.

mana*—power from the spirit world; innate energy of all things animate or inanimate; the grace of god. Mana could be passed on from one person to another, or even stolen. Great care was taken to protect the *ali'i* from having their mana defiled. Commoners were required to lie flat on the ground and cover their faces whenever a great *ali'i* approached. *Kahuna* were often employed in the regaining or transference of mana.

manauahi—free; gratis; extra

manini—stingy; tight; a Hawaiianized word taken from the name of Don Francisco Marin, who was instrumental in bringing many fruits and plants to Hawaii. He was known for never sharing any of the bounty from his substantial gardens on Vineyard Street in Honolulu, therefore his name came to mean "stingy."

mauka*—toward the mountains; used by most islanders when giving directions

mauna—mountain. Often combined with other words to be more descriptive, such as Mauna Kea ("White Mountain").

mele—a song or chant in the Hawaiian oral tradition that records the history and genealogies of the *ali'i*

menehune—the legendary "little people" of Hawaii. Like leprechauns, they are said to have shunned humans and possess magical powers. Stone walls said to have been completed in one night are often attributed to them. Some historians argue that they actually existed and were the aboriginals of Hawaii, inhabiting the islands before the coming of the Polynesians.

moa—chicken; fowl

moana*—the ocean; the sea. Many businesses and hotels as well as places have *moana* as part of their name.

moe—sleep

moolelo—ancient tales kept alive by the oral tradition and recited only by day

muumuu*—a "Mother Hubbard," an ankle-length dress with a high neckline introduced by the missionaries to cover the nakedness of the Hawaiians. It has become fashionable attire for almost any occasion in Hawaii.

nani—beautiful

nui—big; great; large; as in *mahalo nui* (thank you very much)

ohana—a family; the fundamental social division; extended family. Now used to denote a social organization with grassroots overtones, as in the "Protect Kahoolawe Ohana."

okolehau—literally "iron bottom"; a traditional booze made from ti root. *Okole* means "rear end" and *hau* means "iron," which was descriptive of the huge blubber pots in which *okolehau* was made. Also, if you drink too much it'll surely knock you on your *okole*.

ono*—delicious; delightful; the best. *Ono ono* means "extra or absolutely delicious."

opihi—a shellfish or limpet that clings to rocks and is gathered as one of the islands' favorite *pu pu*. Custom dictates that you never remove all of the *opihi* from a rock; some are always left to grow for future generations.

opu—belly; stomach

pahoehoe*—smooth, ropey lava that looks like burnt pancake batter. It is now the correct geological term used to describe this type of lava found anywhere in the world.

pakalolo—"crazy smoke"; grass; smoke; dope; marijuana

pake—a Chinese person. Can be derisive, depending on tone in which it is used. It is a bastardization of the Chinese word meaning "uncle."

pali*—a cliff; precipice. Hawaii's geology makes them quite common. The most famous are the *pali* of Oahu where a major battle was fought.

paniolo*—a Hawaiian cowboy. Derived from the Spanish *espaniola*. The first cowboys brought to Hawaii during the early 19th century were Mexicans from California.

papale—hat. Except for the feathered helmets of the *ali'i* warriors of old Hawaii, hats were generally not worn. However, once the islanders saw their practical uses and how fashionable they were, they began weaving them from various materials and quickly became experts at manufacture and design.

pa'u—long split skirt often worn by women when horseback riding. Last century, an island treat was *pa'u* riders in their beautiful dresses at Kapiolani Park in Honolulu. The tradition is carried on today at many of Hawaii's rodeos.

pau*—finished; done; completed. Often combined into *pau hana*, which means end of work or quitting time.

pilau—stink; bad smell; stench

pilikia—trouble of any kind, big or small; bad times

poi*—a glutinous paste made from the pounded corm of taro which ferments slightly and has a light sour taste. Purplish in color, it's a staple at luaus, where it is called "one-, two-, or three-finger" poi, depending upon its thickness.

pono—righteous or excellent

pua—flower

puka*—a hole of any size. *Puka* is used by all island residents, whether talking about a pinhole in a rubber boat or a tunnel through a mountain.

punalua—a traditional practice, before the missionaries arrived, of sharing mates. Western seamen took advantage of it, leading to the spread of contagious diseases and eventually to the ultimate demise of the Hawaiian people.

punee*—bed; narrow couch. Used by all ethnic groups. To recline on a *punee* on a breezy lanai is a true island treat.

pu pu*—an appetizer; a snack; hors d'oeuvres; can be anything from cheese and crackers to sushi. Oftentimes, bars or nightclubs offer them free.

pupule—crazy; nuts; out of your mind

pu'u—hill, as in Pu'u Ulaula ("Red Hill")

tapa*—a traditional paper cloth made from beaten bark. Intricate designs were stamped in using beaters, and natural dyes added color. The tradition was lost for many years but is now making a comeback, and provides some of the most beautiful folk art in the islands.

taro*—the staple of old Hawaii. A plant with a distinctive broad leaf that produces a starchy root. It was brought by the first Polynesians and was grown on magnificently irrigated plantations. According to the oral tradition, the life-giving properties of taro hold mystical significance for Hawaiians, since it was created by the gods at about the same time as humans.

ti—a broad-leafed plant that was used for many purposes, from plates to hula skirts (never grass). Especially used to wrap religious offerings presented at the *heiau*.

tutu*—grandmother; granny; older woman. Used by all as a term of respect and endearment.

ukulele*—*uku* means "flea" and *lele* means "jumping," so literally "jumping flea"—the way the Hawaiians perceived the quick finger movements used on the banjolike Portuguese folk instrument called a *cavaquinho*. The ukulele quickly became synonymous with the islands.

wahine*—young woman; female; girl; wife. Used by all ethnic groups. When written on a lavatory door it means "Women's Room."

wai—fresh water; drinking water

wela—hot. *Wela kahao* is a "hot time" or "making whoopee."

wiki*—quickly; fast; in a hurry. Often seen as *wiki wiki* (very fast), as in "Wiki Wiki Messenger Service."

USEFUL PHRASES

Aloha ahiahi—Good evening.
Aloha au ia oe—I love you!
Aloha kakahiaka—Good morning.
Aloha nui loa—much love; fondest regards
Hauoli la hanau—Happy Birthday.

Hauoli makahiki hou—Happy New Year.
Komo mai—please come in; enter; welcome
Mele kalikimaka—Merry Christmas.
Okole maluna—bottoms up; salute; cheers; kampai

ACCOMMODATIONS INDEX

RESTAURANT INDEX

GENERAL INDEX

BEACHES

boating: boat ramps 230; canoes 62, 105, 154, 179; 370; excursions/dinner cruises 83-85; fishing boats/charters 87, 89, 329; kayaking 85-86, 105, 130, 241, 300, 329, 355; Makena Boat Landing 253; rafting 85-86; rental boats 83, 241; sail boats 355; tour boats 83-85, 320; yachts 129; *see also* cruises; harbors/marinas; *specific place*
bodysurfing: 81, 141-142, 252
boogie boards: 200, 219-220
botanical gardens: *see* gardens
Boundary Trail (Maui): 72
breadfruit: 114
The Brick Palace (Maui): 177

bugs: 141
Burney, James: 24
bus service: *see* public transportation
Bush, George: 309

C

camping: general discussion 68-71, 74-75, 130; Camp Keanae YMCA (Maui) 285-286; Haleakala National Park (Maui) 272-275; Honomanu County Park (Maui) 285; Kipahulu (Maui) 303; Lanai 325; Molokai 357, 362, 382; permits 69, 71, 170; Polipoli Spring State Recreation Area (Maui) 267; safety 145; Waianapanapa State Park (Maui) 294; what to take 147, 274

FESTIVALS AND EVENTS—MAUI

WHERE TO BUY MOON TRAVEL HANDBOOKS

BOOKSTORES AND LIBRARIES: Moon Travel Handbooks are distributed worldwide. Please contact our sales manager for a list of wholesalers and distributors in your area.

TRAVELERS: We would like to have Moon Travel Handbooks available throughout the world. Please ask your bookstore to write or call us for ordering information. If your bookstore will not order our guides for you, please contact us for a free catalog.

Moon Travel Handbooks
P.O. Box 3040
Chico, CA 95927-3040 U.S.A.
tel.: (800) 345-5473, outside the U.S. (530) 345-5473
fax: (530) 345-6751
e-mail: travel@moon.com

IMPORTANT ORDERING INFORMATION

PRICES: All prices are subject to change. We always ship the most current edition. We will let you know if there is a price increase on the book you order.

SHIPPING AND HANDLING OPTIONS: Domestic UPS or USPS first class (allow 10 working days for delivery): $4.50 for the first item, $1.00 for each additional item.

Moonbelt shipping is $1.50 for one, 50 cents for each additional belt.

UPS 2nd Day Air or Printed Airmail requires a special quote.

International Surface Bookrate 8-12 weeks delivery: $4.00 for the first item, $1.00 for each additional item. Note: We cannot guarantee international surface bookrate shipping. We recommend sending international orders via air mail, which requires a special quote.

FOREIGN ORDERS: Orders that originate outside the U.S.A. must be paid for with an international money order, a check in U.S. currency drawn on a major U.S. bank based in the U.S.A., or Visa, MasterCard, or Discover.

TELEPHONE ORDERS: We accept Visa, MasterCard, or Discover payments. Call in your order: (800) 345-5473, 8 a.m.-5 p.m. Pacific standard time. Outside the U.S. the number is (530) 345-5473.

INTERNET ORDERS: Visit our site at: www.moon.com

MOONBELTS

Looking for comfort and a way to keep your most important articles safe while traveling? These were our own concerns and that is why we created the Moonbelt. Made of heavy-duty Cordura nylon, the Moonbelt offers maximum protection for your money and important papers. Designed for all-weather comfort, this pouch slips under your shirt or waistband, rendering it virtually undetectable and inaccessible to pickpockets. It features a one-inch high-test quick-release buckle so there's no fumbling for the strap nor repeated adjustments. This handy buckle opens and closes with a touch, but won't come undone until you want it to. Moonbelts accommodate traveler's checks, passport, cash, photos, etc. Measures 5 x 9 inches and fits waists up to 48".

MOON TRAVEL HANDBOOKS

Hong Kong Handbook	**$16.95**
Kerry Moran	378 pages, 49 maps
Indonesia Handbook	**$25.00**
Bill Dalton	1,380 pages, 249 maps
Micronesia Handbook	**$14.95**
Neil M. Levy	340 pages, 70 maps
Nepal Handbook	**$18.95**
Kerry Moran	490 pages, 51 maps
New Zealand Handbook	**$19.95**
Jane King	600 pages, 81 maps
Outback Australia Handbook	**$18.95**
Marael Johnson	450 pages, 57 maps
Philippines Handbook	**$17.95**
Peter Harper and Laurie Fullerton	670 pages, 116 maps
Singapore Handbook	**$15.95**
Carl Parkes	350 pages, 29 maps
South Korea Handbook	**$19.95**
Robert Nilsen	820 pages, 141 maps
South Pacific Handbook	**$22.95**
David Stanley	920 pages, 147 maps
Southeast Asia Handbook	**$21.95**
Carl Parkes	1,080 pages, 204 maps
Tahiti-Polynesia Handbook	**$15.95**
David Stanley	380 pages, 35 maps
Thailand Handbook	**$19.95**
Carl Parkes	860 pages, 142 maps
Vietnam, Cambodia & Laos Handbook	**$18.95**
Michael Buckley	760 pages, 116 maps

OTHER GREAT TITLES FROM MOON

"For hardy wanderers, few guides come more highly recommended than the Handbooks. They include good maps, steer clear of fluff and flackery, and offer plenty of money-saving tips. They also give you the kind of information that visitors to strange lands—on any budget—need to survive."

—US News & World Report

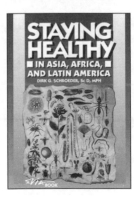

Moon Handbook	**$10.00**
Carl Koppeschaar	141 pages, 8 maps
The Practical Nomad: How to Travel Around the World	**$17.95**
Edward Hasbrouck	575 pages
Staying Healthy in Asia, Africa, and Latin America	**$11.95**
Dirk Schroeder	230 pages, 4 maps

Pennsylvania Handbook	**$18.95**
Joanne Miller	448 pages, 40 maps
Road Trip USA	**$22.95**
Jamie Jensen	900 pages, 165 maps
Road Trip USA: Chicago Getaways	**$9.95**
	60 pages, 1 map
Road Trip USA: Seattle Getaways	**$9.95**
	60 pages, 1 map
Santa Fe-Taos Handbook	**$13.95**
Stephen Metzger	160 pages, 13 maps
South Carolina Handbook	**$14.95**
Mike Sigalas	250 pages, 20 map
Southern California Handbook	**$19.95**
Kim Weir	720 pages, 26 maps
Tennessee Handbook	**$17.95**
Jeff Bradley	530 pages, 44 maps
Texas Handbook	**$18.95**
Joe Cummings	690 pages, 70 maps
Utah Handbook	**$17.95**
Bill Weir and W.C. McRae	490 pages, 40 maps
Virginia Handbook	**$15.95**
Julian Smith	340 pages, 30 maps
Washington Handbook	**$19.95**
Don Pitcher	840 pages, 113 maps
Wisconsin Handbook	**$18.95**
Thomas Huhti	590 pages, 69 maps
Wyoming Handbook	**$17.95**
Don Pitcher	610 pages, 80 maps

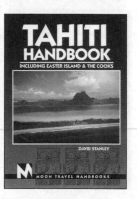

ASIA AND THE PACIFIC

"Scores of maps, detailed practical info down to business
hours of small-town libraries. You can't beat the Asian titles
for sheer heft. (The) series is sort of an American Lonely
Planet, with better writing but fewer titles. (The) individual
voice of researchers comes through."

—Travel & Leisure

Australia Handbook	**$21.95**
Marael Johnson, Andrew Hempstead,	
and Nadina Purdon	940 pages, 141 maps
Bali Handbook	**$19.95**
Bill Dalton	750 pages, 54 maps
Bangkok Handbook	**$13.95**
Michael Buckley	244 pages, 30 maps
Fiji Islands Handbook	**$14.95**
David Stanley	300 pages, 38 maps

Canadian Rockies Handbook	**$14.95**
Andrew Hempstead	220 pages, 25 maps
Colorado Handbook	**$17.95**
Stephen Metzger	480 pages, 59 maps
Georgia Handbook	**$17.95**
Kap Stann	380 pages, 50 maps
Grand Canyon Handbook	**$14.95**
Bill Weir	220 pages, 9 maps
Hawaii Handbook	**$19.95**
J.D. Bisignani	1,030 pages, 90 maps
Honolulu-Waikiki Handbook	**$14.95**
J.D. Bisignani	400 pages, 20 maps
Idaho Handbook	**$18.95**
Don Root	610 pages, 42 maps
Kauai Handbook	**$15.95**
J.D. Bisignani	320 pages, 23 maps
Los Angeles Handbook	**$16.95**
Kim Weir	370 pages, 15 maps
Maine Handbook	**$18.95**
Kathleen M. Brandes	660 pages, 27 maps
Massachusetts Handbook	**$18.95**
Jeff Perk	600 pages, 23 maps
Maui Handbook	**$15.95**
J.D. Bisignani	420 pages, 35 maps
Michigan Handbook	**$15.95**
Tina Lassen	300 pages, 30 maps
Montana Handbook	**$17.95**
Judy Jewell and W.C. McRae	480 pages, 52 maps
Nevada Handbook	**$18.95**
Deke Castleman	530 pages, 40 maps
New Hampshire Handbook	**$18.95**
Steve Lantos	500 pages, 18 maps
New Mexico Handbook	**$15.95**
Stephen Metzger	360 pages, 47 maps
New York Handbook	**$19.95**
Christiane Bird	780 pages, 95 maps
New York City Handbook	**$13.95**
Christiane Bird	300 pages, 20 maps
North Carolina Handbook	**$14.95**
Rob Hirtz and Jenny Daughtry Hirtz	275 pages, 25 maps
Northern California Handbook	**$19.95**
Kim Weir	800 pages, 50 maps
Ohio Handbook	**$15.95**
David K. Wright	340 pages, 12 maps
Oregon Handbook	**$17.95**
Stuart Warren and Ted Long Ishikawa	588 pages, 34 maps

LATIN AMERICA
AND THE CARIBBEAN

"Solidly packed with practical information and full of significant
cultural asides that will enlighten you on the whys and
wherefores of things you might easily see but not easily grasp."

—Boston Globe

Belize Handbook	**$15.95**
Chicki Mallan and Patti Lange	390 pages, 45 maps
Caribbean Vacations	**$18.95**
Karl Luntta	910 pages, 64 maps
Costa Rica Handbook	**$19.95**
Christopher P. Baker	780 pages, 73 maps
Cuba Handbook	**$19.95**
Christopher P. Baker	740 pages, 70 maps
Dominican Republic Handbook	**$15.95**
Gaylord Dold	420 pages, 24 maps
Ecuador Handbook	**$16.95**
Julian Smith	450 pages, 43 maps
Honduras Handbook	**$15.95**
Chris Humphrey	330 pages, 40 maps
Jamaica Handbook	**$15.95**
Karl Luntta	330 pages, 17 maps
Virgin Islands Handbook	**$13.95**
Karl Luntta	220 pages, 19 maps

NORTH AMERICA AND HAWAII

"These domestic guides convey the same sense of exoticism
that their foreign counterparts do, making home-country
travel seem like far-flung adventure."

—Sierra Magazine

Alaska-Yukon Handbook	**$17.95**
Deke Castleman and Don Pitcher	530 pages, 92 maps
Alberta and the Northwest Territories Handbook	**$18.95**
Andrew Hempstead	520 pages, 72 maps,
Arizona Handbook	**$18.95**
Bill Weir	600 pages, 40 maps
Atlantic Canada Handbook	**$18.95**
Mark Morris	460 pages, 61 maps
Big Island of Hawaii Handbook	**$15.95**
J.D. Bisignani	390 pages, 23 maps
Boston Handbook	**$13.95**
Jeff Perk	200 pages, 20 maps
British Columbia Handbook	**$16.95**
Jane King and Andrew Hempstead	430 pages, 69 maps

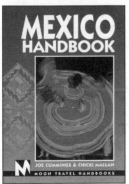

MEXICO

"These books will delight the armchair traveler, aid the undecided person in selecting a destination, and guide the seasoned road warrior looking for lesser-known hideaways."
—*Mexican Meanderings* Newsletter

"From tourist traps to off-the-beaten track hideaways, these guides offer consistent, accurate details without pretension."
—*Foreign Service Journal*

Archaeological Mexico	**$19.95**
Andrew Coe	420 pages, 27 maps
Baja Handbook	**$16.95**
Joe Cummings	540 pages, 46 maps
Cabo Handbook	**$14.95**
Joe Cummings	270 pages, 17 maps
Cancún Handbook	**$14.95**
Chicki Mallan	240 pages, 25 maps
Colonial Mexico	**$18.95**
Chicki Mallan	400 pages, 38 maps
Mexico Handbook	**$21.95**
Joe Cummings and Chicki Mallan	1,200 pages, 201 maps
Northern Mexico Handbook	**$17.95**
Joe Cummings	610 pages, 69 maps
Pacific Mexico Handbook	**$17.95**
Bruce Whipperman	580 pages, 68 maps
Puerto Vallarta Handbook	**$14.95**
Bruce Whipperman	330 pages, 36 maps
Yucatán Handbook	**$16.95**
Chicki Mallan	400 pages, 52 maps

"Beyond question, the most comprehensive Mexican resources available for those who prefer deep travel to shallow tourism. But don't worry, the fiesta-fun stuff's all here too."
—*New York Daily News*

LOSE YOURSELF IN THE EXPERIENCE, NOT THE CROWD

For 25 years, Moon Travel Handbooks have been the guidebooks of choice for adventurous travelers. Our award-winning Handbook series provides focused, comprehensive coverage of distinct destinations all over the world. Each Handbook is like an entire bookcase of cultural insight and introductory information in one portable volume. Our goal at Moon is to give travelers all the background and practical information they'll need for an extraordinary travel experience.

The following pages include a complete list of Handbooks, covering North America and Hawaii, Mexico, Latin America and the Caribbean, and Asia and the Pacific. To purchase Moon Travel Handbooks, check your local bookstore or order by phone: (800) 345-5473 M-F 8 am.-5 p.m. PST or outside the U.S. phone: (530) 345-5473.

"An in-depth dunk into the land, the people and their history, arts, and politics."
—*Student Travels*

"I consider these books to be superior to Lonely Planet. When Moon produces a book it is more humorous, incisive, and off-beat."
—*Toronto Sun*

"Outdoor enthusiasts gravitate to the well-written Moon Travel Handbooks. In addition to politically correct historic and cultural features, the series focuses on flora, fauna and outdoor recreation. Maps and meticulous directions also are a trademark of Moon guides."
—*Houston Chronicle*

"Moon [Travel Handbooks] . . . bring a healthy respect to the places they investigate. Best of all, they provide a host of odd nuggets that give a place texture and prod the wary traveler from the beaten path. The finest are written with such care and insight they deserve listing as literature."
—*American Geographical Society*

"Moon Travel Handbooks offer in-depth historical essays and useful maps, enhanced by a sense of humor and a neat, compact format."
—*Swing*

"Perfect for the more adventurous, these are long on history, sightseeing and nitty-gritty information and very price-specific."
—*Columbus Dispatch*

"Moon guides manage to be comprehensive and countercultural at the same time . . . Handbooks are packed with maps, photographs, drawings, and sidebars that constitute a college-level introduction to each country's history, culture, people, and crafts."
—*National Geographic Traveler*

"Few travel guides do a better job helping travelers create their own itineraries than the Moon Travel Handbook series. The authors have a knack for homing in on the essentials."
—**Colorado Springs** *Gazette Telegraph*

ABOUT THE AUTHORS

J.D. BISIGNANI 1947-1997

Joe Bisignani was a fortunate man because he made his living doing the two things that he liked best: traveling and writing. He will be greatly missed.

A mainstay of Moon Publications since 1979, he was best known in the travel world for his wildly successful, five-volume Hawaii Handbook series, of which *Maui Handbook* won the Hawaii Visitors Bureau's Best Guidebook Award in 1991, while *Hawaii Handbook* earned Best Guidebook as well as the Grand Award for Excellence in 1988. His *Japan Handbook* won the Lowell Thomas Travel Journalism Gold Award in 1993. Together with founder Bill Dalton and other writers, "Joe Biz" profoundly influenced the company's success in the travel publishing world.

ROBERT NILSEN

Robert Nilsen was born and raised in Minnesota. His first major excursion from the Midwest was a two-year stint in South Korea with the Peace Corps. Following that eye-opening service, he stayed on in Korea independently, teaching and traveling for another two years. Setting his sights on other lands and other cultures, he made his way through Asia during 1978-80, first heading south from Seoul to Bali and then west as far as the Kyber Pass before returning home to the United States. Over the intervening years, he has had the good fortune to return five times to various countries in Asia and the Pacific. Robert has written *South Korea Handbook* for Moon Publications, revised *Honolulu-Waikiki Handbook, Kauai Handbook, The Big Island of Hawaii Handbook,* and *Maui Handbook,* and contributed to the *Indonesia Handbook.* Since the passing of his good friend J.D. Bisignani, he has shouldered full responsibility for the revision of the Hawaii series of Moon Travel Handbooks, which also includes *Hawaii Handbook.*

PARKS